COMMENTARY

International
Uniform
Sunday School
Series

EDITOR
Wesley C. Reagan

CONTRIBUTING WRITERS
Ron Durham, Ph.D.
Doug deGraffenried
David Dietzel
William Wharton, Ph.D.
Phil Woodland, Ph.D.
John Wright

ILLUSTRATORS
Billy Ledet – Text
David Chrane – Cover

The **Higley Commentary**, in this sixty-sixth year of its life, renews its commitment to bring you resources that will illuminate and inspire your study and your teaching. We believe that a working knowledge of the Word of God is the foundation of a happy and meaningful life. We are grateful to be a part of the enterprise of broadening that knowledge for hundreds of thousands of students. This volume reaches your hands with our prayer that it will be a great blessing and encouragement to you.

Higley Publishing Corporation
P. O. Box 5398
Jacksonville FL 32247-5398

Foreword

The International Sunday School Outlines are the best efforts of some of the fine biblical scholars of our day. Drawing on their years of training and Bible study, they have provided an outline of balanced study of the Scriptures.

Seven people on **The Higley Lesson Commentary** staff have collaborated to flesh out the skeleton outlines into readily usable form. Each of these writers has years of formal training as well as years of experience practicing a genuine Christian commitment. Each of them also has a library of biblical reference works.

Beginning with the Scripture text itself, the writers select choice materials from their experience, their formal training and their independent research. These materials are arranged into practical illustrations, discussion questions and exposition of the text.

The Higley Lesson Commentary which you now hold in your hand is the highly refined and condensed distillation of this process. In a remarkable way it brings you a tried and true approach to Bible study that will greatly enrich your life.

This volume is sent forth with a prayer that it will result in greater praise to God, a deeper understanding of His Word and a more devout commitment to His way of life.

Wesley C. Reagan, Editor

Copyright©1998 by Higley Publishing Corp.
P. O. Box 5398, Jacksonville, FL 32247-5398 Tel. (904)396-1918

Soft cover ISBN 1-886-763-100 $12.99
Hard cover ISBN 1-886-763-119 $15.99
Large Print Student Book ISBN 1-886-763-127 $11.99

Preface

For years I have appreciated **The Higley Commentary** for its vital mission of involving adults in systematic Bible study. People never outgrow the need to broaden their knowledge of the Scriptures. My own early experience in this great adventure came when a humble salesman began taking me to Sunday School when I was just a boy. I have never outgrown the thrill of discovering new insights into God's Word, and how to apply that Word to my daily life.

When I wrote the book, **The Ten Largest Sunday Schools and What Makes Them Grow** (Regal Books), I was excited to find thousands of adults involved in the enterprise of Bible study. Of course, the **Higley** materials are just as effective in small groups that meet anytime during the week. But it gratifies me that the adult Sunday School is still alive and well in America.

It can be further enlivened by the use of **The Higley Commentary**. I am especially pleased with the way this study guide enables group leaders to present effective lessons regardless of their previous training. The lesson applications show how God's Word speaks to our every day lives, insuring that Bible study doesn't become merely academic.

Let me also note the importance of that word "systematic" in the first paragraph. Every student of the Bible has a favorite passage—classics like the 23rd Psalm, John 3:16, or Romans 8:28. As precious as such texts are, it is also urgent that we explore all the paths God has prepared for us through His Word, instead of "camping out" at just a few spots. Since **Higley** follows the International Sunday School Lessons, study groups that stick to this resource are nourished in an orderly fashion by every part of the life-giving Scriptures.

May God bless you in the lifelong venture of growing in the grace and knowledge of our Lord Jesus Christ through His precious Word!

Elmer L. Towns, D.Min.
Vice President and Dean
School of Religion
Liberty University

FALL QUARTER
God Calls a People to Faithful Living

God Fashions a People (Lessons 1–4)
God Leads in Times of Change (Lessons 5–7)
God Works Through People (Lessons 8–10)
God Judges and Renews (Lessons 11–13)

WINTER QUARTER
God Calls Anew in Jesus Christ

The Good News of Jesus Christ (Lessons 1–4)
Good News for Daily Living (Lessons 5–13)

SPRING QUARTER
That You May Believe

Jesus' Coming Called for Faith (Lessons 1–6)
Jesus Declared God's Message (Lessons 7–9)
Jesus Prepared His Followers (Lessons 10–13)

SUMMER QUARTER
Beginnings

In the Beginning (Lessons 1–4)
The Beginning of a People (Lessons 5–8)
A People Tested (Lessons 9–13

God's Creation Marred by Sin

*N*ow the serpent was more subtil than any beast of the field which the Lord God had made. And he said unto the woman, Yea, hath God said, Ye shall not eat of every tree of the garden?

2 And the woman said unto the serpent, We may eat of the fruit of the trees of the 3 But of the fruit of the tree which is in the midst of the garden, God hath said, Ye shall not eat of it, neither shall ye touch it, lest ye die.

Genesis 3:1-13

4 And the serpent said unto the woman, Ye shall not surely die:

5 For God doth know that in the day ye eat thereof, then your eyes shall be opened, and ye shall be as gods, knowing good and evil.

6 And when the woman saw that the tree was good for food, and that it was pleasant to the eyes, and a tree to be desired to make one wise, she took of the fruit thereof, and did eat, and gave also unto her husband with her; and he did eat.

7 And the eyes of them both were opened, and they knew that they were naked; and they sewed fig leaves together, and made themselves aprons.

8 And they heard the voice of the Lord God walking in the garden in the cool of the day: and Adam and his wife hid themselves from the presence of the Lord God amongst the trees of the garden.

9 And the Lord God called unto Adam, and said unto him, Where art thou?

10 And he said, I heard thy voice in the garden, and I was afraid, because I was naked; and I hid myself.

11 And he said, Who told thee that thou wast naked? Hast thou eaten of the tree, whereof I commanded thee that thou shouldest not eat?

12 And the man said, The woman whom thou gavest to be with me, she gave me of the tree, and I did eat.

13 And the Lord God said unto the woman, What is this that thou hast done? And the woman said, The serpent beguiled me and I did eat.

Memory Selection
Genesis 3:8

Background Scripture
Genesis 3

Devotional Reading
Romans 7:15-25a

Printed Scripture
Genesis 3:1-13

Teacher's Target

Lesson purpose: *To introduce an Old Testament survey with a reexamination of the roots of the universal human problem of sin and shame.*

The apostle Paul wrote that Old Testament events were recorded for our instruction (Rom. 15:4). Today's lesson introduces thirteen lessons in a survey of significant Old Testament events, beginning with the Fall of man in the Garden of Eden.

Of course the Old Testament story begins with the Creation, which God called "very good." Yet our own experience prepares us not to be shocked by Genesis 3. We have only to recall how the best resolutions made at dawn are often broken before the end of the day. This lesson is about where that brokenness began, and its impact even on our everyday life today.

Lesson Introduction

Without some knowledge of the Old Testament, Christians are cut-flower and rootless. To begin this lesson, ask group members to recall Old Testament events and stories that stand out in their minds. Reinforce the significance of these memories as a part of our own story as Christians. Note that one of the earliest stories—the account of the Fall—underlies many of the personal and social problems of our day. What can we learn from this event near the dawn of history?

Some may debate what is literal and what is figurative in this account. (For example, did a literal serpent represent Satan, or are we just to understand that he's a "snake in the grass"?!) Yet the universal experience of "living down" to our potential, of sin and guilt, of shame and hiding from God, all point to the overall truth of this ancient account, which also has such a modern ring.

Teaching Outline

I. The Satanic Confrontation—1-5

    A. An enemy in the Garden, 1

    B. Eve's first response, 2-3

    C. A Satanic half-truth, 4-5

II. The Structure of Temptation—6

III. The Shame of Sin—7-10

    A. Nakedness in a new light, 7

    B. Hiding from God, 9-10

IV. The Searching God, 11-13

Daily Bible Readings

Mon. The Serpent as Tempter
Genesis 3:1-7

Tue. Disobedience Brings Fear
Genesis 3:8-13

Wed. Consequences of Disobedience
Genesis 3:14-19

Thu. Expulsion from the Garden
Genesis 3:20-24

Fri. Who Will Rescue Me?
Romans 7:15-25a

Sat. No Condemnation
Romans 8:1-11

Sun. Alive in Christ
1 Corinthians 15:12-22

Verse by Verse

I. The Satanic Confrontation—1-5

A. An enemy in the Garden, 1

1 Now the serpent was more subtil than any beast of the field which the Lord god had made. And he said unto the woman, Yea, hath God said, Ye shall not eat of every tree of the garden?

The serpent is usually identified as Satan (see Rev. 12:9; 20:2). The account raises several questions that Scripture does not explicitly answer. What's an evil, talking snake doing in the Garden? Why are people who were created "very good" (1:31) so easily tempted by evil? Answers to such questions usually involve the idea that God created both angels and persons with the awesome capacity to choose between good and evil. The view that Satan is a fallen angel is rooted in this view, as is the human tendency to choose evil—to sin. Since God is supremely free, being created in His image (1:27) apparently means that we share that trait to some extent. Being created beings, however, means that we do not always use that freedom like God. The rest of the biblical story is about God's provision to help us deal with this universal weakness.

The King James word "subtil" means "crafty" (see the NIV), which fits what we know about Satan. It is he who uses cunning "devices" in his continual war against the good (2 Cor. 2:11). As verse 6 will show, Satan is darkly skillful in knowing our weaknesses, and how to appeal to them. Here he over-states God's command in 2:16-17. God did not forbid Adam and Eve to eat of "every tree," but only of the tree of the knowledge of good and evil. One of Satan's favorite tricks is to make us feel burdened by God's commands obscuring the fact that even when God says No it is for our good.

B. Eve's first response, 2-3

2 And the woman said unto the serpent, We may eat of the fruit of the trees of the garden:

3 But of the fruit of the tree which is in the midst of the garden, God hath said, Ye shall not eat of it, neither shall ye touch it, lest ye die.

Eve properly corrects the serpent's over-statement. She is a better *hearer* of the word than a *doer* (see James 1:22-24). We wonder whether she grasped the full meaning of the consequences of eating of the forbidden tree. Presumably she did not know about either physical or spiritual death, since these were experienced by humans only after the Fall. On the other hand, animal and plant life in the garden may have been subject to the natural cycles of life and death. Also, God may have taught the man and woman about death as a part of His prohibition against eating of the tree of knowledge.

Recall also that the man and woman

3

apparently were not created to live forever in the first place. They were driven from the Garden before they could eat of the tree of life (3:22). Death, therefore is a natural part of life. Yet because of sin we instinctively cry out against death with terrible questions about punishment in an after-life. Hence, the apostle Paul speaks of sin as the "sting" of death (1 Cor. 15:56).

C. A Satanic half-truth, 4-5

4 And the serpent said unto the woman, Ye shall not surely die:

5 for God doth know that in the day ye eat thereof, then your eyes shall be opened, and ye shall be as gods, knowing good and evil.

Explicitly contradicting God's warning that death would be the consequence of eating the forbidden fruit, the serpent introduces the first lie into human existence. He plants the first insinuation into the human heart that God wants to withhold the good from us. The serpent also tells a half-truth. Eating of the tree *will* give the man and woman the ability to know good from evil; but it will not make them like God.

In fact, Adam and Eve must have already had *some* idea about good and evil, else they would not have been held accountable for listening to the serpent. Perhaps he uses the word "knowing" in the sense of intimate knowledge—much like the word can refer to the sexual relationship (4:1). Merely mentioning the possibility of such intimate acquaintance must have given Eve the thrill of anticipation countless others have experienced amid temptation.

II. The Structure of Temptation—6

6 And when the woman saw that the tree was good for food, and that it was pleasant to the eyes, and a tree to be desired to make one wise, she took of the fruit thereof, and did eat, and gave also unto her husband with her; and he did eat.

In one brief sentence, Scripture records the first sin, the Fall of man that made such an impact that it still echoes in human history. The aged apostle John, in 1 John 2:16, provided a good commentary on the appeal the forbidden fruit (Scripture doesn't say it was an apple) had for Eve—and still has for people today. Sin results from the *lust of the flesh* (the fruit was "good for food"), *the pride of life* (it would "make one wise"). Even today, we fall into sin when we forget that obedience to God is more fulfilling than satisfying these cravings.

III. The Shame of Sin—7-10

A. Nakedness in a new light, 7

7 And the eyes of them both were opened, and they knew that they were naked; and they sewed fig leaves together, and made themselves aprons.

The undraped human figure can be portrayed as beautiful, as countless artists have shown. Since this "original sin," however, such art now easily degenerates to pornography. (The word "apron" means literally a "wrap-around" or cloak.)

B. Hiding from God, 8-10

8 And they heard the voice of the

Lord God walking in the garden in the cool of the day: and Adam and his wife hid themselves from the presence of the Lord God amongst the trees of the garden.

9 And the Lord God called unto Adam, and said unto him, Where art thou?

10 And he said, I heard thy voice in the garden, and I was afraid, because I was naked; and I hid myself.

The author of this ancient account skillfully depicts a scene that is a worthy destination for all humankind: being so at home with God that it's like living with Him in a peaceful garden where we might run into each other on a casual walk! Unfortunately, sin—that of Adam and Eve and our own—injects human fear into the scene. No less than Adam, many today think they can hide themselves and their sin from God, who actually created us to be transparently known to Him and to each other.

We already see here the truth of God's warning that the day Adam and Eve sinned they would "die." When this account was translated into Greek a word was chosen for "death" that also means "separation." Even before God drove Adam and Eve from His presence, they separated themselves from Him by their deliberate disobedience.

IV. The Searching God, 11-13

11 And he said, Who told thee that thou wast naked? Hast thou eaten of the tree, whereof I commanded thee that thou shouldest not eat?

12 And the man said, The woman whom thou gavest to be with me, she gave me of the tree, and I did eat.

13 And the Lord God said unto the woman, What is this that thou hast done? And the woman said, The serpent beguiled me, and I did eat.

Although God knows very well what the first couple did, He must arraign them openly so they also can perceive their guilt, and the justice of the divine sentence. Note that the woman is more forthright in her confession (vs. 13) than is the man, who tries to blame the woman (vs. 12).

As we know from the rest of the story, the door of Paradise slams shut as the result of this "original sin." Yet the God who knows our every thought and deed had already set in motion His plan to redeem His creation through His Son, the Lamb "foreordained before the foundation of the world" (1 Pet. 1:20).

Evangelistic Emphasis

The first sin seemed so trivial in anticipation. Eve listened to the serpent and decided that the fruit from the forbidden tree was indeed good for food, pleasant to the eyes, and could make one wise. The fact that God had expressly forbidden Adam and Eve to eat from that tree was overlooked. Thus, they abandoned the law of God and set out on a tragic course of disobedience rationalized by their own reasoning.

In yielding to temptation, Eve and Adam made a choice not unlike choices people make every day. Even when people know God's law, they often refuse to obey Him.

How can we help people avoid sin? First, we must remember that sin starts in the heart. Jesus made this point several times in His famous Sermon on the Mount (Matt. 5:22,28). Adam and Eve had the wrong motivations of heart and that led to their sin. If we would save a soul from death, we should help that person see clearly what is best for him or her. Looking at the probable consequences of our intentions can have a strong impact on our behavior.

A second thing we can do to protect others from sin is to set the right example. If either Adam or Eve had had the courage to stand up against the serpent's sly temptations, the whole course of human history would have changed. In our age, a Christian can have tremendous impact for good by simply living an exemplary life.

• • • • • • • • • • •

Memory Selection

And Adam and his wife hid themselves from the presence of the Lord God amongst the trees of the garden.—*Genesis 3:8*

Fear caused Adam and Eve to run away from God and try to hide from Him. God had said that they would die if they ate of the tree of knowledge of good and evil. They knew they had sinned by disobeying Him and they feared the consequences. But their efforts to hide from God were not successful.

It is futile to try to hide from God. He sees all and knows all. Yet, there seems to be a tendency in us to try to hide from God. Rather than flee from God when we sin, we should recognize that He is the only One who can restore our relationship with Him. When we know we have sinned, we should confess our sins to God (1 John 1:9). The combination of our acknowledgment of our sinful condition and His grace create a purity that is like the status of Adam and Eve at the beginning.

Weekday Problems

Fred is a bookkeeper for a local firm. He has worked for the same employer for five years and is highly regarded. Unknown to his boss, Fred has been gambling and has built up considerable debt because of his losses. His creditors are pressing him for their money. He has explained to them that he does not have the money and has begged for more time to repay his debt. There have been some threats against his physical well-being if he does not pay up immediately. The person to whom he owes the most has suggested that he can "borrow" the money from his employer and juggle the books so that no one will know about the "loan" before he can pay back his employer. He might even be able to win more through gambling and pay back the "loan" very quickly.

Fred is under great stress and is very tempted to steal the money as suggested. He might get away with the fraud and never be discovered, especially if he could pay back the money quickly. But he also fears that he might be discovered and lose his job, perhaps face a prison sentence.

* What was Fred's first mistake?
* Having made that mistake, what should he have done next?
* What is Fred's concern? What *should* Fred be concerned about?
* What would you advise Fred to do now?

The Crime of PUNishment

"I was a kamikaze piolt during World War II," said a Japanese man named Chow Mein.
"How could that be? That was a suicide squad."
"I know. They called me 'Chicken Chow Mein.'"

* * *

Q: Why did the boy name his rooster "Robinson"?
A: Because he Crusoe.

* * *

Two detectives were standing over a dead man named Juan.
First Detective: He was killed with a golf gun.
Second Detective: What's a golf gun?
First Detective: It's the gun that made a hole in Juan.

* * *

Bill: What's your dog's name?
Jill: Ginger.
Bill: Does Ginger bite?
Jill: No, Ginger snaps.

This Lesson in Your Life

Adam and Eve are not only our original ancestors, they are also eternal symbols of the struggle we have with sin. The same forces are present in our lives as were there in the Garden of Eden: God's desire for our goodness, the tempter's interest in foiling God's will for us and humanity's weighing of the options and choosing a course to follow. As surely as the story of Adam and Eve is tragic, just so is the story of the bad choices we have made in our lives.

When God placed Adam in the Garden of Eden, He gave only one prohibition: "... of the tree of the knowledge of good and evil, thou shalt not eat of it." It seems that it would not be difficult to obey a law as straightforward as that. But the problem was not that God's law was too complicated. The problem was with Adam's and Eve's lack of trust in God. God had placed them in a perfect setting, where all their needs were met by His grace. He had been clear in stating His expectations and in warning them of the consequences of disobedience. But they had not developed a level of appreciation for His grace which equipped them for the trial they were about to experience. So when the tempter appeared, their faith was overwhelmed by the trickery of the serpent. By accepting the serpent's "spin" on the law of God, they actually demonstrated more faith in the tempter than they did in God! When confronted by God, instead of admitting their sin and accepting responsibility, they attempted to pass the blame—Adam to Eve, Eve to the serpent. Of course, as God says so eloquently (Ezek. 18:20), "The soul that sinneth, it shall die." We may wish to "pass the buck" when we are caught in sin, but God knows who is at fault.

No matter how simple the law of God may be, we are unable to keep it if we lack faith. The Old Testament abounds with stories of how God's people abandoned God and sought out gods to worship which were more tangible, made of wood, stone or precious metals. Their memory was short, they forgot all that God had done for them and looked to gods which seemed more contemporary, more popular. They suffered from loss of faith in the one God, thus abandoning the one Deity who could save them from their sins.

We are the children of Adam and Eve. Just as they stumbled because of weak faith and evil motivations, we have done the same. Instead of worshiping idols made of wood and stone, our affections may be centered on other human beings or material items. We may idolize a movie star or some other person. We may become obsessed with our jobs or with sports or with some other pursuit which captures our time and attention. Anything which interferes with our devotion to the one God is extremely dangerous. Just as the tempter was able to deceive Eve and through her ensnare Adam as well, the concerns of this life can be used by Satan to separate us from God. We must build a strong faith in God to enable us to resist the cunning of our enemy (James 4:7).

How can we grow a strong faith? Faith comes through our learning who God is, what He has done for us and what he seeks from us. In seeking to know Him, there is no substitute for dedicated study of God's Word.

Seed Thoughts

1. Name some of the trees that were located in the Garden of Eden.

The tree of life and the tree of knowledge of good and evil. There were other trees which were pleasant to sight, and good for food (v.9).

2. What did God tell Adam he could eat?

"Of every tree of the garden thou mayest freely eat: . . . " (Gen. 3:16). (An exception is noted in verse 17.)

3. What fruit was not permitted as food for Adam and Eve?

Adam and Eve were not permitted to eat of the tree of knowledge of good and evil (v. 17).

4. Who was the first liar?

The serpent (v. 4).

5. How did the tempter convince Eve to disobey God?

He appealed to her ego, promising that she would be like a god, knowing good and evil; and he said that she would not die(vss. 4-5).

---

1. Name some of the trees that were located in the Garden of Eden.

2. What did God tell Adam he could eat?

3. What fruit was not permitted as food for Adam and Eve?

4. Who was the first liar?

5. How did the tempter convince Eve to disobey God?

6. What did God say would happen if they disobeyed Him?

7. Why did Adam and Eve disobey God?

8. How did Adam and Eve deal with their guilt?

9. What was the actual penalty God imposed on Adam and Eve for their sin?

10. What is the penalty for the sins we commit?

(Continued next page)

The tree of life and the tree of knowledge of good and evil. There were other trees which were pleasant to sight, and good for food (v.9).

"Of every tree of the garden thou mayest freely eat: . . . " (Gen. 3:16). (An exception is noted in verse 17.)

Adam and Eve were not permitted to eat of the tree of knowledge of good and evil (v. 17).

The serpent (v. 4).

He appealed to her ego, promising that she would be like a god, knowing good and evil; and he said that she would not die(vss. 4-5).

He said, "In the day that thou eatest thereof thou shalt surely die" (v. 17) .

Eve was deceived by the serpent; Adam was led by Eve to join her in disobedience (1 Tim 2:14). They were not led by faith in God (Rom. 14:23b).

They covered their nakedness, hid from God and, when confronted by God, blamed their sin on someone else (vss. 7-13).

Death was the penalty. God removed Adam and Eve from the Garden so that they no longer had access to the tree of life (vss. 22-24).

Death is the penalty for sin but God will forgive those who repent and obey Him through Christ (Rom. 6:23).

6. What did God say would happen if they disobeyed Him?

He said, "In the day that thou eatest thereof thou shalt surely die" (v. 17) .

7. Why did Adam and Eve disobey God?

Eve was deceived by the serpent; Adam was led by Eve to join her in disobedience (1 Tim 2:14). They were not led by faith in God (Rom. 14:23b).

8. How did Adam and Eve deal with their guilt?

They covered their nakedness, hid from God and, when confronted by God, blamed their sin on someone else (vss .7-13).

9. What was the actual penalty God imposed on Adam and Eve for their sin?

Death was the penalty. God removed Adam and Eve from the Garden so that they no longer had access to the tree of life (vss. 22-24)

10. What is the penalty for the sins we commit?

Death is the penalty for sin but God will forgive those who repent and obey Him through Christ (Rom. 6:23).

Celebrate: God Delivers a People from Slavery

*A*nd it came to pass in processof time, that the king of Egypt died: and the children of Israel sighed by reason of the bondage, and they cried, and their cry came up unto God by reason of the bondage.

24 And God heard their groaning, and God remembered his covenant with Abraham, with Isaac, and with Jacob.

25 And god looked upon the children of Israel, and God had respect unto them.

Exodus 2:23-25; 5:1-2; 12:29-32; 15:1-2

5:1 And afterward Moses went in, and told Pharaoh, Thus saith the LORD God of Israel, Let my people go, that they may hold a feast unto me in the wilderness.

2 And Pharaoh said, Who is the LORD, that I should obey his voice to let Israel go? I know not the LORD, neither will I let Israel go.

12:29 And it came to pass, that at midnight the LORD smote all the firstborn of Egypt, from the firstborn of Pharaoh that sat on his throne unto the firstborn of the captive that was in the dungeon; and all the firstborn of cattle.

30 And Pharaoh rose up in the night, he, and all his servants, and all the Egyptians; and there was a great cry in Egypt; for there was not a house where there was not one dead.

31 And he called for Moses and Aaron

by night, and said, Rise up, and get you forth from among my people, both ye and the children of Israel; and go, serve the LORD, as ye have said.

32 Also take your flocks and your herds, as ye have said, and be gone; and bless me also.

15:1 Then sang Moses and the children of Israel this song unto the LORD, and spake, saying, I will sing unto the LORD for he hath triumphed gloriously: the horse and his rider hath he thrown into the sea.

2 The LORD is my strength and song, and he is become my salvation: he is my God, and I will prepare him an habitation; my father's God, and I will exalt him.

Memory Selection
Exodus 2:23-24

Background Scripture
Exodus 2:23-25; 5:1-2
11:1-8; 12:29-32; 15:1-2

Devotional Reading
Psalm 105:37-45

Printed Scripture
Exodus 2:23-25; 5:1-2;
12:29-32; 15:1-2

Teacher's Target

Lesson purpose: *To examine the roots of freedom as lived out in Israel's release from Egyptian bondage.*

It would be hard to over-emphasize the significance of the exodus—Israel's escape from Egyptian bondage by the mighty hand of God. Before the exodus, Jacob's sons were a loose gathering of clans. The exodus transformed them into a nation, the people of God. Before the exodus, the children of Abraham were slaves. The exodus set them free.

The focus of this lesson can well include both the historical importance of this water-shed event and the way it has become a model for freedom-loving people everywhere. The exodus came to symbolize the yearning—and the right—of all people to be free. At various times on the world stage it has put an end to the kind of slavery that reduces people to chattel. The exodus even echoes in the way Jesus Christ, as the new Moses, leads people out of captivity to sin and into the freedom of salvation.

Lesson Introduction

More than 400 years before the exodus, famine drove the children of Israel from Palestine into Egypt, where there was food. Old Jacob—son of Isaac, son of Abraham—and 11 of his sons were welcomed at first; in fact Joseph, Jacob's next-to-youngest, had himself arisen to a position of leadership. The land was already ancient by the time the Hebrews discovered it. The great pyramids were perhaps a thousand years old.

Gradually, changes in leadership, along with an influx of other foreigners, caused the Egyptians to view the growing Hebrew population as a threat. They were reduced to slavery, and attempts were made to limit their growth. Amid this oppression, however, God selected and prepared a powerful leader, Moses, to lead His people back to the Promised Land. Today's lesson takes up the story with God reasserting His covenant with Father Abraham and sending Moses to confronting the ruler of Egypt with the challenge that still confronts oppressors everywhere: *"Let my people go!"*

Teaching Outline	Daily Bible Readings
I. 'Lord, Hear Our Cry!'—2:23-25 　　A. Reduced to bondage, 23 　　B. Remembered by the Lord, 24-25 II. 'Let My People Go!'—5:1-2 　　A. Request, 1 　　B. Denial, 2 III. 'Lift the Curse!'—12:29-32 　　A. The final plague, 29-30 　　B. Permission to flee, 31-32 IV. 'The Lord Is My Song!'—15:1-2 　　A. Saved through the sea, 1 　　B. A habitation with God, 2	**Mon.** Israelites Enslaved 　　*Exodus 2:11-25* **Tue.** Moses Called 　　*Exodus 3:1-12* **Wed.** "I Am Who I Am" 　　*Exodus 3:13-22* **Thu.** Pharaoh Resists God 　　*Exodus 4:27—5:9* **Fri.** God Repeats the Promise 　　*Exodus 6:1-9* **Sat.** Free at Last! 　　*Exodus 14:19-25* **Sun.** God Remembered the Promise 　　*Psalm 105:23-25*

12

Verse by Verse

I 'Lord, Hear Our Cry!'—2:23-25

A. Reduced to bondage, 23

23 And it came to pass in process of time, that the king of Egypt died: and the children of Israel sighed by reason of the bondage, and they cried, and their cry came up unto God by reason of the bondage.

This verse reminds not only of the death of an Egyptian ruler, but that subsequent rulers "knew not Joseph" (Exod. 1:8). The Hebrews began to be viewed as dangerous aliens, and were pressed into building store-house cities for the government (1:11). Ancient Egyptian records speak of a people called the "Habiru," who are known to be roving bands of Semites. Some scholars think this was an Egyptian form of the term "Hebrews," and that it is a reference from outside of Scripture to Jacob's descendants who were pressed into forced labor for the Egyptians. There are also records of building projects like those described here, under the reign of Pharaoh Seti I, some 1,300 years before Christ. Other biblical references, however, imply that the exodus was earlier; and scholars are not agreed on the dates of these important events.

The fact that the people cry to the true God for relief shows that they had successfully resisted pressures to assimilate with the Egyptians and adopt pagan gods. It is clear that the story of God's Covenant with Abraham and the idea of his descendants as a chosen race had been kept alive by handing it down through several generations.

B. Remembered by the Lord, 24-25

24 And God heard their groaning, and God remembered his covenant with Abraham, with Isaac, and with Jacob.

25 And God looked upon the children of Israel, and God had respect unto them.

To say that God "remembered" the Covenant does not imply that He had forgotten it, but that He decided to act in response to the cry of the people. Perhaps He waited until they cried out to Him because He wanted to test their commitment to Him as a Covenant people. An escape from Egyptian bondage would not be easy, and God would need committed people to accomplish it. This reminds us that the Covenant cut two ways, involving promises to be kept both by God and by His chosen people. (Likewise, to say that God "had respect" for His people does not imply that He formerly did not respect them, but that He cared deeply and compas-

13

sionately about their plight: He was "concerned about them" [NIV].)

II. 'Let My People Go!'—5:1-2

A. Request, 1

1 And afterward Moses went in, and told Pharaoh, Thus saith the Lord God of Israel, Let my people go, that they may hold a feast unto me in the wilderness.

By now, the infant Moses has been rescued from the ban against allowing boy babies among the Hebrews to live. He has grown to manhood, spent 40 years in the nearby wilderness of Midian. He has heard God call him to return to Egypt and lead his people out of captivity. Now, in the court of Pharaoh, he asks permission to take his fellow-Hebrews back to the wilderness for a feast. Although the official Jewish feast days will not be established until the giving of the Law, later in the book of Exodus, Pharaoh knows the Hebrews have a distinctive religion. In other circumstances he might have considered this a reasonable request.

B. Denial, 2

2 And Pharaoh said, Who is the Lord, that I should obey his voice to let Israel go? I know not the Lord, neither will I let Israel go.

Pharaoh rightly suspects that this is no brief excursion, and that Moses has no intention of bringing the people back to Egypt. Knowing that he needs the Hebrews for slave labor, he not only denies Moses' request, but adds to the burden of the people (vss. 6-9).

Also, the author of this ancient text (traditionally supposed to have been Moses himself) is careful to show that Pharaoh's refusal to let the people go is because he is an unbeliever, and holds himself to be above the law of God. In many pagan cultures it was assumed that the ruler could install whatever religion he wished. It is in this very confrontation between Moses and Pharaoh that the world will become heir to the radical view that even the king is subject to the rule of the one true God.

III. 'Lift the Curse!'—12:29-32

A. The final plague, 29-30

12:29 And it came to pass, that at midnight the Lord smote all the firstborn of Egypt, from the firstborn of Pharaoh that sat on his throne unto the firstborn of the captive that was in the dungeon; and all the firstborn of cattle.

30 And Pharaoh rose up in the night, he, and all his servants, and all the Egyptians; and there was a great cry in Egypt; for there was not a house where there was not one dead.

Intervening chapters tell of the horrible plagues God sends upon the Egyptians to convince them to comply with Moses' request. Through them all, Pharaoh alternately hardens his heart (8:15) and in turn has his heart hardened by God (7:13) (reminding us that unless we have a heart for obedience,

God may actually encourage our unbelief (see 2 Thess. 2:11-12).

The final plague, the most terrible of all, is the death of the firstborn among all the Egyptian families, and even among the livestock. We have no way to explain how God would justify the death of the firstborn in an Egyptian peasant's family merely because of their leader's resistance to God's will. Yet it was neither the first nor the last time that innocent citizens have suffered from the decision of irresponsible rulers.

B. Permission to flee, 31-32

31 And he called for Moses and Aaron by night, and said, Rise up, and get you forth from among my people, both ye and the children of Israel; and go, serve the Lord, as ye have said.

32 Also take your flocks and your herds, as ye have said, and be gone; and bless me also.

Finally, the horrors of the last plague persuade Pharaoh to allow Moses and his people to leave. The fact that they are allowed to take their "flocks and herds" indicates that their bondage was not absolute; they were allowed to possess certain property. We also learn from Exodus 12:35-36 that the Egyptians were so eager to have the Hebrews leave that they gave them jewelry, gold, and fine clothing. The final plague did its work well.

IV. 'The Lord Is My Song!'—15:1-2
A. Saved through the sea, 1

1 Then sang Moses and the children of Israel this song unto the Lord, and spake, saying, I will sing unto the Lord for he hath triumphed gloriously: the horse and his rider hath he thrown into the sea.

Both Moses and his sister Miriam were apparently poets, or song-writers (see Miriam's song, 15:21ff.) And who could resist composing a hymn in tribute to one of the world's most astounding events—the parting of the waters that enabled the Hebrews to cross the sea, and the subsequent crashing together of the walls of water that entrapped Pharaoh and his hosts? (Many scholars believe this pharaoh was Rameses II, who reigned from 1299 to 1232 B.C.—although, again, the date may have been much earlier.)

B. A habitation with God, 2

2 The Lord is my strength and song, and he is become my salvation: he is my God, and I will prepare him an habitation; my father's God, and I will exalt him.

The King James reading here includes the idea that the exodus made such an impact on Moses that he determines that freedom from Egypt will not just constitute flight from slavery. It will also be a flight *home*. Rather than implying that he will build a temple for God, the phrase probably refers to making a home for God in his heart—an entirely appropriate response to an exodus from Egyptian slavery or, as in the Lord's prayer, deliverance from evil.

Evangelistic Emphasis

Carolyn Blackman didn't know what to expect when she was invited by her Jewish friend, Rebecca Meir to spend the evening having dinner with her. Rebecca's parents had flown in from New York for the weekend because of the upcoming Passover celebration. It wasn't *just any meal* to which she was being invited, but the Passover Feast. All Carolyn was sure of was that it was a very high honor for her to be invited. Of course, she readily accepted.

Carolyn found herself both fascinated and surprised as the evening's ritual progressed. She was fascinated by "the story" that was so creatively told in the context of the meal. At the same time, she was surprised at how much of the story she knew from her own childhood Sunday School experiences. There were "story details" that caught her attention during this meal that she either had forgotten or that had been omitted in the children's version. Carolyn was not sure which. She had not realized how much she, a Christian, and this non-Christian friend had in common.

Carolyn was also caught off guard by the sensation that impressed itself upon her that *it had been a long time since she had heard the biblical message presented as story*. She hadn't particularly thought of that before. Being actively involved in a conservative Bible church, certainly, she was immersed weekly with Scripture. But it was usually presented as "facts" or "proof" or "systematic doctrine." Carolyn hadn't realized it, but she missed the "story" of the Bible. At the same time, she wondered if perhaps other Christians missed "the story," too.

● ● ● ● ● ● ● ● ● ● ●

Memory Selection

And it came to pass in process of time, that the king of Egypt died and the children of Israel sighed by reason of the bondage, and they cried, and their cry came up unto God by reason of the bondage. And God heard their groaning, and God remembered his covenant with Abraham, with Isaac, and with Jacob. — *Exodus 2:23-24*

Most of us can endure almost any unpleasant experience *for a while.* Even the pangs of childbirth are tolerable if the labor pains do not last too long. And after a while, the young mother may even voluntarily enter into the process of childbirth again.

Yet, there is something about lingering pain, whether physical or emotional, that wears us down. What was at first "not really all that bad" can, in the process of time, come to dominate our lives. It doesn't matter whether it is unresolved grief that weighs upon us or the nagging of a persistent headache. The resources from which we normally draw to see us through difficult times become depleted and our well of faith runs dry.

16

Weekday Problems

Have you ever thought about the fact that often for God to answer your prayer, He must reject someone else's prayer? Perhaps, it's a job that you've desperately wanted. You fervently petition God, "Please, *let me have that job!*" You, *do*n't stop to think about the fact that there are 15 others who feel the same yearning, need, desperation for that job that you feel. For God to say, "Yes" to your prayer, He must say, "No" to each of the others who are praying.

The same night that Israel still celebrates as the time of God's greatest blessing, Egypt grieved for years to follow. For the Israelites, it marked for all time the salvation of God. For the Egyptians, it branded his rebuke bitterly upon the eyes of their memory.

* Other than the matter of "job hunting," what are some examples of times when our prayers potentially conflict with the prayers of others?

* Is it selfish for us to ask God for blessings when we know that his granting our prayer will deprive someone else of his requests? Why?

* Not every time we "compete" with another for God's favor is it an adversarial situation, but sometimes it is. What contemporary situation compares closely with that of Egypt and Israel?

Tall Tales from the Exodus

Biff: A man just sold me the Nile River!
Whiff: Egypt you.

* * *

Joseph, at Pharaoh's Royal Sandwich Shop: Your sign says "50 shekels to anyone who orders anything we can't serve." I want an elephant ear sandwich.
Waiter: Oh, no. Guess we'll have to pay up.
Joseph: Ah ha! No elephant ears, right?
Waiter: Oh we have those all right. It's just that we're out of those really big buns.

* * *

Ahmad: Here's you engagement ring my darling.
Fatima: Why you cheapskate! It has a flaw in it!
Ahmad: But darling, that shouldn't matter—love is blind!
Fatima: Not *stone* blind.

This Lesson in Your Life

Fred Blaylock knows well the truths reflected in Exodus 12–14. He could not possibly count the times that he thought he was finally free of his alcohol addiction. Every time he told himself convincingly that this time he was "dry" *for sure!* Unfortunately, each time "demon rum" blindsided him unexpectedly *one more time*.

Temptation came in many different forms and attacked him on a variety of fronts. Sometimes, its attack was in a crowd, an office party. The weapon of choice in that setting was "peer pressure" echoing the call, *"Ah come on. Don't be a party pooper. Just one won't hurt anything! You're going to ruin the party with this goody-two-shoes routine."*

At other times, the attack came within the privacy of anonymity. It was not necessarily a matter of solitary *aloneness*, as one might find in his closet. Most of the time, the "privacy" came as a result of being surrounded by people who did not know him. *"No one will know,"* whispered the tempter. *"You've been good long enough for one stretch. You deserve a reward."*

Time and time again, Fred fell prey to the tempter's attacks. Just when he thought he was *finally free,* another attack from the enemy would come and Fred would find himself fighting for his survival all over again.

This story of the flight of the Israelites from their bondage reminds Fred so much of his desperate flight from his own. The enemy is different, but the enslavement is just as real. In both situations, a number of false hopes pocked the path of escape. Fred has decided that he will *never* be totally beyond the reach of his attacker—at least not in this life. Even though it has now been five years since he has yielded to the bottle's seductions, he is still aware of the tempter's army of demons breathing down his neck occasionally.

As you and I consider our *deliverance* from bondage, it is not difficult to see a variety of parallels to the story of Israel's rescue. Though we have been *set free* from our slavery to sin that once dominated our lives, *there is a sense* in which we are not yet totally free. Though we have been released from his dungeon with leg-irons that once confined us, Satan has not surrendered. Though we are on the highway to Heaven, Satan's army is very much *in pursuit.* We never know from which side or through what medium the next attack will come. All we know is that it *will* come.

God promises, though, that the time for our need to run will end. Just as Pharaoh's army was destroyed in the sea, so also, Satan will finally come to an end. As the horse and his rider were "thrown into the sea," a time will come when death and hades will be thrown into a lake of fire. When that time comes, we will finally be free. Satan's pursuit of us will end. Meanwhile, Christians, the world over, run and dodge and are wounded occasionally by Satan's sniper fire as they eagerly await that day when the enemy will be no more.

Seed Thoughts

1. Did the Israelites fall immediately into slavery after Joseph's death?

The Bible conveys the idea that the Israelites did not immediately fall into disfavor. Rather, it "it came to pass in process of time."

2. What was it *specifically* that prompted God to respond to the need of the Israelites?

He heard their cries of distress and had "respect" for them.

3. Whom did God send to free the Israelites from their slavery?

God sent Moses and Aaron to deliver them.

4. What was the first step Moses and Aaron took in their attempt to deliver the Israelites from Slavery?

As messengers of God, Moses and Aaron first requested that Pharaoh allow the Israelites to go into the wilderness to worship their God.

5. What was Pharaoh's response to this request?

Pharaoh posed the question, "Who is the LORD that I should obey his voice?" (In other words, "Who is the Lord to tell me what to do?")

1. Did the Israelites fall immediately into slavery after Joseph's death?

2. What was it *specifically* that prompted God to respond to the need of the Israelites?

3. Whom did God send to free the Israelites from their slavery?

4. What was the first step Moses and Aaron took in their attempt to deliver the Israelites from Slavery?

5. What was Pharaoh's response to this request?

6. Did Pharaoh let the Israelites go into the wilderness to worship their God? Why?

7. What incentive did God supply to convince Pharaoh that it would be to his advantage to give the Israelites their freedom?

8. What was the nature of the final plague that finally convinced Pharaoh that Egypt would be better off without the Israelites in the land?

9. What kinds of things were the Israelites allowed to take with them when they left Egypt?

10. At what point did the Israelites know *for sure* that they were finally free?

(Continued next page)

The Bible conveys the idea that the Israelites did not immediately fall into disfavor. Rather, it "it came to pass in process of time."

He heard their cries of distress and had "respect" for them.

God sent Moses and Aaron to deliver them.

As messengers of God, Moses and Aaron first requested that Pharaoh allow the Israelites to go into the wilderness to worship their God.

Pharaoh posed the question, "Who is the LORD that I should obey his voice?" (In other words, "Who is the Lord to tell me what to do?"

No. Pharaoh did not let the Israelites go to worship? He did not know Moses' God, so consequently, he did not see a reason to comply with his demands.

God brought plagues upon the land of Egypt and upon her people until Pharaoh's stubborn will was broken.

Every firstborn offspring in Egypt died-- both animal and human.

They were allowed to take virtually everything they wished to take.

The Israelites knew for sure that they were free when the Egyptian army was destroyed in the sea.

6. Did Pharaoh let the Israelites go into the wilderness to worship their God? Why?

No. Pharaoh did not let the Israelites go to worship? He did not know Moses' God, so consequently, he did not see a reason to comply with his demands.

7. What incentive did God supply to convince Pharaoh that it would be to his advantage to give the Israelites their freedom?

God brought plagues upon the land of Egypt and upon her people until Pharaoh's stubborn will was broken.

8. What was the nature of the final plague that finally convinced Pharaoh that Egypt would be better off without the Israelites in the land?

Every firstborn offspring in Egypt died-- both animal and human.

9. What kinds of things were the Israelites allowed to take with them when they left Egypt?

They were allowed to take virtually everything they wished to take.

10. At what point did the Israelites know *for sure* that they were finally free?

The Israelites knew for sure that they were free when the Egyptian army was destroyed in the sea.

What God Expects

7 am the Lord thy God, which brought thee out of the land of Egypt, from the house of bondage.

7 Thou shalt have none other gods before me.

8 Thou shalt not make thee any graven image, or any likeness of any thing that is in heaven above, or that is in the earth beneath, or that is in the waters beneath the earth:

Deut. 5:6-14a, 16-21

9 Thou shalt not bow down thyself unto them, nor serve them: for I the Lord am a jealous God, visiting the iniquity of the fathers upon the children unto the third and fourth generation of them that hate me.

10 And shewing mercy unto thousands of them that love me and keep my commandments.

11 Thou shalt not take the name of the Lord thy God in vain: for the Lord will not hold him guiltless that taketh his name in vain.

12 Keep the sabbath day to sanctify it, as the Lord thy God hath commanded thee.

13 Six days thou shalt labour, and do all thy work.

14 But the seventh day is the sabbath of the Lord thy God: in it thou shalt not do any work . . . .

16 Honour thy father and thy mother, as the Lord commanded thee; that thy days may be prolonged, and that it may go well with thee, in the land which the Lord thy God giveth thee.

17 Thou shalt not kill.

18 Neither shalt thou commit adultery.

19 Neither shalt thou steal.

20 Neither shalt thou bear false witness against thy neighbour.

21 Neither shalt thou desire thy neighbour's wife, neither shalt thou covet thy neighbour's house, his field, or his manservant or his maidservant, his ox, or his ass, or any thing that is thy neighbour's.

Memory Selection
Deuteronomy 5:6-7

Background Scripture
Deuteronomy 5:1-21

Devotional Reading
Isaiah 49:1-6

Printed Scripture
Deut. 5:6-14a, 16-21

Teacher's Target

Lesson purpose: *To reexamine the Ten Commandments and to reflect on their importance to God's people today.*

The Ten Commandments became so formative to the identity of the Israelites that these profound rules were later called "The Ten Words." Of course God will reveal Himself through many other "words"; and "the Law" will come to refer especially to the first five books of the Old Testament. Yet the Ten Commandments are the foundation of all the rest of these words.

Yet many people in the modern age find rules burdensome. In fact, the apostle Paul himself would later point out inadequacies in "the Law" when people would ask more of it than God intended. Lead your class not only to appreciate each of these "Ten Words," but *the* Word, Jesus Himself, who would come to "fulfill the law" (Matt. 5:17).

Lesson Introduction

When the Israelites escaped from Egypt they were accompanied by the descendants of a "mixed multitude" whose fate had become entwined with the descendants of Abraham (Exod. 12:38). How could a people of such diversity be kept together in the wilderness awaiting them after the exodus? (For that matter, how can such a diverse people as those in the United States bind themselves together in a common cause?)

The answer given in the book of Deuteronomy is: *the Law.* The people could be welded into one nation only by following one set of rules. The Ten Commandments were the foundation of this Law. They became not only Israel's "constitution," but basic to the laws of countless societies since. Far from being a burden, observing such foundational principles is basic to human freedom even today.

Teaching Outline	Daily Bible Readings
I. Obligations to God—6-14a	**Mon.** Deuteronomy 5:1-10
A. Have no other gods, 6-7	*No Other God*
B. Make no images, 8-10	**Tue.** Deuteronomy 5:11-15
C. Don't swear, 11	*Observe the Sabbath*
D. Keep a day for God, 12-14a	**Wed.** Deuteronomy 5:16-21
II. Obligations to People—16-21	*Honor Your Parents*
A. Honor your parents, 16	**Thu.** Deuteronomy 6:1-9
B. Don't murder, 17	*Teach Your Children*
C. Don't commit adultery, 18	**Fri.** Deuteronomy 6:20-25
D. Don't steal, 19	*When Your Children Ask...*
E. Don't lie, 20	**Sat.** Matthew 22:34-40
F. Don't covet, 21	*The Greatest Commandment*
	Sun. Isaiah 49:1-6
	A Light to the Nations

Verse by Verse

I. Obligations to God—6-14a

A. Have no other gods, 6-7

6 I am the LORD thy God, which brought thee out of the land of Egypt, from the house of bondage.

7 Thou shalt have none other gods before me.

If the Ten Commandments were the foundation of God's relationship with His people as He forged them into a new nation, this First Commandment is the foundation of the other nine. The Israelites will confront other people who disapprove of lying and stealing, and who honor their parents; but the concept that there is only One God will be unique.

No wonder later Jews would begin each morning by reciting the "Shemah" (pronounced she-*mah*; it's the first word of this commandment)—"Hear O Israel, the Lord thy God is one God." Even today, this First Commandment should be a reminder that God alone—not wealth, nor our own self-will, nor other people, nor other causes—is worthy of our primary allegiance.

B. Make no images, 8-10

8 Thou shalt not make thee any graven image, or any likeness of any thing that is in heaven above, or that is in the earth beneath, or that is in the waters beneath the earth:

9 Thou shalt not bow down thyself unto them, nor serve them: for I the LORD am a jealous God, visiting the iniquity of the fathers upon the children unto the third and fourth generation of them that hate me.

10 And shewing mercy unto thousands of them that love me and keep my commandments.

Closely related to the First Commandment, the Second safeguards the fact that the One God is invisible. To reduce the God who is everywhere-present to a sculptured or carved representation is not only impossible; it tempts people to worship the representation itself, as in idolatry.

This commandment would later be the basis of opposition to artists such as Michelangelo painting representations of God like that in "The Creation," on the ceiling of the Sistine Chapel in Rome. Even later, the Puritans would object to the statues of Christ and the apostles in Roman Catholic cathedrals. And in America, some strict Protestants would even object to drawings of Jesus in children's Sunday School literature.

C. Don't swear, 11

11 Thou shalt not take the name of the LORD thy God in vain: for the

LORD will not hold him guiltless that taketh his name in vain.

Again, this seemingly straightforward commandment would create surprising conflict when believers tried to practice it consistently. Its most obvious meaning is to forbid using God's name "in vain" by cursing. Later, pious Jews would question whether there is *any* really "worthy" way to use God's name, so they would not even a pronounce the name "Yahweh." Still later, some Christians would wonder whether the commandment also forbids "swearing" in a court of law—affirming that only the truth will be told, "so help me God."

Jesus had this commandment in mind when he warned, in the Sermon on the Mount, against the loose use of God's name (Matt. 5:34-37). Yet the apostle John affirmed the truth of the Revelation by swearing "by him that liveth for ever and ever (Rev. 10:6). The primary meaning of the commandment, however, is clear: we should not use God's name carelessly or loosely.

D. Keep a day for God, 12-14a

12 Keep the sabbath day to sanctify it, as the LORD thy God hath commanded thee.

13 Six days thou shalt labour, and do all thy work.

14 But the seventh day is the sabbath of the LORD thy God: in it thou shalt not do any work . . . .

To "sanctify" something is to set it apart or designate it as holy. Here, this Fourth Commandment is based on Israel's need to set apart a day for the specific purpose of remembering that it was God's mighty hand that rescued the people from Egyptian slavery. In the other primary listing of the Ten Commandments, Exodus 21, keeping the Sabbath is also said to be based on the Creation, when God "rested" from (ceased) His work of creation.

Christians have often debated whether Sunday is a "Christian" Sabbath. The earliest Christians met on "the first day of the week" (Acts 20:7), but there is no evidence that they refrained from working on that day. Many early Christians, being Jews, continued to keep the Sabbath even after converting. The testimony of experience is that people flourish both spiritually and physically when they set aside at least a part of one day each week to tend specifically to worshiping God and learning more of His will and ways.

II. Obligations to People—16-21
A. Honor your parents, 16

16 Honour thy father and thy mother, as the LORD commanded thee; that thy days may be prolonged, and that it may go well with thee, in the land which the LORD thy God giveth thee.

The thrust of the Fifth Commandment is better observed today in the Orient, where old age is respected, than in "Christian" America. Yet this commandment was still important for the apostle Paul, who repeated it as a Christian principle in Ephesians 6:2-3. Paul noted that this is "the first commandment with promise," apparently referring to the promise that (other things being equal) life will go well for those who observe this recognition that godly parents are to be respected for their wisdom and the sacrifices they make for their children.

B. Don't murder, 17

17 Thou shalt not kill.

Some observers have asked whether this commandment strikes a discordant note with the many bloody Old Testament battles in which God's people were ordered to slay their enemies; and with the fact that God ordered capital punishment for some crimes in Old Testament times. Actually, the Hebrew word *ratsach* is used here, meaning "murder" as opposed to several other words meaning "kill" or "slay." This is made clear in the New International Version's translation of this Sixth Commandment: "Thou shalt not murder."

C. Don't commit adultery, 18

18 Neither shalt thou commit adultery.

The Seventh Commandment is perhaps violated with greater abandon than any other in our society. Faithlessness to the marriage vow has become commonplace in media portrayals of "normal" human relationships. The seriousness with which God views this commandment, however, is underscored in the Bible's portrayal of God's people as His bride. If we are careless about observing this commandment, we have good cause to question our commitment to keeping God's bride pure and faithful as well.

D. Don't steal, 19

19 Neither shalt thou steal.

Even secular societies recognize that communities cannot flourish if people do not respect the property of others as off-limits.

E. Don't lie, 20

20 Neither shalt thou bear false witness against thy neighbour.

Again, not only biblical people but all others can affirm that telling the truth is essential to the operation of any society, not only a way to please God.

F. Don't covet, 21

21 Neither shalt thou desire thy neighbour's wife, neither shalt thou covet thy neighbour's house, his field, or his manservant or his maidservant, his ox, or his ass, or any thing that is thy neighbour's.

In the Tenth Commandment, God moves beyond behavior to assert His domain over the human heart and mind. Many a violation of the Seventh Commandment could have been prevented by saying No earlier to covetousness and lust.

Evangelistic Emphasis

It is not unusual to hear someone echo the sentiment, *"This is the '90s! We're not restricted by those same rules that imprisoned our parents."* Whereas such comments were first heard to acknowledge the evolution of clothing styles and customs (i.e., *skirt lengths and heel heights*), they now often reach into the realms of "propriety" and even "morality." By some process of reasoning, the biblical statements establishing the boundaries of good and evil are often perceived as having been directed toward generations of an ancient past *only*. Since "times have changed," it is argued, "certainly those laws could not apply to those of us who live in these more sophisticated times."

Because this trend in society's thinking has thoroughly permeated the Church, the moral behavior of active Christians sometimes strays far beyond the guidelines of God's laws in matters of sexuality, ethics, financial integrity, civil law and family covenants without the least bit of conscience intervention. It is assumed that "That was then, and this is now!"

As Moses addressed the people in this setting recorded in our text, he made it very clear to his listening congregation, "God said it to us. God's covenant is with us. His words cannot be conveniently consigned to some ancient past."

● ● ● ● ● ● ● ● ●

Memory Selection

I am the LORD thy God, which brought thee out of the land of Egypt, from the house of bondage. Thou shalt have none other gods before me.—*Deuteronomy 5:6*

"What right does God have to try to tell me how to live my life?!" Those words rang out with a shock that caught me off guard. I was aware of myself suddenly shrinking back from this 14-year-old, subconsciously expecting lightning to strike at any moment.

"How could *even this kid* be so impious?" I gasped silently. "Hasn't he been taught anything?"

Of course, our God knew before He gave the Law that there would be those who would question its validity. He knew that some would flinch at his directives that attempted to steer them away from trouble and self-destruction. Because God knew this, He alerted them to his good will toward them by reminding them of how He delivered them from slavery. *As their Redeemer, then,* he gives them rules that will guide them to full and profitable lives.

Weekday Problems

Bill and Susan start their day at 4 a.m. every day of the week. Bill drives from their home in Modesto, California, to San Jose every morning. No, he is not one of Silicon Valley's eggheads transforming how America works via computers. Bill manages a Denny's franchise. Though he works seven days each week, he lives in Modesto because of the more affordable housing available. The two-hour drive each morning and evening contributes significantly to the length of his normal workday schedule. Though Susan works only five days each week and commutes a shorter distance (one hour and a half to Fresno), life seems no less hectic for her. The bulk of the parenting responsibilities and the housekeeping chores fall on her. Though they have three children in elementary school, neither Bill nor Susan is satisfied with the perpetual rush their routine of life has come to assume. They both try to give their children "quality time," but there is a haunting voice whispering perpetually to them that their children need *more* of their time.

* Ceremonial questions aside pertaining to the keeping of the Sabbath, what does the fourth commandment have to say to our generation, and to Bill and Susan in particular?

* What is the basic purpose of the Sabbath Law *as it is stated*? How does that purpose still apply today? Or, does it?

* What possible changes could Bill and Susan make to recoup the family life they suspect they are missing?

Another Ancient Law Code

Compare and contrast with the Ten Commandments these excerpts from the Law Code of Hammurabi, from 18th-century Babylon (about the time of Abraham, according to some scholars).

If a citizen . . . has borne false witness . . . and if that case is one warranting the death penalty, that citizen shall be put to death.

If a citizen has stolen property of the temple or of the crown, that man shall die, and whosoever receives the stolen goods from his hand shall die.

If the wife of a citizen is taken cohabiting with another male, they shall both be bound and cast into the water.

If a citizen has destroyed the eye of one of citizen status, they shall destroy his eye.

This Lesson in Your Life

I live in a large farming community of 228,000 with a metropolitan area reaching 350,000. Our total economy is agriculture based—canneries, granaries, and other food-production industries. Our town is surrounded by thousands of acres of farmland. I tell you this, because it is said that such communities are the "best places to raise a family."

Tuesday morning, while making a trip to the Post Office, my attention was caught by the headline of the local newspaper, *"Drive-by Kills Student, Injures 2."* A 15-year-old student was gunned down in front of one of the high schools. I was thankful that my 15-year-old daughter goes to a different high school.

That was not the only such story in Tuesday's paper. Buying and paging through the paper I learned that a 19-year-old person in a small neighboring community was convicted of murdering an 18-year-old "friend." The murder was committed to gain acceptance into the Aryan Brotherhood Chapter 666 *"devil-worshipers."* Also, seven youths, ages 9 to 15were arrested for doing $35,000 worth of vandalism to a local church facility. A 16-year-old was arrested for stabbing his 14-year-old brother. Finally, two 16-year-old boys were arrested for killing a man driving slowly through their neighborhood. They claimed that they thought he was setting up a "drive-by shooting." Apparently, they shot out of fear. Actually, he was driving slowly in order to look for a friend's house.

These were one Tuesday's news stories in one farming town. I can't even imagine how much worse it must be in a large city like York or Chicago or Los Angeles. The world is going insane! Where will it all end? In 1987 a Justice Department study revealed the prediction that *eight out of 10* Americans will be victims of violent crime in their lifetimes.

The problem we are facing as a society is not a "minor social cold." Rather, as one commentator worded it, we as a nation are committing "moral suicide." The words of Judges 17:6 perhaps aptly describe us: *"Every man did that which was right in his own eyes."* Or as Rick Atchley cautioned, "What is truly alarming is that . . . we are approaching the logical end of an every-person-for-himself system of defining morality. We've almost completely lost a shared understanding of what is right. We're not just breaking laws in America anymore; we are denying that anybody has a right to make laws. The only absolute is that everything . . . is relative."

It was for such a time as this that God delivered his Decalogue. He made no attempt to "micro-manage" the multitude of choices of our lives. Instead, our God put into concrete form a few basic principles of right living. Most Christians know them as the "Ten Commandments." Those commandments were never intended to serve as our "savior" or the "means by which we might qualify to be saved." Rather, those commandments were given to provide basic order to life. I don't know about your home town, but my town very much needs such order.

Seed Thoughts

1. Are we listening to live action or a retelling of an earlier event as the Ten Commandments are recited in Deuteronomy 5?

Moses is reminding the people of what they as a nation witnessed 40 years earlier.

2. What is the significance of Moses words, *"The LORD made not this covenant with our fathers, but with us, even us, who are all of us here alive this day."*?

It was important that Israel know that God made the covenant with them, not just with their forefathers.

3. How can Moses speak to these people as though they were all present at the giving of the Law at Horeb 40 years earlier? Were they all there?

In Moses realm of thought, they were. Some witnessed the event as children. Others were present "in the loins of their fathers "(representatively).

4. On what premise did God presume to hand down commandments to these people, expecting them to obey them?

He is the God who not only created them and cares for them (which is left unstated at this point), but who also rescued them out of slavery.

5. Does the wording of the first commandment indicate that it is all right for the Israelites to worship other gods so long as they put the Lord first?

Definitely not. A better reading would perhaps be, "You shall have no other gods *besides* me."

1. Are we listening to live action or a retelling of an earlier event as the Ten Commandments are recited in Deuteronomy 5?

2. What is the significance of Moses words, *"The LORD made not this covenant with our fathers, but with us, even us, who are all of us here alive this day."*?

3. How can Moses speak to these people as though they were all present at the giving of the Law at Horeb 40 years earlier? Were they all there?

4. On what premise did God presume to hand down commandments to these people, expecting them to obey them?

5. Does the wording of the first commandment indicate that it is all right for the Israelites to worship other gods so long as they put the Lord first?

6. Does the second commandment effectively forbid all artistry of the sculptor?

7. How can one be guilty of "taking the Lord's name in vain" besides "cursing"?

8. True or False: The Sabbath Law applied only to the native Israelite, so it was all right for him to hire an alien to do all the work on the Sabbath.

9. True or False: The seventh commandment, "Neither shalt thou commit adultery" does not apply if it involves "two consenting adults."

10. Is it true that, whereas the New Covenant brought by Jesus governs the heart, the Ten Commandments spoke only to "outward conduct?"

(Continued next page)

Moses is reminding the people of what they as a nation witnessed 40 years earlier.

It was important that Israel know that God made the covenant with them, not just with their forefathers.

In Moses realm of thought, they were. Some witnessed the event as children. Others were present "in the loins of their fathers" (representatively).

He is the God who not only created them and cares for them (which is left unstated at this point), but who also rescued them out of slavery.

Definitely not. A better reading would perhaps be, "You shall have no other gods *besides* me."

Apparently not. Moses commanded the making of a "fiery serpent" (Num. 21:8) and there were a variety of sculptures related to the Tabernacle and Temple (i.e. Num. 7:89).

One chief way the Lord's name is "taken in vain" is through empty vows—those made without serious intent to keep them.

False. The commandment applied also to the menservant, maidservant, ox, ass, cattle, and even the "stranger" (alien).

False. Leviticus 18 and 20 spell out a long list of prohibitions involving "consenting adults," and Jesus confirmed this Law as binding (Matt. 1918).

Not true. The 10th commandment forbids one to "desire" ("covet", NIV) any thing that is his neighbor's.

6. Does the second commandment effectively forbid all artistry of the sculptor?

Apparently not. Moses commanded the making of a "fiery serpent" (Num. 21:8) and there were a variety of sculptures related to the Tabernacle and Temple (i.e. Num. 7:89).

7. How can one be guilty of "taking the Lord's name in vain" besides "cursing"?

One chief way the Lord's name is "taken in vain" is through empty vows—those made without serious intent to keep them.

8. True or False: The Sabbath Law applied only to the native Israelite, so it was all right for him to hire an alien to do all the work on the Sabbath.

False. The commandment applied also to the menservant, maidservant, ox, ass, cattle, and even the "stranger" (alien).

9. True or False: The seventh commandment, "Neither shalt thou commit adultery" does not apply if it involves "two consenting adults."

False. Leviticus 18 and 20 spell out a long list of prohibitions involving "consenting adults," and Jesus confirmed this Law as binding (Matt. 1918).

10. Is it true that, whereas the New Covenant brought by Jesus governs the heart, the Ten Commandments spoke only to "outward conduct?"

Not true. The 10th commandment forbids one to "desire" ("covet", NIV) any thing that is his neighbor's.

Remembering What God Has Done

*A*nd it came to pass, when all the people were clean passed over Jordan, that the LORD spake unto Joshua, saying,

2 Take you twelve men out of the people, out of every tribe a man,

3 And command ye them, saying, Take you hence out of the midst of Jordan, out of the place where the priests' feet stood firm, twelve stones, and ye shall carry them over with you, and leave them in the lodging place, where ye shall lodge this night.

8 And the children of Israel did so as Joshua commanded, and took up twelve stones out of the midst of Jordan, as the LORD spake unto Joshua, according to the number of the tribes of the children of Israel, and carried them over with them unto the place where they lodged, and laid them down there.

10 For the priests which bare the ark stood in the midst of Jordan, until every thing was finished that the LORD commanded Joshua to speak unto the people, according to all that Moses commanded Joshua: and the people hasted and passed over.

11 And it came to pass, when all the people were clean passed over, that the ark of the LORD passed over, and the priests, in the presence of the people.

Joshua 4:1-3, 8, 10-11, 20-24

20 And those twelve stones, which they took out of Jordan, did Joshua pitch in Gilgal.

21 And he spake unto the children of Israel, saying, When your children shall ask their fathers in time to come, saying, What mean these stones?

22 Then ye shall let your children know, saying, Israel came over this Jordan on dry land.

23 For the LORD your God dried up the waters of Jordan from before you, until ye were passed over, as the LORD your God did to the Red sea, which he dried up from before us, until we were gone over:

24 That all the people of the earth might know the hand of the LORD, that it is mighty: that ye might fear the LORD your God forever.

Memory Selection
Joshua 4:21-22

Background Scripture
Joshua 3:7–4:24

Devotional Reading
Psalm 78:1-8

Printed Scripture
Joshua 4:1-3, 8,
10-11, 20-24

Teacher's Target

Lesson purpose: *To show how Israel's commemoration of the exodus at the Jordan River can inspire us to pass along to the next generation the values of our own spiritual journey.*

During 40 years of wandering in the wilderness after leaving Egypt, the Israelites traveled in tribes and clans and families. Now, on the verge of entering the Promised Land, it is important to think about handing along the towering experience of the exodus to the next generation. Twelve stones are erected as a memorial of the rescue of the 12 tribes from slavery.

Group members may enjoy sharing what memorials of their own religious experience mean to them. Sometimes youth fail to appreciate the significance of events such as baptism, the Lord's Supper, and familiar patterns of worship. Only if adults are in touch with the meaning of such practices can they answer such questions as Israel's children asked: "What mean these stones" (Josh. 4:21).

Lesson Introduction

Moses, the mighty leader of Israel for so long, is dead. His right-hand man Joshua, better suited to lead the people in the battles ahead, has taken command. Approaching Canaan from the west, Joshua sends spies across the Jordan River to the city of Jericho. They find the people trembling in fear of the approaching armies of Israel.

Joshua tells the people to "sanctify" themselves (3:5), calling for invisible cleansing to prepare them for the visible miracle God will perform the next day. Circumcision is performed on the uncircumcised males. The next day, the waters of the Jordan part. Since most of those who had left Egypt 40 years earlier died because of their rebellion and unbelief, the parting of the Jordan confirmed the stories of the exodus to the new generation. Memorializing the event with a monument of stones will in turn be reassuring to later generations of Israelites. They will testify to an important part of the history of the Chosen People.

Teaching Outline	Daily Bible Readings
I. Memorial in Stone—1-3, 8	**Mon.** Hear the Words of the Lord *Joshua 3:7-13*
A. All tribes represented, 1-2	**Tue.** A Memorial Forever *Joshua 3:14–4:9*
B. Stones from holy ground, 3, 8	**Wed.** The Lord Exalted Joshua *Joshua 4:10-24*
II. Ministry of Priests—10-11	**Thu.** The Conquest of Jericho Begins *Joshua 6:1-7*
A. Standing by to intercede, 10	**Fri.** The Walls Come Tumbling Down *Joshua 6:12-25*
B. Bearing the Ark of the Covenant, 11	**Sat.** God's Covenant Transgressed *Joshua 7:1-9*
III. Meaning Passed Along—20-24	**Sun.** That Others May Know *Psalm 78:1-8*
A. First camp, 20	
B. Testimony of the stones, 21-24	

Verse by Verse

I. Memorial in Stone—1-4, 8
A. All tribes represented, 1-2

1 And it came to pass, when all the people were clean passed over Jordan, that the LORD spake unto Joshua, saying,

2 Take you twelve men out of the people, out of every tribe a man,

The descendants of Jacob's sons had apparently maintained their identity during more than 400 years of Egyptian captivity. Only Joseph, the next to youngest son, lacked a people bearing his name. Instead, his sons Ephraim and Manasseh each headed a half-tribe (See Gen. 46:5-26). Now, as the conquest of the Promised Land begins, it is important to select a representative of each tribe to remind the people that God is fulfilling His promise to Father Abraham that his descendants would inherit the land (see Gen. 35:11-12).

The number twelve, standing for the tribes of Israel, will continue to have symbolic significance. The followers of Christ will be led by twelve apostles—symbolically blending God's original chosen people with Gentiles in the new "Israel of God" (Gal. 6:16). The solidarity of this redefined tribal system is even affirmed in John's vision of the saved in Revelation 7:4-8).

B. Stones from holy ground, 3, 8

3 And command ye them, saying, Take you hence out of the midst of Jordan, out of the place where the priests' feet stood firm, twelve stones, and ye shall carry them over with you, and leave them in the lodging place, where ye shall lodge this night.

8 And the children of Israel did so as Joshua commanded, and took up twelve stones out of the midst of Jordan, as the LORD spake unto Joshua, according to the number of the tribes of the children of Israel, and carried them over with them unto the place where they lodged, and laid them down there.

As long as the priests stood in the midst of Jordan, the waters were held back—exposing the stones the twelve representatives were to carry to Gilgal, "the place where they lodged" (4:19). It must have been emotional to watch the parade of men, each bearing a stone representing each tribe in the watching multitude.

(The way verse 9 is translated in several versions indicates that stones were also set up in the middle of the river Jordan, possibly implying two monuments. The difficulty with this is that a river monument of only twelve stones would have been covered with water when the water returned to its normal bed. The difficulty probably stems from a mis-copying of two Hebrew letters that look very much alike. The NIV solves the difficulty by following an older version that refers to stones "that *had been* in the midst of Jordan.")

II. Ministry of Priests—10-11
A. Standing by to intercede, 10

10 For the priests which bare the ark stood in the midst of Jordan, until every thing was finished that the LORD commanded Joshua to speak unto the people, according to all that Moses commanded Joshua: and the people hasted and passed over.

Israel's priesthood, the "sons of Aaron," Moses' brother, had been installed shortly after the exodus from Egypt. They had been charged with bearing all through the wilderness the Ark of the Covenant that contained The Ten Commandments, a bowl of manna, and Aaron's rod. They also officiated at the Old Covenanted sacrifices, standing as intermediaries between the people and God.

Now, at the momentous entry into Canaan, God signals that the role of the priests will still be prominent. As representatives of the holy God, even their very presence in the stream causes, as it were, a "dam" that holds back the waters even though it was at flood stage and out of its banks (vs. 18). Some archeologists believe they have discovered evidence of an earthquake at about

this time that may have caused a "natural" but temporary dam. The point made by the author of Joshua, however, does not depend on "natural" evidence. He is concerned that readers know that it is the very Creator of the waters Himself who is responsible for the entry of His people into Canaan; and that His priests are His authorized mediators presiding at the event.

B. Bearing the Ark of the Covenant, 11

11 And it came to pass, when all the people were clean passed over, that the ark of the LORD passed over, and the priests, in the presence of the people.

After the last of the general population hurried across on the dry bed of the Jordan, the priests follow, with the ark. The soberness of the situation is indicated by the fact that instead of spreading in all directions after the crossing, the people stand solemnly watching first the troop of men carrying the stones, then the priests carrying the Ark of the Covenant.

III. Meaning Passed Along—20-24
A. The first camp, 20

20 And those twelve stones, which they took out of Jordan, did Joshua pitch in Gilgal.

The name "Gilgal" seems to be related to a Hebrew word for "roll." Joshua 5:9 says the place was given the name at the great circumcision ceremony, when God "rolled away the reproach of Egypt" or sanctified the people for the occupation of the land.

B. Testimony of the stones, 21-24

21 And he spake unto the children of Israel, saying, When your children shall ask their fathers in time to come, saying, What mean these stones?

22 Then ye shall let your children know, saying, Israel came over this Jordan on dry land.

23 For the Lord your God dried up the waters of Jordan from before you, until ye were passed over, as the Lord your God did to the Red sea, which he dried up from before us, until we were gone over:

24 That all the people of the earth might know the hand of the Lord, that it is mighty: that ye might fear the Lord your God for ever.

The Jewish faith has always been related closely to the family system. Generations of Israelites have recited their sacred history at family ceremonies at in which children ask question equivalent to "What do these stones mean?" The answer is far more than a history lesson. Reciting the story honors God for delivering the people from Egypt, protecting them through their wandering exile in the wilderness, and ushering them into the Promised Land.

Even more, the stones and the rituals that would follow are testimony to non-Jews as well. The Gilgal memorial was still standing when the book of Joshua was composed (vs. 9b). As Canaanites passed by the stone would "witness" to them the same message the record of the event tells us: God is with these people.

As "the new Israel," it is equally important for Christian families and fellowships to provide times when God's mighty acts are memorialized and celebrated. The New Testament speaks of this process as "traditioning," using a word that literally means "handing down." Although it warns against the "traditions of men," the Bible urges believers to stand firm in the "handing down" (*paradosis* or tradition) of the true faith (2 Thess. 2:15). It is in this way that "the fear of the Lord" is perpetuated "forever."

Evangelistic Emphasis

Most of us do not have a "photographic memory," remembering everything we read and experience. Though we tell ourselves, "this is something I'll never forget," the chances are better than even that we will. Deep down, we know that. That's why we take notes in class and hide the combination to our locker in a safe place. That's why we carry our camera with us on vacation. That's why we make sure we've hired one of the best photographers in town to shoot our daughter's wedding. We want to preserve the memories.

Class notes are never as complete as "perfect recall" would be, but they serve well to pompt our less-than-perfect memory in valuable ways. Pictures from our summer vacation or our daughter's wedding do not provide "an instant replay" of the experience, but they can come close. In much the same way, we have built into our faith walk "notes," "pictures" and "monuments" to remind us of our experiences with God.

The Israelites erected a monument of stones to remind them of God's awesome intervention into their lives, parting the waters of the Jordan. We erect a Cross on our steeple or at the front of our sanctuary to remind us of that Friday when He intervened for us. As those stones reminded each young child of the place of God in his life, baptism and the Eucharist remind each Christian.

• • • • • • • • • •

Memory Selection

And he spake unto the children of Israel, saying, When your children shall ask their fathers in time to come, saying, What mean these stones? Then ye shall let your children know, saying, Israel came over this Jordan on dry land.—*Joshua 4:21-22*

Henry and Elvira are just beginning their exciting adventure as parents. Their son was born just two weeks ago. They have vacillated between excitement and terror ever since they learned that a child was "on the way." Just now, they are beginning to come down out of the clouds and feel like real parents. As Christians, what Elvira and Henry fear the most is that they will fail to instill adequately faith into the heart of this little one. Their questions are much the same as most other Christian parents

"When is the right time to teach?"

"How much should I try to indoctrinate?"

"What if I drive them away with too much preaching?"

Two clues that Henry and Elvira might gain from this lesson (as well as a variety of other Scriptures) is, <u>first</u>, *the best time to teach is when they ask*. <u>Second</u>, it is important to *plan ahead for occasions that will prompt them to inquire*.

36

Weekday Problems

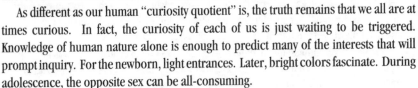

Curiosity is an interesting human component. Some people seem *naturally* to have more of it than others do. One child will ask questions with incredible speed, while another child sits in what seems to be silent disinterest. One child will destroy every one of his toys, taking each apart to see how it works. His playmate shows no interest in *how* it works at all. He is more concerned that it does work.

As different as our human "curiosity quotient" is, the truth remains that we all are at times curious. In fact, the curiosity of each of us is just waiting to be triggered. Knowledge of human nature alone is enough to predict many of the interests that will prompt inquiry. For the newborn, light entrances. Later, bright colors fascinate. During adolescence, the opposite sex can be all-consuming.

* How can we capitalize on the natural curiosity of developing children to introduce them to God?

* How can we build into our lives "monuments" that will prompt questions of curiosity (and so, opportunity for faith to be taught)? Give some examples of such monuments.

* How can we utilize such "monuments" to trigger the curiosity of our unbelieving friends?

Have I Got a Proposal for You!

Boy: Why won't you marry me? Is there someone else?
Girl: There must be.

* * *

Lynn: Jim proposed to me last night!
Friend: Doesn't he do it nicely?!

* * *

Joe: What would you say if I asked you to be my wife?
Flo: Nothing. I can't talk and laugh at the same time.

* * *

Mae: I've been asked to get married lots of times.
Rae: Who asked you?
Mae: Mom and Dad. *Lots* of times.

This Lesson in Your Life

Freda Brandt began university life just three weeks ago. It was both exciting and scary as she drove down that long country lane that leads from the farm house where she grew up to the highway that offers promises of other worlds. Her heart pounded and tears flowed as she turned onto the highway, heading east toward Duke University.

In addition to all of her clothes and dorm-life necessities, Freda also carried with her a suitcase full of memories—tokens of affection that had blessed her growing years. In spite how wonderful Freda knew her family was, she never quite adjusted to their deep-seated German heritage. At least, that was the explanation her mother gave to her one night when she found her sobbing into her pillow, thinking her parents did not love her. She was only 10 years old then.

She had never thought much about it when she was little, because there was nothing with which to compare her family. As Freda got older, however, she saw first-hand the open displays of affection in her friends' homes. An emptiness began to form in her soul. Why was her home not like that? Freda could never remember her dad ever telling her that he loved her. She could not remember the last time her mother wiped away a tear. Never had she been given hugs of affection or kisses good night. Could it be that *they had not wanted her and only tolerated her in their home?* The question began as an occasional, quiet whisper, but gradually grew to dominate her life as a constant scream.

That night, though, Freda's mother explained how, though both she and her father wanted very much to express love to their children, they had never learned how. As she talked, Freda began to notice a tear in her mother's eye—ever so slightly. Then her mother gave her a gift that seemed nonsense at the time, but has come to be one of the greatest treasures of her life. She suggested for Freda to look for other signs of love and tokens of affection to sustain her in the absence of hugs and kisses.

It was on that painful night when Freda was 10 that she began the collection of her suitcase treasures. Every item in it represented a moment of evidenced love. She began with the handkerchief her mother used that night to wipe away her tears. Then there was a western belt her dad proudly made to present to her on her 12th birthday. There was a ticket stub from her 14th summer when the whole family went together to Six Flags Over Georgia. A soda cap reminded her of her dad's good-natured response when she ran over the mailbox during her first driving lesson with him. He brought her the soda from the Exxon station to coax her to stop crying and try again.

Through the years, Freda has grown in understanding of her parent's deep love for her and the quietly subtle ways they more naturally show it. She still hopes to bless her own children (when she has them) with a healthy dose of touching, but for now, she treasures in her dorm room that tangible evidence of her parent's love.

I have no doubt that as Freda matures in life and in faith, she will come to look for those kinds of tangible evidence of God's love, too. Though He does not reach down and hug her, and though Freda's Lutheran heritage has not conditioned her to respond with an outpouring of emotion that seems to come so easily to some of her friends, Freda knows that God loves her. And she loves Him. As life matures for Freda, she will come to collect all kinds of tokens of those moments when He has been near. As she looks back over the years, she will see His fingerprints all over her life.

Seed Thoughts

1. What promise did God make to Joshua that he began immediately to fulfill?

God promised to "magnify" him in the eyes of the people.

2. What was the motive behind God magnifying Joshua in the eyes of the people?

He wanted to make sure that the people understood that He was with Joshua just as he had been with Moses.

3. What unusual instructions were the priests to be given?

The priests were to be told to carry the ark of the covenant into the waters of the Jordan River and stand still.

4. What happened when the priests carried out the instructions just as they had been told?

The water of the Jordan River stopped flowing up-stream from them, forming a wall of water. The water down-stream flowed on, draining the river dry.

5. How many men were to be chosen? From where? For what?

Twelve men were to be chosen, one from each tribe. They were to be asked to carry a stone from the middle of the Jordan River to the place they were to lodge.

1. What promise did God make to Joshua that he began immediately to fulfill?

2. What was the motive behind God magnifying Joshua in the eyes of the people?

3. What unusual instructions were the priests to be given?

4. What happened when the priests carried out the instructions just as they had been told?

5. How many men were to be chosen? From where? For What?

6. What was the *date* when this took place?.

7. What was the name of the place where the Israelites camped?

8. What was the *purpose* of the stones that had been carried? How were they used?

9. To what did Joshua compare the crossing of the Jordan River?

10. What was the ultimate goal of God, as stated by Joshua?

(Continued next page)

God promised to "magnify" him in the eyes of the people.

He wanted to make sure that the people understood that He was with Joshua just as he had been with Moses.

The priests were to be told to carry the ark of the covenant into the waters of the Jordan River and stand still.

The water of the Jordan River stopped flowing up-stream from them, forming a wall of water. The water down-stream flowed on, draining the river dry.

Twelve men were to be chosen, one from each tribe. They were to be asked to carry a stone from the middle of the Jordan River to the place they were to lodge.

It was the first day of the tenth month when these things took place.

The name of the place where the Israelites camped was Gilgal.

The stones were used to establish a monument (a marker) reminding the people of how God had been with them crossing the Jordan River.

Joshua compared the crossing of the Jordan river to their crossing of the Red Sea.

The ultimate goal of Joshua was to have the people fear (*respect/ reverence*) God forever.

6. What was the *date* when this took place?.

It was the first day of the tenth month when these things took place.

7. What was the name of the place where the Israelites camped?

The name of the place where the Israelites camped was Gilgal.

8. What was the *purpose* of the stones that had been carried? How were they used?

The stones were used to establish a monument (a marker) reminding the people of how God had been with them crossing the Jordan River.

9. To what did Joshua compare the crossing of the Jordan River?

Joshua compared the crossing of the Jordan river to their crossing of the Red Sea.

10. What was the ultimate goal of God, as stated by Joshua?

The ultimate goal of Joshua was to have the people fear (*respect/ reverence*) God forever.

Lesson 5

Cycle of Sin and Judgment

*A*nd the children of Israel did evil in the sight of the LORD, and served Baalim:

12 And they forsook the LORD God of their fathers, which brought them out of the land of Egypt, and followed other gods, of the gods of the people that were round about them, and bowed themselves unto them, and provoked the LORD to anger.

13 And they forsook the LORD, and served Baal and Ashtaroth.

14 And the anger of the LORD was hot against Israel, and he delivered them into the hands of their enemies round about, so that they could not any longer stand before their enemies.

15 Whithersoever they went out, the hand of the LORD was against them for evil, as the LORD had said, and as the LORD had sworn unto them: and they were greatly distressed.

16 Nevertheless the LORD raised up judges, which delivered them out of the hand of those that spoiled them.

17 And yet they would not hearken unto their judges, but they went a whoring after other gods, and bowed themselves unto them: they turned quickly out of the way which their fathers walked in, obeying the commandments of the LORD; but they did not so.

18 And when the LORD raised them up judges, then the LORD was with the judge, and delivered them out of the hand of their enemies all the days of the judge: for it repented the LORD because of their groanings by reason of them that oppressed them and vexed them.

19 And it came to pass, when the judge was dead, that they returned, and corrupted themselves more than their fathers, in following other gods to serve them, and to bow down unto them; they ceased not from their own doings, nor from their stubborn way.

20 And the anger of the LORD was hot against Israel. . . .

Judges 2:11-20a

Oct. 4

Memory Selection
Judges 2:16-17

Background Scripture
Judges 2

Devotional Reading
Psalm 78:17-32

Printed Scripture
Judges 2:11-20a

41

Teacher's Target

Lesson purpose: *To discern, from Israel's life under the judges, the pattern of God's response to those who flaunt His will.*

A graph charting the level of faithfulness of many believers would have highs and lows. There would be peaks of glad faithfulness, contrasting with valleys of disobedience.

This pattern is especially apparent in the book of Judges. In response to the people's unfaithfulness, God allows their neighbors to oppress them. They cry out to God, and He sends a judge to deliver them. The consistent theme can be reduced to a three-part outline: *Disobedience, Discipline,* and *Deliverance.*

The purpose of this lesson is both to describe this experience and to apply it to our own lives. Have we also experienced lapses in faithfulness followed by the "oppression" of God's absence; then experienced also His forgiving grace? Can we hope to interrupt such cycles with longer periods of uninterrupted obedience?

Lesson Introduction

The preceding lesson portrayed the transition in Israel's leadership from Moses to Joshua. The setting of today's lesson is the next transition—the period of the judges, after the death of Joshua.

Without a strong leader to uphold the Law, "every man did that which was right in his own eyes" (Judg. 21:25). This individualism left the people vulnerable to the eroding influence of pagan cultures about them. Instead of driving God's enemies from the land, the Jews often chose peaceful co-existence, trade, intermarriage, and idol worship.

God alternately responded by delivering His people to their enemies, then raising up a judge to deliver the people when they cried out in penitence. This pattern of judgment and grace is so real to human experience that it can be seen in the history of God's people throughout the ages.

Teaching Outline	Daily Bible Readings

I. Disobedience—11-13
   A. Evil deeds, 11
   B. Idolatry, 12-13
	Mon. The Risk of Forgetfulness
	Judges 2:1-10
	Tue. A Recurring Pattern Emerges
	Judges 2:11-23
	Wed. The Cycle Continues
	Judges 6:1-10

II. Discipline—14-15
   A. The anger of God, 14
   B. The judgment of God, 15
	Thu. The Saga of Samson
	Judges 13:2-12
	Fri. Samson's 20 Years Ends
	Judges 16:18-31

III. Deliverance—16-20
   A. The grace of God, 16
   B. The cycle continues, 17-20a
	Sat. Sow Wind, Reap the Whirlwind
	Hosea 8:1-10
	Sun. You Reap Whatever You Sow
	Galatians 6:1-10

Verse by Verse

I. Disobedience—11-13

A. Evil deeds, 11

11 And the children of Israel did evil in the sight of the Lord, and served Baalim:

Note that the indictment here against Israel consists both of doing evil and of worshipping foreign gods. The connection between false works and false worship is no accident; and it is a two-way street. The history of religions shows that people tend to become like the object of their worship, so bowing before false gods leads to wrong behavior. Also, practicing evil tends to drive people to seek a god who will justify their life-style, leading to false gods. The modern fascination with devil worship is a good example.

"Baalim," the plural of "Baal," was a generic term referring to any number of false Gods, one of which was a god known by that name (vs. 13). God's decision to allow the Jews to drive out the inhabitants of Israel was based both on Canaanite idolatry and evils such as child sacrifice, injustice and tribal warfare. Now, ironically, His chosen people have stooped to similar levels of evil practices and false worship.

B. Idolatry, 12-13

12 And they forsook the Lord God of their fathers, which brought them out of the land of Egypt, and followed other gods, of the gods of the people that were round about them, and bowed themselves unto them, and provoked the Lord to anger.

13 And they forsook the Lord, and served Baal and Ashtaroth.

The worship of the two gods singled out here for special mention was firmly ingrained in Canaan. Baal was a male deity, and Ashtaroth was his female consort. Baal was the lord of rain and thunder, and Ashtaroth was goddess of war. Both were also fertility gods, and worshiping them was supposed to result in pregnant wives and good harvests.

Why would God's people forsake the One who had delivered them from Egypt? We are not told, but we can imagine a set of complex reasons. Some no doubt wanted to establish trade relations with the Canaanites. There was frequent intermarriage, although God forbade it; and family ties proved stronger than remaining faithful to God.

Some may have tired of worshiping an invisible God, and resorted to idolatry because it appeals to the physical senses. Others may have been lured to paganism by its promise of sexual fertility; and pagan agricultural gods may have appealed to Jewish farmers.

II. Discipline—14-15
A. The anger of God, 14

14 And the anger of the LORD was hot against Israel, and he delivered them into the hands of their enemies round about, so that they could not any longer stand before their enemies.

The anger attributed to God here causes discomfort among some people. Not many years after this period, nearby Greek philosophers would sketch a view of the gods that denied that they had emotional qualities. Instead they were considered "impassible" or without passion. The God of the Bible, however, roars with anger, repents in sorrow (vs. 18), and enjoys gladness as He fellowships with the obedient.

Here God's anger prompts Him to deliver the idolatrous nation of Israel to their enemies. If they choose pagan gods over Him, let their false gods deliver them!

B. The judgment of God, 15

15 Whithersoever they went out, the hand of the LORD was against them for evil, as the LORD had said, and as the LORD had sworn unto them: and they were greatly distressed.

Here is evidence that God not only *allowed* His people to be overrun by their enemies; he took the more active position of being "against them for (the) evil" they had committed. A radical consequence of having the freedom to forsake God is that He may actually "grease the skids" for us! Much later, the apostle Paul will warn Christians that God will send "strong delusion" to those who "believed not the truth, but had pleasure in unrighteousness" (2 Thess. 2:11-12).

This is such a sobering thought that the author of Judges explains twice that God had warned His people of the consequences of unfaithfulness. Delivering them into the hands of their enemies was no more than what "the Lord had sworn to them." This explanation is necessary because God promised in His Covenant with the fathers that He would bless their descendants. But the Covenant had two parties—God and the people. It presumed that the people would be faithful in keeping their part of the agreement. According to the nature of covenants throughout the land, one party's failure to keep the commitment released the other party from obligation.

III. Deliverance—16-20
A. The grace of God, 16

16 Nevertheless the LORD raised up judges, which delivered them out of the hand of those that spoiled them.

God is not only a God of emotions such as anger; He now shows His mercy and compassion by raising up a "deliverer" or "savior" (Heb. *yeshuah*, which is the same as the name "Jesus"; see Matt. 1:21). Both wrath and love are compatible within God's nature.

The "judges" God raised up represent a transition in governance between the previous *"elder statesman"* leadership of Moses and Joshua, and the subsequent *kings* beginning with Saul. A total of 14 judges are mentioned, most having merely local authority which seems to have been laid aside when they had averted a particular crisis.

Although several of these judges receive only a bare mention in the narrative, three of the more memorable examples were Deborah, the only woman judge (chapters 4–5); Gideon, whose army was cut down to a size that would not lead to boasting (5–8); and Samson, the strong man of questionable morals and tragic fate (13–16).

B. The cycle continues, 17-20a

17 And yet they would not hearken unto their judges, but they went a whoring after other gods, and bowed themselves unto them: they turned quickly out of the way which their fathers walked in, obeying the commandments of the LORD; but they did not so.

18 And when the LORD raised them up judges, then the LORD was with the judge, and delivered them out of the hand of their enemies all the days of the judge: for it repented the LORD because of their groanings by reason of them that oppressed them and vexed them.

19 And it came to pass, when the judge was dead, that they returned, and corrupted themselves more than their fathers, in following other gods to serve them, and to bow down unto them; they ceased not from their own doings, nor from their stubborn way.

20 And the anger of the LORD was hot against Israel....

This description forms a tragically repetitive cycle throughout the rest of the book of Judges. The people in general responded to God's blessings by forsaking Him once He delivered them from their immediate danger. Also, the fact that they "ceased not from their own doings, nor from their stubborn way" shows that they were possessed by a destructive spirit of individualism. In a phrase reminiscent of the moral tone in much of our own culture, the book of Judges will end on this note: "In those days there was no king in Israel: every man did that which was right in his own eyes" (21:25).

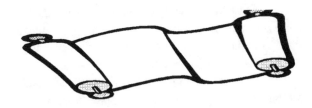

Evangelistic Emphasis

"Hypocrites! They're all a bunch of hypocrites!" Never has there ever been found a more effective battle-cry against faith. It is effective, perhaps, because it contains too much truth. No. We are *not all* a bunch of hypocrites, but some of us are. Perhaps, not all the time, but some of the time.

Perhaps more often though, we just appear to be hypocrites because of our struggle to maintain faithfulness or because of our half-hearted faith. We are so quick to forget the goodness of God. We are so gullible to the deceptions of Satan. Easily we believe his lie that our "little sin" *won't* hurt anyone—nobody will know. Then, when sadly we see the brokenness that our sin brought into our lives and the lives of those about us, we hear the echo of Satan's mocking laughter. Hardly any time passes, though, until we forget again. Before the next sunrise, we are listening again to another convincing lie. Is it any wonder that those who watch our pilgrimage of faith from the sidelines laugh with scorn? What fools we show ourselves to be!

What our critics tend to be blind to, though, is *their own* blatant hypocrisy. Somehow, they have convinced themselves that nobody is lord of their lives—they call the shots for themselves. Yet, as we watch them from the sidelines, we notice easily Satan's marionette strings controlling their every move. They are held so completely under his control, there is no struggle of resistance from them at all.

• • • • • • • • • •

Memory Selection

Nevertheless the LORD raised up judges, which delivered them out of the hand of those that spoiled them. And yet they would not hearken unto their judges, but they went a whoring after other gods, and bowed themselves unto them they turned quickly out of the way which their fathers walked in, obeying the commandments of the LORD; but they did not so.—*Judges 2:16-17*

Teddy Anderson is now 19 years old. Adopted when he was 10 months old, Teddy has never known any parents other than Theodore and Alice. From a neighbor's perspective, it would be difficult to find more loving and committed parents. At first, it appeared as though Teddy more than returned their affection and love.

Unfortunately, for the past five years life has not been so serene at the Anderson house. Teddy's life has been one wild ride through a forest of nightmares. Alice and Theodore have petitioned the Lord's help, time and time again. Every small victory comes with a huge defeat right on its heels (or at least it seems that way). When it is not drugs, it's sex. When it's not sex, it's shoplifting. Add to that truancy, and tattoos and gang rap and outbursts of profanity. It is no wonder the Andersons' hearts break with sorrow. Theodore and Alice have almost reached a point where they are reluctant to hope any longer. Then, they read again the book of Judges.

Weekday Problems

The company Jeremiah Franklin works for is advertised as "A Christian Company." That's the very reason, in fact, Jeremiah was so excited when he received the call that he had gotten the job. He's not so sure anymore.

"Calvary Auto Repair" is not like a religious book store that deals only in religious materials (i.e. repairs only church buses, etc.). Instead, it promotes itself as "A Christian Company" so as to put people's minds at ease, assuring them that they can trust that they will not be "ripped off." Though Jeremiah is fairly comfortable that the owner is honest in his dealings with the customers, he is not always so comfortable with the language or the taste in humor that sometimes permeates the work setting. Immediately after a major "revival" down at church it is much better for a while, but it never takes very long for things to get raunchy again.

* How does what Mr. Franklin witnesses down at the garage relate to the cycle echoed in Judges two?

* What can Mr. Franklin do to improve his work setting? When would be the best time for him to attempt to work toward such improvements?

* If the intent of the "Christian-targeted advertising" is to emphasize *integrity*, and that integrity seems to be maintained, should Jeremiah make an issue of the language of the shop, at all? If so, why? If not, why not?

Be Sure Your Sins Will Find You Out

Wife: Tommorrow's our twenty-fifth wedding anniversary. I think I'll kill the big red rooster and bake him.

Husband: Now, now, honey. Why punish the poor chicken for a mistake made twenty-five years ago?

* * *

Fred: Whaddya know! This article says that they've dug up the petrified remains of prisoners in the jails of ancient Rome.

Red: So *that's* what they mean by "hardened criminals."

* * *

Man: Hi. I was named after my parents. My dad was named Ferdinand and my mom was Liza.

Fran: So what's your name?

Man: Ferdiliza.

This Lesson in Your Life

"Why doesn't God do miracles any more?" six-year-old Tommy asked his dad. Tommy had heard many stories from his Sunday School class teacher about times when God intervened in history "with a mighty hand." Always, though, his teacher was telling something that happened a long, long time ago. Once, Tommy even asked his teacher if she ever saw a dead person come back to life or bread raining down from heaven. She seemed *almost speechless* at the time but then said, *"God doesn't work miracles like that anymore."* Tommy's innocent question was asking his father, *"Why not? Is my teacher right?"*

Of course, Tommy's question is not unique, isolated or trivial. Neither is it merely a child's inquiry. That same question is asked by those we are attempting to lead to faith. They may phrase the question less confrontationally, but the question will predictably be asked in some form. How are we to respond? How are we to respond to Tommy?

Obviously, we Christians do not respond consistently. Some of us will take strong opposition to Tommy's teacher's remark. Others of us will heartily agree. Our response is not necessarily a matter of "liberal" versus "conservative." Other matters tend to play far more important roles. Questions such as:

"What is a miracle?" How flamboyant must God's intervention be to be classified as a miracle? Is His answer to a run-of-the-mill prayer a miracle, or must it be something spectacular?

"What is God's function in the 'normal' events of the day?" Does He just sit on the sideline watching the world go around, or is He intricately involved in the myriad events that transpire day by day? Is He involved in the birth of a baby, or is that merely the "natural law of reproduction" functioning on schedule?

Certainly, today's text seems to indicate that a generation had arisen that had not "seen all the great works of the LORD." During their lifetime, *either* God's involvement in the lives of his people had not been as ostentatious as it once was *or* they had not been as observant to what He was doing. Though both may have been involved, the former seems to be the focus of verse seven. God's obvious intervention into their lives had not been as readily apparent as his activity had been in the lives of their forefathers.

When we are replying to the honest inquiry of a Tommy or a potential believer, we must remember that the question is not really hostile to faith. Rather, it is a stepping-stone toward faith. It seeks to understand, not reject. Rather than being threatened by such inquiries, we ought instead be challenged by them. How do we understand God's involvement in our world and our lives? Have we just taken his involvement for granted? Do we truly believe God responds to prayer, or are our prayers the product of a childhood habit that has become entrenched? Are our eyes and hearts tuned to *see* God's finger-prints in our lives, or have they become glazed over by secular/scientific conditioning? Must we *continually see* God's obvious activity in our lives to maintain our faith in Him, or does our faith reach beyond the demands of sight?

If we are to be successful in helping seekers understand the activity and mystery of God, we must first be comfortable with our own understanding of Him. That is not a demand for total comprehension, but it is a request for a proven faith.

Seed Thoughts

1. What did God promise Israelites that He would never do?

God promised the Israelites that he would *never break his covenant with them*.

2. What relationship were the Israelites *not* to have with the nations around them?

The Israelites were to "make no league with" (no covenant or treaty) the nations around them.

3. What else were they instructed by God to do?

They were to tear down the pagan altars of their godless neighbors.

4. Since the people did not keep their covenant with God, how did He respond to their disobedience?

God responded to their disobedience by allowing their pagan neighbors remain in the land to be thorns in their sides.

5. When the angel of the Lord told the people the Lord's decision, how did they respond?

The people responded to the angel's message with petition and weeping.

---

1. What did God promise Israelites that He would never do?

2. What relationship were the Israelites *not* to have with the nations around them.

3. What else were they instructed by God to do?

4. Since the people did not keep their covenant with God, how did He respond to their disobedience?

5. When the angel of the Lord told the people the Lord's decision, how did they respond?

6. How long did the people continue thereafter to serve the Lord?

7. How old was Joshua when he died?

8. After Joshua's generation had died off, what remained in Israel in regard to faith?

9. Having grown-up without a first-hand knowledge of God, how did this new generation of Israelites respond?

10. Whom did the Lord raise up to deliver his people from their enemies?

(Continued next page)

God promised the Israelites that he would *never break his covenant with them*.

The Israelites were to "make no league with" (no covenant or treaty) the nations around them.

They were to tear down the pagan altars of their godless neighbors.

God responded to their disobedience by allowing their pagan neighbors remain in the land to be thorns in their sides.

The people responded to the angel's message with petition and weeping.

The people continued to serve the Lord as long as Joshua lived *and* as long as the elders remained alive who had seen the great works of God.

Joshua lived to be age 110.

After Joshua's generation died, no one remained who had seen first-hand the mighty work of God, so they forgot and forsook God.

Not knowing God, the younger generation was easily caught up in the religions of their neighbors and began bowing to Baal and Ashtaroth.

The Lord raised up judges to deliver His people from their oppressors.

6. How long did the people continue thereafter to serve the Lord?

The people continued to serve the Lord as long as Joshua lived *and* as long as the elders remained alive who had seen the great works of God.

7. How old was Joshua when he died?

Joshua lived to be age 110.

8. After Joshua's generation had died off, what remained in Israel in regard to faith?

After Joshua's generation died, no one remained who had seen first-hand the mighty work of God, so they forgot and forsook God.

9. Having grown-up without a first-hand knowledge of God, how did this new generation of Israelites respond?

Not knowing God, the younger generation was easily caught up in the religions of their neighbors and began bowing to Baal and Ashtaroth.

10. Whom did the Lord raise up to deliver his people from their enemies?

The Lord raised up judges to deliver His people from their oppressors.

From Judges to Kings

*A*nd Samuel judged Israel all the days of his life.

16 And he went from year to year in circuit to Bethel, and Gilgal, and Mizpeh, and judged Israel in all those places.

17 And his return was to Ramah; for there was his house; and there he judged Israel; and there he built an altar unto the LORD.

8:1 And it came to pass, when Samuel was old, that he made his sons judges over Israel.

2 Now the name of his firstborn was Joel; and the name of his second, Abiah: they were judges in Beer-sheba.

3 And his sons walked not in his ways, but turned aside after lucre, and took bribes, and perverted judgment.

4 Then all the elders of Israel gathered themselves together, and came to Samuel unto Ramah,

5 And said unto him, Behold, thou art old, and thy sons walk not in thy ways: now make us a king to judge us like all the nations.

6 But the thing displeased Samuel, when they said, Give us a king to judge us. And Samuel prayed unto the LORD.

7 And the LORD said unto Samuel, Hearken unto the voice of the people in all that they say unto thee: for they have not rejected thee, but they have rejected me, that I should not reign over them.

8 According to all the works which they have done since the day that I brought them up out of Egypt even unto this day, wherewith

they have forsaken me, and served other gods, so do they also unto thee.

9 Now therefore hearken unto their voice: howbeit yet protest solemnly unto them, and shew them the manner of the king that shall reign over them.

19 Nevertheless the people refused to obey the voice of Samuel; and they said, Nay; but we will have a king over us;

20 That we also may be like all the nations; and that our king may judge us, and go out before us, and fight our battles.

21 And Samuel heard all the words of the people, and he rehearsed them in the ears of the LORD.

22 And the LORD said to Samuel, Hearken unto their voice, and make them a king. And Samuel said unto the men of Israel, Go ye every man unto his city.

1 Samuel 7:15-8:1-9, 19-22

Oct. 11

Lesson 6

Memory Selection
1 Sam. 8:22a (1st sentence)

Background Scripture
1 Samuel 7:15–8:22

Devotional Reading
1 Peter 2:13-17

Printed Scripture
1 Samuel 7:15–8:9, 19-22

51

Lesson purpose: *To learn, from the experience of Israel's demand for a king, the danger of believers' abandoning God's ways in order to copy the culture about them.*

According to a significant phrase that rings continually through the book of Judges, *God*, not the people, raised up successive judges to deliver them from oppression. The present lesson, however, portrays the people clamoring for a change in this system of government. Just as they so often adopted the false gods among the people about them, they now call for a government like the pagan nations of Canaan.

Since only on Judgment Day will God force His sovereign will on people, He reluctantly allows them to abandon His ways and become subject to the oppressive monarchs.

Again we see that God's ways are always best; and that true freedom is found only in submitting to His will instead of our own.

Lesson Introduction

Previous lessons have traced the system of governance in ancient Israel from the "elder statesman" system of leadership under Moses and Joshua to the system of judges such as Deborah, Gideon, and Samson.

Had we been Israelites living under the judges, we might have found several reasons to object to this form of government. Since the authority of most judges was limited to particular times and places instead of spanning across all the tribes, there was little hope for the kind of strong centralized control that would give definitive shape to Israel as a nation. Also, each tribe decided for itself whether to send an army to fight an oppressor attacking another tribe. Wouldn't a system that could raise a national army provide greater security?

Furthermore, the character of some judges, such as Samson and old Eli's sons, provided poor examples for the people. It was all too easy for the people to look at the monarchies in neighboring states and to lift up the cry, "Make us a king!"

Teaching Outline

I. The Last Judges—7:15–8:3
  A. A circuit-riding judge, 7:15-17
  B. His unjust sons, 8:1-3

II. The Lust for a King—8:4-5

III. The Rejection of God—6-9
  A. Personal rejection? 6
  B. A more objective view, 7-9

IV. The Request Granted—19-22
  A. The lust for conformity, 19-20
  B. 'Make them a king' 21-22

Daily Bible Readings

Mon. Hannah Prays for a Male Child
  1 Samuel 1:3-11

Tue. Hannah Did as She Promised
  1 Samuel 1:21-28

Wed. Speak, Your Servant Is Listening
  1 Samuel 3:1-10

Thu. Samuel Administered Justice
  1 Samuel 7:15–8:9

Fri. Samuel Listened
  1 Samuel 8:10-22

Sat. Pray for Kings
  1 Timothy 2:1-7

Sun. Saul Made Israel's First King
  1 Samuel 11:5-15

I. The Last Judges—7:15–8:3
A. A circuit-riding judge, 7:15-17

15 And Samuel judged Israel all the days of his life.

16 And he went from year to year in circuit to Bethel, and Gilgal, and Mizpeh, and judged Israel in all those places.

17 And his return was to Ramah; for there was his house; and there he judged Israel; and there he built an altar unto the LORD.

Samuel had prepared for his career since he was a child, when he was apprenticed to Eli the priest (2 Sam. 2:18ff.). From Gilgal, near the Jordan river, to two other sites probably just north of Jerusalem, his jurisdiction can be compared with those of circuit-riding Methodist ministers in frontier America.

Along with judging from his home at Ramah, Samuel's "circuit" focused on the boundaries traced by these four cities. Like the territories of the other judges, however, the area described here is relatively small compared with the rest of the country. Yet in 7:3, at the beginning of his judgeship, Samuel speaks "unto all the house of Israel." And it is frequently said that he "judged Israel" (7:17). Apparently he had a much wider influence than merely that in his primary territory. Perhaps he had the assistance of the "elders," who will appear later in the account.

B. His unjust sons, 8:1-3

1 And it came to pass, when Samuel was old, that he made his sons judges over Israel.

2 Now the name of his firstborn was Joel; and the name of his second, Abiah: they were judges in Beer-sheba.

3 And his sons walked not in his ways, but turned aside after lucre, and took bribes, and perverted judgment.

When Samuel was a boy working under Eli the priest, old Eli's sons had also been poor models (1 Sam. 2:22). Now history seems to repeat itself, reminding us that a nation usually rises no higher than the character of its public officials. Samuel and Eli's sons would perhaps be termed "PKs" in our day—"preacher's kids." Why they sometimes have difficulty achieving a mature faith has become the subject of some investigation, although there is little solid evidence that they have a more trying time of negotiating these waters than children from other families. We may wonder if Eli and Samuel were too much involved in their careers to tend to their families, but it would be mere speculation.

II. The Lust for a King—8:4-5

4 Then all the elders of Israel gathered themselves together, and came to Samuel unto Ramah,

5 And said unto him, Behold, thou art old, and thy sons walk not in thy ways: now make us a king to judge us like all the nations.

Israel's elders (literally "bearded ones") served as a primary level of informal rulers under the judge, and in areas where the judge did not go. They are first mentioned as far back as the time of Moses, before the exodus (Exod. 4:29). Their duties varied, and sometimes included presiding over civil cases. Often they formed a prominent but informal council, such as those before whom Boaz laid out his claim to marry Ruth (Ruth 4).

Here the elders have enough influence and authority to approach Samuel about their desire to be ruled by a king. Although the low character of his sons are the stated reason, it is also clear that they believe the monarchies around them would be a more preferable form of government than the judges had been.

III. The Rejection of God—6-9
A. Personal rejection? 6

6 But the thing displeased Samuel, when they said, Give us a king to judge us. And Samuel prayed unto the LORD.

In light of the next verse, Samuel's displeasure seems to indicate that he took the elders' request not just as the rejection of God's system, but of himself personally. Anyone who has been dismissed from a job can understand how he felt. The fact that his sons were poor examples of judges no doubt contributed to his despondency.

B. A more objective view, 7-9

7 And the LORD said unto Samuel, Hearken unto the voice of the people in all that they say unto thee: for they have not rejected thee, but they have rejected me, that I should not reign over them.

8 According to all the works which they have done since the day that I brought them up out of Egypt even unto this day, wherewith they have forsaken me, and served other gods, so do they also unto thee.

9 Now therefore hearken unto their voice: howbeit yet protest solemnly unto them, and shew them the manner of the king that shall reign over them.

God reassures Samuel that the elders deeper sin is not in rejecting Samuel but God. Their rejection of their former "theocracy," in which God is king, in favor of a human monarchy is the serious issue. The demand is only an extension of the people's wayward ways in the wilderness and under the judges.

God tells Samuel to "protest solemnly" the people's choice for the very good reason that it will not bring them the relief they envision. "The manner of the king" here and in verse 11 is a play on words. In the original language it is almost sarcastic, meaning something like "You want the judgment of a king over the justice of a judge? Hah!"

IV. The Request Granted—19-22

A. The lust for conformity, 19-20

19 Nevertheless the people refused to obey the voice of Samuel; and they said, Nay; but we will have a king over us;

20 That we also may be like all the nations; and that our king may judge us, and go out before us, and fight our battles.

In the intervening verses (10-18), Samuel runs through a sobering list of the way ruthless kings rule. They press a nation's youth into war, enslave the people, and exact exorbitant taxes. Despite the warning, however, the people back the elders' request. Finally one of their real motives is revealed: they believe kings will provide greater protection against their enemies.

In contrast to the people's willful answer here, they later indicate sorrow over their choice when Samuel gives a farewell speech and concludes by calling down rain at harvest time (12:18-19).

B. 'Make them a king' 21-22

21 And Samuel heard all the words of the people, and he rehearsed them in the ears of the LORD.

22 And the LORD said to Samuel, Hearken unto their voice, and make them a king. And Samuel said unto the men of Israel, Go ye every man unto his city.

Finally the argument is over. The people's stubborn request is to be reluctantly granted. This raises the question of why God would agree to something He knows represents a rejection of Him. Many scholars believe that the earliest parts of 1 Samuel reflect a more positive view of the monarchy, and that only later, after various kings had proved to be tyrants, did editors rework the material and insert the negative views expressed here.

It is also possible that God simply respects the free will of His people. He grants their request because He is the God of the second mile. Instead of abandoning Israel because of a bad choice, He remains to pick up the pieces when the people realize His warnings were not empty.

Evangelistic Emphasis

Alex is only seven years old, a first grader, but he already has strong opinions about where he wants to go to school next year. He wants to go to his neighborhood elementary school, "TCK." Presently, he attends Sierra Christian School where his mother teaches fifth grade. It's not that Alex doesn't like Sierra. He likes it very much. Some of his friends with whom he plays T-Ball, however, go to TCK. Alex wants to be like his T-Ball friends. Consequently, he wants to go to TCK, too. Surely, there must be something *better* about TCK!

Isn't that just like the Israelites! It wasn't that they didn't like judges. Certainly, Samuel had served them well. Nevertheless, it was not like their neighbors. None of their neighbors had a leadership of judges. Their neighbors were led in grandeur by kings. Surely, there must be something *better* about a king.

Just as Alex has parents who care for him and understand his wish to "be like his friends," so also Israel had a God who cared for them and understood their wish for a king. Though it grieved Him, he yielded to their wish and gave them a king. Yes, He warned them sufficiently ahead of time how much it would cost them. Unfortunately, their ears were too full of their fingers to hear his warnings. They had made up their mind what they wanted and didn't wish to be confused by the facts.

Are we any different today?

● ● ● ● ● ● ● ● ● ●

And the LORD said to Samuel, Hearken unto their voice, and make them a king.—*1 Samuel 8:22*

Should it surprise us that God told Samuel to grant Israel their wish, *even though* that was not His wish for them? From the beginning, hasn't God allowed humankind to choose that against which He had warned—*even that which He had forbade?*

In Luke's Gospel is recorded a story about a father who had two sons, the younger of which demanded his inheritance in advance. The father made the proper arrangements necessary and gave his inheritance to him *even though that son would proceed to waste it in shameful choices* (Luke 15). Surely he could have prevented the waste by rejecting the request of which he disapproved. The father in the story, however, wanted more than his son to "respect the value of a dollar." He wanted him to treasure the value of life.

If I understand Jesus' story properly, He is telling us about his heavenly Father. He allows us to leave home, even though, he wants desperately for us to be at home. He will not force us to stay home against our will.

Weekday Problems

Larry Vickers has always had a determined streak in him. His mother called it "stubborn." At age three he would stomp his foot with insistence so as to let his mother know that he intended to have it his way. All his stomping got him nowhere at age three.

Larry is now 28, and the owner of a downtown Radio Shack franchise in Philadelphia. His habit of stomping his foot has not changed. One thing has changed, however. Larry is now old enough and persuasive enough that his stomping now sometimes gets him his way. That is sometimes to his advantage and sometimes to his detriment.

Last week, Larry proposed to his supervisor a promotional scheme he believes will bring major revitalization to the downtown economy, and in the process, boost his business as well. Though his regional supervisor is skeptical and has tried to discourage Larry from the investment, Larry's stomping foot may very well prevail. If his idea is successful, it could profit everybody involved. If he is wrong, it may cost him his business.

* When all-or-nothing decisions like this need to be made in your life, what kind of information do you like to have in hand before deciding?

* What would be a way Larry's wife might help him to evaluate the possible rewards and risks of his decision?

* Is there a possible "test scenario" that would better inform Larry's decision-making process? What such "test scenario" could Israel have used?

The Sport of Kings

The lion went up to the rhinocerous and asked, "Who is king of the jungle?"

"You are, O mighty lion," the rhino said.

The lion asked the hippopotamus, "Who is king of the jungle?

"You are, O great lion," came the answer.

The lion asked the elephant, "Who is king of the jungle. In response, the elephant seized the lion with his trunk, threw him high in the air, caught him on the way down and body-slammed him against a tree.

The lion got up, dazed, shook himself and said weakly, "Just because you don't know the right answer you don't have to get sore."

* * *

King to Queen: I know the baby's giving you trouble, dear, but just remember that the hand that rocks the cradle rules the world.

Q to K: Oh yeah? Well how about taking over the world for awhile so I can go shopping?

This Lesson in Your Life

Rarely does it happen as an emphatic decisive moment. Rejecting God's leadership in our lives usually follows a long process of re-evaluation and assessment. The form that the process assumes is dependent on the context in which it is found.

For the 13-year-old who wants desperately to be accepted by her peers and to fit into the teen culture around her, the process of "rejecting God's leadership" in her life may take the form of social conformity. Probably she does not *immediately* do everything they do. She first observes that what they are doing does not seem to have all the negative consequences that she had been told that they would have. They may use marijuana, but they don't seems to be "strung out" continually as she had imagined. They may be sexually active, but she would not describe any of them as "sluts" or "sex addicts." As far as she knows, not one of her friends is "HIV positive." "What's so bad about fitting in?" she protests to her mother. "What's the big deal about having a little fun?"

For this adolescent, it's not that she wants to rebel against God. She just wants to be like the kids around her. Consequently, a shift takes place in who defines the standards for her actions. Whereas there was a time in her childhood when "pleasing her parents" (and through them, pleasing God) dominated her interests, she has come to be more interested in whatever her friends find acceptable. Of course, once she has allowed them (rather than God) to *take the lead* in her life, it is only a matter of time until she will follow them wherever they go.

For the middle-aged businessman who's beginning to feel the pressures of a waning career, abandoning the leadership of God may be economically motivated in a desperate attempt to revitalize his career. Of course, he won't perceive it that way. It's just that there was a time when he could afford to be outspoken in behalf of ethics and principles. He knew well that the company could not afford to lose him. As the years pass, however, quite a few young professionals have come to breathe down his neck with their higher-level degrees and their sharper skills. They can work longer hours with less family distractions and fewer illness. If he's going to manage to hold onto his position, he's going to have to make some compromises. Gradually *pragmatics* takes priority over *ethics*. *Profit* edges out *principle*.

Was it all that much different for the Israelites? Wasn't the wish to become a monarchy, led by a king, a pragmatics-driven dream? After all, Israel was not faring very well as a loose assortment of tribes with no central authority *on earth*. A familiar refrain that echoed throughout the period of the Judges cried, "In those days there was no king in Israel every man did that which was right in his own eyes" (Judges 17:6; 21:5). *"Surely a monarchy would be better than what we have,"* they thought. *"How could God object to that?"*

Seed Thoughts

1. Had Samuel been a judge in 19th-century America, what phrase would have described his work and territory?

Samuel would have been called a circuit judge since he traveled a circuit each year hearing the cases at hand.

2. What places benefited from Samuel's judgeship first-hand?

The Bible says that "he went from year to year in circuit to Bethel, and Gilgal, and Mizpeh, and judged Israel in all those places."

3. Where was Samuel's home during this tenure of his career?

Samuel's home was in Ramah, so he returned to Ramah at the completion of each circuit.

4. Whom did Samuel appoint to be his eventual replacement?

In his old age, Samuel appointed his two sons as judges—Joel and Abiah.

5. From what location did these men attempt to judge Israel?

They were judges in Beersheba.

1. Had Samuel been a judge in 19th-century America, what phrase would have described his work and territory?

2. What places benefited from Samuel's judgeship first-hand?

3. Where was Samuel's home during this tenure of his career?

4. Whom did Samuel appoint to be his eventual replacement?

5. From what location did these men attempt to judge Israel?

6. How well did these men serve Israel as judges? How would you characterize their leadership?

7. What reasons did the elders of Israel give to Samuel to justify their wish for a king?

8. How did Samuel feel about their wish for a king to rule them?

9. Whom did Samuel tell about his displeasure with the people's request?

10. What did Samuel tell Israel about their wish for a king in an attempt to discourage them?

(Continued next page)

Samuel would have been called a circuit judge since he traveled a circuit each year hearing the cases at hand.

The Bible says that "he went from year to year in circuit to Bethel, and Gilgal, and Mizpeh, and judged Israel in all those places".

Samuel's home was in Ramah, so he returned to Ramah at the completion of each circuit.

In his old age, Samuel appointed his two sons as judges—Joel and Abiah.

They were judges in Beersheba.

They did not serve Israel well, at all. They were "crooked" judges, taking bribes and perverting judgments.

They said that he was old and his sons were crooked.

Their wish for a king displeased him.

He told God.

Samuel tried to discourage Israel from wanting a king by telling them how much it would cost them in taxes and in service.

6. How well did these men serve Israel as judges? How would you characterize their leadership?

They did not serve Israel well, at all. They were "crooked" judges, taking bribes and perverting judgments.

7. What reasons did the elders of Israel give to Samuel to justify their wish for a king?

They said that he was old and his sons were crooked.

8. How did Samuel feel about their wish for a king to rule them?

Their wish for a king displeased him.

9. Whom did Samuel tell about his displeasure with the people's request?

He told God.

10. What did Samuel tell Israel about their wish for a king in an attempt to discourage them?

Samuel tried to discourage Israel from wanting a king by telling them how much it would cost them in taxes and in service.

Jeroboam's Sin

*A*nd it came to pass, when all Israel heard that Jeroboam was come again, that they sent and called him unto the congregation, and made him king over all Israel: there was none that followed the house of David, but the tribe of Judah only.

25 Then Jeroboam built Shechem in mount Ephraim, and dwelt therein; and went out from thence, and built Penuel.

26 And Jeroboam said in his heart, Now shall the kingdom return to the house of David:

27 If this people go up to do sacrifice in the house of the LORD at Jerusalem, then shall the heart of this people turn again unto their lord, even unto Rehoboam king of Judah, and they shall kill me, and go again to Rehoboam king of Judah.

28 Whereupon the king took counsel, and made two calves of gold, and said unto them, It is too much for you to go up to Jerusalem: behold thy gods, O Israel, which brought thee up out of the land of Egypt.

29 And he set the one in Bethel, and the other put he in Dan.

30 And this thing became a sin: for the people went to worship before the one, even unto Dan.

1 Kings 12:20, 25-33

31 And he made an house of high places, and made priests of the lowest of the people, which were not of the sons of Levi.

32 And Jeroboam ordained a feast in the eighth month, like unto the feast that is in Judah, and he offered upon the altar. So did he in Bethel, sacrificing unto the calves that he had made: and he placed in Bethel the priests of the high places which he had made.

33 So he offered upon the altar which he had made in Bethel the fifteenth day of the eighth month, even in the month which he had devised of his own heart; and ordained a feast unto the children of Israel: and he offered upon the altar, and burnt incense.

Oct. 18

Memory Selection
1 Kings 2:28

Background Scripture
1 Kings 12

Devotional Reading
Matthew 27:15-26

Printed Scripture
1 Kings 2:20, 25-33

Teacher's Target

Lesson purpose: *To examine the roots of sectarianism and religious division through the experience of Israel under the leadership of Jeroboam.*

The seeds of religious division come in many forms, several of which are illustrated in the story of Jeroboam. He was "a mighty man of valour" and industrious (1 Kings 11:28), so we may assume he was a natural leader. Yet he was also susceptible to pride, and his vision of himself as a leader was inflated by a prophecy portraying him as elevated from a kind of cabinet member to a king (11:29-39).

Once installed as king over the northern tribes of Israel, Jeroboam sought to consolidate his position by giving the people an alternative to the city of Jerusalem as a place of centralized worship. He deceitfully draped his political ambition in religious garments. His story forms an appropriate set of signs warning us today of the many motives of religious division and strife.

Lesson Introduction

Be sure to prepare for this lesson by reading 1 Kings 11. The evolution of ancient Israel's system of government has been traced from a strong military leader, Joshua, to the judges, then to the people's demand for a king. The setting of this lesson is the period following the reigns of the first kings—Saul, David, and Solomon.

Solomon's son Rehoboam succeeded his father to the throne in Israel. Rash and foolish, Rehoboam refused to follow older and wiser counsel advising him to relax the government's strangle-hold on the people. Instead, he listened to younger men who advised him to levy heavier taxes and install oppressive measures against his political enemies (1 Kings 12:14).

Jeroboam, a widely respected nobleman, is installed as a rival king on a wave of popular resentment of Rehoboam's rule. As we shall see, Jeroboam's pride and his attempt to strengthen his position leads to a tragic and permanent rift in the kingdom.

Teaching Outline	Daily Bible Readings
I. A Division Instituted—20	**Mon.** Jeroboam Bows to Temptation *1 Kings 11:26-35*
II. A Dynasty Established—25	**Tue.** Jeroboam Flees to Egypt *1 Kings 11:36-43*
III. Idolatry Installed—26-33	**Wed.** Advice of Elders Rejected *1 Kings 12:1-19*
A. A separate place, 26-27	**Thu.** Rehoboam Falls, Jeroboam Sins *1 Kings 12:20-33*
B. Separate gods, 28-30	**Fri.** Consequences of Jeroboam's Sin *1 Kings 13:1-10*
C. A separate priesthood, 31	**Sat.** More Consequences of Sin *1 Kings 13:33—14:10a*
D. Separate rites, 32-33	**Sun.** Jeroboam's Son Dies *2 Kings 14:10b-20*

Verse by Verse

I. A Division Instituted—20

20 And it came to pass, when all Israel heard that Jeroboam was come again, that they sent and called him unto the congregation, and made him king over all Israel: there was none that followed the house of David, but the tribe of Judah only.

Jeroboam was the son of one of King Solomon's court officials. The ambitious young man caught Solomon's eye, and he was made superintendent over a labor force (which was probably forced labor) charged with rebuilding part of the wall around the capital city of Jerusalem. (1 Kings 11:28; see the NIV). A prophet fed Jeroboam's ambitions by predicting he would rule over a portion of Israel who would revolt against Solomon (11:30-39). When Solomon heard this he sought to kill Jeroboam, who promptly fled to Egypt (vs. 40).

The present verse shows that Jeroboam's fortunes have begun to reverse. Although Solomon has died, the oppressive rule of his son Rehoboam has angered many in the land. They call Jeroboam out of Egypt to lead a revolt. At first the rebellion consists of "Judah only"; but it is shortly expanded to include the smaller tribe of Benjamin (vs.

21). This insurrection will have far-reaching effects. Although previous tensions have existed between southern and northern Israelites, Jeroboam institutionalizes these differences and will result in a divided kingdom—Judah in the south and Israel in the north.

II. A Dynasty Established—25

25 Then Jeroboam built Shechem in mount Ephraim, and dwelt therein; and went out from thence, and built Penuel.

Like many other ambitious leaders, Jeroboam sought to strengthen his position and commemorate himself with great building programs (compare the Egyptian pharaohs and the pyramids; and Solomon's great projects in Jerusalem). Actually, both Shechem and Penuel already existed; so the NIV more accurately states that Jeroboam only "fortified" and "built up" these areas. Shechem was in an area occupied by the half-tribes of Ephraim and Mannasseh, providing residents who may have previously worked under Jeroboam in the construction project he supervised in Jerusalem (11:28, NIV).

III. Idolatry Installed—26-33
A. A separate place, 26-27

26 And Jeroboam said in his heart, Now shall the kingdom re-

turn to the house of David:

27 If this people go up to do sacrifice in the house of the L_ORD_ at Jerusalem, then shall the heart of this people turn again unto their lord, even unto Rehoboam king of Judah, and they shall kill me, and go again to Rehoboam king of Judah.

Jerusalem had been the religious, political, and trade center of Israel since King David conquered it (2 Sam. 5:6-7). God Himself had promised the people His special presence in the Temple that King Solomon built in Jerusalem (1 Kings 9:3). Going up to Jerusalem, the city built on seven hills, had been a powerful unification force among the Israelites. (How many church splits have been over this "power of place," as people's religious security has been manifested by allegiance to a church building?!). Jeroboam realizes that he must build a worship center elsewhere to counter Jerusalem's unifying influence.

B. Separate gods, 28-30

28 Whereupon the king took counsel, and made two calves of gold, and said unto them, It is too much for you to go up to Jerusalem: behold thy gods, O Israel, which brought thee up out of the land of Egypt.

29 And he set the one in Bethel, and the other put he in Dan.

30 And this thing became a sin: for the people went to worship before the one, even unto Dan.

What a sad day it was for those in Israel who remembered the stories of their fathers having erected the golden calf in the wilderness shortly after fleeing Egypt. In fact, the Jews probably brought the notion with them out of Egypt, where there was a long tradition of worshiping "Apis" the bull—probably because it was a symbol of power and sexual virility. Such animal worship also surrounded the Jews who arrived in Canaan, since some Canaanite gods were also represented by a bull.

Even Moses had praised the majesty of a "first-born bull" (Deut. 33:17). It is barely possible that Jeroboam wanted the calves to represent the majesty of God; but if so, he violated the Second Commandment in erecting the images. Bethel had been an important place of worship since the days of Father Abraham. In placing the calves there, and at Dan, Jeroboam shows he is more interested in the political impact of the images than in whatever religious meaning they may have had.

C. A separate priesthood, 31

31 And he made an house of high places, and made priests of the lowest of the people, which were not of the sons of Levi.

Jeroboam also correctly calculated that a religious people's loyalty can be swayed by creating a new priesthood, since that is their means of accessing God. Since the time of Aaron, in the wilderness, Israel's priests were to come from the tribe of Levi, Aaron's forefather. No doubt worshipers from other tribes wondered why they were excluded from being a priest. Now Jeroboam exploits such ambitions, installing as priests anyone and everyone who would pretend to be intermediaries between the people and God, but whose primary mission was to seal their loyalty to Jeroboam.

D. Separate rites, 32-33

32 And Jeroboam ordained a feast in the eighth month, like unto the feast that is in Judah, and he offered upon the altar. So did he in Bethel, sacrificing unto the calves that he had made: and he placed in Bethel the priests of the high places which he had made.

33 So he offered upon the altar which he had made in Bethel the fifteenth day of the eighth month, even in the month which he had devised of his own heart; and ordained a feast unto the children of Israel: and he offered upon the altar, and burnt incense.

Finally, Jeroboam further ensures his authority over the breakaway tribes by giving them their own rituals. Why should they make annual pilgrimages to Jerusalem to make sacrificial offerings and celebrate religious feast days?

Against God's Law, which required that priests preside over sacrifices, Jeroboam assumes the role of "high priest" by offering them himself. In this

way he hopes to become more than a political ruler. He is positioning himself also as the people's representative with God.

Postscript:

Vestiges of the division between the ten northern tribes under Jeroboam and the two southern tribes that followed Rehoboam were still apparent in the time of Christ. Samaritans, descendants of the northern tribes in Samaria were despised by Jews in Jerusalem.

Unfortunately, religious division among Christians is often fueled by the same factors exploited by Jeroboam. While diversity can be healthy, we are also urged not to allow differences to divide (see 1 Cor. 1:10-13). In extreme cases, the "Jeroboam" syndrome produces tragic results. Only last year, thirty-nine members of the Heavens Gate cult in San Diego were led to commit suicide in the misguided belief it would prepare them for a "higher plane" of existence.

While most Christian divisions have far different roots, we would all do well to take seriously the factors exploited by Jeroboam: those involving place, worship styles and rituals, and self-centered concerns. In light of our Lord's appeal for Christian unity (John 17:20-21), we would do well to focus on the one powerful force we have in common: the high priesthood of Jesus Christ.

Evangelistic Emphasis

One of the remarkable characteristics about the Bible is the way it blatantly tells the truth—*warts and all*. It makes no difference whether they are deeds of God's greatest enemy that are being told or those of His prized hero. Virtue is told as virtue. Vice is candidly displayed as vice. The adultery of King David (the man after God's own heart) is recorded openly. So are the acts of penitence of the one who denied Jesus.

When someone raises questions about the frailties of God's people, perhaps he should highlight the reality that in the Judaeo-Christian scriptures, there is only one hero. That hero is God; first, in living interaction with his people; second, in the presence of Jesus Christ.

Just as there were Rehoboams and Jeroboams in Israel, so there will be their counterparts in Christianity. Let that fact not blind us to the other fact that there will also be Abrahams, Elijahs and Ruths. There will be those who are embarrassingly un-God-like in their lives. Others will prove to be impressively godly. "Faith" has never removed the reality of human frailty. Nor has *the claim* of conviction ever guaranteed authenticity. There will always be pretenders who give those of conviction a bad name.

• • • • • • • • • •

Memory Selection

Whereupon the king took counsel, and made two calves of gold, and said unto them, It is too much for you to go up to Jerusalem behold thy gods, O Israel, which brought thee up out of the land of Egypt.—*1 Kings 12:28*

As a life-long Christian who cut his teeth on the church pews, it is *extremely* difficult for me to imagine how these people could suddenly stop worshiping the Lord whom they had worshiped all their lives and immediately begin worshiping *golden calves*. That would be like a man who has been lovingly devoted to his wife for 25 years suddenly deserting her and running off with the new secretary he hired this morning.

Of course, it doesn't usually happen that way. Probing behind the obvious will invariably unveil that things at home were not nearly as cozy as they seemed. Perhaps, also as a 20th-century Christian, I assume far too much about the *personal* element of their religion. The leader of the people had far more influence in the shaping of the people's religion than the "people in the pew" had. Perhaps my surprise ought to be directed toward Jeroboam. From the story, itself, we learn that for him things at home were not as "cozy" as they ought to have been. Like at Jonestown, Waco, and Heaven's Gate, the people just blindly followed their leader.

Weekday Problems

Most of us are all too aware of the scandals that have plagued the Christian clergy during the past couple of decades. In a high percentage of those scandals, "money and power" were major factors in the clergy's corruption. Nevertheless, this is not exclusively a clergy problem.

Jim serves as pastor of a 700-member church. He is working hard to help it survive the devastating news that one of the deacons embezzled almost a million dollars of the church's building fund. It wasn't that Bill Martin *intended* to rob God's people. He took the position to help. An investment broker by trade, he "knew about accounting and such." Unfortunately, bending ethics came too easily for Bill. Once in a place of absolute trust, he found it easy to bend his ethics absolutely. He wrote himself loans to take care of some personal losses. He had "every intention of paying it all back." Before long, he was in way over his head—far too much to ever think of paying it back.

* Should the church have filed charges against Bill Martin? Should it press for the most severe punishment possible?

* What can a church do to better protect itself from such scandalous outbreaks of humanity (i.e. embezzlement, child molestation, malicious gossip)?

* Since sin sometimes is found to be "comfortably at home in church," should we just gracefully close the doors and admit that it is all a sham? If not, why not?

Discussing Our Differences

Teacher: What's the difference between a porpoise and a dolphin?
Student: That's what I say. What's the difference?

* * *

Wife: Let's don't go to the mountains for our vacation. I'm afraid the air would disagree with me.
Husband (wearily): My dear, it wouldn't care.

* * *

Angry wife to husband: No I won't talk it over. Every time we discuss something sensibly, I lose!

* * *

Prejudice is a great time-saver. It helps us form opinions without bothering to get the facts.

* * *

Glen: Why did the potatoes argue all the time?
Ben: Because they never could see eye to eye.

This Lesson in Your Life

Would you be willing to worship a different God to preserve your position of power or profit? No one would have ever thought Larry Cannon would, either. Yet, it is the painful assessment of some of his friends that he did exactly that. It was not a conscious decision made at some definite point in time. It happened gradually over a period of seven years.

It all began one Thursday evening when Larry and his wife, Brianne, spent the evening at the home of a new couple at church who had invited them for dinner. Casually, during the course of the evening's conversation, Aaron, the host, asked Larry how he survived on a teacher's salary? Larry responded that it wasn't easy. The Detroit School District didn't pay its employees as well as some. Yet, he and Brianne had made the hard decision for her not to work outside the home while their children were still preschool. Aaron told Larry that he, too, once struggled to make ends meet, but not any longer.

In the three hours that followed, Larry and Brianne found themselves swept up into some of the most exciting fantasies they had ever experienced as Aaron skillfully painted for them a full-color picture of how they could own their own business and be debt-free. It was a network marketing enterprise that sounded almost too good to be true, yet Aaron and his wife were "living proof" that the plan worked. Their home, their clothes and the cars they drove all testified to a life of abundance.

That night neither Brianne nor Larry could sleep as they excitedly considered Aaron's offer to sponsor them as new members of the business. How could they say no, since "there was no way they could lose." Larry would continue teaching until his business be-came fully self-supporting. Then he could decide whether to go with the business full-time.

It was slow at first but so exciting, as Larry and Brianne learned how to set up and build their business. Gradually, they learned and came to sponsor other young couples to train and supervise. Some of the ones they tried to nurture did not do well so eventually dropped out. Others did very well. Yet, all of this took time—far more than they had originally imagined.

It was three years before Larry made the decision to leave the classroom. Though he had gone into teaching because of his wish to make a differences in the lives of teenagers, he really couldn't afford the time it required any longer. He now made far more money with his part-time business than he was making teaching. Besides, there were just not enough hours in a day to attend all the seminars and training sessions, and to head the business. Then there was church. They wanted to stay active in church.

Today, the Cannons appear to be doing quite well, *financially*. They have moved several times, each time to a roomier and more luxurious house. Their dress and the cars they each drive testify to affluence. They have also changed churches several times. Church was found to be one of their best sources for "new prospects" for the business. Unfortunately, only a few in their original congregation returned any interest. Easily they have moved their membership from church to church to find a new group of prospects. Besides, it had been emphasized strongly to them, they didn't have time for *losers*. It is very important that they not allow themselves to be influenced by negative thinkers. As a result, the Cannons have cut ties with most of their life-long friends. They serve another God, now—the Almighty Dollar. That's what some of their former friends say, at least. But do their former friends understand?

Seed Thoughts

1. Which son of Solomon was in line to be the next king?

Rehoboam was Solomon's son who was next in line for the throne.

2. Where had Jeroboam been staying and why?

Jeroboam had been living in Egypt, because he had fled from his father.

3. Who were among those who approached Rehoboam regarding his taking the throne?

Jeroboam and all the congregation of Israel came to Rehoboam and spoke to Rehoboam.

4. What request did Jeroboam and the congregation of Israel make of Rehoboam.

Jeroboam and the congregation of Israel asked that Rehoboam make their [tax] burden lighter than it had been with Solomon.

5. Whose counsel did Rehoboam first seek so as to better answer their request? What did they advise?

Rehoboam first consulted with the "old men" who had served his father. They advised him to respond positively to their request.

---

1. Which son of Solomon was in line to be the next king?

2. Where had Jeroboam been staying and why?

3. Who were among those who approached Rehoboam regarding his taking the throne?

4. What request did Jeroboam and the congregation of Israel make of Rehoboam.

5. Whose counsel did Rehoboam first seek so as to better answer their request? What did they advise?

6. Whom did Rehoboam turn to get a second opinion? What advice did he receive?

7. How did the people respond to Rehoboam's harsh response?

8. Of what was Jeroboam particularly afraid?

9. How did Jeroboam address his fear?

10. How were Jeroboam's actions regarded by the biblical text?

(Continued next page)

69

Rehoboam was Solomon's son who was next in line for the throne.

Jeroboam had been living in Egypt, because he had fled from his father.

Jeroboam and the congregation of Israel asked that Rehoboam make their [tax] burden lighter than it had been with Solomon.

Rehoboam first consulted with the "old men" who had served his father. They advised him to respond positively to their request.

Rehoboam then called in his peers to ask what they thought. His peers told him to tell them that they "hadn't seen anything yet!" He would be tougher still.

The people rebelled against the house of David and appointed Jeroboam to lead them.

Jeroboam was afraid that if the people continued to go to Jerusalem to worship they would be won back to the leadership of Rehoboam.

To keep the people from returning to Jerusalem, Jeroboam built altars with golden calves for the people to worship, and established a new priesthood.

Jeroboam's actions were called "sin."

6. Whom did Rehoboam turn to get a second opinion? What advice did he receive?

Rehoboam then called in his peers to ask what they thought. His peers told him to tell them that they "hadn't seen anything yet!" He would be tougher still.

7. How did the people respond to Rehoboam's harsh response?

The people rebelled against the house of David and appointed Jeroboam to lead them.

8. Of what was Jeroboam particularly afraid?

Jeroboam was afraid that if the people continued to go to Jerusalem to worship they would be won back to the leadership of Rehoboam.

9. How did Jeroboam address his fear?

To keep the people from returning to Jerusalem, Jeroboam built altars with golden calves for the people to worship, and established a new priesthood.

10. How were Jeroboam's actions regarded by the biblical text?

Jeroboam's actions were called "sin."

Lesson 8

The Work of Prophets

*A*nd the Syrians had gone out by companies, and had brought away captive out of the land of Israel a little maid; and she waited on Naaman's wife.

3 And she said unto her mistress, Would God my lord were with the prophet that is in Samaria! for he would recover him of his leprosy.

4 And one went in, and told his lord, saying, Thus and thus said the maid that is of the land of Israel.

5 And the king of Syria said, Go to, go, and I will send a letter unto the king of Israel. And he departed, and took with him ten talents of silver, and six thousand pieces of gold, and ten changes of raiment.

6 And he brought the letter to the king of Israel, saying, Now when this letter is come unto thee, behold I have therewith sent Naaman my servant to thee, that thou mayest recover him of his leprosy.

9 So Naaman came with his horses and with his chariot, and stood at the door of the house of Elisha.

10 And Elisha sent a messenger unto him, saying, Go and wash in Jordan seven times, and thy flesh shall come again to thee, and thou shalt be clean.

11 But Naaman was wroth, and went away, and said, Behold, I thought, He will surely come out to me, and stand, and call

2 Kings 5:2-6, 9-14

on the name of the LORD his God, and strike his hand over the place, and recover the leper.

12 Are not Abana and Pharpar, rivers of Damascus, better than all the waters of Israel? may I not wash in them, and be clean? So he turned and went away in a rage.

13 And his servants came near, and spake unto him, and said, My father, if the prophet had bid thee do some great thing, wouldest thou not have done it? how much rather then, when he saith to thee, Wash, and be clean?

14 Then went he down, and dipped himself seven times in Jordan, according to the saying of the man of God: and his flesh came again like unto the flesh of a little child, and he was clean.

Oct. 25

Background Scripture
2 Kings 5:1-19

Memory Selection
2 Kings 5:8b

Devotional Reading
2 Samuel 12:1-14

Printed Scripture
2 Kings 5:2-6, 9-14

Teacher's Target

Lesson purpose: *To take a snapshot of the work of Israel's prophets, focusing especially on the importance of obeying the Word spoken through them.*

This delightful story reminds us of the power of God over creation, particularly as expressed through the prophet Elisha. The same power that formed the worlds is still available today, although God may dispense it in different ways.

A good introduction to the session might be to encourage group members to share experiences when they believe God healed loved ones. Don't limit the discussion to the "miraculous," or get stalled in a debate on whether "faith healing" is operative today. Instead, point out that all healing comes from God, whether it is through God-given medication, professional care and expertise, or simply through prayer.

Use these experiences as a springboard into a discussion of how God also heals the soul of sin—and how this lesson will show that the key to such healing is faith and obedience.

Lesson Introduction

With the rise of Israel's kings came also a new emphasis on the work of another kind of ministry in ancient Israel: that of the prophets.

We usually think of a prophet as someone who foretells the future. Indeed, the English word means literally a "before-sayer." The work of the prophets, however, also included "forth-saying," or even "forthright saying." It was their task to confront Israel's kings and the people with God's word. Just as our government has legislative, judicial and executive branches as a "balance of powers," so the prophets were to boldly proclaim God's word to balance the tendency of kings to assume power for themselves apart from the will of God.

In the process, some prophets such as Elijah and Elisha, also performed miracles as signs that God was truly with them. This lesson is about one of these famous signs, as well as the importance of simple obedience to the prophet's word.

Verse by Verse

I. The Girl Who Knew a Prophet—2-6

A. A Jewish servant in Syria, 2

2 And the Syrians had gone out by companies, and had brought away captive out of the land of Israel a little maid; and she waited on Naaman's wife.

In Old Testament times the land of Syria (also called Aram), was approximately where it is today. Its capital, Damascus, is one of the oldest continuously occupied cities in the world. In Old Testament times it was a storied place with irrigated fields.

Its proximity to the northern tribes of Israel often tempted the powerful nation of Syria to make war on its neighbor to the south. On one of the Syrian raids they took a young Jewish girl captive. She became a servant of Naaman (whose name means "pleasant"). Verse 1 has high praise for this Syrian soldier, but the dread phrase, "he was a leper," would have voided all his virtues in the eyes of most people. (Actually, the word for "leper" is a generic term used for a variety of skin diseases.)

The biblical writer would have us understand that while God sometimes gave Israel over to foreign powers because of disobedience, there were good people in Israel, too—people such as this young maiden who are willing to be used to bless others.

B. A solution for leprosy, 3-4

3 And she said unto her mistress, Would God my lord were with the prophet that is in Samaria! for he would recover him of his leprosy.

4 And one went in, and told his lord, saying, Thus and thus said the maid that is of the land of Israel.

The chronicles of nations usually center on great leaders. Only occasionally does a "nobody" make the history books, as does this unnamed Jewish girl. Although unsung, she knows of the mighty miracles of the prophet Elisha. She is also a strong enough personality to witness to her faith to her Syrian mistress, and is caring enough to show concern for Naaman's dread disease. Designating Elisha's home base as Samaria reminds us that his work was primarily among the ten northern tribes of Israel. Other prophets aimed their testimony to the southern kingdom of Judah.

C. A letter from the king, 5-6

5 And the king of Syria said, Go to, go, and I will send a letter unto the king of Israel. And he de-

parted, and took with him ten talents of silver, and six thousand pieces of gold, and ten changes of raiment.

6 And he brought the letter to the king of Israel, saying, Now when this letter is come unto thee, behold I have therewith sent Naaman my servant to thee, that thou mayest recover him of his leprosy.

The king of Syria was probably Ben-hadad (see 8:7). He had apparently regained some power since his recent defeat in a great battle against the forces of King Ahab (1 Kings 20). He is so concerned about his captain that he sends him to the king of Israel (probably Jehoram; see 3:1), along with a polite letter of introduction, a request—and cash and clothes that must have been worth millions in today's currency.

Ben-hadad speaks of Israel's king as able to cure Naaman, because, after the manner of strong, autocratic rulers, he assumes that Jehoram would issue the order for Elisha to perform the cure. As a matter of fact, verse 7 shows that the letter from the Syrian king drove Jehoram into a fit of terror and rage. He had no control over Elisha, and in fact was an evil idolater who would have borne the brunt of Elisha's stern preaching (3:1-3). Now he wonders if the Syrian king is just trying to pick a fight with him.

II. An Unpretentious Prophet—9-12

A. Small steps, 9-10

9 So Naaman came with his horses and with his chariot, and stood at the door of the house of Elisha.

10 And Elisha sent a messenger unto him, saying, Go and wash in Jordan seven times, and thy flesh shall come again to thee, and thou shalt be clean.

In verse 8 we are told that Elisha heard that the Syrian captain had come to Israel for help. (The "grapevine" was not a modern invention.) He chastises Jehoram for his anger, and offers to see the Syrian captain.

Again we see that one of the intents of this section of Scripture is to show the superiority of Israel's faith over that of the surrounding pagans. Elisha wants to be involved in Naaman's healing so he and the rest of the Syrians "shall know that there is a prophet in Israel." Probably Elisha wants this demonstration to have an impact on Jehoram himself as much as on the Syrians.

Of course since it is God, not Elisha, who will accomplish the healing, Elisha could have "thought" or prayed Naaman's disease away. In prescribing the simple, sevenfold washing in the nearby Jordan River, the prophet seems to be testing the depth of the Syrian officer's willingness to be healed.

B. Great expectations, 11-12

11 But Naaman was wroth, and went away, and said, Behold, I thought, He will surely come out to me, and stand, and call on the name of the Lord his God, and strike his hand over the place, and recover the leper.

12 Are not Abana and Pharpar, rivers of Damascus, better than all the waters of Israel? may I not wash in them, and be clean? So he turned and went away in a rage.

Naaman is incensed by the simplicity of Elisha's "prescription" for his skin disease. No doubt he was accustomed to wild gyrations, shouting, and even some blood-letting accompanying pagan rites back home (see 1 Kings 18, esp. vs. 28). Even today, quiet obedience and prayer are effective in their own way in times of crisis, without sensational displays.

In a way, Naaman is correct: the waters of the rivers near Damascus *did* have as much therapeutic powers as the Jordan. Of course Elisha has another reason in mind for prescribing the Jordan.

III. A Soldier Who Was Healed—13-14

A. Bold servants, 13

13 And his servants came near, and spake unto him, and said, My father, if the prophet had bid thee do some great thing, wouldest thou not have done it? how much rather then, when he saith to thee,

Wash, and be clean?

Just as it was an unknown young girl who put in motion the events that led to Naaman's consultation with Elisha, so it is the captain's unnamed, lowly servants who dared to confront him with the unarguable logic of the situation. "My father" is a term of respect much like "my lord." The servants correctly see that washing in the Jordan is nothing compared to bleeding with leeches or reciting incantations to the gods—"medical" measures that might well have been expected in those days.

B. Healing from God, 14

14 Then went he down, and dipped himself seven times in Jordan, according to the saying of the man of God: and his flesh came again like unto the flesh of a little child, and he was clean.

Condescending to follow the prophet's instructions, the Syrian captain comes up from the Jordan with his disease cured. Apparently he sees clearly that the water is not magic, but served only as the test of his willingness to obey the prophet's God, who actually healed him. He confesses his faith in the one true God (vs. 15), and even asks to take earth from Israel, the special land of this God, back to Syria, perhaps to build an altar on it. From there, who knows how the worship of the true God might have spread in Syria, all from the word of a courageous servant girl.

Evangelistic Emphasis

Henrietta Jackson had worked at Stonewall Jackson Hospital almost four years. She eagerly went about her tasks with a spirit of service and genuine delight to have a part in the field of medicine— even though it was a small part. In her childhood, she had always dreamed of being a nurse, but family finances did not permit her to pursue the education necessary to fulfill her dream. Now as part of the "housekeeping crew" at Stonewall Jackson, she cleaned every room and scoured every washroom with the ever-present awareness that she did it *for the health of the patient*.

One morning while busy at her tasks, she felt her heart tenderly tug for one of "her patients" in hard labor. Though the nursing staff busily scurried about *trying* to attend to everyone, this poor mother-to-be was exceptionally scared about what was happening to her. Quietly, Henrietta exited the room and asked the attending nurse if it would be okay to invite the patient's husband to wash his hands and come into the room to help comfort her. Normally, any recommendation coming from "a maid" would not have been well-received. That particular hectic day, however, *any* suggestion was welcome.

Now, 25 years later, only a few of nurses at Stonewall Jackson Hospital remember that first father-to-be who was allowed to sit with his wife in labor. One nurse and one proud father remember that it was because of a young "maid."

• • • • • • • • • •

Memory Selection

Let him come now to me, and he shall know that there is a prophet in Israel.—*2 Kings 5:8b*

I still remember how arrogant it sounded to me when I first heard a friend express the confident security he knew in Christ. The question had been asked in a classroom of college freshmen, "How many of you *know* that you would spend eternity with the Lord, should you die right now?" Only three hands went up in a class of 45 students. Mine was not one of them. I was aghast that anyone would be so smug about his righteousness. It was not until sometime later that I understood that their confidence had nothing to do with their own righteousness but in Christ's atonement.

In much the same way, Elisha's words at first hearing ring a bit boastful. As one continues to listen in, however, it becomes quite clear that Elisha had no confidence in his own ability to make Naaman well. It was because he served a mighty Lord that he could call confidently for the leper to be sent to him for a cure. He knew the power of his God.

Weekday Problems

The Washingtons and the Franklins have lived next-door to each other for more than 20 years. Their children have grown up together. Every July they have celebrated the Fourth by sharing a picnic at the county park. The stories they could tell would fill a book!

Four months ago Henrietta Franklin, the last of the Franklin children at home, was discovered to have bone cancer. The thought of her 15-year-old body lying in a coffin is too much to bear. Together, the two families have prayed and cried and hoped. Last week, Henrietta's parents were told about a "new Christian clinic" in Mississippi headed by "a prophet," or so he is called. When the Franklins excitedly told the Washingtons, they were unable to conceal their apprehension. Fear gripped them for their dear friends. It sounded too good to be true. Were their comrades buying into a sick scam?

* How can the Washingtons help the Franklins make a decision about the treatment of their daughter that is the product of both wisdom and faith?

* How can the Washingtons support their good friends even if they decide to pursue a course they think unwise? What would you do?

* How can the Franklins best respond to their friends' candid apprehensions about their care for their daughter?

Exceptional Excuses

Jones came into the office in New York City an hour late for the third time in a week. "What's the story this time?" asked his boss.

"Everything went wrong this morning," Jones said. "The wife decided to take me to the station, but it took her ten minutes to get dressed. Then the drawbridge got stuck. Rather than let you down, I swam across the river, ran out to the airport, chartered a helicopter, landed atop Radio City Music Hall, and was carried here piggyback by one of the Rockettes."

"You'll have to do better than that," his boss said. "No woman can get ready in ten minutes."

* * *

The employee arrived late with one eye closed, his left arm in a sling, and his clothes in tatters. "It's 9:30," the boss said, "and you were due at 8:30. What happened?"

"I fell out of a tenth-story window," the employee said.

"What?" the boss said. "It took you a whole hour?"

This Lesson in Your Life

Daniel and his mother moved from New Jersey to California. She had an impressive new job, but Daniel discovered that a dark-haired Italian boy with a Jersey accent can sometimes have difficulty fitting into the blond surfer crowd of the West Coast. That is especially true if he tries to date one of the ace-jock's girl friends.

Though he managed to talk his way out of some of his troubles, Daniel was finally cornered by several boys who belonged to the same karate school. The end result was not pretty. While in the process of mending, Daniel became aware that the elderly gardener working at the apartment complex where he and his mother live was something of a karate expert. Hesitantly, he approached Miyagi, the gardener and asked him to teach him the art.

Miyagi was reluctant at first, but Daniel was not easy to discourage. After much pleading by Daniel, Miyagi agreed to teach Daniel karate, strongly cautioning Daniel that violence is not the answer to life's problems. Even with Miyagi's quiet sermonette, Daniel was thrilled to have a teacher.

His elation at having a personal karate teacher did not last long, however. When Daniel's training began, he couldn't understand what he was being shown. Miyagi seemed more interested in having Daniel paint fences and wax cars than teaching him karate. Daniel impatiently suspected that he was just "being used" to get a few distasteful chores done. As the story line of "The Karate Kid" unfolded, however, it became comically clear that all those seemingly unrelated assignments were developing the very muscles and movements necessary for use in skilled karate.

Naaman's dismay at the simple instruction delivered to him by the servant from Elisha is not really that surprising. Isn't that the way we often are? We expect the spectacular or heroic or flamboyant. The ordinary tends both to disappoint and to surprise us. We listen for God's voice to thunder from the mountain tops, but we hear only "a still small voice" (see 1 Kings 19:12) breaking the silence of our closet. Perhaps we looked for a conversion experience charged with Fourth-of-July fireworks. In reality, our experience may have been more like a gradual awareness of a "warm glow." Often our eager anticipation of thunder and lightening to accompany God's promise has found, instead, a small cloud about the size of a man's hand (see 1 Kings 18:44).

In much the same way, the marriage counselor tells us that *simple kindness of speech* will save our crumbling marriage. The problem is not "a deep-seated neurosis" or "uncorrectable incompatibility" as we had suspected. Somehow his allegation that our marriage is dying from *verbal abuse* angers us. Instead of "filling the doctor's prescription," we find another doctor.

Our visit with the Pastor is equally disappointing. Responding to our search for spiritual depth and richness, he points us to a daily devotional reading schedule and prayer time. We were expecting some "in depth seminar," a Bible College curriculum or some personal guidance into some *supernatural* realm. Is it any wonder that Naaman balked at Elisha's instruction to dip in the Jordan as a cure for his leprosy? Naaman responded much like we do.

Seed Thoughts

1. What king did Naaman serve, and in what capacity?

Naaman served the King of Syria as "captain of the host."

2. What heroic triumph was credited to Naaman because of the Lord's blessing?

The Lord had used Naaman to give deliverance to Syria.

3. What was the outstanding "negative" in Naaman's life?

In spite of Naaman's prestige and success, he was a leper.

4. Who was the person who provided the initial news that *someone* might be able to cure Naaman?

Someone described as "a little maid... [who] waited on Naaman's wife".

5. Whom did this person say could cure Naaman? Where was this *miracle worker* to be found?

At this point he is simply described as "the prophet that is in Samaria."

---

1. What king did Naaman serve, and in what capacity?

2. What heroic triumph was credited to Naaman because of the Lord's blessing?

3. What was the outstanding "negative" in Naaman's life?

4. Who was the person who provided the initial news that *someone* might be able to cure Naaman?

5. Whom did this person say could cure Naaman? Where was this *miracle worker* to be found?

6. To whom was this valuable information delivered that a cure for Naaman might be available?

7. What gifts did the king of Syria send to appeal for a cure for his servant, Naaman, and to whom did he send them?

8. What was his reaction when he receive the letter and gifts from the king of Syria?

9. What did the prophet's servant tell Naaman to do to get rid of his leprosy?

10. How did Naaman receive this prescription for his disease?

(Continued next page)

Naaman served the King of Syria as "captain of the host."

The Lord had used Naaman to give deliverance to Syria.

In spite of Naaman's prestige and success, he was a leper.

Someone described as "a little maid... [who] waited on Naaman's wife".

At this point he is simply described as "the prophet that is in Samaria."

The rumor was taken to the king of Syria, whom Naaman served.

The king of Syria sent 10 talents of silver, 6,000 pieces of gold, and 10 changes of garments to the king of Israel.

He tore his clothes, and said, "Am I God, to kill and to make alive?" He thought the king of Syria was seeking a quarrel against him.

Elisha's servant told him to dip in the Jordan River seven times.

He was very angry. He thought the prophet himself would come to see him and do something spectacular.

6. To whom was this valuable information delivered that a cure for Naaman might be available?

The rumor was taken to the king of Syria, whom Naaman served.

7. What gifts did the king of Syria send to appeal for a cure for his servant, Naaman, and to whom did he send them?

The king of Syria sent 10 talents of silver, 6,000 pieces of gold, and 10 changes of garments to the king of Israel.

8. What was his reaction when he receive the letter and gifts from the king of Syria?

He tore his clothes, and said, "Am I God, to kill and to make alive?" He thought the king of Syria was seeking a quarrel against him.

9. What did the prophet's servant tell Naaman to do to get rid of his leprosy?

Elisha's servant told him to dip in the Jordan River seven times.

10. How did Naaman receive this prescription for his disease?

He was very angry. He thought the prophet himself would come to see him and do something spectacular.

Courage to Speak for God

*W*oe to them that are at ease in Zion, and trust in the mountain of Samaria, which are named chief of the nations, to whom the house of Israel came!

7:7 Thus he shewed me: and, behold, the Lord stood upon a wall made by a plumb-line, with a plumbline in his hand.

8 And the Lord said unto me, Amos, what seest thou? And I said, A plumbline. Then said the Lord, Behold, I will set a plumbline in the midst of my people Israel: and I will rise against the house of Jeroboam with the sword.

9 And the high places of Isaac shall be desolate, and the sanctuaries of Israel shall be laid waste; and I will rise against the house of Jeroboam with the sword.

10 Then Amaziah the priest of Bethel sent to Jeroboam king of Israel, saying, Amos hath conspired against thee in the midst of the house of Israel: the land is not able to bear all his words.

11 For thus Amos saith, Jeroboam shall die by the sword, and Israel shall surely be led away captive out of their own land.

12 Also Amaziah said unto Amos, O thou seer, go, flee thee away into the land of Judah, and there eat bread, and prophesy there:

13 But prophesy not again any more at Bethel: for it is the king's chapel, and it is the king's court.

14 Then answered Amos, and said to Amaziah, I was no prophet, neither was I a prophet's son; but I was an herdman, a gatherer of sycomore fruit:

15 And the Lord took me as I followed the flock, and the Lord said unto me, Go, prophesy unto my people Israel.

Amos 6:1; 7:7-15

Nov. 1

Memory Selection
Amos 7:14-15

Background Scripture
Amos 6—7

Devotional Reading
Acts 4:13-22

Printed Scripture
Amos 6:1; 7:7-15

Teacher's Target

Lesson purpose: *To describe, through the work of the prophet Amos, how the prophetic voice often invades our "comfort zone," and to emphasize the importance of heeding it anyway.*

Continuing our survey of Israel's prophets, we come to one who is famous for his insistence that true faith results in justice and righteousness. Amos was very unpopular for these pronouncements, since, like most of us, the high officials he rebuked were not eagerly seeking someone to correct their ways.

This lesson provides a good opportunity to show that Israel's prophets were not gifted as mere fortune tellers, but with the boldness to speak out against those who were not faithful to the faith.

Lesson Introduction

The prophet Amos is best known for his insistence that public piety is no substitute for treating others as creatures of God who deserve justice. He railed against mistreating the poor and needy, then offering public sacrifices designed to paint a picture of religiosity (4:2-5). He even quoted God as saying, "I hate, I despise your feast days . . . take thou away from me the noise of thy songs; for I will not hear the melody of thy viols. But let judgment run down as waters, and righteousness as a mighty stream" (5:21-24).

Although Amos lived in the southern kingdom of Judah, he aimed his prophetic arrows at the northern kingdom of Israel. A rustic shepherd who had no doubt confronted lions and other predators, he spoke for God in a "roar" (1:2). He portrayed God as burning the walls and palaces of unjust kings (1:10), and sending into captivity those who slept on ornate ivory beds while ignoring the poor (6:4-7). Yet Amos also foresaw that God would bring a remnant back to the Promised Land (9:11-15).

Teaching Outline	Daily Bible Readings
I. Woe to the Complacent!—6:1	**Mon.** Amos Speaks for God *Amos 1:1-8*
	Tue. Transgressing God's Law *Amos 2:4-8*
II. Measuring for Uprightness—7:7-9	**Wed.** Condemning the Complacent *Amos 6:1-7*
III. Warning: Prophet at Work–7:10-11	**Thu.** Turning Justice to Poison *Amos 6:8-14*
IV. Prophet Go Home!—12-13	**Fri.** Setting the Plumb Line *Amos 7:1-9*
	Sat. Invitation to Leave *Amos 7:10-17*
V. The Commission's Priority—14-15	**Sun.** Against Waste and Indifference *Luke 16:19-31*

Verse by Verse

I. Woe to the Complacent!—6:1

6:1 Woe to them that are at ease in Zion, and trust in the mountain of Samaria, which are named chief of the nations, to whom the house of Israel came!

During Amos' time, eight centuries before Christ, both the southern kingdom of Judah and the northern kingdom of Israel were enjoying considerable prosperity (see 2 Kings 14:23-29). They had declined to obey God's stern command to drive out the people of the land, with their false gods, and had settled instead for profitable trade agreements and inter-marriage. Furthermore, many had become rich at the expense of the poor, with the aid of a court system that accepted bribes.

Although Amos is from the southern kingdom, he pronounces woe both on Zion (Jerusalem) in the south and Samaria in the north. He is inspired not to pronounce judgment on people who were enjoying the fruits of hard-earned labor, but on those who by and large had become wealthy at the expense of the poor, and idolatrous at the expense of allegiance to the One God.

The people's wealth had lured them to trust in themselves and in the gods of the nations about them (see 8:14), instead of giving credit to Yahweh for their well-being. The ten northern tribes were especially at fault for attributing their wealth to gods worshiped atop the high places of Samaria.

II. Measuring for Uprightness—7:7-9

7 Thus he shewed me: and, behold, the Lord stood upon a wall made by a plumbline, with a plumbline in his hand.

8 And the LORD said unto me, Amos, what seest thou? And I said, A plumbline. Then said the Lord, Behold, I will set a plumbline in the midst of my people Israel: and I will rise against the house of Jeroboam with the sword.

9 And the high places of Isaac shall be desolate, and the sanctuaries of Israel shall be laid waste; and I will rise against the house of Jeroboam with the sword.

Now Amos focuses specifically on Israel, the northern kingdom led by Jeroboam II, a descendant of the Jeroboam who led the revolt against the southern kingdom of Judah (1 Kings 11:31-32). The vision of the plumbline shows that God is measuring Israel like a carpenter uses a weighted line to "plumb" the walls of a house to ensure that they are precisely vertical.

The measurement shows Israel to be seriously "out of plumb." The nation has oppressed the poor, and, especially mentioned here, it has polluted the pure worship of God with idolatrous worship on the "high places." These were mountains, hilltops, and sometimes elevated platforms, where the people thought to lift themselves closer to pagan gods, who were presumed to inhabit the air. Not only did Israel forsake the One God at these places; it also ignored the importance of Jerusalem as the place where God promised to meet His people (1 Kings 9:3).

III. Warning: Prophet at Work!—7:10-11

10 Then Amaziah the priest of Bethel sent to Jeroboam king of Israel, saying, Amos hath conspired against thee in the midst of the house of Israel: the land is not able to bear all his words.

11 For thus Amos saith, Jeroboam shall die by the sword, and Israel shall surely be led away captive out of their own land.

As a "court priest" in the northern kingdom, Amaziah's job was to promote the worship of the golden calves Jeroboam I had set up at Bethel and Dan (1 Kings 12:28-29). Amaziah was dedicated not only to leading pagan worship but to telling Jeroboam II what the king wanted to hear. He is representative of a strong but unenviable tradition of "false prophets" who became the targets of true prophets such as those who names are attached to several Old Testament writings.

Although true priests in Israel were supportive of true prophets, this scene illustrates the frequent tension between false priests and true prophets. The former were more interested in ritual accuracy and politics, while the latter called both king and subjects to back up true worship with justice and mercy. False prophets can be identified by being popular with wrong-headed kings, and true prophets by the degree of the kings' opposition!

Amaziah is therefore only too happy to report to his king that Amos has been guilty of treason by prophesying that the kingdom will fall because of its rampant, institutionalized sins (7:9). As a matter of historical fact, Amos' prediction about the captivity of Israel soon came true. Soon after the rule of Jeroboam II, many in Israel were carried away by the Assyrians. Other foreigners were imported to Samaria to intermarry with the Israelites who remained, resulting in the mixed race of the Samaritans, toward whom "pure-blooded" Jews in the time of Christ were so prejudiced.

IV. Prophet Go Home!—12-13

12 Also Amaziah said unto Amos, O thou seer, go, flee thee away into the land of Judah, and there eat bread, and prophesy there:

13 But prophesy not again any

more at Bethel: for it is the king's chapel, and it is the king's court.

Jeroboam's priest Amaziah is not content with merely warning the king against Amos. In a direct confrontation, he challenges Amos to go back home and ply the profession of prophet there, instead of preaching in Israel. Perhaps out of feigned respect for Amos, he calls him a "seer," the older name for prophet (1 Sam. 9:9). This term emphasizes the predictive aspect of a prophet's work, while the term "prophet" connotes both that aspect and the work of pronouncing God's Word.

Amaziah implies that Amos should "eat bread" or make a living in the prophecy business in Judah, not at Bethel, in Samaria. For years there had been formal "schools" or "guilds" of prophets" (1 Sam. 10:5-12), who were apparently financially supported as modern churches might support a minister; and it is to this kind of arrangement that Amaziah refers.

We can easily imagine how unwelcome Amos, an outspoken and judgmental foreigner, would have been in Israel. The prophet was about as welcome as a "carpet-bagger" preacher from New England would have been in the south after the Civil War. Bethel, Amaziah holds, is Jeroboam's and the northern tribes' own "chapel" or center of worship. It is out of Amos' territory; and both religious and civil order is threatened by this hell-and-damnation preacher/intruder. Note that Amaziah's primary concern is not that the people conform to God's standards, but to preserve the economic, religious, and political status quo.

V. The Commission's Priority—14-15

14 Then answered Amos, and said to Amaziah, I was no prophet, neither was I a prophet's son; but I was an herdman, a gatherer of sycomore fruit:

15 And the LORD took me as I followed the flock, and the LORD said unto me, Go, prophesy unto my people Israel.

Amos' defense against Amaziah the priest rests on the fact that prophecy is not his profession but his calling. He was not a member of the "seminary-trained" school of the prophets, nor even the son of a prophet who might take on his father's mantle. He was only a shepherd and an orchard-keeper from Tekoa, near Bethlehem, in the southern kingdom (1:1; 7:14). He has no personal stake in whether his message is accepted, but in fact was preach-ing at considerable personal discomfort. God had plucked him out of the bands of sheep he was tending and sent him packing with a divine message. It is this constraint, not self-service, that provides an objective way to distinguish the true prophet from the false.

Evangelistic Emphasis

Twenty years ago when Hank Jefferson moved into his neighborhood in south Dallas, he was part of a cultural migration—though he never thought much about that at the time. The neighborhood was in a state of flux as young families "of color" were rapidly moving into an area that had once been dominated by near-retirement-age, middle-management Caucasians. Whole churches that had once burst with activity were suddenly closing their doors, moving to communities farther out in the suburbs. Hank's own Missionary Baptist Church had purchased one of those abandoned church plants for an unbelievably low price. The unflattering term that was sometimes used for that social phenomenon was "white flight."

Today, the neighborhood where Hank Jefferson raised his family and had planned to spend his retirement years is very much amidst another social change. This time the cultural group moving into the area is Hispanic. One by one, Hank has watched the homes on his block be sold to people of a radically different culture than his own—even of a different language. His once thriving Missionary Baptist Church has come to be a virtual Black island amidst a Hispanic sea. With great anguish he has sat through many deacons' meetings discussing what the church should do. Always, the deacons (against much opposition) have decided to "reach out to the Hispanics" in an attempt to welcome them to their community and their church. Yet, one by one, Hank has watched his own church brothers with their families leave to find a less threatening church home.

● ● ● ● ● ● ●

Then answered Amos, and said to Amaziah, I was no prophet, neither was I a prophet's son; but I was an herdman, and a gatherer of sycamore fruit. And the LORD took me as I followed the flock, and the LORD said unto me, Go, prophesy unto my people Israel.—*Amos 7:14-15*

There is a certain credibility that comes with a long and rich heritage of profession or service. The third-generation attorney in a long-established law firm begins his practice with a level of natural clout that is the envy of the rookie from the ghetto getting his start in the district attorney's office. The same could be said of the surgeon or the police officer or the Air Force pilot that comes to the task from a rich heritage.

At the same time, there is another kind of credibility that blesses the one who arrives on the scene "out of season." It is not at his (or her) own initiative. Instead, the call comes by the circumstances of the moment thrusting onto one the necessity to step up to the line. In the process of arising to the challenge, resources beyond his own experience or internal fortitude are supplied. It is in such moments of crisis that heroes are made. Amos was that kind of hero. He responded to the call of God.

Weekday Problems

When Ted Armstrong's supervisor at Federal Express informed him that he was being transferred from Jacksonville to Salt Lake City, it came as a shock. Even though the move was billed as a "promotion," it seemed like he and Ann, his wife, were being sentenced to an American "Siberia."

As the date for their move approached, however, the Armstrongs' prayer time increasingly focused on their move. The more they prayed about the matter, the more they sensed a *calling of God* at work in this unexpected move. Could it be?

Though the Armstrongs had never thought of themselves as "missionaries," they certainly were strong people of faith. Ever since their marriage they have been aggressively involved in their very active young adults' program at First Church. Their participation included not only Sunday School and socials, but also holding a VBS for some inner-city children, and building a house for Habitat for Humanity.

* What about a move to Salt Lake City might make it seem to be the "call of God"?

* In what ways might the Armstrongs find church to be significantly different in Salt Lake City?

* In what way might we view any such unexpected move to "have God's hand at work in it?" Is this an appropriate or inappropriate question to apply to life's events?

The Other Side of Sanity

Shrink: Now, will you be able to pay for this treatment?
Shrinkee: Don't worry, doc. You'll get your money or my name ain't Henry VIII.

* * *

Shrinkee: You see, doc, my problem is that I like shoes better than boots.
Shrink: That's no problem. Most people prefer shoes.
Shrinkee (elated): That's great! How do *you* like them—fried or   scrambled?

* * *

Wife: My husband thinks he's a refrigerator.
Psychiatrist: Oh, I wouldn't worry as long as he's not violent.
Wife: Oh his delusion doesn't bother me. It's just that when he sleeps with his mouth open the little light keeps me awake.

This Lesson in Your Life

Toby Miller works at Kennimer, Hawkins and Jones Accounting as a "Department Assistant." Though his official title sounds impressive, Toby does not really expect to excel much beyond his current "errand boy" position that he has held since he began with the firm seven years ago. Toby is "intellectually challenged." Though he is thankful for this minimal skills job, it is unlikely that he will ever be able to earn a living wage that would support a family.

Every day Toby delivers coffee and mail to his friends behind their big desks in their plush offices. They are dressed like he only dreams about dressing. They each carry a fine leather attache case and drive a shiny new BMW or Mercedes or Porche. Most of them smile at Toby and have some kind greeting for him. Still, even after seven years, not one seems to know the man full of dreams who lives behind those dull, *I'm-just-an-errand-boy* eyes.

It's not that Toby resents his fellow-workers their big salaries, fine cars and stylish suits. It's just that he wishes they could *really see* him. He overhears them complaining about their investment losses, but they never seem to notice when he is forced to skip lunch because of insufficient funds. They boast to each other about their "new wheels," but four of them passed by him last week when he missed the bus and was forced to walk the three miles to work. Their families are very different from each other—some rich with happiness, others with painful brokenness. Yet, everybody in the building has some kind of family—everyone but Toby. Never has he been invited to share a holiday cookout or Christmas party or even a "night out with the guys." Toby wonders what it would be like to be able to share in such things. He can only dream of them.

Is it possible that Amos was speaking to people very much like those who work at Kennimer, Hawkins and Jones? The people of Israel were not nearly as depraved as they are sometimes painted. There was nothing particularly *wicked* about "beds of ivory" or enjoying the luxury of body lotions. Relaxing on couches and listening to the music of viols was not all that uncommon, either. Basically, the Israelites were "upwardly mobile" people who had prospered enough to "enjoy the good life" (as we are prone to word it). Their sin was not in enjoying the blessings they had been given by God. Their sin consisted in their *forgetting* from where those blessing had come and their *thoughtless unconcern* for the rampant injustice that supported their luxury.

Reflected in the accounting offices of Hawkins and Jones, Amos' message might fall on ears just as deaf as those who first heard it in Israel. Perhaps he would talk about those who complained loudly about the rising price of gasoline but showed no concern about the threat of discontinued public transportation subsidies that would force Toby to have to walk. Or maybe such an "Amos" would talk about those who bewailed the "high price of coffee" but gave no regard to the peasant wages paid to those who picked the coffee beans.

Amos might even have some words of rebuke for the accounting staff who lose themselves in their ladder-climbing ambitions and their social conquests, but fail to have any awareness or thoughtful concern for the "have-nots" of their world. They might even maintain a respectable presence at church, but at the core of their lives, they are consumed with themselves.

Seed Thoughts

1. In whom or what did those who were "at ease in Zion" trust for their security?

They were said to trust in the mountain of Samaria.

2. Is Amos telling the people of Israel that it is wrong to stretch themselves upon their couches or to anoint themselves with ointments, etc.?

No. His point was that they lavished themselves in luxury *without any concern for the injustice in the land.*

3. What are some of the other examples of "luxury" that Amos listed?

Lying upon beds of ivory, eating the lambs of the flock and the calves of the stall, inventing for themselves instruments of music and drinking wine in bowls.

4. What did the Lord say He abhorred? What did He say that He hated?

The Lord said that He abhorred the excellency of Jacob and hate his palaces.

5. What prompted Amos to appeal to the Lord for mercy?

The Lord revealed to him the grasshoppers he had formed to eat the king's harvest.

1. In whom or what did those who were "at ease in Zion" trust for their security?

2. Is Amos telling the people of Israel that it is wrong to stretch themselves upon their couches or to anoint themselves with ointments, etc.?

3. What are some of the other examples of "luxury" that Amos listed?

4. What did the Lord say He abhorred? What did He say that He hated?

5. What prompted Amos to appeal to the Lord for mercy?

6. How did the Lord respond to Amos' appeal?

7. When Amos "saw" the Lord standing on the wall, what did He have in his hand?

8. What did the vision of the plumb line intend to communicate?

9. What accusation did Amaziah, the priest of Bethel make against Amos?

10. What did Amos declare to be his prophetic heritage?

(Continued next page)

They were said to trust in the mountain of Samaria.

No. His point was that they lavished themselves in luxury *without any concern for the injustice in the land*.

Lying upon beds of ivory, eating the lambs of the flock and the calves of the stall, inventing for themselves instruments of music and drinking wine in bowls.

The Lord said that He abhorred the excellency of Jacob and hate his palaces.

The Lord revealed to him the grasshoppers he had formed to eat the king's harvest.

The Lord repented of, or changed His mind about, his plan.

The Lord had a plumb line in his hand.

The message from the Lord was one of judgment rather than tolerance.

Amaziah said that Amos conspired against Jeroboam, the king, in the midst of the house of Israel.

Amos said that he was not a prophet, nor the son of a prophet but a herdsman and a gatherer of sycamore fruit.

6. How did the Lord respond to Amos' appeal?

The Lord repented of, or changed His mind about, his plan.

7. When Amos "saw" the Lord standing on the wall, what did He have in his hand?

The Lord had a plumb line in his hand.

8. What did the vision of the plumb line intend to communicate?

The message from the Lord was one of judgment rather than tolerance.

9. What accusation did Amaziah, the priest of Bethel make against Amos?

Amaziah said that Amos conspired against Jeroboam, the king, in the midst of the house of Israel.

10. What did Amos declare to be his prophetic heritage?

Amos said that he was not a prophet, nor the son of a prophet but a herdsman and a gatherer of sycamore fruit.

Writers of Songs

ruly God is good to Israel, even to such as are of a clean heart.

2 But as for me, my feet were almost gone; my steps had well nigh slipped.

3 For I was envious at the foolish, when I saw the prosperity of the wicked.

12 Behold, these are the ungodly, who prosper in the world; they increase in riches.

Psalm 73: 1-3, 12-13, 16-18, 21-26

13 Verily I have cleansed my heart in vain, and washed my hands in innocency.

16 When I thought to know this, it was too painful for me;

17 Until I went into the sanctuary of God; then understood I their end.

18 Surely thou didst set them in slippery places: thou castedst them down into destruction.

21 Thus my heart was grieved, and I was pricked in my reins.

22 So foolish was I, and ignorant: I was as a beast before thee.

23 Nevertheless I am continually with thee: thou hast holden me by my right hand.

24 Thou shalt guide me with thy counsel, and afterward receive me to glory.

25 Whom have I in heaven but thee? and there is none upon earth that I desire beside thee.

26 My flesh and my heart faileth: but God is the strength of my heart, and my portion for ever.

Memory Selection
Psalm 73:28

Background Scripture
Psalm 73

Devotional Reading
Psalm 27:1-14

Printed Scripture
Psalm 73:1-3, 12-13, 16-18, 21-26

Nov. 8

91

Teacher's Target

Lesson purpose: *To consider frankly certain obstacles to faith, and to affirm with the psalmist that worship is a necessary antidote for doubt.*

Introduce this session by asking group members to share times or events that threw their faith, or that of others, into question. The wicked prosper, a friend or marriage partner betrays us, our business fails, a loved one dies an untimely death, flood or fire destroys our home—such events often create doubt in the strongest believers.

Then point out that the psalmist Asaph knew well the toll such experiences can take on faith. Yet in this Psalm we can also learn about an antidote to doubt: *meeting together with others in worship.* The psalmist found that simply being with God and other believers in the sanctuary, forms a refuge for faith even when "answers" are lacking. Worship protects us from the satanic suggestion that if life "goes wrong" we should stop believing.

Lesson Introduction

The book of Psalms has been called "The Hymnbook of the Second Temple." This description arises from evidence that many of the Psalms were collected and used in Jewish worship after the Jews returned from Babylonian captivity and rebuilt the Temple in Jerusalem (some 500 years B.C.). Although most of these "chantable hymns" were apparently written by King David, some, like Psalm 73 were composed by others.

Some of these "songs" are hymns of joy, and some are outbursts of praise. Yet they also include honest confessions that not all of life prompts feelings of joy. The Psalms also include radically honest elements such as doubt. Psalm 73, along with its numerically reversed "twin," Psalm 37, remind us that God accepts honest questions in the context of worship. In fact, it is in that setting that we experience a depth of assurance that does not require immediate answers to our questions.

Teaching Outline	Daily Bible Readings

I. Confession of Doubt—1-3
  A. The general rule, 1
  B. The exceptions, 2-3
II. Crisis of Evidence—12-13
  A. Why do the ungodly prosper?, 12
  B. What use is righteousness?, 13
III. Coming to Worship—16-18
  A. The weight of the question, 16
  B. The setting of the resolution, 17-18
IV. Confession of Faith—21-26
  A. Grievous questions, 21-22
  B. God's presence is enough, 23-26
	Mon. My Feet Had Almost Stumbled
	  Psalm 73:1-14
	Tue. I Went into the Sanctuary
	  Psalm 73:15-20
	Wed. I Was Stupid and Ignorant
	  Psalm 73:21-28
	Thu. Reassurance Found in Worship
	  Psalm 27:1-14
	Fri. The Fate of the Wicked
	  Psalm 37:1-13
	Sat. Integrity Is Affirmed
	  Psalm 26:1-12
	Sun. The Lord Is Our Protector
	  Psalm 121:1-8

Verse by Verse

I. Confession of Doubt—1-3

A. The general rule, 1

1 Truly God is good to Israel, even to such as are of a clean heart.

These lines reflect God's promise to care for His Covenant people, Israel. When the original Covenant with Abraham was renewed after Israel escaped from Egypt, God promised anew that, for the faithful, "Blessed shall be the fruit of thy body, and the fruit of thy ground, and the fruit of thy cattle, the increase of thy kine (cattle), and the flocks of thy sheep" (Deut. 28:4). In contrast to these blessings, curses were pronounced on those who refused to observe God's commandments (28:15).

All this led some in Israel to assume that a wealthy person who obviously was blessed by God was also a faithful person; and that hard times were automatic evidence of sin. This was the view of Job's friends, who tried to convince this famous sufferer that the trials he was enduring were the result of sin in his life. The same view is expressed in Psalm 37:25: "I have been young, and now am old; yet have I not seen the righteous forsaken, nor his seed begging bread."

B. The exceptions, 2-3

2 But as for me, my feet were almost gone; my steps had well nigh slipped.

3 For I was envious at the foolish, when I saw the prosperity of the wicked.

The psalmist confessed that he almost slipped and fell in his faith-walk when he realized that the wicked weren't always punished after all. He had taken a general rule—that God blesses the righteous and punishes the wicked *in this life*—and turned it into an automatic "deal" with God. Instead, the Covenant is subject to the will of a sovereign Lord.

This Old Testament believer lacked the teaching of Christ that "the rain falls on both the just and the unjust" (Matt. 5:45). He also lacked the example and promise of the resurrection of Christ, which Christians can use as evidence that God *will* bless the righteous and punish the wicked in an after-life. Instead, many Old Covenant believers expected God's approval or disapproval to be made evident in this life by material blessings.

II. Crisis over Evidence—12-13

A. Why do the ungodly prosper?, 12

12 Behold, these are the ungodly, who prosper in the world; they increase in riches.

It seems to the psalmist—as it must

seem to us sometimes—that ungodly people profit the most in life. They seem to believe they can ignore contracts, lie, cheat, and otherwise ignore all moral standards. We want to believe the humble, honest toiler will be blessed, but the fact is we see them often stepped on by the unscrupulous.

B. What profit is righteousness?, 13

13 Verily I have cleansed my heart in vain, and washed my hands in innocency.

To a devout person who has been passed over for a promotion by an ungodly person, doing right may seem useless. He may ask, "What good did it do me to follow the rules?" Although this is a natural reaction, it is dangerously close to the attitude that Satan accused Job of having: "Doth Job fear God for nought?" (Job 1:9). The psalmist is grappling with the question of how believers can love and serve God just for who He is, instead of having our faith attached to material interests.

III. Coming to Worship—16-18
A. The weight of the question, 16

16 When I thought to know this, it was too painful for me;

In our day many people shun serious questions like the one the psalmist is asking because they are painful. We have been promised that Christianity puts a smile on our face and a spring in our step. Although that is a very good general rule, it does not equip us to deal with the exceptions. Like Job, however, the author of this psalm wrestles with the question of why the wicked prosper until he was spiritually weary.

B. The setting of the resolution, 17-18

17 Until I went into the sanctuary of God; then understood I their end.

18 Surely thou didst set them in slippery places: thou castedst them down into destruction.

The questioner's uneasiness is resolved not in the philosopher's study but in a place of worship. An understanding of the true fate of the wicked dawns on him in a setting where the focus of his reflection is shifted from how someone else is prospering to the nature of God. It is in worship where we recall, along with fellow-believers, that over the long run our "story" includes such events as the exodus from Egypt, Israel's supreme evidence that God delivers His people. The big picture is simply more reliable than particular exceptions.

The parallels with the experience of the classic sufferer Job continue. It was after God had revealed Himself to Job, and after Job had worshiped by offering sacrifices and praying for his friends that he was able again to receive God's blessings (Job 42).

IV. Confession of Faith—21-26
A. Grievous questions, 21-22

21 Thus my heart was grieved, and I was pricked in my reins.

22 So foolish was I, and ignorant: I was as a beast before thee.

The word translated "reins" is actually the Hebrew word for "kidneys," meaning that the psalmist was moved "from the gut" or inside out because of his previous doubt. He was ashamed that he did not have a greater level of trust that God would give the wicked but prosperous person his "come-uppance" at an appropriate time. The author knows he is more than an ignorant beast who can trust a person only if it is cared for physically.

B. God's presence is enough, 23-26

23 Nevertheless I am continually with thee: thou hast holden me by my right hand.

24 Thou shalt guide me with thy counsel, and afterward receive me to glory.

25 Whom have I in heaven but thee? and there is none upon earth that I desire beside thee.

26 My flesh and my heart faileth: but God is the strength of my heart, and my portion for ever.

What do believers have to sustain them in times when God's physical blessings are lacking? What keeps the farmer clinging to faith when his crops are destroyed by drought? The awareness that God is present, and that this presence does vary with the ebb and flow of material gain.

The expression in verse 26 expressing confidence that God will "afterward receive me to glory" may be a particularly bold affirmation of an after-life that is relatively rare in the Old Testament. It is also possible that the phrase means "After I have endured a lack of material blessings without losing my faith You will show me your glory." It seems more likely, however, that the psalmist realizes that the injustices in this life call for trust that they will be made right in the next life.

To note again a parallel with the book of Job, this affirmation may be compared with Job 19:25-26: "I know that my redeemer lives, and that in the end he will stand upon the earth. And after my skin has been destroyed, yet in my flesh I will see God."

Evangelistic Emphasis

Andrew Brummett grew up in a rich university setting. His church home benefited both from its rich Lutheran heritage and its abundance of academic superstars.

Worship as Andrew had always known it was an interesting mix of "high church" and "youth church." Though the student body of the university kept the tension taut with contemporary worship expectations, the "old money" paying the parish bills demanded a level of decorum suiting *A Mighty Fortress* dignity.

Coming from such a rich church heritage, it was with genuine dread that

Andrew climbed the front steps of the small church in Middleboro, Kentucky. He had promised one of his college friends, however, that he would stop in to see him, should he be in the area. His friend then agreed to meet him at church Sunday morning. He couldn't imagine getting anything out of the service.

It was the third song that exploded inside his head—the one right before the sermon:

*Tempted and tried we're oft made to
    wonder*
Why it should be thus all the day long,
While there are others living about us,
Never molested, though in the wrong.

Andrew had never heard that song before, but he surely did identify with it! One of his greatest struggles of faith was watching those who seemed so corrupt prosper so abundantly. Now somehow, he found amazing comfort in knowing that others had struggled with this, too.

• • • • • • • •

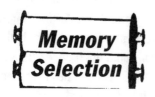

Memory Selection

But it is good for me to draw near to God I have put my trust in the Lord GOD, that I may declare all thy works.—*Psalm 73:28*

Life apart from the presence of God conditions one to forget His goodness. Vision becomes impaired by the forest of luxury (or by the desert of poverty). One's own heart gradually comes to beat in rhythm with the pulse of the masses of people surrounding him. Their cries of despair make us cry. Their cutting cynicism begins to echo from our voice, too. Their flippant vulgarities increasingly flitter about inside our own head, even if they are not yet vocalized. One day, we hear ourselves subconsciously singing the same ballads of self-pity or hatred or Narcissism that once were appalling to us.

Interesting, isn't it—how being again in the presence of meaningful worship has a profound way of refocusing our sights on the heavenly throne. Suddenly, we see beyond the forest or the desert to the Eden of God where the tree of life grows and our heart longs to go.

Weekday Problems

Ellen Baker has been part of the marketing staff at Mishistu Electronics for more than eight years. Though she enjoys her work very much, she has not advanced in the company as rapidly as she had anticipated. Through the years, Ellen has watched several newcomers arrive and quickly move on up in the company ahead of her. She has tried to be patient and understanding about it, but she has begun to wonder if God is punishing her for something. She is the only practicing Christian in the office, and she is the only one in the office who has not moved ahead in her career at a reasonable pace. Somewhere along the way, she got the idea that God blesses the faithful, but it seems to her as though He punishes them.

* Was Ellen correct or misguided in her expectation that God would bless her in her career if she proved faithful to him?

* Is Ellen correct or misguided in her present thoughts that God must be punishing her for something?

* What are some other possible explanations for why Ellen has not progressed in her career as she had expected?

Miss Prints in the News

Item: At the Ladies' Aid Society meeting many interesting articles were raffled off. Every member brought something she no longer needed. Many members brought their husbands.

* * *

First printing: Mr. Janelli was a defective in the police force.
Correction: Mr. Janelli was a detective in the police farce.

* * *

Notice: The Wildwife League will meet tonight.

* * *

Headline: Father of ten shot; mistaken for rabbit.

* * *

Item: Dr. Jeremiah is the author of a brand-new book that is expected to outsmell the two million copies of his first book.

* * *

Headline: Man found dead in cemetery.

This Lesson in Your Life

One term that has come to roll off of the contemporary tongue with ease is the designation, *"real world."* Often it is used to highlight a contrast to what is being taught or experienced in the classroom at school (high school, medical school, Sunday School, etc.). It may be that the person using the term intends to infer that what is being experienced or learned *in the present setting* does not fairly represent "the real world" (i.e., *"That theory sounds great here in the classroom, but it doesn't work like that in the real world!"*).

It must be admitted that classroom theories are at times much more sterile than the operating room procedures. The automotive test laboratory may not accurately simulate the grueling demands of *real world* commuter traffic. Theological platitudes often have great difficulty being fleshed out in life as it is lived in the *real world*.

Though this "real world" distinction has its times of legitimacy, it is perhaps more often used improperly. In the realm of "faith" and "religion" and "holiness," this is most assuredly true. Our reasons for raising this distinction vary.

(1) Sometimes we feel the need to soothe our throbbing conscience because of the severity of our transgression. Consequently, we tell ourselves that, even though we've embraced certain biblical absolutes all of our lives, "God's rules don't work very well *in the real world*."

(2) It may be that in looking for some way to *give ourselves permission* to do what in principle we reject, we appeal to the "real world distinction" in a way that *discounts* our professed principles. The problem in this setting is not a wounded conscience but a tempted and compromising heart.

(3) Perhaps, our most common reason for calling to our circumstance this appeal to the "real world" is because we have become so saturated with the values and mind of the secular world around us that we are no longer able to distinguish between *reality* and *fantasy / illusion*. For example:

Which is *reality*—the popular claim that "living together before marriage" is helpful in making sure two people are a good match, or the statistical evidence that those who "live together before marriage" have a higher divorce rate than those who don't?

Which is *reality*—the claim of Scripture that a person's value does not consist in the abundance of his possessions, or the claim of our contemporary culture that a person's worth is definitely measured by his financial assets?

Which is *reality*—the claims of the secularist that no life exists beyond the grave, or the claims of Scripture that eternal life exists beyond the grave?

Is the "real world" the one that tells us that self-gratification is the highest good or the one that tells us that self-gratification is counter-productive to our highest good?

Is the "real world" the one that tells me that I'm simply the by-product of billions of years of circumstantial accidents or the one that tells me that I am created in the image of God?

Is the "real world" the one that claims that matters relating to spiritual realities come from superstitious illusions, or the one that claims that a spiritual realm exists beyond the physical realm?

Perhaps our most basic question ought to be, "Is the *real world* the one I am confronted with at the office, or the one I am reminded of at church?

Seed Thoughts

1. What almost caused Asaph to slip in his faithfulness to God?

Asaph almost slipped when he looked about and noticed the prosperity of the wicked.

2. What did Asaph notice about the *physical* health of the wicked?

It appeared to Asaph that the wicked were *especially healthy*. Their bodies were healthy and their muscles were firm.

3. What did Asaph notice about the *emotional* health of the wicked?

Asaph noticed that they seemed to be at peace, free of troubles common to other men (NIV uses the term "carefree").

4. What did Asaph notice about the *financial* health of the wicked?

According to Asaph, the wicked seemed to be especially prosperous, increasing in riches.

5. Why did Asaph describe these people as "wicked"?

Asaph described them as wicked because they were proud, violent, oppressive, corrupt, blasphemous, and defiant of God.

1. What almost caused Asaph to slip in his faithfulness to God?

2. What did Asaph notice about the *physical* health of the wicked?

3. What did Asaph notice about the *emotional* health of the wicked?

4. What did Asaph notice about the *financial* health of the wicked?

5. Why did Asaph describe these people as "wicked"?

6. Since Asaph saw so much prosperity among the wicked, how did that make him feel?

7. How did Asaph perceive his own condition?

8. At what point did Asaph begin to see more clearly the condition of his relationship with God?

9. What new insight about the wicked did Asaph gain that he had not seen before?

10. What insight about his own relationship with God was Asaph given in the sanctuary?

(Continued next page)

Asaph almost slipped when he looked about and noticed the prosperity of the wicked.

It appeared to Asaph that the wicked were *especially healthy*. Their bodies were healthy and their muscles were firm.

Asaph noticed that they seemed to be at peace, free of troubles common to other men (NIV uses the term "carefree").

According to Asaph, the wicked seemed to be especially prosperous, increasing in riches.

Asaph described them as wicked because they were proud, violent, oppressive, corrupt, blasphemous, and defiant of God.

The prosperity that Asaph saw among the wicked made him feel as though he had served God *in vain*.

It seemed to Asaph as if life for him was especially difficult, as if he were being punished for something.

Asaph began to understand *when he went into the sanctuary* of god.

In the sanctuary Asaph was reminded that the rewards of the wicked are but momentary. There was nothing in them for him to envy.

In the sanctuary Asaph began to see that God was his best friend, his source of strength and One who would stand by him always.

6. Since Asaph saw so much prosperity among the wicked, how did that make him feel?

The prosperity that Asaph saw among the wicked made him feel as though he had served God *in vain*.

7. How did Asaph perceive his own condition?

It seemed to Asaph as if life for him was especially difficult, as if he were being punished for something.

8. At what point did Asaph begin to see more clearly the condition of his relationship with God?

Asaph began to understand *when he went into the sanctuary* of god.

9. What new insight about the wicked did Asaph gain that he had not seen before?

In the sanctuary Asaph was reminded that the rewards of the wicked are but momentary. There was nothing in them for him to envy.

10. What insight about his own relationship with God was Asaph given in the sanctuary?

In the sanctuary Asaph began to see that God was his best friend, his source of strength and One who would stand by him always.

Lesson 11

False Hopes and Judgment

7 us saith the LORD, Go and get a potter's earthen bottle, and take of the ancients of the people, and of the ancients of the priests;

2 And go forth unto the valley of the son of Hinnom, which is by the entry of the east gate, and proclaim there the words that I shall tell thee,

3 And say, Hear ye the word of the LORD, O kings of Judah, and inhabitants of Jerusalem; Thus saith the LORD of hosts, the God of Israel; Behold, I will bring evil upon this place, the which whosoever heareth, his ears shall tingle.

4 Because they have forsaken me, and have estranged this place, and have burned incense in it unto other gods, whom neither they nor their fathers have known, nor the kings of Judah, and have filled this place with the blood of innocents.

10 Then shalt thou break the bottle in the sight of the men that go with thee,

11 And shalt say to unto them, Thus saith the LORD of hosts; Even so will I break this people and this city, as one breaketh a potter's vessel, that cannot be made whole again: and they shall bury them in Tophet, till there be no place to bury.

21:1 The word which came unto Jeremiah from the LORD, when king Zedekiah sent unto him Pashur the son of Melchiah, and Zephaniah the son of Maaseiah the priest, saying,

2 Inquire, I pray thee, of the LORD for us; for Nebuchadrezzar king of Babylon maketh war against us; if so be that the LORD will deal with us according to all his wondrous works, that he may go up from us.

8 And unto this people thou shalt say, Thus saith the LORD; Behold, I set before you the way of life, and the way of death.

9 He that abideth in this city shall die by the sword, and by the famine, and by the pestilence: but he that goeth out, and falleth to the Chaldeans that besiege you, he shall live, and his life shall be unto him for a prey.

10 For I have set my face against this city for evil, and not for good, saith the LORD: it shall be given into the hand of the king of Babylon, and he shall burn it with fire.

Jeremiah 19:1-4, 10-11; 21:1-2, 8-10

Nov. 15

Memory Selection
Jeremiah 21:8

Background Scripture
Jeremiah 19: 21:1-10

Devotional Reading
Joshua 24:14-28

Printed Scripture
Jeremiah 19:1-4, 10-11;
21:1-2, 8-10

Lesson purpose: *To face squarely, through the work of Jeremiah, the truth that God will hold accountable those who deliberately flaunt His rule over their lives.*

It was noted in the preceding lesson that many people are reluctant to dwell on life's hard questions. Today's lesson confronts us with another truth many would like to avoid:

God's promise to judge the willfully rebellious is no idle threat.

Many in Jeremiah's day stopped up their ears against the prophet's gloomy predictions. So also do many today want only a happy face in the pulpit rather than the thunder of promised judgment. Unlike the case with Israel in Jeremiah's day, we do not always see swift evidence that God means what He says. The evidence in this lesson, however, points up the wisdom of facing the fact that whether in this life or the next, God will keep His promise of judgment as certainly as His promises of blessing.

Lesson Introduction

The prophet Jeremiah bluntly confronted the kings of Judah with God's will some 600 years before Christ. God had grown weary of His people's continual apostasy. Jeremiah saw the reforms of the good king Josiah canceled by a return to idolatry and injustice. Through the prophet, God warned the last four kings of Judah that He would allow the Babylonians to overtake the land if the people's leaders did not lead the nation back to God.

For forty years Jeremiah preached his message of reform and warning. "Court" prophets who were willing to tell the king what he wanted to hear persecuted Jeremiah and threatened his life. Although he tried to suppress the message boiling up in his heart, Jeremiah was constrained to continue to tell the truth. He is often called "the weeping prophet" because of the inner and outer conflicts he endured. In the end, the sad events he predicted came true. Jeremiah was taken to Egypt with a contingent of Israelites who fled Babylon's conquering army.

Teaching Outline	Daily Bible Readings
I. Action Parable of Warning—19:1-4, 10-11	**Mon.** At the Potter's House *Jeremiah 18:1-11*
A. The charge, 1-4	**Tue.** Disaster Predicted *Jeremiah 19:1-9*
B. The sentence, 10-11	**Wed.** The City to Be Broken *Jeremiah 19:10-15*
II. Appeal for Reprieve—21:1-2	**Thu.** Jeremiah Placed in Stocks *Jeremiah 20:1-6*
III. The Way of Life or Death—8-10	**Fri.** Jeremiah's Complaint *Jeremiah 20:7-18*
A. Stay and die, 8-9a	**Sat.** God Will Fight His People *Jeremiah 21:1-10*
B. Surrender and live, 9b-10	**Sun.** The Covenant Abandoned *Jeremiah 22:1-9*

Verse by Verse

I. Action Parable of Warning—19:1-4, 10-11

A. The charge, 1-4

19:1 Thus saith the LORD, Go and get a potter's earthen bottle, and take of the ancients of the people, and of the ancients of the priests;

2 And go forth unto the valley of the son of Hinnom, which is by the entry of the east gate, and proclaim there the words that I shall tell thee,

3 And say, Hear ye the word of the LORD, O kings of Judah, and inhabitants of Jerusalem; Thus saith the LORD of hosts, the God of Israel; Behold, I will bring evil upon this place, the which whosoever heareth, his ears shall tingle.

4 Because they have forsaken me, and have estranged this place, and have burned incense in it unto other gods, whom neither they nor their fathers have known, nor the kings of Judah, and have filled this place with the blood of innocents.

The proclamations of Old Testament prophets were sometimes illustrated by action parables. God had earlier told Jeremiah to bury a garment and leave it in the ground until it was rotten, to show how "good for nothing" faithless Israel had become (13:1-11). The prophet also placed an ox yoke on his neck to demonstrate the coming captivity by the Babylonians (27:1-8); and bought a field near Jerusalem as an investment to reassure the people that after serving their captivity a remnant would be allowed to return to Jerusalem (32:6-15).

Here God tells Jeremiah to take a clay vase or bottle and, accompanied by several elders from among the people and the priests, to a valley near one of the gates of Jerusalem. Although the KJV calls this the "east gate," the NIV's identification of it as the "Potsherd Gate" is probably correct, since this fits Jeremiah's use of the clay pot to demonstrate his message. The gate was probably so named because potters went through it on the way to the nearby valley where they dumped their broken pottery and clay refuse.

The valley of Hinnom (or the sons of Hinnom) had been the site of idolatrous worship that included child sacrifice—so it was a very appropriate place to demonstrate the charge that the people had been horribly unfaithful to God. The reform king Josiah had filled it in and made it a city dump (2 Kings 23:10). It was also known as "Tophet" (vs. 11). By the time of Christ, the ever-burning fires at the dump made it a suitable symbol of hell, and its name had been changed to Gehenna, a New Testament term for hell (Matt. 5:22; James 3:6).

In emphasizing that this false worship, which shed "the blood of innocents," did not come from these elders' forefathers, Jeremiah is accusing the elders of importing it from the surrounding pagans.

B. The sentence, 10-11

10 Then shalt thou break the bottle in the sight of the men that go with thee,

11 And shalt say to unto them, Thus saith the LORD of hosts; Even so will I break this people and this city, as one breaketh a potter's vessel, that cannot be made whole again: and they shall bury them in Tophet, till there be no place to bury.

No wonder Jeremiah was an unpopular prophet! Here he would be viewed as both a religious heretic and a national traitor. Dramatically breaking the clay jar, he maintains that God will similarly smash the people and the city of Jerusalem beyond repair. In the verses to follow, Jeremiah takes this message of doom and gloom straight to the ruling priests at the Temple. In return, Pashur the priest struck Jeremiah and had him placed in stocks (20:1-2).

II. Appeal for Reprieve—21:1-2

21:1 The word which came unto Jeremiah from the LORD, when king Zedekiah sent unto him Pashur the son of Melchiah, and Zephaniah the son of Maaseiah the priest, saying,

2 Inquire, I pray thee, of the LORD for us; for Nebuchadrezzar king of Babylon maketh war against us; if so be that the LORD will deal with us according to all his wondrous works, that he may go up from us.

Zedekiah was the last king in Judah. No friend of Jeremiah, Zedekiah would later have the prophet imprisoned, although he would not allow him to be killed (32:2-3; 38:16). Here, however, the king sends envoys to Jeremiah to enlist his endorsement of a plan to resist an attack by King Nebuchadnezzar (or Nebuchadrezzar, a variant spelling), king of Babylon. The king compliments Jeremiah's God by referring to "all his wondrous works" because he wants God's support in repelling the invader.

Neither Jeremiah nor God, however, is impressed. The prophet tells the king in no uncertain terms that not only should the invading Babylons not be resisted, but God Himself will fight against His own people because they have rejected Him (vss. 4-6). Again, Jeremiah is cast in the role of a traitor for supporting a foreign nation.

III. The Way of Life or Death—8-10

A. Stay and die, 8-9a

8 And unto this people thou shalt say, Thus saith the LORD; Behold, I set before you the way of life, and the way of death.

9a He that abideth in this city shall die by the sword, and by the famine, and by the pestilence:

Continuing bravely to assert a message that would be perceived as unpatriotic, Jeremiah counsels the people to submit to the invading Babylonians (called here by the synonym "Chaldeans") and allow themselves to be taken captive. This would have made the prophet about as popular as former President Reagan would have been had he counseled the U. S. to submit to Russian threats and allow them to invade during the Cold War.

The alternative to surrendering to the invaders, Jeremiah says, is certain death. They will fall either to the sword or to the effects of the siege that would be laid against the city.

B. Surrender and live, 9b-10

9b but he that goeth out, and falleth to the Chaldeans that besiege you, he shall live, and his life shall be unto him for a prey.

10 For I have set my face against this city for evil, and not for good, saith the LORD: it shall be given into the hand of the king of Babylon, and he shall burn it with fire.

Imagine how a patriotic Israelite who believes that he is a part of the Chosen Race would react to this counsel. For one's life to be given him as a "prey" is to receive it as the spoils of war, instead of giving it up to the enemy as a part of the spoils earned by capturing the city.

Of course the reason for such radical and "unpatriotic" counsel is that God Himself has become the real enemy. The Babylonians are only God's instrument of punishment. Because of Israel's idolatry and faithlessness, God has donned as it were the armor of war and taken up arms against His own people. Resisting Nebuchadnezzar's armies would be as futile as resisting God.

History proved the validity of Jeremiah's doleful prophecy. King Zedekiah was apprehended by the Babylonians while trying to escape during the siege. His sons were slain before his very eyes, then he was blinded and deported to Babylon (39:4-7) along with most of the other residents of Jerusalem. After years of siege, Jerusalem was finally destroyed by fire in 587 B.C.

After 70 years of captivity, a remnant of the people was allowed to return—an event which Jeremiah, "the weeping prophet" who predicted the captivity, had also foreseen (25:11-12).

Evangelistic Emphasis

Isn't it amazing how we always think of God as being on *our* side! It doesn't matter whether we're going to war against a foreign nation or embroiled in litigation involving our next-door neighbor and his barking dog. Invariably, we perceive our view of "right" to be God's view of right. Few of us, if it is merely a interpersonal matter, would be bold enough to say, *"God is on my side in this dispute."* Yet we often assume that He is. We're not even bashful about *saying* it in matters of war or religion.

Imagine how shocked King Zedekiah must have been when he received back the message from Jeremiah that the Lord was *not* on his side but on the side of the pagan king, Nebuchadrezzar. Zedekiah expected some special help from the Lord— another one of "his wondrous works" that would annihilate the enemy. What he didn't realize was that in God's perception of things he, Zedekiah, was the enemy.

Perhaps we should proceed more humbly whenever we find ourselves in an altercation with another. There is almost always a reason for disagreements. Much of the time, both parties involved claim to be justified in their positions. Rarely is that true. Though I resist admitting it with all that is within me, sometimes I am the one in the wrong.

● ● ● ● ● ● ● ● ●

Memory Selection

And unto this people thou shalt say, Thus saith the LORD; Behold, I set before you the way of life, and the way of death.—*Jeremiah 2:18*

A couple of years ago the Thomas Nelson publishing firm published a book by Dr. Jan Dargatz entitled, *Simple Truths*. It carried the subtitle, *"How You Can Teach Your Children the 12 Most Important Lessons of Life."* Lesson No.10 in Dr. Dargatz's list was, "You Always Have A Choice." In other words, each child needs to learn not to blame "fate" or "luck" or "somebody" for his negative experiences of life. Almost always, life is a matter of *our choosing*. I must take responsibility for the choices I have made.

Isn't that the basic plan God lays before his people? He places before us life and death and then calls us to choose. This message was echoed by both Moses (Deut. 30:19) and Joshua (Josh. 24:15). In the early church when problems arose, the people were even challenged to choose whom they trusted to answer fairly their dissatisfaction (Acts 6).

Should it surprise us that the demands of life today call upon us to make tough choices? Sometimes those choices are basic to survival.

Weekday Problems

Certain doom cannot be an enjoyable problem to face. Surely it leaves a sinking feeling deep inside. Those who remained on the Titanic after all the lifeboats had been launched knew keenly that feeling. So have unfortunate travelers who agonized through long moments as their commercial airline carrier dropped from the sky.

Brenda Walker experienced that feeling when the two officers walked into her office and began their conversation with the words, *"You have a right to remain silent."* Brenda managed the accounts for Charter Automotive. One month ago, she had "borrowed" some money from the company to keep from losing her house. She really had planned to replace the money but had not yet been able to raise it. The fact of the money's absence had been discovered. Brenda knew that *certain doom* awaited her.

* How can Brenda Walker best respond to this major trauma in her life? Should she play ignorant and hope that they can't trace the money to her? Or, should she surrender and confess everything?

* If Brenda's employer is a Christian, how can he best respond to Brenda's situation?

* At what point should Brenda trust her employer to understand? At what point should she hire an attorney?

Comely Comebacks

Millie: You know girls, I'll make a lot of men miserable when I marry.
Tillie: Really? How many men are you going to marry?

* * *

Sassy: I want you to know that the president has asked me to help beautify the United States.
Lassie: Really? And to which country have you decided to move?

* * *

Actor: As a matter of fact, I have received letters from ladies in almost every place where I've appeared.
Rival: Landladies, I presume.

* * *

Two married girls were gouging a young woman who hadn't married. "Be truthful," they said scornfully. "Have you ever really had a chance to marry?"
With a withering glance she retorted, "Suppose you ask your husbands?"

This Lesson in Your Life

One of the things that the U.S. Postal Service and this newfangled "e-mail" have in common is *junk mail*. It comes in all forms. Travel agencies send me notices about "special promotions" that certain tour agencies or selected airlines are having. Computer companies attempt to entice me with an *"unbelievable sale!"* at least once each week. Financial organizations want to let me know that a new, *fully approved* "Platinum Master Card" has been reserved in my name. To receive it, all I need to do is log onto the World-wide Web and fill out an information form.

There is a positive aspect to e-mail, though. It also blesses me occasionally with a real letter from a friend or a well-crafted article that a friend thought I might enjoy. Such was the case this morning when I found in my "mailbox" a moving story that began with the began as follows:

Jerry was the kind of guy you love to hate. He was always in a good mood and always had something positive to say. When someone would ask him how he was doing, he would reply, *"If I were any better, I would be twins!"*

The writer behind this electronic blessing, Francie Baltazar-Schwartz, went on to tell how Jerry, a restaurant manager, was a contagious optimist. He had several waiters who had followed him around from restaurant to restaurant because of his uplifting attitude. He was a natural motivator. If an employee was having a bad day, Jerry was there telling the employee how to look on the positive side of the situation.

When asked the secret of his incurably positive spirit, he replied by saying, "Each morning I wake up and say to myself, *'Jerry, you have two choices today. You can choose to be in a good mood or you can choose to be in a bad mood.'* I choose to be in a good mood. Each time something bad happens, I can choose to be a victim or I can choose to learn from it. I choose to learn from it."

The bottom line of Jerry's philosophy of life was that *life is all about choices*. When you cut away all the junk, every situation is a choice. You choose how you react to situations. You choose how people will affect your mood. You choose to be in a good mood or bad mood. The bottom line is it is your choice how you live life.

Of course, the challenge that naturally arises in our minds says, *"Sure, that works fine as long as life runs smoothly. But, life does not come so carefully packaged as the Pollyannas of the world would like us to believe."*

That of course is true. It is also true, however, that those we label as "Pollyannas" are not always so naive and protected from the "real world" as we would like to believe. Certainly, such is not so of restaurant manager Jerry Bernstein. One morning in preparation for opening for business he left the back door unlocked. Just a few minutes later three armed robbers surprised him at gun point. While trying to open the safe, his hand, shaking from nervousness, slipped off the combination. The robbers panicked and shot him. Fortunately, Jerry was found relatively quickly and rushed to the local trauma center.

Later Jerry recounted his immediate reaction, *"The first thing that went through my mind was that I should have locked the back door,"* he said. *"Then, as I lay on the floor, I remembered that I had two choices. I could choose to live, or I could choose to die. I chose to live."*

Seed Thoughts

1. What *visual aid* was Jeremiah to use in his communication to the Judah? To what people was he to take this message?

Jeremiah's visual aid was an "earthen bottle" that he was to use when delivering God's message to the elders.

2. Where was Jeremiah told to deliver this message to the people of Judah?

Jeremiah was told to go to the valley of the son of Hinnom, which is by the entry of the east gate and to deliver his message there.

3. What was the message from God that Jeremiah was to deliver?

Basically, the message from God that Jeremiah was to deliver was that because of Jerusalem's sin, she would be destroyed.

4. What *specifically* did God declare that He would bring upon Jerusalem?

God declared, "I will bring evil upon this place."

5. What is meant by the threat that God would bring "evil" upon Jerusalem? Is God capable of evil?

Perhaps the New King James Version provides a better contemporary translation. Instead of "evil," it uses the word, "catastrophe."

---

1. What *visual aid* was Jeremiah to use in his communication to the Judah? To what people was he to take this message?

2. Where was Jeremiah told to deliver this message to the people of Judah?

3. What was the message from God that Jeremiah was to deliver?

4. What *specifically* did God declare that He would bring upon Jerusalem?

5. What is meant by the threat that God would bring "evil" upon Jerusalem? Is God capable of evil?

6. What sins of the people of Judah were mentioned by the prophet?

7. By what designation would the Valley of son of Hinnom come to be known after God's justice was delivered?

8. What was Jeremiah to do with the earthen bottle? What message was it to convey?

9. Who was king of Judah during this period of time?

10. What was stated as the only chance of survival for those who were in the city at the time?

(Continued next page)

Jeremiah's visual aid was an "earthen bottle" that he was to use when delivering God's message to the elders.

Jeremiah was told to go to the valley of the son of Hinnom, which is by the entry of the east gate and to deliver his message there.

Basically, the message from God that Jeremiah was to deliver was that because of Jerusalem's sin, she would be destroyed.

God declared, "I will bring evil upon this place."

Perhaps the New King James Version provides a better contemporary translation. Instead of "evil," it uses the word, "catastrophe."

Judah had forsaken God, worshiped other gods, built temples to other gods, and burned their children as offerings.

The prophet said that the valley of the son of Hinnom would come to be known as the valley of slaughter.

Jeremiah was to break the earthen bottle and tell the people that because of their sins, God would break them.

Zedekiah.

The people's only chance of surviving the destruction of Jerusalem was through surrender.

6. What sins of the people of Judah were mentioned by the prophet?

Judah had forsaken God, worshiped other gods, built temples to other gods, and burned their children as offerings.

7. By what designation would the valley of son of Hinnom come to be known after God's justice was delivered?

The prophet said that the valley of the son of Hinnom would come to be known as the valley of slaughter.

8. What was Jeremiah to do with the earthen bottle? What message was it to convey?

Jeremiah was to break the earthen bottle and tell the people that because of their sins, God would break them.

9. Who was king of Judah during this period of time?

Zedekiah.

10. What was stated as the only chance of survival for those who were in the city at the time?

The people's only chance of surviving the destruction of Jerusalem was through surrender.

God's Vision for Exiles

7 he hand of the L0RD was upon me, and carried me out in the spirit of the L0RD, and set me down in the midst of the valley which was full of bones,

2 And caused me to pass by them round about: and, behold, there were very many in the open valley; and, lo, they were very dry.

3 And he said unto me, Son of man, can these bones live? And I answered, O Lord G0D, thou knowest.

4 Again he said unto me, Prophesy upon these bones, and say unto them, O ye dry bones, hear the word of the L0RD.

5 Thus saith the Lord G0D unto these bones; Behold, I will cause breath to enter into you, and ye shall live:

6 And I will lay sinews upon you, and will bring up flesh upon you, and cover you with skin, and put breath in you, and ye shall live; and ye shall know that I am the L0RD.

7 So I prophesied as I was commanded: and as I prophesied, there was a noise, and behold a shaking, and the bones came together, bone to his bone.

8 And when I beheld, lo, the sinews and the flesh came up upon them, and the skin covered them above: but there was no breath in them.

9 Then said he unto me, Prophesy unto the wind, prophesy, son of man, and say to the wind, Thus saith the Lord G0D; Come from the four winds, O breath, and breathe upon these slain, that they may live.

10 So I prophesied as he commanded me, and the breath came into them, and they lived, and stood up upon their feet, an exceeding great army.

11a Then he said unto me, Son of man, these bones are the whole house of Israel:

25a And they shall dwell in the land that I have given unto Jacob my servant, wherein your fathers have dwelt; . . . .

26 Moreover I will make a covenant of peace with them; it shall be an everlasting covenant with them: and I will place them, and multiply them, and will set my sanctuary in the midst of them for evermore.

27 My tabernacle also shall be with them: yea, I will be their God, and they shall be my people.

Ezekiel 37:1-11a, 25a, 26-27

Memory Selection
Ezekiel 37:27

Background Scripture
Ezekiel 37

Devotional Reading
Jeremiah 29:4-14

Printed Scripture
Ezekiel 37:1-11a, 25a, 26-27

Nov. 22

111

Lesson purpose: *To show, through Israel's return from Babylonian captivity, that God stands waiting to receive those who return to Him.*

The role of the prophets in denouncing the sin of Israel was sampled in the last lesson on the work of Jeremiah. Despite the stern warnings of the prophets, Israel persisted in faithlessness, and God allowed them to be captured by their enemies.

Many of the prophets, however, also foresaw that God would allow a remnant of Judah, the southern kingdom, to return from captivity and rebuild Jerusalem. The present lesson focuses on this glad prospect, when God would breathe new life into the "bones" of His people and restore them to the Promised Land.

The principle applies not only to Israel but to believers today. While the preceding lesson emphasized God's certain judgment against the impenitent, focus today on His grace which is just as surely available to anyone who will return to Him.

Lesson Introduction

Ezekiel, a younger contemporary of Jeremiah, was among the Jews who were carried away into Babylonian during the decline of the southern kingdom of Judah. While Jeremiah was denouncing Israel's sins during the siege of Jerusalem, Ezekiel was already in Babylon.

Although Ezekiel was charged with being a bold watchman on guard against apostasy, he was also given the picture in this lesson of Israel's coming to life. This hopeful vision was supplemented by a tender exhortation not to "pine away" out of guilt but to respond to God's gracious invitation to return to Him (33:10).

Ezekiel was profoundly affected by the revelations God gave him. Once he was struck dumb by their weight (Ezek. 3:26). He was even unable to mourn for his wife when she died unexpectedly (24:15-17). Yet he faithfully delivered this vision of hope for the restoration of his people.

Teaching Outline	Daily Bible Readings
I. The Disjointed Nation—1-2	**Mon.** The Spirit Entered Me *Ezekiel 3:22-27*
	Tue. The Spirit Lifted Me Up *Ezekiel 8:1-13*
II. A Different Possibility—3-6	**Wed.** Can These Bones Live? *Ezekiel 37:1-14*
III. From Disjointed to Connected—7-8	**Thu.** I Will Make Them One Nation *Ezekiel 37:15-23*
IV. The Divine Spirit—9-11a	**Fri.** David Shall Be Their King *Ezekiel 37:24-28*
V. The Dwelling Place—25a, 26-27	**Sat.** In Visions of God *Ezekiel 40:1-4*
	Sun. Glory Fills the Temple *Ezekiel 43:1-9*

Verse by Verse

I. The Disjointed Nation—1-2

1 The hand of the LORD was upon me, and carried me out in the spirit of the LORD, and set me down in the midst of the valley which was full of bones,

2 And caused me to pass by them round about: and, behold, there were very many in the open valley; and, lo, they were very dry.

We learn from Ezekiel 1:1-3 that he began to see visions from God at the river Chebar in Chaldea (or Babylonia), where many Israelites had been taken captive. It is this dimension of the work of Israel's prophets that earned them the title "seer"—they saw into the mind of God through the visions He provided.

Yet the content of this vision indicates that the prophet was taken "in the spirit," or in a vision, to a valley back in Judah. It is there that God had promised to gather His people, and it was there that they had fallen into idolatry, injustice, and disobedience.

This state of spiritual "death" or disarray is portrayed by a landscape of bleached bones, disjointed and lifeless, strewn over the valley like the literal remains of the Jews defeated by the armies of Nebuchadnezzar. The description of the bones as "very dry" conveys the sense that they lack all the "juices" of the life force that makes the difference between a living body and a mere skeleton.

II. A Different Possibility—3-6

3 And he said unto me, Son of man, can these bones live? And I answered, O Lord GOD, thou knowest.

4 Again he said unto me, Prophesy upon these bones, and say unto them, O ye dry bones, hear the word of the LORD.

5 Thus saith the Lord GOD unto these bones; Behold, I will cause breath to enter into you, and ye shall live:

6 And I will lay sinews upon you, and will bring up flesh upon you, and cover you with skin, and put breath in you, and ye shall live; and ye shall know that I am the LORD.

God's prophets did not always immediately understand the visions and revelations they received. As the apostle Peter would write many years later, they sometimes "inquired and searched diligently" before the meaning came clear. When an elder caught up in the visions of the book of Revelation asked the apostle John what one scene meant, John had to reply honestly, "Sir, thou knowest"! So

113

Ezekiel, here, pleads understandable ignorance of whether the dead bones in the panorama before him could ever live. The answer to such questions and the meaning of all such visions lie with God, not man. In this instance, however, God provides an immediate answer (although the identity of the bones as Israel is not stated until verse 11).

The Lord tells Ezekiel that the bones—wonder of wonders!—can live if he *prophesies* to them. Recall that "prophecy" has as much to do with "forth-telling" or proclaiming the Word as with foretelling the future. We learn here that God's people can be enlivened only by the prophetic proclamation of the Word. In Israel's case, false prophets had told its kings what they wanted to hear instead of what God had to say. The result—a dead and disjointed people—lies before Ezekiel now.

The reason God's Word can enliven these bones is that it is "enbreathed" or inspired by God's Spirit (2 Tim. 2:16). The Hebrew word translated "breath" in these verses can also mean, wind, the human spirit, or the Holy Spirit. Apparently we are to understand it in a double sense here. It is God's Spirit enlivening the human spirit that makes the difference between a skeleton and a live body with tissue and flesh, as described in verse 6.

III. From Disjointed to Connected—7-8

7 So I prophesied as I was commanded: and as I prophesied, there was a noise, and behold a shaking, and the bones came together, bone to his bone.

8 And when I beheld, lo, the sinews and the flesh came up upon them, and the skin covered them above: but there was no breath in them.

The meaning of this intermediate state between disjointed bones and a live body is not made explicit. Perhaps the vision is intended to convey the way the work of false prophets in Israel had resulted in a mere "mannequin" like the wood-carved Pinocchio before he magically came to life. Perhaps we are to distinguish between merely "prophesying" to people in the sense of preaching *at* them, and allowing our proclamation to be truly Spirit-filled. At any rate, the hopeless ring of the last line of verse 8—"but there was no breath in them"—is unmistakable. Neither the "body" of believers in Ezekiel's day nor the Body of Christ today can function without God's animating Spirit.

IV. The Divine Spirit—9-11a

9 Then said he unto me, Prophesy unto the wind, prophesy, son of man, and say to the wind, Thus saith the Lord God; Come from the four winds, O breath, and breathe upon these slain, that they may live.

10 So I prophesied as he commanded me, and the breath came into them, and they lived, and stood up upon their feet, an exceeding great army.

11a Then he said unto me, Son of man, these bones are the whole house of Israel: . . .

In verses 9-10 the Hebrew word *ruach* appears with a bewildering variety of meanings. In the KJV it is translated first "wind," then, in the plural, "winds," and finally "breath." The NIV reads, "Prophesy to the *breath* . . . Come from the four *winds*, O *breath* . . . ." The Contemporary English Version probably gives the sense most clearly: "Say to the wind, 'The Lord God commands you to blow from every direction and to breathe life into these dead bodies, so they can live again.' "

Verses 10-11 help us conclude that the call to the four winds here is to the exiled children of Israel wherever they were. Some had stayed in Egypt, toward the south, declining to take part in the exodus. Many in the northern kingdom of Israel had been taken north into Assyrian captivity in the eighth century B.C., and others from the southern kingdom of Judah had accompanied Ezekiel into Babylon, to the southeast, a hundred years later. Archeological evidence also shows that Jews lived in the Mediterranean lands to the west.

V. The Dwelling Place—25a, 26-27

25a And they shall dwell in the land that I have given unto Jacob my servant, wherein your fathers have dwelt; . . . .

26 Moreover I will make a covenant of peace with them; it shall be an everlasting covenant with them: and I will place them, and multiply them, and will set my sanctuary in the midst of them for evermore.

27 My tabernacle also shall be with them: yea, I will be their God, and they shall be my people.

This call for God's people to reassemble in the Promised Land seems to have had its first fulfillment some 70 years after Judah was taken captive into Babylonia. It was then that Cyrus, the new king of Persia who conquered Babylon, allowed a remnant of the people to return to their homeland and rebuild Jerusalem.

Some interpreters see a secondary fulfillment of this prophecy as the gathering, beginning in 1948, of Jews from throughout the world to re-establish the Jewish state of Israel in 1948. Still others see the fulfillment yet to come, in either a more triumphant gathering of Jews in Palestine, or in a spiritual gathering of all of God's people in heaven.

The anguished history of Jewish and Arab disputes and bloodshed since 1948 shows that whatever the ultimate meaning of Ezekiel's vision, the "covenant of peace" of verse 26 has yet to be realized.

Evangelistic Emphasis

Preaching from this text one Thursday evening, the great Charles Spurgeon observed that "we may learn, from the action of Ezekiel on this occasion, that *we may so act as to have the Holy Spirit.*" He was alluding to the fact that when Ezekiel first saw the dry bones, there was no life nor breath. Yet, upon obeying the voice of the Lord in the vision, the breath came, and life followed. "How, then, shall we act?" Spurgeon asked.

Eloquently, he advised, "If we want the Holy Spirit to be surely with us, to give us a blessing, we must, in the power of the Spirit, realize the scene in which we are to

labor." In Ezekiel's vision the Holy Spirit took the prophet, carried him out and set him down in the midst of the valley which was full of bones. "This is just a type of what will happen to every man whom the Spirit means to use." challenged Spurgeon.

In other words, if a person wants to save the poor of the inner-city, then he must go to the inner-city. If your heart is burdened for the plight of homeless children, do not be surprised if you become aware of circumstances (*"luck," "chance," "the turn of events," "the Spirit of God"*) carrying you to where homeless children are abundantly available for your hands-on caring. Once you have allowed God to "plant you where He wants you to be," you would do well to carry out your ministry with the awareness that He *even raises the dead.*

● ● ● ● ● ● ● ●

Memory Selection

My tabernacle also shall be with them, yea, I will be their God, and they shall be my people.—*Ezekiel 37:27*

The affectionate refrain that sings throughout Robert Munsch's classic children's book echoes its title sentiment

I'll love you forever,
I'll like you for always,
As long as I'm living
my baby you'll be.

Without any obvious intent, Munsch vividly captured the sentiment found in Ezekiel 37:27 that echoes from the

beginning of Scripture to it's end. It is the Lord's ever present *and repeatedly expressed* desire to have a relationship with his people that is based on mutual love and affection. If poetically arranged in Munsch-like verse, his words of affection might sound like this:

I'll love you forever,
I'll care for you always,
As long as I'm living
my children you'll be.

Weekday Problems

During most of Gertrude's growing years, she dreamed of having a loving, happy Christian family. Never did she even consider dating a non-Christian, because her determination to have a Christian mate was strong. She did not want to give herself a chance of "falling in love" with a non-Christian.

Indeed, Gertrude married a Christian, and together they began their Christian family. For awhile, her dream could hardly have been more beautifully fulfilled. Gertrude's husband became a deacon. They and their five children filled a pew every Sunday. Unfortunately, then came the church split.

It was an ugly division that tore friendships apart. Cruel words were spoken on both sides. Many of them were shouted. In the midst of it all, Gertrude's husband had a massive heart-attack. After two weeks in a coma, he died. The two children, who were teens at the time, have not darkened the church door since. The other three dropped out as soon as they were on their own.

It has now been 20 years since Gertrude became a widow. The prospects of *any* of her children ever being Christians seem hopeless to her.

* What are some of the factors that possibly contributed to the "faithlessness" of Gertrude's children?

* Did Gertrude do anything wrong that contributed to her children's departure? If so, what?

* What element of *hope* can there be seen in Gertrude's "family of dry bones"?

Out of the Mouths of Sunday School Students

What songs did you sing at Sunday School?

We sang a song about Andy: "Andy walks with me, Andy talks with me, Andy tells me I am his own."

We sang a Christmas song about "Round John Virgin."

We sang a Christmas song about shepherds doing their laundry: "Shepherds were washing their socks by night."

We sang about a cross-eyed bear named Gladly: "Gladly the Cross-eyed Bear."

* * *

What is the Fifth Commandment?

Humor thy father and thy mother.

* * *

Mom: I love this picture about the birth of Jesus—Mary and Joseph and the animals around the manger. But who is this in the airplane flying overhead?

Tom: Oh, that's Pontius the Pilot."

This Lesson in Your Life

At night the sirens howl with an eerie quality even more pronounced than that of a coyote or a wolf. There is a certain "darkness" linked with their howling that is absent from the animals of the forest. Police cars rush from one burglary to another. Next it is a domestic disturbance. Then a mugging on Fifth Street. Prostitutes ply their trade all along Montrose Street—both male and female. Gangs prowl some of the neighborhoods into the wee hours of the morning.

Inner-city Houston is not all that different from most other large cities of the late 20th century. What was once a thriving community of families and businesses, school yards filled with laughing children, and church bells that happily announced Sunday morning's assembly, has become what seems to many a wilderness of hopelessness.

Churches aren't to be found in prominence in downtown Houston anymore. There is "Old Church," standing quaintly in Sam Houston Memorial Park, serving as a painful reminder that years ago faith lived strongly there. It has been decades since worshipers actually gathered in that building, though. Candidly, it stands as a relic, symbolizing a holy but distant past. On one side of the park, tall bank buildings reflect an economy built on what is now a waning oil industry. On the other side of the park, across the freeway, stands one of the largest and most controversial public housing projects in the state.

Yes, there are plenty of parking lots, bars, night clubs, bridges and elevated freeways (under which countless homeless people sleep). Any early morning trip to the court house will take one past a dozen or so slumbering bundles of humanity curled up on a cardboard palate on the sidewalk near the courthouse itself.

The churches, however, are gone. One by one, they each found the darkness of the inner-city to be greater than it could bear. Whereas churches in the suburbs were holding their own (some even growing), the churches "inside the loop" were dying a painful death. Once all of them had left, all hope seemed to be gone, too. Downtown Houston, like the downtown of so many of our American cities, has become a valley of dry bones.

The apparent hopelessness of an inner-city arises from a variety of sources. Some of the carcasses lying amidst this valley of bones are the product of organized crime and drug traffic. Some are there because of domestic abuse and the deterioration of the home. Without question, poverty and academic deprivation have played some role, contributing more casualties. All of these factors are readily cited anytime the "problems" of the inner-city are mentioned.

There are other factors that have contributed measurably to the downtown area's decline, however, that are not as quickly recognized. Perhaps chief among these has been the enthronement of Almighty Dollar. The most public form of this has often been reflected in the sacrifice of "historic landmarks" (bearing community pride and identity) for the sake of "economic progress." A not-so-public reflection of this enthronement was the quiet dismissal of a near-retirement custodian. It was "documented" as a case of his "neglecting his duty," but the charge was falsified to save the company some money. On the street, of course, the exchange of human life for dollars happens regularly, in a much seedier and blatantly evil context. In each of the incidents, though, human sacrifices are offered at that same altar of the monetary god.

Seed Thoughts

1. What enticed Ezekiel to go out to that valley in the first place?

The text says that the hand of the Lord was upon him, and carried him out in the spirit of the Lord, and set him down in the midst of the valley.

2. What was the name of the valley to which Ezekiel was taken?

The Bible does not give the name of the valley.

3. What did Ezekiel see when he arrived at this unusual valley?

He saw that the valley "was full of bones."

4. What was particularly noticeable to Ezekiel about the bones?

Ezekiel noticed that the bones were "very dry."

5. What did the Lord ask Ezekiel about the bones, and how did he answer?

The Lord asked Ezekiel if the bones could live. Ezekiel replied, "O Lord GOD, thou knowest."

---

1. What enticed Ezekiel to go out to that valley in the first place?

---

2. What was the name of the valley to which Ezekiel was taken?

---

3. What did Ezekiel see when he arrived at this unusual valley?

---

4. What was particularly noticeable to Ezekiel about the bones?

---

5. What did the Lord ask Ezekiel about the bones, and how did he answer?

---

6. What unusual instruction did the Lord then give Ezekiel regarding the bones?

---

7. What message did the Lord want Ezekiel to communicate to the bones?

---

8. What began to happen when Ezekiel obeyed the Lord?

---

9. What was still lacking, and what did the Lord tell Ezekiel to do about it?

---

10. Who did the Lord say this valley of dry bones represented? Why?

(Continued next page)

The text says that the hand of the Lord was upon him, and carried him out in the spirit of the Lord, and set him down in the midst of the valley.

The Bible does not give the name of the valley.

He saw that the valley "was full of bones."

Ezekiel noticed that the bones were "very dry."

The Lord asked Ezekiel if the bones could live. Ezekiel replied, "O Lord GOD, thou knowest."

The Lord told him to prophesy upon the bones (in other words, to preach to them).

Ezekiel was to tell the bones that the Lord would make them live.

There was a noise, a shaking, and the bones came together. Then, sinews and flesh came up upon them, and skin covered them above.

The bones now were fully bodies but lacked breath. The Lord told Ezekiel to prophesy to the wind, telling it to breathe on them.

The Lord said that these dry bones were the whole house of Israel, because they felt their hope to be lost. He promised to make them live again.

6. What unusual instruction did the Lord then give Ezekiel regarding the bones?

The Lord told him to prophesy upon the bones (in other words, to preach to them).

7. What message did the Lord want Ezekiel to communicate to the bones?

Ezekiel was to tell the bones that the Lord would make them live.

8. What began to happen when Ezekiel obeyed the Lord?

There was a noise, a shaking, and the bones came together. Then, sinews and flesh came up upon them, and skin covered them above.

9. What was still lacking, and what did the Lord tell Ezekiel to do about it?

The bones now were fully bodies but lacked breath. The Lord told Ezekiel to prophesy to the wind, telling it to breathe on them.

10. Who did the Lord say this valley of dry bones represented? Why?

The Lord said that these dry bones were the whole house of Israel, because they felt their hope to be lost. He promised to make them live again.

Renewal and Worship

*A*nd on the second day were gathered together the chief of the fathers of all the people, the priests, and the Levites, unto Ezra the scribe, even to understand the words of the law.

14 And they found written in the law which the LORD had commanded by Moses, that the children of Israel should dwell in booths in the feast of the seventh month:

15 And that they should publish and proclaim in all their cities, and in Jerusalem, saying, God forth unto the mount, and fetch olive branches, and pine branches, and myrtle branches, and palm branches, and branches of thick trees, to make booths, as it is written.

16 So the people went forth, and brought them, and made themselves booths, every one upon the roof of his house, and in their courts, and in the courts of the house of God, and in the street of the water gate, and in the street of the gate of Ephraim.

17 And all the congregation of them that were come again out of the captivity made booths, and sat under the booths: for since the days of Jeshua the son of Nun unto that day had not the children of Israel done so. And there was very great gladness.

Nehemiah 8:13-93

18 Also day by day, from the first day unto the last day, he read in the book of the law of God. And they kept the feast seven days; and on the eighth day was a solemn assembly, according unto the manner.

9:1 Now in the twenty and fourth day of this month the children of Israel were assembled with fasting, and with sackclothes, and earth upon them.

2 And the seed of Israel separated themselves from all strangers, and stood and confessed their sins, and the iniquities of their fathers.

3 And they stood up in their place, and read in the book of the law of the LORD their God one fourth part of the day; and another fourth part they confessed, and worshipped the LORD their God.

Memory Selection
Nehemiah 9:6

Background Scripture
Nehemiah 8-9

Devotional Reading
Galatians 3:23-29

Printed Scripture
Nehemiah 8:13-9:3

Nov. 29

Teacher's Target

Lesson purpose: *To celebrate the spirit of renewal that keeps calling believers back to their roots, as when the Jews were restored to the Promised Land under the leadership of Nehemiah and Ezra.*

The celebration of "Advent" among many churches this time of the year renews faith in the advent or coming of Christ into the world.

Such remembrances point out the importance of celebrating historical events of the faith with festivals and other activities. Among practicing Jews, Passover, the Day of Atonement, Hanukkah, and Rosh Hashanah are examples of annual celebrations. Among Christians, the "feast" of the Lord's Supper remains the oldest festival, followed by Easter observances.

Encourage a discussion of the most joyous religious celebrations in group members' memory as a means of leading into today's lesson. Set the stage for the mixture of joy among the Jews of Nehemiah's day at returning to their homeland, with sadness at having gone so long without such renewals of faith.

Lesson Introduction

Although the book of Nehemiah is placed near the end of the "historical" books of the Old Testament, it describes scenes that followed by only a few years the preceding lessons from Jeremiah and Ezekiel.

Along with Ezra, Nehemiah was a leader in the restoration of the Jews from Babylonian captivity and the rebuilding of Jerusalem. Ezra, a priest, returned to the city about 458 B.C., and Nehemiah, appointed governor of the returning colony, followed about 13 years later. The two worked together to organize a new government and to restore the people's allegiance to God by restoring their respect for His Law.

The events recorded in Nehemiah take on special importance when we realize that they comprise the last recorded Bible history of God's people before the New Testament period, when the story is taken up with a focus on the coming of Messiah.

Teaching Outline	Daily Bible Readings
I. Recovery of the Word—8:13	**Mon.** The Gathering of the People *Nehemiah 8:21-12*
A. Reestablishing leadership, 13a	
B. Convening for Bible study, 13b	**Tue.** The Study of the Law *Nehemiah 8:13-18*
II. Restoration of a Festival—14-18	**Wed.** Confession of Sin *Nehemiah 9:1-5*
A. The Feast of Booths, 14-15	
B. Camp-outs of testimony, 16-18	**Thu.** You Are the Lord! *Nehemiah 9:6-15*
III. Renewal of Commitment—9:1-3	**Fri.** Forgiveness and Grace *Nehemiah 9:16-25*
A. Repentance, 1	
B. Identity, 2	**Sat.** You Have Been Just *Nehemiah 9:26-37*
C. Confession and worship, 3	**Sun.** Peace Be Unto You *Psalm 122:1-9*

Verse by Verse

I. Recovery of the Word—8:13

A. Reestablishing leadership, 13a

13a And on the second day were gathered together the chief of the fathers of all the people, the priests, and the Levites, unto Ezra the scribe,

The prophet Jeremiah had predicted that although God would allow His people to be captured by the Babylonians, they would be allowed to return after 70 years (Jer. 25:11-12). This prophecy began to be fulfilled during the reign of Cyrus, king of Persia, who had finally conquered the proud armies of Babylon. A later king, Artaxerxes, commissioned Ezra the priest (here called a scribe), to assist with the rebuilding of the Temple (Ezra 7).

It is important to note that the system of "elders" that formed the backbone of local leadership in Israel had been preserved as much as possible during the captivity. The long lists in Ezra 2 show that a careful census was maintained, as though in preparation for the opportunity to reorganize Israel. This verse shows that Jewish leadership was finally reestablished. As we shall see, these leaders took seriously the task of restoring not just the structure but the heart and soul of Israel's worship as well. This reminds us of the importance of dedicated leaders in any attempt at renewal among God's people.

B. Convening for Bible study, 13b

13b even to understand the words of the law.

The people had requested that Ezra bring out the treasured scrolls of the Law which had somehow been preserved during both the destruction of Jerusalem and the subsequent years in Babylon (Neh. 8:1). The solemn reading of God's way that had been so long neglected moved the people to tears; but Ezra and Nehemiah reassured them that a new day was dawning, and that it was a time not for tears but for festivities (vss. 9-12).

Now, the people gather again to hear and understand more about God's will. Although the phrase "the law" (Heb. *ha torah*) often refers only to the Ten Commandments, it is used in a broader sense here. As the verses to follow indicate, here the term includes other statutes in the Law of Moses such as the feast of booths.

This renewed interest in the Scriptures went beyond the legalism that sometimes accompanies attention to the Bible. Verse 8 has emphasized that the material was placed in its proper context and its true meaning explained. Although mere outward rigidity sometimes results from a renewed emphasis on paying heed to Scripture, it is obvious here that genuine spiritual renewal arose when the people regained respect not merely for the words of Scripture but for their intent and spirit as well.

II. Restoration of a Festival—14-18

A. The Feast of Booths, 14-15

14 And they found written in the law which the LORD had commanded by Moses, that the children of Israel should dwell in booths in the feast of the seventh month:

15 And that they should publish and proclaim in all their cities, and in Jerusalem, saying, Go forth unto the mount, and fetch olive branches, and pine branches, and myrtle branches, and palm branches, and branches of thick trees, to make booths, as it is written.

On the first day of this remarkable revival in Bible study, the people had recovered the feast of the new moon, which was on the first day of the month, with the most important of this series being in the seventh month (8:1; cp. Lev. 23:23-25).

Next, as the present verses show, the people rediscover the feast of booths (or tabernacles). This joyous observance had been instituted to commemorate the way God had protected people during their wandering in the wilderness, when they lived in "booths" made of tree boughs, or else tents (which gave the feast-day the name "tabernacles"). The phrase "As it is written" apparently indicates that the text read

before the people here was Leviticus 23:39-43.

The feast of booths was also associated with harvest-time, with a festival celebrating the ingathering of crops (Exod. 23:16; Deut. 16:13). Sill later, the prophet Zechariah used this feast to describe the "harvest" or ingathering of all believers (Zech. 14:16).

B. Camp-outs of testimony, 16-18

16 So the people went forth, and brought them, and made themselves booths, every one upon the roof of his house, and in their courts, and in the courts of the house of God, and in the street of the water gate, and in the street of the gate of Ephraim.

17 And all the congregation of them that were come again out of the captivity made booths, and sat under the booths: for since the days of Jeshua the son of Nun unto that day had not the children of Israel done so. And there was very great gladness.

18 Also day by day, from the first day unto the last day, he read in the book of the law of God. And they kept the feast seven days; and on the eighth day was a solemn assembly, according unto the manner.

The people participate widely and whole-heartedly in the joyous occasion. We can compare the scene on the housetops to July 4 parades in America when people sit under colorful umbrellas on their porches and atop buildings in a public demonstration of patriotism. The priests also erect the symbolic booths in the Temple, and others are placed at two important gates in the city wall. The water gate is thought to have been at a point in the southeast wall, and the gate of at the north end of the city.

The gala also spills out of the city into the countryside to include "all the congregation" that had come out of captivity. The feast therefore becomes a symbol of national solidarity, not just a local celebration in the capital.

The lack of observance of this important feast "since the days of Jeshua" (Joshua), mentioned in verse 17, probably refers to this nationwide aspect of the celebration, since what was apparently a more limited version had in fact been observed earlier (Ezra 3:4). Throughout the week-long festival and during the great assembly on the next day, the attention to the Scriptures is maintained.

III. Renewal of Commitment—9:1-3

A. Repentance, 1

9:1 Now in the twenty and fourth day of this month the children of Israel were assembled with fasting, and with sackclothes, and earth upon them.

Two days after the celebration of the feast of booths the mood grows more somber. The people realize that this is a time not only to rejoice in their restoration to the land but to repent of the sins that had caused their captivity. The sackcloth is thought to have been made of animal hair to prickle the skin

as a symbol of a pricked conscience— like the hair cloths among some penitents in the middle ages. Even today, renewal without repentance can smack of superficial enthusiasm without underlying commitment.

B. Identity, 2

2 And the seed of Israel separated themselves from all strangers, and stood and confessed their sins, and the iniquities of their fathers.

The people's renewal also includes the recognition that their previous idolatry came from the nations about them. Here their spirit seems not so rooted in arrogant exclusiveness but in the realization that their identity as the people of God will require a continued recognition that their chosenness implies the responsibility to live above any godless standards of the surrounding culture.

C. Confession and worship, 3

3 And they stood up in their place, and read in the book of the law of the Lord their God one fourth part of the day; and another fourth part they confessed, and worshipped the Lord their God.

Confession is a corollary to repentance. Note that it is not merely personal, but includes the "iniquities of the fathers." It is also made in the context of corporate worship, indicating the people's intent to include the whole body of believers in the great revival or renewal.

Evangelistic Emphasis

...ny value in special festivals. That was true for Isaac Erickson. At age 57, he had never been to even one family reunion, even though for more than 25 years the Erickson family had not let even one year go by without one. Each year Isaac received a reunion notice but tried to throw it into the trash before his wife, Carolyn, saw it. If Carolyn got the mail with the notice first, she nagged him for weeks wanting to go.

The summer Isaac turned 58, all that changed. That previous winter Isaac became a grandfather for the very first time. His daughter and military son-in-law blessed them with a granddaughter. Even though the baby was born in February, Isaac had still not seen the baby in June at family-reunion time because his new granddaughter was born in Germany. On May 15, Isaac's daughter called home to let them know that she and their new granddaughter were going to be in the states (on the West Coast) in June for a few days *at the family reunion*. In talking with her daddy, she told him she really hoped that he could come.

Isaac was in Oregon that June for the Erickson family reunion. It was the first time, but it was not the last. He learned that he had missed a lot over the years by staying away. Somehow, those times of special feasting and laughter and light visiting, ministered to his soul.

● ● ● ● ● ● ● ●

Memory Selection

Thou, even thou, art LORD alone; thou hast made heaven, the heaven of heavens, with all their host, the earth, and all things that are therein, the seas, and all that is therein, and thou preservest them all; and the host of heaven worshippeth thee.—*Nehemiah 9:6*

God, as the Holy Scriptures introduce Him, is Creator of heaven and earth. Dodge and squirm as we may, it is difficult to continue to affirm that we believe in the "God of the Bible" while, at the same time, forsaking the belief that He created the worlds. His role in the creation process is not merely an incidental *sideline* of his divinity. More than 150 times (from Genesis 1 to Revelation 17) this dimension of His Personhood is highlighted.

Not only is God of the Bible perceived as "the original Cause." He is also regarded as the One who sustains the world that He created. He provides the laws that give our universe its order. He contributes the life that enables every living thing to keep breathing. He gives the Spirit that makes it possible for the believer to become.

126

Weekday Problems

Martha cut her teeth on the church pews at Second Street Church. Her memories of Sunday School and of Vacation Bible School stand as some of the greatest treasures of her heart. Never in her 31 years had there been as much as a ripple of contention in the church that she was aware of—until six months ago.

It was then that, one Sunday morning, the new minister decided that the best illustration for the message he wanted to communicate that morning needed to be *acted out*. So, right in the middle of his sermon, two members of the youth group (one being the minister's daughter) "came out of nowhere" onto the pulpit and began to echo the conversation of Jesus and "the woman at the well."

Though it surprised everyone, some were strongly offended. Three families stomped out. Ever since that day, the whole congregation has been in an uproar about "drama in church."

* How would today's Bible text contribute (positively and negatively) to the discussion about the matter of "drama in church"?

* What New Testament examples do we have of the Word of God either *presented* **or** *sustained* with the use of drama?

* What contemporary practice captures some of the same spirit as the Israelite's making and sitting in booths to remind them of their blessings?

Major Feasts of the Old Testament

Religious observances among the Jews included hearty feasts and celebrations. Four "pilgrimage feasts" ordinarily required all circumcised males to make three pilgrimages to the Temple in Jerusalem.

Passsover, on the fourteenth day of the first month (Abib), celebrated the exodus from Egypt, when the angel of death "passed over" Jewish homes. The next day, the feast of *Unleavened Bread* began, commemorating the bread of the Passover (Exod. 12:15). Eventually these two feasts were combined.

Pentecost or the *Feast of Weeks* was celebrated fifty days after Passover (the word "pentecost" is from the Greek word for "fiftieth.") This feast celebrated harvest time.

The feast of *Booths* or *Tabernacles*, as in today's lesson, commemorated the days when Israel dwelt in temporary shelters during the forty years of wandering in the wilderness after leaving Egypt. This celebration also lasted seven days, beginning on the fifteenth day of the seventh month.

This Lesson in Your Life

Had Solomon been present to hear the words spoken by Nehemiah, Ezra and the Levites, he likely would have said, *"I told you so."* When the people began to weep upon hearing the Law being read, they were told it was *not the time*. Weeping was out of place, even though it was in sorrowful repentance responding to their new consciousness of sin. In the words of Solomon, there is *"a time to weep and a time to laugh, a time to mourn and a time to dance."* This was the time "to dance," to celebrate the blessings of God.

You probably have known people who got lost along the way in the process of repentance. Somehow, they got bogged down in "sorrow" for their sins and never got past that point. Their whole Christian lives have been steeped in sorrow. There is no laughter or joy or celebration in Christ, because they are so overcome by their burden of guilt. It's not that they do not understand the nature of forgiveness. In fact, they may very well articulate quite well that God has forgiven them. That does not, however, lift from them the burden and shame they feel for *needing* forgiveness. Though they acknowledge God's forgiveness, they are unable to forgive themselves. Perpetually, they berate themselves. In fact, they may feel *obligated* to do so. It might be O.K. for others to "rejoice in the Lord always," but it certainly wouldn't be appropriate for them. So penance is done daily by living under the cloud of gloom, comprised of all of their terrible past sins.

Those Israelites are to be commended for responding so readily to the instruction they received to *stop weeping and start feasting*. Had only a few persisted in their grieving, it could have turned the festival into a lament. It appears as though, however, they all participated in the celebration. The instruction of Nehemiah, Ezra and the Levites needs to be remembered in the life of the church today.

(1) After the death of a prominent and much loved church member, there is an appropriate time to mourn the loss of a loved one. Sunday morning, week after week, is *not* that time, however, even though we are reminded again of the loss because the pew that he or she once occupied now sits empty.

(2) The Lord's Supper has often assumed the tone of "a funeral" as the church gets lost in the process of mourning the death of the Son. Should onlookers interpret the gospel message by our Holy Communion, they might conclude that Jesus didn't rise from the dead since Christians still seem to be grieving His death.

In contrast to that, the term "Eucharist," given to that special meal very early in Christian history, means *thankfulness*. For those early Christians, it was clearly understood that Jesus arose from the dead. The time for grieving His death is past. Now is the time to anticipate thankfully His return.

(3) Worship itself, perhaps, needs to be completely re-evaluated in some of our churches. Sunday after Sunday, the preacher bewails the waywardness of the people—their poor attendance, their pitiful giving, their woeful evangelism practice. Week after week, their singing mourns the dying church and the dying faith. Rather than celebrating their salvation and eagerly anticipating their coming Lord, the people are overwhelmed with discouragement and sorrow. They never celebrate. The prophet standing watch, unlike Nehemiah and Ezra, does not call them to feast!

Perpetual grieving over sin destroys. It doesn't heal.

Seed Thoughts

1. Who called the people of Israel together for the meeting—Nehemiah or Ezra or someone else?

It seems from the text that it was a *spontaneous gathering*. The people called the meeting.

2. Where, *precisely*, did this gathering take place?

The people gathered in the street before the Water Gate.

3. What did the people request of Ezra?

The people asked that Ezra bring the Book of the Law that Moses had given. They wanted him to read it.

4. For how long did Ezra read the book of the Law? How did the people respond?

Ezra read the first day from morning until noon and the people listened attentively.

5. What accompanied the word-for-word reading of the Law?

Ezra and those assisting him also "gave the sense" and helped them to understand the reading.

1. Who called the people of Israel together for the meeting—Nehemiah or Ezra or someone else?

2. Where, *precisely*, did this gathering take place?

3. What did the people request of Ezra?

4. For how long did Ezra read the book of the Law? How did the people respond?

5. What accompanied the word-for-word reading of the Law?

6. How did the people respond to this reading of Scripture and preaching?

7. What did Nehemiah, Ezra and the Levites tell the people when they observed their weeping?

8. What was the subsequent spirit of the day after the admonition from Nehemiah, Ezra and the Levites?

9. Beginning the second day of the reading, what did the people add to their celebration? Why?

10 On the 24th day of the month, what was the mood of the assembled nation?

(Continued next page)

It seems from the text that it was a *spontaneous gathering*. The people called the meeting.

The people gathered in the street before the Water Gate.

The people asked that Ezra bring the Book of the Law that Moses had given. They wanted him to read it.

Ezra read the first day from morning until noon and the people listened attentively.

Ezra and those assisting him also "gave the sense" and helped them to understand the reading.

All the people wept when they heard the words of the Law.

They told the people, "This day is holy unto the LORD your God; mourn not, nor weep."

The time of mourning was changed into a time of feasting, celebration and sharing.

The people built booths (tents) of branches and leaves on the roofs of their houses. They did this to remind them of their homelessness and God's provision.

On the 24th day of the month the people assembled with fasting, sackcloth and dirt on their heads, and confessed their sins.

6. How did the people respond to this reading of Scripture and preaching?

All the people wept when they heard the words of the Law.

7. What did Nehemiah, Ezra and the Levites tell the people when they observed their weeping?

They told the people, "This day is holy unto the LORD your God; mourn not, nor weep."

8. What was the subsequent spirit of the day after the admonition from Nehemiah, Ezra and the Levites?

The time of mourning was changed into a time of feasting, celebration and sharing.

9. Beginning the second day of the reading, what did the people add to their celebration? Why?

The people built booths (tents) of branches and leaves on the roofs of their houses. They did this to remind them of their homelessness and God's provision.

10 On the 24th day of the month, what was the mood of the assembled nation?

On the 24th day of the month the people assembled with fasting, sackcloth and dirt on their heads, and confessed their sins.

Lesson 1

Who Is This?

𝒢od, who at sundry times and in divers manners space in time past unto the fathers by the prophets,

2 Hath in these last days spoken unto us by his Son, whom he hath appointed heir of all things, by whom also he made the worlds;

3 Who being the brightness of his glory, and the express image of his person, and upholding all things by the word of his power, when he had by himself purged our sins, sat down on the right hand of the Majesty on high;

4 Being made so much better than the angels, as he hath by inheritance obtained a more excellent name than they.

Matthew 16:13-23

13 When Jesus came into the coasts of Cæsarea Philippi, he asked his disciples, saying, Whom do men say that I the Son of man am?

14 And they said, some say that thou art John the Baptist: some, Elias; and others, Jeremias, or one of the prophets.

15 He saith unto them, But whom say ye that I am?

16 And Simon Peter answered and said, Thou art the Christ, the Son of the living God.

17 And Jesus answered and said unto him, Blessed art thou, Simon Bar-jona: for flesh and blood hath not revealed it unto thee, but my Father which is in heaven.

18 And I say also unto thee, That thou art Peter, and upon this rock I will build my church; and the gates of hell shall not prevail against it.

19 And I will give unto thee the keys of the kingdom of heaven: and whatsoever thou shalt bind on earth shall be bound in heaven: and whatsoever thou shalt loose on earth shall be loosed in heaven.

20 Then charged he his disciples that they should tell no man that he was Jesus the Christ.

21 From that time forth began Jesus to shew unto his disciples, how that he must go unto Jerusalem, and suffer many things of the elders and chief priests and scribes, and be killed, and be raised again the third day.

22 Then Peter took him, and began to rebuke him, saying, Be it far from thee, Lord: this shall not be unto thee.

23 But he turned, and said unto Peter, Get thee behind me, Satan: thou art an offence unto me: for thou savourest not the things that be of God, but those that be of men.

Hebrews 1:1-4; Matthew 16:13-23

Memory Selection
Matthew 16:16

Background Scripture
Hebrews 1:1-4; Matthew 16:13-26

Devotional Reading
Isaiah 11:1-10

Printed Scripture
Hebrews 1:1-4; Matt. 16:13-23

Teacher's Target

Lesson purpose: *To learn, from two classic New Testament passages, about the nature and purpose of Jesus Christ.*

"Christ is the answer" has become a standard cliché and even a bumper sticker for many Christians. During the unrest of the '60s, however, some witty critic designed a counter-culture bumper sticker that replied, "What is the question?"

The New Testament does not resort to clichés because its authors took seriously the right and the need for unbelievers to know something about the nature and work of their Lord. The two passages for today's study discuss important questions about the qualifications of Jesus to offer salvation, and about His determination to do so. They lay a solid groundwork for urging others to accept Christ as the answer.

Lesson Introduction

Just as the first quarter's lessons offered a brief survey of important Old Testament high points, so this quarter's New Testament survey focuses on central themes of the New Covenant.

In perfect symmetry, the Old Testament begins with the story of creation, and the New Testament with the story of the New Creation,the opportunity for renewed life in Christ. In the first passage, of today's lesson, Jesus' authority to offer this "rebirth" of creation is based on the fact that in some pre-existent state He was present at the first creation; and on the fact that He shares the same nature of the Creator.

The second passage presents a shocking paradox. Jesus proved His authority and His divine nature not by exerting kingly might but by insisting that He would give up His life for others. In proving His love for all people in this way, He also taught His followers that the proof of their loyalty to Him is their willingness to give of themselves for others.

Teaching Outline	Daily Bible Readings

I.The Nature of Christ,Heb. 1:1-4
  A.The nature of revelation, 1
  B.Christ's role at creation, 2
  C.Sharing God's character, 3
  D.Sharing God's name, 4
 	
II.The Work of Christ,Matt. 16:13-23
  A.What some say about Jesus, 13-14
  B.The "Good Confession," 15-17
  C.The Church's foundation, 18-20
  D.The suffering Christ, 21-23
	Mon. She Shall Name Him Immanuel
	Isaiah 7:10-17
	Tue. A Child Has Been Born to Us
	Isaiah 9:1-7
	Wed. A Vision of Peace
	Isaiah 11:1-10
	Thu. Wounded for Our Transgressions
	Isaiah 53:1-12
	Fri. Arise, Your Light Has Come
	Isaiah 60:1-7
	Sat. God Has Spoken by His Son
	Hebrews 1:1-4
	Sun. You Are the Messiah!
	Matthew 16:13-26

Verse by Verse

I. The Nature of Christ—Heb. 1:1-4

A. The nature of revelation, 1

1 God, who at sundry times and in divers manners space in time past unto the fathers by the prophets,

Because we are blessed with the Scriptures in the form of a single, bound book, it would be easy to think of God's revelation as having suddenly dropped out of heaven in its present form. The Hebrew writer, however, reminds us that it came "at many times and in various ways" (NIV). Revelation burst forth at various periods in Israel's history, "line upon line, here a little there a little" (Isa. 28:10, 13).

God also revealed His will in "sundry" ways (the word still means "a variety," as in the "sundries" department of a variety store). Although the focus here is on the role of the prophets in revealing God's will, it also came in such diverse ways as visions (Gen. 15:1); angels appearing as men (18:10); and even through a donkey (Num. 22:28)!

B. Christ's role at creation, 2

2 Hath in these last days spoken unto us by his Son, whom he hath appointed heir of all things, by whom also he made the worlds;

The phrase "these last days" does not necessarily refer to the belief that the end of the world was near, but may simply mean "lately," referring to God's latest or recent revelation through the event of Christ.

The Hebrew writer will place special emphasis on the importance of accepting the authority of Jesus as God's Son over that of angels (vs. 4ff.), Moses (3:5-6), and the Jewish priesthood(5:1ff.) None of these lesser channels of God's revelation is the very Son and heir of the Father,and even the means of creation! Here is a brief reference to the profound truth that the Son was somehow with the Father from the very beginning, when the worlds were formed (see also Col. 1:16-17; John 1:1-3). This is an important part in the Hebrew writer's overall argument, since it shows that Jesus' authority preceded that of Moses and the Law.

The word "son" also affirms the deity of Christ, since the son of a king was considered to be endowed with kingly authority. The Jews in John 5:18 took the term to mean that Jesus was "equal with God."

C. Sharing God's character, 3

3 Who being the brightness of his glory, and the express image of his person, and upholding all things by the word of his power, when he had by himself purged our sins, sat down on the right hand of the Majesty on high;

The author also exalts Jesus by saying He shares the nature of God like a ray of light shares the nature of the sun. More than simply "reflecting" God's glory, Jesus *is* that glory! Perhaps this is why His garments appeared so bright on the Mount of Transfiguration, and why Saul was blinded by his vision of Christ on the road to Damascus.

Further, Jesus' divine nature is underscored by saying He is the "express image" of God. These two words translate a single Greek word that gives us our word "character." The next word, "person" (Gk. *hypostasis*) would later lead to debates about what came to be called the "Trinity," or God in "three persons."

Finally, this tightly-packed verse exalts the work of Jesus on the Cross, after which he assumed His rightful place with God on the heavenly throne. Everyone in the ancient world knew that sitting at a king's "right hand" was a sign that a person shared the power of the king himself.

D. Sharing God's name, 4

4 Being made so much better than the angels, as he hath by inheritance obtained a more excellent name than they.

The superiority of Christ over angels will occupy the Hebrew writer through chapter 2. The argument is that while the angels were created beings, the pre-existent Son, as the agent of creation, was actually the creator of the angels as well. Angel worship was a persistent temptation (Col. 2:18), but this passage shows that Jesus was even more excellent because He shared God's very "name." This may be an astounding affirmation that Jesus is qualified to share the name "Jehovah" (or Yahweh); or it may refer to the title "Messiah" or one of the other exalted names Christ earned by His death and resurrection (see Isa. 7:14; 9:6).

II. The Work of Christ—Matt. 16:13-23

A. What some say about Jesus, 13-14

13 When Jesus came into the coasts of Cæsarea Philippi, he asked his disciples, saying, Whom do men say that I the Son of man am?

14 And they said, some say that thou art John the Baptist: some, Elias; and others, Jeremias, or one of the prophets.

Our lesson now moves from the Epistles to the Gospels, where Jesus is demonstrating by His actions the divinity ascribed to Him in Hebrews 1. He has laid out the way of life expected of His followers (Matt. 5+7), and has worked mighty signs and wonders that show both His divine power and His love for people. Now, as He journeys from His home in the north toward Jerusalem, it is time to test the impact of all this on His disciples. (The town was north of Jerusalem, not the Caesarea on the Mediterranean coast. The word translated "the coasts" was a term that meant something like the Old West phrase "these parts.")

Jesus' followers report various beliefs among the people who have seen or heard of this Wonder Worker. Their perceptions reflect the common expectation that the Messiah would come as a prophet. They are especially centered on Elijah (Elias), since the prophet Malachi had predicted that God would send Elijah before the "day of the Lord" (Mal. 4:5). Actually, Jesus had said that this prophecy was fulfilled in the coming of John the Baptist (Matt. 11:14-15).

B. The "Good Confession," 15-17

15 He saith unto them, But whom say ye that I am?

16 And Simon Peter answered and said unto him, Thou art the Christ, the Son of the living God.

17 And Jesus answered and said unto him, Blessed art thou, Simon Bar-jona: for flesh and blood hath not revealed it unto thee, but my Father

which is in heaven.

Although Jesus no doubt knows who His followers believe Him to be, it is urgent that they hear themselves confess their faith—or lack of it. Outspoken Peter seems to speak for them all when He confesses His faith that Jesus is precisely who He has presented Himself to be. He is the Christ, which is the Greek term for "Messiah," or the Anointed One, and God's own Son. Jesus' response that the Father has revealed this to Peter may simply refer to the fact that Peter has learned of Jesus' true identity through the words and works God has enabled Jesus to do as Peter listened and watched.

C. The Church's foundation, 18-20

18 And I say also unto thee, That thou art Peter, and upon this rock I will build my church; and the gates of hell shall not prevail against it.

19 And I will give unto thee the keys of the kingdom of heaven: and whatsoever thou shalt bind on earth shall be bound in heaven: and whatsoever thou shalt loose on earth shall be loosed in heaven.

20 Then charged he his disciples that they should tell no man that he was Jesus the Christ.

"This rock" on which Christ says He will build His Church probably refers to the foundational truth that Jesus is the Messiah of God, which Peter has just confessed, rather than on Peter Himself as Roman Catholic interpreters hold. Also, most Protestants hold that Peter is given "the keys of the kingdom" only as a representative of the rest of the apostles, not because Christ is elevating Peter himself to a position of authority over others. Yet it was Peter who first used these keys, when he preached the first sermon after the ascension of Christ and opened the doors of the Church.

Christ's promise that the apostles' preaching would be "bound" or "loosed" in heaven is intended to reassure them that when they proclaimed Christ's forgiving grace and divine authority, their message would be the word of God, not just the word of men.

D. The suffering Christ, 21-23

21 From that time forth began Jesus to shew unto his disciples, how that he must go unto Jerusalem, and suffer many things of the elders and chief priests and scribes, and be killed, and be raised again the third day.

22 Then Peter took him, and began to rebuke him, saying, Be it far from thee, Lord: this shall not be unto thee.

23 But he turned, and said unto Peter, Get thee behind me, Satan: thou art an offence unto me: for thou savourest not the things that be of God, but those that be of men.

Peter obviously finds Jesus' prediction that He will die to be unbecoming of the Messiah. Apparently he has the mistaken but popular notion that Messiah would take up the sword and lead a revolt against the oppressive Romans who occupied the land. Jesus' stern rebuke lays down two laws: that His death was necessary in God's plan to offer Himself as a sacrifice for sin, and that Jesus' followers are most like their Lord when they too are self-giving instead of self-serving.

Evangelistic Emphasis

Peter declared that Jesus is the Son of God, but he likely did not understand the significance of Who Jesus is. His confusion is obvious in Matthew 17, where Jesus' transfiguration is recorded. Neither Peter, James nor John seemed to grasp the significance of the declaration by God that Jesus is His Son. This fact continued to elude the disciples even through the crucifixion. Only after His resurrection and His appearance to them on numerous occasions does the truth begin to take on reality to them. Thus, fifty days after Jesus' resurrection, Peter declared, "... God hath made that same Jesus, whom ye have crucified, both Lord and Christ."

The apostles' slow realization of Jesus' divinity should be comforting to us who attempt to convince unbelievers. Not everyone is ready to accept our testimony that Jesus is Christ and that all should become His disciples. The reality of His divine nature can be communicated only through sharing the Good News revealed in God's Word. As the Apostle Paul explained to the Corinthian Christians, he had "planted," "Apollos watered; but God gave the increase" (1 Cor 3:6). That is, God is the one who causes our teaching to bear fruit. So we should not get discouraged when we share the Gospel with others and they seem not to be moved by God's grace. Instead, we should remember that God—in His time—will give the increase.

● ● ● ● ● ● ● ●

Memory Selection

And Simon Peter answered and said, Thou art the Christ, the Son of the living God. — *Matthew 16:16*

One day Jesus asked His disciples what other people were saying about Him. He knew what the people were speculating: Had Elijah returned from his fiery trip to Heaven? Was He Jeremiah, back to continue his lament for God's people? Or maybe He was John the Baptist, who had recently been calling the people to repentance.

Then Jesus asked His disciples plainly, "Whom say ye that I am?" That is when Peter said, "Thou art the Christ, the Son of the living God." Jesus immediately pronounced a blessing on Peter and went on to make a promise that the confession Peter had just made would serve as the bedrock for His church.

If Jesus is an impostor, our faith in Him is meaningless and so is our religion (see 1 Cor. 15:12-20). But if He is the Son of God, we owe Him total allegiance. The decision each of us makes about Who Jesus is is the most important decision of our lives.

Weekday Problems

David is a young employee of a major company. He is making a good start on the corporate ladder and he is expected to rise rapidly through the ranks. He has a wife and two children, a nice house in the suburbs and two cars. But he seldom spends time with his family because he is very busy in his job. He is determined to become a major executive in the company by the age of forty.

His life took an unexpected turn when he awakened late one night in the middle of a dream and could not remember who he was. It was a fleeting sensation but it troubled him. During the following day, he began asking himself, "Who am I, really?" He started thinking about his various roles — husband, father, employee — and realized that he had been neglecting his family and his own soul as he relentlessly pursued his career. What should he do?

Jesus had no doubts about His identity. He had been with the Father from before the beginning of time and had been an active participant in the creation of the world. When the time came for Him to come to this earth and redeem mankind, He accepted His role and poured His entire life into meeting that purpose.

* Have you ever had doubts about your own identity?
* Can we be like Jesus?
* What causes us to be confused about our purpose in life?

Bible Quiz

Q: What common ailment caused the death of Samson?
A: Fallen arches.

* * *

Q: Who's the best financial manager in Scripture?
A: Noah. He floated his stock while the whole world was in liquidation.

* * *

Q: Who was the straightest man in the Bible?
A: Joseph. Pharaoh made a ruler out of him.

* * *

Q: Where is tennis mentioned in the Bible?
A: When Joseph served in Pharaoh's court.

* * *

Q: What animal took the most baggage on the ark?
A: The elephant. He took his trunk, while the fox and the rooster only took a brush and comb.

* * *

Q: What man in the Bible had no parents?
A: Joshua. He was the son of Nun.

This Lesson in Your Life

Simon Peter's declaration that Jesus is the Christ, the Son of the living God, was not the product of Peter's reasoning power. Nor was he simply repeating what he had been hearing from others. Rather, Jesus told him that the fact of His identity had been revealed to him by God the Father.

There was plenty of evidence that Jesus was more than a man. He had been performing all sorts of miracles—healing the sick, casting out demons, even raising the dead! He taught the people as One Who had authority (Matt. 7:29). But some of the Old Testament prophets had done similar things.

What was the unique quality about Jesus? That was the essence of Jesus' question to His disciples: "Whom say ye that I am?" The uniqueness of Jesus is Who He is. As the writer of Hebrews says, "God . . . hath in these last days spoken unto us by His Son" (Heb. 1:2).

Jesus' Sonship has application to our everyday life.

First, we can confidently accept His word as authoritative. God has spoken to mankind through Him, so we must accept His teaching as from God. Contrary to the teachings of some, Jesus was not "just a good teacher." He was not "just one of the prophets." His Word stands out from all the teachings of all the great teachers. As God thundered out on the Mount of Transfiguration, "Hear ye Him!" Jesus did not leave us with only the few words which sometimes are printed in red in our Bibles. Through the Holy Spirit, He guided the disciples in their teaching and writings so that we could have a broad spectrum of teaching for everyday living. Thus, in our everyday lives, we need to study and then remember what Jesus and His inspired disciples taught and apply these teachings to our lives.

Second, we can joyfully accept forgiveness of our sins through Him. It was Jesus who declared that He had come into the world, not to condemn mankind, but to save (John 3:16-17). His life demonstrated that purpose. He came in fulfillment of the prophecy that "good news" would be preached to the poor, that healing would come to the broken-hearted and that deliverance would be preached to the captives (Luke 4:16-21). Ultimately, His death was the culmination of His mission to save, for it was on the cross that our sins were finally taken away (Col. 1:20). And He has promised to continue to cleanse our souls of sin if we maintain our fellowship with Him (1 John 1:7).

Third, we can pray to God, knowing that Jesus is sitting at His right hand serving as our intercessor. We need no other priest, for "He ever liveth to make intercession" for us (Heb. 7:25). As One Who lived on this earth and was tempted just as we are (Heb. 4:15), He is in the unique position to serve as our perfect intermediary before the God of the universe.

Finally, we can have a steadfast hope for eternity. God has promised eternal life to the followers of His Son Jesus. Jesus' own resurrection is the proof that God will indeed raise those who have been faithful to enjoy everlasting life with Him.

The confession that Jesus is the Christ, the Son of the living God, is one which we make when we commit ourselves to Him; but we should be making that same confession every day in the character of our lives and in the testimony to those we meet.

Seed Thoughts

1. Who did the people of Jesus' day think He was?

They thought he was John the Baptist, Elijah, Jeremiah or one of the prophets (Matt. 16:14).

2. What was the great confession Simon Peter made concerning Jesus?

"Thou art the Christ, the Son of the living God" (Matt. 16:16).

3. How did Peter know who Jesus was?

God had revealed Jesus' identity to him (Matt. 16:17).

4. What does the word, "Christ," mean and why was that term significant?

"Christ" is a Greek word meaning "anointed." It is equivalent to the Hebrew word "Messiah," referring to the promised deliverer of Israel.

5. Why did the Jewish leaders refuse to accept Jesus as the Christ/Messiah?

They had a preconception that the Messiah would be a political or military leader, much different from what Jesus was.

---

1. Who did the people of Jesus' day think He was?

2. What was the great confession Simon Peter made concerning Jesus?

3. How did Peter know who Jesus was?

4. What does the word, "Christ," mean and why was that term significant?

5. Why did the Jewish leaders refuse to accept Jesus as the Christ/Messiah?

6. Upon what did Jesus promise to build His church?

7. Peter was promised the keys of the kingdom of heaven. What does that promise signify?

8. Why did Jesus rebuke Peter when he protested the announcement that Jesus would be killed?

9. Who is ranked higher—Jesus or the angels? How does this affect our concept of heavenly beings?

10. Why is it important to confess that Jesus is the Christ, the Son of the living God?

(Continued next page)

They thought he was John the Baptist, Elijah, Jeremiah or one of the prophets (Matt. 16:14).

"Thou art the Christ, the Son of the living God" (Matt. 16:16).

God had revealed Jesus' identity to him (Matt. 16:17).

"Christ" is a Greek word meaning "anointed." It is equivalent to the Hebrew word "Messiah," referring to the promised deliverer of Israel.

They had a preconception that the Messiah would be a political or military leader, much different from what Jesus was.

Upon the "rock" of His identity as the Christ, the Son of the living God (Matt. 16:18).

He was authorized to use the keys to open the kingdom, which he did for the Jews (Acts 2) and the Gentiles (Acts 10).

Peter was applying human reasoning to the right way for Jesus to accomplish His mission, rather than accepting God's plan which Jesus had announced.

Jesus is "so much better than the angels" (Heb. 1:4). His authority, His word excels beyond the messages of angels (see Heb. 2:1-4 and Gal. 1:8).

If we confess Him, He will confess us before the Father (Matt. 10:32).

6. Upon what did Jesus promise to build His church?

Upon the "rock" of His identity as the Christ, the Son of the living God (Matt. 16:18).

7. Peter was promised the keys of the kingdom of heaven. What does that promise signify?

He was authorized to use the keys to open the kingdom, which he did for the Jews (Acts 2) and the Gentiles (Acts 10).

8. Why did Jesus rebuke Peter when he protested the announcement that Jesus would be killed?

Peter was applying human reasoning to the right way for Jesus to accomplish His mission, rather than accepting God's plan which Jesus had announced.

9. Who is ranked higher—Jesus or the angels? How does this affect our concept of heavenly beings?

Jesus is "so much better than the angels" (Heb. 1:4). His authority, His word excels beyond the messages of angels (see Heb. 2:1-4 and Gal. 1:8).

10. Why is it important to confess that Jesus is the Christ, the Son of the living God?

If we confess Him, He will confess us before the Father (Matt. 10:32).

Good News: Spoken and Written

Forasmuch as many have taken in hand to set forth in order a declaration of those things which are most surely believed among us,

2 Even as they delivered them unto us, which from the beginning were eyewitnesses, and ministers of the word;

3 It seemed good to me also, having had perfect understanding of all things from the very first, to write unto thee in order, most excellent Theophilus,

4 That thou mightest know the certainty of those things, wherein thou hast been instructed.

Luke 1:1-4
1 Cor. 15:1-4
1 John 1:1-4

1 Corinthians 15:1-4

1 Moreover, brethren, I declare unto you the gospel which I preached unto you, which also ye have received, and wherein ye stand;

2 By which also ye are saved, if ye keep in memory what I preached unto you, unless ye have believed in vain.

3 For I delivered unto you first of all that which I also received, how that Christ died for our sins according to the scriptures;

4 And that he was buried, and that he rose again the third day according to the scriptures:

1 John 1:1-4

1 That which was from the beginning, which we have heard, which we have seen with our eyes, which we have looked upon, and our hands have handled, of the Word of life;

2 (For the life was manifested, and we have seen it, and bear witness, and shew unto you that eternal life, which was with the Father, and was manifested unto us:)

3 That which we have seen and heard declare we unto you, that ye also may have fellowship with us: and truly our fellowship is with the Father, and with his Son Jesus Christ.

4 And these things write we unto you, that your joy may be full.

Memory Selection
1 John 1:3
Background Scripture
Luke 1:1-4; 1 Cor. 15:1-4;
1 John 1:1-4
Devotional Reading
Colossians 1:15-20
Printed Scripture
Luke 1:1-4; 1 Cor. 15:1-4
1 John 1:1-4

Teacher's Target

of the Gospel, the Good News about Jesus, through the eyes of those who personally observed His ministry.

Compared to many books, the New Testament isn't a huge volume. On the other hand, it may be viewed as a mini-library of 27 books. They comprise a mass of information about the life and teaching of Jesus and His apostles, designed to meet the needs of cross-cultural readers consisting of both Jews and Greeks. Isn't there a concise summary of the saving message of Jesus, a "core curriculum" that applies to all readers?

Fortunately there is. Each of the four Gospels is a condensation of His life and teachings; and Paul's first letter to the church at Corinth summarizes the core of the message. This lesson is especially important because it presents the essence of the most important teaching the world has ever known.

Jesus burst upon the ancient world with

Lesson Introduction

the brightness of the star of Bethlehem. Lest the event die with the star's fading, God took measures to preserve the light for all the ages.

At first, the message was repeated orally as early Christians gathered to hear the apostles and other traveling preachers. Then, eye-witnesses and others committed the Good News to writing. Just as the Old Testament came about as "holy men of God spake as they were moved by the Holy Ghost" (2 Pet. 1:21), so New Testament authors were inspired to record the story. Letters such as Galatians and the Thessalonians are generally regarded as the earliest. Then came the Gospels and the rest of the Epistles.

This priceless material was produced and preserved so that generations to follow, including ourselves, might "have fellowship" with those who personally sat at the feet of Jesus (see 1 John 1:3). This lesson is a summary of their message.

Teaching Outline	Daily Bible Readings
I. An Eyewitness Account, Luke 1:1-4 　A. Footprints of faith, 1-2 　B. The story " in order," 3-4 II. The Basic Message—1 Cor. 15:1-4 　A. A saving message, 1-2 　B. The core content, 3-4 III. Seen, Heard, and Handled—1 John 1:1-4 　A. First-hand faith, 1 　B. Life made manifest, 2 　C. Fellowship in the faith, 3-4	**Mon.** An Orderly Account 　*Luke 1:1-4* **Tue.** Paul's Proclamation 　*1 Corinthians 15:1-4* **Wed.** Seen, Heard, and Handled 　*1 John 1-4* **Thu.** Those Who Do God's Will 　*1 John 2:15-29* **Fri.** We Are Children of God 　*1 John 3:1-10* **Sat.** Love One Another 　*1 John 3:11-24* **Sun.** God Is Love 　*1 John 4:13-21*

Verse by Verse

I. An Eyewitness Account—Luke 1:1-4
A. Footprints of faith, 1-2

1 Forasmuch as many have taken in hand to set forth in order a declaration of those things which are most surely believed among us,

2 Even as they delivered them unto us, which from the beginning were eyewitnesses, and ministers of the word;

Many world religions can be taught merely by discussing their ideas, apart from history. Biblical faith insists that its ideas are grounded in historical events. The author of the third Gospel, widely believed to be Paul's physician-companion Luke (see Col. 4:14), realizes the importance of writing down "in order" the basics of what happened, as a firm base for what is believed.

Although Luke was not one of the original apostles, he knows of many other accounts from which he no doubt drew. These accounts apparently included "declarations" or oral accounts, but Luke may also have had access to earlier written accounts such as the Gospel of Mark. Also, he must have learned much about Christ's work from his travels with Paul, who was instructed by the Lord Himself in the "Damascus Road" vision and in his sojourn in the Arabian desert (Acts 22:7-9; Gal. 1:17). Notice that this material was already considered "the word" of God.

B. The story "in order," 3-4

3 It seemed good to me also, having had perfect understanding of all things from the very first, to write unto thee in order, most excellent Theophilus,

4 That thou mightest know the certainty of those things, wherein thou hast been instructed.

If the author here is indeed Luke the physician, we see his "scientific method" at work as he commits himself to arrange in sequence the important events and teachings of Jesus. His qualifications include the fact that he has followed these things closely from the beginning.

The identity of "Theophilus" is unknown. The name tells us more about the author's own work. It is widely believed that Luke also wrote the book of Acts, since that work is also addressed to Theophilus (Acts 1:1). The name literally means "friend of God"; and the title "most excellent" may suggest that he was a nobleman who had become a believer. He may even have subsidized Luke's work as a "patron" of early Christian writings. Luke writes not just to inform Theophilus (and ages to come) but to confirm the "certainty" of his faith.

II. The Basic Message—1 Cor. 15:1-4
A. A saving message, 1-2

1 Moreover, brethren, I declare unto you the gospel which I

preached unto you, which also ye have received, and wherein ye stand;

2 By which also ye are saved, if ye keep in memory what I preached unto you, unless ye have believed in vain.

We now move from Luke's reasons for and method of writing His Gospel to a nutshell version of the Good News as formulated by the apostle Paul. This passage comes toward the end of the apostle Paul's powerful letter to the church at Corinth. It includes some "hard sayings" and even rebuke, since there were several deficiencies in the church there. Now Paul wants to ground his exhortations in the basic facts of the Gospel. The reforms he calls for are not arbitrary; they grow out of the authority of Jesus Himself, who validated His own message through the events Paul describes.

Furthermore, the Corinthians are not to think that moral reform alone will save them. They are saved by the grace of God in the self-giving acts Paul will list here, as long as they "keep in memory" or maintain their allegiance to their Lord. Otherwise, like the devils who believe, but tremble (James 2:19), their faith will have been in vain.

B. The core content, 3-4

3 For I delivered unto you first of all that which I also received, how that Christ died for our sins according to the scriptures;

4 And that he was buried, and that he rose again the third day according to the scriptures:

Paul's term for "I delivered" will later

be used to describe the handing along of the central core of the gospel. It is "tradition" in the sense of the classic, unchanging essence of Christ's work and words, as opposed to the contingent parts of the New Covenant. It the central "preaching" (Gk.. *kerygma*) without which Christianity cannot be genuine, as opposed to less basic "teaching" (*didache*) which, while important, is not the central thrust Paul has in mind here.

Many Christians will recognize in these words the basis of what is commonly called "The Apostles' Creed." The first plank in this platform of faith is the vicarious atonement of Christ, who "died for our sins." Note that this claim is rooted not only in the historical event of the cross, but in "the Scriptures",which in this context refers to Old Testament predictions (such as Isa. 53:1-11).

The second important part of this Gospel summary is the burial of Christ. Some taught (as some still teach) that Jesus only fainted on the cross and somehow revived in the tomb. Paul will have none of this attempt to explain away Christ's death because the next point he makes depends on Jesus' actually having died.

"He rose again" is the capstone of this basic Christian statement of faith. This too was predicted in the Old Testament Scriptures according to a common Christian interpretation of Hosea 6:2. Paul will elaborate on this point throughout 1 Corinthians 14, arguing that "If Christ be not raised, your faith is vain; ye are yet in your sins" (vs. 17).

III. Seen, Heard, and Handled—1 John 1:1-4

A. First-hand faith, 1-2

1 That which was from the beginning, which we have heard, which we have seen with our eyes, which we have looked upon, and our hands have handled, of the Word of life;

2 (For the life was manifested, and we have seen it, and bear witness, and shew unto you that eternal life, which was with the Father, and was manifested unto us:)

Moving again to another important fundamental way of stating the Good News, we enter the late first-century world of the aged apostle John. By now, opposition to the "Christ event" has taken the form of early "gnostic-like" teachings. Some forms of this teaching held that since "the flesh" is inherently evil, Jesus could not have had a fleshly body and at the same time been one with God the Father. Thus they held Jesus only "seemed" to have a body.

John rebukes this view by saying not only that he heard and saw Jesus teach; he actually touched or handled Him. Even after His resurrection, Jesus insisted that "a spirit hath not flesh and bones, as ye see me have" (Luke 24:39).

Yet John affirms that Jesus was much more than a man of flesh. He was also the "Word" or supernatural communication of God. He was the Word-made-flesh (John 1:14). It is this dual insistence that Jesus is "very God and very man" that the historic Church has clung to as a basic doctrine through the ages, against frequent attempts to deny one aspect or the other of the nature of Christ.

C. Fellowship in the faith, 3-4

3 That which we have seen and heard declare we unto you, that ye also may have fellowship with us: and truly our fellowship is with the Father, and with his Son Jesus Christ.

4 And these things write we unto you, that your joy may be full.

Why is it important to maintain allegiance to the foregoing summaries of the Gospel? John has something more than a mere doctrinaire significance in mind. Affirming the basic facts about Jesus' life, death, burial, and resurrection is key to relating to Him today. Having fellowship with Christ through these truths is far different than having a mere historical memory that He lived long ago. Those who accept the truth of Jesus' bodily resurrection know that Jesus still lives. John is eager that we make his faith in that event our own, since it is that level of fellowship with God through Christ that is the path to true joy.

Evangelistic Emphasis

We often judge news by the source delivering the news. When the people at CNN talk news we tend to listen. When we read a headline on the cover of that magazine for "inquiring minds" we tend to ignore the outrageous claims. The source of the information often gives validity to the information being shared.

Luke and John wrote to the ancient world about the nature of Jesus' ministry on earth. They wrote as persons who have considered the evidence. The author of 1 John wrote as an eyewitness to the life of Jesus Christ. As 1 John was read in the ancient world, the epistle had weight because of John's eyewitness status. He could write about good news because he had experienced good news.

Who we are as Christians validates or invalidates our witness for Jesus Christ. If our words and our deeds have consistency then our witness will have power. Our witness is weakened when we don't live up to the bold words we proclaim. The good news is that each of us can be powerful witness for Jesus Christ. Today the news is judged by the integrity of the messenger.

The one irrefutable argument I can make is my experience. No one can argue when I say I have experienced God's love and mercy in my life. No one can argue with you as you express how you have experienced God's presence in your life.

Be careful my brothers and sisters, people are watching your witness.

● ● ● ● ● ● ●

Memory Selection

That which we have seen and heard declare we unto you, that ye also may have fellowship with us: and truly our fellowship is with the Father, and with his Son Jesus Christ.—*1 John 1:3*

Think about the nativity scenes that you are experiencing this time of year. There may be one in your home and in your church. Whether they are contemporary or a family heirloom, they share one thing in common. The nativity scenes that decorate our Christmas season are silent.

That first Christmas was anything but silent. The baby Jesus spent some time crying. Mary and Joseph had whispered conversations about their son and His special place in God's plan. The shepherds came. Shepherds have never been quiet. They are outdoor people who bring their "outdoor" noises with them, even at the manger. Bethlehem was a buzz with the noise of strangers coming for the census. Jesus Christ was born into a real world full of sound and sight.

The first Christians gave weight to eyewitness accounts of Jesus' life. At the end of this century we give weight to persons who have first-hand experiences with the risen Christ. Most of those people testify to the fact that God is not silent, but in Christ is speaking words of comfort and calling to those who will listen.

So on Christmas morning listen to the sound of a child's laughter and joy, in it you may just hear the voice of God.

Weekday Problems

Shanna was livid about the Christmas card she had recently received from her missionary uncle. It was the same card every year. Shanna's aunt would sit down at the computer and write a one-page diary of the events in her family's life. Aunt Billie would always brag on Shanna's cousins and her uncle. There was never any bad news reported in Aunt Billie's Christmas letter. There were a couple of other people in the office who agreed with Shanna's chagrin over the form letter Christmas card tradition that had recently developed. Marcie was even complaining that her family had taken to sending e-mail Christmas cards.

Shanna's response was predictable for her. She picked out the prettiest Christmas card she could find. It was a rather large card too. She began by writing Aunt Bille and Uncle Ted. In her card she wrote about the struggles her family had endured. With lofty words filled with joy she wrote how even through struggles God had been good to her family. She wrote about discovering a renewed sense God's presence sustaining her in her troubles. She concluded by saying that while others might not see her year as a good one, she thought that it had been one of the best yet. With words expressing her prayer for Aunt Billie's family, Shanna closed her personalized Card.

On Christmas Eve, Aunt Billie called Shanna to say Merry Christmas and to talk about Uncle Ted's recent bad medical news.

* How does being "real" often open the doors to ministry and service to others?

Creeds in Christendom

Doctrinal diversity prompted many attempts in the early church to standardize the basics of the faith into a creed. The oldest is the "Old Roman Creed," later known as "The Apostles' Creed." It reads:

I believe in God Almighty, and in Christ Jesus, his only son our Lord, who was born of the Holy Spirit and Mary the Virgin, who, under Pontius Pilate, was crucified and buried, and on the third day rose from the dead, ascended into heaven and sitteth on the right hand of the Father, whence he shall come to judge the living and the dead, and in the Holy Spirit, the holy church (later amended to "holy *catholic* [worldwide] church), the remission of sins, the resurrection of the flesh, and life everlasting.

Such statements have served both to unite and to divide Christians. Do you believe they should have a place in the Church today?

This Lesson in Your Life

God saved the world in plain sight. The Christmas season is our celebration that God came to be born as one of us. Jesus Christ was God in the flesh. Beyond all the commercial trappings of Christmas there is this basic message. God did this wonderful thing where not only could humanity reach out and touch His son, humanity could comment on His ministry.

Think about all the things that happen in our world in secret. Why must a School Board have an executive session? Aren't they about providing for a good education for our children? Why should that be a cause for secrecy? What about Congress, why would our elected officials have to keep information from those who elected them? It seems the longer we live in the information age the more the need for secrecy.

The writer of Hebrews says in chapter 1 that God had always been speaking to His children. In the last days God spoke in Son talk. Son talk is the language of incarnation. God coming to earth in the person of Jesus Christ. It was a language that was hard to argue with. Jesus not only talked about love he modeled love. Not only did he preach about forgiveness, he offered forgiveness to those who sought it. He lived a life centered in God's will just as he talked about centering in God's will. His words were spoken to be heard. His deeds were done to be seen. Jesus didn't do things secretly.

Christianity is a faith that is best shared in the open. The church can never create a "secret conclave" because it would be contrary to the public nature of the faith. We are a "see and be seen" church! We are a talking and noise-making community. We should claim the language of Son talk and be making God-like noises all over our planet. The church is called to be as visible all year as we are at this time of the year.

The life of Jesus Christ was filled with sights and sounds. His life touched many people and they, in turn, spread the gospel to the ends of the earth. We follow in their steps as witnesses to what Jesus has done in our lives. We have words to share. We have deeds of love and service to be spread in our world.

As we talk about what God has done in our lives, we become effective witnesses. We make Christmas real to the next generation by showing how Jesus has been born in each of us. Even after 2,000 years, the best way to share God's love is to mimic Jesus. The simple act of inviting a friend to a meal will get his attention. Helping someone decorate a home for Christmas or helping a homebound person shop will get his or her attention. These are the noises the church and individual believers need to make. Too often, however, in the face of great pain and suffering the church has been silent.

People in the throws of agony or darkness doesn't need a sermon. They need to look into the eyes and hold the hands of a person who can say, "I was where you are." When you can identify with that pain and have a story of redemption you will have a captive audience. Christmas is a great time to share your faith. There are so many excuses during this season to invite a friend over and share with them that "which we have seen with our eyes . . . and touched with our hands" (1 John 1:1). People are looking for the words of life and you have those very words dwelling in your heart. Don't miss this wonderful seasonal opportunity to share God's love with a friend.

I write this so that your joy would be complete. The greatest gift you can share is the gift of Jesus Christ. Seeing a person coming to faith in Christ is a thrill that can't be matched by anything in this world.

Seed Thoughts

1. In the first verses of Luke's gospel, Luke indicates his reason for writing. What was his reason?

Luke was writing because others were also writing accounts of Jesus' life.

2. Why would Luke be a person qualified to write the story of Jesus?

Luke may not have been an eyewitness to the life of Jesus, but he had close association with eyewitnesses to Jesus' life.

3. To whom was Luke addressing his book?

The book of Luke was written to Theophilus. The name Theophilus means, "friend of God."

4. Why do you suppose Luke addressed this gospel to Theophilus?

Luke wanted Theophilus to know about Jesus so that Theophilus might believe in Jesus.

5. What other book in the New Testament was written by Luke?

The Acts of the Apostles is the other work Luke wrote. It was also addressed to Theophilus.

---

1. In the first verses of Luke's gospel, Luke indicates his reason for writing. What was his reason?

2. Why would Luke be a person qualified to write the story of Jesus?

3. To whom was Luke addressing his book?

4. Why do you suppose Luke addressed this gospel to Theophilus?

5. What other book in the New Testament was written by Luke?

6. Verse one of 1 John sounds like the opening of two other books in the Bible, which two books?

7. The word of life was experienced in three ways by the author of 1 John, what were those ways?

8. What was the purpose of the writing of this work of 1 John?

9. What two words in this passage describe the way the gospel message was spread?

10. What is the essence of the word fellowship?

(Continued next page)

Luke was writing because others were also writing accounts of Jesus' life.

Luke may not have been an eyewitness to the life of Jesus, but he had close association with eyewitnesses to Jesus' life.

The book of Luke was written to Theophilus. The name Theophilus means, "friend of God."

Luke wanted Theophilus to know about Jesus so that Theophilus might believe in Jesus.

The Acts of the Apostles is the other work Luke wrote. It was also addressed to Theophilus.

First John 1:1 sounds like Genesis 1:1 and John 1:1. All these books stress God's activity "from the beginning."

The word of life was heard. The word of life was seen. The world of life was touched.

First John was written so that persons reading or hearing the message might believe and have fellowship with the author.

The author testified to Jesus. He also proclaimed the message of Jesus.

Fellowship means, "sharing in common." In Christ we share "in common" with God and each other.

6. Verse one of 1 John sounds like the opening of two other books in the Bible, which two books?

First John 1:1 sounds like Genesis 1:1 and John 1:1. All these books stress God's activity "from the beginning."

7. The word of life was experienced in three ways by the author of 1 John, what were those ways?

The word of life was heard. The word of life was seen. The world of life was touched.

8. What was the purpose of the writing of this work of 1 John?

First John was written so that persons reading or hearing the message might believe and have fellowship with the author.

9. What two words in this passage describe the way the gospel message was spread?

The author testified to Jesus. He also proclaimed the message of Jesus.

10. What is the essence of the word fellowship?

Fellowship means, "sharing in common." In Christ we share "in common" with God and each other.

The Birth of Jesus

*A*nd it came to pass in those days, that there went out a decree from Cæsar Augustus, that all the world should be taxed.

2 (And this taxing was first made when Cyrenius was governor of Syria.)

3 And all went to be taxed, everyone into his own city.

4 And Joseph also went up from Galilee, out of the city of Nazareth, into Judæa, unto the city of David, which is called Bethlehem; (because he was of the house and lineage of David:)

Luke 2:1-17

5 To be taxed with Mary his espoused wife, being great with child.

6 And so it was, that, while they were there, the days were accomplished that she should be delivered.

7 And she brought forth her firstborn son, and wrapped him in swaddling clothes, and laid him in a manger; because there was no room for them in the inn.

8 And there were in the same country shepherds abiding in the field, keeping watch over their flock by night.

9 And, lo, the angel of the Lord came upon them, and the glory of the Lord shone round about them: and they were sore afraid.

10 And the angel said unto them, Fear not: for behold, I bring you good tidings of great joy, which shall be to all people.

11 For unto you is born this day in the city of David a Saviour, which is Christ the Lord.

12 And this shall be a sign unto you; Ye shall find the babe wrapped in swaddling clothes, lying in a manger.

13 And suddenly there was with the angel a multitude of the heavenly host praising God, and saying,

14 Glory to God in the highest, and on earth peace, good will toward men.

15 And it came to pass, as the angels were gone away from them into heaven, the shepherds said one to another, Let us now go even unto Bethlehem, and see this thing which is come to pass, which the Lord hath made known unto us.

16 And they came with haste, and found Mary, and Joseph, and the babe lying in a manger.

17 And when they had seen it, they made known abroad the saying which was told them concerning this child.

Memory Selection
Luke 2:11

Background Scripture
Luke 2:1-20

Devotional Reading
Isaiah 9:2-7

Printed Scripture
Luke 2:1-17

Teacher's Target

Lesson purpose: *To examine anew the "glad tidings", the timeless story of the birth of Jesus, reminding ourselves of our spiritual roots, and the appropriate response to this unique event.*

Children are often fascinated by stories about family events that concern them, but that occurred when they were too young to remember. One child insisted on asking his parents to "Tell me again about the time when Aunt Mary came to see us right after I was born and I spit up on her." Such events help us establish ourselves in the family, giving us a sense of roots.

As children of God, we also never tire of hearing the story of the birth of the Christ-Child. In a profound sense this story is not only about the entrance of our Lord into human history, but about our place in His family as well. It is at once the story both of the Babe of Bethlehem, of the birthing of our faith, and of our spiritual roots.

Lesson Introduction

One way to bring a fresh note to Luke's familiar story of the birth of Jesus is to introduce it by encouraging group members to share joyful stories about the birth of children in their own families. Are any families present who rejoiced when they had a baby after going childless for years? Are there stories of mother or child surviving despite high-risk births? Are there any unusual circumstances to share, such as the mom who gave birth in the hospital hallway because she couldn't convinced the staff she was ready to go into the delivery room?

Such stories become a part of the lore of our families because they are about significant beginnings. They stick in our minds because they are about the way God brings new beginnings to families through the miracle of birth. And for members of the family of God, no story is more significant than Luke's account of the birth of this unique Child.

TeachingOutline	Daily Bible Readings	
I. A Taxing Trip—1-5	**Mon.**	John's Birth Foretold *Luke 1:15-17*
A. The Roman tax, 1-3	**Tue.**	Gabriel Visits Mary *Luke 1:24-38*
B. Prophecy fulfilled, 4-5	**Wed.**	'My Spirit Rejoices!' *Luke 1:39-55*
II. An Inn with No Room, 6-7		
III. Applause in Heaven—8-14	**Thu.**	What Manner of Child! *Luke 1:57-66*
A. Good tidings of joy, 8-12	**Fri.**	Strong in the Spirit *Luke 1:67-80*
B. Glory to God!, 13-14	**Sat.**	From Nazareth to Bethlehem *Luke 2:1-7*
IV. Adoration on Earth—15-17	**Sun.**	Good News of Great Joy *Luke 2:8-20*

Verse by Verse

I. A Taxing Trip—1-5
A. The Roman tax, 1-3

1 And it came to pass in those days, that there went out a decree from Cæsar Augustus, that all the world should be taxed.

2 (And this taxing was first made when Cyrenius was governor of Syria.)

3 And all went to be taxed, everyone into his own city.

Luke is the only Gospel writer to record these details surrounding the birth of Christ. With his usual eye for tying spiritual events to "real time" or history, Luke is careful to note that the awesome entrance of God's Son into this world occurred at a specific, and in some ways quite ordinary, point in time. It was during the days when Judea was controlled by the mighty Roman empire, and specifically under Caesar Augustus' rule.

"All the world" was a common way of referring to the far-flung Roman empire, which at the time was spread out over "all the world" known by common people (see the NIV, "the entire Roman world"). The Jewish historian Josephus tells us that Judea had only recently been made a sub-province of Syria. This is why the Syrian governor Cyrenius (NIV "Quirinius") is mentioned here. Appar-

ently the reorganization of the area prompted Augustus to take a new census and assess a new tax. (The word translated "to be taxed" means "to enroll" or "register," which preceded being taxed.) The tax census would more accurately reflect the make-up of the population if all registered in the city of their birth.

B. Prophecy fulfilled, 4-5

4 And Joseph also went up from Galilee, out of the city of Nazareth, into Judæa, unto the city of David, which is called Bethlehem; (because he was of the house and lineage of David:)

5 To be taxed with Mary his espoused wife, being great with child.

Luke has introduced us to Joseph in 1:26-27 as a descendant of King David who lived in the village of Nazareth in the north country near the Sea of Galilee. Why then are we told again of Joseph's connection with the house of David? Because we are to understand that the child about to be born in the manger of Bethlehem is none other than the Messiah.

Several prophets had predicted that the Messiah would be a descendant of David (Isa. 9:6-7); and the prophet

Micah had even specified that He would be born in David's home town, Bethlehem (Mic. 5:2). This connection between Joseph as the surrogate father of Jesus and the house of David will be made again in Luke's account of Christ's family tree (Luke 3:31-32).

No biblical story more strongly affirms God's sovereignty over history. Although Rome has been, and will continue to be, a frequent oppressor of God's people, God is able to use the Roman Caesar's census and tax as a means of arranging for this Messianic prophecy to be fulfilled in Bethlehem.

II. An Inn with No Room—6-7

6 And so it was, that, while they were there, the days were accomplished that she should be delivered.

7 And she brought forth her firstborn son, and wrapped him in swaddling clothes, and laid him in a manger; because there was no room for them in the inn.

Mary had become pregnant "of the Holy Ghost" while she was engaged to Joseph (Matt. 1:18-20). Jewish custom made the engagement period more binding than in our own culture, but the pregnancy was still of some embarrassment to Joseph. Here, however, he is bravely shouldering the responsibility of a father and caring tenderly for his wife, who is about to deliver the child.

In one sense it seems a supreme injustice for the King of kings not to be born in a palace nursery, much less a cozy inn, and to settle instead for a rude stable. Yet the picture fits the nature of Christ's role as a Servant, just as Isaiah had predicted. In a supreme moment of giving up His pre-existent heavenly status, God's Son becomes a human son. The "swaddling clothes", clean cloths used as a warm wrap for a new-born infant, become His royal mantle.

III. Applause in Heaven—8-14

A. Good tidings of joy, 8-12

8 And there were in the same country shepherds abiding in the field, keeping watch over their flock by night.

9 And, lo, the angel of the Lord came upon them, and the glory of the Lord shone round about them: and they were sore afraid.

10 And the angel said unto them, Fear not: for behold, I bring you good tidings of great joy, which shall be to all people.

11 For unto you is born this day in the city of David a Saviour, which is Christ the Lord.

12 And this shall be a sign unto you; Ye shall find the babe wrapped in swaddling clothes, lying in a manger.

Continuing the theme of understated royalty, the first people to learn of the Messiah's birth are not fellow-kings but humble shepherds in the nearby fields. The picture symbolizes both the role of the Good Shepherd that Jesus will play, and the fact that "not many wise men after the flesh, not many mighty, not many noble, are called" (1 Cor. 1:26).

The "angel of the Lord" and the "glory of the Lord" are frequent Old Testament indications of God's presence. The glory appeared as a cloud and fire at the giving of the Law, and hovered over the tabernacle, then the Temple. No wonder the shepherds are afraid, it is fearful to stand this close to the divine Power!

The angel, however, reassures the shepherds that this is a joyful, not a judgmental, manifestation. He emphasizes once again that this Miracle-Child fits the Messianic prophecies that He would be a descendant of David and born in David's city, Bethlehem. The angel knows that the shepherds will hasten to welcome the Infant-King; and since there may have been more than one babe born in the crowded town that night, he tells the shepherds how to identify the Child they seek.

B. Glory to God!, 13-14

13 And suddenly there was with the angel a multitude of the heavenly host praising God, and saying,

14 Glory to God in the highest, and on earth peace, good will toward men.

The announcement of Messiah's birth is too momentous to limit to a single angel. The "heavenly host" consists perhaps not only of other angels but cherubim and seraphim, the entire heavenly court who are attendants at God's throne. The darkness must have literally glowed with their shining presence, and the ordinary hush of night broken with divine song and the glad announcement that this Birth signals God's peace and favor to all.

IV. Adoration on Earth—15-17

15 And it came to pass, as the angels were gone away from them into heaven, the shepherds said one to another, Let us now go even unto Bethlehem, and see this thing which is come to pass, which the Lord hath made known unto us.

16 And they came with haste, and found Mary, and Joseph, and the babe lying in a manger.

17 And when they had seen it, they made known abroad the saying which was told them concerning this child.

Now it is humanity's turn to rejoice. The shepherds make their way to Bethlehem where they are rewarded with the sight that made angels burst into song. Their making known "abroad" the good news of the coming of the Savior is a response that is still enjoined on those who have the privilege of learning of this wondrous Birth.

Evangelistic Emphasis

The account of the first Christmas is loaded with irony. The good news that Mary was having a baby was not really good news. She and Joseph struggled with the news until Joseph was reassured by an angel. The census was bad news. The reason for a census in the ancient world was to determine the amount of tax. Taxes are not good news. Because of the census, Mary and Joseph had to take a trip. To add to their bad news, the inn in Bethlehem was full. It all worked out the way that God wanted. That is why, what should have been bad news turned out to be good news for you and me.

How would you want your Savior born?

Would you feel comfortable with a Savior who was born in a palace and raised to be royalty? What about a Savior who was born among the aristocratic and had all the luxuries of life? Could you approach that kind of Savior with your daily problems? How about a Savior who was born, out back in the barn?

I can approach a Savior who had such humble beginnings. I can relate to that kind of Savior. The good news of Jesus Christ is that He came as one of us for us. His life was filled with the kind of irony that surrounds Christmas. He loved sinners and that made religious people hate Him. He never committed a sin, yet died a sinner's death. He never owned a home, yet prepared a home for us in heaven. One whose life began in a cave and ended on a cross is our Savior. His life was so full of contradictions and irony that He surely can understand our confusion and forgive our sin.

• • • • • •

Memory Selection

For unto you is born this day in the city of David a Savior which is Christ the Lord.— *Luke 2:11*

Names are important. Names evoke a response. To prove this, find a child under the age of six and watch his or her face as you say Santa Claus. His face will light up and he will start looking for Santa.

Your name is important. Your parents gave you the name you have for a very important reason. Perhaps there is a tradition behind your name. In church, the minister called your name before he said, "I baptize you in the name of the Father, Son and Holy Spirit." We identify each other by name. God also has called each of us by name. We are individually important to Him.

This verse is filled with names. An important one is missing, yours. I want you to make a substitution as you read the verse. Try reading it like this: "For unto *your name* is born this day in the city of David a Savior which is Christ the Lord." He came to this earth to be YOUR Savior! While your name might not be in the verse, you were in the heart of God as He planned for Jesus' life and ministry. To think God did all of this for you.

Weekday Problems

Shirlene was in a state. Something was going on in the office and she wasn't in on the secret. Telephone calls were being made and when she would walk into the room the person on the phone would grow silent. She could hear whispering in the other offices when certain phone calls were made. When Shirlene inquired about the secrecy the secretaries simply gave her an incredulous look and went about their business. That was not so far out of the ordinary, since Shirlene was not the most popular executive in the firm. She wondered if a Christmas party was being planned without her being on the guest list. She often felt left out, especially at Christmas time. Shirlene was one of those persons whose birthday fell a couple of days before Christmas. She never had a party on her birthday, it was always "too close to Christmas." With all the secret office shenanigans, Shirlene was certain that her birthday would be forgotten and she would be excluded from any Christmas party now being planned.

On a Saturday night, Shirlene and her husband Mike attended the Christmas play at their daughter's school. It was a pageant complete with sheep, shepherd, Magi, the Holy Family and even old St. Nick. Their daughter was the star of the show. She played Mary. On the way home Shirlene began reflecting on all the goings on at the office. When she walked in the house that night thirty people from her office yelled, "Happy Birthday!"

* When have you ever felt "left out"?

* Have you included everyone in your Christmas celebration?"

Taxing Times

Sunday School teacher: Now who decreed that all the world should be taxed?
Pupil: The Democrats.

* * *

God couldn't do without the IRS. He loves the poor, and the IRS creates them for Him to love.

* * *

Hope: What's the difference between a taxidermist and the tax collector?
Dope: No difference at all. Both of them skin the victim.

* * *

I'm going to invest in the IRS. Taxes are the only commodity guarantee to go up.

* * *

Jack: Did you know that some presidents gave their salaries back to the government?
Zack: Yeah, and now they have us all doing it.

This Lesson in Your Life

"In those days a decree went out from Caesar Augustus." (Luke 2:1) We have heard the words so often they don't register with us. The decree caused chaos. Persons had to pack up their homes and move to strange cities. These displaced pilgrims were forced to live with relatives. They had to find work in strange job markets. Children had to make adjustments and find new friends. When the decree went out the world fell apart for many persons including Joseph and Mary. Have you wondered why Joseph's relatives didn't make room for him in their ancestral home of Bethlehem? Could it be that they had already made room for a bunch of other strange cousins?

It was out of this chaos that God brought His Son into the world. Think about your life. We go to great lengths to avoid unpredictability in our lives. Many of your friends won't go out of the house without a planner. They want to control every moment of life. Ask your friends about how their lives are working out with their planners. They will tell you that the unexpected and unplanned activities change their agendas. This happens almost daily. In the unexpected we often find God. Elijah didn't find God in all the expected places. He was not in the wind, the earthquake or in the fire. God came to Elijah in "sheer silence" (1 Kings 19: 11-13). As a person who plans worship I can testify that God comes more in the unplanned moments than in those that are carefully worked out. He turned the world upside down for the birth of His Son. Jesus would turn His world upside down as well. The first impulse of this lesson is that God is found in the surprises of life, if you are looking for Him.

Think about the shepherds watching their flocks. They had not planned on an angelic choir singing to them. The message the choir gave was important: "Fear not!" (Luke 2: 10) The second impulse of this passage is the call to fearless living. The shepherds had much to fear. They had to keep watch over sheep. The sheep could be stolen by other shepherds. They could be attacked by wild animals. They could become lost and hurt themselves. Then there were all the strangers coming to town. Strange shepherds bringing strange flocks of sheep to graze on their lands. Right in the middle of the shepherd's chaos came the message, "Fear not."

Change often brings fear. We are such creatures of habit that when something is different we are thrown. Ask your class members if they drove to church the same way that they always do. Ask them if anything in this past week has been new or different. You will find that we are creatures of habit and newness is often frowned upon. The shepherds needed to be reminded that there was nothing to fear. Even as this "new thing" was announced to them.

Christmas challenges the church to practice fearless living in a frightening world. We can do that only as we are anchored to Jesus Christ. Jesus was born into a world like ours. It was a world that had been thrown into chaos by the capricious dictates of a world ruler. People had been displaced. They were afraid. They had the sense of being lost. Imagine all the people around that manger in Bethlehem. Do you think any of them were afraid?

Jesus came into that kind of world. It doesn't sweem to have been that much different from the world in which we live. Yet, as you let your spirit dwell on the manger, don't you find a sense of peace? It is safe and silent there with the Christ. He brings peace . . . even with the chaos that we have brought to Christmas.

Seed Thoughts

1. Jesus was born at a specific time in world history. What historical figures are mentioned by Luke?

Caesar Augustus was the emperor of the Roman Empire. Quirinius was the governor of Syria.

2. What was the essence of the decree that had been issued?

The decree was a call for a census of the Roman Empire. Each member of the empire had to register.

3. What was the purpose of the trip that Joseph and Mary made from Nazareth to Bethlehem?

Joseph was going to Bethlehem to pay his taxes. Taxes were collected according to tribes or families.

4. What was the importance of Bethlehem?

Bethlehem was the ancestral home of David and it was prophesied as the birth place of the Messiah.

5. Tracing the lineage of Jesus in Matthew 1: 1-17 and Luke 3: 23-38, what do you notice?

Matthew traces the genealogy back to Abraham. Luke traces the genealogy back to God.

1. Jesus was born at a specific time in world history. What historical figures are mentioned by Luke?

2. What was the essence of the decree that had been issued?

3. What was the purpose of the trip that Joseph and Mary made from Nazareth to Bethlehem?

4. What was the importance of Bethlehem?

5. Tracing the lineage of Jesus in Matthew 1: 1-17 and Luke 3: 23-38, what do you notice?

6. What other interesting difference is there between the two genealogies of Jesus?

7. According to Luke, were Joseph and Mary married when they traveled to Bethlehem?

8. We have many Christmas traditions based on Scripture. What verse mentions the innkeeper?

9. The long-awaited Savior of the Jews had come. To whom was the great event first announced?

10. What was the significance of the announcement of the birth to the shepherds?

(Continued next page)

Caesar Augustus was the emperor of the Roman Empire. Quirinius was the governor of Syria.

The decree was a call for a census of the Roman Empire. Each member of the empire had to register.

Joseph was going to Bethlehem to pay his taxes. Taxes were collected according to tribes or families.

Bethlehem was the ancestral home of David and it was prophesied as the birth place of the Messiah.

Matthew traces the genealogy back to Abraham. Luke traces the genealogy back to God.

Matthew traces the genealogy through Joseph. Luke gives Mary's genealogy.

According to Luke, Mary and Joseph were still engaged when they made the journey to Bethlehem (Luke 2:5b).

The innkeeper is never mentioned in any Scripture. This scrooge-like person is not in the Bible.

The announcement was first made to shepherds who watched the flocks at night.

Jesus came for all people. No one was to be excluded from His love, not even lowly shepherds.

6. What other interesting difference is there between the two genealogies of Jesus?

Matthew traces the genealogy through Joseph. Luke gives Mary's genealogy.

7. According to Luke, were Joseph and Mary married when they traveled to Bethlehem?

According to Luke, Mary and Joseph were still engaged when they made the journey to Bethlehem (Luke 2:5b).

8. We have many Christmas traditions based on Scripture. What verse mentions the innkeeper?

The innkeeper is never mentioned in any Scripture. This scrooge-like person is not in the Bible.

9. The long-awaited Savior of the Jews had come. To whom was the great event first announced?

The announcement was first made to shepherds who watched the flocks at night.

10. What was the significance of the announcement of the birth to the shepherds?

Jesus came for all people. No one was to be excluded from His love, not even lowly shepherds.

Christ's Presence Continues

Dec. 27

*A*nd as they thus spake, Jesus himself stood in the midst of them, and saith unto them, Peace be unto you.

37 But they were terrified and affrighted, and supposed that they had seen a spirit.

38 And he said unto them, Why are ye troubled? and why do thoughts arise in your hearts?

39 Behold my hands and my feet, that it is I myself: handle me, and see; for a spirit hath not flesh and bones, as ye see me have.

40 And when he had thus spoken, he shewed them his hands and his feet.

41 And while they yet believed not for joy, and wondered, he said unto them, Have ye here any meat?

42 And they gave him a piece of a broiled fish, and of an honeycomb.

43 And he took it, and did eat before them.

44 And he said unto them, These are the words which I space unto you, while I was yet with you, that all things must be fulfilled, which were written in the law of Moses, and in the prophets, and in the psalms, concerning me.

45 Then opened he their understanding, that they might understand the scriptures,

Luke 24:36-53

46 And said unto them, Thus it is written, and thus it behooved Christ to suffer, and to rise from the dead the third day:

47 And that repentance and remission of sins should be preached in his name among all nations, beginning at Jerusalem.

48 And ye are witnesses of these things.

49 And, behold, I send the promise of my Father upon you: but tarry ye in the city of Jerusalem, until ye be endued with power from on high.

50 And he led them out as far as to Bethany, and he lifted up his hands, and blessed them.

51 And it came to pass, while he blessed them, he was parted from them, and carried up into heaven.

52 And they worshiped him, and returned to Jerusalem with great joy:

53 And were continually in the temple, praising and blessing God. Amen.

Memory Selection
Luke 24:49

Background Scripture
Luke 24:13-53

Devotional Reading
John 16:1-11

Printed Scripture
Luke 24:36-53

Teacher's Target

Lesson Purpose: *To describe the impact of Christ's death, resurrection, and ascension on the earliest disciples, and to apply lessons from these events to our own lives.*

C. S. Lewis, the late British author and defender of the faith, married late in life. Then, tragically, in only a few years his beloved wife Joy died. For months Lewis felt bereft of God's presence as well as that of his wife.

Jesus' disciples could relate. Many of them had been awaiting the Messiah for years. Imagine their joy when He finally came, then their grief when he was crucified early in life.

The startling news that He had risen from the dead was reassuring. Then they were again left alone when He returned to the Father. In this lesson note the role of *biblical teaching* as a means of controlling roller-coaster emotions as we seek to be faithful disciples in the face of unanswered questions and disillusionment.

Lesson Introduction

Thirty-three years have elapsed since Christ's birth, the setting of our previous lesson in this brief New Testament survey. Jesus' short life on earth has come to an abrupt end with a mock trial and a cruel crucifixion.

Although Jesus had predicted His death, Peter no doubt spoke for most of the disciples when he protested that such a fate did not become a Messiah (Mark 8:32). When Christ was actually crucified, the event brought disillusionment and questioning among the disciples (see Luke 24:13-35). When He appeared to the two disciples on the Emmaus Road, He tried again to explain that His death was a fulfillment of prophecy and thus the will of God. Yet "seeing is believing"; so in this lesson we see Jesus condescending to make yet another appearance and offer further proof and reassurance that God's plan of salvation is being unfolded through Him.

Teaching Outline	Daily Bible Readings
I. Believing by Seeing—36-40	**Mon.** Jesus Himself Came Near *Luke 24:13-27*
II. Reassured at a Meal—41-43	**Tue.** 'Stay with Us' *Luke 24:28-35*
III. Understanding Scripture—44-49	**Wed.** 'Peace Be with You' *Luke 24:36-43*
A. Listening to the text, 44	**Thu.** All Must Be Fulfilled *Luke 24:44-53*
B. Tuning the heart, 45	**Fri.** 'I Will Not Abandon You' *John 14:15-24*
C. Preparing for mission, 46-49	**Sat.** The Holy Spirit Promised *John 14:25-31*
IV. Worshiping with Joy—50-53	**Sun.** Jesus Speaks in Riddles *John 16:12-28*

162

Verse by Verse

I. Believing by Seeing—36-40

36 And as they thus spake, Jesus himself stood in the midst of them, and saith unto them, Peace be unto you.

37 But they were terrified and affrighted, and supposed that they had seen a spirit.

38 And he said unto them, Why are ye troubled? and why do thoughts arise in your hearts?

39 Behold my hands and my feet, that it is I myself: handle me, and see; for a spirit hath not flesh and bones, as ye see me have.

40 And when he had thus spoken, he shewed them his hands and his feet.

Luke has just recorded Jesus' appearance to two disciples on the road to Emmaus (24:13ff.). In that incident He proved He had risen from the grave by *appearing*, *eating*, and *teaching* from the Scripture, and He continues that pattern of reassurance in this scene before a larger group of followers.

Jesus goes to such lengths because He has to overcome centuries of misunderstanding about what Messiah would do when He came. Most of Jesus' followers expected Him to restore the earthly kingdom of Israel, which would have required Him to lead a revolt against the occupation armies of Rome.

When in fact the Messiah allowed Himself to be killed, all hope seemed lost.

The way Jesus suddenly "stood in the midst of them" implies a miraculous appearance without bothering to enter the room through a door (see also John 20:19). Apparently Jesus' resurrected body was not limited by the physics of ordinary mortals. So, in addition to seeing a figure of a man who had been killed and buried, it's understandable that the disciples would think they were beholding a ghost. Jesus counters their speculation and fear by showing them the physical wounds He had so recently received, adding the common-sense observation that ghosts lack such physical characteristics.

II. Reassured at a Meal—41-43

41 And while they yet believed not for joy, and wondered, he said unto them, Have ye here any meat?

42 And they gave him a piece of a broiled fish, and of an honeycomb.

43 And he took it, and did eat before them.

Now the reason for the disciples' disbelief moves from fear to joy, as when something is "too good to be true." This time Jesus counteracts their doubts with an "action parable." He shares a meal with them, just as he had done at Emmaus (vs. 30). This also, the disciples are to understand, is uncharacteristic of a ghost, which has neither body nor bodily functions.

In later years, both of these demonstrations of the reality of Christ's resurrected body would become useful arguments against "gnostics." Some of these early heretics considered the flesh to be evil, and taught that Messiah could only have *seemed* to have a real body. Against this view, true believers argued that the wounds in Christ's flesh and the fact that He fed His body with food were proof that He had an actual body of flesh, however much it may have changed in ways that allowed it to appear in a room with locked doors. Such "appearances" after His resurrection were so important that the apostle Paul would include them in his list of Gospel fundamentals in 1 Corinthians 15:3-7.

III. Understanding Scripture—44-49
A. Listening to the text, 44

44 And he said unto them, These are the words which I space unto you, while I was yet with you, that all things must be fulfilled, which were written in the law of Moses, and in the prophets, and in the psalms, concerning me.

By Jesus' day, Jewish scholars had divided the Old Testament into the Law (the first five books of the Bible), the Prophets, and the Psalms or "Hagiographa," which came to be known as "Psalms" because that was the largest book in the collection.

To correct His followers' understanding of the nature and role of the Messiah, perhaps Jesus chose from the Law such passages as Genesis 12:3, which predicts that through the seed of Abraham all nations of the earth would be blessed. From the prophets Jesus may have spoken of how Isaiah 53 predicts the coming Servant of God who would suffer for others. And from the Psalms He may have taken texts such as 16:10—"For thou wilt not leave my soul in hell; neither wilt thou suffer thine Holy One to see corruption." (The apostle Paul actually used this verse in Acts 13:35 as a prophecy of Christ's resurrection.)

B. Tuning the heart, 45

45 Then opened he their understanding, that they might understand the scriptures,

Many of the Old Testament passages used in the New Testament as prophecies about Jesus are not immediately obvious references to Him. They become so only after the heart is attuned to accepting them as such; and here this "heart-tuning" is supplied by Jesus.

It is important to note the high priority Jesus places here on Scripture. Like the disciples, we too are often susceptible to attacks of doubt. At such times it is important to give more weight to the unchanging testimony of Scripture to the truth of Christ, than to our ever-changing emotions.

C. Preparing for mission, 46-49

46 And said unto them, Thus it is written, and thus it behooved Christ to suffer, and to rise from the dead the third day:

47 And that repentance and remission of sins should be preached in his name among all nations, beginning at Jerusalem.

48 And ye are witnesses of these things.

49 And, behold, I send the promise of my Father upon you: but tarry ye in the city of Jerusalem, until ye be endued with power from on high.

Now that the disciples are better grounded in the biblical basis of their faith, they are commissioned to go preach the Good News to which they were "witnesses" (Gk.. *martyres*; the fact that so many early witnesses were killed for their conviction forms the background of our word "martyr".)

It was also a matter of prophecy that this world-wide mission would begin at Jerusalem (see Joel 3:16). This emphasis is repeated in Luke's introduction to the book of Acts,which is one reason for considering Acts a kind of "Luke, Volume 2" (see Acts 1:1-8).

The power for which the disciples are to "tarry" or wait for in Jerusalem is the Holy Spirit. Luke also records in Acts 2 the Spirit's promised descent on and filling of the disciples.

IV. Worshiping with Joy—50-53

50 And he led them out as far as to Bethany, and he lifted up his hands, and blessed them.

51 And it came to pass, while he blessed them, he was parted from them, and carried up into heaven.

52 And they worshiped him, and returned to Jerusalem with great joy:

53 And were continually in the temple, praising and blessing God. Amen.

Jesus' final personal act on earth is to bless His disciples, providing perfect "closure" to a life that had begun with blessing the world by coming as the Babe of Bethlehem. Then, in a triumphant return to His rightful place at God's right hand, Jesus ascends into heaven. Referring again to this awe-inspiring event, Luke adds in Acts 1:11 that two divine beings appear at this point to remind the disciples not to stand staring open-mouthed into the heavens, but to get busy with the task of world evangelism.

While they wait for the outpouring of the Spirit, the disciples nourish themselves for the work ahead by worship. The fact that they do this in the Temple indicates that they still envision that the new movement will be widely accepted by Jews as the fulfillment of their Messianic hopes instead of becoming a separate movement with its own churches.

Evangelistic Emphasis

With Jesus life gets better and better.

About March of last year my wife and I were moving some furniture so we could do our spring cleaning. When we slid the bed to the side of the room we discovered something under it. We had bought our son a big model airplane for Christmas. We had hidden this plane under our bed and intended to give it to him on Christmas morning. With all the other stuff we had for our son, we both forgot about the airplane hidden under our bed. It was quite a moment when we found the ungiven gift. We called Andrew into our room and in the middle of March told him, "Merry Christmas." He was thrilled to get a gift at a time when he wasn't expecting a gift.

With Christmas only a few days in the past, it seems strange to be thinking about Easter. This is the nature of God's gift. The shepherds couldn't conceive of anything better than the announcement of the birth of Jesus. All the people listening to the Sermon on the Mount couldn't conceive of anything better than listening to this inspired Rabbi. All the people Jesus healed couldn't think of anything better than the miracle God had given them.

The disciples gathered in that Upper Room couldn't conceive of anything thing better than what had happened to those Emmaus bound disciples. When they couldn't imagine anything better, Jesus appeared. They couldn't think of anything better than that, until they experienced the Holy Spirit on Pentecost. With God things get better and better.

The best day of your life is today. Because God is with you today, can you think of anything better?

And behold, I send the promise of my Father upon you.—*Luke 24: 49*

We are wary of promises. The three "promises" that are most dubious are: "The check is in the mail." "I will call you back." "I'm from the government and I'm here to help you." It is no wonder that we don't believe some promises that are made to us. Our problem has less to do with human doubt than with the failure of persons to keep their word. Many persons have decided that if a politician's mouth is moving then he is lying. It is an unfortunate impression of the cynical world in which we live. It makes us dubious of all promises, even those that were made by our Lord.

Jesus Christ kept His word. He was the promise of God to humanity. He also made promises to His disciples about his continuing presence. He promised to be present with them in the person of the Holy Spirit. Jesus kept His promise. He keeps all of His promises. You can trust Him.

Whether it is for salvation, the answer to prayer or the need of His presence in a situation, you can live with the knowledge that Jesus will never break a promise. He said so. Trust His word!

Weekday Problems

Charles had been a walking miracle for four years. He had been diagnosed with a rare and insidious form of cancer four years ago. After major surgery and a round of potent chemotherapy the doctors decided that Charles didn't have much hope of living longer than a year. Charles believed in prayer. He had every church he'd ever been associated with praying for him. He attended weekly prayer meetings with other people who believed in prayer. He did everything that the doctors told him to do. He tried everything that persons in his prayer groups told him to do. He participated in and started a cancer support group in his church. Charles lived much longer than his physician believed was possible. The cancer never completely disappeared. For a time it remained dormant. The doctors treating him marveled at his progress. One, who didn't really believe in God, admitted that prayer was certainly working in his case.

Toward the end of the fourth year, the cancer started growing again. The doctors were baffled. Because of many factors including Charles' weakness, the doctors told the family there was no further treatment available. In talking to his minister, Charles tried to be optimistic. He did admit that he wondered why prayer wasn't working. He also admitted that he wasn't ready to die. While saying all of that he also confided he was tired of fighting for each breath he took. He said, "Pastor I am beginning to doubt my faith."

* How is the resurrection of Jesus Christ the ultimate answer to all human doubt?

* What would you say to Charles? What do you think God wants him to hear?

Angles on Aging

You know you're reaching middle age when all your energy goes to waist.

* * *

"I'm just as young as I ever was. It just takes a lot more effort."

* * *

"I still have that old spark, but it takes more to light it."

* * *

They call it middle age because that's where it shows up first.

* * *

Old age is the time of life when you know all the answers but nobody asks you the questions.

* * *

A sure sign of growing older is when the narrow waist and the broad mind begin to change places.

This Lesson in Your Life

As these lessons were being written the announcement was made that a sheep had been successfully cloned in England. By the time you read these lessons progress in human cloning will be in the news. Although we usually ask only, "Can we?", with the cloning issue the more appropriate question is, "*Should* we?" Technology has made almost anything possible. We no longer marvel at "medical miracles." They are common place.

The universe is shrinking as science unlocks the mysteris of its orign and age. Although scientists may figure out the age and origin of the universe, they can never answer the *why* of the universe. Our universe was created to glorify God. "The heavens are telling the glory of God; and the firmament proclaims his handiwork" (Ps. 19:1). The creation points toward the Creator. Scientists are now starting to delve into that part of astronomy.

The other thing scientists will never do is cause a resurrection. The resurrection of Jesus Christ is something only God could do. Our resurrection as disciples of Jesus Christ is something that only God will do. In a age where "miracles" can be explained scientifically, we have a miracle that can't be explained apart from faith.

Resurrection is the ultimate truth of the Christian faith. We are Easter people. As our celebration of Christmas concludes we are reminded of what happened at the end of the gospel story. The birth of Jesus took all involved by surprise. The resurrection of Jesus was just as surprising. Jesus had predicted His death and promised His resurrection, still the disciples did not understand.

As we face a new year and think about new beginnings, it is important to do so in the context of resurrection. The resurrection of Jesus Christ places the events of our lives into proper focus and context. If God orchestrates the events of our lives then each is important. Have you ever noticed a darkened stained glass window? You might be able to detect some of the beauty of the window at night. You will never appreciate fully it's beauty until that window is bathed in light. The same is true of our lives. They may have beauty and meaning, but until the light or resurrection glows in our lives that beauty is hidden. Resurrection is the powerful continuation of our lives in the presence of God.

That means that our death is not final. Paul wrote to the early church, "Where, O death, is your victory? Where, O death, is your sting?" (1 Cor. 15:55). The resurrection of Jesus Christ makes death a moot point for the Christian. Our lives are only complete as we stand bathed in the presence of Jesus Christ.

The resurrection gives us hope. It gives us hope that the days spent on earth are pilgrim days. We are all "just passing through." Our home is with the Lord. That promise frees us to live daily without fear. The promise of resurrection keeps us from being bound by the concerns of this earth. It lets us keep our heads high and our hearts hopeful even as others fear tomorrow. The resurrection challenges us to spread this good news to others.

Because of the resurrection of Jesus no situation is hopeless. Our faith is that death is not the permanent condition of the Christian. Birth is to early existence what death is to eternal life, a portal though which we all will travel.

Are you facing this new year with resurrection faith? Do you see signs where God is bringing life out of death? Can you imagine a day when pain and suffering will be no more? As the song says, "What a day of rejoicing that will be. When we all see Jesus. We will sing and shout, the VICTORY."

Seed Thoughts

1. What were the disciples discussing when Jesus appeared to them?

They were talking about the events that were reported by the two disciples on the way to Emmaus.

2. When Jesus appeared to His disciples in Jerusalem what was the greeting He offered them?

His first words were "Peace be with you." The Hebrew word is Shalom. It was used as both a greeting and a benediction.

3. What was the response of the disciples to the sudden appearance of Jesus?

They were startled and frightened. They believed they were seeing a ghost.

4. How did Jesus respond to their fear?

He asked them why they were troubled and why they were letting their minds cause them to doubt (Luke 24: 38).

5. What did Jesus offer the disciples as proof that He was not an apparition?

Jesus showed them his hands and feet as proof. He told them that ghosts don't have flesh and bones.

---

1. What were the disciples discussing when Jesus appeared to them?

2. When Jesus appeared to His disciples in Jerusalem what was the greeting He offered them?

3. What was the response of the disciples to the sudden appearance of Jesus?

4. How did Jesus respond to their fear?

5. What did Jesus offer the disciples as proof that He was not an apparition?

6. What did Jesus do next that indicated the physical nature of the resurrection?

7. What was the essence of the message that Jesus presented to the disciples?

8. How did Jesus describe the writings you and I call the Old Testament?

9. What did He command the disciples to do?

10. How do you understand this "promise of the Father" that will come to the disciples?

(Continued next page)

They were talking about the events that were reported by the two disciples on the way to Emmaus.

His first words were "Peace be with you." The Hebrew word is Shalom. It was used as both a greeting and a benediction.

They were startled and frightened. They believed they were seeing a ghost.

He asked them why they were troubled and why they were letting their minds cause them to doubt (Luke 24: 38).

Jesus showed them his hands and feet as proof. He told them that ghosts don't have flesh and bones.

He asked the disciples if they had something to eat. He ate a piece of fish.

Everything He had told them had come true. The Scriptures had been fulfilled by His life, death and resurrection.

He referred to them as the "Law of Moses, the Prophets and the Psalms."

He told them to wait in Jerusalem until the promise of the Father was sent to them.

Jesus was referring to the Holy Spirit, who was given to the disciples on Pentecost.

6. What did Jesus do next that indicated the physical nature of the resurrection?

He asked the disciples if they had something to eat. He ate a piece of fish.

7. What was the essence of the message that Jesus presented to the disciples?

Everything He had told them had come true. The Scriptures had been fulfilled by His life, death and resurrection.

8. How did Jesus describe the writings you and I call the Old Testament?

He referred to them as the "Law of Moses, the Prophets and the Psalms."

9. What did He command the disciples to do?

He told them to wait in Jerusalem until the promise of the Father was sent to them.

10. How do you understand this "promise of the Father" that will come to the disciples?

Jesus was referring to the Holy Spirit, who was given to the disciples on Pentecost.

People of Love

*A*nd one of the scribes came, and having heard them reasoning together, and perceiving that he had answered them well, asked him, Which is the first commandment of all?

29 And Jesus answered him, The first of all the commandments is, Hear, O Israel; The Lord our God is one Lord:

30 And thou shalt love the Lord thy God with all thy heart, and with all thy soul, and with all thy mind, and with all thy strength: this is the first commandment.

31 And the second is like, namely this, Thou shalt love thy neighbour as thyself. There is none other commandment greater than these.

32 And the scribe said unto him, Well, Master, thou hast said the truth: for there is one God; and there is none other but he:

33 And to love him with all the heart, and with all the understanding, and with all the soul, and with all the strength, and to love his neighbour as himself, is more than all whole burnt offerings and sacrifices.

34 And when Jesus saw that he answered discreetly, he said unto him, Thou art not far from the kingdom of God. And no man after that durst ask him any question.

Luke 6:27-31

27 But I say unto you which hear, Love your enemies, do good to them which hate you,

28 Bless them that curse you, and pray for them which despitefully use you.

29 And unto him that smiteth thee on the one cheek offer also the other; and him that taketh away thy cloke forbid not to take thy coat also.

30 Give to every man that asketh of thee; and of him that taketh away thy goods ask them not again.

31 And as ye would that men should do to you, do ye also to them likewise.

John 13:34-35

34 A new commandment I give unto you, That ye love one another; as I have loved you, that ye also love one another.

35 By this shall all men know that ye are my disciples, if ye have love one to another.

Mark 12:28-34
Luke 6:27-31
John 13:34-35

Memory Selection
John 13:35

Background Scripture
Mark 12:28-34;
Luke 6:27-36; John 13:31-35

Devotional Reading
1 John 4:7-12

Printed Scripture
Mark 12:28-34;
Luke 6:27-31; John 13:34-35

Teacher's Target

Lesson purpose: *To identify the most basic characteristic of the teachings of Jesus, and to discuss how to make that trait a part of our own character.*

Tradition has it that when the apostle John was too old and senile to say much of anything he would mouth over and over, "My little children, love one another." Yet if Christians were to lose all language but that one phrase, they would capture and cap-sule the essence of the teachings of Jesus.

The passages in today's lesson show Jesus' emphasis on loving God and others. This focus so captivated the apostle Paul that he was led to pen the justly famous hymn to love in 1 Corinthians 13.

Because the concept of love is so romanticized in our culture, and so limited to the arena of *feelings*, emphasize in this lesson the active nature of love as Jesus used the term. As John himself wrote, "As for the well-to-do man who sees his brother in want but shuts his eyes, and his heart, how could anyone believe that the love of God lives in him?" (1 John 3:17. *Phillips*).

Lesson Introduction

The Greeks were not as limited in the language of love as are English speakers. We use the same word to say we love ice cream that we use when we fume through gritted teeth, "I'd love to get my hands on him."

Ancient Greeks, however, had the word *eros* for "attraction," especially that between the sexes; *philos* for the affection between friends; and *storge* (STOR-gay) for love for family members. Then, some three centuries B.C., Greek-speaking Jews translating the Old Testament used a virtually new word, *agape* (ah-GAS-pay). They used this word to describe the selfless love of God for man, and the love His followers should have for Him and for other people.

The authors of the New Testament used this term in similar ways, and it is this word that is the prominent theme of today's lesson. *Agape* describes not simply an emotion but attitudes and actions that show we have another's highest interest at heart.

Teaching Outline	Daily Bible Readings
I. Love and the Law—Mark 12:28-34	**Mon.** Which Commandment Is First? *Mark 12:28-34*
A The first commandment, 28-30	**Tue.** Love Your Enemies *Luke 6:27-36*
B. The second commandment, 31	
C. Implications, 32-34	**Wed.** Evidence of Discipleship *John 13:31-35*
II. Loving Above and Beyond—Luke 6:27-31	**Thu.** Rooted in Love *Ephesians 3:14-19*
A. Loving our enemies, 27-29	**Fri.** Love Fulfills the Law *Romans 13:1-10*
B. The Golden Rule, 30-31	**Sat.** Love Builds Up *1 Corinthians 8:1-6*
III. Loving Each Other—John 13:34-35	**Sun.** God Abides in Those Who Love *1 John 4:7-12*

172

Verse by Verse

I. Love and the Law—Mark 12:28-34

A. The first commandment, 28-30

28 And one of the scribes came, and having heard them reasoning together, and perceiving that he had answered them well, asked him, Which is the first commandment of all?

29 And Jesus answered him, The first of all the commandments is, Hear, O Israel; The Lord our God is one Lord:

30 And thou shalt love the Lord thy God with all thy heart, and with all thy soul, and with all thy mind, and with all thy strength: this is the first commandment.

"Scribes" in Israel and other societies of the ancient near-East were educated men who functioned much like modern attorneys. They were schooled in either civil or religious law, or both; and the fact that they could read and write in a day when illiteracy was widespread made them highly influential. Older biblical references to scribes include Ezra, who was an effective leader in the return of God's people from captivity (Ezra 7).

In the New Testament, however, scribes are usually portrayed as opposing Jesus and His work. The authority with which He taught seemed to have threatened them (see Matt. 7:29).

Scribes are often mentioned in the same breath with the sect of the Pharisees, who specialized in challenging Jesus. He once pronounced judgment on the two groups jointly (Matt. 23:13).

The honesty and openness of the scribe in this passage stands in sharp contrast to the general rule. He comes upon a semi-public discussion in which Jesus had successfully dealt with a trick question posed by the Sadducees (John 12:18-27). Intrigued by what he hears, the scribe asks whether, out of the more than 600 laws in the Old Testament, one commandment can be singled out as the basis for all the others.

Jesus answers by quoting Deuteronomy 6:4-5, the "Shemah" (meaning "Hear," the first word of the passage in Hebrew), which is still recited daily by faithful Jews. This skillfully frames Jesus' teaching in a way that shows He is not contradicting, but fulfilling, the Old Testament Law. Only later would the Jewish insistence on circumcision and other points of the Old Law result in a sharp separation between Jewish and Christian teaching.

The first or most important commandment, Jesus says, is to honor God as One (as opposed to the many gods of paganism), and to love Him with the total being, heart, soul, mind, and strength. It is important to note that in Jesus' teaching loving others, or relating "horizontally" to people, depends first on getting this "vertical" or God-related commandment down right. This is the difference between basing ethics on theology, and mere humanism.

B. The second commandment, 31

31 And the second is like, namely this, Thou shalt love thy neighbour as thyself. There is none other commandment greater than these.

Following quickly on the emphasis on loving God is the requirement to love others as we love ourselves. Again, Jesus quotes from the Old Testament, this time from Leviticus 19:18. Note that loving others "as (we love) ourselves" assumes what is missing in many personalities these days: a healthy self-image. Persons who lack a healthy respect for themselves have difficulty loving others, especially in intimate relationships.

Remarkably, Jesus has laid down the two most important "commandments" without quoting the most famous of all, the Ten Commandments. Actually He is maintaining that keeping all other commandments depends on these two, loving God and loving others. He says as much in Matthew's version of this incident: "On these two commandments hang all the law and the prophets" (Matt. 22:40).

C. Implications, 32-34

32 And the scribe said unto him, Well, Master, thou hast said the truth: **for there is one God; and there is none other but he:**

33 And to love him with all the heart, and with all the understanding, and with all the soul, and with all the strength, and to love his neighbour as himself, is more than all whole burnt offerings and sacrifices.

34 And when Jesus saw that he answered discreetly, he said unto him, Thou art not far from the kingdom of God. And no man after that durst ask him any question.

The scribe's question obviously grew out of previous thoughtful consideration of its answer, for he recognizes immediately the truth in Jesus' reply. He has found an echo of the teaching of prophets such as Amos, who insisted that love for God must include justice for others, else all sacrifices and other religious rituals are useless (Amos 5:21-24). Jesus applauds the scribe's recognition of this truth by saying he is at the very door of the kingdom,which will be built on the twin commandments of loving God and others.

II.Loving Above and Beyond—Luke 6:27-31

A. Loving our enemies, 27-29

27 But I say unto you which hear, Love your enemies, do good to them which hate you,

28 Bless them that curse you, and pray for them which despitefully use you.

29 And unto him that smiteth

thee on the one cheek offer also the other; and him that taketh away thy cloke forbid not to take thy coat also.

Our summary of the heart of Jesus' teaching moves now to Luke's account of the "Sermon on the Plain" (which may or may not be the same incident as the more famous Sermon on the Mount, Matt. 5+7). Here is the familiar but challenging code of not simply loving "others" as ourselves, but our enemies as well.

The Old Covenant had moved in this direction when it said "A soft answer turneth away wrath" (Prov. 15:1). Now Jesus makes it explicit that loving our enemies is not just a way of defusing their anger; it is the real mark of a Christian as opposed to "sinners" (vss. 32-34). It is human nature to love those who love us; it requires super-human resources to love our enemies. (See Matthew's version of this teaching, which includes the "second mile" dimension of this lofty command-ment, Matt. 5:41.)

B. The Golden Rule, 30-31

30 Give to every man that asketh of thee; and of him that taketh away thy goods ask them not again.

31 And as ye would that men should do to you, do ye also to them likewise.

Loving others is broadened here from enemies to anyone who has needs. These teachings have prompted endless questions about how literally we are to take them. For example, how could we lend to everyone who asks, while still caring for our own families? And does the "turn the other cheek" ethic apply to warfare between nations? Like all lofty ethical challenges, it is wise not to soften their difficulty by endless qualifications. Otherwise the rule that is "Golden" can be cheapened to tin! Still, we must seek to apply such standards to specific situations with wisdom and discernment.

III. Loving Each Other—John 13:34-35

34 A new commandment I give unto you, That ye love one another; as I have loved you, that ye also love one another.

35 By this shall all men know that ye are my disciples, if ye have love one to another.

After focusing on Christ's teaching about loving God and others, then on loving our enemies, this text shows the importance of loving brothers and sisters in Christ. Ironically it is sometimes easier to love people on the other side of the earth than it is to act lovingly toward those with whom we go to church.

Since, as we have noticed, Leviticus 19:18 teaches us to love our neighbors as ourselves, in what sense is Jesus' exhortation a "new commandment"? Perhaps because He elevates this teaching from one commandment among many to the status of the one distinguishing mark of believers in the New Order He is establishing.

Evangelistic Emphasis

The only way to defuse the bomb that our sinful nature has planted in our world is to love. Love is the most powerful force in our universe. It is not a mushy ethereal good feeling. It is a way of living defined in the person of Jesus Christ. The kind of love that Jesus modeled was love that was involved with persons where they were. It was a love that was not satisfied until the bondage of sin was broken in a life. It was a stubborn love. A love that traveled all the way up Calvary's mountain to rescue and redeem that which was lost.

It is this unconditional unbounded love that Jesus commanded His disciples to live in our world. Those words don't seem to belong do they? "Commanded" and "love" almost don't belong in the same sentence. Our Lord did command us to love one another. Until you have given or received an act of unconditional love you can only speculate as to its power. Once you experience unconditional love, you can't keep it to yourself. It must be shared. Love compels us to love others. It is following that compulsion to love that brings joy.

Jesus Christ loved you so much that He died for your sins. He removed the stain and the power of sin from your life. He did that so that you could experience God's perfect love. It is that experience that compels His children to love others. It is that experience of being loved that compels us all to share the gospel. What have you done about sharing the good news that, "God loved the world so much that He gave His only Son"?

• • • • • • • •

Memory Selection

By this shall all men know that ye are my disciples, if ye have love one to another. — *John 13: 35*

What is important in your faith? We have all met people who thought it was most important to be right. They carried a reference Bible and were ready to debate at a moments notice. Others in the church have deemed social justice the most important aspect of Christian living. Still others call for a renewed sense of personal piety and moral righteousness. All of these are important elements of a deep faith.

Jesus Christ would call the members of His church to be loving above all else. If we remove love from doctrinal standards, social justice, personal piety or morality we end up with the religion of the Pharisees. Love is the force of faith that keeps everything else in balance and creative tension. It is the driving power behind what we try to do as Christians. It is the emotion that makes faith most appealing to our world.

In our day, there are many people who claim to be right. We have a host of persons clamoring for social justice. Groups sue so that moral righteousness can be adjudicated by courts. What we don't have an abundance of is love.

Weekday Problems

Jacob Mills had been a minister for forty years. He was the pattern for a loving and caring pastor. Jacob carried his ministry home. He was a devoted husband. He was a good parent. He loved his family as much as he loved his calling.

Jacob's two children were very different from each other. His daughter, the youngest, was a school teacher and a mom. Everything she did seemed to work out. Jacob's son was another story. John Wesley Mills had been "trouble" from the day he was born.

Now as an adult, J.W. had managed to have two children before his life fell apart. He was a drinker. He had been drinking since he was in High School. He had learned to conceal it well. Neither the people of the church nor his father knew of his early drinking exploits. J.W's. marriage had broken up. He had lost his job. He was broke. At the age of forty he moved back home.

Jacob Mills confided that he didn't know what to do with his son. J.W. had lost both jobs that dad arranged for him. He had managed to get arrested for drunken and disorderly behavior. He had wrecked a car. He had been arrested for DWI. Jacob confided in a minister friend that he didn't know whether to hug J.W. or "whip him good." Jacob didn't know how much more he and his wife could endure. It seemed that J.W. was not getting any better.

* Can J.W. be redeemed? What must happen?

* How do you feel about the "tough love" movement and what of it's teachings apply to this situation?

This Is Love?

Dad: How dare you, young man! What do you mean, smooching with my daughter?

Lad: I,I,I was just doing what the Bible says: "Hold fast that which is good."

* * *

She: Will you love me when I'm old?

He: I will love you always. I will cherish the ground you walk on. I will,er, you won't turn out to look like your mother, will you?

* * *

He: If you'll give me your phone number, I'd give you a call.

She: It's in the phone book.

He: Good. What's your name?

She: It's in the book, too.

* * *

He: If I tried to kiss you, would you call for help?

She: Do you need help?

This Lesson in Your Life

The Weekday Problem raised the issue of tough love. It is a concept that is often mentioned when one is discussing a problem person. A well-meaning soul will offer the solution to a dilemma by saying, "That person would straighten out with some tough love." Some people swear by it and they can show you examples where it has "worked." I'll confess to you that I am skeptical.

To modify love with the word "tough" doesn't fit. I can understand better if one modifies the world love with the word "sacrificial." The Weekday Problem is a true story. It is being played out right now in your church. Jacob Mills has two options. He can give his son "the boot," throwing him out and letting him wallow in the gutter until something or someone straightens him out. Or Jacob Mills can love J.W. in such a way that his problem is healed. Which one will cost Jacob Mills the most? Which one is showing sacrificial love? Are you leaning toward the second one yet?

The kind of love Jesus shared with us is astounding. We can't really understand it. Without understanding it, all of us have experienced it. We have experienced it directly from God and from other members of the body of Christ. It is the kind of love that challenges belief systems. It is the kind of love that breaks down barriers. It is the kind of love that can bring healing to any broken life.

I maintain that only the disposable, self-centered culture of 1970s America could have dreamed up a harsh concept and called it "tough love." When did we ever read of Jesus turning a person away? Jesus never turned anyone away. There were, howeve,r persons who chose not to follow Him. Even at that, His love was absolute. He loved the world so much that He gave His life for us. The demands He placed on us were to love God and love one another. Our love is to extend to friends *and enemies*. If we are to love our enemies, certainly we are to love those difficult persons in our lives. We are to love them unconditionally. It is not tough love. The truth is love is tough. It can't happen apart from the presence of Jesus Christ.

That is why love is the distinguishing mark of the Christian. You can fake everything else about the Christian faith. The one thing that can't be forged is love. Genuine love comes from God. It is a love that we don't have, but that is reflected though us. It is not in my nature to love certain kinds of people; but as I allow Christ to love them through me, I can genuinely love even those I would otherwise find unlovable.

Love, as Jesus shared it, is tough for another reason. The kind of love we are to have for one another and for God is the kind of love that won't let go. Paul wrote of this love. "Love is patient; love is kind; love is not envious or boastful or arrogant or rude. It does not insist on its own way; it is not irritable or resentful; it does not rejoice in wrongdoing, but rejoices in the truth. It bears all things, believes all things, hopes all things, endures all things" (1 Cor. 13: 4-8). This isn't tough love, it's *agape* love. It is only that kind of love that makes the world go round.

Seed Thoughts

1. In the passage from Mark, what stirred the teacher of the Law to ask Jesus the question about the commandments?

This teacher had obviously heard Jesus debating with the Sadducees over the issue of resurrection.

2. How did Jesus answer the teacher of the Law's question about the greatest commandment?

Jesus' answer comes from the *shema*, which is not a part of the Ten Commandments (Deut. 6:4).

3. What was the response of the teacher of the Law to Jesus' answer about the commandments?

The teacher of the Law was impressed by the answer that Jesus gave him.

4. What did Jesus say about the religious life of the teacher of the Law?

This person's understanding of the Law had brought him "not far from the kingdom of God."

5. As a class, why do you think Jesus could sum up the Ten Commandments with only two?

The Ten Commandments are naturally divided into two sections, one about loving God and one about loving others.

---

1. In the passage from Mark, what stirred the teacher of the Law to ask Jesus the question about the commandments?

2. How did Jesus answer the teacher of the Law's question about the greatest commandment?

3. What was the response of the teacher of the Law to Jesus' answer about the commandments?

4. What did Jesus say about the religious life of the teacher of the Law?

5. As a class, why do you think Jesus could sum up the Ten Commandments with only two?

6. How did Jesus want His people to treat their enemies?

7. What was the essence of the golden rule and where was it found?

8. What is different about the love sinners have and a disciple's love?

9. According to the passage in John what was Jesus' new commandment?

10. How were people to distinguish a disciple from other people?

(Continued next page)

179

This teacher had obviously heard Jesus debating with the Sadducees over the issue of resurrection.

Jesus' answer comes from the *shema*, which is not a part of the Ten Commandments (Deut. 6:4).

The teacher of the Law was impressed by the answer that Jesus gave him.

This person's understanding of the Law had brought him "not far from the kingdom of God."

The Ten Commandments are naturally divided into two sections, one about loving God and one about loving others.

We are to love, do good to, bless and pray for those persons who mistreat us.

The "golden rule" is to do unto others as you want done to yourself. It is found in Luke 6:31.

Even sinners love those who love them. Disciples are different because of the love we have for our enemies.

He commanded His people to "love one another."

"By this all men will know you are my disciples if you love one another" (John 13:35).

6. How did Jesus want His people to treat their enemies?

We are to love, do good to, bless and pray for those persons who mistreat us.

7. What was the essence of the golden rule and where was it found?

The "golden rule" is to do unto others as you want done to yourself. It is found in Luke 6:31.

8. What is different about the love sinners have and a disciple's love?

Even sinners love those who love them. Disciples are different because of the love we have for our enemies.

9. According to the passage in John what was Jesus' new commandment?

He commanded His people to "love one another."

10. How were people to distinguish a disciple from other people?

"By this all men will know you are my disciples if you love one another" (John 13:35).

180

Kingdom Priorities

*A*nd one of the company said unto him, Master, speak to my brother, that he divide the inheritance with me.

14 And he said unto him, Man, who made me a judge or a divider over you?

15 And he said unto them, Take heed, and beware of covetousness: for a man's life consisteth not in the abundance of the things which he possesseth.

16 And he spake a parable unto them, saying, The ground of a certain rich man brought forth plentifully:

17 And he thought within himself, saying, What shall I do, because I have no room where to bestow my fruits?

18 And he said, This will I do: I will pull down my barns, and build

greater; and there will I bestow all my fruits and my goods.

19 And I will say to my soul, Soul, thou hast much goods laid up for many years; take thine ease, eat, drink, and be merry.

20 But God said unto him, Thou fool, this night thy soul shall be required of thee: then whose shall those things be, which thou has provided?

21 So is he that layeth up treasure for himself, and is not rich toward God.

Luke 12:13-21

Memory Selection
Luke 12:15

Background Scripture
Luke 12:13-34

Devotional Reading
Habakkuk 3:17-19

Printed Scripture
Luke 12:13-21

Teacher's Target

Lesson purpose: *To explore Jesus' teaching on material possessions with a view to ordering our priorities after His will.*

If acting lovingly toward others is the most basic feature of Jesus' teaching, as the previous lesson indicated, the proper view of material possessions is a close second.

Why does Jesus place such a high priority on this issue? Probably because wealth so often competes with God for first place in our lives. Christ taught in Matthew 6:24, "Ye cannot serve God and mammon (possessions that have a damaging influence)." This way of stating the issue indicates that wealth is easily elevated to the status of a god. Paul will later say that this is equivalent with idolatry (Col. 3:15).

Use this lesson to put wealth in its place. Instead of becoming an idol that demands our constant attention, possessions should serve us in our attempts to serve God.

Lesson Introduction

The poet's statement that "The world is too much with us" accurately describes the widespread fascination in our society for the material over the spiritual. While a few good souls seem "so spiritual they are of no earthly good," most of us need constant encouragement to keep the spiritual as a high-priority dimension of our lives. Jesus frequently provided this encouragement in His teaching.

Yet, as a Jew, Jesus placed this teaching within the context of a healthy appreciation for the material world. Land and cattle, property and wealth, are a part of the creation that God pronounced "good" and "very good" at creation. The New Covenant Scriptures therefore do not enjoin on us "asceticism",severe denial of the material. However, their uncompromising affirmation of the priority of the spiritual comprises a challenging confrontation to our materialistic society.

Teaching Outline	Daily Bible Readings	
	Mon.	Guard Against Greed *Luke 12:13-21*
I. A Feud over Money—13-14	Tue.	Don't Worry About Life *Luke 12:22-34*
II. The Folly of Things—15	Wed.	Greed Robs Us of Life *Proverbs 1:8-19*
III. The Fool and His Money—16-21	Thu.	Money Alone Doesn't Satisfy *Eccles. 5:1-10*
A. From blessing to curse, 16	Fri.	Wealth Can Be Hazardous *Jeremiah 17:5-11*
B. Riches in the wrong place, 17-21	Sat.	Beware of Covetousness *Micah 2:1-5*
	Sun.	Greed Is Self-defeating *James 5:1-6*

Verse by Verse

I. A Feud over Money—13-14

13 And one of the company said unto him, Master, speak to my brother, that he divide the inheritance with me.

14 And he said unto him, Man, who made me a judge or a divider over you?

Among the many contexts in which Jesus taught the priority of the spiritual over the material, none strikes home more realistically than this. Anyone who has been involved in a dispute over an inheritance knows how it can transform loving family relationships into feuds fueled by greed.

"Company" is from the Greek word for "the many," indicating that the man bringing the complaint is not from the "company" of the disciples who were closest to Jesus but from the crowds that frequently gathered to hear His teaching (12:1).

Jesus' blunt retort indicates unusual impatience. This probably stems from His strong feelings against covetousness, which leads to the parable to follow; but it may also arise from some impatience that the man would interrupt His teaching mission with such a trivial and self-centered request. Jesus indicates that His mission does not in-clude making rulings on such personal, and perhaps civil, issues. He takes a similar "non-position" in the case of the woman taken in adultery (John 8:3-11), and when asked about paying taxes (Matt. 22:17). This does not mean that our Lord has no interest in such issues, but that He expects us to use our own judgment, guided by His teachings, in such cases.

II. The Folly of Things—15

15 And he said unto them, Take heed, and beware of covetousness: for a man's life consisteth not in the abundance of the things which he possesseth.

As the Lesson Introduction indicated, Jesus does not teach that having possessions is foolish, but that it is folly to allow them to be the definition of the good life. To do so is "covetousness," He warns.

Covetousness is greed, or an unjustified desire for "more." Although we usually think of this as a problem mainly of the wealthy, unjustifiably wanting "more" afflicts people at any income level. Again, the problem is not that what we want more of is evil. Jesus does not say that "things" in themselves are evil, but that thinking that having them in "abundance," or more than we need, is the primary goal of

183

life. It is in having Christ at the heart of our existence that defines the "abundant life" (John 10:10). Placing things at the heart of life displaces Christ from His rightful throne there, making covetousness equal to idolatry (Col. 3:15).

The true place of *things* is also illuminated by noting that the word for "life" in this verse is *zoe* (ZO-ay, from which we get our word "zoology"). This is the part of life in which we are to enthrone Christ. On the other hand, *bios* (as in "biology") is the Greek word for mere existence. Jesus is not saying that it is wrong to have enough "things",food, clothing, and shelter,to maintain *bios*; but that things are inadequate to maintain *zoe,* the spiritual dimension of life. This is why the spiritual is to have priority over the material.

III. The Fool and His Money—16-21

A. From blessing to curse, 16

16 And he space a parable unto them, saying, The ground of a certain rich man brought forth plentifully:

Turning to His favorite method of teaching, Jesus now tells the famous parable of the rich fool. Note that the story begins at the level of *bios*,the man was blessed with farmland rich enough to provide the basics that sustain life. Unfortunately, he will turn this blessing into a curse by expecting mere property to sustain *zoe* and his quest for meaning and purpose in life.

The man was not a fool because he was rich,his wealth could have supplied the needs of many who were less fortunate. It is right to gain in order to meet our basic needs and to give to those who lack them (Eph. 4:28); the sin is in gaining in order to satisfy our lust for "more" (James 4:3).

The word translated "brought forth" is, ironically, related to our word "euphoria",the feeling of elation or well being. It is enough to feel "euphoric" or blessed that our "ground" or occupation provides the basics for life. Unfortunately we too often go for even more "euphoria" by seeking more and more things that require larger and larger "barns."

B. Riches in the wrong place, 17-21

17 And he thought within himself, saying, What shall I do, because I have no room where to bestow my fruits?

18 And he said, This will I do: I will pull down my barns, and build greater; and there will I bestow all my fruits and my goods.

19 And I will say to my soul, Soul, thou hast much goods laid up for many years; take thine ease, eat, drink, and be merry.

20 But God said unto him, Thou fool, this night thy soul shall be required of thee: then whose shall those things be, which thou has provided?

21 So is he that layeth up treasure for himself, and is not rich

toward God.

"What shall I do?", to increase my wealth and standing, is, unfortunately, life's most important question for many people. If the rich man had a more appropriate set of priorities he might have asked, "How can I share the wealth I have gained from the rich land and bountiful crops God gave to me?" Since his question, however, is materialistic and self-centered, his answer will also be of a materialistic nature. Also notable is that "I" or "my" form the man's main concern. These pronouns appear ten times in the man's dialogue with his "soul" or self.

The larger barns the man plans to build are as much of a symbol of his priorities as having more things. They would stand as an emblem of his wealth for all to see, just as do the larger house we buy or build for ourselves, even when our present house is very adequate. Jesus pointedly notes that instead of "bestowing" part of his wealth on the poor, the man can only bestow it to a mere barn.

The rich fool's "self-talk" in verse 19 provides a window into his heart. He is consumed with thoughts of a secure future, a life of ease, and a lifestyle like that of the "rich and famous." Many a retired person who thought that wealth alone can provide "the good life" can testify that trying to enjoy doing nothing can be less satisfying than staying engaged with pursuits more meaningful than material goods.

Finally, God calls the rich fool up short with the message that his death is eminent, reminding us that the lease we have on life has been signed by God, not ourselves. The folly of the rich man is in seen in two areas: (1) Not preparing for his death by investing in the spiritual, being "rich toward God", instead of the material; and (2) Not being able to enjoy the estate he has amassed, but instead having to leave it to others, who may squander it.

As a postscript to this parable, Jesus will go on to elaborate on the principles He has taught here. As evidence that we can well afford to give higher priority to the spiritual over the material, He notes that since God cares for the birds of the air and the lilies of the field, He certainly will care for the needs of those who give Him first place in their lives (vss. 24-28).

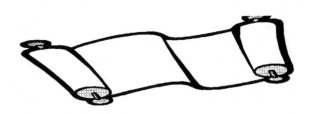

Evangelistic Emphasis

Sunday is under assault from all sides. It seems like every store is open now on Sunday. The malls are open for at least part of the day. In my community, the church competes with Sunday morning soccer leagues and T-Ball leagues. For most of our culture, Sunday has become another day of busy activity.

Sunday is under assault because it is no longer a priority for God's people. That is what happens when priorities are mixed up. We will look in this lesson about a man who came to Jesus with a misplaced set of priorities. Jesus' response to this man was the parable of the Rich Fool. It was a story about another man with misplaced priorities.

Think about priorities and what is really important to your church. In your congregation, is leading the lost to Jesus Christ an activity that is a priority? Does your church concern itself with all of those lost souls living around the church? Do you concern yourself with the lost souls living near you? Evangelism is a matter of priority. Christ called us to be evangelists all the time. We are preachers and teachers of the gospel. Sometimes when we don't make Christ's priorities our own, we accidentally pervert the gospel.

What is important according to Jesus, are those matters that relate to the soul. A man came to Jesus with a question and Jesus' answer reflected what our Lord thought was important.

Do you think that Jesus has changed His mind about searching for lost sheep? If He hasn't, why have we?

● ● ● ● ● ● ● ●

Take heed, and beware of covetousness: for a man's life consisteth not in the abundance of the things which he possesseth.—*Luke 12: 15*

How do you measure your success? Is it in terms of the number of things that you have? Is it the location and size of your house? Is it in the number of cars that you own? How about the size of your savings account?

We live in a world in which we are judged on the acquisition of things. Each day on television and radio, in the print media and on the Internet, we are bombarded with the message that we are what we own. If we want to be persons of substance we need to live at the right address, drive the right kind of car and wear certain perfumes. Billions are spent each year to convince us that we are what we possess.

I have a friend who has started giving things away. She isn't in bad health and has had no harbinger of doom. She decided that she didn't need all the stuff she thought she needed. What she discovered is that she needed a relationship with Christ and with all other pilgrims on the road to Heaven. She is teaching us to live like Jesus lived...simply and with Godly priorities.

Weekday Problems

Don was a very successful person in the Financial industry. He had worked his way up through a couple of investment firms and now found himself being hired as the Executive vice-president for Acme Investments. It was a prestigious job.

Don was also active in his church. Since he had skill in money matters he naturally served on every Finance Committee the church had. He was involved annually in the stewardship campaign. He gave testimonies in the pulpit about the importance of tithing. God seemed to be blessing Don and he was good at passing those blessings on.

Don was known at all levels of his church for his financial acumen and generosity. Don was known for buying expensive suits for his pastor. He would give the pastor and his family trips to Disney World or to Washington D.C. He not only shared generosity with the pastor, but with his friends and family as well.

As Don rose in various firms so did his standard of living. Don and his family had moved a couple of times. Each time they moved it was into a larger home and a more prestigious area of town.

The shock rippled though the community when Don suddenly lost his job. It was not because of anything illegal or immoral at work, it was because of Don's lifestyle away from work. Don had to confess to his pastor that he was broke, that he'd actually borrowed the money to pay his large pledge to the church. Don had to confess that he was greedy and it cost him his job and eventually his wife and children.

* Do you know any "Don's" in your community? What would Jesus say to them?

Money Matters

A man visited a crystal gazer and was shocked to learn that the fee was $50. "That entitles you to two questions," she added.
"Isn't that pretty steep for just two questions?" the man asked.
"Pretty steep. Now what's your second question?"
"You mean you're going to count the question about your price?"
"Yep, and that's the second."

* * *

The latest gift for the man who has everything is a calendar to remind him of when the payments on everything are due.

* * *

"Don't forget, son," said the wealthy banker. "Money isn't everything. There's also stocks and bonds and debentures and Certificates of Deposit, travelers checks, bank drafts. . . ."

This Lesson in Your Life

Greed and covetousness are things that are easy to see in your life and easily overlooked in mine. The popular bumper sticker is tragic, though to our culture it rings true: "The one that dies with the most toys, wins." Some churches have even bought into "success theology." The idea is put forth that if you are faithful to God, He will bless your life with the "things of this world." I have heard preachers in the pulpit claim that Christians deserve the best of cars, homes, boats and anything else. Sounds like we have dressed up greed and brought it to church.

I remember when we were studying this passage in seminary. The professor was talking about greed and coveting the things of this world. He was getting some hearty "amens." We were agreeing with him until he started talking about books. Most ministers have an ample supply of theological books. We refer to our books as our "library." This professor said that he no longer wrote his name in his books. Most of us students had those stamps which embossed *our* names in *our* books. We wanted the world to know that these were our books. He said that he didn't believe anything on this earth could be possessed. Everything, according to this professor, was on loan from God, even preachers' books.

I went home that afternoon still thinking about what he had said. Seminary professors should stick to lecture and not upset students with timely preaching. I was doing research for another class and consulted a book in my fledgling "library." There in the cover page were the names of at least four other preachers. Four others had "owned" my book before it became a part of my "library."

I have yet to bury anyone who has "taken it with them." The things we spend our time and life working for will end up in someone's garage sale or in a landfill. Someone we don't know will one day drive our car. Someone not related to us will live in the house we have slaved to build. Someone other than us will spend all of the money we have worked hard to earn and save. If we say we are making a nest-egg for our spouses or children, they won't keep the stuff either.

Beyond greed this lesson focuses on the whole concept of stewardship. The Rich Fool tried to take credit for and ownership of something that was not his. Everything in our world belongs to God. He has simply lent us what we have to better serve Him. When we understand God's ownership and our stewardship then we can leave possessions in God's hands. We don't have to spend time in acquiring stuff. If we understand it is God's world, then we won't become slaves to the things of this world.

True wealth is found in God. He gives value to our lives. He abundantly provides the things that we need. Isn't it ironic that when people talk about the good old days they talk about a simpler time, when possessions were as few as responsibilities? I wonder what God would have us learn from those simpler days.

Trusting God's provisions, you can return to that simple style of living.

Seed Thoughts

1. What issue was raised which caused Jesus to tell the story of the Rich Fool?

A person in the crowd was having a problem settling an estate with his brother.

2. What was Jesus' immediate reply to the request to act as a mediator in this situation?

He would not put Himself in the position of solving a trivial problem, but addressed the real issue in this person's life.

3. What issue did Jesus address in the Parable of the Rich Fool?

Jesus addressed the issue of greed and covetousness. He used the parable to show that "things" don't bring happiness.

4. How would you infer that Jesus' hearers defined the "good life?"

The "good life" was measured by the amount of things a person possessed. The Rich Fool echoed this in his soliloquy.

5. The Rich Man was a farmer. Who was given credit for the abundant crop that was produced?

Jesus said, "the ground" produced abundantly, but the Rich Man contributed nothing to the good harvest.

1. What issue was raised which caused Jesus to tell the story of the Rich Fool?

2. What was Jesus' immediate reply to the request to act as a mediator in this situation?

3. What issue did Jesus address in the Parable of the Rich Fool?

4. How would you infer that Jesus' hearers defined the "good life?"

5. The Rich Man was a farmer. Who was given credit for the abundant crop that was produced?

6. What was the response of the Rich Man to the abundant crop?

7. What did the Rich Man decide to do about the storage problem caused by his crop?

8. What was the Rich Fool's goal in building these bigger barns?

9. Because the abundant crop brought him security, what was the Rich Man planning to do for the next few years?

10. What happened to the Rich Man and his stuff?

(Continued next page)

189

A person in the crowd was having a problem settling an estate with his brother.

He would not put Himself in the position of solving a trivial problem, but addressed the real issue in this person's life.

Jesus addressed the issue of greed and covetousness. He used the parable to show that "things" don't bring happiness.

The "good life" was measured by the amount of things a person possessed. The Rich Fool echoed this in his soliloquy.

Jesus said, "the ground" produced abundantly, but the Rich Man contributed nothing to the good harvest.

Rather than thanking God for the bounty, the Rich Man was worried about where to store the crop.

He decided to enter a building campaign. He tore down his old barns and built new and bigger ones.

By storing his abundance in the barns, he planned to take his ease and enjoy the "good life."

His plans were to eat, drink and be merry.

He died, and his stuff ended up in the hands of a stranger. Jesus said he was a fool.

6. What was the response of the Rich Man to the abundant crop?

Rather than thanking God for the bounty, the Rich Man was worried about where to store the crop.

7. What did the Rich Man decide to do about the storage problem caused by his crop?

He decided to enter a building campaign. He tore down his old barns and built new and bigger ones.

8. What was the Rich Fool's goal in building these bigger barns?

By storing his abundance in the barns, he planned to take his ease and enjoy the "good life."

9. Because the abundant crop brought him security, what was the Rich Man planning to do for the next few years?

His plans were to eat, drink and be merry.

10. What happened to the Rich Man and his stuff?

He died, and his stuff ended up in the hands of a stranger. Jesus said he was a fool.

Reversing the World's Standard

*A*t the same time came the disciples unto Jesus, saying, Who is the greatest in the kingdom of heaven?

2 And Jesus called a little child unto him, and set him in the midst of them,

3 And said, Verily I say unto you, Except ye be converted, and become as little children, ye shall not enter into the kingdom of heaven.

4 Whosoever therefore shall humble himself as this little child, the same is greatest in the kingdom of heaven.

20:17 And Jesus going up to Jerusalem took the twelve disciples apart in the way, and said unto them,

18 Behold, we go up to Jerusalem; and the Son of man shall be betrayed unto the chief priests and unto the scribes, and they shall condemn him to death,

19 And shall deliver him to the Gentiles to mock, and to scourge, and to crucify him: and the third day he shall rise again.

20 Then came to him the mother of Zebedee's children with her sons, worshiping him, and desiring a certain thing of him.

21 And he said unto her, What wilt thou? She saith unto him, Grant that these my two sons may sit, the one on thy right hand, and the other on the left, in thy kingdom.

22 But Jesus answered and said, Ye know not what ye ask. Are ye able to drink of the cup that I shall drink of, and to be baptized with the baptism that I am baptized with? They say unto him, We are able.

23 And he saith unto them, Ye shall drink indeed of my cup, and be baptized with the baptism that I am baptized with: but to sit on my right hand, and on my left, is not mine to give, but it shall be given to them for whom it is prepared of my Father.

24 And when the ten heard it, they were moved with indignation against the two brethren.

25 But Jesus called them unto him, and said, Ye know that the princes of the Gentiles exercise dominion over them, and they that are great exercise authority upon them.

26 But it shall not be so among you: but whosoever will be great among you, let him be your minister;

27 And whosoever will be chief among you, let him be your servant:

28 Even as the Son of man came not to be ministered unto, but to minister, and to give his life a ransom for many.

Matt. 18:1-4; 20:17-28

Jan. 17

Memory Selection
Matthew 20:26

Background Scripture
Matthew 18:1-4; 20:17 -28

Devotional Reading
Galatians 5:13-15

Printed Scripture
Matthew 18:1-4; 20:17-28

Teacher's Target

Lesson purpose: To *contrast the basic qualifications for leadership in the Kingdom of God with the standards often seen in worldly realms.*

Is music really the "universal language," as we sometimes hear, or is it really *power*? When we think of the ruling majority in a country's politics, we think of those "in power." In con-frontations between nations, we instinctively expect the victor to be the nation with the most "fire-power."

In this lesson Jesus contrasts these views of power with His own definition of power and leadership in *His* Kingdom. He will ask us to remember two traits of a truly powerful leader: *humility* and *service.*

Since worldly power-plays seem to work so well, it is tempting for even Christian leaders to adopt such tactics. Those who remember their true calling, however, lead in ways that reflect the leadership style of Him who showed He was a King by being a Servant.

Lesson Introduction

In this passage Jesus continues to turn worldly values upside down, just as He had in the Sermon on the Mount." He served notice that His "Kingdom values" were distinctive when He prefaced them by saying "You have heard it said...but I say." (See a Bible dictionary under "Kingdom of God.")

Although many people identify the Kingdom of God with the Second Coming, many biblical passages show its immediate relevance as well. Wherever Christ is enthroned as Lord, there will the Kingdom be found (Luke 17:21). This implies that to live by "Kingdom ethics" is a way of realizing many of the fruits of the Kingdom in the present. Applied to the text for today, this means that leaders who rise to Christ's challenge to lead by humility and service instead of by force are impacting society in ways that reflect the "ideal world" that will one day be the rule, rather than the exception.

Teaching Outline	Daily Bible Readings	
I. Who Is the Greatest?—Matt. 18:1-4	**Mon.**	Matthew 18:1-4 *A Child Among Them*
A. The "changed," 1-3	**Tue.**	Matthew 20:17-28 *To Serve, not to Be Served*
B. The humble, 4	**Wed.**	I Have Set You An Example *John 13:1-5*
II. Who Reigns in the Kingdom?—20:17-28	**Thu.**	The Strong to Help the Weak *Romans 15:1-6*
A. The Suffering Servant, 17-19	**Fri.**	I Am Not Worthy *Genesis 32:3-12*
B. Not the glory-seekers, 20-23	**Sat.**	Humility Goes Before Honor *Proverbs 15:25-33*
C. Not the power-hungry, 24-28	**Sun.**	Humble in Spirit *Isaiah 57:15-21*

Verse by Verse

I. Who Is the Greatest?—Matt. 18:1-4

A. The "changed," 1-3

1 At the same time came the disciples unto Jesus, saying, Who is the greatest in the kingdom of heaven?

2 And Jesus called a little child unto him, and set him in the midst of them,

3 And said, Verily I say unto you, Except ye be converted, and become as little children, ye shall not enter into the kingdom of heaven.

The "kingdom of heaven" (or kingdom of God) is one of the most prominent themes in the teaching of Jesus. He seems to have used the phrase to refer not so much to a faraway heavenly realm as to wherever His rule is acknowledged. He could therefore say "The kingdom of God is within (or among) you" (Luke 17:21). Thus Jesus' teaching on power here, like the lofty standards He taught in the Sermon on the Mount, are to be considered a statement of how His followers are called to live *now* under His rule.

Since the disciples knew that earthly kingdoms are run "from the top down," it was natural for them to suppose Jesus' realm is similar; and they want to have chief places in it. Jesus surprises them by using not another king but a child for a model of who is the greatest in His kingdom. "Converted" here is more accurately rendered "changed." How should Jesus-style leaders change back into a child? This question will be answered in the next verse.

B. The humble, 4

4 Whosoever therefore shall humble himself as this little child, the same is greatest in the kingdom of heaven.

Jesus doesn't have in mind choosing leaders who lack experience or knowledge, but who have child-like humility. This word, in English, comes from the same root as "humus," or soil. Humility does not mean a hang-dog embarrassment at being called to lead, but the ability to acknowledge frankly that we are made of earth, with feet of clay. Humble leaders are those who aren't too good to provide the "ground" on which others stand.

Jesus is calling for leaders who are willing to approach the task of leadership as "powerless" in worldly ways as a child. Perhaps He is also calling for leaders to have a child-like willingness to learn, instead of assuming they are always correct. Finally, He is preparing His followers for the teaching on service in chapter 20.

II. Who Reigns in the Kingdom?— 20:17-28

A. The Suffering Servant, 17-19

17 And Jesus going up to Jerusalem took the twelve disciples apart in the way, and said unto them,

18 Behold, we go up to Jerusalem; and the Son of man shall be betrayed unto the chief priests and unto the scribes, and they shall condemn him to death,

19 And shall deliver him to the Gentiles to mock, and to scourge, and to crucify him: and the third day he shall rise again.

Matthew inserts this profound and, to the disciples, shocking teaching between Jesus' comment praising childlike humility and another request, in verses 20-21, for prominence in the Kingdom. He does so in order to model for His misguided and power-seeking followers the kind of servant leadership He urges them to adopt.

The disciples were expecting their Messiah to assume ruling power along the same lines as the power and prominence they sought. Imagine their dismay when He says, instead, that He is going to give Himself up to the authorities to be killed! Peter was so stunned by a similar announcement that he rebuked His Master (Matt. 16:21-22).

Jesus, however, is determined to be the "Suffering Servant" predicted in Isaiah. The Hebrew word for "servant" in such passages as Isaiah 42:1-4 can also be translated "son" or "child," showing the connection between this passage and Matthew 18:1-4. Jesus will be as obedient to His heavenly Father as a child obeying his earthly father or a servant obeying his master. Again, when leaders today can exert their leadership in service to others instead of for their own glory, a bit of the Kingdom can be seen in everyday life.

Jesus' statement here also speaks to modern discussions of who was responsible for His death. Some anti-Semitic statements tend to implicate only the Jews. Jesus, however, places responsibility not on a race but on unbelievers, both Roman and Jewish. In other words, *sinners* (a class of people that includes ourselves), not a particular race, are responsible for Jesus' death.

B. Not the glory-seekers, 20-23

20 Then came to him the mother of Zebedee's children with her sons, worshiping him, and desiring a certain thing of him.

21 And he said unto her, What wilt thou? She saith unto him, Grant that these my two sons may sit, the one on thy right hand, and the other on the left, in thy kingdom.

22 But Jesus answered and said, Ye know not what ye ask. Are ye able to drink of the cup that I shall drink of, and to be baptized with the baptism that I am baptized with? They say unto him, We are able.

23 And he saith unto them, Ye shall drink indeed of my cup, and be baptized with the baptism that I am baptized with: but to sit on my right hand, and on my left, is not mine to give, but it shall be given to them for whom it is prepared of my Father.

The right and the left hand of a king were positions of prominence (see Hebrews 1:3). The sons of Zebedee are James and John, who are really putting their mother up to this request (see Mark 10:35). She seems as glad to make the appeal as parents who want their Little League child to win at any cost, or their daughter to have an unfair advantage in a beauty pageant.

Jesus' first response is based on His prophetic knowledge that anyone considered a leader in the movement He established would risk being given the same treatment He has just indicated He would undergo at the hands of enemies. Are James and John ready to endure the baptism of fire and the cup of suffering that awaited Jesus? Their answer, "We are able," indicates that they probably did not realize the implications of Jesus' statement.

No sooner do the disciples claim they are "able" but Jesus admits an inability! In verse 23 He says He is unable to assign places of rank in the kingdom because that is the Father's role. This is a problem only for people who claim more for Jesus in His humanity than Scripture does. Remember that Jesus deliberately subjected Himself to human limitations when He took on flesh (Philip. 2:5-9). (He also confessed that He did not know the date of the end of the world,24:36.)

C. Not the power-hungry, 24-28

24 And when the ten heard it, they were moved with indignation against the two brethren.

25 But Jesus called them unto him, and said, Ye know that the princes of the Gentiles exercise dominion over them, and they that are great exercise authority upon them.

26 But it shall not be so among you: but whosoever will be great among you, let him be your minister;

27 And whosoever will be chief among you, let him be your servant:

28 Even as the Son of man came not to be ministered unto, but to minister, and to give his life a ransom for many.

The other ten apostles resent the audacity of James and John,not because the two haven't learned that Kingdom leadership is defined by service, but because the ten did not think to ask for first place first! So Jesus draws the point home in painful detail: His followers are to leave power struggles to "Gentiles",meaning unbelievers here. In the Kingdom, the best leadership takes on the form of a servant, just as Jesus did.

Evangelistic Emphasis

Christ gave His life for you! He gave His life as a ransom for a bunch of other unsavory characters as well. Think about those disciples who came to Jesus asking who would be the greatest in the kingdom of heaven. They were really asking Jesus to do a favor for them. They wanted to rule with Him when the earthly Messianic kingdom arrived. Even though Jesus had predicted His passion twice, they still were thinking in terms of overthrowing the Roman Empire and setting up a nation. Jesus gave His life for those disciples.

He gave His life for the mother of James and John. For some reason, Matthew has their mother ask the question the other gospels attribute to James and John. What would they have done to attain the seats of honor next to Jesus? Jesus told the little family that was not a gift He could give. Despite their ambition, Jesus died for them.

He died for the bickering disciples. Those that were upset about the question coming from the Zebedee family. He died for the Zebedee brothers who wanted places of honor.

He died for that child He sat on His lap as an example of childlike faith. That child who served as a pointed example to the proud disciples of the humility that is the cornerstone of faith.

So, Jesus died for the characters in the New Testament. According to Matthew, Jesus died for all. That means that He died for YOU. There is no escaping it. Jesus death was on your behalf.

Can you think of others who need to know that Jesus died for them, too?

● ● ● ● ● ● ● ●

Memory Selection

But whosoever will be great among you, let him be your minister.—*Matthew 20: 26*

My list of great persons is an unusual one. I have no stars, athletes or ministers on my list of great persons. I have simple people on the list.

My list of great persons includes those Christians I have seen on their knees praying for men and women they will never meet. Praying that God would bring redemption, healing or the miracle of love into a life. My list of great persons includes people who visit in hospitals and with the home bound members of the Body of Christ. It has listed persons who work in clothes closets and food distribution centers. I list those volunteers who go all over this country rebuilding after disasters. I must include those persons who build homes with Habitat for Humanity.

You see my list includes people like you. People who are so filled with the love of Jesus Christ that they want others to know about that love. The best way to communicate love is in simple acts of loving kindness and charity. Thank you for being the hands and feet of Jesus. You are on my list of great persons.

Weekday Problems

Julia started her faith well. She grew up in First Church and was one of those bright children who is a blessing to Sunday School teachers. She was active in the youth group. She struggled early in her college career with a call to be a missionary. That call, was ill defined and she got busy in her chosen major.

Julia was on the cutting edge of Internet technology. She knew about the Net when it a tool for the military and scientists only. She had gone from the university to a major national computer company all in the span of five years. Now with a Master's degree, Julia was starting her own company.

She had appeared on the cover of a major national news magazine as a model "woman." She gave thanks to her parents and to her church for raising her the way they did. What she didn't reveal was that she had gone years without ever attending a church service. The light of her faith in Christ was fading fast.

The new pastor of First Church asked to make an appointment with Julia. He wanted to talk to her about beginning a class in computer literacy for the single mothers of the community. He was hoping that Julia could give some advice on where to start and how to structure the program to best help the mothers.

He got a less that courteous response from Julia. To the contrary she was rude to him. "I don't have time for that stuff. Can't you see that I'm doing important business?"

* How is it that when some persons "make it to the top" they forget the church?
* How can Julia be shepherded back into the fold?

Power Points

The most striking defect of our system of government is that it divides political power and thereby conceals political responsibility.—*Carl Lotus Becker*

* * *

Even in war, moral power is to physical as three parts out of four.—*Napoleon*

* * *

If ever this free people, if this government itself, is ever utterly demoralized, it will come from this incessant human wriggle and struggle for office, which is but a way to live without work.—*Abraham Lincoln*

* * *

The measure of a man's greatness is not the number of servants he has, but the number of people he serves.—*Anon.*

* * *

The one power greater than personal might is the power to give up power and to serve others.—*Anon.*

This Lesson in Your Life

An important distinction needs to be made. It is the difference between child*ish* and child*like*. Childish is what happens on that long trip you take in the back seat. You know, that argument when Johnny touches Susie's side of the car. It happens when a parent foolishly asks, "Kids, where do you want to eat." Johnny will want a Pizza and Susie will want a hamburger.

Childishness is not limited to children. Adults are childish, but we do it in an adult fashion. Large children in adult bodies act like small children in the back seat of a car. Turf wars, and skirmishes over personal agendas. Adults scrambling over one another trying to be king of the hill. It even happens in church meetings.

Like most things, we have a New Testament pattern for it—James and John and Mrs. Zebedee who innocently came to Jesus with a request. Mom wanted her boys to be at the right and left of Jesus. That is what any good mother wants for her children, the best. The problem was that the rest of the disciples had mothers too, who wanted *their* little boys to have those positions of power. So there was a childish fight.

Child*like* behavior stands in stark contrast to child*ish* behavior. Childlikeness is open, honest, hopeful and faithful. Jesus lifted up childlikeness as the example of kingdom faith. All children care about is showing love. They are giving of their love and affection without bounds. They believe— in Jesus and angels and goodness and miracles. If you have lost your sense of childlikeness, ask a teacher in the Primary Department if your class can observe the children for a while. In them you will see the brightness and love that Jesus wanted His followers to have for one another.

True greatness is childlike. True greatness is found in serving others for the Kingdom of God. The Son of God did not come as a powerful person. Paul wrote that "He humbled himself taking on the form of a servant" (Phil. 2: 5-11). It was that servant attitude that was an example for the disciples. True greatness is found in persons who willingly serve others.

Jimmy Carter served as President in tempestuous times in America. It is not clear how history will judge his presidency. What is clear is that Carter is a great human being. Since leaving politics, he has been actively involved in the Habitat for Humanity program, which builds homes for people of little means (who are asked to contribute their own "sweat equity." Imagine receiving that act of servant love. Imagine what pride a person takes in a home built by a former President.

That is the whole point of the servant activity that Jesus modeled. The person receiving the act of servant ministry experiences personally the love of God through another human being. That is why the servant image is powerful.

Only as we give our love freely and openly, like children, do we win people to Christ. Lording it over others or trying to prove themwrong doesn't win converts. We point to Jesus most clearly when we humble ourselves in acts of obedient service.

Seed Thoughts

1. According to Matthew the disciples came to Jesus asking a question. What was that question?

The disciples asked Jesus who would be the greatest in the kingdom of heaven.

2. What was Jesus' response to this question?

He had a child stand among them. As the child stood he commanded them to be childlike in their dealings with others.

3. According to Jesus what is the essence of true greatness?

A disciple becomes truly great when that disciple is willing to humble himself as a child.

4. Where was Jesus traveling when He turned and predicted His death a third time?

Jesus was on his way to Jerusalem. On that journey He took the twelve aside to tell them about His death.

5. According to Jesus what groups would be involved in His execution?

The chief priests and the teachers of the law as well as the Gentiles would be involved in His death.

---

1. According to Matthew the disciples came to Jesus asking a question. What was that question?

2. What was Jesus' response to this question?

3. According to Jesus what is the essence of true greatness?

4. Where was Jesus traveling when He turned and predicted His death a third time?

5. According to Jesus what groups would be involved in His execution?

6. Who would condemn Jesus to death?

7. Who would actually carry out the death sentence?

8. Who came to Jesus asking a favor on behalf of others?

9. What favor did she ask of Jesus?

10. What did Jesus do with this request?

(Continued next page)

The disciples asked Jesus who would be the greatest in the kingdom of heaven.

He had a child stand among them. As the child stood he commanded them to be child-like in their dealings with others.

A disciple becomes truly great when that disciple is willing to humble himself as a child.

Jesus was on his way to Jerusalem. On that journey He took the twelve aside to tell them about His death.

The chief priests and the teachers of the law as well as the Gentiles would be involved in His death.

Jesus would be condemned to death by the Jews. The Sanhedrin would pass the death sentence.

The Romans (Gentiles) crucified Jesus, since the Jews had no power to execute to carry out a death sentence.

The mother of James and John, the sons of Zebedee, came to Jesus with a request on behalf of her sons.

She wanted Him to grant her sons seats of power, one on His right hand and one on His left, in His Kingdom.

He explained that this request was not something He could grant.

6. Who would condemn Jesus to death?

Jesus would be condemned to death by the Jews. The Sanhedrin would pass the death sentence.

7. Who would actually carry out the death sentence?

The Romans (Gentiles) crucified Jesus, since the Jews had no power to execute to carry out a death sentence.

8. Who came to Jesus asking a favor on behalf of others?

The mother of James and John, the sons of Zebedee, came to Jesus with a request on behalf of her sons.

9. What favor did she ask of Jesus?

She wanted Him to grant her sons seats of power, one on His right hand and one on His left, in His Kingdom.

10. What did Jesus do with this request?

He explained that this request was not something He could grant.

Forgiving Each Other

7 hen came Peter to him, and said, Lord, how oft shall my brother sin against me, and I forgive him? till seven times?

22 Jesus saith unto him, I say not unto thee, Until seven times: but, Until seventy times seven.

23 Therefore is the kingdom of heaven likened unto a certain king, which would take account of his servants.

24 And when he had begun to reckon, one was brought unto him, which owed him ten thousand talents.

25 But forasmuch as he had not to pay, his lord commanded him to be sold, and his wife, and children, and all that he had, and payment to be made.

26 The servant therefore fell down, and worshiped him, saying, Lord, have patience with me, and I will pay thee all.

27 Then the lord of that servant was moved with compassion, and loosed him, and forgave him the debt.

28 But the same servant went out, and found one of his fellow servants, which owed him an hundred pence: and he laid hands on him, and took him by the throat, saying, Pay me that thou owest.

29 And his fellow servant fell down at his feet, and besought him, saying, Have patience with me, and I will pay thee all.

30 And he would not: but went and cast him into prison, till he should pay the debt.

31 So when his fellow servants saw what was done, they were very sorry, and came and told unto their lord all that was done.

32 Then his lord, after that he had called him, said unto him, O thou wicked servant, I forgave thee all that debt, because thou desirest me:

33 Shouldest not thou also have had compassion on thy fellow servant, even as I had pity on thee?

34 And his lord was wroth, and delivered him to the tormentors, till he should pay all that was due unto him.

35 So likewise shall my heavenly Father do also unto you, if ye from your hearts forgive not every one his brother their trespasses.

Matt. 18:21-35

Jan. 24

Memory Selection
Matthew 6:14-15
Background Scripture
Matthew 18:6-35

Devotional Reading
Psalm 103:6-14

Printed Scripture
Matthew 18:21-35

Teacher's Target

Lesson purpose: *To probe Jesus' teaching on forgiveness, recalling the joy of being forgiven and experiencing the freedom of being forgiving persons.*

Some topics, such as angels, are "heavenly," while others, such as family relationships, are "earthly." Forgiveness is one of those topics that stands squarely between heaven and earth, immediately making us aware of both its divine and human aspects.

The sensitive Christian cannot say the word without the double awareness that God has graciously released us from our own sin, and that we are to extend this graciousness to others. Forgiveness is therefore a conduit between God and sinners, with the Christian being responsible for receiving it with joy and passing it along to others.

The Good News (gospel) about forgiveness is also twofold: We do not have to struggle under the burden of sin, nor do we have to carry the burden of grudges and an unforgiving spirit toward others.

Lesson Introduction

This lesson portrays Jesus employing two of His methods of teaching: confronting His followers with a radical standard of behavior, and reinforcing it with a parable.

Some scholars have pictured Jesus as a sadly mistaken visionary whose dream of setting up an earthly kingdom was shattered by the crucifixion. His followers then organized the Church as an after-thought, to revise the dream and keep it alive. Matthew, however, has focused since chapter 13 on how His followers should act after His departure. In fact, chapter 18 has the distinction of being the only place in the Gospels that mentions the word "church." Jesus apparently envisioned the Church as a phase of the Kingdom of God in which His followers would be called on to live the "Kingdom ethic," including extending to others the forgiveness they experienced from God.

Teaching Outline	Daily Bible Readings
	Mon. No Stumbling Blocks! *Matthew 18:6-14*
I. Crucial Question—21-22	**Tue.** Dealing with Church Members *Matthew 18:15-20*
A. Limited generosity, 21	**Wed.** How Often Must I Forgive? *Matthew 18:21-35*
B. Unlimited grace, 22	**Thu.** Restore Transgressors! *Galatians 6:1-5*
II. Penetrating Parable—23-34	**Fri.** Be Kind and Forgiving *Ephesians 4:25-32*
A. A debt forgiven, 23-27	**Sat.** God Forgives; So Should We *Psalm 103:6-14*
B. An obligation enforced, 28-34	**Sun.** Remembering Sin No More *Hebrews 10:11-25*
III. Incisive Application—35	

Verse by Verse

I. Crucial Question—21-22
A. Limited generosity, 21

21 Then came Peter to him, and said, Lord, how oft shall my brother sin against me, and I forgive him? till seven times?

Jesus has been teaching on the importance of having a compassionate attitude. We are to be as accepting and innocent as children (18:1-5, 10), to be willing to leave ninety-nine safe "sheep" just to save a single one that is lost (11-14), and to negotiate harmony among brothers and sisters in the church (15-17). Significantly, such attitudes and behavior are a reflection of the compassionate standards in heaven (18-20).

All this stands in contrast to some strict interpretations of the Law of Moses, with its "eye for an eye" ethic. Yet Christ's more compassionate message has begun to penetrate the hearts of His disciples. So Peter, in what he must have thought was a generous gesture, goes so far as to suggest that this radical new teaching might involve foregoing the right of taking an eye for an eye. He may be able even to *forgive* a sinner, and not just once but *seven times!*

The Greek word for "forgive" comes

from a root that means to "release." Being able to forgive someone who offends us not only means releasing them from having to "pay" for the offense; it also releases us from the burden of bearing a grudge.

Yet, as generous as Peter thought he was being, his capacity to forgive is limited to "seven times." After all, what would happen to standards if Christ's followers placed no limitations on forgiveness? Peter seems to be both challenged by his Lord's great-hearted spirit, and concerned about where it might lead.

B. Unlimited grace, 22

22 Jesus saith unto him, I say not unto thee, Until seven times: but, Until seventy times seven.

No, Peter, Jesus replies: You must place no limits on your capacity to forgive. This is indicated by the use of the number seven, which often stands for perfection or infinity. Whether we are to read "seventy times seven" (490) as in the KJV, or "seventy-seven" (as in the NIV), Jesus transforms Peter's understanding of a generous spirit into God's concept of unlimited grace.

Just as Jesus' lofty statements in the Sermon on the Mount ("Resist not evil,"

"Turn the other cheek," etc.) raise tough questions, so does this radical concept of unlimited forgiveness. Does Jesus mean that a professional thief who commits fifty robberies should be forgiven just as freely as the youth who steals a piece of candy?

Two qualifications must guide our response. First, Jesus assumes that the sinner here *repents,* which is explicitly stated in Luke's version of this incident (Luke 17:4). Repentance also implies that the sinner must "bring forth fruits meet (or fit) for repentance" (Matt. 3:8).

Second, forgiveness for the *sin* involved, and declining to hold a grudge, do not necessarily mean that punishment should be withheld. A murderer, for example, may repent and experience full forgiveness from both God and the Church; but he still has to live with the consequence of having taken a life, which might mean punishment through the judicial process.

Yet such qualifications should not dull the radical nature of Jesus' teaching. The parable to follow shows how much personal stake we have in adopting an attitude of infinite forgiveness.

II. Penetrating Parable—23-34
A. A debt forgiven, 23-27

23 Therefore is the kingdom of heaven likened unto a certain king, which would take account of his servants.

24 And when he had begun to reckon, one was brought unto him, which owed him ten thousand talents.

25 But forasmuch as he had not to pay, his lord commanded him to be sold, and his wife, and children, and all that he had, and payment to be made.

26 The servant therefore fell down, and worshiped him, saying, Lord, have patience with me, and I will pay thee all.

27 Then the lord of that servant was moved with compassion, and loosed him, and forgave him the debt.

Everything in Jesus' parable about forgiveness is "over-sized" for emphasis. Ten thousand talents (a money-weight) in our money would amount to from six to ten million dollars, a debt few working people could ever repay. The threatened punishment of selling the debtor's family into slavery is also hopeless, since they would never bring enough to repay the debt.

All this, of course, is exactly Jesus' point. We are like the hopelessly indebted servant, in that our debt of sin is too great for us to repay. We can only throw ourselves on His mercy. When we do, the King doesn't grant us permission to work off the debt, as the servant offered. Instead the huge debt is totally wiped off the books.

It is important that we appreciate this part of the parable, both for our own sense of security and gratitude for the free, saving grace of God, and because if we do not appreciate the cost of the forgiveness God has extended to us it will be difficult for us to forgive others. "To whom little is forgiven, the same loveth little" (Luke 7:47).

B. An obligation enforced, 28-34

28 But the same servant went out, and found one of his fellow servants, which owed him an hundred pence: and he laid hands on him, and took him by the throat, saying, Pay me that thou owest.

29 And his fellow servant fell down at his feet, and besought him, saying, Have patience with me, and I will pay thee all.

30 And he would not: but went and cast him into prison, till he should pay the debt.

31 So when his fellow servants saw what was done, they were very sorry, and came and told unto their lord all that was done.

32 Then his lord, after that he had called him, said unto him, O thou wicked servant, I forgave thee all that debt, because thou desirest me:

33 Shouldest not thou also have had compassion on thy fellow servant, even as I had pity on thee?

34 And his lord was wroth, and delivered him to the tormentors, till he should pay all that was due unto him.

Continuing the parable, Jesus shows the folly of *forgiven* people refusing to be *forgiving* people. The fellow-servants who reported the amazingly harsh action of the forgiven servant (vs. 31) may reflect what Jesus had taught in verses 15-17: the Christian community has a role in the process of restoring members who sin against each other.

The exaggeration continues when we compare the paltry amount owed the servant with the huge amount he had owed the king. Sin is always more of an offense against God than it is against us. King David made this clear in an astounding confession after his sin with Bathsheba. Even after committing adultery with her, and having her husband murdered, David said to God, "Against thee, thee only, have I sinned" (Ps. 51:4). We can forgive others more easily when we understand that their offense hurts God more than ourselves.

III. Incisive Application—35

35 So likewise shall my heavenly Father do also unto you, if ye from your hearts forgive not every one his brother their trespasses.

Finally, Jesus draws the application so clearly no one can misunderstand. Forgiveness is at first a grace and gift from God to us, then an obligation for us to extend to others. Note also that it is to be more than disdain, more than lip-service. Forgiveness is to be "from the heart."

Evangelistic Emphasis

There is no sin too great for God's forgiveness. The only sin ever mentioned in the New Testament that is unforgivable is blasphemy against the Holy Spirit. That particular sin is the ultimate and final rejection of God. As long as we are willing, God forgives our sins.

Today few people talk seriously about sin. That is the bad news. Sin is rampant. We have called it other things. "Individual expression" and "alternative lifestyles" may sound harmless but in most cases they are euphemisms for sin. Only when persons confess their sins and repent of their sins can God's forgiveness cleanse their sins. The problem in today's culture is not God's unwillingness to forgive our sins. The modern problem is that we don't think sin exists, really. When the church points out moral depravity or sin we are subsequently called bigoted and narrow-minded by the persons trying to advocate this behavior.

The good news is that God can forgive sin. As we make friends with persons who don't know Christ we can offer them the abundant love, grace and forgiveness of God. As we become instruments of God's love, the Holy Spirit will do the convicting of sin. As the Spirit brings conviction of sin, we can offer God's mercy.

When surrounded by abounding love and in a trusting relationship people are free to admit their faults. When they do, be an instrument of God's forgiveness.

God forgives all sins, if we ask. For people burdened with guilt this is good news. For people lost and looking for a new beginning this is good news. For members of the Body of Christ who have sinned, this is good news!

• • • • • •

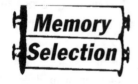

Memory Selection

For if ye forgive men their trespasses, your heavenly Father will also forgive you: But if ye forgive not men their trespasses, neither will your Father forgive your trespasses.—*Matt.hew 6: 14-15*

God is faithful! Another way of saying that is, God is consistent. The truth of this text is startling. It says that you can't hold a grudge and expect God to forgive your sins. There is no way to theologize around the words of this passage. I don't think that it is God's unwillingness to forgive. I rather think that when we are unforgiving we close to door to forgiveness possibilities.

You might ponder the following image to help you understand this. Imagine you are carrying a heavy sack of rocks on your back. Those rocks represent grudges and persons you are unwilling to forgive. After a while, you become resentful of carrying that load. Resentment grows as you believe everyone else seems to be without a heavy sack of rocks. You can't let go of that bag. You ask God to help, but even as you pray you tighten your grip on your resentments. It is only in letting go and forgiving persons (even if they wronged you) that you will find healing.

Weekday Problems

Andrea was having a difficult time. She had been a member of Grace Church for fifteen years. She and her husband Buddy had four children. They were doing their best to raise their four children in church. Andrea and Buddy were one of those young couple who love the church and the fellowship of its members. However, their attendance was not consistent. Buddy owned his own company. Andrea was an executive at an architectural firm. Their four children would be in church when the parents were in church. The problem was that the parents started missing church more often.

The pastor went to talk to Buddy and Andrea. They apologized and promised to be more faithful. A couple of days later Andrea stopped by to talk privately with the pastor. In that conversation Andrea confided that she had been unfaithful in her marriage. Buddy knew about the situation and had forgiven her. She said that recently coming to church had made her feel uncomfortable. She didn't feel worthy to be sitting in a pew or participating in a Sunday School class. She knew that what she had done was very wrong and had hurt Buddy. She was worried it was about to happen again. There was a man in her firm who had caught her eye.

* How is complete forgiveness contingent on true repentance?

* Do you think Andrea has repented of her sins and been forgiven?

* If she feels unforgiven, is she more or less likely to sin again? If you were her pastor what would you advise her to do?

Forgive Me, but . . .

A worker was shorted two dollars in his pay envelope, and complained to the paymaster. "Hey," the paymaster said,"You were *over*paid two dollars last week and you never said anything."

"I know," said the employee. "I don't mind overlooking one mistake, but when it happens the second time I think it's time to complain."

* * *

Judge: You've admitted that you stole those eggs. What's your defense?

Defendant: I took them by mistake, your honor.

Judge: How's that?

Defendant: I mistook them for fresh eggs.

* * *

Mac: The way to avoid having to ask for forgiveness is never to make a mistake.

Jack: You mean you've never been wrong?

Mac: Well there *was* that time I thought I was wrong and I was right.

This Lesson in Your Life

An unforgiving spirit might be the major cause that persons drop out of the church. While it is true that some people are slighted or hurt in the church, an unforgiving spirit keeps them from reconciling the situation. Most of the members of your group can tell stories about people who have stopped coming to church because they weren't asked to serve "high tea" to some visiting dignitary in the congregation. Another favorite is when church members play "hide-and-seek" and the minister fails to "discover" they have had an illness. The person can then boast that the pastor didn't visit them. They get mad and leave the church.

What would happen if forgiveness were offered and accepted? The church could reclaim many former members. Forgiveness is a radical concept of the church, isn't it?

In an earlier lesson a reference was made to "tough love." The idea of forgiveness as Jesus lived it precludes any notion that we can turn people out. Forgiveness according to Jesus should come freely and abundantly. It is something that we offer to all who confess and repent of their sins. It is not our position to judge the sincerity of that confession or repentance.

Forgiveness is reciprocal in nature. It is only given to those willing to practice forgiveness in their lives. Holding grudges shuts off the pipeline through which God brings forgiveness in our lives. The notion that two people can sit across the aisle from one another in church and hold a grudge against each other is contrary to the New Testament. In that scenario there are two unforgiven people sitting in church. The only way for them to receive the forgiveness of God is to be willing to forgive one another.

Forgiveness is complete. We use the image of burying the hatchet to describe forgiveness. The old joke is that we need to bury the hatchet but remember where the handle is. Forgiveness involves forgetting. The Old Testament often pictures God's forgiveness of our sins in terms of forgetting sin. "Do not remember the sins of my youth or my transgressions; according to your steadfast love remember me, for your goodness' sake, O Lord!" (Ps 25: 7, NRSV). It is only in forgetting the wrongs done to us that we can have a new start. When we hold onto hurts, grudges, slights, even wrongs done to us, we are carrying that person or event as an emotional burden. It is only in giving that situation and person to God in loving ways that we are freed from the burden of that memory.

Forgiveness is something God must do through us. Forgiveness and the ability to forgive must come from God. It is not in our power to forgive certain people of certain heinous acts. In those difficult situations we must trust that God is acting through us. Forgiveness is impossible unless we trust God to lead us in the process. When we refuse to forgive we are subtly hoping and praying that God will not forgive the person either. Our human nature wants to hold on to grudges. We like our pet hates. We long to see the unjust receive retribution from the Lord. We are comfortable with this position as long as we feel that God understands our position and is also forgiving us even as we are holding a grudge.

Forgiveness opens the door to renewed relationships. Saying "forgive me" is an act of childlike humility. Offering forgiveness is an act of Christ-like compassion. In either case the results are graceful in nature. Forgiveness and reconciliation are powerful forces in renewing severed relationships. Most of all, forgiveness opens up a new door between you and your God. The forgiveness of sins is why Jesus came to earth. He has called us to "follow Him" even if it means praying, "Father, forgive them."

Seed Thoughts

1. What question did Simon Peter ask of Jesus in this lesson?

Simon Peter wanted to know how many times he should forgive a brother who sinned against him.

2. How many times was Simon Peter willing to forgive?

Peter was willing to forgive a persons who had sinned against him seven times.

3. Do you know the significance of being willing to forgive seven times?

Jewish Rabbis taught that a persons was only required by the Law to forgive three times. Peter was showing his "long-suffering."

4. What was Jesus' response to Peter's willingness to forgive a person seven times?

Jesus taught that His disciples should be willing to forgive seventy times seven.

5. What might be the significance of being willing to forgive seventy times seven?

The number seven and its multiples are perfect numbers. Forgiveness is "perfectly unlimited."

---

1. What question did Simon Peter ask of Jesus in this lesson?

2. How many times was Simon Peter willing to forgive?

3. Do you know the significance of being willing to forgive seven times?

4. What was Jesus' response to Peter's willingness to forgive a person seven times?

5. What might be the significance of being willing to forgive seventy times seven?

6. Is there someone in your faith community that needs to receive your forgiveness? Are you holding any grudges?

7. What was the point of the parable that Jesus told in response to Peter's inquiry?

8. How did the Master in the parable respond to the servant refusing to forgive a debt?

9. What was the point of throwing the man in prison until he worked off the debt?

10. In light of this parable what do you think about God and forgiveness?

(Continued next page)

209

Simon Peter wanted to know how many times he should forgive a brother who sinned against him.

Peter was willing to forgive a persons who had sinned against him seven times.

Jewish Rabbis taught that a persons was only required by the Law to forgive three times. Peter was showing his "long-suffering."

Jesus taught that His disciples should be willing to forgive seventy times seven.

The number seven and its multiples are perfect numbers. Forgiveness is "perfectly unlimited."

This might be a good question with which to begin your class. It will stir discussion!

A man who was forgiven a great debt in turn refused to forgive a very small debt.

The first servant was thrown into prison and forced to stay there and work off the original debt.

Jesus was teaching that we can't work off our sins. The debt we owe God is bigger than we can pay.

God is a forgiving God. Through Jesus Christ we are called to be ambassadors of that forgiveness and grace in our world.

6. Is there someone in your faith community that needs to receive your forgiveness? Are you holding any grudges?

This might be a good question with which to begin your class. It will stir discussion!

7. What was the point of the parable that Jesus told in response to Peter's inquiry?

A man who was forgiven a great debt in turn refused to forgive a very small debt.

8. How did the Master in the parable respond to the servant refusing to forgive a debt?

The first servant was thrown into prison and forced to stay there and work off the original debt.

9. What was the point of throwing the man in prison until he worked off the debt?

Jesus was teaching that we can't work off our sins. The debt we owe God is bigger than we can pay.

10. In light of this parable what do you think about God and forgiveness?

God is a forgiving God. Through Jesus Christ we are called to be ambassadors of that forgiveness and grace in our world.

The Gospel Has No Boundaries

*7*hen Paul stood in the midst of Mars' hill, and said, Ye men of Athens, I perceive that in all things ye are too superstitious.

23 For as I passed by, and beheld your devotions, I found an altar with this inscription, TO THE UNKNOWN GOD. Whom therefore ye ignorantly worship, him declare I unto you.

24 God that made the world and all things therein, seeing that he is Lord of heaven and earth, dwelleth not in temples made with hands;

25 Neither is worshipped with men's hands, as though he needed any thing, seeing he giveth to all life, and breath, and all things;

26 And hath made of one blood all nations of men for to dwell on the face of the earth, and hath determined the times before appointed, and the bounds of their habitation;

27 That they should seek the Lord, if haply they might feel after him, and find him, though he be not far from every one of us:

28 For in him we live, and move, and have our being; as certain also of your own poets have said, For we are also his offspring.

29 Forasmuch then as we are the offspring of God, we ought not to think that the Godhead is like unto gold, or silver, or stone, graven by art and man's device.

30 And the times of this ignorance God winked at; but now commandeth all men every where to repent:

31 Because he hath appointed a day, in the which he will judge the world in righteousness by that man whom he hath ordained; whereof he hath given assurance unto all men, in that he hath raised him from the dead.

32 And when they heard of the resurrection of the dead, some mocked: and others said, We will hear thee again of this matter.

33 So Paul departed from among them.

34 Howbeit certain men clave unto him, and believed: among the which was Dionysius the Areopagite, and a woman named Damaris, and others with them.

Acts 17:22-34

Jan. 31

Memory Selection
Acts 17:30-31

Background Scripture
Acts 17:16-34

Devotional Reading
Psalm 96:1-13

Printed Scripture
Acts 17:22-34

Teacher's Target

Lesson purpose: *To reflect, from Paul's sermon in Athens, on God as a universal Sovereign even over people who do not know Him.*

The diversity of the world's cultures and national heritages adds to the world's richness. Yet all people everywhere have in common at least three traits, whether they acknowledge them or not. (1) They came from God. (2) They are responsible to Him, not to idols. (3) They are infinitely loved by Him and invited to come to Him.

It was the apostle Paul's mission to bring these truths to the awareness of "the Jew first, and also to the Greek," or Gentile. Here we see him busy at this work in the Greek city of Athens. His message is also the central theme in modern missions. It raises questions such as how the identity of this God can best be presented, what relationship He has to deities worshipped by non-Christians, and even how we ourselves should serve this One God.

Lesson Introduction

Paul is on his second missionary journey. For the first time in recorded Bible history, the gospel is being preached on European soil. God has chosen His messenger carefully for this task of preaching to Gentiles. As a Jew, Paul knows well that there is only one true God. As an educated man, he can respect the learning of Greek philosophers. As a Christian, he can compare and contrast Jesus and His unique work on the Cross with the practice of pagan sacrifices to idols.

Acts 17:16 notes that when Paul entered Athens, the philosophical center of the Greek world, he went first to the local synagogue. This is in keeping with his mission to go "to the Jew first" (Rom. 1:16). Moved by the idolatry in the city, he next faces off with the Athenian philosophers. Can the gospel gain a foothold here? How can Paul approach sincere seekers in a way that leads them to confess Jesus as Lord?

Teaching Outline	Daily Bible Readings	
I. The Athenian Gods—22:23	Mon.	All Must Repent *Acts 17:16-34*
II. The Actual God—24-28	Tue.	Instructed by an Angel *Acts 10:1-8*
A. Services He doesn't need, 24-25	Wed.	Peter's Vision *Acts 10:9-16*
B. Extent of His rule, 26-28	Thu.	Peter Has Visitors *Acts 16:17-23a*
III. The Appropriate Response—29-31	Fri.	No One Is "Unclean" *Acts 10:23b-33*
IV. The Actual Response—32-34	Sat.	No Partiality *Actds 10:34-38*
	Sun.	Salvation Is for All *Romans 1:8-17*

Verse by Verse

I. The Athenian Gods—22-23

22 Then Paul stood in the midst of Mars' hill, and said, Ye men of Athens, I perceive that in all things ye are too superstitious.

23 For as I passed by, and beheld your devotions, I found an altar with this inscription, TO THE UNKNOWN GOD. Whom therefore ye ignorantly worship, him declare I unto you.

Faithful to his mission to proclaim the gospel first to the Jews, Paul had begun his important mission in Athens at the local synagogue (vs. 17). The city had declined since the "Golden Age of Greece" some three centuries earlier, when it was the center of Greek learning and the arts. Here Socrates, Plato and Aristotle and the various schools of Greek philosophy, including the Epicureans and Stoics of verse 18, had flourished, then waned.

From the synagogue, Paul had moved to the bustling *agora* or marketplace (vs. 17). There his reference to the resurrection of Jesus had created such a hubbub that he was escorted to the quieter and more dignified setting of "the hill of Mars," or the Areopagus (the same word is used in both verses 19 and 22). Paul has been asked to appear before a kind of court or council that at times considered criminal charges; but the scene here seems to be more of a courtesy hearing than an arraignment. The council seems genuinely interested in what this teacher has to say (see vss. 19-20).

The term translated "superstitious" in the KJV also means "religious," and Paul probably means it in the latter sense, as somewhat of a compliment (see the NIV). Although his message certainly challenges the *kind* of religion practiced in Athens, it is more characteristic of Paul to begin on a more conciliatory note.

Next Paul explains that he is not really setting forth a "strange" god (as charged in vs. 18). He is championing the cause of the God the Athenians had labeled "Unknown." The statue Paul saw may have been erected in vague acknowledgment that Zeus, Apollo, Athena and the myriad other Greek gods were simply inadequate to explain the divine nature. Or the idol may have been worshiped as a safeguard against failing to mention some god.

Again, the KJV "ignorant" implies a harshness not found in the original. Paul is actually making a play on the title "Unknown God" by saying "Although you were unknowing of it, 'The Unknown God' is the real God." Like any good missionary, Paul seizes on a point familiar to his audience and uses it as a springboard to the Good News.

II. The Actual God—24-28

A. Services He doesn't need, 24-25

24 God that made the world and all things therein, seeing that he is Lord of heaven and earth, dwelleth not in temples made with hands;

25 Neither is worshipped with men's hands, as though he needed any thing, seeing he giveth to all life, and breath, and all things;

Now Paul challenges t he way his audience has worshiped "The Unknown God." Above Paul stood the magnificent temple of Athena, Athens' patron goddess. All around him were numerous statues of other gods. At various times, worshipers would leave garlands and gifts of food at the feet of these statues and in the temples and shrines of the gods and goddesses. Such "service" at the hands of mere humans is not what the True God needs or wants, Paul says. It is God who gives *us* food and shelter, life and breath; and it is demeaning to consider Him as Someone who needs our care.

B. The extent of His rule, 26-28

26 And hath made of one blood all nations of men for to dwell on the face of the earth, and hath determined the times before appointed, and the bounds of their habitation;

27 That they should seek the Lord, if haply they might feel after him, and find him, though he be not far from every one of us:

28 For in him we live, and move, and have our being; as certain also of your own poets have said, For we are also his offspring.

Here Paul states a truth it took medical science centuries to rediscover: all races on earth have the same lifeblood flowing in their veins. Paul uses this fact as a two-edged sword. On the one hand it indicates that all people share a common origin and are therefore "kin" to each other. On the other hand this commonality shows that not just Christians but even unbelievers are subject to their Creator's rule. They should therefore worship Him, not the pagan gods.

The orderly and helpful progression of the "seasons" is one way that God's universal providence can be seen. The "bounds" are not to be understood as zones foreordained for certain races to occupy, but the "setting" of the good, green earth God gave to all. Paul's point is that people of good hearts can come part-way to God through nature; although it takes the gospel to complete the journey back to Him (see also Rom. 1:19-20).

Again showing his skill at using an argument from a people's own culture, Paul shows that one of the Athenians' own poets made a similar point. Scholars trace this saying to a poem written in 310 B.C. by one Aratus. This poet also affirmed that all people grew out of the human race created by God. The quotation reinforces Paul's point that his message is not in behalf of a "strange" god; it is a reminder of the God the Athenians had forgotten.

III. The Appropriate Response—29-31

29 Forasmuch then as we are the offspring of God, we ought not to think that the Godhead is like unto gold, or silver, or stone, graven by art and man's device.

30 And the times of this ignorance God winked at; but now commandeth all men every where to repent:

31 Because he hath appointed a day, in the which he will judge the world in righteousness by that man whom he hath ordained; whereof he hath given assurance unto all men, in that he hath raised him from the dead.

Now Paul aims drives his point home. If the "Godhead" (meaning "the Divine," not necessarily a reference to the Trinity), is the true God, we should not be expressing allegiance to false gods by making idols in their honor. Although God tolerated such ignorant worship in previous ages, the coming of His Son Jesus constituted not only salvation but judgment on such false worship (see John 16:7-11), requiring repentance from both false worship and false deeds.

The judgment "in principle" seen in the entrance of Christ into the world will be judgment "in fact" at the Last Day. To assure his hearers that Jesus can in fact return for this Day, Paul returns to the theme that had so excited the mob in the marketplace: the resurrection of Christ. Paul proclaims this crowning fact of the gospel, instead of arguing philosophy with his audience (see 1 Cor. 15:1-4).

IV. The Actual Response—32-34

32 And when they heard of the resurrection of the dead, some mocked: and others said, We will hear thee again of this matter.

33 So Paul departed from among them.

34 Howbeit certain men clave unto him, and believed: among the which was Dionysius the Areopagite, and a woman named Damaris, and others with them.

Some Athenians may have mocked the idea of the resurrection because it cannot be tested by experience. Others may have rejected it simply because they were only dabblers in religion, more interested in entertaining new ideas (vs. 21) than in exerting the effort to discern truth and personally commit to it. Still, Paul's message is accepted by a member of the "Areopagus" or Mars Hill council, and by a woman and others who go unnamed.

Despite this modest response from Paul's message, the seed of the gospel has now been sown in Europe. It will take root and grow far beyond the results reported here.

Evangelistic Emphasis

We live in a religious nation where people are starving for the Word of God. Those two images don't seem to go together, but it is true. There are very few atheists in the nation. Surveys indicate that more than 90 percent of our people believe in and practice prayer. Almost 95 pecent of persons surveyed say they believe in God. Yet if we are so religious why is our nation in such a fix? The answer is found in the fact that we live in a religious nation that is no longer a Christian nation.

Religion has become a multi-billion dollar a year industry. The major bookstores all have large sections dedicated to the study of religion. The personal enrichment section and the religious section are often indistinguishable. Folks who are good members of your church read their horoscope, believe in channeling and perhaps have crystals in their homes. We have believed all of the hype that has come our way. So much of this religious salesmanship is done under the name and banner of Jesus. Much of it is leading people down the path of deception.

Our world is much like first century Athens. They had many gods. They had a statue to the "unknown god," so they would not offend any god by omission. Paul defined for the Athenians who that God was. We are called as Christians to proclaim Jesus Christ as THE way, THE truth and THE life. It is a message our world is waiting to hear. We don't need any more religions. We must offer persons a personal relationship with a living Lord.

Memory Selection

God . . . commandeth all men every where to repent: Because he hath appointed a day, in the which he will judge the world in righteousness by that man whom he hath given assurance unto all men, in that he hath raised him from the dead.—*Acts 17: 30-31*

God is very clear about His expectations for us. He sent His Son Jesus Christ to die for our sins. He pointed the way to eternal life. Through the power of the Holy Spirit we are given all the tools and gifts we need to live faithfully for Christ. All this was done on our behalf. God placed us in the fields to tend and harvest the crop. He left us to complete His work of sharing God's love and justice with our world.

His expectations are clear because one day the world will be judged by Christ. All of your words, deeds, thoughts and motivations will come under the scrutiny of God's eye. This might make some members of the Body of Christ nervous. With judgment day coming, God is preparing us for that day. His call to the church and to the world is to repent. The word "repent" means "to turn around."

God warned us that if we continue on the path of self-centeredness we are on the wrong path. Self-centeredness is a sin. We are called to make God a priority. He will judge. He will also forgive and restore. Don't you want to face judgment day with a clean conscience? You can if you will fall on your knees before God and repent of your sins.

Weekday Problems

Larry Maxwell was a good old boy. He could fix anything that had a motor. If you had a car or a boat that wouldn't run, Larry could make it run. He knew where to hunt, too. He was an avid dear hunter. He spent most of the time between October and January in the woods hunting deer. When the summer rolled around, Larry was on the banks of the local pond fishing. Larry was a good husband and a loving father. He never met a stranger and would do anything in the world for anyone. That is what his wife told James Martin who was the pastor of Faith Church.

"Did your husband attend church?" asked Rev. Martin.

"No," said Jenny Maxwell, "he didn't much believe in organized religion. He was a good man. I know that he is with Jesus."

"Did he read the Bible?"

"No, Larry said he learned from God through nature."

James Martin tried one more question in preparing to preach Larry Maxwell's funeral. "Did your husband ever make a profession of faith in Jesus?"

"No," said Jenny. "I'm sorry I haven't been much help to you. I know you'll preach Larry a fine funeral."

James Martin left the Maxwell home shaking his head. What could he say about Larry? How could he maintain integrity and still comfort the family? What if someone asked him what he believed about Larry's eternal destiny?

*If you were Pastor Martin how would you handle this funeral?

*Do you believe that everyone is judged equally?

*Would you talk to this family about judgment? If so, when?

This Lesson in Your Life

Paul faced a most difficult audience in Athens. They were religious philosophers. They were like some audiences ministers preach to in our day. Much like the ancient Greeks, the modern American doesn't wish to offend any god. So sitting on the pew with you this day are people who don't really believe all the tenets of the faith. They treat religion like it is some grand Cafeteria. If love and grace are needed, these persons find a church that offers an abundance of love and grace. If direction and rigidity are needed there are several congregations that fill that need.

The average church member did not grow up in the church which he now attends. Many didn't grow up in the denomination with which their current church is affiliated. Paul warned Timothy about a time that was coming when "people will not put up with sound doctrine, but having itching ears, they will accumulate for themselves teachers to suit their own desires" (2 Tim. 4:3, NRSV). The average preacher stays a little under eighteen months in a church. Can you see what one of the problems might be? With pastoral and lay mobility, proper theology often suffers.

So many people are close to the cross and yet far from the Christ. They have enough religion to make them comfortable. They don't see the need for repentance. They are not sure that church attendance is that important. They long for a minister who won't make them uncomfortable, while comforting them in their afflictions.

When the faith of the church doesn't suit their fancy they go after all of our cultural "gods." Persons will try many things to be happy. They will hinge their happiness on the acquisition of things. They will worship at the throne of pleasure. They will feast at the meal of self-gratification. They will profess to be good and religious persons.

Their comfort is that they don't really believe in a judgment. The only one capable of judging our world rightly is Christ. Paul proclaimed to the Athenians that Jesus, because of the resurrection, was deemed worthy to judge humanity. What most of the religious people miss is that one day we will all stand in judgment for our words as well as our deeds.

The gods we have formed from our savings accounts or our seeking to have our own way will not serve us well in that day. Judgment will be based upon our faithfulness to Jesus the Christ. Unlike the Athenians who were afraid of offending the "UNKNOWN GOD," we might turn our attention to not offending the Lord God.

He calls us all to repentance. That call to repentance is a call to come home. We are all like wandering sheep. We must see what is beyond the next hill. We have to look in the next valley. Before we are aware of being lost, we are lost. Our only hope is to turn in repentance back to our Creator and Redeemer. That is all that Christ demands.

Repentance is an act of humility. It is admitting that life cannot be lived without a Savior. That admission is hard for people trained in a self-satisfying religion. So many of the "pop spiritualities" begin with the notion that we all are "little gods." How strange it is that if we are all "little gods" we are so very lost. Repentance is an admission that salvation is not something we can accomplish, no matter how hard we work. It acknowledges that we are the creatures and God is the Creator. Salvation is a gift which is freely given, not earned. That gift cost God his only Son. It won for us the opportunity to experience the new birth and eternal life. Our only hope at Judgment is to be clothed in His righteousness and love.

Seed Thoughts

1. What was different about the "men of Athens" in relationship to the other groups to which Paul preached?

These people were Gentiles. There were no Jews in the audience.

2. How did the audience affect the way Paul delivered his message?

Paul didn't begin with a rehearsal of Jewish history, but with where these people were. They were "religious" people.

3. What had Paul noticed as he walked around the city of Athens?

He had seen all of the shrines and temples dedicated to the various "gods."

4. Which altar caught Paul's attention and how did he use that altar?

Paul saw an altar dedicated to the "UNKNOWN GOD." In his message he said that this was actually the true God.

5. What was Paul's first affirmation about the nature of this UNKNOWN GOD?

The God that Paul was describing was the God who had created the world and everything in it.

---

1. What was different about the "men of Athens" in relationship to the other groups to which Paul preached?

2. How did the audience affect the way Paul delivered his message?

3. What had Paul noticed as he walked around the city of Athens?

4. Which altar caught Paul's attention and how did he use that altar?

5. What was Paul's first affirmation about the nature of this UNKNOWN GOD?

6. According to Paul where does this Creator God reside?

7. What was the next major point in Paul's message to the men of Athens?

8. According to Paul what was the purpose behind creation?

9. If we are the offspring of God, what should we assume is true about God?

10. What was the proof, according to Paul, that this God should be worshiped as the only true God?

(Continued next page)

219

These people were Gentiles. There were no Jews in the audience.

Paul didn't begin with a rehearsal of Jewish history, but with where these people were. They were "religious" people.

He had seen all of the shrines and temples dedicated to the various "gods."

Paul saw an altar dedicated to the "UNKNOWN GOD." In his message he said that this was actually the true God.

The God that Paul was describing was the God who had created the world and everything in it.

This God did not live in temples made with human hands. He didn't need anything made from human hands.

This creator God also make mankind. He started human creation with only one man, i.e., Adam.

God created mankind so that they would come to know Him and His love for them.

God is not made of gold or silver or stone. He is not the reflection of any object made by a human.

Paul pointed to the resurrection of Jesus Christ as the evidence that God is Lord above all.

6. According to Paul where does this Creator God reside?

This God did not live in temples made with human hands. He didn't need anything made from human hands.

7. What was the next major point in Paul's message to the men of Athens?

This creator God also make mankind. He started human creation with only one man, i.e., Adam.

8. According to Paul what was the purpose behind creation?

God created mankind so that they would come to know Him and His love for them.

9. If we are the offspring of God, what should we assume is true about God?

God is not made of gold or silver or stone. He is not the reflection of any object made by a human.

10. What was the proof, according to Paul, that this God should be worshiped as the only true God?

Paul pointed to the resurrection of Jesus Christ as the evidence that God is Lord above all.

Civic Responsibility

*L*et every soul be subject unto the higher powers. For there is no power but of God: the powers that be are ordained of God.

2 Whosoever therefore resisteth the power, resisteth the ordinance of God: and they that resist shall receive to themselves damnation.

3 For rulers are not a terror to good works, but to the evil. Wilt thou then not be afraid of the power? do that which is good, and thou shalt have praise of the same:

4 For he is the minister of God to thee for good. But if thou do that which is evil, be afraid; for he beareth not the sword in vain: for he is the minister of God, a revenger to execute wrath upon him that doeth evil.

5 Wherefore ye must needs be subject, not only for wrath, but also for conscience sake.

6 For this cause pay ye tribute also: for they are God's ministers, attending continually upon this very thing.

7 Render therefore to all their dues: tribute to whom tribute is due; custom to whom custom; fear to whom fear; honour to whom honour.

8 Owe no man any thing, but to love one another: for he that loveth another hath fulfilled the law.

9 For this, Thou shalt not commit adultery, Thou shalt not kill, Thou shalt not steal, Thou shalt not bear false witness, Thou shalt

not covet; and if there be any other commandment, it is briefly comprehended in this saying, namely, Thou shalt love thy neighbour as thyself.

10 Love worketh no ill to his neighbour: therefore love is the fulfilling of the law.

11 And that, knowing the time, that now it is high time to awake out of sleep: for now is our salvation nearer than when we believed.

12 The night is far spent, the day is at hand: let us therefore cast off the works of darkness, and let us put on the armour of light.

13 Let us walk honestly, as in the day; not in rioting and drunkenness, not in chambering and wantonness, not in strife and envying.

14 But put ye on the Lord Jesus Christ, and make not provision for the flesh, to fulfil the lusts thereof.

Feb. 7

Memory Selection
Romans 13:1

Background Scripture
Romans 12:9+13:14

Devotional Reading
Psalm 15:1-5

Printed Scripture
Romans 13

221

Teacher's Target

Lesson purpose: *To explore Paul's teaching on how Christians are to relate to the society about them.*

The great Christian teacher Augustine described Christians as inhabitants of "The City of God." He and many others since asked how residents of this "city" should relate to those in "The City of Man"—the political and social structures about them.

Although Romans 13 does not claim to be a comprehensive treatise on the subject, it raises several crucial issues. Paul is mainly concerned to prescribe a Christian life-style that makes a positive impact on the world.

You may want to allow the issues Paul touches on to become a springboard for discussions on contemporary topics. For example, What are Christians to do when civil law opposes Christian principles? And does Paul's teaching about government's "bearing the sword" support capital punishment? Guard against allowing such discussions to stray too far from Paul's central point: Christians are to be salt and leaven in the world about them.

Lesson Introduction

Paul's letter to the Romans follows his typical approach: *theology* first, and *Christian living* second. In Romans theology comes first because Paul wants us to understand that we are saved by grace, not by works.

Yet he is equally insistent that Christians live in a way that shows they have been touched by God's grace. Here Paul's ethical teaching counters some Jewish and Christian revolutionary tendencies that caused them to despise current Roman rule. Some may have drawn from Christ's statement, "My kingdom is not of this world?" that Christians are so otherworldly they can ignore secular civil power. Others may have drawn the same conclusion from their belief that Christ's second coming was just on the horizon.

Paul, however, affirms the necessity of civil order and the authority of the state, regardless of any delay in the Second Coming. Unbelievers are watching, and Paul wants them to see that Christians take Christ's ethical message as seriously as they do His message of salvation.

Teaching Outline	Daily Bible Readings
I. Respecting the Government—1-7 　A. The state's power, 1-4 　B. The conscience's call, 5-7 II. Living in Love—8-10 　A. The unpaid debt, 8a 　B. Love and the Law, 8b-10 III. Walking in the Light—11-14 　A. Noting the time, 11-12 　B. Walking the talk, 13-14	**Mon.** Hate the Evil, Do the Good 　*Romans 12:9-21* **Tue.** Be Subject to the State 　*Romans 13:1-7* **Wed.** Love Does No Wrong 　*Romans 13:8-14* **Thu.** Walking Blamelessly 　*Psalm 15:1-5* **Fri.** Accept Authority 　*1 Peter 2:11-17* **Sat.** For Life and Godliness 　*2 Peter 1:2-11* **Sun.** A Living Sacrifice 　*Romans 12:1-8*

Verse by Verse

I. Respecting the Government—1-7
A. The state's power, 1-4

1 Let every soul be subject unto the higher powers. For there is no power but of God: the powers that be are ordained of God.

2 Whosoever therefore resisteth the power, resisteth the ordinance of God: and they that resist shall receive to themselves damnation.

3 For rulers are not a terror to good works, but to the evil. Wilt thou then not be afraid of the power? do that which is good, and thou shalt have praise of the same:

4 For he is the minister of God to thee for good. But if thou do that which is evil, be afraid; for he beareth not the sword in vain: for he is the minister of God, a revenger to execute wrath upon him that doeth evil.

"Soul" simply stands for "person"; and every person exists in relationship with certain structures such as the family, the fellowship of believers, and, here, the nation. As corrupt as Roman rule could be, Paul teaches that the power of the state is better than anarchy. Virtually all forms of government have laws based on universal principles of morality, and God has ordained them for the good of society. Paul himself had occasion to call on these laws to rescue him from unjust treatment (see Acts 26:9-12).

Of course even devout believers have found it difficult to obey this counsel to the letter. Indeed, when the laws of the "powers that be" conflict with the laws of God, "We ought to obey God rather than men" (Acts 5:29). The revolutionaries in the American colonies felt they were rebelling not against the authority of legitimate government but against tyranny. They believed that English rule had become a terror to the good instead of to the evil.

Still, Rome was also tyrannical; and the overall thrust of New Testament teaching is that believers are to submit to governmental powers (see also 1 Tim. 2:1-2; Tit. 3:1; 1 Pet. 2:13-17). In our own country we are blessed with a government that is committed to the democratic process, offering avenues of change that avoid violent rebellion.

Verse 4 seems to authorize capital punishment, if it is the outcome of due process under the law. As a Jew, Paul is guided by the Old Testament rule against murder ("Thou shalt not kill"), while recognizing that some deeds rightly earn the death sentence (see Exod. 21:14).

B. The conscience's call, 5-7

5 Wherefore ye must needs be subject, not only for wrath, but also for conscience sake.

6 For for this cause pay ye tribute also: for they are God's minis-

ters, attending continually upon this very thing.

7 Render therefore to all their dues: tribute to whom tribute is due; custom to whom custom; fear to whom fear; honour to whom honour.

Despite Paul's teaching that the state "beareth not the sword in vain," Christians should obey the laws of the land for a higher motive: for conscience's sake. While others do right for fear of being punished, Christians are to make just laws a part of their inner law, the consciousness of sin.

In verses 6 and 7, Paul extends this principle to paying "tribute" or taxes. The U. S. income tax laws depend heavily on this exhortation, counting on the trustworthiness of people who simply choose to report earnings not recorded by employers. The breakdown of this "honor system" would plunge the nation into financial and moral chaos.

II. Living in Love—8-10
A. The unpaid debt, 8a

8 Owe no man any thing, but to love one another:

While some have taken this teaching to forbid borrowing money, Paul is no doubt commanding Christians not to default on debts. They are not to refuse to pay taxes and other obligations. The exception arises from "the law of love." The fact that God is love, and has loved us supremely in the gift of His Son, creates a debt we can never repay but can gladly keep on paying on.

B. Love and the Law, 8b-10

8b for he that loveth another hath fulfilled the law.

9 For this, Thou shalt not commit adultery, Thou shalt not kill, Thou shalt not steal, Thou shalt not bear false witness, Thou shalt not covet; and if there be any other commandment, it is briefly comprehended in this saying, namely, Thou shalt love thy neighbour as thyself.

10 Love worketh no ill to his neighbour: therefore love is the fulfilling of the law.

Although we can never fulfill, or cease paying on, our debt to love others, Paul, as a Jew, is concerned to show that we can fulfill the Law of Moses by loving. Then he summarizes sketchily the Ten Commandments to show that each one is based on, and fulfilled by, Christ's "new commandment" that we love one another (John 13:34). It would be impossible truly to love God and others while living in continuous disobedience to these fundamental laws of godly behavior. Therefore "love is the fulfilling of the law."

III. Walking in the Light—11-14
A. Noting the time, 11-12

11 And that, knowing the time, that now it is high time to awake out of sleep: for now is our salvation nearer than when we believed.

12 The night is far spent, the day is at hand: let us therefore cast off the works of darkness, and let us put on the armour of light.

Now Paul adds the urgency of *time* to his teaching on the need for Christians to support the powers that be. Ethical exhortations in the New Testament are typically accompanied by this reminder that we live in view of the Day of Judgment. This is not done to create a sense of guilt but of *urgency* and *consistency*.

The urgency arises in view of the Second Coming. When Paul says that salvation is "nearer than when we believed" (vs. 11b), he means that "We are farther down the road toward the End than we were when we became Christians" (as in the NIV), rather than indicating that "It's later than we thought." Although many early Christians expected Christ's return to be immediate, every day it is postponed means that we have that much less time to honor the Name of Christ by the way we live.

Putting on the armor of God, or practicing Christian ethics, is also the only consistent way to live. Since initial salvation is a coming into the light, it is inconsistent to continue to walk in the darkness (see also Eph. 5:8-14). In view of the approaching Dawn of Christ's Second Coming, Christians have no business living in the darkness of sin.

B. Walking the talk, 13-14

13 Let us walk honestly, as in the day; not in rioting and drunkenness, not in chambering and wantonness, not in strife and envying.

14 But put ye on the Lord Jesus Christ, and make not provision for the flesh, to fulfil the lusts thereof.

Again we see the theme of living honestly, in the full light of the gospel, instead of partaking of wickedness for which people often seek the cover of darkness. Six acts of wickedness are specifically named, perhaps because they were special temptations in the Roman and Greek communities of Paul's day. "Rioting" refers not just to civil disobedience but to any loud revelry. "Drunkenness" is from a word that also gives us *methyl* as in methyl alcohol. "Chambering" is from the Greek word for "bed," and refers especially to sexual immorality (as in the NIV).

"Wantonness" (NIV "debauchery") refers to licentious or indecent conduct in general. "Strife" is from the Greek word *eris*, after the goddess of discord, reminding us that stirring up needless strife among people is as serious as the other forms of immorality listed here. Finally, "envying" or jealousy, often the root of strife,is also included in this list of forbidden ethical traits.

There is a more positive way to "walk in the light" than trying to remember a list of forbidden steps. Paul completes the passage by reminding us that "putting on" Christ as one would don a garment is like "dressing for success" in living the Christian life.

Evangelistic Emphasis

Scripture was given for our instruction in faithful discipleship. Being a faithful disciple of Jesus Christ can mean doing things we don't like to do. Paul wrote, "Pay to all what is due them—taxes to whom taxes are due, revenue to whom revenue is due, respect to whom respect is due, honor to whom honor is due" (Rom. 3:7). That verse brings under the lamp of conviction several "soap boxes" that preachers like to climb upon. Faithful discipleship involves being a good citizen.

As the church reaches out to this nation we must remember that being a good neighbor has a positive influence. There are civic areas in which the church is called to be prophetic, even called to protest. The church can only be prophetic from within the civic community. Only as we act responsibly as citizens will our calls for change be heard and heeded.

Storm clouds are on the horizon. The church and the nation are headed for a clash. The good news is that God will still be God no matter what a government might dictate to the church. God and His people will always find a way to share the love of Christ with a world desperately in need of Him. The good news personally is that if a nation can't stop God, then neither can any problem in your life.

Live as a victorious Christian and a good American.

• • • • • • • • • •

Memory Selection

Let every soul be subject unto the higher powers. For there is no power but of God: the powers that be are ordained of God.—*Romans 13:1*

Someone has to be in charge. Paul states that all authority is of God and from God. The Apostles' words, "Let every soul be subject unto the higher powers. . ." rub against some other natural inclinations of our souls. The whole notion of being subject to anyone or anything is foreign to the American psyche. The history books tell us that on July 4, 1776, our forefathers formally declared a mutiny from England. We are a nation of fiercely independent rebels.

The notions of authority and obedience are under attack in our time, Engaged couple routinely ask before the wedding ceremony, "Do we have to promise to obey?" Ministers have their authority challenged openly in churches. We challenge the government's right to deny us our rights. We are a rebellious bunch!

Yet, at the heart of our faith is the called to be "subject" to authority. Our authority is ultimately God. The next time you feel your rebellious side boiling over ask, "against whom am I rebelling?"

Weekday Problems

The reactions from members of the Finance Committee ranged from resignation to outrage. The financial secretary at Big Church had spent an hour going over the ways in which the church was in violation of current tax law. The indiscretions of Big Church ranged from not reporting income for teenagers working in the nursery to "money laundering."

The main problem as Frank Johnson saw it was how the new laws would hurt Mrs. Theo Wallace. Miss Theo, as everyone knew her, was a widowed saint of Big Church. Her husband Harry had been the church organist for as long as anyone could remember. When he died, members of the church felt compelled to supplement Theo's meager pension. They gave donations to the church in Theo's name. The church treasurer wrote a check from these donations to Miss Theo. For years the members had taken a tax deduction on the amount they gave the church for Miss Theo. Miss Theo never felt like she had to claim this gift income from the church. The financial secretary told the finance committee that this practice was at best not good business and at worst, illegal.

There were other issues that were tax related and had the committee all stirred up. "Why do we have to obey the tax laws? We are a church!" Those sentiments were expressed by the chairman as the meeting got real hot.

*Ask the minister to share with your class what laws a church must obey.

*Do you think the church should be required to obey tax laws?

*Do you think the church should be regulated by the government?

Statements on the State

The object of government in peace and in war is not the glory of rulers or of races, but the happiness of the common man.—*William, Lord Beveridge*

* * *

Everything goes wrong for a government which is going wrong.—*Richard Crossman*

* * *

Governments never learn. Only people learn.—*Milton Friedman*

* * *

Any woman who understands the problems of running a home will be nearer to understanding the problems of running a country.—*Margaret Thatcher*

* * *

You should esteem the sword or governmental authority as highly as the estate of marriage, or husbandry, or any other calling which God has instituted.—*Martin Luther*

This Lesson in Your Life

On the surface this appears to be a straight forward lesson. Paul wrote, "Be subject to the higher powers" (Rom.13:1). Yet his teaching suggests at least three major areas for discussion.

The first has to do with how the Bible views governments and governing authorities. Paul in Romans was speaking personally and historically. The church was only a few short years away from a major outbreak of systematic persecutions. Church tradition says that Peter and Paul both died in the persecution instituted by Nero. Until that time, the Roman Empire largely ignored the church.

By the time the Revelation was given to John, the view of governments had changed. Many scholars identify the beast in Revelation as an evil governmental system, with Christians called to withstand its evil powers. This raises such questions as: Should a Christian ever rebel against authority? Or become involved with a para-military group that protrets governmental policy?

The second area of discussion might be the understanding of democracy as it is connected to Christianity. After World War II, America tried to introduce democracy into conquered nations. The two greatest experiments in American democracy were in Japan and Italy. Both of these experiments in democracy failed miserably, and for the same reason. Neither country had the theological foundation necessary to build a democracy. A democracy is built upon certain assumptions about the nature of humanity, keeping laws and involving God in the process of government. You might spend some time reflecting on how our nation has changed in your lifetime in terms of our democratic freedoms.

As the church is less able legally to influence society, we see society changing in subtle ways. Rather than individual responsibility, our government is in the process of creating a cradle-to-grave care system. A church that once enjoyed complete freedom in this country is seeing that freedom eroded. More than a few cases are pending in Federal Tax Courts challenging the church's non-profit status. Our failing is that we are not keeping up on what the government is doing to limit the access the church has to society. Paul clearly states that authorities exist and were instituted by God. If the government turns against the church would that mean that God is using the government to bring judgment on the church? Or is God calling the church to challenge what the government is doing to the church and to society?

The third issue is the the entire area of church-state relations, and the Christian's involvement in politics. Many Christians have not been involved in politics because they believe it is dirty business. We, as a church, fail to understand political power and how it relates to our continued freedom in ministry. We fail to organize to influence government policy. We fear controversy. We fear the compromises necessary in the political process. Too often the church emphasizes personalities and single issues rather than looking at a broad sweep of political issue. And, finally, we misunderstand historically the doctrine of separation of church and state. Did the founding fathers mean by this doctrine that our laws should not be based on religious foundations? Are churches to be subject to the same rules as other institutions in our society?

Seed Thoughts

1. What did Paul state is the origin and authority for all civil government?

Governing authorities exist and have been instituted by God. God is the ultimate authority behind all other authority.

2. What should be the Christian's response to the authority of government?

As a good Christian a person should also be a good citizen. A good Christian citizen submits to the authority of the government.

3. What, according to Paul, was the penalty for not obeying the authority of government?

By implication the person would receive not only the wrath of the government, but would receive the judgment of God.

4. What two motivating factors does Paul give for the Christian to obey governmental authority?

The Christian is compelled by both the fear of wrath and because of conscience to obey government.

5. What four specific civic duties are spelled out in Romans 13?

Christians are to pay taxes, pay all revenue that is due and show respect and honor where those are due.

1. What did Paul state is the origin and authority for all civil government?

2. What should be the Christian's response to the authority of government?

3. What, according to Paul, was the penalty for not obeying the authority of government?

4. What two motivating factors does Paul give for the Christian to obey governmental authority?

5. What four specific civic duties are spelled out in Romans 13?

6. What other personal advice did Paul give to the church?

7. Which commandments did Paul list?

8. Why do you think Paul emphasized these commandments?

9. What behaviors were the Christians to avoid?

10. Why were Christians called to avoid such behavior?

(Continued next page)

Governing authorities exist and have been instituted by God. God is the ultimate authority behind all other authority.

As a good Christian a person should also be a good citizen. A good Christian citizen submits to the authority of the government.

By implication the person would receive not only the wrath of the government, but would receive the judgment of God.

The Christian is compelled by both the fear of wrath and because of conscience to obey government.

Christians are to pay taxes, pay all revenue that is due and show respect and honor where those are due.

Paul admonished the people in the church to "owe no one anything."

He listed the commandments prohibiting adultery, murder, stealing and coveting.

These four commandments specifically deal with personal interaction. They were vital in keeping the fellowship unified.

The were to avoid reveling, drunkenness, debauchery, licentiousness, quarreling and jealousy.

These behaviors gratify the flesh. The Christian was to make no provision for the flesh.

6. What other personal advice did Paul give to the church?

Paul admonished the people in the church to "owe no one anything."

7. Which commandments did Paul list?

He listed the commandments prohibiting adultery, murder, stealing and coveting.

8. Why do you think Paul emphasized these commandments?

These four commandments specifically deal with personal interaction. They were vital in keeping the fellowship unified.

9. What behaviors were the Christians to avoid?

The were to avoid reveling, drunkenness, debauchery, licentiousness, quarreling and jealousy.

10. Why were Christians called to avoid such behavior?

These behaviors gratify the flesh. The Christian was to make no provision for the flesh.

Caring Community

*W*hen ye come together therefore into one place, this is not to eat the Lord's supper.

21 For in eating every one taketh before other his own supper: and one is hungry, and another is drunken.

22 What? have ye not houses to eat and to drink in? or despise ye the church of God, and shame them that have not? What shall I say to you? shall I praise you in this? I praise you not.

1 Cor. 11:20-34

23 For I have received of the Lord that which also I delivered unto you, That the Lord Jesus the same night in which he was betrayed took bread:

24 And when he had given thanks, he brake it, and said, Take, eat: this is my body, which is broken for you: this do in remembrance of me.

25 After the same manner also he took the cup, when he had supped, saying, This cup is the new testament in my blood: this do ye, as oft as ye drink it, in remembrance of me.

26 For as often as ye eat this bread and drink this cup, ye do shew the Lord's death till he come.

27 Wherefore whosoever shall eat this bread, and drink this cup of the Lord, unworthily, shall be guilty of the body and blood of the Lord.

28 But let a man examine himself, and so let him eat of that bread, and drink of that cup.

29 For he that eateth and drinketh unworthily, eateth and drinketh damnation to himself, not discerning the Lord's body.

30 For this cause many are weak and sickly among you, and many sleep.

31 For if we would judge ourselves, we should not be judged.

32 But when we are judged, we are chastened of the Lord, that we should not be condemned with the world.

33 Wherefore, my brethren, when ye come together to eat, tarry one for another.

34 And if any man hunger, let him eat at home; that ye come not together unto condemnation. And the rest will I set in order when I come.

Feb. 14

Memory Selection
1 Corinthians 11:28-29

Background Scripture
1 Corinthians 11:17-34

Devotional Reading
1 Corinthians 12:14-27

Printed Scripture
1 Corinthians 11:20-34

Teacher's Target

Lesson purpose: *To examine the roots of the Lord's Supper, with an eye to learning basic attitudes that contribute to the formation of genuine community.*

The early Christians were a diverse lot. They consisted of Jew and Gentile, the poor and the rich, male and female, Roman soldiers and Jewish zealots. Yet the apostle Paul was charged with welding all such factions into "one body." Where in the world could they all come together as one?

Only at the foot of the Cross could it happen. It was there that all kinds of people confessed that they were part of the same race—sinners. It was also at the Cross that they claimed the common hope of salvation, the sacrifice of Christ.

The Lord's Supper was instituted as a feast commemorating this sacrifice. Note in this lesson how the Supper, properly observed, serves to form Christians into a caring community; and how treating this historic rite carelessly contributes also to careless human relationships.

Lesson Introduction

Since Christ instituted the Lord's Supper during a Jewish Passover Feast, the historic Christian meal shares in the spiritual force that unified the Jews Moses led out of Egyptian captivity. Sharing the Passover lamb and marking their doorposts with blood helped transform the people into a nation. By participating in the feast, descendants of Abraham and a motley collection of other slaves confessed their common need for deliverance. Fellow slaves who may have been quarreling the day before the exodus were bound together in both a fellowship of suffering and of hope.

As we shall see, the Christians at Corinth had allowed the way they celebrated the Supper to obscure this sense of community. Their practice emphasized their differences instead of their likenesses. Paul's approach to the problem provides a good opportunity for Christians today to ask: Does the way we celebrate communion foster community?

Teaching Outline	Daily Bible Readings
I. Inappropriate Meal—20-22	**Mon.** For Better, Not Worse
A. Impossible possibility, 20-21	*1 Corinthians 11:17-22*
B. Hungry? Try home! 22	**Tue.** In Remembrance of Me
II. Institution of the Supper—23-25	*1 Corinthians 11:23-24*
A. The bread, the body, 23-24	**Wed.** Origin of the Passover
B. The wine, the blood, 25	*Exodus 12:1-13*
III. Improvements Required—26-34	**Thu.** Day of Remembrance
A. Partaking worthily, 26-28	*Exodus 12:14-28*
B. The health of judgment, 29-34	**Fri.** For All the Congregation
	Exodus 12:43-51
	Sat. Remember this Day
	Exodus 13:1-16
	Sun. One Body, Many Members
	1 Corinthians 12:14-27

232

Verse by Verse

I. Inappropriate Meal—20-22

A. Impossible possibility, 20-21

20 When ye come together therefore into one place, this is not to eat the Lord's supper.

21 For in eating every one taketh before other his own supper: and one is hungry, and another is drunken.

From our earliest record, Christians met regularly on the first day of the week, apparently to commemorate Christ's resurrection in the Lord's Supper ("breaking bread," Acts 20:7). Although this was also the purpose of the assemblies at Corinth, their practice was in fact opposed to the true meaning of the Supper. Hence the KJV footnote: "Ye cannot eat the Lord's Supper."

The possibility of genuine "communion" was rendered impossible because the Corinthians were treating the Supper as a common meal. Some sources, such as Jude 12, indicate that this meal was called the "agape" (a-GAH-pe), or love feast. Like "pot-luck" suppers today, everyone brought food from home. But instead of pooling what they brought, the wealthy brought a bounteous feast of rich foods (including too much wine), the poor brought little, and each family ate separately.

From time immemorial, eating together has been a sign of fellowship. This was especially true of the Passover, the Jewish feast at which Christ instituted the Lord's Supper. Passover was a part of the miracle of Jewish unity, as thousands from throughout the world were caught up in the same sense of peoplehood, recognizing the common history and religious experience they shared. While the Lord's Supper was intended to create similar community among Christians, the way the Corinthians practiced it emphasized the participants' differences instead of what they had in common.

B. Hungry? Try home! 22

22 What? have ye not houses to eat and to drink in? or despise ye the church of God, and shame them that have not? What shall I say to you? shall I praise you in this? I praise you not.

Although common usage refers to "the church" as a building, it is actually "the body of Christ" or His people (Eph. 1:22-23). Here, therefore, "despising the church of God" means showing disrespect for the *people* of God, in this case the poor who brought little to the Sunday Supper, not to the place where they meet. Paul cannot praise the Corinthians for substituting gourmet dining and gluttony for the Lord's Supper.

II. Institution of the Supper—23-25

A. The bread, the Body, 23-24

23 For I have received of the Lord that which also I delivered unto you,

That the Lord Jesus the same night in which he was betrayed took bread:

24 And when he had given thanks, he brake it, and said, Take, eat: this is my body, which is broken for you: this do in remembrance of me.

These famous "words of institution" have appropriately become the foundation of Christian observance of the Lord's Supper. The fact that Paul received instructions for the Supper directly from Christ is evidence of his apostolic authority. The words of Jesus Paul quotes from the Last Supper differ slightly when we compare them with the Gospels (see Matt. 26:26-28; Luke 22:16-20), indicating that they are not a magical saying that must be repeated verbatim at communion. They are, however, a sacred foundation for the Christian celebration of the Supper.

The term "eucharist" for the Lord's Supper grew out of the Greek word for "giving thanks" which Paul notes here. The well-known difference between Roman Catholic and Protestant thought is highlighted by the simple words of Christ, "This is my body." Reading this literally forms the basis of the doctrine of "transubstantiation," in which the substance of the bread and wine are thought to be changed at the priest's blessing into the literal body and blood of Christ. (Luther taught the doctrine of "consubstantiation," in which the body and blood are present "with, in and under" the bread and wine, while other Protestants usually understand the "ele-

ments" to be merely symbols of Christ's body and blood.)

B. The wine, the blood, 25

25 After the same manner also he took the cup, when he had supped, saying, This cup is the new testament in my blood: this do ye, as oft as ye drink it, in remembrance of me.

The author of Hebrews dwells extensively on the importance of blood in the sealing of a covenant (Heb. 9:11-12; 10:16-19). Just as the blood of animal sacrifices was a sign of the Old Covenant (or Testament), so Jesus' death testifies to God's New Covenant promise through Christ. The cup in the Lord's Supper is therefore not a symbol of drinking blood, but of the high price God paid in sending His Son to die for our sins.

The phrase "In remembrance of me" indicates the "vertical" dimension of the Lord's Supper, just as the overall teaching of this passage indicates the Supper's "horizontal" or people-recognizing dimension. Unfortunately, in our time the vertical has virtually overwhelmed the horizontal. Communion for most Christians is a time of silent meditation and inwardness,which Paul affirms here to be vitally important, but not to the exclusion of the community-building importance of the Supper.

III. Improvements Required— 26-34

A. Partaking worthily, 26-28

26 For as often as ye eat this bread and drink this cup, ye do shew the Lord's death till he come.

27 Wherefore whosoever shall

eat this bread, and drink this cup of the Lord, unworthily, shall be guilty of the body and blood of the Lord.

28 But let a man examine himself, and so let him eat of that bread, and drink of that cup.

To "show the Lord's death" is to proclaim it. This points up an often overlooked aspect of the Lord's Supper, its evangelistic dimension. Unbelievers observing Christians partaking of the feast have a visible demonstration of a basic fact of the Gospel: Christ died for our sins (1 Cor. 15:3).

Unfortunately, misunderstanding the word "unworthily" here causes many Christians to labor under the mistaken notion that they must somehow become "worthy" before partaking of the communion. The NIV helps correct this misunderstanding with the reading "in an unworthy manner." No one is "worthy" to partake of this sacred feast, but anyone can partake in a worthy *manner* by following Paul's instructions to (1) examine oneself; and (2) discern the body. The Corinthians could discern neither what the bread and wine stand for nor the plight of the poor in the body, the church, because they had perverted the Supper into a mere banquet.

B. The health of judgment, 29-34

29 For he that eateth and drinketh unworthily, eateth and drinketh damnation to himself, not discerning the Lord's body.

30 For this cause many are weak and sickly among you, and many sleep.

31 For if we would judge ourselves, we should not be judged.

32 But when we are judged, we are chastened of the Lord, that we should not be condemned with the world.

33 Wherefore, my brethren, when ye come together to eat, tarry one for another.

34 And if any man hunger, let him eat at home; that ye come not together unto condemnation. And the rest will I set in order when I come.

The language of judgment Paul uses here indicates the seriousness of the abuse of the Supper. Two things are said to be "damnable": (1) failing to discern in the bread and wine the body and blood of Christ; and (2) failing to discern the needs of "the body",other Christians.

The abuses at Corinth had left deeply damaging scars on the church. It is unclear whether the people's becoming "weak and sickly" refers to spiritual or physical problems, and whether the result was spiritual or physical "sleep" or death. What is clear is that true health could be regained only by correcting problems that had reduced true, community-building communion to revelry. Judging themselves and correcting the situations was the only way to avoid the more serious judgment of God.

235

Evangelistic Emphasis

With all the conveniences to keep us connected, most people live with a nagging sense of isolation. Behind closed doors with technology bringing the world to a television or computer screen, people live without ever knowing or being known by their neighbors. There are few places that the shy or fearful can go for social interaction. Technology can take a person around the world, yet isolation keeps us from knowing our neighbors. That is the paradox in which the church finds its ministry at the sunset of the twentieth century. We have a challenge before us to take the good news of Jesus to people who will never enter the doors of our church. One possible way of connecting to these cyber-dropouts is through the use of computer technology. Unknown ten years ago by most of us, the Internet has become a household word.

The church should claim the new technology in the spreading of the "old, old story of Jesus and His love." We have good news to tell the world. In the body of Christ persons can find meaning, belonging and community. People long for community where they can participate and contribute. The church offers an isolated world the good news that Jesus has created and is creating a community of faith. Paul's concern was that no one was left out of the community. The church is that special place where everyone should be treated equally. It is a place where all belong.

• • • • • •

Memory Selection

But let a man examine himself, and so let him eat of that bread, and drink of that cup. For he that eateth and drinketh unworthily, eateth and drinketh damnation to himself, not discerning the Lord's body.—*1 Corinthians 11:28-29*

Not so long ago, I decided to replace one of the flood lights on the outside of my house. Light fixtures purchased from hardware stores come with a warning that they are only to be installed by professional electricians. The same box will give instructions and a list of items necessary for installing the light. I picked the best time of the day to install this flood light. It was late in the afternoon, after a thunderstorm. The sky was clear. The ground on which I was standing was wet. I had my arms up to the elbows in electrical wiring. I felt no fear because I had turned off the switch to this flood light. I knew better than to try to work on a light with the switch on. However, I didn't turn the circuit breaker off. Can you see what is about to happen? I am lucky that I am not a statistic. I have developed a healthy respect for electricity and for professional electricians.

My point? The Lord's Supper is a powerful time in the worshiping community. Celebrating this rite of the church can bring great joy. It is also a dangerous thing to take unworthily. Much the same as working on a light fixture while standing in wet grass.

Weekday Problems

Randy Jackson found himself at the center of a Communion storm that he never intended to start. Randy was the summer youth director for a church near his college town. He had enjoyed the summer activities with the youth. The group had grown in number. Some profound spiritual changes had occurred in the young people. Randy was thrilled with what God had done. The last weekend before he returned to college the youth had an overnight canoe trip scheduled. It was on this canoe trip that the Lord's Supper was observed.

Randy was not an ordained minister. He had several youth on the outing who were not members of that particular church. He even had a couple of kids on the trip who had made no profession of faith in Jesus. At the campfire Randy talked about the Last Supper of Jesus. He asked the group then to share communion. The communion elements consisted of coke and a hot dog bun. The kids took communion, sang a song and started roasting marshmallows.

Before the youth group arrived back at the church news of the fireside communion service had hit the front steps of the church. Church officials greeted the group. There was also a group ready to read young Mr. Randy Jackson the riot act.

* In your opinion what did Randy Johnson do wrong?

* In your church tradition are there limits to where and when the Lord's Supper may be observed?

Wit and Wisdom

Why doesn't the guy who says "I'm no speech maker" let it go at that instead of giving a demonstration?

* * *

Many can rise to the occasion, but few know when to sit down.

* * *

Two feet on the ground are worth one in the mouth.

* * *

Many a child who watches TV for hours will go down in history, not to mention arithmetic, English, and geography.

* * *

People seldom think alike until it comes to buying wedding presents.

* * *

A halo has to fall only 11 inches to become a noose.

* * *

A man's horse sense deserts him when he's feeling his oats.

This Lesson in Your Life

Christians all over this world celebrate the Lord's Supper. It is variously called the Eucharist, Holy Communion and the Lord's Supper. Traditions surrounding the observance of this act of worship vary by denomination. The supper is variously considered a sacrament, an ordinance, a ritual and a rite of the church. All the traditions about the Lord's Supper contain both a biblical foundation and certain social and theological customs.

The problem in Corinth was not so much in the way the Lord's Supper was observed as it was in the attitude of those coming to the Supper. There are indications from this text that the Lord's Supper was once more of a meal than it is now. Some scholars suggest that the *agape* or love feast is a closer parallel to the Supper than what we observe in a church today with crackers and grape juice. So the Corinthians came to church expecting some sort of a meal. Those who arrived early were not leaving food for the ones to come after them. Paul warned against taking the Supper with a wrong attitude. The warning about observing the Supper lightly is still very appropriate, though it is rarely celebrated as part of a meal.

There are many ways to celebrate the Supper. One way is to make it a memorial of what Christ did for us. "This do in remembrance of me." Looking back at the Last Supper and Christ's final hours we are reminded of His humiliation and His love for us. The Supper keeps us focused on the great sacrifice Jesus made for us and for our salvation. In that spirit, the Lord's Supper is a solemn time. Preceding the Supper in many traditions is a time of confession, which provides opportunity to enter into the proper attitude before receiving the elements.

The Lord's Supper is also a celebration of Jesus' victory which overcame sin and death. While there is a solemn note to the service, it should also possess elements of celebration. We are reminded that on the cross Jesus paid our sin debt. In his sacrifice we are free to experience a new relationship with our Heavenly Father. We are reminded that our burdens have been lifted by His atoning work.

Finally, the Lord's Supper reminds us in bold ways that we are all equal in the community of faith. As we take communion we experience becoming "one with Christ, one with each other and one in ministry to all the world." Some Corinthians viewed this act as a time to feed their bellies and drink until drunk. They ate and drank judgment on themselves because of their egotistical sinfulness. They came to worship not to celebrate Jesus, but to fulfill their own physical desires. It was that attitude that caused them to be judged.

The time of the Lord's Supper is an opportunity for individuals to examine their lives under the light of Christ's love. It is a time to remember His sacrifice. It is a time to proclaim His rising again. It is a time to be strengthened in the Lord. The Supper is a very public act of obedience as well as a very private time of examination.

Seed Thoughts

1. Which prob lem in the church at Corinth did Paul address in 1 Corinthians 11?

The immediate problem addressed in 1 Corinthians 11 was division in the church.

2. What was the underlying cause of the divisions in the Corinthian church?

The divisions were a result of heresies in the church.

3. According to Paul, why did the divisions and factions exist in the church?

They existed so that the true believers would be seen by their actions and their beliefs.

4. What was happening in Corinth at the Lord's Supper?

Some members of the church were overeating and becoming drunk.

5. What was Paul's complaint about the church gathering for the Lord's Supper?

He was warning them that they were not treating the supper with proper respect.

---

1. Which prob lem in the church at Corinth did Paul address in 1 Corinthians 11?

2. What was the underlying cause of the divisions in the Corinthian church?

3. According to Paul, why did the divisions and factions exist in the church?

4. What was happening in Corinth at the Lord's Supper?

5. What was Paul's complaint about the church gathering for the Lord's Supper?

6. Where was this lack of respect being shown?

7. Where did Paul receive his instructions about how the Supper was to take place?

8. What was the order of the Lord's Supper, according to this passage?

9. What proclamation is made through the eating of bread and drinking of the cup?

10. What does Paul say of those who ate and drank unworthily?

(Continued next page)

The immediate problem addressed in 1 Corinthians 11 was division in the church.

The divisions were a result of heresies in the church.

They existed so that the true believers would be seen by their actions and their beliefs.

Some members of the church were over-eating and becoming drunk.

He was warning them that they were not treating the supper with proper respect.

The people in Corinth, who come to eat and drink were not showing respect for the Lord or for other members of the church.

"For I received from the Lord what I also handed on to you" (1 Cor. 11: 23).

The Lord took bread blessed it, broke it and gave it to His disciples. After the supper, He repeated the actions with the cup.

Each time the Supper iscelebrated it pro-claims "the Lord's death until He comes."

Those persons would be answerable for the body and the blood of the Lord.

6. Where was this lack of respect being shown?

The people in Corinth, who come to eat and drink were not showing respect for the Lord or for other members of the church.

7. Where did Paul receive his instructions about how the Supper was to take place?

"For I received from the Lord what I also handed on to you" (1 Cor. 11: 23).

8. What was the order of the Lord's Supper, according to this passage?

The Lord took bread blessed it, broke it and gave it to His disciples. After the supper, He repeated the actions with the cup.

9. What proclamation is made through the eating of bread and drinking of the cup?

Each time the Supper iscelebrated it proclaims "the Lord's death until He comes."

10. What does Paul say of those who ate and drank unworthily?

Those persons would be answerable for the body and the blood of the Lord.

Reconciling the World to Christ

$\mathcal{K}$nowing therefore the terror of the Lord, we persuade men; but we are made manifest unto God; and I trust also are made manifest in your consciences.

12 For we commend not ourselves again unto you, but give you occasion to glory on our behalf, that ye may have somewhat to answer them which glory in appearance, and not in heart.

2 Cor. 5:11-21

13 For whether we be beside ourselves, it is to God: or whether we be sober, it is for your cause.

14 For the love of Christ constraineth us; because we thus judge, that if one died for all, then were all dead:

15 And that he died for all, that they which live should not henceforth live unto themselves, but unto him which died for them, and rose again.

16 Wherefore henceforth know we no man after the flesh: yea, though we have known Christ after the flesh, yet now henceforth know we him no more.

17 Therefore if any man be in Christ, he is a new creature: old things are passed away; behold all things are become new.

18 And all things are of God, who hath reconciled us to himself by Jesus Christ, and hath given to us the ministry of reconciliation;

19 To wit, that God was in Christ, reconciling the world unto himself, not imputing their trespasses unto them; and hath committed unto us the word of reconciliation.

20 Now then we are ambassadors for Christ, as though God did beseech you by us: we pray you in Christ's stead, be ye reconciled to God.

21 For he hath made him to be sin for us, who knew no sin; that we might be made the righteousness of God in him.

Memory Selection
2 Corinthians 5:19

Background Scripture
2 Corinthians 5:11-21

Devotional Reading
1 Peter 2:18-25

Printed Scripture
2 Corinthians 5:11-21

Feb. 21

Teacher's Target

Lesson purpose: To catch the apostle Paul's sense of urgency about the need for reconciliation, both with God and with others.

Modern means of communication and transportation have in one sense made the world smaller, and put people in closer touch with each other. Ironically, however, the more we learn about others, the more suspicious some people become about those who are different. This lesson might well be introduced by a discussion of how the modern world has also brought heightened tensions between Muslims and Jews in Israel, Protestants and Catholics in Ireland, blacks and Koreans in south Los Angeles, Anglos and Hispanics on the border between the U. S. and Mexico.

The Bible maintains that such tensions among people are rooted in our tension with God. When his Jewish and Gentile hearers settled their differences with God they were welded into one Body, the Church. Inspire your class with this portrait of Paul as an ambassador for God, who also laid the foundation for us to be reconciled with other people as well.

Lesson Introduction

Despite its size and complexity, the Bible can in one sense be described as a story with three chapters,and this lesson is "Chapter 3."

Chapter 1 can be titled "Creation." Out of nothing, God made a world that provided for our every need, and stamped it with His approval: "It is very good."

Chapter 2 is titled "Fall." It describes the tragic story of Adam and Eve and their descendants choosing to forsake God and to go their own way,prodigals all.

Chapter 3, however,"Reconciliation",has a theme as joyous as chapter 2 is bleak. It is about Paul's affirmation: "God was in Christ, reconciling the world unto himself." It is a theme accompanied by an invitation: "Be ye reconciled to God."

There is also an Epilogue to the story, an ending that consists of a call to the reconciled to hand along "the word of reconciliation."

Teaching Outline	Daily Bible Readings

I. Selfless Motives—11-15
  A. Transparent before God, 11-12
  B. Impelled by love, 13-15
II. New Creation—16-17
  A. Transformed view, 16
  B. New creation in Christ, 17
III. Challenging Mission—18-21
  A. Reconciled to God, 18-19a
  B. Ambassadors for Christ,
    19b-21
	Mon. Love Urges Us On
	  2 Corinthians 5:11-15
	Tue. There's a New Creation!
	  2 Corinthians 5:16-21
	Wed. Justification and Life
	  Romans 5:18+6:4
	Thu. Alive to God in Christ
	  Romans 6:5-11
	Fri. Eternal Life: God's Gift
	  Romans 6:12-23
	Sat. Taught by Law, Saved by Grace
	  Romans 7:1-13
	Sun. Thanks Be to God!
	  Romans 7:14-25a

Verse by Verse

I. Selfless Motives—11-15

A. Transparent before God, 11-12

11 Knowing therefore the terror of the Lord, we persuade men; but we are made manifest unto God; and I trust also are made manifest in your consciences.

12 For we commend not ourselves again unto you, but give you occasion to glory on our behalf, that ye may have somewhat to answer them which glory in appearance, and not in heart.

"Terror" somewhat overstates the original word, which is actually "fear" (Grk. *phobos*). Especially in the Old Testament, "the fear of the Lord" refers not to fright but to awe at God's might and authority, along with a commitment to obey Him. It produces an understanding of true religion and even holy boldness, rather than dread (Prov. 2:1-5). Paul is saying that his earlier sharpness grew out of obedience to this awesome God and his concern for the Corinthians, not out of personal anger or arrogant exercise of his apostolic authority.

This passage reflects the tension between Paul and the Christians at Corinth. The rebuke and correction he had offered in previous correspondence (perhaps 1 Corinthians) had made some "sorry" and resentful (7:8). Over and over, in this letter, the apostle

appeals to them to realize that his correction is for their sake. Here he affirms that his motive is to give them an occasion to glory by obeying God's will. Paul's heart is "manifest" to God, and he is eager for the Corinthians to know it as well. Obviously he hopes that the following teaching on the need to be reconciled to God will establish a basis for reconciliation between himself and the Corinthians as well.

B. Impelled by love, 13-15

13 For whether we be beside ourselves, it is to God: or whether we be sober, it is for your cause.

14 For the love of Christ constraineth us; because we thus judge, that if one died for all, then were all dead:

15 And that he died for all, that they which live should not henceforth live unto themselves, but unto him which died for them, and rose again.

Apparently some of the Corinthians had accused Paul of being insane with power; but he replies that even if he is out of his mind it is for their benefit. In a sense, all of God's true prophets were "out of their mind," for the essence of inspiration is to be caught up in a revelation from a source outside of or above the human mind. As Paul affirms, such messages are for our good.

The true motive for Paul's sternness is stated in verse 14: "Christ's love compels us" (NIV). While we were in sin, Christ died for us (Rom. 5:8), granting us new life. Now we have the tremendous responsibility to live not for ourselves but for Him. Christ's special commission to Paul was to speak His truth to complete the process of reconciling the Corinthians to Him. So Paul would be doing them no favor to soft-pedal his rebuke when their lives did not reflect their new position in Christ.

II. New Creation—16-17
A. Transformed view, 16

16 Wherefore henceforth know we no man after the flesh: yea, though we have known Christ after the flesh, yet now henceforth know we him no more.

People who have experienced the new birth have a new perspective on life, and on other people. For example, Paul had once considered Christ to be an enemy of the truth, and persecuted His followers to the death (Acts 22:4). However, the Damascus Road experience lifted the scales from Paul's eyes and enabled him to know Christ as He truly is, God's Son.

Likewise, Paul could no longer view the Corinthians with the eyes of flesh. It would be easy for him to overlook their sins and shortcomings, and to curry their favor on the human level. Instead, his view of their "new humanity" impelled him to challenge them to live up to their calling.

B. New creation in Christ, 17

17 Therefore if any man be in Christ, he is a new creature: old things are passed away; behold all things are become new.

What a sensitive psychology of change Paul's new view gave him! He does not simply rebuke people who need to improve; he gives them a view of who they really are in Christ. If they can catch a vision of how Jesus has transformed them and placed them in Himself, where they are safe, protected and enabled, they will "become who they are."

One of America's most gifted counselors once said he formerly focused on healing the emotions of troubled people by casting evil spirits from them. Eventually, however, he noticed that this sensational approach brought many people back again and again. They needed a "supernatural fix." The counselor then adopted the less spectacular but longer-lasting approach of *teaching Christians who they are in Christ*. Out of the recognition and acceptance of their new identity, they were better able to conquer their problems. Such is the power and the promise of realizing the truth Paul states here.

III. Challenging Mission—18-21
A. Reconciled to God, 18-19a

18 And all things are of God, who hath reconciled us to himself by Jesus Christ, and hath given to us the ministry of reconciliation;

19 To wit, that God was in Christ, reconciling the world unto

himself, not imputing their trespasses unto them;

The "things" mentioned here are probably the tense exchanges and relationships between Paul and his opponents at Corinth. All this will be shown to be from God if they will but accept the truth he teaches and the sincerity of his motives. Every time this kind of reconciliation occurs, we can be sure God is involved.

"Reconciliation" is one of the most important words in the vocabulary of salvation, as well as in human relationships. The original meaning of the term had to do with a change or alteration. In our context, it refers to the changed relationship between God and people because of the sacrifice of Christ. The animal sacrifices among the Jews and pagans were put forward by sinful people themselves. In Christ, however, God, the offended party, put forward the sacrifice. Reconciliation is therefore to be *received*; it does not occur because of an offering we make, as though to alter God's mind about our worth (see Rom. 5:11).

Significantly, "reconciliation" also describes restored relationships between people as well as between people and God. The reconciling work of Christ in behalf of all people provides a common meeting ground on which to accept each other despite our differences. Paul's mission was to reconcile both Jew and Greek to each other because both had been reconciled to God (Eph. 2:11-21).

On a more personal level, to these very Corinthians Paul writes of the need for an estranged husband and wife to be "reconciled" to each other" (1 Cor. 7:11).

B. Ambassadors for Christ, 19b-21

19b and hath committed unto us the word of reconciliation.

20 Now then we are ambassadors for Christ, as though God did beseech you by us: we pray you in Christ's stead, be ye reconciled to God.

21 For he hath made him to be sin for us, who knew no sin; that we might be made the righteousness of God in him.

The story of reconciliation is too important to keep to ourselves. Paul was so gripped by the changed relationship he enjoyed with God after the Damascus Road experience that he committed his life to preaching the word of reconciliation to others. "Us" probably refers first to the apostles' commission to spread the word; but they were to teach others to do the same (Matt. 28:18), so the commission is extended to all the reconciled.

Paul closes this profound and fundamental teaching by repeating the basic motivation for the work of reconciliation. It stems from the grand action of the sinless Son of God in bearing our sins, transferring God's righteousness to people who had none of their own.

Evangelistic Emphasis

When you see a person drive up to your church in a flashy new car, don't you make certain assumptions about that person? The media is in business to tell us what makes a positive impression on another person. Impressing a client, a boss, a personnel manager, a lover, a parent or a spouse is the major driving force of every commercial on the airwaves today. We need to impress others because they are making a value judgment about us.

There are also instances in which the church makes value judgments. Not all of the judgments are correct or helpful to the person being judged. A judgmental spirit, even if we are correct in our judgment, drives people from the doors of our congregations. A judgmental spirit is against the spirit and the teachings of Jesus' love.

Paul wrote to the Corinthians that God had made a value judgment about all of humanity. In Jesus Christ, God proved that we are valuable and precious to Him. He sent His Son to bring reconciliation between a holy God and sinful humanity. The good news is that this happened, "while we were yet sinners."

God doesn't wait for you to clean up your act before He invites you home. God is out prowling the "gutters" of life looking for those persons who are in greatest need of His love. It doesn't matter what you have done, Jesus is ready to receive you. His grace is scandalous in its absolute pursuit of wayward persons.

Indeed, we have a message that the world is waiting to hear.

To wit, that God was in Christ, reconciling the world unto himself, not imputing their trespasses unto them; and hath committed unto us the word of reconciliation.—*2 Corinthians 5:19*

Trust is a major issue in our day. There are questions about our politicians, about our school leaders, about any leader, even about those representatives of Christ on earth. We don't trust because our trust has been betrayed many times by those claiming to deserve it.

We are given the ministry of reconciliation. Those are big words which simply mean we are called to put the pieces back together. The role of each Christian, each church, is to bring back together those persons and elements of society that are estranged. This ministry can only take place as we are confident that we have been reconciled to our Father. When we sense the great love He has brought to our lives, we can then share that love with others. The power of God's love to break down barriers and bring healing is beyond the ability of people to explain. God's kind of healing love must be experienced. Let someone experience that love through you as you continue the ministry of reconciliation in your life.

Weekday Problems

Ted Melton found himself in an uncomfortable position at work. Ted was rarely uncomfortable in any situation, but this one was bothering him. Ted found himself in the middle of a feud. The parties involved were both his dear friends. Melanie was the CPA at the firm. She knew all there was to know about accounting. Randy was the firm's lawyer. He knew about tax laws and felt himself accomplished enough to speak on accounting issues. Ted was the office manager in this firm. Randy and Melanie had several projects that demanded their combined attention and expertise. Because they were forced to deal with each other on a daily basis sparks flew, regularly. Both of them would come to Ted and complain about the other. Ted didn't take sides. He tried to be a friend to both of them.

After a couple of months of office combat between Randy and Melanie, Ted was growing weary of work. His wife noticed the change. His children were afraid to speak to him. His church attendance became irregular. Diane, Ted's wife listened patiently to the saga of the office wars. She then suggested Ted talk to their pastor.

The Minister's advice was simple. Christ has given every member of the church the ministry of reconciliation. It was Ted's responsibility as a Christian to try and bring about reconciliation between Randy and Melanie. Ted was not sure his minister understood the realities of the corporate world.

*   What would you do if you were in Ted's position?

*   How can we "mind our own business" and still be involved in the ministry of reconciliation?

The Vocabulary of Salvation

Several Bible words contribute to a New Covenant language of salvation. Here is a short list.

Reconciliation—The changed, newly harmonious relationship between people and God created by Christ's work on the Cross.

Justification—A judicial term referring to God's having pronounced guilty people innocent in Christ.

Atonement—A term growing out of the Old Testament and referring to God's "covering" our sin out of His love.

Redemption—God's work in "buying us back" from slavery to sin, as He redeemed Israel from Egypt.

Propitiation or *expiation*—Word pictures portraying God as a great King who accepts Christ's death in place of that of sinners.

Mediator—Christ as a "go-between" between God and sinful humanity.

247

This Lesson in Your Life

After the Lord's Supper debacle focused on last week, doesn't this passage sound strange? The very people who had defamed the Lord's Table were given in this text the ministry of reconciliation. You might ask your class, "What happened between the writing of first and second Corinthians?" "How can people who were obvious sinners be given the ministry of reconciliation?" One of the things that confounds us is that persons who don't deserve God's love and grace freely receive it.

The whole point of this lesson is the truth that God through Jesus Christ has brought reconciliation to us. In His sacrifice on the cross, the rift between humanity and God was bridged. God gave us the gift of a new start, even though we did not deserve it. That is why reconciliation is a moving force in the cosmos. When we are forgiven, we start all over with God. Our past sins and failures are forgiven and forgotten. Our selfish and willful nature is replaced by the Holy Spirit.

A new creation in Christ can become a person who can participate in the ministry of reconciliation. In most cases, people are estranged from God and each other because of an event in the past. Many people who continue feuding over the years have long forgotten the original fight. They are mad at each other and intend to stay mad at each other. The gift of reconciliation is the gift of a new start with a person. It helps us erase past hurts. That is a miracle that only God can accomplish.

This ministry of reconciliation is powerful and personally challenging. We are challenged to look past behavior to a soul that God loves. Jesus didn't count our trespasses against us. Hanging on the cross, Jesus wiped those sins away. We can come to Him seeking love and mercy, without worrying that He will hold our sins against us. Once we have asked forgiveness for our sins, they are forgiven. We, as Christians are challenged to be as forgiving to others as Christ was to us. Offering Christ openly and lovingly takes the Holy Spirit working in us. Our temptation is always to judge the sins of a person before we offer him the message of God's love in Jesus Christ. As God's people we should see other people as He sees them. A divine perspective helps us see a person that God loves. It keeps us from focusing on the behaviors of that person that we might find offensive.

As those persons who are charged with the ministry of reconciliation, we are called to be ambassadors of Christ. Much like political ambassadors we are called to go into strange lands with the message of God's love. Being an ambassador for Christ is not a title. It is a call to hard work.

The ministry of reconciliation is radical in its goodness. People suffer an epidemic of estrangement from God and from one another. The church holds a very powerful antidote to that emotional bondage. The love of God shown through you can bring all the factions in our society together. We can change our world by loving, forgiving and ministering in the name of Jesus Christ—the one who "reconciled us to God . . .and gave us the ministry of reconciliation" (2 Cor. 5:19).

Seed Thoughts

1. There are many motivations for sharing the gospel of Jesus Christ. Which one did Paul mention?

Paul tried to persuade others "knowing the fear of the Lord." The word fear here means reverence and respect.

2. What was Paul's hope as he wrote this second letter to the Corinthians?

Paul hoped that he was well known to their consciences. He hoped they were following his moral leadership.

3. Paul seems to be defending something to the Corinthians. What was it?

Paul may have been defending his called to be an apostle. That was a constant conflict in his ministry.

4. What failure in judgment did the critics of Paul's apostleship have?

They boasted in outward appearances and gave no thought to what was in a person's heart.

5. From reading verse 6, what might you assume was one of the attacks on Paul's character?

His critics might have been saying to the people in Corinth that Paul was "not in his right mind."

1. There are many motivations for sharing the gospel of Jesus Christ. Which one did Paul mention?

2. What was Paul's hope as he wrote this second letter to the Corinthians?

3. Paul seems to be defending something to the Corinthians. What was it?

4. What failure in judgment did the critics of Paul's apostleship have?

5. From reading verse 6, what might you assume was one of the attacks on Paul's character?

6. What was the power that urged Paul on in his ministry to the church?

7. Since we are raised with Christ, how does that change our perspective on the world?

8. What is the promise for all people who are in Christ Jesus?

9. As a result of our being made a new creation, what ministry have we been given?

10. Why is the invitation to come to Jesus Christ appealing?

(Continued next page)

Paul tried to persuade others "knowing the fear of the Lord." The word fear here means reverence and respect.

Paul hoped that he was well known to their consciences. He hoped they were following his moral leadership.

Paul may have been defending his called to be an apostle. That was a constant conflict in his ministry.

They boasted in outward appearances and gave no thought to what was in a person's heart.

His critics might have been saying to the people in Corinth that Paul was "not in his right mind."

Paul had a deep sense of God's love for all persons in Jesus Christ. It was that deep love that kept Paul going.

Persons who are living for Christ no longer look on the world from the human perspective.

"Anyone in Christ . . . is a new creation . . . everything has become new."

We are given the ministry of reconciliation, and the message of reconciliation.

We are offered in Christ the promise that our sins are taken away and we become the righteousness of God.

6. What was the power that urged Paul on in his ministry to the church?

Paul had a deep sense of God's love for all persons in Jesus Christ. It was that deep love that kept Paul going.

7. Since we are raised with Christ, how does that change our perspective on the world?

Persons who are living for Christ no longer look on the world from the human perspective.

8. What is the promise for all people who are in Christ Jesus?

"Anyone in Christ . . . is a new creation . . . everything has become new."

9. As a result of our being made a new creation, what ministry have we been given?

We are given the ministry of reconciliation, and the message of reconciliation.

10. Why is the invitation to come to Jesus Christ appealing?

We are offered in Christ the promise that our sins are taken away and we become the righteousness of God.

Confident Hope

or the grace of God that bringeth salvation hath appeared to all men,

12 Teaching us that, denying ungodliness and worldly lusts, we should live soberly, righteously, and godly, in this present world;

13 Looking for that blessed hope, and the glorious appearing of the great God and our Saviour Jesus Christ;

14 Who gave himself for us, that he might redeem us from all iniquity, and purify unto himself a peculiar people, zealous of good works.

Titus 2:11-14
Heb. 12:26-29
Rev. 1:17-20;
11:15

Hebrews 12:26 Whose voice then shook the earth: but now he hath promised, saying, Yet once more I shake not the earth only, but also heaven.

27 And this word, Yet once more, signifieth the removing of those things that are shaken, as of things that are made, that those things which cannot be shaken may remain.

28 Wherefore we receiving a kingdom which cannot be moved, let us have grace, whereby we may serve God acceptably with reverence and godly fear:

29 For our God is a consuming fire.

Revelation 1:17 And when I saw him, I fell at his feet as dead. And he laid his right hand upon me, saying unto me, Fear not; I am the first and the last:

18 I am he that liveth, and was dead; and, behold, I am alive for evermore, Amen; and have the keys of hell and of death.

19 Write the things which thou hast seen, and the things which are, and the things which shall be hereafter;

20 The mystery of the seven stars which thou sawest in my right hand, and the seven golden candlesticks. The seven stars are the angels of the seven churches: and the seven candlesticks which thou sawest are the seven churches.

11:15 And the seventh angel sounded; and there were great voices in heaven, saying, The kingdoms of this world are become the kingdoms of our Lord, and of his Christ; and he shall reign for ever and ever.

Memory Selection
Titus 2:13
Background Scripture
Titus 2:11-14; Heb.12:18-29
Rev. 1:14-20; 11:15-19
Devotional Reading
1 Peter 1:3-9
Printed Scripture
Titus 2:11-14; Heb. 12:26-29;
Rev. 1:17-20; 11:15

Teacher's Target

Lesson purpose: *To grasp anew the living hope offered by Christ not only for abundant li ing in the present but in the after-life as well.*

In our day, Christianity's major appeals are based on what the faith offers for this life, better self-esteem, higher moral standards, workable principles for strong marriages and families, peace of mind, etc.

While all this is part of the abundant life Jesus promised, there is more. When we fail so miserably that we have no more self-esteem, when we lose our jobs or our loved ones, when this life seems to have nothing left to offer, what then? The medley of Scriptures for today's lesson answer with one voice: hope for a better life in the world to come.

As you present this lesson, guard against a "pie in the sky by and by" emphasis by showing the connection the Bible makes between accepting God's grace in this life and the next. Note that mere death does not change the "covering" of grace found in Christ. God's love forms a bridge between the seen and the unseen worlds.

Lesson Introduction

Today's lesson title, "Confident Hope," points out a basic difference between the way the Bible uses the word "hope" and the way we often hear it used in everyday life.

"Will it rain today?" a farmer asks.

"I *hope* so," his friend replies, even if it hasn't rained for a month and none is in the forecast. We hope the plane leaves and arrives on time, that taxes don't go up, and that we win the Reader's Digest Sweepstakes.

In contrast, biblical hope for the future is *confident* hope. It differs in two ways: (1) It depends not on passing luck but the eternal God; and (2) it is grounded in past realities. God delivered His people from Egypt, Daniel from the lions' den, and Jesus from the tomb. Biblical hope *knows* Him in whom we believe, that he is able to keep that which we have committed unto him (2 Tim. 1:12).

Teaching Outline	Daily Bible Readings

I. The Unflappable Life—Titus 2:11-14
  A. Graceful living, 11-12
  B. Hopeful living, 13-14
II. The Unshakable Kingdom—Heb. 12:26-29
  A. Certain judgment, 26
  B. A permanent abode, 27-29
III. The Eternal Christ, Revelation—1:17-20; 11:15
  A. From beginning to end, 17
  B. From life to life, 18
  C. From light to light, 19-20
  D. Forever and ever, 11:15
	Mon. The Blessed Hope
	  Titus 2:11-14
	Tue. What Cannot Be Shaken
	  Hebrews 12:18-29
	Wed. Do Not Be Afraid
	  Revelation 1:12-20
	Thu. He Will Reign Forever
	  Revelation 11:15-19
	Fri. A Living Hope
	  1 Peter 1:3-9
	Sat. The Hope God Promises
	  Ephesians 1:15-23
	Sun. New Heavens, New Earth
	  Revelation 21:1-8

Verse by Verse

I. The Unflappable Life—Titus 2:11-14

A. Graceful living, 11-12

11 For the grace of God that bringeth salvation hath appeared to all men,

12 Teaching us that, denying ungodliness and worldly lusts, we should live soberly, righteously, and godly, in this present world;

The short letter to Titus was apparently Paul's next-to-last epistle, written nearly a generation after the death of Christ, about A.D. 67 or 68. There are numerous indications that many Christians who had expected Christ to return in their lifetime had "grown weary in well-doing" (2 Thess. 3:13). Their initial excitement at being forgiven by God's grace had waned. Some even returned to pagan standards of morality, and they were in danger of forgetting that Christ expected their lives to reflect His grace, regardless of when He returns.

Here Paul reminds such believers that the grace of Christ not only forgives people but calls them to a higher plane of living. It reflects badly on Jesus for those He saves from lust, for example, to return to lustful living. It also shows a lack of awareness that this life is a "proving ground" for the next. Paul's reference to "this present world" implies a future world as well. He wants Christians to be unflappable and unfazed by the temptations of this temporary realm in order to be prepared for eternal Kingdom.

B. Hopeful living, 13-14

13 Looking for that blessed hope,
and the glorious appearing of the great God and our Saviour Jesus Christ;

14 Who gave himself for us, that he might redeem us from all iniquity, and purify unto himself a peculiar people, zealous of good works.

The future world, Paul teaches, will be inaugurated by the Second Coming, a time of "blessed hope" for those who look forward to it as evidenced by the way they live in this world. In contrast to the Old Testament prohibition against setting eyes on divinity, "every eye shall see him" on that great day (Rev. 1:7).

The NIV identifies the divine Personage we will see on that day as "our great God and Savior, Jesus Christ"—identifying Jesus with God Himself. A similar confession of the complete unity of the Son with the Father appears in 2 Peter 1:1. It is also possible, however, that the phrase here refers to God and Jesus separately. This reading would seem to be strengthened by verse 14, since Scripture usually speaks of the sacrifice of Christ, not of the Father (although in a sense God gave Himself in the giving of His Son).

Verse 14 explains what being redeemed from sin really involves. We are not just saved *from* past iniquity; we are saved *for* right living, purity, and good works. We are saved to be part of "God's very own people—the meaning of the King James word "peculiar" (see the NIV). In 17th century England, "peculiar" meant "exclusively belonging to," as when we say, "The kangaroo is peculiar to Australia" to mean it is native only to the island continent.

II. The Unshakable Kingdom—Heb. 12:26-29

A. Certain judgment, 26

26 Whose voice then shook the earth: but now he hath promised, saying, Yet once more I shake not the earth only, but also heaven.

The book of Hebrews shares Paul's concern that people not become so discouraged by persecution or the delay of Christ's return that they lapse into the sinful ways from which their Lord redeemed them. The audience here consists of Jewish Christians, many of whom felt the pressure to return to Jewish practices. Some had been persecuted, and others derided by their Jewish friends.

We take up the letter in chapter 12, which exalts Yahweh as a God fully as awesome under the New Covenant as the Old. We are not to mistake salvation by grace to mean that God will not punish the unfaithful. Just as God's thundering voice shook Mt. Sinai when the people committed idolatry while Moses was receiving the Law, we can count on His character remaining unchanged today. There is now this difference, however: the thunder at the Last Judgment will shake both heaven and earth as God winnows out the chaff of professed but professed Christians.

B. A permanent abode, 27-29

27 And this word, Yet once more, signifieth the removing of those things that are shaken, as of things that are made, that those things which cannot be shaken may remain.

28 Wherefore we receiving a kingdom which cannot be moved, let us have grace, whereby we may serve

God acceptably with reverence and godly fear:

29 For our God is a consuming fire.

The Hebrew writer fully understands the view of the Greek philosopher Plato, who taught that behind the visible world stands a more permanent reality. The writer explains that the reference to shaking the earth implies the removal of the very entity that many people think is most real—the material universe. That world, however, is merely "made," while the spiritual world is eternal. When earth and sky have been "shaken" at the Second Coming, it will be that spiritual realm that remains.

Although verse 29 reminds us that we serve the same God who destroyed the disobedient and unbelieving under the Old Covenant, rather than cowering in fear at His nature we should be inspired to live grace-filled lives in this world. While the prospect of Judgment Day should rightfully strike terror in the hearts of the deliberately disobedient and stubbornly evil, it produces reverential awe in the heart of those who not only know God's power, but His love and grace as well.

"Let us have grace" is used in the sense of "saying grace" at a meal, and means "Let us be thankful (as the NIV reads). No one can be more thankful for the opportunity of remaining faithful than those who have been redeemed from faithlessness and who look forward to the Second Coming as a time of final deliverance instead of judgment.

III. The Eternal Christ—Rev. 1:17-20; 11:15

A. From beginning to end, 17

17 And when I saw him, I fell at

his feet as dead. And he laid his right hand upon me, saying unto me, Fear not; I am the first and the last:

Our final texts, from the book of Revelation, emphasize the fact that for the faithful the Last Judgment will consist of the inexpressible joy of being with Christ, rather than the morbid fear of being condemned. The "Son of man" figure—no doubt Jesus Himself—offers His presence instead of condemnation as John falls at His feet.

It is for this moment of ultimate fulfillment that we are so concerned to live pure lives. It is this joyful end that enables us to endure trials and to live in hope. "All good things must come to an end" is a common adage for this life. In the next life, however, the eternal Good that set life into motion at the beginning will be seen to also be the Living End.

B. From life to life, 18

18 I am he that liveth, and was dead; and, behold, I am alive for evermore, Amen; and have the keys of hell and of death.

The faithful are further encouraged to live in hope because of the knowledge that just as Jesus once lived, was crucified, and raised again, so they will follow Him up from the grave. What more substantial hope could anyone have than the confidence that they follow Him who has the key to release us from the bonds of death? ("Hell" here is literally *hades*, and refers not to the hell that is final banishment from God but to the temporary lodging place where souls await judgment.)

C. From light to light, 19-20

19 Write the things which thou hast seen, and the things which are, and

the things which shall be hereafter;

20 The mystery of the seven stars which thou sawest in my right hand, and the seven golden candlesticks. The seven stars are the angels of the seven churches: and the seven candlesticks which thou sawest are the seven churches.

The vision here of the seven stars, representing the seven churches of Asia (chaps. 2-3), links the faithful life being urged in all these texts to life in the Church. How can this be, when the Church itself is full of sinful people? Hope is appropriate for them because Jesus places the saved in His Body, the Church (Eph. 5:23). Hope is appropriate for members of the Body because they trust not in their own righteousness—even though they are enjoined to be righteous—but in the righteousness of Christ.

D. Forever and ever, 11:15

15 And the seventh angel sounded; and there were great voices in heaven, saying, The kingdoms of this world are become the kingdoms of our Lord, and of his Christ; and he shall reign for ever and ever.

The constant ebb and flow of life, fortune followed by misfortune, can cause hope to wane. Christians, however, remember that they are members of a kingdom that "cannot be moved" (Heb. 12:28, above). They inhabit a realm that will one day be shown to be greater than any earthly kingdom, because it is ruled by the King of kings and the Lord of lords. Unlike earthly rulers who flourish, then fall, this King will reign eternally.

What promises could produce more confident hope?

Evangelistic Emphasis

Have you begun practicing writing "2000" yet? In a few short months, most of us will begin referring to our birthday which took place "last century." The various writers of this commentary live with confident hope. We began writing these lessons way back in the spring of 1997. Do you remember 1997? The good news is that our confident hope in Jesus Christ allows us to write these lessons. We all believe that the church of Jesus Christ will still be spreading the gospel message into the twenty-first century. You will still be studying God's Word in Sunday School.

As you stand at the dawn of the next millennium, which really begins on January 1, 2001, you can be confident that God stands with you. The writer of Hebrews made the bold proclamation that God is the same yesterday, today and forever. That means that no matter what we face, we can turn to Him in faith. He will be faithful to His children and will always deliver us. The "old, old story of Jesus and His love" will be just as appealing, just as vital in a new century as it is today.

Persons all around you are looking into the future with trepidation. They are afraid of what the future holds. Perhaps they are more fearful because of all the dire predictions made about things that would happen on or before January 1, 2000. The church is called to proclaim the good news that New Year's Day, 2000, will be like any other. God is still on His throne. God is still in control of history. We can continue to believe and to have hope because Jesus is the same yesterday, today and forever.

● ● ● ● ● ● ● ●

Memory Selection

Looking for that blessed hope, and glorious appearing of the great God and our Savior Jesus Christ.— *Titus 2: 13*

My three dogs know when I am on the way home. I have a suspicion that they can hear my truck coming from a block away. They are always there to greet me at the door of their dog pen. They are always happy to see me. I am the one who usually lets them out of their pen. After they have run in the yard a minute or two they are ready to go into the house. Our dogs are spoiled. They stay outside under a shade tree all day. They stay in the house all night. They don't have it bad at all.

We don't have it bad, either. We live on this earth with the blessings and the care of Jesus Christ. He allows us to participate in some very, very interesting moments. He calls us to be involved with people. He invites us to His Table. We have it made on earth.

One day, Jesus will bring us all home. The glory and joy we have experienced here will pale in comparison to the hope and glory of heaven. When you think about our life in Jesus Christ, we have it good! Thanks be to God for His blessings, here and hereafter!

Weekday Problems

Scott Beasley put the paper down with a mixture of disgust and chagrin. The second page of the morning paper told the story of another teen suicide. This made the third one that year among students from one particular High School. Scott was disgusted because the paper sensationalized the story. He was worried because his two children Allison and Andrew attended the very same high school. Both of his children knew the three teens who had committed suicide. Scott wondered why these young people took their lives.

That night he and his wife decided to have a family meeting with Allison and Andrew about their concerns. It was an idea the newspaper and his pastor had encouraged. "Why do young people feel hopeless?" Scott began. Allison, the oldest, chimed right in.

"Did you read the paper?" was her reply.

"Of course they printed all the grisly details."

"No, Dad. Did you read the rest of the paper?"

Allison went on to articulate what was happening in the world. Wars and uprisings in third world nations had caused the economic situation in this country to become unstable. There was a dire forecast for Social Security. There was a gloomy forecast for job opportunities. The kids went to school in deplorable conditions. Adults were always criticizing their clothes, hair, friends, music, grades, choices and anything else they could think of.

Andrew, the quiet one said, "I thought Jesus would help us with our problems."

* How do you respond when young people tell you there is no hope?

Handfuls of Hope

Hope springs eternal in the human breast; man never is, but always to be blest.—*Alexander Pope*

* * *

The world dares say no more than "while I live, I hope"; but the children of God can add by virtue of a living hope, "While I expire, I hope."—*Robert Leighton*

* * *

The hours we pass with happy prospects in view are more pleasing than those crowded with fruition.—*Oliver Goldsmith.*

* * *

You cannot put a great hope into a small soul.—*J. L. Jones*

* * *

Hope is the only good that is common to all; those who have nothing else possess hope.—*Thales*

This Lesson in Your Life

The "weekday problem" section of this lesson is almost true. In the community where I pastor and where my children go to school, tragedy has struck our youth. In the high school there have been three suicides, multiple suicide attempts and one student murdered by a classmate. That is not good news. The good news happened months later when the principal gathered the community for a town meeting about those issues. One of the things that was striking was the fact that teens feel there is "no hope" for tomorrow. They don't see a bright future ahead of them.

They don't fear forfeiting the American dream. Their lack of hope is a result of their failure to understand matters of the soul. Somehow we have managed to raise up a whole generation that is bereft of soul. They feel passionate about many things. They are emotional about everything from music to curfews. Somewhere the church missed "Generation X" as we tried to share with them the truth of Jesus Christ. We, as a church, did not instill in our youth the belief that in Christ the future is already victoriously won for us. We have a generation of young people who are silently living with the fear that tomorrow will not be as good as today.

The texts from Titus, Hebrews and the Revelation describe a hope for tomorrow that is unshakable. That hope is not based on any external circumstance. The hope the Bible describes is found in the person of Jesus Christ. It is a hope fashioned on the cross and validated by the resurrection. Our hope is as real as the person of Jesus. He understands the struggles we face. Death itself has been faced by our Lord, and He enables us to face it with the assurance that heaven is our home. He also assures us that our loved ones are safe in a place and time at which we haven't arrived.

Our hope is in His presence with us. More than simply understanding what we suffer, Jesus is present with us. He will never leave us. His presence comforts us as we face daily tasks. He also gives us guidance as we look for solutions to our problems.

Perhaps the church has tried to sell to much psychological snake oil disguised as "enlightened faith" to our members. The hard answer is that psychology and self-esteem can't give persons hope. The only hope our young people can hold without fear is Jesus. He can and will provide them with the help and hope they need for living.

We should never make the assumption that our young people are simply too pessimistic about their world. The children of today live in a world we can't imagine. They hunger for our attention and love. They are starving for affection right in the midst of the church.

Hopelessness among young people is startling because they should have everything to live for. They have youth and vitality. They have time and energy. They have the things for which many of us long. With all they seem to have, many youth lack a basic hope that life in Christ is good. Many of your church youth will tell you their future looks bleak. I can't imagine what a child without Christ thinks about their future.

To change this we need to practice our hope before our young people. Does your life reflect an uncompromising trust that Jesus will take care of the future? If you don't have hope, how can the young people watching you have it?

Seed Thoughts

1. What is your hope for the future of the church?

This question might be a good opening question. The answers are as varied as the members of your class.

2. What do you think is the meaning of the phrase, "the grace of God has appeared" (Titus 2: 11).

The grace of God was not merely a concept. The grace of God was made real in the person of Jesus Christ.

3. According to Titus 2: 11, to whom was salvation offered?

The clear implication of this verse is that salvation is offered to all.

4. The grace of God which brings salvation trains a Christian to do what?

The grace of God trains a Christian to renounce impiety and worldly passions.

5. What else did the grace of God train the Christian to do?

Christians are also trained to live self-controlled, upright and godly lives in this present age.

---

1. What is your hope for the future of the church?

2. What do you think is the meaning of the phrase, "the grace of God has appeared" (Titus 2: 11).

3. According to Titus 2: 11, to whom was salvation offered?

4. The grace of God which brings salvation trains a Christian to do what?

5. What else did the grace of God train the Christian to do?

6. While Christians are living godly lives, what else were they suppose to do?

7. What does Hebrews affirm about the nature of the kingdom of God?

8. How do we give thanks for God's unshakable kingdom and His invitation to us to join that kingdom?

9. How is acceptable worship described? Why is that so?

10. What was the proclamation made by the seventh angel of the Revelation?

(Continued next page)

This question might be a good opening question. The answers are as varied as the members of your class.

The grace of God was not merely a concept. The grace of God was made real in the person of Jesus Christ.

The clear implication of this verse is that salvation is offered to all.

The grace of God trains a Christian to renounce impiety and worldly passions.

Christians are also trained to live self-controlled, upright and godly lives in this present age.

Christians are to "wait for the blessed hope and manifestation of the great God and Savior, Jesus Christ."

The kingdom of God cannot be shaken. The things that can't be shaken remain.

We give thinks to God for our place in His kingdom by offering acceptable worship.

Worship is acceptable if it is done with awe and reverence. God, who is a consuming fire, is worthy of awe and reverence.

The angel declared that "the kingdom of the world has become the kingdom of our Lord."

6. While Christians are living godly lives, what else were they suppose to do?

Christians are to "wait for the blessed hope and manifestation of the great God and Savior, Jesus Christ."

7. What does Hebrews affirm about the nature of the kingdom of God?

The kingdom of God cannot be shaken. The things that can't be shaken remain.

8. How do we give thanks for God's unshakable kingdom and His invitation to us to join that kingdom?

We give thinks to God for our place in His kingdom by offering acceptable worship.

9. How is acceptable worship described? Why is that so?

Worship is acceptable if it is done with awe and reverence. God, who is a consuming fire, is worthy of awe and reverence.

10. What was the proclamation made by the seventh angel of the Revelation?

The angel declared that "the kingdom of the world has become the kingdom of our Lord."

Lesson 1

The Word Became Flesh

I n the beginning was the Word, and the Word was with God, and the Word was God.

2 The same was in the beginning with God.

3 All things were made by him; and without him was not any thing made that was made.

4 In him was life; and the life was the light of men.

5 And the light shineth in darkness; and the darkness comprehended it not.

6 There was a man sent from God, whose name was John.

7 The same came for a witness, to bear witness of the Light, that all men through him might believe.

8 He was not that Light, but was sent to bear witness of that Light.

9 That was the true Light, which lighteth every man that cometh into the world.

10 He was in the world, and the world was made by him, and the world knew him not.

11 He came unto his own, and his own received him not.

12 But as many as received him, to them gave he power to become the sons of God, even to them that believe on his name:

13 Which were born, not of blood, nor of the will of the flesh, nor of the will of man, but of God.

14 And the Word was made flesh, and dwelt among us, (and we beheld his glory,

John 1:1-18; 20:30-31

the glory as of the only begotten of the Father,) full of grace and truth.

15 John bare witness of him, and cried, saying, This was he of whom I space, He that cometh after me is preferred before me: for he was before me.

16 And of his fulness have all we received, and grace for grace.

17 For the law was given by Moses, but grace and truth came by Jesus Christ.

18 No man hath seen God at any time; the only begotten Son, which is in the bosom of the Father, he hath declared him.

20:30 And many other signs truly did Jesus in the presence of his disciples, which are not written in this book:

31 But these are written, that ye might believe that Jesus is the Christ, the Son of God; and that believing ye might have life through his name.

Memory Selection
John 1:1-18; 20:30-31

Background Scripture
John 1:14

Devotional Reading
Psalm 33:1-9

Printed Scripture
John 1:1-18; 20:30-31

Teacher's Target

Lesson purpose: *To introduce the Gospel of John, to grasp the purpose of the book, and to draw closer to the Christ portrayed there.*

This quarter's study focuses on the Gospel of John, one of the most profound word portraits of Christ ever "painted." From the beginning we sense that we are being treated not just to the words and deeds of Jesus but to an "insider's" description of His nature.

Enliven what may be familiar territory for many in your group by reminding them that the term "gospel" means "good news." John's Gospel provides something new and good each time we read it. Challenge your group members to look both for new insights and new ways this timeless message can be called "good."

That word "timeless" is important in today's lesson, since John begins by emphasizing the eternal nature of Christ. In an uncertain world of change, the unchanging nature of Christ is itself good news.

Lesson Introduction

For centuries, the Gospel of John has been thought to have been written by the apostle "whom Jesus loved" (13:23), in his old age. The story does not intend to trace the life of Christ from birth to death and resurrection, as the other three Gospels. Instead, John paints a more impressionistic portrait of His Lord--a "spiritual" Gospel as opposed to one that deals only with "external facts."

This inner, spiritual quality is especially apparent in John 1:1-18, often called "The Prologue." Here we learn nothing of Jesus' birth in Bethlehem, but profound truths about His nature and His existence before time began.

This selectivity in what John reports is explained in 20:30-31, the final verses in today's lesson. Here we discover not only John's purpose in writing, but an invitation both to the Gospel's original readers and to your group to believe, unto eternal life.

Teaching Outline	Daily Bible Readings
I. The Word of Creation—1:1-3 　A. Relationship to God, 1-2 　B. Relationship to creation, 3 II. The Light of Life—4-9 　A. The Light's power, 4-5 　B. The Light's witness, 6-9 III. The Power of Faith--10-13 　A. Rejection, 10-11 　B. Reception, 12-13 IV. The Word Made Flesh—14-18 V. The Reason for Writing—20:30-31	**Mon.** In the Beginning Was the Word 　*John 1:1-5* **Tue.** The Witness of John 　*John 1:6-9* **Wed.** John Baptizes Jesus 　*Mark 1:1-15* **Thu.** To All Who Received Him 　*John 1:10-13* **Fri.** Believe on the Lord Jesus 　*Acts 16:25-34* **Sat.** The Word Became Flesh 　*John 1:14-18* **Sun.** Chosen Before Creation 　*Ephesians 1:3-14*

Verse by Verse

I. The Word of Creation—1:1-3
A. Relationship to God, 1-2

1 In the beginning was the Word, and the Word was with God, and the Word was God.

2 The same was in the beginning with God.

John's Gospel begins with a hymn of praise set to a "tune" well-known in the philosophical climate of the day. Some 500 years before Christ, Greek philosophers had speculated that the unifying principle of the universe is "the word" (Grk. *logos*). This force came to be known as a "spark of divinity" running through all creation. Now John reveals that this unifying "spark" is in fact a divine Person—Jesus of Nazareth (vss. 14-17).

Proclaiming Christ as the *Logos* has some astounding implications. As the *Logos* He existed from the beginning. As the *Logos* He is also "the speech of God," and in that sense He and God are one. This implies that we can learn God's will by listening to Christ, not to human philosophy.

B. Relationship to creation, 3

3 All things were made by him; and without him was not any thing made that was made.

As the *Logos* Jesus also participated in the creation of the world. This bold claim identifying Christ with the Creator protects the important concept of monotheism. Some later teachings will claim that Jesus was the first created being, and others that He only *became* God's Son at His birth, or at His baptism. John, however, asserts with Paul that Christ existed before He became the Babe of Bethlehem, and that "by him (Christ) were all things created" (Col. 1:16).

The importance of identifying Christ with the Creator is seen in His sacrificial death. Since humans cannot put forth a worthy sacrifice for sin, God sent Himself in the form of Jesus of Nazareth as a perfect sacrifice. Our only hope of being delivered from the sinfulness of our humanity lies in the divinity of the sacrifice for our sins.

II. The Light of Life—4-9
A. The Light's power, 4-5

4 In him was life; and the life was the light of men.

5 And the light shineth in darkness; and the darkness comprehended it not.

Just as sparks from a fire provide light, Christ as the divine spark running through creation also brings light. Human religions attempt to find God by reason, or by good works. The New Covenant claims that we can discover Him only by standing in the light of His Son Jesus Christ. Since Christ is somehow identified with God, this amounts to God's revealing *Himself* instead of expecting us to find Him on our own.

As various translations indicate, verse 5 can mean either that in its darkness the world did not "understand" Christ (NIV; see also vs. 10); or that the light was so bright that the darkness could not "overpower" it (*New Century Version*). Either reading shows the superior "wattage" of Christ as the Light.

B. The Light's witness, 6-9

6 There was a man sent from God, whose name was John.

7 The same came for a witness, to bear witness of the Light, that all men through him might believe.

8 He was not that Light, but was sent to bear witness of that Light.

9 That was the true Light, which lighteth every man that cometh into the world.

The apostle John now explains how the news that Jesus of Nazareth was "the Word" came to be made known. He refers specifically to the work of another John, John the Baptist, the "voice crying in the wilderness, Make straight the way of the Lord" (vs. 23). It was important to affirm John the Baptist's work because he was, in a spiritual sense, the "Elijah" who was prophesied to come usher in the Messiah (Mal. 4:5; Matt. 11:14).

As necessary as John the Baptizer's role was, the author includes an aside that "puts him in his place." Some of John's followers mistook him for the Messiah, later even forming a sect about him. So the author takes pains to note that John was the *witness* of the Light, not the Light Himself.

Everyone born can be said to be endowed with the light for two reasons.

First, since all were created by the Light who was also somehow Christ, they have enough light within to yearn for more, and to recognize it when they see it. Second, unlike some pagan religions in which salvation is a hidden secret revealed only to a few, the death, burial, and resurrection of Christ occurred in the full light of history—during the specific reigns of specific rulers (Luke 1:5).

III. The Power of Faith—10-13
A. Rejection, 10-11

10 He was in the world, and the world was made by him, and the world knew him not.

11 He came unto his own, and his own received him not.

John consistently affirms that God's love is made manifest by the awesome fact that He as Creator condescended to enter the world of the created. The tragic irony is that so many refused to look for Him by the light said in verse 9 to be available to everyone. The first use of the phrase "his own" in verse 11 is in a form that means "his own *things*," referring to His own creation; and the second use means "his own people"—no doubt referring to those among the Jews who rejected Christ as Messiah (see the NIV).

B. Reception, 12-13

12 But as many as received him, to them gave he power to become the sons of God, even to them that believe on his name:

13 Which were born, not of blood, nor of the will of the flesh, nor of the will of man, but of God.

Many Jews and Gentiles alike did accept Christ's claims. To these people God gave the power to take on something like the divine nature of Christ—to become in a secondary sense "sons of God." While couched in the language of privilege, this must have been an affront to Jews who thought they were children of God by virtue of birth. John would revise this view by saying that *faith in Christ*, not being born of a certain blood line, enables people to become children of God. The "seed" is not of man, but the Word of God (Luke 8:11). This in fact is the "new birth" Jesus will explain in John 3:3-6.

IV. The Word Made Flesh—14-18

14 And the Word was made flesh, and dwelt among us, (and we beheld his glory, the glory as of the only begotten of the Father,) full of grace and truth.

15 John bare witness of him, and cried, saying, This was he of whom I space, He that cometh after me is preferred before me: for he was before me.

16 And of his fulness have all we received, and grace for grace.

17 For the law was given by Moses, but grace and truth came by Jesus Christ.

18 No man hath seen God at any time; the only begotten Son, which is in the bosom of the Father, he hath declared him.

Now John brings his point out of the philosophical arena to say plainly that the *Logos* is no mere speculative "force"; it is Immanuel, God with us—God Himself enfleshed in the person of Jesus (the Incarnation). By speaking of beholding Christ's glory, John probably has in mind the event of Jesus' baptism, which will be described later in this chapter. As essential as was the Law of Moses, mankind's desperate need for grace is met only in Christ.

IV. The Reason for Writing—20:30-31

30 And many other signs truly did Jesus in the presence of his disciples, which are not written in this book:

31 But these are written, that ye might believe that Jesus is the Christ, the Son of God; and that believing ye might have life through his name.

Moving toward the end of John's Gospel, our text reveals clearly that the apostle's purpose in writing is to produce faith, which in turn brings eternal life. There would not be space in all the books of the known world of John's day to record all the marvelous events in the life of Christ (21:25). The events and interpretation John does offer, however, are absolutely sufficient to create faith in those who read.

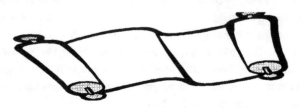

Evangelistic Emphasis

The stated purpose of the Gospel of John is to report some of the things Jesus did in His personal ministry so "that ye might believe . . . and have life through His name" (John 20:30-31).

At the time Jesus was on earth, He taught mainly Jews who professed faith in God. So the apostle John does not dwell on proofs for the existence of God; rather, he assumes the reader already believes in Him. The main burden of his Gospel is that Jesus is God, a full partner with God the Father, and that faith in Him will save.

John declares that the book is his personal testimony. He walked with Jesus throughout His time of ministry, having left his family fishing business to become one of Jesus' first disciples. He became one of Jesus' most trusted friends, chosen by Him to witness the Transfiguration and to be present when He was betrayed. It would have been a great loss to future generations if John had failed to author this book.

What has been your experience with Jesus? What do you know about Him? Is there someone who could benefit from hearing what you have to say about Jesus? In the world around us, there are many who need to know the wonderful saving power of Jesus. We praise John and the other authors of the Bible for taking the trouble to write what they knew for the benefit of posterity. We should be as thoughtful of the needs of others and share Jesus with the lost.

● ● ● ● ● ● ● ● ●

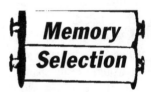

Memory Selection

And the Word was made flesh, and dwelt among us, (and we beheld His glory, the glory as of the only begotten of the Father,) full of grace and truth.—*John 1:14*

What is your concept of God? A stern old man who should be feared? A Santa Claus, a jolly old man who gives gifts to people who ask? Some say He was the Creator, but now is distant, no longer active. Some cannot imagine what God is like.

If you want to know God, know His qualities, know His interests, know Jesus. Jesus has always been with God and is the embodiment of all that God is (see Hebrews 1:1-4). When He came to earth, He could have come in any form He chose. He could have been a giant, intimidating everyone who saw Him. He could have come as an angel, having only heavenly qualities, rather than human characteristics.

John, however, declares that God came to earth as a human being, with the glory of the Father. Moreover, He entered this world as a baby, rather than as an imposing adult. He came with grace rather than with judgment. Our God is a gracious, loving God and He has shown us His face through the Christ.

Weekday Problems

Sally's life has been in a tailspin recently. She was divorced by her husband, who has made no effort to help support their two children. Her teenage son was picked up by the police after he and a friend allegedly stole a car and went joy-riding. Sally is desperate for friends, but also thinks that most people look down her because of the things that have been happening. She has been away from the church for some time—she doesn't have time to go to church and also hold down her job. What can she do?

Sally's dilemma is not unique. Many people in America struggle with circumstances quite similar. Unfortunately, there are no easy solutions to these problems. A person who has lost contact with Jesus and His church is an easy mark for Satan.

As Christians we need to maintain constant communication with God by studying His Word and by prayer. It is not shameful to ask God's aid when we are down, even if we have not been doing His will in our lives. In fact, as someone has said, "Man's extremity is God's opportunity." We know that God and His angels rejoice when we acknowledge our sin and negligence to Him.

* What would you advise someone in circumstances similar to Sally's?

* What are the ingredients of a healthy relationship with God and His church?

* Does God hear the prayers of sinners?

Thoughts on the Incarnation

The Word of God, Jesus Christ, on account of his great love for mankind, became what we are in order to make us what he is himself.—*Irenaeus, c. A.D. 130-200*

* * *

The wonder of the Incarnation is not that God got himself embodied, but that he got himself expressed—expressed in the wonderful life and character of Christ.—*William Newton Clarke*

* * *

God is in our midst; He is now here . . . . Our very bodies become His temples, and our lives must be daily fashioned after the pattern of His presence.—*J. C. Massee*

* * *

Only the Word made flesh can give any sort of hope in a world as grim and ugly and hard and sordid as ours.—*Lynn Harold Hough*

This Lesson in Your Life

What kind of standard are you following in your life? Many say, "I keep the Ten Commandments—that's all I need to do to please God." But is that true? Indeed, Moses delivered the Law of God to the Israelites at Mt. Sinai. It should be noted, however, that the Law consisted of much more than the Ten Commandments. True, the two tables of stone God gave Moses contained the Ten Commandments, but God also commanded obedience to a veritable library of laws which are recorded in the books of Exodus, Leviticus, Numbers and Deuteronomy. All of these laws were intended for the Israelites to obey. Their history reveals that they seldom obeyed the law, but the law was theirs to keep if they would please God.

It would be unfortunate if we were limited to the Ten Commandments as a standard in our lives. As John says so eloquently, "the Law was given by Moses, but grace and truth came by Jesus Christ." The Apostle Paul says in Romans 6:14, "ye are not under the law, but under grace." The Law of Moses was fulfilled in Christ and was taken out of the way at His crucifixion (Col. 2:13-17). Jesus abolished the law of Moses and instituted His own, the law of grace and truth.

This is not a license to violate every law given by God through Moses. In fact, nearly every one of the Ten Commandments can be found in the writings of the New Testament. So Christ has not called people to be lawless. Rather, we must recognize that the law of Moses was given for a limited time and that we are now under a different kind of dispensation with different laws.

Jesus gave some insight into this change when He spoke to the disciples on the mountain (Matt. 5–7). He warned them that hating was equivalent to murder; and lusting is equivalent to fornication. In other words, the law we are under now is one of the heart, not just a law of external behavior. Yes, we are under grace and truth. Does that mean that behavior is unimportant? Of course not. God calls us to control the intents of our hearts so that our behavior will be upright. For example, we are to hate sin, we must not do harm to anyone and we must love everyone, even our enemies. Jesus has high expectations for His followers, even higher than Moses expected from the Israelites. As the writer of Hebrews points out, we have a better covenant with better promises (Heb. 8:6).

What does John mean when he says that "grace and truth came by Jesus Christ"? While God has never suggested that mankind must earn salvation, the Israelites seemed never to understand that their relationship with God was based on His grace rather than their works. God freely gives salvation to those who believe Him and turn their lives over to Him. Their lives will be free from the evil of Satan, and they will "do truth." That is, they will do the things which God has asked them to do. That was the message of Christ (see John 3:16-21).

If we will accept God's grace and let Him mold our lives according to His will, the quality of our lives will exceed anything that was possible under the law of Moses.

Seed Thoughts

1. Who is the Word introduced in verse 1 of John 1?
The Word is Jesus Christ (John 1:14-15; 29-30).

2. Jesus came to the world and to His own. Who were "His own?"
The Jews, who were expecting a Messiah, but did not accept Jesus because they were expecting Him to be a political leader.

3. Why was it important for the Christ to come as a human?
To show how a human could deal successfully with temptation; to die on the cross for our sins and to qualify to be our intercessor with God.

4. What was John the Baptist's role?
John was sent "to bear witness of the Light" and to prepare the people for the coming of the Christ.

5. Has anyone ever seen God?
No (John 1:18).

---

1. Who is the Word introduced in verse 1 of John 1?

2. Jesus came to the world and to His own. Who were "His own?"

3. Why was it important for the Christ to come as a human?

4. What was John the Baptist's role?

5. Has anyone ever seen God?

6. How does one get the power to become a child of God?

7. Why was the Gospel of John written?

8. Is there sufficient information in the Bible to support faith in Jesus as the Son of God?

9. Are all of the miracles Jesus performed recorded in the Bible?

10. Why do you think it took so long for Jesus' disciples to accept Him as the Christ?

(Continued next page)

The Word is Jesus Christ (John 1:14-15; 29-30).

The Jews, who were expecting a Messiah, but did not accept Jesus because they were expecting Him to be a political leader.

To show how a human could deal successfully with temptation; to die on the cross for our sins and to qualify to be our intercessor with God.

John was sent "to bear witness of the Light" and to prepare the people for the coming of the Christ.

No (John 1:18).

Believe on His Name and He will give you the "power to become the sons of God" (John 1:12).

That the reader might believe in Jesus and have eternal life (John 20:30-31).

Yes, the Bible documents His birth, temptations, miracles, teaching, death, burial, resurrection and ascension back to heaven.

No (John 20:30).

They had the same misunderstanding of the prophecies about the Christ as the other Jews, as well as delusions about status in His kingdom.

6. How does one get the power to become a child of God?

Believe on His Name and He will give you the "power to become the sons of God" (John 1:12).

7. Why was the Gospel of John written?

That the reader might believe in Jesus and have eternal life (John 20:30-31).

8. Is there sufficient information in the Bible to support faith in Jesus as the Son of God?

Yes, the Bible documents His birth, temptations, miracles, teaching, death, burial, resurrection and ascension back to heaven.

9. Are all of the miracles Jesus performed recorded in the Bible?

No. (John 20:30)

10. Why do you think it took so long for Jesus' disciples to accept Him as the Christ?

They had the same misunderstanding of the prophecies about the Christ as the other Jews, as well as delusions about status in His kingdom.

The Witness of John the Baptist

A nd this is the record of John, when the Jews sent priests and Levites from Jerusalem to ask him, Who art thou?

20 And he confessed, and denied not; but confessed, I am not the Christ.

21 And they asked him, What then? Art thou Elias? And he saith, I am not. Art thou that prophet? And he answered, No.

22 Then said they unto him, Who art thou? that we may give an answer to them that sent us. What sayest thou of thyself?

23 He said, I am the voice of one crying in the wilderness, Make straight the way of the Lord, as said the prophet Esaias.

24 And they which were sent were of the Pharisees.

25 And they asked him, and said unto him, Why baptizest thou then, if thou be not that Christ, nor Elias, neither that prophet?

26 John answered them, saying, I baptize with water: but there standeth one among you, whom ye know not;

27 He it is, who coming after me is preferred before me, whose shoe's latchet I am not worthy to unloose.

28 These things were done in Bethabara beyond Jordan, where John was baptizing.

29 The next day John seeth Jesus coming unto him, and saith, Behold the Lamb of God, which taketh away the sin of the world.

30 This is he of whom I said, After me cometh a man which is preferred before me: for he was before me.

31 And I knew him not: but that he should be made manifest to Israel, therefore am I come baptizing with water.

John 1:19-34

32 And John bare record, saying, I saw the Spirit descending from heaven like a dove, and it abode upon him.

33 And I knew him not: but he that sent me to baptize with water, the same said unto me, Upon whom thou shalt see the Spirit descending, and remaining on him, the same is he which baptizeth with the Holy Ghost.

34 And I saw, and bare record that this is the Son of God.

Memory Selection
John 1:29

Background Scripture
John 1:19-42

Devotional Reading
Ephesians 4:25–5:2

Printed Scripture
John 1:19-34

Teacher's Target

Lesson purpose: *To introduce the work of John the Baptist in preparing the way for Jesus, and in bearing witness to Him as the Messiah.*

While we may not think of it often, much of life revolves around "testimonials." We present an ID card to the bank teller to testify to our identity. A witness to an accident testifies to what she saw. People testify to the effectiveness of commerical products, from roofing to refrigerators, medicines to make-up, cars to soft drinks. Many Christians have important testimonials about how God has worked in their lives.

Ask members of your study group what they feel strong enough about to "bear witness" or testify to. Will some testify to the superiority of their favorite grocery store? To the value of the being a Democrat over a Republican? To the quality of the weather in Florida over that in Texas?

Of all the convictions to which we might testify, none is as important as our testimony that, in John's words, "This (Jesus) is the son of God."

Lesson Introduction

John the Baptist was a relative of Jesus (Luke 1:36, 60). After the style of some Old Testament prophets, he had a desert ministry and a rough-hewn style, wearing a camel-cloak and leather belt, and dining on locusts and wild honey (Mark 1:6). He was a bold preacher, dared to baptize people in preparation for the new day dawning, and had his own disciples (3:23-25).

When all this suggested to some that John was the Messiah, he set them straight: he was only a witness to the Christ. Yet his ministry was crucial: he was a forerunner preparing the way for Messiah. He was even the figurative reincarnation of the prophet Elijah, whose reappearance would herald the coming of the Christ (Mal. 4:5; Matt. 11:14).

After a courageous preaching career, John was arrested and beheaded by King Herod for daring to question the king's morality (Matt. 14:11-12). Jesus' epitaph was fitting: "There hath not risen a greater than John the Baptist" (Matt. 11:11).

Teaching Outline	Daily Bible Readings
I. The Interrogation—19-22	**Mon.** John's Testimony *John 1:19-23*
A. The inquisitors, 19	**Tue.** I Baptize with Water *John 1:24-28*
B. The questions, 20-22	**Wed.** Here Is the Lamb of God *John 1:29-34*
II. The Answers—23-28	**Thu.** What Are You Looking For? *John 1:35-42*
A. To prepare the way, 23	**Fri.** Jesus Commends John *John 3:22-36*
B. To baptize, 24-28	**Sat.** Jesus Must Increase *Luke 7:18-28*
III. The Testimony—29-34	**Sun.** John Is Beheaded *Mark 6:14-29*
A. 'Behold the Lamb!' 29-30	
B. The sign of the Spirit, 31-34	

Verse by Verse

I. The Interrogation—19-22
A. The inquisitors, 19

19 And this is the record of John, when the Jews sent priests and Levites from Jerusalem to ask him, Who art thou?

Here we are told that John's inquisitors consist of priests and Levites from Jerusalem, the center of Jewish religious authority, and verse 24 notes that the Pharisees sent them. We are to gather from this that these are not friendly questioners, but representatives of the Jewish establishment who are threatened by John's work. As in many Old Testament incidents, this is an encounter between the "prophetic" interest in radical commitment —represented here by John the Baptist—and priestly concerns that religion be done "correctly." Many reform movements since the time of Christ—in both religious and political settings— have reenacted this tension between conservative forces in control and reformation-minded advocates of change.

In this case, the Jewish authorities in Jerusalem were concerned that radical movements like John's might upset their uneasy truce with the occupying forces of Rome. The function of priests and Levites was no longer just to preside over sacrifices and Temple worship. They had become skilled politicians. Despite the superficial courtesy of their questions, their real mission is to keep this upstart wilderness preacher from upsetting the balance of power that kept Rome from crushing Judaism.

B. The questions, 20-22

20 And he confessed, and denied not; but confessed, I am not the Christ.

21 And they asked him, What then? Art thou Elias? And he saith, I am not. Art thou that prophet? And he answered, No.

22 Then said they unto him, Who art thou? that we may give an answer to them that sent us. What sayest thou of thyself?

John's consistent witness since 1:8 has been to deny that he is the Christ ("the Anointed One," the Messiah). It is possible, however, that his interrogators press the question because they want to convict him of being a false messiah, so they can arrest him.

Other possibilities John's opponents suggest had probably been circulating as rumors. Perhaps this Elijah-like figure is in fact Elijah "reincarnated." Jerusalem was boiling with messianic excitement and expectations that "the Day of the Lord" had arrived; and the prophet Malachi had predicted that Elijah would reappear to herald the event (Mal. 4:5). Or perhaps John was "that prophet"—

the one like Moses whom God had also promised to send (Deut. 18:15). John answers No to all these possibilities, then proceeds to explain his real identity and mission.

II. The Answers—23-28
A. To prepare the way, 23

23 He said, I am the voice of one crying in the wilderness, Make straight the way of the Lord, as said the prophet Esaias.

John explains that he is "only" the one designated to prepare the way of the Lord. However, quoting "Esaias" or Isaiah (40:3) in support of this role would have been cause for concern to any questioner who knew his Old Testament. For Isaiah was predicting the return of the Jews who had been taken captive to Babylon. In true prophetic fashion, his message was both comforting and stern. Only if the people would repent—make their own paths straight —would God restore them to the land. By implication John was charging that the current level of faith and commitment in Israel was so uneven that a radical "leveling" was needed to make way for the Holy One of Israel. This is further shown by John's work as a baptizer, described below.

B. To baptize, 24-28

24 And they which were sent were of the Pharisees.

25 And they asked him, and said unto him, Why baptizest thou then, if thou be not that Christ, nor Elias, neither that prophet?

26 John answered them, saying,

I baptize with water: but there standeth one among you, whom ye know not;

27 He it is, who coming after me is preferred before me, whose shoe's latchet I am not worthy to unloose.

28 These things were done in Bethabara beyond Jordan, where John was baptizing.

The Pharisees' spokesmen see correctly that John's practice of baptizing those who respond to his preaching is an accusation that they need to be "washed" from their sins. In addition to the political issues at stake, John's opponents resent being charged with allowing Judaism to sink so low spiritually and morally that a reformation-baptizing movement is needed.

Yet John again speaks of his own work as being secondary to that of the Messiah. While he baptized people with water, Messiah would baptize them with the Holy Spirit and with fire, as Matthew's account adds (Matt. 3:11)—another retort not designed to passify John's questioners. They must have had visions of people seized by an uncontrollable spirit and shouting "Burn, baby burn!"

This one with the superior baptism, John goes on to say, was among them now as an unrecognized Messiah. Although His ministry will come "after" John's, it will be as superior to John's work as a shoe is to a shoe-string.

III. The Testimony—29-34
A. 'Behold the Lamb!' 29-30

29 The next day John seeth Jesus

coming unto him, and saith, Behold the Lamb of God, which taketh away the sin of the world.

30 This is he of whom I said, After me cometh a man which is preferred before me: for he was before me.

The stage has been set and the characters introduced. It is now time for Jesus Himself to emerge from His incognito status, to be revealed as the Word made flesh, and to begin His own ministry. John's dramatic, "Behold the Lamb!" is breath-taking in scope: This is the one who will not simply reform Israel but bear the sins of the entire world. It is this role that earns Jesus the title "Lamb of God." He will be the fulfillment of the Old Testament's sacrificial system.

John's confessional outburst quoted here may not have occurred until after the scene to follow, which indicates that he did not know of Jesus' identity as the Christ until the Spirit descended upon Him—which the other Gospels say occurred at His baptism. The next day, John will repeat his acclaim that Jesus is the Lamb of God (vs. 36).

B. The sign of the Spirit, 31-34

31 And I knew him not: but that he should be made manifest to Israel, therefore am I come baptizing with water.

32 And John bare record, saying, I saw the Spirit descending from heaven like a dove, and it abode upon him.

33 And I knew him not: but he that sent me to baptize with water, the same said unto me, Upon whom thou shalt see the Spirit descending, and remaining on him, the same is he which baptizeth with the Holy Ghost.

34 And I saw, and bare record that this is the Son of God.

Scholars have looked in vain for earlier descriptions of the Holy Spirit appearing as a dove, to explain why John would have recognized the dove as the Spirit in this scene. All we know is that the same God who commissioned John told him to watch for this sign. Verse 31 indicates that John's mission of baptism was not only to call people to repentance in preparation for the Messianic Age, but also as the means by which he would recognize Jesus when He too came to be baptized.

Since Jesus and John were relatives (perhaps cousins), it would be strange if John did not know Him. Perhaps John means that he did not recognize that his kinsman Jesus was God's Son and the long-awaited Messiah until this dramatic sign was given.

The main point of the passage is John's faithfulness in bearing witness that Jesus is the Son of God. The terms "record" in verses 19, 32, and 34 ("testimony" and "testify" in the NIV) all come from the Greek *martys*—reminding us that confessions of faith like John's will later cost many testifiers their lives.

• • • • • • • • •

Evangelistic Emphasis

I became a Christian in 1972 just a month short of my twenty-first birthday. The Lord got my attention through a Lay Witness Mission, a spiritual program going through our denomination at the time. Lay Witness Missions are built around personal testimony. There is no preaching. There are no preachers. The weekend consists primarily of non-ordained folks sharing with other folks what Christ has meant in their lives.

God used the Lay Witness Mission in a mighty way in my life and in the lives of many others. I may never have become a Christian without the Lay Witness Mission. God got my attention through the testimonies of regular folks who had given their lives to Him.

In this passage John is giving His testimony. He is simply telling what he has seen and heard and experienced. Our Heavenly Father asks for that from us. Could we simply tell folks what we have seen and heard and experienced from the Lord in our own lives? We do not have to preach. We do not have to be Bible scholars. All we have to do is give testimony of what God has done in our lives. When we share our testimony, God will do the rest. Be willing to share with others what God has done for you, please.

● ● ● ● ● ● ● ● ●

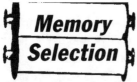

The next day John seeth Jesus coming unto him, and saith, Behold the Lamb of God, which taketh away the sin of the world.— *John 1:29*

There is a legend associated with the angels' appearance to shepherds on the first Christmas night. It has been said that the shepherds were the keepers of a flock that was specifically bred for sacrifice. The shepherds were careful to develop animals without blemish or spot. They had the very best flock in all the land.

One night an angel came. He told the shepherds of a baby, a Savior, born in the city of David. Suddenly the sky was filled with angels praising God.

Then the angels left, all except one. The lone angel came close to the keepers of the sacrificial flock and spoke to them, "By the way, fellows, you guys are out of business. The Lamb of God, the perfect sacrifice to take away the sin of the world, has been born."

That is just a story. Yet, truth is told. In Christ Jesus' atoning, sacrificial death our sins are taken away. No more sacrifice is needed.

Weekday Problems

Jon waited for Ray to respond. It seems the Lord was urging him, "Say something, Ray. This is what I have prepared you for."

Ray had noticed something was bothering Jon. Lately Jon had become withdrawn. Today, while they were taking a break from working on Ray's car, Jonathan opened up. He had been molested as a child by one of his mother's boyfriends. He had told his mom, but she simply told Jon to keep his mouth shut. Jon lived with that pain until it turned into a cold, hard stone of seething anger in his soul. The anger affected his relationships. It seems Jon could never connect with anyone. It was killing him inside.

Jon's revelation shocked Ray. Ray was shocked, not because of Jon's past, but that Jon's story was exactly like his own. He was molested as a youngster. No one came to his defense. Anger and bitterness dogged him. The anger came out in his relationships, preventing him from ever really being close to anyone.

Yet, for Ray there was a change. A woman he was dating asked Ray to go to church with her. There Ray met Christ. Christ's forgiveness for Ray allowed Ray to forgive those who had hurt him in the past. Ray was born again. "Just tell him what I did for you," God's voice whispered to Ray.

* How might Ray's story help Jon?

* Have you ever been called to share personal testimony? What happened?

Ministry Madness

Q: Who can stay single even if he marries many women?
A: The minister, of course.

* * *

Q: What is a "prime minister"?
A: A preacher at his best, of course.

* * *

Fay: How did you like the sermon this morning?
Kay: Not as much last Sunday's. Then he finished up by saying "In conclusion," and he concluded. Today he said "Lastly"— and he lasted and lasted.

* * *

"How do you like the new minister?" a customer asked the store-keeper.

"Well, I ain't heard him, but I like him fine."

"How can you say that?"

"I like the way folks have been comin' in here payin' their bills since he started preachin'."

This Lesson in Your Life

Bearing Witness

The New King James Version begins this passage with these words, "Now this is the testimony of John . . . ." John was a great prophet. Things were happening in John's ministry. People were flocking to hear him. Yet when the priests and Levites went to John to see why this unauthorized teacher was causing such a commotion, John took the opportunity to point to the Messiah. His testimony pointed folks to Jesus. That is what a Christian testimony should always do.

Our testimony is a powerful thing. In a court of law, testimony should be what one has witnessed, what one knows, that of which one is sure. Our Christian testimony is much the same. We tell of that which we have experienced and witnessed. We testify about that which we know. We share that of which we are sure.

In Revelation 12:11. The saints of God have been saved. The one (Satan) who accused the saints before God had been thrown down. The Bible says Satan was defeated by the saints. "They overcame him by the blood of the Lamb and by the *word of their testimony*" (italics mine). Our testimony is a powerful tool in God's hand.

We remember that the last thing Jesus said while on this earth, was "You will receive power when the Holy Spirit comes on you; and you will be my witnesses in Jerusalem, and in all Judea and Samaria, and to the ends of the earth." We are commissioned to be witnesses. We are instructed to tell others about Jesus.

That should not be hard to do. We Christians know the Savior of the world. We Christians know the One who gives eternal life. We Christians know the One who is "the Way, the Truth and the Life." We will testify of Him, won't we?

Suppose I had cancer and I was dying. Further suppose that you had discovered the cure for cancer. The treatment was without side effects and it had a proven 100 percent cure rate. If you had the cure for what was killing me, you would tell me, wouldn't you? Well, friends, Christians do have the way to life eternal. It just makes sense that we would share that way with one who has not found it yet.

You may also remember that Jesus declared that He is the Bread of Life (John 6:35). Bread is the staff of life. Bread will sustain the hungry as nothing else will. We Christians must point others to the Bread of Life. We live in a world of people hungering for something that will give their lives meaning and significance. People are starving for relevance and purpose in their lives. May we help feed a soul-hungry world by simply sharing with others the Bread of Life.

Jesus said, "Let your light shine before men, that they may see your good deeds and praise your Father in heaven" (Matt. 5:16). Our very lives must be our witness. However, we must be careful. If we live our lives to bring glory to ourselves, we have erred.

A powerful testimony is one that points others toward Christ, the Messiah. That is what John's testimony did. May we do the same.

Seed Thoughts

1. John said, "I am not the Christ." What does the word "Christ" mean?

The word "Christ" is the Greek word used to translate the Hebrew, "Messiah." Both words mean "the anointed One."

2. The Jews asked John if he was Elijah. Why might they have thought he was Elijah?

Because Elijah had not died. He was taken up into heaven. The Jews believed that Elijah would come back to announce the end time.

3. Who did John claim to be, according to Isaiah's prophecy?

John identified himself as "the voice of one calling in the desert, 'Make straight the way for the Lord.'"

4. How did the baptism of John differ from the baptism of Jesus?

John baptized with water. Jesus baptizes with the Holy Spirit.

5. How do we know John believed the Messiah was greater than he was?

John said he was unworthy to untie the thongs of the sandals of the One who was coming after John.

1. John said, "I am not the Christ." What does the word "Christ" mean?

2. The Jews asked John if he was Elijah. Why might they have thought he was Elijah?

3. Who did John claim to be, according to Isaiah's prophecy?

4. How did the baptism of John differ from the baptism of Jesus?

5. How do we know John believed the Messiah was greater than he was?

6. How could the one to come after John be before him? See John 1:30. Refer back to John 1:1-5.

7. John called Jesus "the Lamb of God, who takes away the sin of the world." What did he mean?

8. Where did Jesus' baptism and this particular encounter between John and the Jews take place?

9. How did John know for sure that Jesus was the one who would baptize with the Holy Spirit?

10. What was John's testimony as recorded in verse 34?

(Continued next page)

279

The word "Christ" is the Greek word used to translate the Hebrew, "Messiah." Both words mean "the anointed One."

Because Elijah had not died. He was taken up into heaven. The Jews believed that Elijah would come back to announce the end time.

John identified himself as "the voice of one calling in the desert, 'Make straight the way for the Lord.'"

John baptized with water. Jesus baptizes with the Holy Spirit.

John said he was unworthy to untie the thongs of the sandals of the One who was coming after John.

John recognized the truth of John 1:1-5. Jesus was with God. Jesus was God. Jesus was with God from before the beginning of time.

John was saying that Jesus would be the sacrifice that would atone for the sin of the world.

"This all happened at Bethany on the other side of the Jordan, where John was baptizing" (vs. 28).

God told John that the Spirit Baptizer would be identified by the Spirit coming down as a dove and resting on the Chosen One.

"I have seen and I testify that this (meaning Jesus Christ) is the Son of God."

6. How could the one to come after John be before him? See John 1:30. Refer back to John 1:1-5.

John recognized the truth of John 1:1-5. Jesus was with God. Jesus was God. Jesus was with God from before the beginning of time.

7. John called Jesus "the Lamb of God, who takes away the sin of the world." What did he mean?

John was saying that Jesus would be the sacrifice that would atone for the sin of the world.

8. Where did Jesus' baptism and this particular encounter between John and the Jews take place?

"This all happened at Bethany on the other side of the Jordan, where John was baptizing" (vs. 28).

9. How did John know for sure that Jesus was the one who would baptize with the Holy Spirit?

God told John that the Spirit Baptizer would be identified by the Spirit coming down as a dove and resting on the Chosen One.

10. What was John's testimony as recorded in verse 34?

"I have seen and I testify that this (meaning Jesus Christ) is the Son of God."

Nicodemus Visits Jesus

There was a man of the Pharisees, named Nicodemus, a ruler of the Jews:

2 The same came to Jesus by night, and said unto him, Rabbi, we know that thou art a teacher come from God: for no man can do these miracles that thou doest, except God be with him.

3 Jesus answered and said unto him, Verily, verily, I say unto thee, Except a man be born again, he cannot see the kingdom of God.

John 3:1-17

4 Nicodemus saith unto him, How can a man be born when he is old? can he enter the second time into his mother's womb, and be born?

5 Jesus answered, Verily, verily, I say unto thee, Except a man be born of water and the the the Spirit, he cannot enter into the kingdom of God.

6 That which is born of the flesh is flesh; and that which is born of the Spirit is spirit.

7 Marvel not that I said unto thee, Ye must be born again.

8 The wind bloweth where it listeth, and thou hearest the sound thereof, but canst not tell whence it cometh, and whither it goeth: so is every one that is born of the Spirit.

9 Nicodemus answered and said unto him, How can these things be?

10 Jesus answered and said unto him, Art thou a master of Israel, and knowest not these things?

11 Verily, verily, I say unto thee, We speak that we do know, and testify that we have seen; and ye receive not our witness.

12 If I have told you earthly things, and ye believe not, how shall ye believe, if I tell you of heavenly things?

13 And no man hath ascended up to heaven, but he that came down from heaven, even the Son of man which is in heaven.

14 And as Moses lifted up the serpent in the wilderness, even so must the Son of man be lifted up:

15 That whosoever believeth in him should not perish, but have eternal life.

16 For God so loved the world, that he gave his only begotten Son, that whosoever believeth in him should not perish, but have everlasting life.

17 For God sent not his Son into the world to condemn the world; but that the world through him might be saved.

Memory Selection
John 3:17

Background Scripture
John 3:1-21

Devotional Reading
1 Corinthians 15:17 -22

Printed Scripture
John 3:1-17

Teacher's Target

Lesson purpose: *To affirm the power of God to impart new life through the new birth, as described in Jesus' encounter with Nicodemus.*

This lesson might well be introduced by asking those in your group to recall an experience when they or someone they know has ever *changed*—really had a life-changing turn-around. The point is to challenge the cynical view that "people don't change." Negative experiences easily cause us to grow callous and hardened. Many are trapped by the sentiment, "What has been will be again . . . there is nothing new under the sun" (Eccles. 1:9, NIV).

Solomon could conclude this because he was looking only at things "under the sun"—what is humanly possible. In Jesus' conversation with Nicodemus, however, He opens up heavenly possibilities. Challenge learners to be open to the possibility of second chances and new beginnings. They are possible for those who choose to be twice-born!

Lesson Introduction

In our last lesson we noted that many of the priests and Pharisees of Jerusalem were concerned about political unrest stemming from the people's expectation of the Messiah. In this lesson, Jesus' conversation with the Jewish official Nicodemus shows that He was more concerned in changing the human heart than in political changes.

This does not mean that we do not expect faith to make an impact on society. It means that this impact is to begin at the personal level. It means that people discouraged by habits they have been unable to break, or burdened by a sense of guilt, can expect supernatural release when they commit themselves to the One who promises "new birth"—and who, through the ever-widening effects of His ministry, really did change the world, one heart at a time.

Teaching Outline	Daily Bible Readings

I. An Evening Visit—1-2
  A. A Jewish ruler, 1
  B. Tentative respect, 2
II. An Impossible Possibility—3-8
  A. Being born again, 3-4
  B. Being born of the Spirit, 5-8
III. An Answer from Heaven—9-13
IV. A God Who Loves and Saves—14-17
  A. Moses raised a serpent, 14-15
  B. God sent His Son, 16-17
	Mon. Nicodemus Visits Jesus
	    John 3:1-10
	Tue. God So Loved the World
	    John 3:11-21
	Wed. Nicodemus Takes a Stand
	    John 7:45-52
	Thu. Jesus' Body Is Claimed
	    John 19:38-42
	Fri. A Contrasting Response
	    Matthew 19:16-22
	Sat. Another Contrasting Response
	    Acts 24:22-27
	Sun. God Cares for All
	    Psalm 91:1-16

Verse by Verse

I. An Evening Visit—1-2

A. A Jewish ruler, 1

1 There was a man of the Pharisees, named Nicodemus, a ruler of the Jews:

Nicodemus, mentioned only in John's Gospel, is a rare exception to the New Testament's usually negative picture of Pharisees. They were a sect of Jews known for their careful study and protection of Jewish laws and traditions, but not for their consistent application of them to their lives. Although Nicodemus comes to Jesus with honest and open questions, Pharisees are more often described as hypocrites who "draw nigh unto me with their mouth, and honour them with their lips; but their heart is far from me" (Matt. 15:7-8).

As a "ruler of the Jews," Nicodemus may have been a member of the Sanhedrin, a council given considerable authority over internal Jewish affairs by the occupying Roman forces. Although he does not come to faith here, he later defends Jesus against condemnation without a hearing (7:50-51); and anoints Jesus' body for burial after His crucifixion (19:39).

B. Tentative respect, 2

2 The same came to Jesus by night, and said unto him, Rabbi, we know that thou art a teacher come from God: for no man can do these miracles that thou doest, except God be with him.

Nicodemus probably approached Jesus at night because coming openly might compromise his position as a ruler of the Jews. His defense of Christ in 7:50-51 earned suspicion that he was loyal to the Galilean. At least he indicates a willingness to learn the truth about this teacher for himself.

Nicodemus' confession that Jesus is a teacher come from God stemmed from the miracles Jesus has been performing. This is exactly the basis of faith Jesus calls for in John 10:38: "Though ye believe not me, believe the works." Yet there must be more to saving faith than marveling at the signs and wonders Christ performed. Nicodemus is a remarkable illustration of the fact that we are saved by faith, not by sight; for the miracles he acknowledged that Jesus performed were not enough to bring the new birth Jesus says is required for salvation.

II. An Impossible Possibility—3-8

A. Being born again, 3-4

3 Jesus answered and said unto him, Verily, verily, I say unto thee, Except a man be born again, he cannot see the kingdom of God.

4 Nicodemus saith unto him, How can a man be born when he is old? can he enter the second time into his mother's womb, and be born?

"Verily" is from the Greek *amen*, and simply means "truly." Jesus begins this sentence and the one in verse 5 in this way to emphasize the importance and truth of what He is about to say.

This teaching on the need to be "born again" possibly arose because Jesus perceives that Nicodemus' faith lies in his being born a Jew. After all, the Messiah was a Jewish Savior; and many even among Jesus' followers were slow to grasp the concept that non-Jews might be "grafted" into God's family by some means other than being physically born into it.

Jesus, however, insists that people now enter the Kingdom by a spiritual birth. The word for "again" can also mean "from above"—indicating that God, not human parents, "births" people into His true spiritual Family. Nicodemus' question about whether this means repeating the physical birth process indicates that he simply cannot grasp the spiritual dimension of Jesus' teaching.

B. Being born of the Spirit, 5-8

5 Jesus answered, Verily, verily, I say unto thee, Except a man be born of water and of the Spirit, he cannot enter into the kingdom of God.

6 That which is born of the flesh is flesh; and that which is born of the Spirit is spirit.

7 Marvel not that I said unto thee, Ye must be born again.

8 The wind bloweth where it listeth, and thou hearest the sound thereof, but canst not tell whence it cometh, and whither it goeth: so is every one that is born of the Spirit.

Jesus explains that the new birth involves water and Spirit—two common Old Testament concepts of coming into a new and living relationship with God. Through the prophet Ezekiel God said

"Then will I sprinkle clean water upon you, and ye shall be clean . . . and a new spirit will I put within you" (Ezek. 36:25-26).

Although water seems to symbolize cleansing and Spirit the infusion of God's Spirit into ours, the exact way these elements comprise the new birth is widely debated. Some authorities say the water refers to the water that accompanies physical birth, and that Jesus is showing Nicodemus that his natural birth as a Jew was a necessary but insufficient start toward a new relationship with God. Most scholars, however, hold that the water refers to baptism. If this is so, verse 5 is virtually a commentary on the way water and Spirit are related in Acts 2:38: "Repent, and be baptized . . . and ye shall receive the gift of the Holy Ghost."

To further help Nicodemus understand the role of the Spirit in the new birth, Jesus compares it to the wind. While we cannot see wind, we see and hear its results. Simply because the Holy Spirit is also unseen should be no grounds for doubting that He can initiate spiritual birth just as human seed was responsible for Nicodemus' having been born a Jew.

III. An Answer from Heaven—9-13

9 Nicodemus answered and said unto him, How can these things be?

10 Jesus answered and said unto him, Art thou a master of Israel, and knowest not these things?

11 Verily, verily, I say unto thee, We speak that we do know, and testify that we have seen; and ye receive not our witness.

12 If I have told you earthly things, and ye believe not, how shall

ye believe, if I tell you of heavenly things?

13 And no man hath ascended up to heaven, but he that came down from heaven, even the Son of man which is in heaven.

Despite the help in understanding the new birth Jesus has offered, Nicodemus cannot grasp the concept. There is an edge of accusation in Jesus' response: How can a person claim to be a spiritual teacher (the meaning of the word "master"), with such a limited capacity for understanding spiritual truths?

Having "told" Nicodemus "earthly things" may refer to the way Jesus had "communicated" His divinity through His publicly performed miracles, which Nicodemus himself had admitted were an indication that God was with Him. Seeing water changed into wine, for example, should have been an adequate basis for believing that God could also perform the inner, unseen miracle of salvation in the new birth.

Verse 13 indicates that the miracle of the new birth is not something that could be accomplished by a human being, even though he claimed to have ascended to heaven and received such power. Rather, it is an event made possible only by the Son, who *descended* from heaven to reveal it to lost mankind.

IV. A God Who Loves and Saves—14-17

A. Moses raised a serpent, 14-15

14 And as Moses lifted up the serpent in the wilderness, even so must the Son of man be lifted up:

15 That whosoever believeth in him should not perish, but have eternal life.

The apostle John may turn here from his account of Jesus' encounter with Nicodemus, since Jesus' comments now seem to be more of a discourse to anyone listening. Just as He had *descended* with word of the new birth, so He will be lifted up—on the Cross, then into heaven again. In this way He will save those who come to Him just as Old Testament believers were saved from snakebite when they looked with faith on the serpent Moses raised on the pole (see Num. 21:6-9).

B. God sent His Son, 16-17

16 For God so loved the world, that he gave his only begotten Son, that whosoever believeth in him should not perish, but have everlasting life.

17 For God sent not his Son into the world to condemn the world; but that the world through him might be saved.

"Everlasting life" in verse 16, so justly famous as a favorite Bible passage, is the same as "eternal life" in verse 15 and being "saved" in verse 17. Eternal life refers to the kind of life God has, as opposed to the temporary life of created beings. Thus, believing in the only-begotten Son, or being born again, imparts God's life into ours even now, in addition to promising that we will live forever with Him.

Evangelistic Emphasis

Jesus said to Nicodemus, "You must be born again" (v. 7). What Jesus did *not* say is just as important as what He did say. Notice, Jesus did not say, "Nicodemus, you have to get hold of yourself." No, Nicodemus was a successful man. He was a member of the Jewish ruling council. Nicodemus already had it all together.

Jesus did not say to Nicodemus, "It's time you turned over a new leaf." Again, Nicodemus was not a bad man. He did not need to be rehabilitated for anything, as far as we know. He was a decent, up-standing, church-going human being.

Yet, Nicodemus needed a rebirth. Birth is a funny thing. A person cannot "birth" themselves. Birth, both physical and spiritual, is beyond our personal power and ability. It must be done for us by a power greater than ourselves.

There are many in our world today who need to be born again. As a matter of fact, every person who has not been born again needs to be. Regardless of whether or not that person is a fine, upstanding citizen, if he has not been born again he needs to be. Regardless of whether or not that person is a leader in the church, if he has not been born again he needs to be. The new birth in Christ Jesus is the beginning of the Christian life. Without it, one remains unchristian still.

• • • • • • • • • •

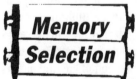

Memory Selection

For God sent not his Son into the world to condemn the world; but that the world through him might be saved.—*John 3:17*

Christians today are viewed in a negative light by many in our society. Part of the reason for that perception is because we Christians always seem to speak out against so many things the world considers acceptable. Christians speak out against activity that degrades or destroys the family. We fight against pornography in movies and books and on the Internet. We warn society of the destructive effects of alcohol and drug consumption. You know, on the surface, it does look like we do condemn many things non-Christians accept.

Yet, the condemnation of destructive life-styles can be lifesaving. If a man were driving his car at breakneck speed toward a bridge that had been washed away, the sweetest words he could hear would be, "Hey! Look out! Stop!!"

Jesus did not come to condemn the world. He came to save the world. Sometimes the words "Stop that!" are words that save.

Weekday Problems

Roger pushed the button marked "12" on the elevator. He was lost in thought as he waited. He had just encountered a man on the street who handed him a printed tract. What the man said disturbed Roger. He told Roger, "You must be born again."

Whish. The elevator doors opened and Roger stepped in for the ride up to his corner office on the top floor. Again, his thoughts flooded in. Roger had heard those "born again" words before.

Roger was a successful business man. He worked his way up to become president of the company. He was active in Kiwanis. He coached Little League baseball. He had a decent marriage and two lovely children.

He was active in the church. When they moved into town he and his wife realized the church would be a good place to meet new friends and business contacts. In his career he made good decisions, worked well through committees and handled large sums of money. The folks at church asked Roger to serve on several committees in which those skills would be helpful. Yet, even in the midst of all the work at the church, Roger could not truthfully say he had been born again.

*   Do you know anyone who is like Roger?

*   What would you say to Roger if he shared this story with you? What might Jesus say to him?

Notes on New Beginnings

I felt that I was altogether born again and had entered paradise itself through open gates.—*Martin Luther, on his discovery of justification by grace.*

* * *

I felt my heart strangely warmed. I felt I did trust in Christ, Christ alone for salvation; and an assurance was given me that He had taken away *my* sins, even *mine*, and saved *me* from the law of sin and death.—*John Wesley.*

* * *

The recognition of the reality of Sin is a New Life.—*T. S. Eliot.*

* * *

Men often take their imagination for their heart; and they believe they are converted as soon as they think of being converted.—*Blaise Pascal*

* * *

I stayed there in the car, wet-eyed, praying, thinking, for perhaps half an hour, perhaps longer, alone in the quiet of the dark night. Yet for the first time in my life I was not alone at all.—*Watergate conspirator Chuck Colson, after being invited to accept Christ.*

This Lesson in Your Life

Seeking Answers for Life's Questions

A song written by Andre Crouch says, "Jesus is the answer for the world today. Above Him there's no other. Jesus is the Way." When it comes to the deep questions of life, Jesus is the answer. When it comes to those questions that touch our heart of hearts, Jesus is the answer.

I love this passage of scripture from John 3. In it Jesus compares himself to the serpent Moses lifted up in the wilderness. You can read this story in Numbers 21. It seems the Israelites were on their way to the Promised Land. For some reason, the Israelites began to complain against Moses and God.

"No good food. No water," they grumbled. "It looks like you brought us out of Egypt so we could die in the desert."

Well, God heard this and their complaints perturbed Him. God allowed some poisonous snakes loose in the Israelite camp. Lots of folks were bitten and many died. It did not take long for people to catch on that they had spoken against God and lost their protection. They went to Moses to ask him to ask God to take away the snakes. So Moses prayed and God said, "Make a snake and put it up on a pole; anyone who is bitten can look at it and live." Moses did as God said and the bronze snake acted as anti-venom. If a person was bitten, all that person had to do was look at the snake and that person would live.

Now, can you imagine anyone in that camp not going to look at that snake after being bitten? A man would be a fool just to sit around and let himself die when the cure was within a few hundred yards, wouldn't he?

Here is Jesus comparing Himself to that snake. "Just as Moses lifted up the snake in the desert, so the Son of Man must be lifted up, that everyone who believes in him may have eternal life" (John 3:14-15, NIV).

God did not tell Moses to make the snake so that those who were bitten and refused to look at it would die. Indeed not! God provided the snake bite remedy so that all who did look at it would *live*. Jesus reminds us of that. He is the *remedy* for judgment, not the cause. He did not come to bring death, but to provide a way for us to live, and to live forever. Jesus said, "I don't condemn you, but you are condemned already." Paul reminds us that "all have sinned and fall short of the glory of God" (Rom. 3:23). Friends, we are snake-bit already. Jesus came not to let us die in our sins. He came to give us life.

There is a slight condition. We must believe in Him. The Israelites had to believe that a look at the snake would keep them from dying. They had to believe that or they would never run to that snake to get a glimpse. In the same sense, we must believe that the Savior will give us eternal life before we will seek Him.

Jesus is the provision for the deepest of our questions and problems. He truly is the answer for the world today.

Seed Thoughts

1. John chapter 3 begins with an encounter between Jesus and a man. Who was the other man?

The other man is Nicodemus, a Pharisee, a member of the Jewish ruling council.

2. At what time of day did Nicodemus come to Jesus?

We are not sure of the exact time, but we are sure he came at night.

3. What convinced Nicodemus that Jesus was a teacher sent from God?

The miracles. "For no one could perform the miraculous signs you are doing if God were not with him" (John 3:2).

4. What is the requirement for seeing and entering the Kingdom of God according to John 3?

One must be born again—born of water and the Spirit—to enter the Kingdom of God.

5. In verse 7 the word "you" in "You must be born again" is plural. To whom does this refer?

In that case Jesus is not referring only to Nicodemus. Jesus is referring to everyone, then and now.

---

1. John chapter 3 begins with an encounter between Jesus and a man. Who was the other man?

2. At what time of day did Nicodemus come to Jesus?

3. What convinced Nicodemus that Jesus was a teacher sent from God?

4. What is the requirement for seeing and entering the Kingdom of God according to John 3?

5. In verse 7 the word "you" in "You must be born again" is plural. To whom does this refer?

6. What does Jesus mean in verse 8?

7. When Jesus says in verse 14, "the Son of Man must be lifted up," to what is He referring?

8. Why are the words "everyone" in verse 15 and "whoever" in verse 16 so important?

9. What motivated God to send Jesus into the world?

10. Why was Jesus sent into the world?

(Continued next page)

The other man is Nicodemus, a Pharisee, a member of the Jewish ruling council.

We are not sure of the exact time, but we are sure he came at night.

The miracles. "For no one could perform the miraculous signs you are doing if God were not with him" (John 3:2).

One must be born again—born of water and the Spirit—to enter the Kingdom of God.

In that case Jesus is not referring only to Nicodemus. Jesus is referring to everyone, then and now.

He means we can control neither the wind nor the Spirit. Yet, we certainly can see the effects of the wind and of the Spirit in the lives of believers.

Jesus is referring to His death on the cross. Our faith and trust in His atoning death is crucial to salvation.

They remind us that salvation is open to all. The Jews thought the Messiah was only for them. The Messiah brings salvation to all who believe.

God was motivated by love. He loved the world so much that He gave His only Son to provide for believers' salvation.

God sent Jesus not to condemn all humanity, but that all humanity might be saved through Christ.

6. What does Jesus mean in verse 8?

He means we can control neither the wind nor the Spirit. Yet, we certainly can see the effects of the wind and of the Spirit in the lives of men.

7. When Jesus says in verse 14, "the Son of Man must be lifted up," to what is He referring?

Jesus is referring to His death on the cross. Our faith and trust in His atoning death is crucial to salvation.

8. Why are the words "everyone" in verse 15 and "whoever" in verse 16 so important?

They remind us that salvation is open to all. The Jews thought the Messiah was only for them. The Messiah brings salvation to all who believe.

9. What motivated God to send Jesus into the world?

God was motivated by love. He loved the world so much that He gave His only Son to provide for believers' salvation.

10. Why was Jesus sent into the world?

God sent Jesus not to condemn all humanity, but that all humanity might be saved through Christ.

A Woman Brings a Village to Jesus

There came a woman of Samaria to draw water: Jesus saith unto her, Give me to drink.

8 (For his disciples were gone away unto the city to buy meat.)

9 Then saith the woman of Samaria unto him, How is it that thou, being a Jew, askest drink of me, which am a woman of Samaria? for the Jews have no dealings with the Samaritans.

10 Jesus answered and said unto her, If thou knewest the gift of God, and who it is that saith to thee, Give me to drink; thou wouldest have asked of him, and he would have given thee living water.

11 The woman saith unto him, Sir, thou hast nothing to draw with, and the well is deep: from whence then hast thou that living water?

12 Art thou greater than our father Jacob, which gave us the well, and drank thereof himself, and his children, and his cattle?

13 Jesus answered and said unto her, Whosoever drinketh of this water shall thirst again:

14 But whosoever drinketh of the water that I shall give him shall never thirst; but the water that I shall give him shall

be in him a well of water springing up into everlasting life.

15 The woman saith unto him, Sir, give me this water, that I thirst not, neither come hither to draw.

28 The woman then left her waterpot, and went her way into the city, and saith to the men,

29 Come, see a man, which told me all things that ever I did: is not this the Christ?

30 Then they went out of the city, and came unto him.

39 And many of the Samaritans of that city believed on him for the saying of the wo-man, which testified, He told me all that ever I did.

40 So when the Samaritans were come unto him, they besought him that he would tarry with them: and he abode there two days.

John 4: 7-15, 28-30, 39-40

Memory Selection
John 4:14

Background Scripture
John 4:1-42

Devotional Reading
Revelation 7:13-17

Printed Scripture
John 4:7-15, 28-30, 39-40

291

Teacher's Target

Lesson purpose: *To reflect, through the story of Jesus' encounter with the woman at Jacob's Well, on the potential impact of telling others about Him.*

The late Dr. Elton Trueblood once said that "There is something faintly embarrassing about all evangelism." The problem isn't helped by modern caricatures of the man on the corner with a sign that says "Jesus is coming soon."

Use this lesson to challenge members of your group to reflect on a more bibilical image of what it means to share the story of Jesus. Encourage them to share stories of lives that have been changed—perhaps their own—by someone caring enough to share with them what Christ has done. Note especially the way this lesson challenges us to be willing to cross racial and class barriers to share the greatest story ever told.

Lesson Introduction

The previous lesson mentioned the difficulty some Jews had in accepting a Messiah for all nations. Christ's confrontation with the woman at the well in Samaria seems to have been included in John's Gospel as deliberate evidence that the message of salvation was too large to be contained in a single race.

The Samaritans were the descendants of mixed races resulting from the settling of the area by Jews and non-Jews after the northern kingdom of Israel was captured in 722 B.C. (see 2 Kings 17:24-41). Jews with purer blood-lines traceable to Father Abraham therefore looked down on Samaritans as half-breeds. They were also considered unfaithful because they had founded their own worship center in competition with Jerusalem.

Today Christians are called to follow Jesus' example of calmly surmounting such cultural barriers in behalf of spreading His Word.

Teaching Outline	Daily Bible Readings
I. Samaritan Water—7-9	**Mon.** Jesus in Samaria *John 4:1-6*
A. A 'chance' meeting, 7-8	**Tue.** Encounter at the Well *John 4:7-15*
B. Crossing lines, 9	**Wed.** 'I am the Messiah' *John 4:16-26*
II. Living Water—10-15	**Thu.** Astonished Disciples *John 4:27-42*
A. Greater than Jacob, 10-12	**Fri.** Sharing the Water *Matthew 10:37-42*
B. The water of life, 13-15	**Sat.** The Gift of Life *Revelation 22:16-21*
III. Sharing the 'Water'—28-30, 39-40	**Sun.** Entering Jerusalem *Mark 11:1-11*
A. 'Come see a man,' 28-30	
B. 'Come stay with us,' 39-40	

Verse by Verse

I. Samaritan Water—7-9
A. A 'chance' meeting, 7-8

7 There came a woman of Samaria to draw water: Jesus saith unto her, Give me to drink.

8 (For his disciples were gone away unto the city to buy meat.)

The apostle John has set the stage for this famous encounter in verses 1-6. Jesus, who has been preaching in and around Jerusalem, has attracted more disciples than John the Baptist. This creates a stir among the Pharisees. Not yet ready for a confrontation with Jewish and Roman authorities that might bring a premature end to His ministry, Jesus retreats north toward Galilee. The disdain many Jews had for the Samaritans (see the Introducton) prompted them to go around the area when business took them north; but Jesus has spiritual business: His disciples must begin to realize that His message is for all people, regardless of race.

Verse 6 has also told us that Jesus and His followers stop at Jacob's well for a break in their journey. Travelers may still see this ancient landmark, which is under an unfinished Greek Orthodox church.

Now John continues to prepare us for Jesus' conversation with the Samaritan woman with a note that Jesus' disciples went into the village of Sychar to get "meat" (lit. "food"). Only Jesus and the woman will occupy center stage for the important conversation to follow.

B. Crossing lines, 9

9 Then saith the woman of Samaria unto him, How is it that thou, being a Jew, askest drink of me, which am a woman of Samaria? for the Jews have no dealings with the Samaritans.

The woman is properly surprised, because Jesus crosses at least two cultural boundary lines. The first was the barrier of race. So prejudiced were the Jews against their neighbors to the north that, in their anger, they once hurled the name "Samaritan" at Jesus (8:48), although He was actually a Galilean, from farther north.

The second cultural barrier surmounted by Jesus was the fact that male Jews of the day were expected not to speak directly to women in a place as public as this community well. The Lord is giving a preface to the later unfolding of the gospel story in the life of the non-Jewish Ethiopian in Acts 8; and among women, who constituted an op-

293

pressed class in many ways, especially in Jewish circles.

II. Living Water—10-15

A. Greater than Jacob, 10-12

10 Jesus answered and said unto her, If thou knewest the gift of God, and who it is that saith to thee, Give me to drink; thou wouldest have asked of him, and he would have given thee living water.

11 The woman saith unto him, Sir, thou hast nothing to draw with, and the well is deep: from whence then hast thou that living water?

12 Art thou greater than our father Jacob, which gave us the well, and drank thereof himself, and his children, and his cattle?

Since Jesus was not first a social reformer, He chooses to lead the woman into a spiritual conversation instead of dealing with the cultural issue she raises. "The gift of God" is an implied term for the Messiah in prophecies such as Isaiah 42:6. If the woman but knew it, she could draw from Jesus sustenance more valuable than the ordinary water in Jacob's well.

Like many people, however, her mind is on more material concerns, and misses the spiritual analogy. "Living water" can also mean "running water," and we can imagine the woman gazing first into the deep, still waters of the well, then looking around for the running stream this stranger seemed to speak of. Did he actually think he could create such running water in a miracle that showed him to be greater than Father Jacob?

B. The water of life, 13-15

13 Jesus answered and said unto her, Whosoever drinketh of this water shall thirst again:

14 But whosoever drinketh of the water that I shall give him shall never thirst; but the water that I shall give him shall be in him a well of water springing up into everlasting life.

15 The woman saith unto him, Sir, give me this water, that I thirst not, neither come hither to draw.

Bread and water are often used as symbols of the spiritual nourishment to be found in Christ (see 6:35; 7:38). If the Samaritan woman contents herself with the water in Jacob's well, she will have to continue the tiresome chore of coming daily to the well. The "water" Jesus offers would be a long term solution to the woman's spiritual needs.

In the intervening verses, the woman begins to see both the spiritual analogy Jesus is making, and the fact that he is a "prophet" or seer—since He can peer into her marital history and note her promiscuity (verses 16-18). She was also treated to Jesus' frank claim that "salvation is of the Jews," not the Samaritans (vs. 22). Ironically, however, this truth leads to the broader principle that the Messiah's ministry will be limited to neither the true

Temple at Jerusalem nor Samaria's rival worship center on Mt. Gerizim (vss. 20). The "temple" Jesus erects is in the heart of anyone, Jew, Samaritan or Gentile, who is a true worshiper (vss. 23-24).

III. Sharing the 'Water'—28-30, 39-40

A. 'Come see a man,' 28-30

28 The woman then left her waterpot, and went her way into the city, and saith to the men,

29 Come, see a man, which told me all things that ever I did: is not this the Christ?

30 Then they went out of the city, and came unto him.

These verses seem to indicate that the Samaritan woman bases her growing conclusion that Jesus is the Christ only on Jesus' ability to see into her past. However, fortune-tellers and other "seers" were as common in her day as ours. Her faith is also built on the theological part of Jesus' conversation with her—especially His open confession that He is the Messiah (vss. 25-26).

Unlike many who accept Jesus' insights into their life and needs only to keep them to themselves, the woman shares her experience with her fellow villagers. Unlike many who remain unmoved by such testimonials, the villagers turn out in force to verify the woman's witness for themselves.

B. 'Come stay with us,' 39-40

39 And many of the Samaritans of that city believed on him for the saying of the woman, which testified, He told me all that ever I did.

40 So when the Samaritans were come unto him, they besought him that he would tarry with them: and he abode there two days.

Jesus' works did not always earn Him such gracious invitations. When he cast demons out of the herd of swine, the local residents begged him to leave—perhaps because they resented the loss of livelihood from raising pigs.

John, however, is especially eager for readers to know of the positive reception the Samaritans give to Christ. Their reaction is set in glaring opposition to the way official Jewry, who looked down on the Samaritans, rejected their Messiah.

Verses 40-41 add that while many of the Samaritans believed on the Lord because of the witness of the woman, many others accepted Him after going to hear Him "for ourselves." While testimonials from others about what Christ has done for them can be valuable and supportive, there is no substitute for daring to examine personally His claims.

Evangelistic Emphasis

I have done a bit of independent research concerning grandparents. One thing I noticed about grandparents, especially new grandparents, is that you never have to beg them to tell you about their grandchildren. If you just mention grandchildren they will bring out photo after photo. They will go on and on about the grandchild's first tooth or first step or first word or first haircut.

Do you know any grandparents? Aren't they like that? Grandparents are willing, in fact they are excited, to tell you everything about their grandkids.

Grandparents aren't the only ones like that. I've discovered that most folks are more than willing to talk about things that bring joy and fulfillment to their lives.

This Samaritan woman in our scripture passage was eager to tell everyone in her town about her encounter with Jesus. John 4:39 says, "Many of the Samaritans from that town believed in Him because of the woman's testimony."

Meeting Jesus is the greatest thing any person can experience. Meeting Jesus is even greater than grandchildren. Shouldn't we be as excited about Jesus as we are about our grand-children? Shouldn't we be as willing to tell others about how we met Jesus as this Samaritan woman was?

● ● ● ● ● ● ● ●

Memory Selection

But whosoever drinketh of the water that I shall give him shall never thirst; but the water that I shall give him shall be in him a well of water springing up into everlasting life.—*John 4:14*

When I played high school basketball, one of my favorite times of practice was when coach let us take a water break. We would practice about an hour before our break. We were hot and sweaty. The inside of my mouth felt like cotton. We would hustle to the water cooler and gulp down that clear, cold elixir.

Many times, if I was especially thirsty, there would be a place way back in my throat that the cold water never seemed to touch. I just couldn't seem to get enough water.

There are people in our world today that have a dry, thirsty place in their lives that never seems to be satisfied. Folks are looking for a drink of something that will slake that thirst. Jesus is the only one who can quench the deep-down thirsting that occurs in a person's soul. It is His living water all folks are looking for, whether they know it or not.

Weekday Problems

Marge was confused as she came out of the Evangelism Committee meeting. Her pastor had just outlined a plan in which every member of the church could be trained in evangelism. The training would teach every person the communication and interpersonal skills needed to equip each individual with the ability to talk to other people about the Christian faith.

Marge had been brought up in a strict church-going home. She had been a Christian since she was a child. However, Marge's parents had impressed upon her, "A person's religion is a private thing. It is not polite to try to push your religion off on someone else." Thus, Marge had never talked to anyone about her faith. Furthermore, she thought it rude to do so.

Yet, tonight Pastor Taylor indicated talking about one's faith should be as natural and as open as talking about the weather over a cup of coffee. He pointed out scripture after scripture that confirmed his viewpoint.

He seemed to be right. Marge was nervous.

* Is Christianity a private religion? What would you say to someone who believes as Marge's parents did?

* Why do you think Jesus stressed the importance of telling others about Him?

Where Is God?

Two young boys were forever swiping small items and otherwise getting into trouble. Their mother asked her minister to talk to them. Instead of scolding them, he decided to try to help them see that God is everywhere, aware of their misdeeds, and disappointed in them.

"Young men," he intoned, I have a question for you. Where is God?"

The pair just sat there, unsure how to answer.

"I repeat!" the minister said. "Where is God?"

The boys looked uneasily at each other, but still remained silent.

"I'll ask one more time," said the minister, and raised his voice: *"Where is God?"*

At that the older boy jumped up and whispered to his friend: "C'mon, let's get outta here. God's missing and they think we did it!"

This Lesson in Your Life

Choose Life

Psychologists tell us that deep within every human being there is a need for self-fulfillment. Now, I hold no degree in psychology, yet I know the truth of that statement. People have a need to be involved with something they feel is significant. We all need to be part of something bigger than we are. We all need to be part of something that is making life better. That basic need within us all is part of the power of the Christian walk. Gaining a personal relationship with Jesus us the ultimate fulfillment in any human being's life.

In our passage this week, we see a woman who has a personal encounter with Jesus. When they met they talked about water. Then Jesus confronted her about her many husbands. Then she tries to change the subject by talking about acceptable places of worship. Eventually, she says, "I know that Messiah is coming. When he comes, he will explain everything to us."

Do you see what is happening? Obviously, the woman has questions about life or she would not need the Messiah to explain everything. Isn't it something? She was speaking directly to the answer to all life's questions. She was speaking to Jesus.

Jesus is the real thing. He is the goal of all our searching. In Him we find fulfillment. In Him we find love, joy, peace, patience, kindness, goodness, faithfulness, gentleness and self-control (Gal. 5:22-23). Jesus is all we need for the deep-down thirsting of our souls. There is a chorus we sing in our church that goes, "You are my strength when I am weak. You are the treasure that I seek. You are my all in all." Jesus is all that . . . and more.

Knowing that Jesus is the ultimate goal of life, it would be the right thing to do as the Samaritan woman did. We should tell all our friends about Him. The scholars that study church growth tell us that the overwhelming majority of people who come to church and eventually join do not do so because of a great preacher, a great program, a convenient location or even because it is of a particulary denomination. The overwhelming majority of people come to a church and eventually join because a friend or relative invites them.

That is what happened in the case of the Samaritan woman. She told people she knew about Jesus. They came to see for themselves, and they believed as well. Once the other Samaritans met Jesus, they no longer had to take the woman's word for who He was. They made their own confession, "We know that this man really is the Savior of the world."

He really is. Jesus is all that. He is all we need. People need Jesus that do not even know they need Him. Jesus fills our lives with Himself, thus fulfilling our lives. He puts color where there was once only black and white. He puts music where there was once only motion. He puts a cool drink where there was once only desert.

It is true. "Whoever drinks the water I give him will never thirst" (John 4:14a).

Seed Thoughts

1. Of what nationality was the woman at the well?

The woman at the well was a Samaritan.

2. Why was it unusual that Jesus asked the woman for a drink?

Jews did not normally associate with Samaritans.

3. What effect did Christ's request for water have on this Samaritan woman?

It aroused her curiosity. His request caused her to ask questions and engage in a conversation with Jesus.

4. Who was it that dug the well around which Jesus and the woman were visiting?

Jacob dug the well. Jacob was one of the patriarchs of the Jews. God gave Jacob the name "Israel."

5. In verse 10 Jesus uses the term "living water." What effect did this have on the chat?

Again, it aroused her curiosity. Her questions then allowed Jesus to move the conversation from the physical to the spiritual realm.

---

1. Of what nationality was the woman at the well?

2. Why was it unusual that Jesus asked the woman for a drink?

3. What effect did Christ's request for water have on this Samaritan woman?

4. Who was it that dug the well around which Jesus and the woman were visiting?

5. In verse 10 Jesus uses the term "living water." What effect did this have on the chat?

6. Why did Jesus speak to this woman about thirsting and drinking and wells?

7. What was the miraculous event the woman told her village about?

8. The woman suspected that Jesus was someone special. Who did she think He might be?

9. What effect did the woman's testimony have on her town?

10. What event led to many more from the town becoming believers?

(Continued next page)

The woman at the well was a Samaritan.

Jews did not normally associate with Samaritans.

It aroused her curiosity. His request caused her to ask questions and engage in a conversation with Jesus.

Jacob dug the well. Jacob was one of the patriarchs of the Jews. God gave Jacob the name "Israel."

Again, it aroused her curiosity. Her questions then allowed Jesus to move the conversation from the physical to the spiritual realm.

He was using terms and objects with which she was familiar to help make a connection with her. He is leading her to salvation.

She told them to come and see a man who told her everything she ever did.

She wondered if Jesus might be the Christ, that is, the Messiah.

Many people in her town believed in Jesus because of her testimony that He knew everything she had done.

When the Samaritans met Christ for themselves and heard His words, many more became believers.

6. Why did Jesus speak to this woman about thirsting and drinking and wells?

He was using terms and objects with which she was familiar to help make a connection with her. He is leading her to salvation.

7. What was the miraculous event the woman told her village about?

She told them to come and see a man who told her everything she ever did.

8. The woman suspected that Jesus was someone special. Who did she think He might be?

She wondered if Jesus might be the Christ, that is, the Messiah.

9. What effect did the woman's testimony have on her town?

Many people in her town believed in Jesus because of her testimony that He knew everything she had done.

10. What event led to many more from the town becoming believers?

When the Samaritans met Christ for themselves and heard His words, many more became believers.

Lesson 5

Jesus Crucified and Resurrected

April 4

Then delivered he him therefore unto them to be crucified. And they took Jesus, and led him away.

17 And he bearing his cross went forth into a place called the place of a skull, which is called in the Hebrew Golgotha:

18 Where they crucified him, and two other with him, on either side one, and Jesus in the midst.

28 After this, Jesus knowing that all things were now accomplished, that the scripture might be fulfilled, saith, I thirst.

John 19: 16-18, 28-30; 20:11-18

29 Now there was set a vessel full of vinegar: and they filled a spunge with vinegar, and put it upon hyssop, and put it to his mouth.

30 When Jesus therefore had received the vinegar, he said, It is finished: and he bowed his head, and gave up the ghost.

20:11 But Mary stood without at the sepulchre weeping: and as she wept, she stooped down, and looked into the sepulchre,

12 And seeth two angels in white sitting, the one at the head, and the other at the feet, where the body of Jesus had lain.

13 And they say unto her, Woman, why weepest thou? She saith unto them, Because they have taken away my Lord, and I know not where they have laid him.

14 And when she had thus said, she turned herself back, and saw Jesus standing, and knew not that it was Jesus.

15 Jesus saith unto her, Woman, why weepest thou? whom seekest thou? She, supposing him to be the gardener, saith unto him, Sir, if thou have borne him hence, tell me where thou hast laid him, and I will take him away.

16 Jesus saith unto her, Mary. She turned herself, and saith unto him, Rabboni; which is to say, Master.

17 Jesus saith unto her, Touch me not; for I am not yet ascended to my Father: but go to my brethren, and say unto them, I ascend unto my Father, and your Father; and to my God, and your God.

18 Mary Magdalene came and told the disciples that she had seen the Lord, and that he had spoken these things unto her.

Memory Selection
Mark 16:6

Background Scripture
John 18:1+20:18

Devotional Reading
Acts 2:32-39

Printed Scripture
John 19:16-18, 28-30;
20:11-18

301

Teacher's Target

Lesson purpose: *To focus again on the keystone event of the Christian faith: the death, burial, and resurrection of Jesus.*

Once again, people in the northern hemisphere are treated to the annual rite of Spring. The earth, planning its own "Easter parade," dresses itself in new greenery, with tulips and crocuses as gaily-colored accessories. Easter eggs, chicks, and bunnies add to nature's new lease on new life.

Although the resurrection of Christ also reminds us of new life, in some ways it is in remarkable contrast to the renewal of nature this time of year. Resurrection is far from "natural." The natural sequence is for the death that follows life to be the last word. We conduct a funeral, and that's that.

The Easter story, however, is about a magnificent and surprising exception to the rule. We conduct not a funeral but a celebration. We cry not with grief but with joy: "He is not here! His is risen!"

Lesson Introduction

John's Gospel contains some unique facts about Jesus' death and resurrection: (1) Jesus' appears before Annas, father-in-law of the high priest Caiphas, in addition to the other trials before the Sanhedrin, Pilate, and Herod. (2) Pilate presents the accused man to the crowd with the dramatic words "Behold the man" (19:1-5). (3) The superscription above Jesus' head is described (vss. 19-22). (4) The curious detail that Jesus' robe was "without seam" is included (19:23). Since the garment of the high priest was also required to be seamless, John is showing that Jesus Himself is the true High Priest. (5) Jesus' commends the care of His mother to John (19:26-27). (6) John describes the blood and water from Jesus' side, and the sparing of His legs from being broken (19:32-37). Nicodemus prepares Jesus' body for burial (19:39).

Teaching Outline	Daily Bible Readings

I. Sentenced Unjustly—19:16-18
  A. Deliverance to death, 16
  B. The Cross, 17-18
II. Scripture Fulfilled—19:28-30
  A. The fulfillment, 28
  B. The death throes, 29-30
III. Seeing the Unascended—20:11-18
  A. The word of angels, 11-13
  B. The word of the Lord, 14-17
  C. Sharing the word, 18
	Mon. Judas Betrays Jesus
	    John 18:1-14
	Tue. Peter's Denial
	    John 18:15-27
	Wed. The Choice
	    John 18:28-40
	Thu. Jesus Is Condemned
	    John 19:1-16a
	Fri. Jesus Is Crucified
	    John 19:16b-30
	Sat. The Day of Preparation
	    John 19:31-42
	Sun. 'I Have Seen the Lord!'
	    John 20:1-18

Verse by Verse

I. Sentenced Unjustly—19:16-18
A. Deliverance to death, 16

16 Then delivered he him therefore unto them to be crucified. And they took Jesus, and led him away.

It is Pontius Pilate, the Roman governor of Judea, who "delivers" Jesus to the Jews to be crucified. Under Roman law the Jewish rulers were not allowed to carry out the death sentence, so Pilate's authority was necessary. Throughout the account, Pilate is shown to be reluctant; "he sought to release him" (vs. 12). Other sources portray Pilate as very insensitive to the Jews, whom he apparently despised, so his resistance to their clamoring for the life of this just man is doubly understandable. Finally, however, Pilate's resistance crumbles under the Jewish threat to report him as no friend of Caesar.

B. The Cross, 17-18

17 And he bearing his cross went forth into a place called the place of a skull, which is called in the Hebrew Golgotha:

18 Where they crucified him, and two other with him, on either side one, and Jesus in the midst.

Apparently Jesus carried His own cross part of the way toward Golgotha, since John does not mention Simon of Cyrene, whom the other Gospels say helped with the burden. Later tradition held that John emphasizes Christ's bearing of His own cross to show the parallel with Isaac, who bore the wood of his own near-sacrifice. The "place of the skull" is thought to have received the name because hollow places in the hill gave it the appearance of a human skull; but many archeologists deny that the hill in present-day Jerusalem that some say resembles a skull is actually Golgotha.

John states simply that Jesus was crucified between two other condemned men, perhaps because Jewish tradition required that in a public appearance by three persons the most important should be in the middle. Luke adds the interesting scenario of one thief joining those who railed against Jesus, and the other, who defended Him, apparently being promised salvation (Luke 23:43).

II. Scripture Fulfilled—19:28-30
A. The fulfillment, 28

28 After this, Jesus knowing that all things were now accomplished, that the scripture might be fulfilled, saith, I thirst.

John now adds an important note showing that God's sovereign will has been over-riding even the unjust treatment of His Son. The word for "accomplished" implies that all the preceding events have been moving toward a prearranged point. Of course the "point" is the sacrifice of Christ for the sins of

303

the world, which God had planned from the beginning, and which had been predicted in the Old Testament. The riotous crowd, the high priests, Herod, Pilate—all have been playing into the hands of God in His scheme of redemption.

Of course this does not excuse the unjust sentence and the blatant tragedy that the Jews are executing their own Messiah. The apostle Peter affirms that both the divine plan and evil men were at work in this scene, telling the Jews: "him being delivered by the determinate counsel and foreknowledge of God, ye have taken, and by wicked hands have crucified and slain" (Acts 2:23).

Yet John does not neglect the very painful human dimension of this awesome scene. The long ordeal has wracked Jesus' body; he thirsts.

B. The death throes, 29-30

29 Now there was set a vessel full of vinegar: and they filled a spunge with vinegar, and put it upon hyssop, and put it to his mouth.

30 When Jesus therefore had received the vinegar, he said, It is finished: and he bowed his head, and gave up the ghost.

With his love of analogies and parallels, John says that the sponge of vinegar-wine was hoisted to Jesus' lips not just on a reed, as the other Gospel writers say, but specifically on a *hyssop* reed—perhaps to recall the hyssop plant's role in the sprinkling of blood on the doorposts at the exodus (Exod. 12:22). We are to understand from this that Jesus is the true Lamb of God, who takes away the sins of the world.

Jesus' final cry "It is finished!" takes up the same word translated "accomplished" in verse 28, showing again the cosmic significance of Christ's death. The crucifixion-resurrection is in fact so central to accomplishing God's plan of salvation that it can be considered "the hinge of history."

"Ghost" simply meant "spirit" when the KJV was translated, coming from the German word Geist for spirit. The phrase simply means "He died." The other Gospels add that this "setting of the Son" was an event so black and bleak that the sun was darkened in appropriate acknowledgment.

III. Seeing the Unascended—20:11-18

A. The word of angels, 11-13

11 But Mary stood without at the sepulchre weeping: and as she wept, she stooped down, and looked into the sepulchre,

12 And seeth two angels in white sitting, the one at the head, and the other at the feet, where the body of Jesus had lain.

13 And they say unto her, Woman, why weepest thou? She saith unto them, Because they have taken away my Lord, and I know not where they have laid him.

Although Mary the mother of Jesus and Mary the mother of James were also at the tomb, this Mary is Mary Magdalene (or Mary of [the town of] Magdala, 20:1). She was one of several women who ministered to Jesus both during His travels and ministry, and who finally assembled at the Cross and came to tend to His body after His death. Her prominence here in being the first to be told of the risen Christ, and in then telling the other disciples, may have led to some ancient traditions that she was named an apostle.

In addition to her sadness about the Lord's death, Mary may have been weeping out of fear that grave-robbers have been at work. The angels' question, "Why weepest thou?" is to be taken as a gentle "set-up"—they are preparing Mary for what they already know: there is no reason to weep because Jesus is alive!

B. The word of the Lord, 14-17

14 And when she had thus said, she turned herself back, and saw Jesus standing, and knew not that it was Jesus.

15 Jesus saith unto her, Woman, why weepest thou? whom seekest thou? She, supposing him to be the gardener, saith unto him, Sir, if thou have borne him hence, tell me where thou hast laid him, and I will take him away.

16 Jesus saith unto her, Mary. She turned herself, and saith unto him, Rabboni; which is to say, Master.

17 Jesus saith unto her, Touch me not; for I am not yet ascended to my Father: but go to my brethren, and say unto them, I ascend unto my Father, and your Father; and to my God, and your God.

Jesus is said more than once to have been unrecognized in His resurrection appearances. Some have suggested that His face would have been emaciated after the ordeal of the trials, beating, and crucifixion. Here it may also be possible that Mary is simply blinded by her tears. Jesus reveals Himself to her first by repeating the angels' question; then by the dramatic speaking of her name.

Wheeling around, Mary realizes that the figure is not the gardener but the Lord! In her joy and relief she apparently throws herself on Him, only to be told not to touch Him. At first this seems strange, since others touched Him before He ascended; and Thomas was even urged to do so (vs. 27). Perhaps Mary is not just touching Jesus but clinging to Him as though to keep Him from disappearing again; and Jesus is saying "Don't hinder me from my destiny; instead, go tell my followers that I am about to leave again."

C. Sharing the word, 18

18 Mary Magdalene came and told the disciples that she had seen the Lord, and that he had spoken these things unto her.

We can well imagine the joy with which Mary accepts this first commission to spread the Good News of Christ's triumph over the grave and will soon ascend to be with the Father. According to Mark 16:10, they were at first reluctant to accept such news; so Jesus will soon supplement the women's testimony by making several personal appearances.

Evangelistic Emphasis

According to John's gospel, the first message delivered after the resurrection of Jesus was, "I have seen the Lord!" That was the great news. Jesus was alive. He had been dead. He had been buried. He had lain in the tomb for three days. Now He is alive.

The resurrection of Christ validated everything He had taught while He was alive on the earth. The resurrection confirmed all that the prophets had written about Him. The resurrection was the greatest event in all of history, for it meant (and means) that Christians do not simply follow a philosophy or adhere to a particular ideology. Christians follow a living person.

Meeting the living Lord transforms lives. One cannot come face to face with Jesus and not be changed. The disciples' encounter with the risen Lord changed them from the cowards of Good Friday to the bold preachers of Pentecost.

They told the story. The apostles and the women told the story. They told it to all who would listen and to some who refused to listen. They told the story in the same city that had sought to destroy the Christ, right at the doorstep of the stronghold of the priests.

Eventually all who saw the risen Christ told the story. Have you met the risen Christ?

• • • • • • • •

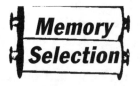

Memory Selection

And he saith unto them, Be not affrighted: Ye seek Jesus of Nazareth, which was crucified: he is risen; he is not here: behold the place where they laid him.—*Mark 16:6*

Paul wrote in Romans 10:9, "...if you confess with your mouth, 'Jesus is Lord,' and believe in your heart that God raised Him from the dead, you will be saved." One of the criteria for salvation is the conviction that the resurrection really happened. We are convinced our faith is based not upon simply a magnificent philosophy, but a living truth. We are convinced our faith is not in an abstract, academic theory but in a living Person.

The first witnesses of the empty tomb had every opportunity to be frightened. Had someone stolen the body? Had the Romans pulled some cruel joke? Had the body of Jesus been desecrated? These questions may have raced through their minds when they saw the abandoned sepulcher.

Yet the basis for our faith hinges upon the empty tomb. There was no reason to be alarmed. The greatest event in all eternity had happened.

Weekday Problems

"It's funny how things work out," Kay thought as she drove home from the elementary school where she volunteered as a reading tutor. It was only last year that disaster struck. She and her husband, David, were both on the fast track in their careers with the same computer company. They were bright, well educated and driven.

Both lived for their work. It was not unusual for them to spend seventy to eighty hours a week at their jobs. Because of the success in their professions, they had plenty of money. From all outward appearances, they had it made.

Kay chuckled to herself, "Nobody could see what was really going on." David was battling high blood pressure at only thirty years old. Their marriage was in shambles because they poured all their energy into their careers. They never went to church. They were completely self-absorbed.

One day the unthinkable happened. The company was downsizing. "I'm sorry, but you know how it is," the company vice-president shrugged as he fired them both. They were forced to re-evaluate their lifestyle and their lives.

He was able to get a job with less stress at another firm. She discovered she could work at home. They found time to rediscover their love for each other. They began to attend church. Now, they were happier than they had ever been.

*Have you ever experienced good things coming from disasters? Explain. (Consider Romans 8:28.)

Observations on Easter

The Easter message tells us that our enemies, sin, the curse and death, are beaten. Ultimately they can no longer start mischief. They still behave as though the game were not decided the battle not fought; we must still reckon with them, but fundamentally we must cease to fear them any more.—*Karl Barth*

* * *

The great Easter truth is not that we are to live newly after death . . . but that we are to be here and now by the power of the resurrection; not so much that we are to live forever as that we are to, and may, live nobly now because we are to live forever.—*Phillips Brooks*

* * *

One trouble with the churches is that too many people want to have Easter without Calvary.—*Lawrence Pearsall Jacks*

This Lesson in Your Life

From Death to Life

Apparently neither John nor Jesus' other disciples ever expected to see their Lord alive again. Yet, seeing Him alive again changed all their lives.

The behavior of the disciples during the arrest and trial of Jesus was somewhat less than impressive. They had not been courageous. In truth, they had all either fled the scene to save their own necks or they followed and watched the proceedings at a safe distance. Peter was so fearful that he denied ever having known the Nazarene. All the disciples, after their Master's death, stayed in hiding with the doors locked "for fear of the Jews."

Yet, after that first Easter morning, we find these same men who had been timid, frightened and ineffective, preaching openly with fear of no one. Their personal conviction burned like a magnesium fire—hot, bright and unquenchable. John said, "That which was from the beginning, which we have heard, which we have seen with our eyes, which we have looked at and our hands have touched--this we proclaim concerning the Word of life"(1 John 1:1).

Of what were the disciples so sure? That Jesus Christ was alive! He was not "spiritually alive" or alive "by faith," He was alive!

When the Scripture speaks of the resurrection, it means that on a certain Sunday, sometime between sunset and dawn, in a new tomb which had belonged to Joseph of Arimathea, there had been a rustling sound as the Spirit of God moved through the cemetery. Life was breathed back into the dead body of Jesus that had lain upon a cold stone slab. Then the formerly dead man rose up and emerged from the tomb, alive forevermore.

The apostles and the women told the story to all who would listen and to some who refused to listen. They had seen the Lord! Once Simon Peter actually stood before Caiaphas and the Sanhedrin, the same group who said Jesus should be condemned to death, and nothing but fiery words of courage came from his lips: "Judge for yourselves whether it is right in God's sight to obey you rather than God. For we cannot help speaking about what we have seen and heard" (Acts 4:19-20). It takes a powerful convicting force to change folks so dramatically. They had seen the Lord. He was (and is) living proof that we do not follow a dead philosophy. We worship a Living Savior.

Through the centuries people in every nation on the earth have encountered the Living Savior and experienced the same fellowship the apostles experienced. People have felt the same power in their lives, had the same peace and inner serenity, the same joy and victory. They too came face to face with the Living Lord. These people are not crackpots or morons or lunatics. Included among them are great minds, brilliant thinkers, philosophers, scientists and scholars.

"I have seen the Lord!" That statement is more than your everyday Elvis sighting. It is the testimony of a life changed forevermore. We serve a risen Savior! He is alive!

Seed Thoughts

1. What is the name of the place where Jesus was crucified?

It was a place outside of Jerusalem called The Skull. In Aramaic the name is Golgotha. Calvary is the Latin term.

2. According to John's gospel, what were the last words Jesus uttered on the cross?

Jesus said, "It is finished."

3. To what did the phrase, "It is finished," refer?

Probably both to Jesus' earthly ministry (see vs. 28) and to His life.

4. According to John's gospel, who was the woman who looked into the empty tomb of Jesus?

It was Mary Magdalene.

5. The scripture says she was weeping. Why was she crying?

The tomb was empty. She was afraid someone had come and taken the body of Jesus away.

---

1. What is the name of the place where Jesus was crucified?

2. According to John's gospel, what were the last words Jesus uttered on the cross?

3. To what did the phrase, "It is finished," refer?

4. According to John's gospel, who was the woman who looked into the empty tomb of Jesus?

5. The scripture says she was weeping. Why was she crying?

6. The resurrected Jesus spoke to Mary. Why do you think she did not recognize Him at first?

7. Jesus said to Mary, "Do not hold on to me." What was the next command He gave to her?

8. Can you think of other times Jesus commanded His followers to go and spread the Good News?

9. What was the first message Mary Magdalene gave to the disciples?

10. Why is the death and resurrection of Jesus so important to the Christian faith?

(Continued next page)

It was a place outside of Jerusalem called The Skull. In Aramaic the name is Golgotha. Calvary is the Latin term.

Jesus said, "It is finished."

Probably both to Jesus' earthly ministry (see vs. 28) and to His life.

It was Mary Magdalene.

The tomb was empty. She was afraid someone had come and taken the body of Jesus away.

His resurrected body may have looked different. He may intentionally have prevented recognition. We are not absolutely sure why.

"Go to my brothers and tell them, 'I am returning to my Father and your Father, to my God and your God.'"

He gave this command several times in several ways: Matthew 28:19-20—the Great Commission; Mark 16:15; Acts 2:8.

Mary's first message was not the one Jesus told her to give. Her first message was, "I have seen the Lord!"

Jesus died on the cross for our sins. His resurrection validates all that He taught and promised, and guarantees us eternal life.

6. The resurrected Jesus spoke to Mary. Why do you think she did not recognize Him at first?

His resurrected body may have looked different. He may intentionally have prevented recognition. We are not absolutely sure why.

7. Jesus said to Mary, "Do not hold on to me." What was the next command He gave to her?

"Go to my brothers and tell them, 'I am returning to my Father and your Father, to my God and your God.'"

8. Can you think of other times Jesus commanded His followers to go and spread the Good News?

He gave this command several times in several ways: Matthew 28:19-20—the Great Commission; Mark 16:15; Acts 2:8.

9. What was the first message Mary Magdalene gave to the disciples?

Mary's first message was not the one Jesus told her to give. Her first message was, "I have seen the Lord!"

10. Why is the death and resurrection of Jesus so important to the Christian faith?

Jesus died on the cross for our sins. His resurrection validates all that He taught and promised, and guarantees us eternal life.

Jesus Appears to His Disciples

7hen the same day at evening, being the first day of the week, when the doors were shut where the disciples were assembled for fear of the Jews, came Jesus and stood in the midst, and saith unto them, Peace be unto you.

20 And when he had so said, he shewed unto them his hands and his side. Then were the disciples glad, when they saw the Lord.

21 Then said Jesus to them again, Peace be unto you: as my Father hath sent me, even so send I you.

22 And when he had said this, he breathed on them, and saith unto them, Receive ye the Holy Ghost:

23 Whose soever sins ye remit, they are remitted unto them; and whose soever sins ye retain, they are retained.

24 But Thomas, one of the twelve, called Didymus, was not with them when Jesus came.

25 The other disciples therefore said unto him, We have seen the Lord. But he said unto them, Except I shall see in his hands the print of the nails, and put my finger into the print of the nails, and thrust my hand into his side, I will not believe.

26 And after eight days again his disciples were within, and Thomas with them: then came Jesus, the doors being shut, and stood in the midst, and said, Peace be unto you.

27 Then saith he to Thomas, Reach hither thy finger, and behold my hands; and reach hither thy hand, and thrust it into my side: and be not faithless, but believing.

28 And Thomas answered and said unto him, My Lord and my God.

29 Jesus saith unto him, Thomas, because thou hast seen me, thou hast believed: blessed are they that have not seen, and yet have believed.

John 20:19-29

April 11

Memory Selection
John 20:29

Background Scripture
John 20:19-29

Devotional Reading
Mark 9:14-24

Printed Scripture
John 20:19-29

Teacher's Target

Lesson purpose: *To recap some of the appearances of Jesus after His resurrection, focusing especially on the need to overcome doubt with faith, after the example of "Doubting Thomas."*

It isn't unusual for some Christians to experience a "slump" after the drama and excitement of Easter. What better way to deal with this syndrome than to revisit some of Jesus' post-resurrection appearances? There too we find some disciples still basking in the after-glow of the resurrection—and one named Thomas in a slump of doubt.

Like Thomas, many modern Christians need to reflect on the validity of their own faith. Do we go through the motions of formal Christianity while, inside, doubt is gnawing away? This lesson would be a good time to invite group members to face questions they may have about faith . . . and to encourage them to be among the "blessed" who "have not seen, and yet have believed."

Lesson Introduction

From the beginning, Christ's disciples had found it hard to accept His predictions that He would die (Mark 8:31-33). Little in the Old Testament prophecies concerning the coming of the Messiah could have prepared them for the awful tragedy of the crucifixion. After Jesus' death and burial, His disciples were therefore left in a state of confusion, despite word from some that they had found his tomb empty.

The several "appearances" Jesus made to His disciples between His resurrection and ascension were designed to strengthen their faith. Showing them His wounds would reassure them that He was not a ghost. Promising them the continuing presence of the Spirit would ease their disappointment that He was not to remain an earthly Messiah. Perhaps of equal importance, commissioning the disciples to "Go ye into all the world and preach the gospel" would give them a high purpose and calling worthy of their most heroic efforts.

Teaching Outline	Daily Bible Readings
	Mon. Peace Be with You *John 20:19-23*
	Tue. Unless I See *John 20:24-29*
I. The Peace of His Presence—19-20	**Wed.** On the Road to Emmaus *Luke 24:13-27*
II. The Power and the Mission—21-23	**Thu.** Their Eyes Were Opened *Luke 24:28-35*
III. The Problem of Doubt—24-25	**Fri.** Touch Me and See *Luke 24:36-43*
IV. The Prints of His Wounds—26-29	**Sat.** He Opened Their Minds *Luke 24:44-52*
	Sun. He Appeared Again *John 21:1-14*

Verse by Verse

I. The Peace of His Presence–19-20

19 Then the same day at evening, being the first day of the week, when the doors were shut where the disciples were assembled for fear of the Jews, came Jesus and stood in the midst, and saith unto them, Peace be unto you.

20 And when he had so said, he shewed unto them his hands and his side. Then were the disciples glad, when they saw the Lord.

"The same day at evening" must have been late on the first day of the week after Jesus' tomb had been found empty (20:1). We can imagine how dispirited the disciples were at the death of their Messiah, and they probably gathered for mutual encouragement. Yet the fact that they re-assembled on the same day of the next week (vs. 26) reminds us of how quickly our Sunday became a regular day for Christian worship. Of course many Christian Jews also continued for some time to attend Temple and synagogue services on the Jewish Sabbath, or Saturday.

Suddenly, although fear of persecution has caused the disciples to meet behind closed doors, Jesus appears among them. His greeting of peace and His vulnerability in showing them His wounds must have revived their spir-

its—John is remarkably restrained to say merely that they were "glad."

Jesus repeats the greeting, "Peace be unto you," three times in this passage (vss. 19, 21, 26). The fact that John reports it in this way may indicate that the saying was well on the way to becoming a somewhat fixed part of early Christian liturgy by the time the apostle wrote.

II. The Power and the Mission—21-23

21 Then said Jesus to them again, Peace be unto you: as my Father hath sent me, even so send I you. 22 And when he had said this, he breathed on them, and saith unto them, Receive ye the Holy Ghost:

23 Whose soever sins ye remit, they are remitted unto them; and whose soever sins ye retain, they are retained.

Not claiming to be writing a verbatim report, John recounts "the Great Commission" more briefly than the other Gospel writers (see Matt. 28:18-20; Mark 16:15-16; Luke 24: 45-48). John is more concerned with how Jesus deals with the disciples' need for peace and power and faith as He sends them out on their world-wide mission—

which is to be patterned after His own.

Jesus' "breathing on" the discplies to symbolize the imparting of the Holy Spirit is an echo of God's breathing the spirit of life into Adam (Gen. 2:7), and of the life breathed into the dry bones in Ezekiel's vision (Ezek.37:9-10). "Breathing on" someone to impart the Spirit is a highly appropriate "parabolic act," since "spirit" and "breath" are the same in Greek (pneuma). Later, the giving of the Spirit will be symbolized by the laying on of hands (Acts 8:17).

Jesus had promised that this gift of the Spirit would enable His disciples to remember His teachings (14:26), and bear witness of their truth (15:26-27). Since this work was hardly necessary as long as Jesus was present with the disciples, He had noted that the Spirit's presence would not be fully realized until after His departure (16:7). This "gift of the Holy Spirit" is expanded in Acts 2, when the disciples are empowered to speak to a multi-cultural audience in languages they had not previously studied (see esp. vss. 1-6).

Accompanying the Spirit was the authority to bind or remit the sins of those to whom the disciples preached (see also Matt. 16:19). The usual Roman Catholic interpretation of this authority is that it was transmitted to the apostles' successors and thence through the Popes. Protestants generally hold that the apostolic power was necessary only until the appearance of the written Word, which is the ultimate witness on guilt and forgiveness.

III. The Problem of Doubt—24-25

24 But Thomas, one of the twelve, called Didymus, was not with them when Jesus came.

25 The other disciples therefore said unto him, We have seen the Lord. But he said unto them, Except I shall see in his hands the print of the nails, and put my finger into the print of the nails, and thrust my hand into his side, I will not believe.

Although Thomas "the Twin" (Grk. *didymos*) is listed as an apostle in all four Gospels, only John adds details about his struggle with faith. At one point he seems ready to die like Lazarus if it will mean that Jesus would somehow use his death to create faith (11:15-16). Later, he professes not to know Jesus' destiny, and hence how to follow Him (14:4-5).

The death of Christ seems—understandably—to have increased this tendency to doubt, for here Thomas lays down almost stubbornly the only conditions that could lead him to believe. They go beyond the insistence that faith come by sight, and extend to the assertion that his faith can only come by touch as well. In Thomas' defense, however, it should be recalled that he was absent at the first assembly at which Jesus appeared (vs. 24). The other disciples have had the advantage of actually laying eyes, if not hands, on the risen Lord.

IV. The Prints of His Wounds—26-29

26 And after eight days again his disciples were within, and Thomas with them: then came Jesus, the doors being shut, and stood in the midst, and said, Peace be unto you.

27 Then saith he to Thomas, Reach hither thy finger, and behold my hands; and reach hither thy hand, and thrust it into my side: and be not faithless, but believing.

28 And Thomas answered and said unto him, My Lord and my God.

29 Jesus saith unto him, Thomas, because thou hast seen me, thou hast believed: blessed are they that have not seen, and yet have believed.

A week after the previous scene, the disciples are assembled again, and this time Thomas is among them. Jesus grants them a repeat appearance, apparently in a form that can again join them without being encumbered by the necessity of entering through a door.

After the same greeting of peace, Jesus goes directly to the point, and to Thomas' aid, inviting him to touch His wounds and to believe. The tender tolerance of Jesus in not rebuking Thomas, or even dismissing him from his apostolic office, for his initial disbelief is remarkable. Thomas also is to be commended for continuing to assemble with the other disciples despite his struggle with faith—a lesson modern doubters should not overlook.

Christ's appearance seems sufficient for Thomas, and apparently without having actually to touch Christ's wounds he confesses his faith. In fact, Thomas not only expresses belief in Jesus as Lord, but somehow as God as well. He goes beyond the faith of some who can believe in Jesus as an authoritative Teacher, but struggle with accepting His divinity.

Thomas' confession earns not only the Lord's immediate blessing on him, but on all who will ever accept Christ merely on the basis of the testimony of others. The last line of verse 29 has been called "the last beatitude," and serves both as an invitation and a challenge to everyone born after the ascension of Christ, whose faith must be to some degree "second-hand."

Later tradition has it that Thomas proved faithful to his profession of faith, going as far as India to spread the Word and establish churches. Although a "Gospel of Thomas" has also been preserved, its teachings espouse the heresy of "gnosticism," denying many of the truths the apostle John affirms in his authentic Gospel. It can hardly be considered to have been written by Thomas.

Evangelistic Emphasis

All the disciples except Thomas were together when Jesus appeared to them. When Thomas got back with the disciples, they immediately told him their good news, "We have seen the Lord!"

However, Thomas did not believe them. "Unless I see the nail prints and put my finger where the nail was and put my hand on the wound in His side, I will not believe." That was Thomas. He wanted some proof.

There are people in our world today that want to see proof of the Living Savior. They may not ask to see the nail prints or the spear wound, but they want proof all the same. They want to see in the lives of Christians the evidence of a living faith based upon a Living Lord.

I suspect that the greatest damage to the Christian faith comes not from honest doubt but from dishonest belief. People these days want to see evidence that Christ is alive in the lives of His people. Folks these days will not be convinced that Jesus is the Way, the Truth and the Life unless and until those who call upon His name live their lives as living proof of the life-changing power of the Risen Lord.

It is our duty and privilege to be the visible, living proof that Jesus changes lives.

● ● ● ● ● ●

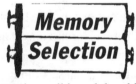

Memory Selection

Jesus saith unto him, Thomas, because thou hast seen me, thou hast believed: blessed are they that have not seen, and yet have believed.—*John 20:29*

We have all heard the old saying, "Seeing is believing." But in reality, we believe in many things we cannot see. For instance, we believe in gravity. We see the effects of gravity, but we cannot see the force.

We believe in atoms. Have you ever seen an atom? I certainly have not. They are too small to see. Yet, we know they are there.

We believe in the universe. Scientists and mathematicians calculate distances in the universe in light years. A light year is the distance light can travel at 186,000 miles per second in one year. Most of us cannot comprehend that.

We often believe in things we cannot see. We believe because we see evidence.

When it comes to things of God, we do not have to see God to believe in Him. We can believe the testimony of others. We can see the evidence of His working. We can see the proof in the lives of Christians.

Weekday Problems

Marty had a great plan for evangelism in the community. At least, he thought it was a great plan. He had read about it in one of the monthly newsletters he received.

Tonight, he was going to present it to the Board. "Brothers and sisters," Marty began. "Here is a simple plan to get people to become a part of our church. When people show an interest in our church, we go visit them and give them a loaf of home-baked bread and a brochure outlining the ministries and programs of our church. All we need are eight volunteers to visit in teams of two. One team will visit every week. We also need only four folks to bake the bread or to buy it freshly baked. Last, and most importantly, we need a coordinator to get the names of prospects from the attendance registration pads or from present members. Studies have shown that most people who visit a church and are followed up with a visit from lay people of the church return to that church. Many of them join. It's a plan that is working all over the nation."

"Can you name a church it's working in?" Mr. Thomas queried. "I don't believe it will work. I've never seen a plan like that work," Sister Stuck commented.

*How will this congregation ever know if the plan will work or not?

*How does "stepping out in faith" fit in Marty's plan?

Declarations on Doubt

The trouble with the world is that the stupid are cocksure and the intelligent full of doubt.—*Bertrand Russell*

* * *

Doubt is part of all religion. All the religious thinkers were doubters.—*Isaac Singer*

* * *

"What kind of flower is that?"
"It's a chrysanthemum."
"Looks like a rose to me."
"No, I believe it's a chrysanthemum."
"Oh yeah? Spell it."
"K-r-y . . . K-r-i-s . . . C-h-r-i-s . . . . You know, you're right. It's a rose."

* * *

A man struggling with faith was asked to write his church preference on a form. Finally he scrawled, "red brick."

This Lesson in Your Life

Believing Without Seeing

If Missouri is the "Show Me" state, then Thomas must have been from Missouri. He always seemed to say, "Show me. Prove it to me." Thomas seemed to have been a guy who always looked before he leaped. He would not take the other disciples' word for the fact that Jesus had been raised from the dead. Thomas had to see Jesus for himself. Thomas probably considered himself a realist. He was probably very practical. But notice that Jesus, though He proved Himself to Thomas, chided His doubting disciple. Jesus let Thomas know that people would one day believe without seeing.

We have Thomases in our churches today, don't we? Thomas is the one who crosses his arms after the discussion about the new church sanctuary and says, "That's all well and good. How are we going to pay for it?" Thomas is the one who speaks up at the board meeting and tells us how we need to get more young parents with children into the church, but balks at all those "new-fangled ideas." Thomas' litany always seems to be, "We've never done it that way before."

Alas, we all know there are some things that cannot be demonstrated beforehand. There are some things we do in the Kingdom of God that require faith and trust beforehand in order for them ever to get done.

I was a pharmacist when I felt the call to the ministry. I loved my job. I was making a good salary. My wife and I use the expression, "I could see all the way to my retirement." But God had other plans for me. I decided to quit my job, go to seminary and become a fully ordained, full-time pastor.

Some people asked me, "How did you know God was calling you?" My answer is always the same, "I just knew." However, God did not clearly confirm my call until my wife, kids and I stepped out in faith. I quit my job and went to seminary. Once we made that step of faith, God put confirmation after confirmation, sign after sign in our path. He made it very clear. Yet, I am convinced that we would never have received the confirmations nor the blessings if we had simply said, "Well, God, we won't believe we are supposed to go to seminary until you show us something up front." I know God will do that if we earnestly ask Him to. Look at the encounter between Jesus and Thomas. But notice, Jesus said, "blessed are those who believe without seeing."

Do you find yourself telling God, "If you'll just show me, I'll believe you can do it?" If that sounds like you, then you are missing some of the greatest blessings of God. Our motto must eventually become as the old song, "I don't know what tomorrow holds, but I know who holds my hand." We do not have to see all the way down the road into the future to believe. All we have to do is look back at how God has worked in our lives in the past. That is enough to make us believe before we see what is coming tomorrow.

Seed Thoughts

1. What day was it that Jesus first appeared to all the disciples except Thomas?

It was the evening of the first day of the week. That would make it on a Sunday.

2. The disciples were huddled together in a locked room. Why was that?

They were afraid of the Jews. The Jews had arrested Jesus and brought Him to trial and the disciples were scared they would come after them next.

3. Why do you think Jesus showed them His hands and His side?

He wanted clearly to identify Himself. Remember that Mary did not recognize Jesus at first.

4. What was the command Jesus gave the disciples in verse 21?

He said, "As the Father has sent me, I am sending you." He was telling the disciples to go out into the world and spread the good news.

5. What was the message the disciples gave to Thomas when they saw him?

Their message was the same one Mary shared, "We have seen the Lord!"

---

1. What day was it that Jesus first appeared to all the disciples except Thomas?

2. The disciples were huddled together in a locked room. Why was that?

3. Why do you think Jesus showed them His hands and His side?

4. What was the command Jesus gave the disciples in verse 21?

5. What was the message the disciples gave to Thomas when they saw him?

6. What were the first words Jesus said each time He appeared to the disciples in the locked room?

7. Why do you think He said, "Peace be with you!"

8. What confession did Thomas make when He realized Jesus was alive?

9. What do we receive when we believe in Jesus without the same proof Thomas had?

10. Why did John record so many of Jesus' miraculous signs?

(Continued next page)

It was the evening of the first day of the week. That would make it on a Sunday.

They were afraid of the Jews. The Jews had arrested Jesus and brought Him to trial and the disciples were scared they would come after them next.

He wanted clearly to identify Himself. Remember that Mary did not recognize Jesus at first.

He said, "As the Father has sent me, I am sending you." He was telling the disciples to go out into the world and spread the good news.

Their message was the same one Mary shared, "We have seen the Lord!"

He said, "Peace be with you!"

It was probably a startling sight to see Jesus appear in a locked room.

Thomas professed, "My Lord and my God!"

Jesus said, "Blessed are those who have not seen and yet have believed." We receive blessings upon blessings.

So that we "may believe that Jesus is the Christ, the Son of God, and that by believing (we) may have life in His name."

6. What were the first words Jesus said each time He appeared to the disciples in the locked room?

He said, "Peace be with you!"

7. Why do you think He said, "Peace be with you!"

It was probably a startling sight to see Jesus appear in a locked room.

8. What confession did Thomas make when He realized Jesus was alive?

Thomas professed, "My Lord and my God!"

9. What do we receive when we believe in Jesus without the same proof Thomas had?

Jesus said, "Blessed are those who have not seen and yet have believed." We receive blessings upon blessings.

10. Why did John record so many of Jesus' miraculous signs?

So that we "... may believe that Jesus is the Christ, the Son of God, and that by believing (we) may have life in His name."

Lesson 7

Jesus, the Bread of Life

*A*nd Jesus took the loaves; and when he had given thanks, he distributed to the disciples, and the disciples to them that were set down; and likewise of the fishes as much as they would.

12 When they were filled, he said unto his disciples, Gather up the fragments that remain, that nothing be lost.

14 Then those men, when they had seen the miracle that Jesus did, said, This is of a truth that prophet that should come into the world.

26 Jesus answered them and said, Verily, verily, I say unto you, Ye seek me, not because ye saw the miracles, but because ye did eat of the loaves, and were filled.

27 Labour not for the meat which perisheth, but for that meat which endureth unto everlasting life, which the Son of man shall give unto you: for him hath God the Father sealed.

35 And Jesus said unto them, I am the bread of life: he that cometh to me shall never hunger; and he that believeth on me shall never thirst.

36 But I said unto you, That ye also have seen me, and believe not.

37 All that the Father giveth me shall come to me; and him that cometh to me I will in no wise cast out.

38 For I came down from heaven, not to do mine own will, but the will of him that sent me.

39 And this is the Father's will which hath sent me, that of all which he hath given me I should lose nothing, but should raise it up again at the last day.

40 And this is the will of him that sent me, that every one which seeth the Son, and believeth on him, may have everlasting life: and I will raise him up at the last day.

47 Verily, verily, I say unto you, He that believeth on me hath everlasting life.

48 I am that bread of life.

49 Your fathers did eat manna in the wilderness, and are dead.

50 This is the bread which cometh down from heaven, that a man may eat thereof, and not die.

51 I am the living bread which came down from heaven: if any man eat of this bread, he shall live for ever: and the bread that I will give is my flesh, which I will give for the life of the world.

John 6:11-12, 14, 26-27, 35-40, 47-51

April 18

Memory Selection
John 6:51

Background Scripture
John 6:1-59

Devotional Reading
Isaiah 55:1-11

Printed Scripture
John 6:11-12, 14,
26-27, 35-40, 47-51

Teacher's Target

Lesson purpose: To reaffirm Jesus' teaching that the true benefits of faith lie in accepting Him as spiritual nourishment—not in reaping self-serving benefits.

Each Sunday faithful Christians and their families stir around early enough and expend enough effort to attend church. Some disagree with the sermon or the general stance of their denomination, and experience congregational quarrels. In some countries, believers even practice the faith at the risk of being jailed, or even killed. Why do millions of Christians "hang in" despite such challenges?

A few may do so because the church offers good business contacts. The fellowship and social life attracts many. Some attend store-front churches and soup kitchens just for the food.

In this lesson, call your group to higher motivation. Emphasize that the "benefits" of Christianity are ultimately to be found not in any social or physical advantages, but in the opportunity to walk intimately with Christ.

Lesson Introduction

Although John relates none of the parables of Jesus as recorded in the other three Gospels, he makes a point to quote Jesus' parable-like "word pictures" of Himself: "I am the door . . . the way . . . the truth . . . the life . . . the vine . . . the good shepherd . . . the light of the world . . . ," and, here, "I am the bread of life."

Some authorities tie this repetition of "I am" with John's emphasis on Jesus as being one with the Father—the great "I am" (Exod. 3:14). Certainly the present topic, "I am the bread of life," identifies Jesus as the Source of spiritual nourishment, just as we view the Father as the Source of all life.

Note also that Jesus was willing to be broken, as the bread of the Passover Feast, in the offering of His body on the Cross. Here is a call for Christ's followers also to give themselves in service to others.

Teaching Outline	Daily Bible Readings

I. A Miracle of Feeding—11-12, 14
  A. Thousands are fed, 11-12
  B. Believers—of a sort, 14
	Mon. There Is a Boy Here
	John 6:1-15
	Tue. It Is I; Do Not Fear
	John 6:16-24

II. 'Meat' that Endures—26-27
  A. A warning about motives, 26
  B. A word about purpose, 27
	Wed. Give Us This Bread
	John 6:25-40
	Thu. I Am the Bread of Life
	John 6:41-51

III. The Mission of Jesus—35-40, 47-51
  A. To feed the called, 35-40
  B. To be true 'Bread'—47-51
	Fri. The Bread from Heaven
	John 6:52-59
	Sat. Bread for Israel
	Nehemiah 9:6-15
	Sun. The Bread of Angels
	Psalm 78:17-29

Verse by Verse

A Miracle of Feeding—11-12, 14

A. Thousands are fed, 11-12

11 And Jesus took the loaves; and when he had given thanks, he distributed to the disciples, and the disciples to them that were set down; and likewise of the fishes as much as they would.

12 When they were filled, he said unto his disciples, Gather up the fragments that remain, that nothing be lost.

Although, as the Introduction notes, John records none of Jesus' "story" parables, he has a keen eye for action parables or "signs." These are miraculous events that point to the authenticity of Christ as the Messiah. Here the sign is of the feeding of 5,000 people by the multiplication of seven loaves and two small fishes (vs. 9; the number 5,000 is supplied in Matt. 14:21). We should also note from the introduction to this parable that Jesus intends for it to be a test of His own disciples' awareness of who He is and why He came (see vss. 6-7).

In our day of critical environmental concerns, the Lord's command to gather up the twelve baskets of leftovers "that nothing be lost" has been applied to the need to conserve food and clean up our messes. In its original setting, however, it is more likely that this is another "action parable," illustrating what Jesus will teach in verses 37 and

39: Jesus will preserve all of the "fragments" of humanity who are called to be saved.

B. Believers—of a sort, 14

14 Then those men, when they had seen the miracle that Jesus did, said, This is of a truth that prophet that should come into the world.

In Lesson 2 we noted that one expectation among many Jews was that the Messiah would come as a prophet in the spirit of Moses, as predicted in Deuteronomy 18:15. Just as Moses worked miracles before Pharaoh to convince him to release the Hebrews from captivity, perhaps the Messiah would work similar miracles to herald the New Age, and release the Jews from Roman domination. The feeding of the multitudes convinced some that Jesus was that wonder-working prophet. In verse 15, they became so excited about the possibilities of this "prophet" fulfilling all their material hopes that Jesus had to flee when He realized they were about to crown Him "king"—prematurely, and for all the wrong reasons.

II. 'Meat' that Endures—26-27

A. A warning about motives, 26

26 Jesus answered them and said, Verily, verily, I say unto you, Ye seek me, not because ye saw the miracles, but because ye did eat of the loaves, and were filled.

The people caught up with the expectation that Jesus would become their earthly king followed Him across the Sea of Galilee after He fled (vss. 24-25). Now Jesus must confront their misplaced hopes. Knifing to the core of their material motivation, He charges that they sought Him not because His signs showed His spiritual authority, but because of their lust for a full belly.

B. A word about purpose, 27

27 Labour not for the meat which perisheth, but for that meat which endureth unto everlasting life, which the Son of man shall give unto you: for him hath God the Father sealed.

These Galileans, like common people everywhere, expended a great deal of effort to earn their daily bread. They were in a frenzy about the possibility of Jesus, as a "new Moses," releasing them from this struggle, worsened as it was by the oppression of Rome. Jesus reminds them that that sort of food only nourishes until the next day, and He tries to revise the focus of their efforts to the securing of spiritual food. He alone can offer this kind of "meat" or food, because God has, through the very miracles they were witnessing, set His seal of approval on Jesus.

III. The Mission of Jesus—35-40, 47-51

A. To feed the called, 35-40

35 And Jesus said unto them, I am the bread of life: he that cometh to me shall never hunger; and he that believeth on me shall never thirst.

36 But I said unto you, That ye also have seen me, and believe not

37 All that the Father giveth m shall come to me; and him tha cometh to me I will in no wise cas out.

38 For I came down from heaven, not to do mine own wil but the will of him that sent me.

39 And this is the Father's wil which hath sent me, that of al which he hath given me I shoul lose nothing, but should raise i up again at the last day.

40 And this is the will of hin that sent me, that every one whicl seeth the Son, and believeth o him, may have everlasting life: an I will raise him up at the last day

Jesus speaks first to the materialis here. He has spoken of "true bread, and some of those who followed Hin for the loaves and fishes perceive i speaking figuratively. Apparently, how ever, they are merely turning fron bread made of flour to the kind of po litical sustenance they think an earthl Messiah might provide. To correct thei misunderstanding, Jesus calls then again to a higher view of "bread"— accepting Him as the One whose nou ishment is more permanent than eithe literal bread or an earthly King wh might supply them with both food an freedom.

Then, turning to the issue of wh anyone would choose mere physica bread or an earthly King over Him Jesus says He can save only those whon the Father has "given" Him. At firs glance, this may seem to require th view that God has selected only a ce tain number of people to be saved, an has condemned out of hand the rest of humanity. In fact, the statement only implies that God has foreknown, not fore-ordained, those who would respond to Christ. As Jesus will say in verse 45, "Every man therefore that hath heard, and hath learned of the Father, cometh unto me."

Christ is not personally hurt by those who had rather have literal bread than the spiritual life He offers. He came not to do His own will, but the Father's. So He promises safe passage and a resurrection to life for all those whom the Father has foreseen would respond to His message. He would dare not cast out any among that group.

3. To be true 'Bread'—47-51

47 Verily, verily, I say unto you, He that believeth on me hath everlasting life.

48 I am that bread of life.

49 Your fathers did eat manna in the wilderness, and are dead.

50 This is the bread which cometh down from heaven, that a man may eat thereof, and not die.

51 I am the living bread which came down from heaven: if any man eat of this bread, he shall live for ever: and the bread that I will give is my flesh, which I will give for the life of the world.

What does it take to choose the eternal nourishment offered by Christ instead of literal bread, or an earthly Messiah? Verse 47 answers with the same call to faith we noted in John 3:16: truly believing. As is often noted, this means more than mere "mental assent," since "the devils also believe, and tremble" (Jas. 2:19). True faith in Christ

as Savior prompts people to respond to Him as Lord.

Jesus' claim to be the bread of life causes His opponents to grumble (vs. 43): "How can this young man, whose father Joseph we know, claim to have come down from heaven? Is He asserting that He is greater than Moses, who gave our fathers the manna in the wilderness?" (See vss. 31-33.)

Jesus had at first answered by pointing out that it was God, not Moses, who gave "the fathers" manna in the wilderness (vs. 32). Now He also notes that the manna fell far short of delivering eternal nourishment: the fathers who ate it died. In contrast, the "true bread" that consists of Christ Himself is the only eternally-sustaining "food" available.

In the last part of verse 51, Jesus gives a new twist to the meaning of the term "bread," applying it not just to Himself, or His Word, but to "my flesh." In verse 53 He will also refer to "drinking" His blood. There is little doubt that these references forecast the early Church's observance of the Lord's Supper. It is that "meal" at which Christians are reminded of the true significance of Christ's sacrifice of Himself. Around the Lord's Table we are treated anew to the fact that no earthly food and no earthly king can comprise the true bread of life.

Evangelistic Emphasis

I heard of a medical case once in which a man was starving to death, although he was eating. It seems this man had some kind of digestive disorder that inhibited his body from absorbing any nutrients from his food. In laymen's terms, the food would simply pass right through him. It mattered little what he ate. He could put food in his mouth. He could chew and swallow. Yet, the digestive problem allowed no nourishment from what he ate. He lost weight daily. He was starving to death. He could eat but he was never nourished.

There are those in our world today who are like that. Now, I am not referring to physiological problems within the human race. I mean there are those who are starving spiritually. They may be looking. They may even be taking in ideas and teachings that look nourishing, but within they are famished still

Folks need to feast upon the Bread of Life. That is the banquet upon which we can all be filled. The Bread of Life will nourish us. In this passage, Jesus calls Himself the Bread of Life. D. T. Niles, a Christian from India, was credited with saying, "Evangelism is simply one beggar telling another beggar where to find bread." I believe that is true. One of our tasks as Christians is to show others where to find the Bread of Life. We must, for the world around us is starving spiritually.

Memory Selection

I am the living bread which came down from heaven: if any man eat of this bread, he shall live for ever: and the bread that I will give is my flesh, which I will give for the life of the world.—*John 6:51*

What a beautiful and poetic verse of scripture! Bread has been called the staff of life. It is the basic staple for existence. Bread was a necessity in Jesus' day. It still is in many cultures today. One can hardly live without bread.

What bread is to the physical body, Jesus is to the soul. Jesus is necessary for life. It is "in Him we live and move and have our being" (Acts 17:28). Therefore, to refuse the invitation and command of Jesus is to miss life and die. Without the Living Bread, our souls starve in this life. Without the Living Bread, our souls die an eternal death in the life to come.

Now hear the good news. To refuse the offer of Jesus is to miss life in this world and the world to come. To accept His offer is to find real life, abundant life in this world and glory in the world to come.

Weekday Problems

Kate stood with the refrigerator door wide open. She heard
the program come back on the television. She realized she had
been standing there in front of the open refrigerator for the full
commercial time. "It's funny," she said out loud to no one, "I'm
hungry but I don't know what I want."

She found a slice of sausage and mushroom pizza. She added a little leftover potato
salad. She reached into the cabinet and dug out some cheese crackers. She counted out
four fat-free cookies as an afterthought.

As she sat down to resume watching her program she noticed how her diet was so
much like her life. Just like her refrigerator, her life was full of good things, but nothing
really got her excited. "My life is filled full," she mused, "but it's just not fulfilling." She
had a good job, a nice house and two Siamese cats. She crocheted, did pen-and-ink art
and even found time to work out three times a week at the gym. Still, there was a hole in
her life somehow.

"Oh well," she thought as she munched on the cheese crackers and pointed the
remote at the flickering screen.

* Have you ever felt that your life was empty? Did Jesus fill the void? If so, how?

* How would you explain to Kate about real meaning and purpose in life?

Speaking of Eating

You know it's time to diet when you step on one of those talking
scales and it says, "One at a time, please."

* * *

He has Dunlap's disease. It's when your stomach done-laps
over your belt.

* * *

Their diets seem to be working. He's so thin that when he
stands sideways and sticks out his tongue, he looks like a zipper . .
.

And she's so thin that when she wears a fur coat she looks like
a pipe cleaner.

* * *

The man was on a strict diet, and dreamed one night that
marshmallows were all he was allowed to eat. In his dream he
became so obsessed with marshmallows that he ate more and
more, cramming so many into his mouth that the bag was soon
empty. When he awoke, his pillow was gone.

This Lesson in Your Life

Bread that Lasts Forever

Have you ever heard someone say, "My God is still in the need-meeting business!" When that is said in a church service the congregation comes alive with "Amen" and "Praise God" and "That's right, Brother!" The fact that God meets needs is as true today as it was when John recorded the miracle of the feeding of the 5,000 with five loaves and two fish. God will provide all that we need. In fact, the Scripture tells us that God "is able to do immeasurably more than all we ask or imagine, according to his power that is at work within us" (Eph. 3:20); and that "God will meet all your needs according to his glorious riches in Christ Jesus" (Phil. 4:19). We know God is in the need-meeting ministry. To be honest, we rely on the fact that God will meet our needs.

Yet, we must be careful that we do not begin to seek the gift more than the Giver. It seems that some in this crowd of 5,000 were seeking Jesus for what He could do for them. Jesus chided them for that when He said, "Do not work for food that spoils, but for food that endures to eternal life, which the Son of Man will give you" (John 6:27). They had been fed. They saw Jesus as the source of that miracle. They followed to have their needs met again.

Following Jesus for the primary purpose of having our needs met is treading on dangerous ground. If we believe in Christ solely for what He can do for us we are in trouble. If we seek Him only for what He can do for us, we cease to seek when the blessings slow down. If we seek the blessing first, it is easy to fall into the trap of asking, "What have you done for me *today*, Jesus?"

Therefore, it is important to seek the face of Jesus, not just His hand.

William Barclay shares this story in his commentary of John. In the years just after A.D. 60 the luxury of Roman society was unparalleled. They served feasts of peacocks' brains and nightingales' tongues. It was told that a Roman lady was married in a robe so richly jeweled and gilded that it cost the equivalent of 432,000 English pounds. There was a reason for all this. The reason was a deep dissatisfaction with life. There was a hunger that nothing could satisfy. They would try anything for a new thrill, because they were both appallingly rich and appallingly hungry.

That could be our world today. We hear of young men who can hit a baseball or dunk a basketball or run a football who have everything in life: money, fame, power and all that those things bring. Many who are fabulously wealthy but still seeking another thrill, folks who are fabulously wealthy, yet with an inner hunger still.

There are hungers that can be satisfied only by Jesus. There is the hunger for truth—in him alone is the truth of God. There is the hunger for life—in Him alone is life more abundant. There is the hunger for love—in Him alone is the love that outlasts sin and death. There is the hunger for meaning—in Christ alone can one find meaning by giving oneself to Him. Jesus is the Bread of Life. He alone can satisfy the hunger of the human heart and soul.

Seed Thoughts

1. Knowing that the bread and fish were limited, did Jesus limit the amount each person received?

No, the passage says Jesus distributed to those who were seated as much as they wanted.

2. How many barley loaves did they start with? How much was left over?

Before the blessing there were five barley loaves. There were twelve baskets full of pieces left over after everyone had eaten.

3. When Jesus speaks of "food that endures to eternal life" (v.27) what is He talking about?

He is referring to spiritual things, things that will live forever as the spirit does. Things that are of God which only Christ can give.

4. What was Jesus Christ's purpose for coming down from heaven?

Verse 38 tells us that Jesus came not to do His own will but the will of the Father, the one who sent Jesus.

5. What was the will of God as described in this passage?

That Jesus should lose none of those God has given Him, and God will raise them up at the last day. All who believe will have eternal life.

1. Knowing that the bread and fish were limited, did Jesus limit the amount each person received?

2. How many barley loaves did they start with? How much was left over?

3. When Jesus speaks of "food that endures to eternal life" (v.27) what is He talking about?

4. What was Jesus Christ's purpose for coming down from heaven?

5. What was the will of God as described in this passage?

6. Why does Jesus mention the manna the Israelites ate in the wilderness after the exodus from Egypt?

7. What was the big difference between eating manna and eating the Living Bread?

8. What does Jesus mean by, "This bread is my flesh, which I will give for the life of the world"?

9. Jesus asserts repeatedly that He has come down from heaven. Why is this important?

10. Which is more important, life on this earth or eternal life? Why?

(Continued next page)

329

No, the passage says Jesus distributed to those who were seated as much as they wanted.

He is referring to spiritual things, things that will live forever as the spirit does. Things that are of God which only Christ can give.

Before the blessing there were five barley loaves. There were twelve baskets full of pieces left over after everyone had eaten.

Verse 38 tells us that Jesus came not to do His own will but the will of the Father, the one who sent Jesus.

That Jesus should lose none of those God gave Him, and that God will raise them up at the last day. All who believe will have eternal life.

He is showing the connection between God's provision in temporal things and eternal things (manna vs. Bread of Life).

Those who ate the manna died. Those who partake of the Living Bread will live forever.

He is referring to His atoning death on the cross. It is His death and resurrection that gives us eternal life.

He reminds us over and over that He is no ordinary human. He is both human and divine. He was sent directly from God.

Eternal life is more important. Life on this earth will end for each of us. Eternal life is lived forever in God's presence.

6. Why does Jesus mention the manna the Israelites ate in the wilderness after the exodus from Egypt?

He is showing the connection between God's provision in temporal things and eternal things (manna vs. Bread of Life.)

7. What was the big difference between eating manna and eating the Living Bread?

Those who ate the manna died. Those who partake of the Living Bread will live forever.

8. What does Jesus mean by, "This bread is my flesh, which I will give for the life of the world"?

He is referring to His atoning death on the cross. It is His death and resurrection that gives us eternal life.

9. Jesus asserts repeatedly that He has come down from heaven. Why is this important?

He reminds us over and over that He is no ordinary human. He is both human and divine. He was sent directly from God.

10. Which is more important, life on this earth or eternal life? Why?

Eternal life is more important. Life on this earth will end for each of us. Eternal life is lived forever in God's presence.

Truth That Sets People Free

7nen spake Jesus again unto them, saying, I am the light of the world: he that followeth me shall not walk in darkness, but shall have the light of life.

21 Then said Jesus again unto them, I go my way, and ye shall seek me, and shall die in your sins: whither I go, ye cannot come.

22 Then said the Jews, Will he kill himself? because he saith, Whither I go, ye cannot come.

23 And he said unto them, Ye are from beneath; I am from above: ye are of this world; I am not of this world.

24 I said therefore unto you, that ye shall die in your sins: for if ye believe not that I am he, ye shall die in your sins.

25 Then said they unto him, Who art thou? And Jesus saith unto them, Even the same that I said unto you from the beginning.

26 I have many things to say and to judge of you: but he that sent me is true; and I speak to the world those things which I have heard of him.

27 They understood not that he spake to them of the Father.

28 Then said Jesus unto them, When ye have lifted up the Son of man, then shall ye know that I am he, and that I do nothing of myself; but as my Father hath taught me, I speak these things.

29 And he that sent me is with me: the

John 8:12, 21-36

Father hath not left me alone; for I do always those things that please him.

30 As he spake these words, many believed on him.

31 Then said Jesus to those Jews which believed on him, If ye continue in my word, then are ye my disciples indeed;

32 And ye shall know the truth, and the truth shall make you free.

33 They answered him, We be Abraham's seed, and were never in bondage to any man: how sayest thou, Ye shall be made free?

34 Jesus answered them, Verily, verily I say unto you, Whosoever committeth sin is the servant of sin.

35 And the servant abideth not in the house for ever: but the Son abideth ever.

36 If the Son therefore shall make you free, ye shall be free indeed.

April 25

Memory Selection
John 8:31-32

Background Scripture
John 8:12-59

Devotional Reading
Psalm 51:1-9

Printed Scripture
John 8:12, 21-36

Teacher's Target

Lesson purpose: *To raise our commitment to truth to a higher level by building our confidence in Jesus Himself as the Truth and the Light.*

Few people are willing to say they do not love the truth. "The truth, the whole truth, and nothing but the truth" has become not just a statement made by witnesses in a court of a law; it is affirmed as a life-goal by virtually everyone.

Fewer people, however, have the commitment to follow the truth wherever it leads. Lying to protect self-interest is epidemic. Even in the courts, perjury is not uncommon.

The fact is, many people are bound by commitments that take precedence over the truth. In today's lesson, Jesus promises freedom from those bonds. Will we have the courage to let the fetters fall? Challenge your group to dare to take Christ seriously when He promises, "The truth shall make you free."

Lesson Introduction

John's Gospel is known for its long accounts of Jesus' "discourses." The present discourse deals with another "I am"—this time His claim to be "the light of the world." His opponents see immediately that this claim implies Christ's authority, as the Light, to expose the darkness of error as well as to shed the light of truth.

"Truth" is a topic that is easily lost in the heady atmosphere of philosophy. As a Jew, Jesus would have been more interested in the truth as exhibited in one's life than in Greek philosophers' endless arguments about truth in the abstract. For example, He knows that a majority of those He speaks to here will falsely accuse Him and call for His death (vs. 28). Yet He deals sensitively with some among them who are brave enough to accept His claims at least to some extent. With gentle firmness, Jesus leads us to the realization that if He indeed embodies "truth," then "doing the truth" by following Him is more important than philosophical arguments.

Teaching Outline	Daily Bible Readings		
I. The Light of Life—12	**Mon.**	The Light of the World	*John 8:12-20*
II. Living a Lie—21-24	**Tue.**	Many Believed in Him	*John 8:21-30*
A. Seeking but not finding, 21-22	**Wed.**	If You Remain in My Word	*John 8:31-38*
B. A matter of origins, 23-24			
III. Linked to the Father, 25-29	**Thu.**	Being Abraham's Children	*John 8:39-47*
A. Speaking God's truth, 25-27			
B. Deny Jesus, deny God, 28-29	**Fri.**	How to Live Forever	*John 8:48-59*
IV. Living the Truth—30-36	**Sat.**	Live in the Light	*Ephesians 5:1-14*
A. Freed by truth, 30-32			
B. Bound by sin, 33-36	**Sun.**	Led by Light and Truth	*Psalm 43:1-5*

Verse by Verse

I. The Light of Life—12

12 Then spake Jesus again unto them, saying, I am the light of the world: he that followeth me shall not walk in darkness, but shall have the light of life.

The story of Jesus and the adulterous woman has interrupted a scene that found Jesus teaching at the Jewish Feast of Tabernacles (7:2). This celebration came to be called the Feast of Lights as well, since part of its tradition was the nightly lighting of lamps commemorating the pillar of fire that provided light for the Jews fleeing Egypt. In yet another "I am" statement, Jesus uses this Feast as an object lesson for claiming to be not just a reflection of that light in the wilderness, but light for the whole world.

One of the unique features of biblical religion is that God Himself offers the light of revelation to assist those who want to find Him, in contrast to other religions that conceive enlightenment as a goal to be worked for. The symbolism of Jesus as Light will also have special application when the discussion turns toward *truth*—implying that those who really want the truth will accept the aid of this Light for finding it.

II. Living a Lie—21-24

A. Seeking but not finding, 21-22

21 Then said Jesus again unto them, I go my way, and ye shall seek me, and shall die in your sins: whither I go, ye cannot come.

22 Then said the Jews, Will he kill himself? because he saith, Whither I go, ye cannot come.

Jesus' language is blunt here because since proclaiming Himself to be the Light of the world, the Pharisees have bluntly rejected Him (vs. 13). Although they will seek the salvation He offers, and although "whosoever will" may come, these opponents of the truth and the light do not seek the truth earnestly enough to identify it with Jesus. "Ye cannot come" is therefore a self-imposed judgment.

Taking Jesus' reference to be a euphemism for dying, the Jews wonder if He is thinking of taking His own life. Ironically, *they* will soon be the ones clamoring for His death. He is really referring to returning to the Father, where His opponents' unbelief will not allow them to come.

B. A matter of origins, 23-24

23 And he said unto them, Ye are from beneath; I am from above: ye are of this world; I am not of this world.

24 I said therefore unto you, that ye shall die in your sins: for if ye believe not that I am he, ye shall die in your sins.

The choice these Jews have made not

333

to believe marks them as people of "worldly" origins. They cannot follow Jesus because He is of heavenly origins. In verse 44 the Lord will use even stronger language: the willfully unbelieving "are of your father the devil." People who have deliberately shut their eyes against the Light, who have made up their minds not to believe, will, if they persist in such as state at death will die in their sins.

III. Linked to the Father, 25-29
A. Speaking God's truth, 25-27

25 Then said they unto him, Who art thou? And Jesus saith unto them, Even the same that I said unto you from the beginning.

26 I have many things to say and to judge of you: but he that sent me is true; and I speak to the world those things which I have heard of him.

27 They understood not that he spake to them of the Father.

Jesus' reference to being "from above" pricks the curiosity of His opponents—and their question probably goes no deeper than curiosity. Who is this man who makes such radical claims, and speaks with such scathing judgment against them? Jesus calmly replies that He is who He—and John the Baptist— have said He is all along: the Son of God, the Word made flesh.

Consistent with His origins in the bosom of the Father, Jesus says He has no agenda other than speaking the Word He heard from His Father to a world lying in darkness. His opponents, however, are deaf to the fact that "he that sent me" is God the Father (vs. 27).

B. Deny Jesus, deny God, 28-29

28 Then said Jesus unto them, When ye have lifted up the Son of man, then shall ye know that I am he, and that I do nothing of myself; but as my Father hath taught me, I speak these things.

29 And he that sent me is with me: the Father hath not left me alone; for I do always those things that please him.

For many, it would take the awful scene at Golgotha to convince them of Jesus' origin and their own hope for a safe destiny with Him. Christ's prediction that they will know who He is seems to contain a glimpse of the coming Judgment as well as the possibility of these opponents' salvation. Although those who witnessed the crucifixion "smote their breasts," we are not told of mass conversions of the Jews who put Christ to death. The knowledge of the divinity of the One they put to death may not dawn until judgment. Christ's statement sounds very much like the prophet Zechariah's warning that at the Last Judgment "they shall look upon me whom they have pierced, and they shall mourn" (Zech. 12:10).

Regardless of whether those who claim to seek salvation recognize Jesus, He is comforted by the assurance that He has only spoken the words given Him by the Father, who will never forsake Him. It will only be under the pain of the Cross that in His humanity Jesus' confidence will lapse for a moment in the "cry of dereliction": "My God, my God, why hast thou forsaken me" (Matt. 27:46).

IV. Living the Truth—30-36
A. Freed by truth, 30-32

30 As he spake these words, many believed on him.

31 Then said Jesus to those Jews which believed on him, If ye continue in my word, then are ye my disciples indeed;

32 And ye shall know the truth, and the truth shall make you free.

The KJV does not bring out the tense of the verb in verse 31. These Jews are some who "*had* believed" in Jesus, but whose faith had not yet germinated and produced the new birth. The good news is that not all of the Jews challenging the truth of Jesus' claims were so hard-hearted they could not take a tentative step toward faith. The bad news is that they had yet to "continue" (literally *remain*) in faith to the point of discipleship. As John had said in chapter 1, the first blush of faith merely gives us the "power" or capacity to become children of God (1:12). These few Jews who believed had yet to act on the truth to be able to accept true freedom.

Verse 32 has become famous as a proof-text for the importance of all learning. It is true that arriving at any truth frees us from the bondage of ignorance. Specifically, however, Jesus is probably referring to the truth of His Sonship and divinity. His opponents were laboring under the chains of salvation by Law. The truth that would set them free was the free gift of God's grace through faith and obedience to Jesus—as the next exchange will explain.

B. Bound by sin, 33-36

33 They answered him, We be Abraham's seed, and were never in bondage to any man: how sayest thou, Ye shall be made free?

34 Jesus answered them, Verily, verily I say unto you, Whosoever committeth sin is the servant of sin.

35 And the servant abideth not in the house for ever: but the Son abideth ever.

36 If the Son therefore shall make you free, ye shall be free indeed.

It is a tribute to the fierce, freedom-loving spirit of the Jews that they could deny having been in bondage. The truth is that the Jewish nation was born only as they were being freed from bondage in Egypt, in the exodus. By the time of Christ they had also fallen captive to Babylonians, Assyrians, Egyptians, Greeks, and Romans. Their denial of such oppression is based more on God's promise that they would be *His* people, rather than on historical fact.

Furthermore, Jesus states the deeper truth that regardless of a people's political situation, they dwell in bondage to sin unless they choose to be "free-born" in the new birth. Only by pledging allegiance to the Son can we really be free.

335

Evangelistic Emphasis

The people asked Jesus, "Who are you?" Jesus answered, "I am who I claimed I was all along." Friends, the world today is asking of Christians almost the same question, "Who is Jesus?" People want to know Jesus. They want to know who He is. They want to know about His character. They want to know about His power. They want to know about His love. They want to know how He helps those who need help. They want to see Him as He really is. People want to know who Jesus is.

I am convinced that if people today could see Jesus Christ in all His glory,

splendor, majesty and power that every knee would immediately bow and every tongue would instantly confess that Jesus Christ is Lord. Though Jesus will reveal Himself in that fashion at the end times, He seldom does that now. In fact, one of the ways Jesus tends to show folks who He is by revealing Himself through the lives of Christians. If the world today does not know who Jesus is, part of the reason is that we Christians have done a less than adequate job of revealing Him to the world.

People will die in their sins if they go to their graves without knowing who Jesus is. Will we let Christ shine clearly through us? Will we walk with Him so intimately that people will see Him and know Him?

• • • • • •

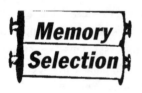

Memory Selection

Then said Jesus to those Jews which believed on him, If ye continue in my word, then are ye my disciples indeed; And ye shall know the truth, and the truth shall make you free.—*John 8:31-32*

Have you ever heard someone say, "I can't help it. That's just the way I am." I have heard Christians make that statement after they have repeated an act which they knew was wrong. We tend to shrug our shoulders and make excuses when we continue to mess up over and over in the same areas of our lives. Because the action does not cease, we convince ourselves it cannot cease.

In that sense we become slaves to those actions. "I can't help it," we hear ourselves saying. We have become victims.

Yet, we must always hear the truth about our sin. Jesus gives us victory over sin. Through the power of the Holy Spirit, we are no longer victims. We are victorious! We are no longer compelled to sin. When we recognize the truth of the power of Jesus to free us from sin, we become free indeed.

Weekday Problems

"Hummph!" Gary groused as he drove out of the factory parking lot. "I don't need anybody telling me how to live my life! I sure don't need some Christian goody-two-shoes saddling me with a bunch of outdated moral rules!" It seems that a Christian co-worker of Gary's had suggested that Gary clean up his language a bit after Gary told an off-color joke in front of several women who were offended. The Christian gave Gary a tract , "The Four Spiritual Laws," and asked himto read it .

Gary was still talking to himself as he drove toward an empty house. His wife had left last month after years of verbal and physical abuse. Gary had pleaded with her, "Please stay. It's just that when I get mad I can't control myself." She had heard that story dozens of times. She left anyway.

"I'm so mad at that guy my hands are shaking," Gary fumed. "I can hardly light my cigarette." About that time he passed the local bar. "I'll stop by, have a few drinks and forget all about what happened at work." With that he pulled into the bar's parking lot just as he did every day after work.

* Gary thinks he is his own man. Some may think he is a slave to sin. What do you think?

* Are the teachings of Jesus designed to spoil our fun or to make life more enjoyable? Explain.

Perspectives on Freedom

Freedom can be best understood ultimately as the freedom of the person who belongs wholly to no social group, who is a citizen of two cities, who is responsible to God.—*John C. Bennett*

* * *

God has laid upon man the duty of being free, of safeguarding freedom of spirit, no matter how difficult that may be, or how much sacrifice and suffering it may require.—*Nicolas Berdyaev*

* * *

Sound the loud timbrel o'er Egypt's dark sea!
Jehovah hath triumphed—his people are free.
　　　　　　　—*Lord Byron*

* * *

Oh, Lord, I want to be free, want to be free;
Rainbow 'round my shoulder, wings on my feet.
　　　　　　　—*Black American hymn*

* * *

Congress shall make no law respecting an establishment of religion, or prohibiting the free exercise thereof.—*U. S. Constitution*

This Lesson in Your Life

How to Know the Truth

Not long ago a video came out entitled, "A Few Good Men." Much of the movie was shot in a courtroom during the debate concerning the court-martial of two young U.S. Marines. In one scene the defense attorney is cross-examining a tough Marine colonel concerning his command. The questioning gets heated. Tempers flare. The colonel rages something like, "What do you want from me?!"

The attorney shouts back, "I want the truth!"

The colonel thunders, "You can't handle the truth!"

Sometimes we are like the attorney. We say we want the truth, but in reality we cannot handle it. Picture this scene. A forty-five-year-old accountant walks by the full-length mirror. He weighed 170 pounds when he got married. Now he is up to 221. He looks in the mirror, sucks in his gut and strikes a body builder's pose. "You're still as fit as always," he gloats. The mirror is telling the truth, but can this man handle it?

Sometimes we cannot handle the truth. There are times in a person's life when Jesus confronts that person with the truth of her/his sin. We can say to Jesus, "Well, don't I look good?" Or, we can say to Jesus, "I see my sin. Clean me up."

Jesus shows us the truth about ourselves. Even more than that, Jesus is the truth. Every search for the truth ends at Jesus Christ.

The search for the truth begins with discipleship. Just listen to Jesus: "So Jesus said to the Jews who had come to believe in Him, 'If you remain in my word, you are truly my disciples: and you will know the truth: and the truth will make you free'" (John 8:31-32).

Discipleship begins with belief. The beginning is the moment one accepts what Jesus says as true. All that He says about the love of God is true. All that He says about the terror of sin is true. All that He says about the real meaning of life is true.

Discipleship means constantly remaining in the word of Jesus. It means we constantly listen to and for the word of Jesus. It means we are always learning from Jesus, regardless of how long we have been disciples. It involves constantly digging deeper into the words of Jesus. It involves obeying the words of Jesus. The disciple does not learn the words simply for academic satisfaction. The disciple knows the words in order to put them into practice.

Discipleship issues in knowledge of the truth. To learn from Jesus is to learn the truth. What is that truth? One way to word an answer to that question is that the truth which Jesus brings shows us the real values of life. The fundamental question in every human life is this: "To what am I to give my life? To a career? To amassing a fortune? To pleasure? To the service of God?" In the truth of Jesus we see which things are really important and which are not.

Discipleship results in freedom. In the service of Christ is perfect freedom. It is freedom from fear, for the disciple never again has to walk alone. It is freedom from ourselves, for the power and presence of Christ can make a person brand new. It brings freedom from others, for we are no longer manipulated by fear of what others think or say. Most important of all, discipleship brings freedom from sin. Many a person comes to the place where he sins, not be-cause he wants to, but because he cannot help it.

The truth of Jesus Christ through discipleship breaks all chains which bind us and en-ables us to be the people we ought to be. Free!

338

Seed Thoughts

1. When Jesus claimed to be the light of the world, what was He saying about Himself?

He was saying that He is the Messiah. Isaiah 9:2 notes that the Messiah will be the "great light."

2. When Jesus said He was going away, to what was He referring?

He was referring to His death on the cross.

3. When Jesus said his listeners could not come where He was going, to what was He referring?

He was referring to His ascension into Heaven to His place at the right hand of the Father.

4. What did the Jews think Jesus was talking about?

They thought Jesus was talking about committing suicide.

5. Why could the Jews not understand what Jesus was talking about?

They did not understand because they were from below, Satan's domain, and Jesus was from above, God's domain.

1. When Jesus claimed to be the light of the world, what was He saying about Himself?

2. When Jesus said He was going away, to what was He referring?

3. When Jesus said his listeners could not come where He was going, to what was He referring?

4. What did the Jews think Jesus was talking about?

5. Why could the Jews not understand what Jesus was talking about?

6. According to verse 26, who was the source for Jesus' message?

7. What happens to folks who will not believe that Jesus is the Messiah?

8. When Jesus uses the term "lifted up" in verse 28, what is He talking about?

9. How do others know if we are disciples of Jesus?

10. How can we be set free from slavery to sin?

(Continued next page)

He was saying that He is the Messiah. Isaiah 9:2 notes that the Messiah will be the "great light."

He was referring to His death on the cross.

He was referring to His ascension into Heaven to His place at the right hand of the Father.

They thought Jesus was talking about committing suicide.

They did not understand because they were from below, Satan's domain, and Jesus was from above, God's domain.

God was the author of Christ's message. Jesus said, "what I have heard from Him I tell the world."

Those people will die in their sins. They will be lost forever.

He is not talking about the Jews exalting Him. He is speaking of His being lifted up on the cross at His crucifixion.

They know we are disciples when we follow or "hold to" the teachings of Jesus.

We can only be set free by the Son, Jesus Christ. When the Son sets you free, you are free indeed.

6. According to verse 26, who was the source for Jesus' message?

God was the author of Christ's message. Jesus said, "what I have heard from Him I tell the world."

7. What happens to folks who will not believe that Jesus is the Messiah?

Those people will die in their sins. They will be lost forever.

8. When Jesus uses the term "lifted up" in verse 28, what is He talking about?

He is not talking about the Jews exalting Him. He is speaking of His being lifted up on the cross at His crucifixion.

9. How do others know if we are disciples of Jesus?

They know we are disciples when we follow or "hold to" the teachings of Jesus.

10. How can we be set free from slavery to sin?

We can only be set free by the Son, Jesus Christ. When the Son sets you free, you are free indeed.

If I am lifted up from earth I will draw all men to myself.

The Purpose of Jesus' Death

*A*nd Jesus answered them saying, The hour is come, that the Son of man should be glorified.

24 Verily, verily, I say unto you, Except a corn of wheat fall into the ground and die, it abideth alone: but if it die, it bringeth forth much fruit.

25 He that loveth his life shall lose it; and he that hateth his life in this world shall keep it unto life eternal.

26 If any man serve me, let him follow me; and where I am, there shall also my servant be: if any man serve me, him will my Father honour.

27 Now is my soul troubled; and what shall I say? Father, save me from this hour: but for this cause came I unto this hour.

28 Father, glorify thy name. Then came there a voice from heaven, saying, I have both glorified it, and will glorify it again.

29 The people therefore, that stood by, and heard it, said that it thundered: others said, An angel spake unto him.

30 Jesus answered and said, This voice came not because of me, but for your sakes.

31 Now is the judgment of this world: now shall the prince of this world be cast out.

32 And I, if I be lifted up from the earth, will draw all men unto me.

33 This he said, signifying what death he should die.

34 The people answered him, We have heard out of the law that Christ abideth forever: and how sayest thou, The son of man must be lifted up? who is this Son of man?

35 Then Jesus said unto them, Yet a little while is the light with you. Walk while ye have the light, lest darkness come upon you: for he that walketh in darkness knoweth not whither he goeth.

36 While ye have light, believe in the light, that ye may be the children of light. These things spake Jesus, and departed, and did hide himself from them.

37 But though he had done so many miracles before them, yet they believed not on him:

42 Nevertheless among the chief rulers also many believed on him; but because of the Pharisees they did not confess him, lest they should be put out of the synagogue;

43 For they loved the praise of men more than the praise of God.

John 12: 23-37, 42-43

May 2

Memory Selection
John 12:32

Background Scripture
John 12:20-50

Devotional Reading
Romans 5:1-11

Printed Scripture
John 12:23-37, 42-43

Teacher's Target

Lesson purpose: *To evaluate the effect of Jesus' affirmation that He must die— both on His original hearers and on believers today as we are called to follow Him.*

The action of God in the world is rarely just what we expect. His ways are not our ways, nor are His thoughts our thoughts (Isa. 55:8-9). No one expected a miracle as huge as the exodus from Egypt. Later, after Israel proved unfaithful and were carried away into captivity, who would have predicted that God would then rescue them from their captivity?

None of the divine surprises, however, was more mysterious than Jesus' announcement that He would die. Explore with your class why this was so. Was it all because they expected Messiah to live forever, or partly because His followers are fearful of death themselves? Is Christ's challenge that we give ourselves away more than we can bear?

Lesson Introduction

More than one "Messianic hope" circulated among the Jews in the time of Christ. Some looked forward to a "prophetic Messiah," one who would be a new Moses and fulfill the prophecy in Deuteronomy 18:15. Another set of expectations centered on a "Davidic" Messiah, one who would restore the kingdom to the glory it enjoyed under King David. He was also expected as the "Son of man" in Daniel and Ezekiel—a figure of awesome, divine power. Still others looked for a "priestly Messiah" who would restore faithful worship.

Jesus came as prophet, priest, and king, fulfilling many of these expectations. Yet He disappointed many because He was no warlike king, and because He did not intend to reign forever in a visible kingdom—He would die. This was unacceptable both to His opponents (vss. 33-34) and to some of His own disciples (Mark 8:31-32). Jesus' response to this disappointment was to promise the abiding presence of the Holy Spirit, and to urge His followers to walk in the light.

Teaching Outline	Daily Bible Readings
	Mon. We Wish to See Jesus *John 12:20-26*
I. Dying to Live—23-26	**Tue.** For This Reason I Came *John 12:27-36b*
II. Reassuring the People—27-30	**Wed.** Who Has Believed? *John 12:36c-43*
III. Questioning the Christ—31-34	**Thu.** Whoever Believes in Me *John 12:44-50*
IV. Walking in the Light—35-37	**Fri.** The Mind of Christ *Philippians 2:1-11*
V. Bowing to Pressure—42-43	**Sat.** In the Image of God *Colossians 1:9-20*
	Sun. Knowledge of God's *Mystery* Colossians 2:1-15

Verse by Verse

I. Dying to Live—23-26

23 And Jesus answered them saying, The hour is come, that the Son of man should be glorified.

24 Verily, verily, I say unto you, Except a corn of wheat fall into the ground and die, it abideth alone: but if it die, it bringeth forth much fruit.

25 He that loveth his life shall lose it; and he that hateth his life in this world shall keep it unto life eternal.

26 If any man serve me, let him follow me; and where I am, there shall also my servant be: if any man serve me, him will my Father honour.

Jesus' prediction of His death seems to have been triggered by a visit from several Greek-speaking Jews who were in Jerusalem for the Passover Feast (vss. 1, 20-23). We can imagine that their view of the Messiah would have been influenced by such Greek ideas as "the ideal man." Perhaps they hoped to find in Jesus the embodiment of the ideal Greek philosopher-king who would live forever. Jesus abruptly relieves them of such notions by announcing that He must die like a seed in order to produce fruit—a far cry from the Greek ideal of immortality.

To make matters worse, Jesus warns that anyone who seeks to protect his life instead of giving it in behalf of others will, ironically, lose it. He even implies that if these Greeks—or people today—really want to be His disciples they must be prepared to follow Him to their own "cross." Of course He is referring to self-giving acts of service, not literal crucifixion, since it is only *His* death that is required for the redemption of sin. This "death by service" will be rewarded with its own kind of "resurrection"—special honor from God.

II. Reassuring the People—27-30

27 Now is my soul troubled; and what shall I say? Father, save me from this hour: but for this cause came I unto this hour.

28 Father, glorify thy name. Then came there a voice from heaven, saying, I have both glorified it, and will glorify it again.

29 The people therefore, that stood by, and heard it, said that it thundered: others said, An angel spake unto him.

30 Jesus answered and said, This voice came not because of me, but for your sakes.

Jesus' approaching rendezvous with death was both a willing act of obedience to the Father and a profoundly agonizing prospect. Troubled as He was, however, how could he plead for the Father to save Him from His freely-chosen destiny? Turning His back on this tempting thought, He prays instead that He might simply "glorify" God.

The word "glorify" comes from the same root that gives us "doxology," reminding us that each time we sing this time-honored praise-song we are glorifying Him "from whom all blessings flow." This is the same life-goal reflected in the Westminster Shorter Catechism, which affirms that "The chief end of life is to glorify God and enjoy Him forever." Jesus' determination to exalt God is an inspiring example to us: whether we live or die, our aim should be not self-preservation but exalting God.

We can understand that the people could not understand mere words amid the awesome sound made by God's divine voice! Even so, Jesus said it was for their benefit. He may have interpreted for them what the voice said, or perhaps the mere supernatural nature of the sound communicated heaven's approval of the approaching sacrifice of Christ.

III. Questioning the Christ—31-34

31 Now is the judgment of this world: now shall the prince of this world be cast out.

32 And I, if I be lifted up from the earth, will draw all men unto me.

33 This he said, signifying what death he should die.

34 The people answered him, We have heard out of the law that Christ a abideth for ever: and how sayest thou, The son of man must be lifted up? who is this Son of man?

How did Christ's approaching death on the Cross constitute "judgment of this world"? This supreme act of love would condemn by its very nature all the world's hatred, injustice, and unbelief. Once Jesus affirmed His own destiny, the destiny of "the prince of this world," Satan, was also sealed.

Jesus had had a prophetic glimpse of the doom of evil when He sent out the seventy disciples on the "limited commission." Hearing His disciples report excitedly on the miracles, including casting out demons, that had accompanied their preaching, Jesus said, "I beheld Satan as lightning fall from heaven" (Luke 10:18).

All this is lost on Christ's hearers. Their ideal of a "Christ" (Heb. *messiah*) was like that of the Greek expectation of an ideal king who would never die but "abide" forever. How could Jesus be the Son of man, as He claimed, and be lifted up on a Cross?

We may also ask why evil still seems to reign from time to time even after Christ's death and resurrection. The situation has been aptly compared to the decisive events toward the end of World War II. When Allied troops landed in Europe on D-Day, the fall of the Axis forces was assured: V-Day would follow after a few months' mopping-up operations. The Cross is the Christian D-Day, assuring victory to follow. Present evils are only the death-throes of Satan.

IV. Walking in the Light—35-37

35 Then Jesus said unto them, Yet a little while is the light with you. Walk while ye have the light, lest darkness come upon you: for he that

walketh in darkness knoweth not whither he goeth.

36 While ye have light, believe in the light, that ye may be the children of light. These things spake Jesus, and departed, and did hide himself from them.

37 But though he had done so many miracles before them, yet they believed not on him:

Jesus has exhausted all possible avenues of communicating the truth that the Son of man must die. He resorts to focusing on the behavior of His hearers. If they fail to grasp the concept of the Suffering Servant-Messiah, at least they can "live in the light" while He is among them, keeping their hearts open to allowing the truth eventually to dawn.

Although "light" is a universal symbol of the divine, Jesus' use of the concept no doubt comes from His familiarity with the Old Testament Scriptures. He was the living fulfillment of God's promise that He would give the Messiah "for a covenant of the people, for a light of the Gentiles" (Isa. 42:6). Several saw in Christ's birth the fulfillment of this promise (Luke 1:76-79; 2:30-32). Now Jesus calls on His followers to be "children of light"—that is forsaking the darkness in favor of walking in the light of His Word.

V. Bowing to Pressure—42-43

42 Nevertheless among the chief rulers also many believed on him; but because of the Pharisees they did not confess him, lest they should be put out of the synagogue;

43 For they loved the praise of men more than the praise of God.

The "nevertheless" here is a postscript to John's sad report in verses 37-40 that despite the voice from heaven, Jesus' miracles, and His stirring preaching, most of those at this scene "believed not on him" (vs. 37). Here we learn that, "nevertheless," several Jewish leaders were in fact convicted in their hearts that the claims of Jesus were true. Yet they bowed to social, religious, and political pressure and declined to confess their faith for fear of being excommunicated.

Before rushing to heap judgment on these Jews and their less-than-bold response to Jesus, we would do well to consider how much our own boldness of faith is tempered by our fear of what family, friends, or business associates would think of us if we were as outspoken as our hearts often tell us to be. No one lives in a vacuum; and the believer faces the continual challenge both to "live peaceably with all men" (Rom. 12:18), and to love the praise of God more than the praise of others.

Evangelistic Emphasis

A few summers ago I was a counselor at church camp for junior high kids. We had a rule that the lights went out at 10:00 PM. The time rolled around and, after much complaining from the boys, the lights were turned off. Things got quiet—too quiet.

All of a sudden there was a loud bump and the stifled sounds of an adolescent boy in pain. I turned on the light to discover that one of our mischief makers had tried to sneak to my bed with shaving cream for a practical joke. However, his bare toe struck the leg of one of the bunks. His plan was foiled.

That just goes to show you that a person can see to avoid danger and pain better when in the light. We know that in our lives the darkness hides danger. The darkness hides mischief and evil. The darkness obscures the safe path.

Jesus is the light of the world. When walking in his light we avoid much danger and pain. We avoid falling into the clutches of evil. We see more clearly the path to follow.

However, Jesus reminds us that, just as in summer camp at 10 p.m., there will a time when one may be unable to walk in the light. Those of us who know Jesus as Savior must make it our goal to lead all that we can to the light of Jesus Christ while there is still time.

● ● ● ● ● ● ● ●

Memory Selection

And I, if I be lifted up from the earth, will draw all men unto me.—*John 12:32*

This verse is significant in two ways. First, Jesus was speaking of His death on the cross when He said, "if I be lifted up." What was thought to be the ultimate humiliation in human terms, turned out to be the supreme exaltation in God's eyes. It was and is Christ's suffering, death and resurrection that draws us to His side. The cross is the ultimate demonstration of His love for us.

The second significant thing is found in the two words, "all men." Of course, Christ did not mean that only men would come to Him. What He meant was that all could come to Him. Every human being, regardless of ethnic origin or economic background or education, is welcome into the Kingdom. All humans are welcome at the foot of the cross. Jesus died for all.

Weekday Problems

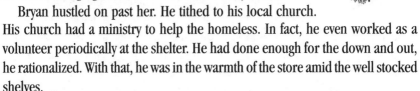

Bryan got out of his car in the crowded mall parking lot. "It's beginning to look a lot like Christmas," Bryan thought wryly. "There's a sure sign Christmas is near." It was a cheerful woman ringing a bell over a Salvation Army kettle.

Bryan hustled on past her. He tithed to his local church. His church had a ministry to help the homeless. In fact, he even worked as a volunteer periodically at the shelter. He had done enough for the down and out, he rationalized. With that, he was in the warmth of the store amid the well stocked shelves.

Bryan looked down his shopping list. It was a long one. He loved buying gifts for his family and friends. He went up and down the aisles filling his basket. "How blessed I am to have so many loved ones," Bryan reflected. "How blessed I am to have a good job that I can afford to buy gifts for everybody."

Then Bryan thought about the Salvation Army woman outside. Feeling sheepish, Bryan rang up his purchases and walked out the door. "God thank you for your many blessings to me," he prayed as he put two twenty dollar bills in the kettle. "I guess sometimes self-sacrifice does a lot of good," Bryan thought as he walked to his car.

* Share some times in your life when self-sacrifice benefitted others.

* What are some ways Jesus Christ sacrificed to benefit us?

Natural Laws

Murphy's Law—If anything can go wrong, it will.

O'Toole's Commentary on Murphy's Law—Murphy was an optimist.

The Unspeakable Law—As soon as you mention something, if it's good it goes away. If it's bad, it happens.

Howe's Law—Everyone has an idea of how something should work, but it doesn't.

The Unfailing Law of the Supermarket—The other line moves faster.

Law of Selective Gravity—Every object accidentally dropped will fall in a way that does the most possible damage.

Solomon's Corollary—The chance of the bread falling buttered-side down is directly proportionate to the cost of the carpet.

Einstein's Law of Experiments—If a research project is not worth doing at all, it is not worth doing well.

347

This Lesson in Your Life

Finding Life in Death

Every farmer knows that the seed of any plant must be buried in the earth for it to fulfill its ultimate purpose. Please let me attribute human qualities to an inanimate seed. That is, if a seed wants to be ultimately fulfilled, it must be willing to die from being a seed in order to become a plant, which in turn produces more seed.

Could we go so far as to say that for something truly to live to the fullest, it must be willing to die? It has always been because men have been prepared to die for a cause that great things have lived. Sometimes it is only when a person buries his/her own personal ambitions and aims that one can be of greatest use to God. Henri Nouwen was a professor in a prestigious Ivy League seminary in New England. He taught some of the best and brightest minds in the world. He was highly sought after as a speaker and seminar leader throughout academia. Yet, after years of teaching, he was led by God to become a worker at a home for mentally and physically challenged men. He went from teaching the best and the brightest to bathing the handicapped and just being a friend. Whatever personal ambitions Dr. Nouwen had, he gave to God. He died to self, if you will. Only by the death of personal desire and personal ambition can a person become a true servant of God.

It is also true that only by spending one's life can one save it. We used to sing a song which contained the chorus, "Love's just like a magic penny. Hold it tight and you won't have any. Spend it and you'll have so many they'll roll all over the floor." The world owes much to folks who have generously spent their strength and given themselves to God and to others. We might just exist longer if we made up our minds to take life easy, never to risk anything for another, to look out for "number one" first and foremost. We may exist longer . . . but it will not be living.

However, there are those who cannot receive this truth. Our scripture tells us of those who believed in Jesus, who knew His words were the truth. Yet, those would not confess their faith because they wanted to be accepted by men more than they wanted praise from God. That mind set is still around today. There are those who know that giving of ourselves is still the best way. They see the merits of self-sacrifice. They know that a person should give to others and do for others and consider the feelings and well-being of others as a priority. Yet, some of those same people are afraid of giving up the ways of the world to trust the higher ways of God. As Jesus put it, they do not "trust the light" as much as they trust conventional wisdom. They cannot move themselves to die to self. Thus, they fail to live fully.

An elementary student was asked what parts of speech "my" and "mine" were. He thought a minute before he said, "Those are *aggressive* pronouns." There is truth to the mistake. "My" and "mine" can focus aggressivley on ourselves.

Only by giving our lives to others do we truly live. Only by spending our lives do we truly retain it. Only by serving others comes true greatness.

Seed Thoughts

1. Of what was Jesus speaking when He said it was time for the Son of Man to be glorified?

He was speaking of His death on the cross and his subsequent resurrection and ascension into heaven.

2. Jesus refers to His followers as servants. What are some characteristics of a servant?

A servant does what the master wants him to do. A servant puts his master's desires above his own. A servant is obedient.

3. Jesus uses a word picture about a kernel of wheat here. He used word pictures often. Why?

He used examples and illustrations familiar to His listeners in order to help them understand exactly what He was talking about.

4. Jesus considered asking God to keep Him from the crucifixion but He did not ask. Why?

Because by this time He knew that the very reason He had come to the earth was to die for the sins of the world.

5. Who is the "prince of this world" to whom Jesus refers in verse 31?

The devil; Satan.

---

1. Of what was Jesus speaking when He said it was time for the Son of Man to be glorified?

2. Jesus refers to His followers as servants. What are some characteristics of a servant?

3. Jesus uses a word picture about a kernel of wheat here. He used word pictures often. Why?

4. Jesus considered asking God to keep Him from the crucifixion but He did not ask. Why?

5. Who is the "prince of this world" to whom Jesus refers in verse 31?

6. What event ultimately defeated the devil and drove him from power?

7. Who is the Son of Man?

8. When Jesus speaks of the Son of Man being lifted up, is He referring to His return to heaven or His death on the cross?

9. When Jesus speaks of those who walk in the dark, to whom is He referring?

10. Why did some leaders who believed in Christ fail to confess their faith?

(Continued next page)

He was speaking of His death on the cross and his subsequent resurrection and ascension into heaven.

A servant does what the master wants him to do. A servant puts his master's desires above his own. A servant is obedient.

He used examples and illustrations familiar to His listeners in order to help them understand exactly what He was talking about.

Because by this time He knew that the very reason He had come to the earth was to die for the sins of the world.

The devil; Satan.

It was Jesus' death on the cross. What seemed to be Satan's triumph was actually his defeat.

Jesus Christ.

His death on the cross. His sacrificial love will draw all people to Him.

Jesus is referring to any and all who fail to believe in Him and fail to put their trust in Him.

They were afraid the Pharisees would put them out of the synagogue if they confessed their faith.

6. What event ultimately defeated the devil and drove him from power?
It was Jesus' death on the cross. What seemed to be Satan's triumph was actually his defeat.

7. Who is the Son of Man?
Jesus Christ.

8. When Jesus speaks of the Son of Man being lifted up, is He referring to His return to heaven or His death on the cross?
His death on the cross. His sacrificial love will draw all people to Him.

9. When Jesus speaks of those who walk in the dark, to whom is He referring?
Jesus is referring to any and all who fail to believe in Him and fail to put their trust in Him.

10. Why did some leaders who believed in Christ fail to confess their faith?
They were afraid the Pharisees would put them out of the synagogue if they confessed their faith.

Lesson 10

Jesus Taught About Servanthood

*N*ow before the feast of the passover, when Jesus knew that his hour was come that he should depart out of this world unto the Father, having loved his own which were in the world, he loved them unto the end.

2 And supper being ended, the devil having now put into the heart of Judas Iscariot, Simon's son, to betray him;

3 Jesus knowing that the Father had given all things into his hands, and that he was come from God, and went to God;

John 13:1-17

4 He riseth from supper, and laid aside his garments; and took a towel, and girded himself.

5 And after that he poureth water into a bason, and began to wash the disciples' feet, and to wipe them with the towel wherewith he was girded.

6 Then cometh he to Simon Peter: and Peter saith unto him, Lord, doest thou wash my feet?

7 Jesus answered and said unto him, What I do thou knowest not now; but thou shalt know hereafter.

8 Peter saith unto him, Thou shalt never wash my feet. Jesus answered him, If I wash thee not, thou hast no part with me.

9 Simon Peter saith unto him, Lord, not my feet only, but also my hands and my head.

10 Jesus saith to him, He that is washed needeth not save to wash his feet, but is clean every whit: and ye are clean, but not all.

11 For he knew who should betray him; therefore said he, Ye are not all clean.

12 So after he had washed their feet, and had taken his garments, and was set down again, he said unto them, Know ye what I have done to you?

13 Ye call me Master and Lord: and ye say well; for so I am.

14 If I then, your Lord and Master, have washed your feet; ye also ought to wash one another's feet.

15 For I have given you an example, that ye should do as I have done to you.

16 Verily, verily, I say unto you, The servant is not greater than his lord; neither he that is sent greater than he that sent him.

17 If ye know these things, happy are ye if ye do them.

May 9

Memory Selection
John 13:16
Background Scripture
John 13:1-35
Devotional Reading
Matthew 25:31-40
Printed Scripture
John 13:1-17

Teacher's Target

Lesson purpose: *To learn, from Jesus' interaction with the apostles at the Last Supper, the meaning and importance of true servanthood.*

The emphasis on individual freedom and human rights in today's world is light years away from the world in which Jesus gave this teaching. His was a realm of lords and servants, kings and subjects, masters and slaves.

A bridge can be built between these two worlds by reminding your group of the difference between serving Jesus and a tyrant. Introduce the lesson by asking about how Jesus exerts His authority over us. Instead of making decisions merely in his own self-interest, this "slave-holder" has *our* best interest in mind. Instead of ruling over us as a tyrant, "His banner over us is love." His "rule" in our hearts is actually the only way to freedom.

Lesson Introduction

The word for "servant" in today's lesson also meant "slave." In Jesus' day, this cut two ways. On the one hand a slave had no rights. He was chattel, human merchandise, and could be bought and sold at the will of his owner. On the other hand, it was an honor to be owned by certain masters, and to serve, for example, in the court of a king.

We also, on the one hand, are to obey Jesus without reservation, since He "owns" us. Also, since no one can serve two masters, we give exclusive allegiance to Him. Yet we can also be thankful that we are not servants of a tyrant but of a Benevolent King. As Paul wrote, we are all governed by our orientation toward life or death; we do not have absolute freedom, but only the choice of masters (Rom. 6:16-18). Furthermore, as servants of the Great King, we also recall that in another sense the King has set us *free*, through the truth (John 8:31-32). We do not grovel and simper as though we had no will of our own, but stand as those who have freely chosen, with open-eyed awareness, to love and serve Jesus as Lord.

Teaching Outline	Daily Bible Readings

I. Preparations for a Journey—1-3
  A. Leaving in love, 1
  B. Awareness of betrayal, 2-3
 	
II. Parable of Servanthood—4-9
  A. Washing feet, 4-5
  B. Peter's reaction, 6-9
 	
III. Practicing the Model—10-17
  A. Refining the notion, 10-11
  B. Explaining the role, 12-17
	Mon. Washing the Disciples' Feet
	  John 13:1-11
	Tue. Do You Know What I've Done?
	  John 13:12-20
	Wed. One of You Will Betray Me
	  John 13:21-30
	Thu. Not Long for this World
	  John 13:31-35
	Fri. Here Is My Servant
	  Isaiah 42:1-9
	Sat. To Be Great, Serve
	  Matthew 23:1-11
	Sun. Follow in Christ's Steps
	  1 Peter 2:18-25

Verse by Verse

I. Preparations for a Journey—1-3

A. Leaving in love, 1

1 Now before the feast of the passover, when Jesus knew that his hour was come that he should depart out of this world unto the Father, having loved his own which were in the world, he loved them unto the end.

This verse serves to introduce the second major part of John's Gospel. From here through chapter 17 John will report on several lengthy and profound "speeches" Jesus makes to the Twelve at the Last Supper.

The verse also includes a great deal of information about Jesus, as though John is summarizing much of what has gone before and drawing a deep breath before continuing. He notes that (1) Jesus knew that His "moment of truth" had arrived, when His death would accomplish the will of the Father; (2) He was aware of His pre-existence with the Father (as in John 1), and was confident of His return to that safe haven; (3) while loving all the world (3:16), He had a special love for these twelve men who were His inner circle of disciples; and (4) He would show this love "to the full extent" (the NIV rendering of "unto the end")—probably a reference to sending them the Holy Spirit in His absence (16:13).

B. Awareness of betrayal, 2-3

2 And supper being ended, the devil having now put into the heart of Judas Iscariot, Simon's son, to betray him;

3 Jesus knowing that the Father had given all things into his hands, and that he was come from God, and went to God;

The role of Satan in prompting Judas Iscariot to betray his Lord brings together the twin mysteries of predestination and the freedom of persons. Did "the devil make him do it"? Some have also defended Judas on the ground that God had foreordained him to perform the "service" of betrayal, without which Jesus would not have been put to death for our sins. They emphasize the truth stated by Peter in Acts 2:23: Jesus was slain "by the determinate counsel and foreknowledge of God."

Yet it was also Peter who boldly assigned the responsibility of Jesus' death not to God or Satan but to those, including Judas, who "denied the Holy One and the Just" (Acts 3:14). One way to view these two poles of the same reality is to affirm that God knew before the beginning of time that *someone* would betray Jesus, but that Judas and others freely chose to play that role. Similarly, God prepared salvation for "the elect" from before the worlds were created, but allows us free will to decide whether we will be a part of that Body.

II. Parable of Servanthood—4-9
A. Washing feet, 4-5

4 He riseth from supper, and laid aside his garments; and took a towel, and girded himself.

5 And after that he poureth water into a bason, and began to wash the disciples' feet, and to wipe them with the towel wherewith he was girded.

In an "action parable" with at least two levels of meaning, Jesus assumes the role He requires of His followers—that of a servant. At the first level, he "arises" from the low middle-eastern-style table at which people sat on the floor or on pillows, and proceeds to perform a task of menial service. With few stone pavements, people would often arrive as guests at meal-time with dirty feet. Servants and urns of water were stationed in many households of the day to wash the guests' feet—and Jesus serves as that servant at the Last Supper.

Foot-washing was such a lowly task that later tradition would not require it of Jewish slaves (only of Gentile slaves, children and wives!). Yet Jesus girds Himself with a towel to serve in this way. This was itself a sign of service, much like a manual laborer today, in cool weather, will tie the arms of a sweat-shirt around his waist when he doesn't need it immediately. Again from Jewish tradition, it was held that when Abraham sent Hagar away to keep peace with Sarah, he bound her shawl about her waist so

people would consider her a mere slave and not his wife.

A second level of meaning from this scene will appear in the next act of the drama.

B. Peter's reaction, 6-9

6 Then cometh he to Simon Peter: and Peter saith unto him, Lord, doest thou wash my feet?

7 Jesus answered and said unto him, What I do thou knowest not now; but thou shalt know hereafter.

8 Peter saith unto him, Thou shalt never wash my feet. Jesus answered him, If I wash thee not, thou hast no part with me.

9 Simon Peter saith unto him, Lord, not my feet only, but also my hands and my head.

We can imagine that all the apostles felt awkward at the sight of their Lord stooping to wash the feet of His servants. It was Simon Peter who voiced the silent protest of the others. Surely it should be the other way around, with the disciples washing Jesus' feet.

Verses 7-8 reveal the deeper meaning in Jesus' deed. Cleansing the feet of His closest followers is symbolic of the cleansing that will shortly be accomplished in the blood flowing from His Cross. Although the disciples have not yet understood the necessity of this "service," the events during the next several days will finally enable them to see the point.

This is why the Lord gently rebukes Peter for at first refusing to allow his feet to be washed by Christ. "If I wash thee ot, thou hast no part with me" refers not to the literal foot-washing, but to Christ in His role of the Suffering Servant, prophesied in Isaiah 53:1-6). In dying on the Cross He would wash away the sins of the world—including Peter's. The word for "part" was used to describe the portion of a will or inheritance doled out to each of the surviving children. While He does not yet grasp the full meaning of what Jesus is doing, Peter sees the urgency of being included in whatever spiritual legacy His Lord might leave. So, in his typical all-or-nothing style, he blurts out, "Then give me a bath, Lord!"

II. Practicing the Model—10-17

A. Refining the notion, 10-11

10 Jesus saith to him, He that is washed needeth not save to wash his feet, but is clean every whit: and ye are clean, but not all.

11 For he knew who should betray him; therefore said he, Ye are not all clean.

Subtly correcting Peter's exuberant response, Jesus patiently explains that Peter doesn't need to be given a bath. Having committed himself to Jesus, He will be "clean every whit" (lit. "wholly clean") because of the cleansing power of the blood soon to flow from the Cross. It will only remain to perform acts of kindness like foot-washing for each other.

The exception, of course is Judas. "Ye are clean, but not all" injects the tragic fact that one of the apostles will soon betray his Lord.

B. Explaining the role, 12-17

12 So after he had washed their feet, and had taken his garments, and was set down again, he said unto them, Know ye what I have done to you?

13 Ye call me Master and Lord: and ye say well; for so I am.

14 If I then, your Lord and Master, have washed your feet; ye also ought to wash one another's feet.

15 For I have given you an example, that ye should do as I have done to you.

16 Verily, verily, I say unto you, The servant is not greater than his lord; neither he that is sent greater than he that sent him.

17 If ye know these things, happy are ye if ye do them.

The supreme "service" of the Cross now illustrated by washing His disciples' feet, Jesus emphasizes the importance of their following His example. Earlier, the disciples had argued about who would be the greatest in the Kingdom of heaven (Mark 9:34); and the mother of James and John had begged that her sons be given prominence (Matt. 20:20-21).

In the act of foot-washing Jesus shows how He turns the world's standards of "greatness" upside down. Instead of His disciples washing His feet, He washes theirs. If we want to be great in His Kingdom, we must serve others, not exalt ourselves above them. Knowing this, we can be happy only if we act accordingly.

Evangelistic Emphasis

The good news of the gospel is that God loved the world so much that He gave His only Son to die as a substitutionary sacrifice to erase our sins. Whoever believes that Jesus can do that will have his sins forgiven and that person's soul will live forever with God in heaven, even though that person may die a physical death on this earth.

John tells us in this passage that Jesus was about to show the full extent of His love. Thus Jesus took a towel and basin and washed the feet of the disciples. The washing was both impor-tant and symbolic, but the fact that Jesus, the Son of God in the flesh, did a servant's job was also important.

Paul tells us, "Your attitude should be the same as that of Christ Jesus: Who, being in very nature God, did not consider equality with God something to be grasped, but made himself nothing, taking the very nature of a servant, being made in human likeness. And being found in appearance as a man, he humbled himself and became obedient to death-- even death on a cross! (Phil. 2:5-8).

The fact that Jesus emptied Himself of many of His divine qualities and gave up His throne in heaven is good news. We can tell others that precious story. We can pattern our lives by His and be the servant of our brothers and sisters.

• • • • •

Verily, verily, I say unto you, The servant is not greater than his lord; neither he that is sent greater than he that sent him.—*John 13:16*

"God is God and I am not." That certainly sounds like a statement with whic we would all agree, does it not? Yet, I am afraid there are times I begin to think am God. Well, not really, but there are times I argue with God. There are times think I know better how to do things than God does. Sometimes I feel that Go really does not have all the facts, or He would not want me to do certain things i certain ways at certain times. "Lord, you don't know how that person hurt me! can't love that person!"

God instructs every believer to do things God's way. When we refuse or argu with God or try to find a better way (which is not better at all), what we are reall doing is putting our-selves above God. Remember, God is God and you are no

Weekday Problems

"Come in, David," Pastor Wink stood to shake hands as David came through the door. "Have a seat. As you know, David, we are about to begin a contemporary worship service in our church. One of the new things we will do in the service is have a worship team rather than a choir. I know that you have a marvelous voice. Your guitar playing is professional quality."

David was sitting on the edge of his chair. He had heard about the worship team. He knew he was the one to lead it. "I am good," David thought. "I am the best qualified in the church to do that." David could already see himself in front of the whole church leading crowds of people in worship. He could already hear his marvelous voice escorting all in attendance to the throne of God's grace in praise.

Pastor Wink continued, "So our pastoral staff feels you would be perfect to be a member of that worship team under the direction of our Music Minister."

"What!?" David thought. "I should be the leader! If I can't lead, I won't participate." David spoke aloud, "I'm sorry Pastor Wink. I simply do not have the time for an additional commitment.

* If you were a Christian friend of David's how would you counsel him?

* What does it mean to have a servant's heart?

The Marks of a Leader

Scars are the authenticating marks of a true spiritual leader. The only thing Jesus took pains to show after His resurrection were His scars. The disciples on the Emmaus road did not recognize Him until He broke bread with His nail-scarred hands.

Nothing moves people more than the print of the nails and the mark of the spear. Those marks are tests of sincerity that none can challenge, as Paul knew well. "Let no one cause me trouble," he wrote, "for I bear on my body the marks of Jesus" (Gal. 6:17).

A song by Amy Carmichael says it well:

Hast thou no scar?
No hidden scar on foot, or side, or hand?
I hear thee sung as mighty in the land,
I hear them hail thy bright ascendant star:
Hast thou no scar?

—Adapted from the book *Spiritual Leadership,* by J. Oswald Sanders

357

This Lesson in Your Life

Living as Servants

As a pastor, I regularly have opportunity to perform weddings. In the pre-marital counseling I usually have the couples fill out a survey called "Role Model Comparison." Several of the questions have to do with the division of labor in the home. That is, who is going to do what after marriage. Some of the questions deal with housework. I know a marriage is in deep trouble before it ever begins if the future husband says, "I don't do housework. That's woman's work."

I do not want to make a statement about marriage. I want to look rather at how true love and a servant's heart are related. When a person loves another, neither lords it over the other. When persons love each other there is a mutual submission to one another. Each person considers the well-being of the other as primary.

That is one of the things Jesus demonstrated when He took the towel and the basin and washed the disciples' feet. To wash one's dusty, dirty feet was servant's work. Jesus knew that. Therefore, He demonstrated the full extent of His love. He was willing to be a servant. Can we do any less?

So often, even in churches, trouble arises when someone does not get the recognition from others he thinks he deserves. Some years back I was helping with a laymen's gathering at our church by taking up the money for registration. A distinguished gentleman in a dark suit came up to register and I asked him for the fee. He straightened up and asked, "Do you know who I am?" Well, I certainly did. He was the pastor of the largest church in our district.

"Yes, pastor, I know who you are. Is there a problem?" I asked.

"Well, I shouldn't have to pay," he sniffed.

I believe Pastor Bigchurch needed a lesson on being a servant. In God's eyes, there is only one type of greatness and that is the greatness of service. The world is full of people who are standing on their dignity when they ought to be kneeling at the feet of their brothers and sisters.

In every walk of life the desire for prominence and the unwillingness to take a subordinate role wreck the scheme of things. A player who has to sit on the bench one day quits the team. A member of the choir does not get the solo and refuses to sing anymore. A church leader is not chosen to head a prestigious committee and resigns from all committees. When we are tempted to think of our own dignity, our prestige and our rights, we should consider the picture of the Son of God Himself, wrapping a towel around His waist, kneeling on the floor and washing the disciples' feet.

A servant's heart is hard to come by. As a matter of fact, it does not come naturally. It comes supernaturally. In the world the great ones are the most powerful, the richest or the most famous. In God's Kingdom the great ones are the servants of others. May we always be great in God's eyes first.

Seed Thoughts

1. When did this scene occur according to the Jewish timetable?

It was just before the Passover Feast, during the Jewish month Abib, later called Nisan. It was in the springtime.

2. John's gospel does not tell us of the Lord's Supper in the Upper Room. What does he describe?

John tells us about Jesus washing the disciples' feet.

3. Who was the one who betrayed Jesus to the authorities? Who was that man's father?

The betrayer was Judas Iscariot. Verse tells us Judas' father was named Simon.

4. Whose job was it normally to wash the feet of the guests at a meal?

Normally, this menial and lowly task was performed by a servant.

5. How did Jesus show "them the full extent of His love?" (vs.2)

By His act of servanthood by washing feet. Even more, His act of washing sin by the cross and His blood showed the full extent of His love.

---

1. When did this scene occur according to the Jewish timetable?

2. John's gospel does not tell us of the Lord's Supper in the Upper Room. What does he describe?

3. Who was the one who betrayed Jesus to the authorities? Who was that man's father?

4. Whose job was it normally to wash the feet of the guests at a meal?

5. How did Jesus show "them the full extent of His love?" (vs.2)

6. What was Peter's reaction to Christ's action of foot washing?

7. Why did Jesus say, "You are clean, though not every one of you?"

8. What did Jesus instruct the disciples to do in verse 14?

9. When Jesus told the disciples to wash each other's feet, was He speaking literally? Explain.

10. When do the blessings of servanthood come to the believer?

(Continued next page)

It was just before the Passover Feast, during the Jewish month Abib, later called Nisan. It was in the springtime.

John tells us about Jesus washing the disciples' feet.

The betrayer was Judas Iscariot. Verse 2 tells us Judas' father was named Simon.

Normally, this menial and lowly task was performed by a servant.

By His act of servanthood by washing feet. Even more, His act of washing sin by the cross and His blood showed the full extent of His love.

At first, he did not want Christ to wash his feet. Then he wanted Jesus to wash his hands and head as well.

Jesus knew that Judas had already made up his mind to betray Christ. Judas was the unclean one.

He instructed them to wash one ano-ther's feet.

Yes and no. He was telling them to be as a servant to one another. He was telling them not to think themselves better than one another.

The blessings come not by knowing how to be a servant but by the practical perfor-mance, the doing, of servanthood

6. What was Peter's reaction to Christ's action of foot washing?

At first, he did not want Christ to wash his feet. Then he wanted Jesus to wash his hands and head as well.

7. Why did Jesus say, "You are clean, though not every one of you?"

Jesus knew that Judas had already made up his mind to betray Christ. Judas was the unclean one.

8. What did Jesus instruct the disciples to do in verse 14?

He instructed them to wash one another's feet.

9. When Jesus told the disciples to wash each other's feet, was He speaking literally? Explain.

Yes and no. He was telling them to be as a servant to one another. He was telling them not to think themselves better than one another.

10. When do the blessings of servanthood come to the believer?

The blessings come not by knowing how to be a servant but by the practical performance, the doing, of servanthood.

Jesus, the True Vine

1 am the true vine, and my Father is the husbandman.

2 Every branch in me that beareth not fruit he taketh away: and every branch that beareth fruit, he purgeth it, that it may bring forth more fruit.

3 Now ye are clean through the word which I have spoken unto you.

4 Abide in me, and I in you. As the branch cannot bear fruit of itself, except it abide in the vine; no more can ye, except ye abide in me.

John 15:1-17

5 I am the vine, ye are the branches: He that abideth in me, and I in him, the same bringeth forth much fruit: for without me ye can do nothing.

6 If a man abide not in me, he is cast forth as a branch, and is withered; and men gather them, and cast them into the fire, and they are burned.

7 If ye abide in me, and my words abide in you, ye shall ask what ye will, and it shall be done unto you.

8 Herein is my Father glorified, that ye bear much fruit; so shall ye be my disciples.

9 As the Father hath loved me, so have I loved you: continue ye in my love.

10 If ye keep my commandments, ye shall abide in my love; even as I have kept my Father's commandments, and abide in his love.

11 These things have I spoken unto you, that my joy might remain in you, and that your joy might be full.

12 This is my commandment, That ye love one another, as I have loved you.

13 Greater love hath no man than this, that a man lay down his life for his friends.

14 Ye are my friends, if ye do whatsoever I command you.

15 Henceforth I call you not servants; for the servant knoweth not what his lord doeth: but I have called you friends; for all things that I have heard of my Father I have made known unto you.

16 Ye have not chosen me, but I have chosen you, and ordained you, that ye should go and bring forth fruit, and that your fruit should remain: that whatsoever ye shall ask of the Father in my name, he may give it you.

17 These things I command you, that ye love one another.

Memory Selection
John 15:5

Background Scripture
John 15:1-17

Devotional Reading
Job 23:1-12

Printed Scripture
John 15:1-17

May 16

Teacher's Target

Lesson purpose: *To explore the nature of the Christian life through Jesus' image of Christians as branches attached to Himself as the Vine.*

Many people in today's world feel restless and rootless, adrift and unattached. Some say the feeling results from the fast pace of modern life. Others point to the fragility of marriage and friendships, and still others to the way some businesses move employees from city to city, allowing little chance to put down roots.

In this lesson, Jesus offers a solution: remain attached to Him as a branch is attached to a vine. Firmly secured to the ultimate Source of nourishment, people not only can cope, but flourish. They not only are nourished to a healthy state as a branch; they go ahead to produce fruit—in the form of service to others, good parenting, enjoyable hobbies, long-lasting relationships, fulfilled lives.

Help your group apply this privileged relationship to Christ as the Vine to practical ways they can bear fruit—wherever they live.

Lesson Introduction

Here is another of the remarkable "I am's" in John's Gospel. Jesus affirms that He is the door, the good shepherd, the light of the world, the way, the truth, the bread of life, and, in the last of these images, "the vine."

We can imagine that Jesus' followers related this last image to His teaching on Himself as "the fruit of the vine" in the context of the Lord's Supper (see Mark 14:25; John omits the institution of the Supper in his Gospel). There is an obvious parallel between the unity of Christians when they gather around the Lord's table and the common nourishment they can share if they all remain attached to Christ as the Vine.

This parable-like saying cuts two ways. While it is a privilege to be attached to Christ as a branch to a vine, it carries with it the responsibility of doing what vines are expected to do: bear fruit.

Teaching Outline	Daily Bible Readings
I. The Vine and the Farmer—1	**Mon.** I Am the True Vine *John 15:1-11*
II. The Value of Fruit-bearing—2-8	**Tue.** Love As I Loved You *John 15:12-17*
A. Expectation of fruit, 2-5	**Wed.** O, to Find Him! *Job 23:1-12*
B. Judgment and glory, 6-8	**Thu.** Saul, God's Messenger *Acts 9:10-19a*
III. The Vitality of Love—9-17	**Fri.** God's Goodness and Severity *Romans 11:13-24*
A. Loving to obey, 9-14	**Sat.** By the Mercy Shown to You *Romans 11:25-36*
B. Friendship and mission, 15-17	**Sun.** God Sent His Son *Mark 12:1-12*

Verse by Verse

I. The Vine and the Farmer—1

1 I am the true vine, and my Father is the husbandman.

Even though He describes Himself as "the vine," the source of the branches' nourishment, Jesus here defers to the source of His own nourishment—the Father, depicted here as a "husbandman" or farmer. The imagery of God's people as a vine would have been familiar to the disciples, since Israel was often compared to a vineyard in the Old Testament. Usually it is a negative reference. Although it was a well-tended "vineyard," Israel bore no fruit (Isa. 5:1ff.). In Hosea 10:1 "Israel is an empty vine." Mark records a parable of Jesus in which Israel is an unfaithful tender of God's vineyard (Mk. 12:1-11. Here Jesus claims that He, not Israel, is the true vine. He is therefore the leader of a new, true Israel—people who draw their nourishment from Him.

II. The Value of Fruit-bearing—2-8

A. Expectation of fruit, 2-5

2 Every branch in me that beareth not fruit he taketh away: and every branch that beareth fruit, he purgeth it, that it may bring forth more fruit.

3 Now ye are clean through the word which I have spoken unto you.

4 Abide in me, and I in you. As the branch cannot bear fruit of itself, except it abide in the vine; no more can ye, except ye abide in me.

5 I am the vine, ye are the branches: He that abideth in me, and I in him, the same bringeth forth much fruit: for without me ye can do nothing.

The privilege of being "the new Israel" is accompanied by the responsibility of bearing the fruit Israel failed to produce. What does it mean to bear fruit in a spiritual sense? One answer comes from Paul: "The fruit of the Spirit is love, joy, peace, longsuffering, gentleness, goodness, faith, meekness, temperance" (Gal. 5:22-23). This fruit consists of personal traits, while a more external kind of fruit will be referred to in verse 16.

Jesus does not stop with the positive point that His followers must bear fruit. He warns that failing to do so will mean being cut from the vine. Even those who do bear fruit can expect to be "purged" (NIV "pruned"). Without being pruned, branches tend to put out more leaves than fruit, and are thus more showy than nourishing. So, contrary to our frequent desire for faith to solve all our problems, Christ promises some pain! Always, however, it is for the purpose of constructive discipline, that we might bear more fruit and produce "a harvest of righteousness and peace" (see Heb. 12:6-11).

Unfortunately, some irresponsible teaching demands fruit-bearing without showing that Jesus promises the sustenance to make it possible. Jesus has two warnings in verses 4-5. (1) It is futile (and, as we know, guilt-producing) to attempt to exhibit the fruits of the Christian life without being attached to Him as the nourishing vine; and (2) no other "vine" can provide true nourishment. The warning to "abide" (or remain) in Him, or else suffer being "cut off," may reflect Jesus' foreknowledge that many who became His followers in the excitement of the resurrection would later fall away under pressure.

B. Judgment and glory, 6-8

6 If a man abide not in me, he is cast forth as a branch, and is withered; and men gather them, and cast them into the fire, and they are burned.

7 If ye abide in me, and my words abide in you, ye shall ask what ye will, and it shall be done unto you.

8 Herein is my Father glorified, that ye bear much fruit; so shall ye be my disciples.

The judgment promised here against not "abiding" in Jesus shows how serious a responsibility it is to be grafted

onto Jesus, the Vine. Not abiding, and not bearing fruit, constitute more than personal failure on the part of the branch. They are also a poor reflection on the Vine. God is glorified (vs. 8) only when His branches prove they are attached to the vine by bearing fruit.

The promise in verse 7 that whatever "ye will" to pray for will be granted is tempered in the Lord's Prayer by the reminder that our wills must always be subject to God's: "Thy will be done."

III. The Vitality of Love—9-17
A. Loving to obey, 9-14

9 As the Father hath loved me, so have I loved you: continue ye in my love.

10 If ye keep my commandments, ye shall abide in my love; even as I have kept my Father's commandments, and abide in his love.

11 These things have I spoken unto you, that my joy might remain in you, and that your joy might be full.

12 This is my commandment, That ye love one another, as I have loved you.

13 Greater love hath no man than this, that a man lay down his life for his friends.

14 Ye are my friends, if ye do whatsoever I command you.

Now Jesus explains clearly that keeping His commandments is what constitutes "abiding" in Him and bearing fruit. These commandments are not a burden but a joy—because they can be summarized as the commandment to love, just as He explained in Mark 12:30-31.

Jesus says that His own "love life" illustrates this love in two ways: He showed His love for the Father by keeping His commandments; and He has loved these disciples—even to the point of being willing to give up His life. As the Greek philosopher Plato said, "Only those who love wish to die for others."

B. Friendship and mission, 15-17

15 Henceforth I call you not servants; for the servant knoweth not what his lord doeth: but I have called you friends; for all things that I have heard of my Father I have made known unto you.

16 Ye have not chosen me, but I have chosen you, and ordained you, that ye should go and bring forth fruit, and that your fruit should remain: that whatsoever ye shall ask of the Father in my name, he may give it you.

17 These things I command you, that ye love one another.

Jesus expands on his reference to the disciples as "friends" in verse 14 by calling attention to the evidence of His friendship. He does not mean that they are no longer also servants, but that they are not merely servants. Good friends share with each other in depth; and the sign of the disciples' new status is that Jesus is willing to share with them the truths He brought from heaven.

This privileged status was conferred on them out of sheer grace. However, as in the case of Judas in Lesson 10, this "election" coincided with the condition and volition of the heart of each disciple. In addition to bearing the fruit of godly character traits, above, the apostles are ordained (appointed) to produce the fruit of conversions to their preaching.

This commission was accompanied by apostolic authority. Verse 7 contains the general promise that their prayers will be answered; the promise in verse 17 seems to relate specifically to prayers they will raise in their evangelistic commission, which was accompanied by the authority to cast out demons. A parallel is found in Matthew 16:19: "Whatsoever thou shalt bind on earth shall be bound in heaven: and whatsoever thou shalt loose on earth shall be loosed in heaven."

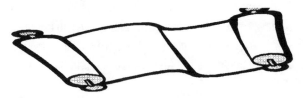

Evangelistic Emphasis

As I write this, I am returning home from a Florida vacation. On the highway we passed several orange groves. There were rows and rows and rows of trees. There is a reason the orange grower has orange trees. He plans to reap a harvest of oranges. An orange tree produces more oranges.

The orange trees must produce fruit. If they do not, the orange grower is out of business. He is bankrupt. Thus, if a tree does not bear fruit it has to be replaced with one that does.

We Christians are called to produce fruit. That is, we are to produce after our own kind. A Christian is to produce more Christians. That is what Jesus was telling us in the last chapter of Matthew when He told us to go and make disciples.

Jesus gives us an ominous warning here in John. If a branch fails to bear fruit, it is cut off. If a branch does not produce fruit, it is not doing its job. Jesus then becomes the orange grower, pruning the tree that is not doing its job.

One of our "jobs" as Christians is to produce fruit, that is, to make new Christians. We must perform that function. It is not optional. We must make disciples. If not, our relationship with the Lord cools. If disciples of Christ refuse to produce fruit, we run the risk of being cut off. I never want that to happen. Do you?

● ● ● ● ● ●

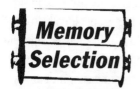

Memory Selection

I am the vine, ye are the branches: He that abideth in me, and I in him, the same bringeth forth much fruit: for without me ye can do nothing.—*John 15:5*

Sometimes we Christians forget who our source is. We read so much these days about self-esteem. It is taught almost as a religion in our elementary schools. Our society tells us that we can achieve anything if we work hard enough at it. We tell each other, "Anything's possible." Generally, those mantras are true. Success and achievement tend to be first cousins of effort, diligence and commitment.

However, in the spiritual realm, we must never forget that nothing of eternal value can be achieved through human effort alone. We can tell the story. We can make the calls. We can stay extremely busy. Yet, if we do it under our own strength, we will soon discover that our strength is exhausted and the results of our labor are temporary.

Jesus is our source. He will provide the strength to do all He calls us to do. He is responsible for the results. Abide in Him.

Weekday Problems

"Beth, how is it that you always seem to be happy?" Kay wondered aloud to Beth over a cup of coffee.

Beth smiled as she formulated an answer. Beth's older child had been born with a birth defect called spina bifida. She was confined to a wheelchair. The financial problems were never ending, but Beth and her husband took care of their daughter without a whine or a whimper.

"Well, Kay, I owe it all to the Lord," Beth answered. "He always seems to sustain us. He always seems to take care of us, even in the darkest times. I don't think we are anything special. If we looked around at our problems, we'd quickly fall into self-pity. We just keep our eyes on Jesus and He takes care of us."

"What do you mean, 'keep your eyes on Jesus?'" Kay asked.

"Well, we go to Sunday School and church every Sunday. I take some quiet time every morning to study my Bible and to pray. I try to listen for God's direction for my life every day. I try to show my love for God and others by doing things for people. When I focus on God and others, I feel happier myself," Beth explained.

Kay nodded, deep in thought.

* Are there times in your life when you felt joy even in desperate times?

* Did your spiritual disciplines help you during that time? Explain.

A's to All Your Q's

Q: What animal has two humps and can be found in Alaska?
A: A lost camel.

Q: What's a Grecian urn?
A: Depends on what kind of work he does.

Q: What's the greatest invention in the world?
A: Venetian blinds. If it weren't for them, it would be curtains for us.

Q: Why do bees hum?
A: Because they don't know the lyrics.

Q: How long is a minute?
A: Depends on which side of the bathroom door you happen to be on.

Q: What do you get when you cross a praying mantis with a termite?
A: A bug that says grace before eating your house.

This Lesson in Your Life

Fruitful Christians

Not long ago a lady came to our house to demonstrate a vacuum cleaner. She put it together and plugged it in. She asked us to clean a section of our carpet with our old vacuum cleaner. "Vacuum until you think it is clean," she told us. We ran our vacuum until we were sure every grain of dirt was gone from our floor. Then she took her vacuum, ran it over the same section of carpet five times—then showed us how much dirt her cleaner took from what we thought was an already clean floor. She sold us a vacuum cleaner.

However, we discovered something about our new vacuum. It will not work at all . . . if it is not plugged in. We can take it out and put it together. We can put the power head on the carpet. We can move the brush bar all over the floor. But if it is not plugged into the power source, it will never do what it is designed to do.

Our spiritual lives are very similar to that vacuum cleaner. If we are not plugged into our Power Source, we will never be able to do what we are supposed to do. Jesus said, "If a man remains in me and I in him, he will bear much fruit; apart from me you can do nothing" (John 15:5b). We must plug into the power of Christ.

The secret of the power-filled, fruit-bearing Christian life is in our constant contact with God. Jesus knew that. He withdrew often to a solitary place to meet with God. We must do the same. We must stay in contact with Jesus. We cannot do that unless we intentionally take steps to do it. A mature life in Christ does not come by accident. It grows as we take time to be with Christ. For example, when we take time to read God's Word and pray in the morning, we seem to stay near Him all day long.

When we stay in Christ our lives are more fruitful. In the Christian life there are two kinds of fruit. First, there is the fruit in the sense that disciples make more disciples. That is, in an agricultural sense, producing fruit after our own kind. That is the fulfillment of the Great Commission from Matthew 28. Disciples are to go out and make other disciples. We are to win people to Jesus. We are to introduce people to the life saving knowledge of Jesus, then to nurture them in their Christian growth. That produces a multiplication effect, as any good farmer knows.

There is another fruit the Bible speaks of. This other fruit is to be present and growing in every Christian's life. That is the fruit of the Holy Spirit. Paul writes, "But the fruit of the Spirit is love, joy, peace, patience, kindness, goodness, faithfulness, gentleness and self-control" (Gal. 5:22-23a). This fruit must grow in the Christian's life. The fruit of the Spirit is the true mark of the Christian. Jesus said, "This is to my Father's glory, that you bear much fruit, showing yourselves to be my disciples" (John 15:8). When a person's life is filled with love, joy, peace, patience, kindness, goodness, faithfulness, gentleness and self-control, everybody who sees that person knows he is a disciple of Christ. Folks know that person is a Christian because that person bears the fruit of the Christian life. The fruit of the Spirit is the character of God.

Seed Thoughts

1. Who is the true vine? Who is the gardener?

Jesus is the true vine. God, the Father, is the gardener.

2. What does Jesus say is the condition for bearing fruit?

A believer must remain in Jesus Christ, the true vine, in order to bear fruit. One cannot bear fruit by oneself.

3. What warning does Jesus gives us about the judgment (vs. 6)?

He warns us that if we fail to remain in Him we wither. Eventually the withered branch is thrown into the fire and burned.

4. Why is it so important to know God's Word and keep it in our hearts?

If we do we have the promise that we can ask whatever we wish in God's will and it will be given us.

5. What is one way we show that we are disciples of Jesus, according to John 15:8?

We show ourselves to be disciples of Jesus by bearing much fruit.

---

1. Who is the true vine? Who is the gardener?

2. What does Jesus say is the condition for bearing fruit?

3. What warning does Jesus gives us about the judgment (vs. 6)?

4. Why is it so important to know God's Word and keep it in our hearts?

5. What is one way we show that we are disciples of Jesus, according to John 15:8?

6. What is the guarantee that the believer will remain in Christ's love?

7. What is the greatest love a person can show for another?

8. What is the proof that we are friends of Jesus?

9. What is one privilege we have as friends of Christ rather than servants only?

10. What command does Jesus give in verse 12 and repeat in verse 17?

(Continued next page)

Jesus is the true vine. God, the Father, is the gardener.

A believer must remain in Jesus Christ, the true vine, in order to bear fruit. One cannot bear fruit by oneself.

He warns us that if we fail to remain in Him we wither. Eventually the withered branch is thrown into the fire and burned

If we do we have the promise that we can ask whatever we wish in God's will and it will be given us.

We show ourselves to be disciples of Jesus by bearing much fruit.

Jesus said as we obey His commands, we remain in His love.

Jesus said the greatest love one can have for another is the willingness to lay down one's life for a friend.

We are friends of Christ when we do what He commands.

Everything Jesus learned from His Father has been made known to His friends.

Jesus tells us to love each other as He has loved us.

6. What is the guarantee that the believer will remain in Christ's love?

Jesus said as we obey His commands, we remain in His love.

7. What is the greatest love a person can show for another?

Jesus said the greatest love one can have for another is the willingness to lay down one's life for a friend.

8. What is the proof that we are friends of Jesus?

We are friends of Christ when we do what He commands.

9. What is one privilege we have as friends of Christ rather than servants only?

Everything Jesus learned from His Father has been made known to His friends.

10. What command does Jesus give in verse 12 and repeat in verse 17?

Jesus tells us to love each other as He has loved us.

The Spirit Empowers for Loving Obedience

*I*f ye love me, keep my commandments.

16 And I will pray the Father, and he shall give you another Comforter, that he may abide with you for ever;

17 Even the Spirit of truth; whom the world cannot receive, because it seeth him not, neither knoweth him: but ye know him; for he dwelleth with you, and shall be in you.

18 I will not leave you comfortless: I will come to you.

24 He that loveth me not keepeth not my sayings: and the word which ye hear is not mine, but the Father's which sent me.

25 These things have I spoken unto you, being yet present with you.

26 But the Comforter, which is the Holy Ghost, whom the Father will send in my name, he shall teach you all things, and bring all things to your remembrance, whatsoever I have said unto you.

16:7 Nevertheless I tell you the truth; It is expedient for you that I go away: for if I go not away, the Comforter will not come unto you; but if I depart, I will send him unto you.

8 And when he is come, he will reprove the world of sin, and of righteousness, and of judgment:

9 Of sin, because they believe not on me;

10 Of righteousness, because I go to my Father, and ye see me no more;

11 Of judgment, because the prince of this world is judged.

12 I have yet many things to say unto you, but ye cannot bear them now.

13 Howbeit when he, the Spirit of truth, is come, he will guide you into all truth: for he shall not speak of himself; but whatsoever he shall hear, that shall he speak: and he will shew you things to come.

14 He shall glorify me: for he shall receive of mine, and shall shew it unto you.

15 All things that the Father hath are mine: therefore said I, that he shall take of mine, and shall shew it unto you.

John 14:15-18, 24-26; 16:7-15

Memory Selection
John 14:26

Background Scripture
John 14:15-31; 16:4b-15

Devotional Reading
Hebrews 2:10-18

Printed Scripture
John 14:15-18, 24-26; 16:7-15

May 23

371

Teacher's Target

Lesson purpose: *To reaffirm the living presence of Christ among His people today through the Comforter, the Holy Spirit.*

Perhaps several in your study group have felt bereft by the death of a loved one. After the welcome company of mourners at the funeral, they have entered a room containing reminders of life and love no longer present, and the loneliness washes over them like a wave. They wonder where they will get the strength to carry on.

Jesus knew that His followers would face such issues after His death. In addition to their feelings of personal loss, there would be questions. How can we recall all that He said and taught? And even if we could, how will we be able to follow His commandments without His empowering presence?

This lesson focuses on how our Lord prepared His closest followers for His absence. "I will not leave you alone," he promises. "You will be taught and empowered by the Holy Spirit."

Lesson Introduction

The setting of this lesson follows the question raised by "Doubting Thomas": If Jesus "goes away," how can the disciples find Him? (John 14:1-5). Christ's answer is given in the promise of the "Comforter," or Holy Spirit, who would guide the apostles into all truth (16:13).

Of course the Holy Spirit was not a new topic for the disciples. Knowing their Old Testaments, they knew of the Spirit's work at creation, and of His empowerment of the prophets. At Jesus' baptism the Spirit was present in the form of a dove to designate Him as the Messiah.

This lesson, however, introduces a new chapter in the story of the Spirit. He will be a comfort in the absence of Christ, a reminder of His teachings, and an energizing power (as in giving the gift of tongues in Acts 2) to inspire and teach the followers of Jesus. In short, from this point on, the story of faith might be titled "The Acts of the Holy Spirit."

Teaching Outline	Daily Bible Readings
I. Promise of the Spirit—14:15-18	**Mon.** Obey Me if You Love Me *John 14:15-24*
A. Loving and obeying, 15	**Tue.** The Spirit Will Teach You *John 14:25-31*
B. Receiving the Comforter, 16-18	**Wed.** When the Spirit Comes . . . *John 16:4-15*
II. Power in the Promise—24-26	**Thu.** The Spirit Brings Freedom *2 Corinthians 3:12-18*
III. Plan for the Future—16:7-15	**Fri.** From Slavery to Sonship *Galatians 4:1-7*
A. Universal presence, 7	**Sat.** Empowered by His Spirit *Ephesians 3:14-19*
B. Convicting power, 8-11	**Sun.** We Are Children of God *Romans 8:12-17*
C. Guide to the truth, 12-15	

Verse by Verse

I. Promise of the Spirit—14:15-18
A. Loving and obeying, 15

15 If ye love me, keep my commandments.

Tradition has it that when the apostle John grew old and senile he continued to summarize both the gospel and the purpose of his long life by repeating over and over, "My little children, love one another." Some people find this emphasis on love contradictory to the repeated call in John's writings to keep God's commandments. Actually, John would have found it odd for anyone to separate love from obedience. The connection appears again in 1 John 5:2: "By this we know that we love the children of God, when we love God, and keep his commandments." While "love is the fulfilling of the law" (Rom. 13:10), John no doubt refers here to the importance of following all the ethical teachings of Jesus.

B. Receiving the Comforter

16 And I will pray the Father, and he shall give you another Comforter, that he may abide with you for ever;

17 Even the Spirit of truth; whom the world cannot receive, because it seeth him not, neither knoweth him: but ye know him; for he dwelleth with you, and shall be in you.

18 I will not leave you comfort-

less: I will come to you.

A common failing in some Christian circles is to call for "keeping the commandments" without also noting God's provision that enables us to obey Him. This provision Jesus promises in the form of the Holy Spirit. He is not only a "Comforter," as in the KJV. The original word (parakletos) meant literally "one called alongside." It referred to the kind of comforter who would support an accused person in court—an advocate or "counselor" (NIV). Since Jesus Himself is the great Mediator or Counselor, the Spirit will be "another Comforter."

According to verse 17, the Spirit was already dwelling with Jesus' followers; but with the departure of Christ the Spirit will take on an expanded role. That role and mission will be explained further in the verses to follow.

The world cannot receive "the Spirit of truth" because the worldly mind is not attuned to the truth, much less to supernatural power. There can be no Christian boasting over this fact, since "the world" often exists in the hearts of Christians as well. Even believers are able to be "comforted" or guided by the Spirit only to the extent that the desire to know and obey the truth.

Verse 18's promise that "I (Jesus) will come to you" may mean that He will be present in the form of the Spirit who has just been promised. In light of verses 19-20, however, this is more likely referring to Christ's Second Coming.

II. Power in the Promise—24-26

24 He that loveth me not keepeth not my sayings: and the word which ye hear is not mine, but the Father's which sent me.

25 These things have I spoken unto you, being yet present with you.

26 But the Comforter, which is the Holy Ghost, whom the Father will send in my name, he shall teach you all things, and bring all things to your remembrance, whatsoever I have said unto you.

This statement is in response to Judas' question in verse 22. He seems to sense unfairness in Christ's statement that only His followers can receive the Spirit. Jesus answers that those who do not have an earnest desire for the truth send the signal that they do not love Him and would not keep His commandments. Always deferring to the Father, Jesus adds that "His" commandments are actually the Word of the Father.

In verses 25-26 Jesus elaborates on the role of the Holy Spirit. ("Ghost" here is from the Greek word pneuma, spirit or breath, as in verse 17. The ĸᴊᴠ often renders it "ghost" because that word comes from the German word for spirit—Geist). While Jesus was present in the flesh His words were sufficient. After He returns to heaven, however, the Holy Spirit will be not only a Comforter but a Teacher, reminding Christ's apostles of all that He taught while He was with them.

This "anointing" is usually taken to refer first to the apostles and others whom God authorized to communicate His words in ways that eventually would be written down and become the New Testament documents. Yet to a lesser degree the Spirit dwelling in the hearts of all believers is also a witness to the truth. John will also write to believers in general that "The anointing which ye have received of him abideth in you, and ye need not that any man teach you" (1 John 2:27). It should be apparent that this does not mean that Christians will not have to study to gain a knowledge of the truth. It is rather a reassurance that their study will not be fruitless, and that if they sincerely desire the truth the Spirit's inner witness will authenticate or give the lie to what they study.

Verse 26 also is remarkable in that it brings together all three persons of the Godhead. The Spirit is sent by the Father in the name of the Son. Christ seems intent on seeing that His disciples do not feel alone. Whether we experience losses, face ethical challenges, or long to know more of the truth, we live in the confidence that Father, Son, and Holy Spirit are present to us as a source of encouragement and strength.

III. Plan for the Future—16:7-15
A. Universal presence, 7

7 Nevertheless I tell you the truth; It is expedient for you that I go away: for if I go not away, the Comforter will not come unto you; but if I depart, I will send him

unto you.

Although the Spirit has been present all along (see verse 17, and the Lesson Introduction), His new role will be more clearly seen only if Jesus returns to the Father. As long as God's Words are confined to the lips of Jesus in human form, they are limited in time and space to the Man of Galilee. When those Words are carried far and wide by the Spirit, who is not confined to a body, they become universally accessible. This saying was fulfilled when the disciples who had been filled with the Spirit in Acts 2 "went everywhere preaching the word" (Acts 8:1-4).

B. Convicting power, 8-11

8 And when he is come, he will reprove the world of sin, and of righteousness, and of judgment:

9 Of sin, because they believe not on me;

10 Of righteousness, because I go to my Father, and ye see me no more;

11 Of judgment, because the prince of this world is judged.

Yet another role of the Holy Spirit is outlined here. While Jesus was on earth, the world put Him on trial, "reproving" or convicting Him of claiming falsely to be a king. With His return to heaven, however, and with the Spirit's work guiding the disciples to proclaim the truth, the facts are exposed: It is really the world who is on trial.

A good illustration of this occurred when the apostle Paul preached to the Roman ruler Felix, who was convicted when Paul boldly "reasoned of righteousness, temperance, and judgment to come" (Acts 24:24-25).

C. Guide to the truth, 12-15

12 I have yet many things to say unto you, but ye cannot bear them now.

13 Howbeit when he, the Spirit of truth, is come, he will guide you into all truth: for he shall not speak of himself; but whatsoever he shall hear, that shall he speak: and he will shew you things to come.

14 He shall glorify me: for he shall receive of mine, and shall shew it unto you.

15 All things that the Father hath are mine: therefore said I, that he shall take of mine, and shall shew it unto you.

These concluding verses repeat the theme that the Spirit will assist the apostles in remembering, understanding and proclaiming the words of Christ. In John 15:15 Jesus said he had made known "all things" He had heard from the Father. Why does He say here in verse 12 that He had more to tell them but that they "cannot bear them now"? Jesus is probably referring to their full understanding of the meaning of His death and resurrection. Although He had tried repeatedly to help them understand His mission on the Cross, they could not grasp it. Only after it had occurred could the truth of how His death purchased salvation come clear—and then only with the guidance of the Spirit.

Evangelistic Emphasis

Leprosy is a dreaded condition that appears often in the pages of Scripture. Leprosy attacks the extremities in an especially vicious manner. One of the effects of the condition is the loss of feeling in the hands and feet. This loss of sensation is extremely damaging. When one has no feeling in the extremities, one feels no pain to warn of a possibly worse effect. For example, if a person's hand was affected by leprosy, that person could accidentally let his hand come in contact with fire and not feel pain. He would not know his hand was being scorched until he smelled the flesh burning. This could lead to infection and further degeneration of the limb.

The Holy Spirit acts as a pain receptor in our spirits. He tells us, "Don't touch that! Stay away from that! You shouldn't do that!" That ministry of the Spirit may sound negative. Yet it keeps us from further spiritual damage.

The Spirit convicts us of sin, not to lay a guilt trip on us, but to keep us out of trouble and away from further damage to our souls. Jesus sent the Holy Spirit as a ministry of grace to walk along side of us. He helps us walk in God's way.

• • • • • •

Memory Selection

But the Comforter, which is the Holy Ghost, whom the Father will send in my name, he shall teach you all things, and bring all things to your remembrance, whatsoever I have said unto you.—*John 14:26*

Last year I attended an evangelism convention sponsored by my denomination. We spent almost a full week in seminars and worship services. We were taught by some of the brightest minds and finest preachers in the United States. When the week was over I was so full of new knowledge and concepts I thought my head would burst. I was almost overwhelmed. Yet in the weeks and months afterward I would remember what one of the speakers said. I would remember a point one of the preachers made. That was the Holy Spirit's ministry in my life.

Jesus knew there was no earthly way His disciples could recall all the wondrous things He had taught them. The concepts were just too deep. There was just too much. Thus, they needed the Holy Spirit to be a divine computer for them, calling to their consciousness His teaching at the proper times. The Holy Spirit still does that today. He teaches us and prompts us in God's way.

Weekday Problems

Bob poured himself another glass of water from the crystal pitcher. He put the replaced the pitcher on its tray and surveyed the men around the mahogany conference table. He nervously fingered his diamond cuff links. Bob was uncomfortable but he wasn't sure why.

Bob had recently attended a Promise Keepers rally. He had heard men testify how God had changed their lives. He had heard how God had healed marriages and families. He had heard men testify how God had led them in business dealings. Bob had been in business a long time. He was now very successful. Many breadwinners depended on a paycheck from his company to feed their families. He had been a reasonably good church member for most of his adult life. Still, he had never been challenged to allow Jesus to take over his business. He had never been challenged to allow the Holy Spirit to guide his business dealings. He wondered as he adjusted his tie, "Could this be the Holy Spirit trying to tell me this deal is not right?"

Bob looked around the table at the powerful men there. Would they understand if he called off the deal because of the Holy Spirit's guidance?

* Can we trust the Holy Spirit to guide us in every area of our lives? Explain.

* Share an experience in which you felt the guidance of the Spirit.

Speaking of the Spirit

I should as soon attempt to raise flowers if there were no atmosphere, or produce fruits if there were neither light nor heat, as to regenerate men if I did not believe there was a Holy Ghost.—*Henry Ward Beecher*

* * *

The word "Comforter" as applied to the Holy Spirit needs to be translated by some vigorous term. Literally, it means "with strength." Jesus promised His followers that "The Strengthener" would be with them forever. This promise is no lullaby for the faint-hearted. It is a blood transfusion for courageous living.—*E. Paul Hovey*

* * *

The Spirit of God first imparts love; he next inspires hope, and then gives liberty; and that is about the last thing we have in many of our churches.—*Dwight L. Moody*

This Lesson in Your Life

Help in Time of Need

According to Matthew's gospel, the very last words the risen Lord Jesus spoke while on this earth were, "And surely I am with you always, to the very end of the age." He promised all believers, present and future, that His presence would be with them always. When Christ was called back to Heaven to sit at the right hand of the Father, He sent us His Holy Spirit. One of the difficulties Christ took on when He accepted an earthly body was that He could not be everywhere at once. He gave up His omnipresence. Yet, when He ascended to heaven He became omnipresent again through the Spirit He sent to be with us always and everywhere. On the day of Pentecost, the Spirit was poured out upon and into all who would receive Him. Luke describes the experience by saying, "All of them were filled with the Holy Spirit." The Spirit fills us. He gets within us. He becomes a part of us.

When the Holy Spirit fills us we are able to tap into the power of God. Listen to the words of Jesus: "I am going to send you what my Father has promised; but stay in the city until you have been clothed with *power* from on high" (Luke 24:49, emphasis mine). The risen Lord is quoted again in Acts 2:8: "But you will receive *power* when the Holy Spirit comes on you." When we open our lives to the Holy Spirit and are thus filled, we have the power of God within us. Furthermore, by the power of the Holy Spirit within us, we can do anything God calls us to do. By the power of the Holy Spirit we can find the strength to face and gain victory over any of life's challenges.

The Holy Spirit is our guide. Jesus said, "I have much more to say to you, more than you can now bear. But when he, the Spirit of truth, comes, he will guide you into all truth. He will not speak on his own; he will speak only what he hears, and he will tell you what is yet to come" (John 16; 12-13). Our vision is limited. We cannot see over the hilltop or around the corner. There are times we are unable to see the light at the end of the tunnel. The Spirit can be our guide. He will show us the way when we cannot see it.

The Holy Spirit grows the character of God within us. Paul tells us in Galatians 5:22-23, "But the fruit of the Spirit is love, joy, peace, patience, kindness, goodness, faithfulness, gentleness and self-control." When one sees this fruit evident in the life of another person, one has no trouble accepting that person as a Christian. The fruit of the Holy Spirit is the mark of the Christian life. When the Spirit fills our lives the fruit grows.

The Holy Spirit not only fills a person with the character of God, He fills a person with the power to do God's work. Paul lists gifts of the Holy Spirit, the "charismata," in several places in the New Testament. In Romans 12 he lists prophecy, teaching, serving, encouragement, leadership and mercy. In 1 Corinthians 12:4-11; 28 and Ephesians 4:11 Paul adds to that list. Read those passages. These gifts of the Holy Spirit are given to build up the body of Christ. They are given to enable us and empower us to be the Church to the world. Through the Holy Spirit we can be the hands of Jesus, relieving suffering in the world. Through the Holy Spirit we can be the voice of Jesus spreading the good news to a lost and dying world.

The Holy Spirit is the manifestation of the promise Jesus gave—"And surely I am with you always, to the very end of the age."

Seed Thoughts

1. According to verse 15, how do we show our love for Jesus?

We show our love for Christ by obeying that which He commands.

2. Why does the world not accept the Spirit of truth?

The world cannot accept Him because the world is not aware of Him, does not know Him, see Him or experienced Him.

3. Upon whose authority does both the Holy Spirit and Jesus speak?

They both speak by the authority of the Father. See John 14:24 and 16:13.

4. According to John 14:26, what are two ministries of the Holy Spirit?

The Spirit will teach us and remind us of things Jesus has already taught us.

5. Why are these two ministries of the Holy Spirit so important?

Because Jesus is no longer with us in body to teach us. In addition, He taught so much that we are unable to remember it all without assistance.

---

1. According to verse 15, how do we show our love for Jesus?

2. Why does the world not accept the Spirit of truth?

3. Upon whose authority does both the Holy Spirit and Jesus speak?

4. According to John 14:26, what are two ministries of the Holy Spirit?

5. Why are these two ministries of the Holy Spirit so important?

6. Concerning the Holy Spirit, why was it so important that Jesus leave this earth?

7. According to John 16:18, what are some ministries of the Holy Spirit?

8. According to John 16:13, what is one of the ministries of the Holy Spirit?

9. Will the Holy Spirit "invent" any new theology or teachings? Explain.

10. How does the Holy Spirit bring glory to Christ?

(Continued next page)

We show our love for Christ by obeying that which He commands.

The world cannot accept Him because the world is not aware of Him, does not know Him, see Him or experienced Him.

They both speak by the authority of the Father. See John 14:24 and 16:13.

The Spirit will teach us and remind us of things Jesus has already taught us.

Because Jesus is no longer with us in body to teach us. In addition, He taught so much that we are unable to remember it all without assistance.

Because the Holy Spirit would not be sent unless Jesus went to be with the Father.

He convicts the world of guilt in regard to sin, righteousness and judgment.

The Holy Spirit, the Spirit of Truth, will guide us into all truth.

No, the Spirit will not speak on His own. He will speak only what He hears from the Father and the Son.

He brings glory to Jesus by revealing or making known the things of Christ to believers.

6. Concerning the Holy Spirit, why was it so important that Jesus leave this earth?

Because the Holy Spirit would not be sent unless Jesus went to be with the Father.

7. According to John 16:18, what are some ministries of the Holy Spirit?

He convicts the world of guilt in regard to sin, righteousness and judgment.

8. According to John 16:13, what is one of the ministries of the Holy Spirit?

The Holy Spirit, the Spirit of Truth, will guide us into all truth.

9. Will the Holy Spirit "invent" any new theology or teachings? Explain.

No, the Spirit will not speak on His own. He will speak only what He hears from the Father and the Son.

10. How does the Holy Spirit bring glory to Christ?

He brings glory to Jesus by revealing or making known the things of Christ to believers.

Jesus Prayed for His Disciples

7 hese words spake Jesus, and lifted up his eyes to heaven, and said, Father, the hour is come; glorify thy Son, that thy Son also may glorify thee.

2 As thou hast given him power over all flesh, that he should give eternal life to as many as thou hast given him.

3 And this is life eternal, that they might know the only true God, and Jesus Christ, whom thou hast sent.

4 I have glorified thee on the earth: I have finished the work which thou gavest me to do.

5 And now, O Father, glorify thou me with thine own self with the glory which I had with thee before the world was.

9 I pray for them: I pray not for the world, but for them which thou hast given me; for they are thine.

10 And all mine are thine, and thine are mine; and I am glorified in them.

11 And now I am no more in the world, but these are in the world, and I come to thee. Holy Father, keep through thine own name those whom thou hast given me, that they may be one, as we are.

15 I pray not that thou shouldest take them out of the world, but that thou shouldest keep them from the evil.

16 They are not of the world, even as I am not of the world.

17 Sanctify them through thy truth: thy word is truth.

18 As thou hast sent me into the world,

*John 17:
1-5, 9-11,
15-24*

even so have I also sent them into the world.

19 And for their sakes I sanctify myself, that they also might be sanctified through the truth.

20 Neither pray I for these alone, but for them also which shall believe on me through their word;

21 That they all may be one; as thou, Father, art in me, and I in thee, that they also may be one in us: that the world may believe that thou hast sent me.

22 And the glory which thou gavest me I have given them; that they may be one, even as we are one:

23 I in them, and thou in me, that they may be made perfect in one; and that the world may know that thou hast sent me, and hast loved them, as thou hast loved me.

24 Father, I will that they also, whom thou hast given me, be with me where I am; that they may behold my glory, which thou hast given me: for thou lovedst me before the foundation of the world.

Memory Selection
John 17:11
Background Scripture
John 17
Devotional Reading
Ephesians 6:10-20
Printed Scripture
John 17:1-5, 9-11, 15-24

May 30

Lesson purpose: *To examine Jesus' "High Priestly Prayer" with an eye on improving our own awareness of the power of intercessory prayer.*

When the apostle Paul sought to send someone to tend to the needs of Christians at Philippi, he could find only one person—Timothy. Everyone else, Paul said, "looks after their own interests" (Philip. 2:21).

Could this be said of many of us today? Even Christians are often so caught up with their own problems, careers, and recreation that they have little time to think of the needs of others.

Of course there are many needs we cannot meet. We can, however, pray for others. We can intercede in their behalf before God's throne, as Jesus does in today's lesson. Invite discussion of specific ways group members might pray for others, both within and without the fellowship of believers.

Lesson Introduction

Jesus' prayer in John 17 is often called His "high priestly" prayer since He intercedes for others after the manner of an Old Testament priest. This, the longest prayer attributed to Jesus, comes near the end of His life. Although He does include a prayer for Himself, the major focus is remarkably other-centered—an orientation required of believers today if they are to follow Christ's example.

As is the case with all prayer, we are faced here with the mystery of human interaction before an all-powerful and all-knowing God. God knows our needs, and the needs of others before we pray. He wants to bless us in far more ways than we can think to pray about. He is not withholding blessings until we remember to ask for them. Yet, in the mystery of His will, Jesus taught that we "ought always to pray" (Luke 18:1). Jesus' high priestly prayer is a classic on what to pray about.

Teaching Outline	Daily Bible Readings
I. A Prayer for Himself—1-5	**Mon.** This Is Eternal Life *John 17:1-5*
A. The hour is come, 1	
B. To glorify God, 2-5	**Tue.** Your Name Made Known *John 17:6-10*
II. A Plea for His Own—9-11, 15-19	**Wed.** Your Word Proclaimed *John 17:11-19*
A. 'Keep them,' 9-11	
B. 'Sanctify them,' 15-19	**Thu.** That They May Be One *John 17:20-26*
III. A Petition for Unity—20-24	**Fri.** I Have Prayed for You *Luke 22:24-32*
A. As the Son and the Father, 20-23	**Sat.** Could You Not Watch? *Matthew 26:36-46*
B. In glory with Him, 24	**Sun.** Nothing Can Separate *Romans 8:31-39*

Verse by Verse

I. A Prayer for Himself—1-5
A. The hour is come, 1

1 These words spake Jesus, and lifted up his eyes to heaven, and said, Father, the hour is come; glorify thy Son, that thy Son also may glorify thee.

Throughout His ministry, Jesus has had a divine sense of timing. Early on, when crowds who were dazzled by His miracles wanted to make Him king, he slipped away—perhaps to avoid fomenting so much political strife that he would be arrested and executed before He had fully developed His teaching. Now, however, toward the end of the third year of His work on earth, He has accomplished the mission given Him by the Father. Here He repeats in prayer what He had known since gathering the apostles together for the Last Supper: His hour of destiny has come (see also 13:1). Both He and the Father will be glorified as Jesus receives the strength to complete His ascent to the Cross.

B. To glorify God, 2-5

2 As thou hast given him power over all flesh, that he should give eternal life to as many as thou hast given him.

3 And this is life eternal, that they might know the only true God, and Jesus Christ, whom thou hast sent.

4 I have glorified thee on the earth: I have finished the work which thou gavest me to do.

5 And now, O Father, glorify thou me with thine own self with the glory which I had with thee before the world was.

Jesus customarily refers to Himself not as "I" and "me" but as "he" and "him"—although He does use the first person in verses 4-5. The more frequent use of the third person is probably a touch of humility, calling attention more to His role as the Christ, God's only Son, than to Himself personally as Jesus. Jesus takes no personal pride in having been empowered by the Father to grant eternal life to the called. As noted earlier, being "given" to Christ, or elected, can be harmonized with the doctrine of free will by envisioning the saved as an elect group, in which individuals may choose to be added by their faithful response to Christ.

If eternal life is gained by knowing God and His Son, then those who give themselves to God through Jesus experience eternal life in one sense even before death and resurrection. More than life unending, eternal life is the divine quality of life God grants when we come to Him in faith. The joy of salvation will merely be extended into timelessness at the Last Judgment.

Committed to the Cross, Christ has glorified God by completing the mission the Father gave Him. Now He appeals to be glorified by the Father by the return of the Son to the heavenly glory He enjoyed before His earthly sojourn.

II. A Plea for His Own–9-11, 15-19
A. 'Keep them,' 9-11

9 I pray for them: I pray not for the world, but for them which thou hast given me; for they are thine.

10 And all mine are thine, and thine are mine; and I am glorified in them.

11 And now I am no more in the world, but these are in the world, and I come to thee. Holy Father, keep through thine own name those whom thou hast given me, that they may be one, as we are.

Jesus is not indicating indifference to outsiders by saying that He prays for His inner circle of disciples. Indeed, "God so loved the world that He gave His only begotten Son" for them. Jesus is focusing on His followers here because it is they, rather than others, who will be shattered and scattered by His approaching death. It is the disciples who will need God's special Fatherly protection to keep them from discouragement and faithlessness in the absence of their Lord.

God can offer this kind of "keeping" because these people belong to Him as children belong to their father. Yet, while not of the world, they are still in the world (see also vs. 16). By praying that God will keep them "through thine own name," Jesus asks that His followers remain faithful to the teaching He gave them—teaching offered "in the name of" or by the authority of Yahweh. The plea is that by remaining faithful the disciples will not blaspheme "the name of God and his doctrine" (Tim. 6:1).

B. 'Sanctify them,' 15-19

15 I pray not that thou shouldest take them out of the world, but that thou shouldest keep them from the evil.

16 They are not of the world, even as I am not of the world.

17 Sanctify them through thy truth: thy word is truth.

18 As thou hast sent me into the world, even so have I also sent them into the world.

19 And for their sakes I sanctify myself, that they also might be sanctified through the truth.

The term "sanctify" is given special theological weight in the teaching of some churches. Originally the term simply meant to be set apart, consecrated, and dedicated for holy service to God. This is implied in verses 15, 16, as Jesus refers to His specially chosen disciples as being separate and apart from "the world." That "sanctified" does not always mean "made holy" is seen in Jesus' statement that He sanctifies Himself (vs. 19). He had no sin to leave behind, but deliberately dedicated Himself especially to God.

Of course people hear many calls to be separate from others. In Jesus' day and ours, political parties, differing religious views, and competing moral standards divide society. Yet Jesus will call for unity in the verses to follow. It is therefore important to note here that He prays for His followers to be sanctified, or consecrated, by the truth of God's Word. This is roughly equivalent to asking that they be kept "through thine own name" (vs. 11). Remaining faithful to the Word and to the Name becomes the way to unity for the sanctified.

III. A Petition for Unity—20-24

A. As the Son and the Father, 20-23

20 Neither pray I for these alone, but for them also which shall believe on me through their word;

21 That they all may be one; as thou, Father, art in me, and I in thee, that they also may be one in us: that the world may believe that thou hast sent me.

22 And the glory which thou gavest me I have given them; that they may be one, even as we are one:

23 I in them, and thou in me, that they may be made perfect in one; and that the world may know that thou hast sent me, and hast loved them, as thou hast loved me.

One of the tragedies of the history of God's people is their inability to more nearly realize their Lord's impassioned plea for their unity. Just as this unified spirit was to testify to the truth of Jesus as being sent from God, so division detracts from the glory of God. Note that Jesus envisions Christian unity like the unity between the Father and the Son. Although each has a different identity, role, and mission, they are together in spirit. Christ's prayer is that this unity-in-diversity will be the model for Christian oneness as well.

B. In glory with Him, 24

24 Father, I will that they also, whom thou hast given me, be with me where I am; that they may behold my glory, which thou hast given me: for thou lovedst me before the foundation of the world.

Jesus' final petition is that the followers God has given Him will not only share the oneness that exists between the Father and the Son, but also the glory God is about to bestow on Him. Ultimately this seems to be another prayer that His disciples will be faithful and thus allowed entrance to heaven to be with their Lord. However, Jesus said in verse 4 that He glorified God by finishing the work God gave Him. Thus, for the Christian, "beholding Christ's glory" can also mean sticking with our own charge to be faithful to the end.

Evangelistic Emphasis

Jesus said, "Now this is eternal life; that they may know you . . . ." It is a funny thing, this knowing God. I submit to you, there are many more people who know *about* God than there are who know God Himself.

My life is an example. As a boy, my parents saw to it that I was in church every Sunday, twice. I never missed Sunday School. I never missed youth group. But I did not know Christ. I knew a lot about Him, but I did not know Him. My early relationship with Jesus was like my present relationship with President Bill Clinton. I know much about Bill Clinton. The newspapers and television news shows insure that I know volumes about President Clinton. I know the names of his wife and his daughter. I know about his mother. I know about his birthplace. Yet, I have never personally met President Bill Clinton.

Are you like that with Jesus? Are there those around you who have that same type relationship with Jesus? Are there folks with whom you come in contact who know about Jesus but have never met Him personally? Jesus told us that eternal life was linked with *knowing* Him, not knowing *about* Him. May we meet Jesus personally. May we know God intimately, for only in the knowing is there eternal life.

• • • • •

Memory Selection

And now I am no more in the world, but these are in the world, and I come to thee, Holy Father, keep through thine own name those whom thou hast given me, that they may be one, as we are.—*John 17:11*

When Jesus left this earth, He left us in charge of His ministry. When Jesus left, He sent His Holy Spirit to enable us and empower us to do the work of Christ. One of the most important things Christ prayed was for us to be in the unity of the Spirit. In fact, He compared the relationship He desired for His followers to the relationship He had with His Father.

Too often we allow our differences to divide us. We in the church sometimes become simply separate groups, squabbling for dominance of the Body. Jesus prayed that we would be in unity: united in love, united in mission, united in Christ. His prayer was not that we simply ignore our differences. He prayed that our love for Him and desire for unity make our dividing differences seem less and less important.

Weekday Problems

Ginny was sitting in church. The pastor was actually an excellent preacher, but Ginny was not really listening to his message. It was just that Ginny had other things on her mind.

She was back in church for the first time in six months. Six months ago Ginny had disagreed with Darlene at a Board meeting. Somehow the issue became bigger than it deserved to be. The discussion degenerated into an argument. Battle lines were drawn. Hot words flew. Mean things were said. At the end of the meeting Ginny walked through the doors of the church and did not return until today.

And there was Darlene. It was the first time they had seen each other since the argument. Their eyes met when Ginny came in the sanctuary. Old feelings flooded to the surface. As she sat through the sermon without listening, Ginny prayed. She knew the incident was blown out of proportion. She just never could work up enough courage to go to Darlene.

Now the sermon was over. Ginny had not noticed before that it was Communion Sunday. They lined up to go to the chancel rail. As she shuffled down the aisle she realized that she would be kneeling next to Darlene at the altar.

* How does Christ's love working in our hearts heal hurts?

* Is there anyone you need to forgive and/or ask forgiveness today?

Odds and Ends

Biff: My brother's working for an electrician, and one day he grabbed hold of a live wire.
Whiff: What happened?
Biff: I'm not sure, but this is the only job he's ever held on to.

* * *

Lady to panhandler: I'm going to give you a quarter, not because you deserve it but because it pleases me to do so.
Panhandler: Thanks, but why not make it a dollar so you can really enjoy yourself?

* * *

Fay: I once sang for the king of Siam. At least he told me that's who he was.
Mae: Sure you did. The guy said, "If you're a singer then I'm the king of Siam."

* * *

Joe: Did you know that it takes a dozen sheep to make a sweater?
Moe: No! I didn't even know sheep could knit.

This Lesson in Your Life

Interceding in Prayer

In John chapter 17 we read Jesus' longest recorded prayer. Jesus is praying for us. He knows He is about to be separated in body from His followers. He knows His death is imminent. Thus, He prays for His "children" for the time they will be apart. We do the same thing in different ways.

Our daughter just graduated from high school. She is about to go to the university. There she will be challenged with new and different ideas. There she will be challenged by the reality of living with the results of her own decisions. She will not have her mother and me within arm's reach to bail her out of trouble, to protect her, to act as a buffer between her and harsh realities of life. Thus, we pray for her—for her protection, that she will do right, that she will remember what she has been taught and be able to stand upon those convictions. We pray for her trusting the Father to do what we cannot.

Jesus knew about praying for others. He prayed for His disciples. He prayed for us. He prayed for unity among future believers.

Dr. Lovett Weems tells of a pastor who felt the Lord's leading to have a rally among all the Christians in his community. He spoke to several leaders. All said, "That's a good idea."

He went to the pastor of the largest church in the community and said, "Pastor, we want to have a rally among Christians in our community.

"My that's a wonderful idea," the big-church pastor said.

"And," the first pastor continued, "we need to use your church."

"W-e-l-l," the pastor of the big church said, stroking his chin. "That could be a problem. Our constitution states that we our forbidden to fellowship with others outside our body. We just can't do that."

The pastor then went to another large church. He explained the plan.

"That's a wonderful idea," the pastor exclaimed.

"And," the first pastor continued, "we would like to use your church."

"Are *all* groups going to be there?"

"Why, yes. All Christian groups will be there," the first pastor responded.

"Then I don't think that will work. I'm afraid my congregation would not accept every group," the pastor apologized.

The first pastor, undaunted, went to see if they could get the VFW hall. The head of the VFW in that town was a tavern owner. The pastor walked into the tavern and explained the plan and the fact that the rally would need the VFW hall.

"That's a wonderful idea!" the VFW leader/tavern owner exclaimed. "We'll have the hall ready."

The rally was held. Christians gathered from all over the community. It was a marvelous time. However, the rally of Christians from all over town was held in a VFW hall with the permission of a tavern owner. It was not held in a church.

Seed Thoughts

Why did Jesus want to be glorified by the Father?

He wanted to be glorified in order that he might glorify the Father.

What was one of the purposes the Son was given authority over all people?

The Son was given authority that He might give eternal life to all those God had given Him.

How did Jesus define the source of eternal life?

He said the source of eternal life is knowing the only true God and Jesus Christ, who was sent by the Father.

How did Jesus glorify the Father while Jesus was on earth?

He glorified the Father by completing the work God gave Him to do.

How might we also glorify our heavenly Father while we are on the earth?

We should follow Christ's example and glorify God by doing the work God gave us to do.

---

1. Why did Jesus want to be glorified by the Father?

2. What was one of the purposes the Son was given authority over all people?

3. How did Jesus define the source of eternal life?

4. How did Jesus glorify the Father while Jesus was on earth?

5. How might we also glorify our heavenly Father while we are on the earth?

6. Why did Jesus ask for God's protection of Christ's followers?

7. Did Jesus pray for our deliverance from the evils of the world? Explain.

8. What is it that sanctifies us and makes us holy?

9. According to verse 23, how will the world know that God sent Christ into the world?

10. In verse 24, what was Jesus prayer for the believers?

(Continued next page)

He wanted to be glorified in order that He might glorify the Father.

The Son was given authority that He might give eternal life to all those God had given Him.

He said the source of eternal life is knowing the only true God and Jesus Christ, who was sent by the Father.

He glorified the Father by completing the work God gave Him to do.

We should follow Christ's example and glorify God by doing the work God gave us to do.

He asked for God's protection for His followers so they might be one as God and Jesus are one.

No. Jesus prayed not that we be taken out of the world, but protected from Satan's power while we are on earth.

It is the truth that sanctifies us. God's word is truth. Note that Jesus is the Truth (John 14:6), and also the Word (John 1:1).

The world will know that God sent Christ through the complete unity of the church, the believers.

Jesus prayed that we would be with Him in glory. He prayed that we would see Him in His full glory.

6. Why did Jesus ask for God's protection of Christ's followers?

He asked for God's protection for His followers so they might be one as God and Jesus are one.

7. Did Jesus pray for our deliverance from the evils of the world? Explain.

No. Jesus prayed not that we be taken out of the world, but protected from Satan's power while we are on earth.

8. What is it that sanctifies us and makes us holy?

It is the truth that sanctifies us. God's word is truth. Note that Jesus is the Truth (John 14:6), and also the Word (John 1:1).

9. According to verse 23, how will the world know that God sent Christ into the world?

The world will know that God sent Christ through the complete unity of the church, the believers.

10. In verse 24, what was Jesus prayer for the believers?

Jesus prayed that we would be with Him in glory. He prayed that we would see Him in His full glory.

Lesson 1
God's Good Creation

*I*n the beginning God created the heaven and the earth.

2 And the earth was without form, and void; and darkness was upon the face of the deep.

20 And God said, Let the waters bring forth abundantly the moving creature that hath life, and fowl that may fly above the earth in the open firmament of heaven.

21 And God created great whales, and every living creature that moveth, which the waters brought forth abundantly, after their kind, and every winged fowl after his kind: and God saw that it was good.

22 And God blessed them, saying, Be fruitful, and multiply, and fill the waters in the seas, and let fowl multiply in the earth.

23 And the evening and the morning were the fifth day.

24 And God said, Let the earth bring forth the living creature after his kind, cattle, and creeping thing, and beast of the earth after his kind: and it was so.

25 And God made the beast of the earth after his kind, and cattle after their kind, and every thing that creepeth upon the earth after his kind: and God saw that it was good.

29 And God said, Behold, I have given you every herb bearing seed, which is upon the face of all the earth, and every tree, in the which is the fruit of a tree yielding seed to you it shall be for meat.

30 And to every beast of the earth, and to every fowl of the air, and to every thing that creepeth upon the earth, wherein there is life, I have given every green herb for meat: and it was so.

31 And God saw every thing that he had made, and, behold, it was very good. And the evening and the morning were the sixth day.

Genesis 1: 1-2, 20-25, 29-31

Memory Selection
Genesis 1:31a

Background Scripture
Genesis 1:1–2:4a

Devotional Reading
Psalm 104:24-35

Printed Scripture
Genesis 1:1-2, 20-25, 29-31

Teacher's Target

Lesson purpose: *To reaffirm our conviction that the world about us testifies to the goodness of God and to His loving provision for all people.*

This lesson introduces the quarter's thirteen studies in the book of Genesis. The series appropriately "begins with the beginning"—the majestic account of the creation in Genesis 1.

The fact that this text has become a battleground between science and religion must not obscure the basic purpose of the lesson: to build trust in the goodness of God and of His creation. Two extremes should be avoided: (1) Not allowing any science-based questions to be raised, and (2) Becoming bogged down in the creation/evolution argument. You could spend all your time on questions Scripture does not answer, while neglecting to praise God for the magnificence of creation and its provision.

Complex though these issues are, Genesis 1 is well summarized in the child's prayer: *God is great/God is good/Let us thank Him/for our food.*

Lesson Introduction

Most cultures have their ancient accounts of how the earth was formed. The Bible creation account is more concerned about the *who* than the *how.* Pagan peoples surrounding Israel had their legends about various gods' involvement in creation. In the animistic views, nature seemed alive with these deities.

Against such views, Genesis 1 made two assertions: (1) The one God, not many gods, created the world and all that is in it. The material world is evidence of His love and provision for people. In other words, the universe is "friendly." (2) This God is above and separate from His creation. In the musical, Maria may sing, "The hills are alive with the sound of music"; but the hills themselves are not alive. God's people therefore do not worship mountains or trees or rocks; they worship the God who made them—the Creator rather than the creation.

Teaching Outline	Daily Bible Readings

I. God Brings Order—1-2
  A. The starting point, 1
  B. Order from chaos, 2
II. God Creates Life—20-25
  A. Swimmers and fliers, 20-23
  B. Creepers and crawlers, 24-25
III. God Sustains Life—29-31
  A. The provision, 29-30
  B. The pronouncement, "Good," 31
	Mon. Day One of Creation
	Genesis 1:1-5
	Tue. Days Two and Three
	Genesis 1:6-13
	Wed. Day Four of Creation
	Genesis 1:14-19
	Thu. Day Five of Creation
	Genesis 1:20-23
	Fri. Day Six of Creation
	Genesis 1:24-31
	Sat. The Last Day of Creation
	Genesis 2:1-4a
	Sun. "How Wondrous Thy Works!"
	Psalm 104:24-35

Verse by Verse

I. God Brings Order—1-2
A. The starting point, 1

1 In the beginning God created the heaven and the earth.

When did God make the heavens and the earth? How did He make it? How long did it take? Despite the arguments that have swirled around such questions, especially since the evolutionary theory put forward by Charles Darwin, Scripture does not answer these questions. (Although many King James Bibles confidently place the date 4004 B.C. at Gen. 1:1, it is not a part of the original text.)

As stated in the Lesson Introduction, the author of Genesis (traditionally held to be Moses) is mainly concerned to affirm that the one true God was at the beginning of things. Creation did not stem from the accidental spilling of blood or sperm by a mythical god, as in some ancient accounts, but from the purposeful and artful hand of the God who breathed the breath of life into the first man.

The skies were not constructed as a home for pagan gods, but by a God who knew His animate creation would need to breathe oxygen. The earth was not the frightening abode of spirit-beings who in the rocks, trees, and hills; it was created by the same God, and thus contained no evil spirits to demand devotion or sacrifices from persons, who will be the crowning act of creation.

B. Order from chaos, 2

2 And the earth was without form, and void; and darkness was upon the face of the deep.

Although this classic account makes no attempt to fit itself into modern scientific theory, it is remarkable how this description fits some scientific theories. An earth consisting mainly of swirling gases that blotted out the sun—the result of a "big bang"—seems very much like the chaos described here.

Since some of the Hebrew words used here are very much like the names of pagan gods, some scholars believe the Genesis account is deliberately refuting pagan versions of creation. For example, "the deep" here is *tehom,* thought to be related to *tiamat,* the ancient Sumerian god of the sea. Genesis tells us that the sea is not a god, but merely "the deep." Despite its wild waves, the ocean is not to be worshipped or appeased by sacrifice; it is under the authority of the Creator by right of creation.

II. God Creates Life—20-25
A. Swimmers and fliers, 20-23

20 And God said, Let the waters bring forth abundantly the moving creature that hath life, and fowl that may fly above the earth in the open firmament of heaven.

21 And God created great whales, and every living creature that

moveth, which the waters brought forth abundantly, after their kind, and every winged fowl after his kind: and God saw that it was good.

22 And God blessed them, saying, Be fruitful, and multiply, and fill the waters in the seas, and let fowl multiply in the earth.

23 And the evening and the morning were the fifth day.

The creation of the inanimate world during Days One through Four occupied verses 3-19. There God created light; the sky (firmament); the seas, dry land, and plant life; and the greater light of the sun and the lesser light of the moon.

Now the stately account describes the creation of life—in the seas and on the land. Again, the order of these "creative days" is remarkably like the best evidence from paleontology—the study of "old things." Since the sun, which determines earth's "days," was not created until Day 4, some authorities believe these "days" of creation were ages or stages—which would account for the apparent fact that the earth is much older than the date of 4004 in many King James Bibles.

Once more, however, the point is not to write a scientific treatise on the creation of life, but to assert that all life is created by God as a part of a creation He says is "very good." Of course after the Fall in Genesis 3, the earth will not always live up to its original potential. People die in the oceans by drowning. There are fatal earthquakes and tornadoes and other "natural calamities." Yet it is important for Genesis to describe the original creation as good, since God will later promise that the defects of a fallen earth will one day be redeemed in the "new heaven and a new earth" (Rev. 21:1). We can trust God to one day restore the earth to work *for* us instead of *against* us because it worked that way at creation.

As the next verse will also state, verse 21 tells us that these swimming and flying creatures were made after their "kind." Among the arguments of evolutionists is the laboratory evidence that fruit flies and other kinds of life can be bred to change, or "evolve." Genesis doesn't deny this; it merely affirms that God created the primary *kinds* of animal life—another fact that is borne out in the fossil record. The account here makes no comment on how animals may have evolved within their own kind.

B. Creepers and crawlers, 24-25

24 And God said, Let the earth bring forth the living creature after his kind, cattle, and creeping thing, and beast of the earth after his kind: and it was so.

25 And God made the beast of the earth after his kind, and cattle after their kind, and every thing that creepeth upon the earth after his kind: and God saw that it was good.

Following the pattern of the creation of flying and swimming creatures, the account moves on to the creation of land animals. The recurring terms "every" and "every thing" (vss. 21, 25) testify that no part of the created world came into existence apart from the loving hand of God. Long before people learned to catalogue and identify most species of life, believers in God could dwell securely in the knowledge that there were no beasts or creatures in the air, on land, or in the sea, that God did not create. Of course we sometimes wish that *fewer* species had been created—as when mosquitoes or bears attack us. Scripture explains such ills as a result of the Fall of Man as recorded in Genesis 3.

III. God Sustains Life—29-31
A. The provision, 29-30

29 And God said, Behold, I have given you every herb bearing seed, which is upon the face of all the earth, and every tree, in the which is the fruit of a tree yielding see; to you it shall be for meat.

30 And to every beast of the earth, and to every fowl of the air, and to every thing that creepeth upon the earth, wherein there is life, I have given every green herb for meat: and it was so.

Moving now beyond the intervening verses (26-28) that describe the creation of mankind, it may seem strange for God to say that plant life was given for *meat*. This word had a broader meaning than animal flesh for the King James translators; it simply means "food."

This description does not necessarily mean that people were originally vegetarians. It merely reflects the truth that all life, including animal life, depends on plant life. This generalized nature of the passage is seen again when the text says that "every" kind of plant is for our consumption. It is a grand statement of the Creator's care for people's every need, not an assertion that every form of vegetation is suitable for humans to eat.

B. The pronouncement, "Good," 31

31 And God saw every thing that he had made, and, behold, it was very good. And the evening and the morning were the sixth day.

Finally, the pronouncement of the goodness of creation should be contrasted with pagan views that both good and evil deities had a hand in forming the world. This "endorsement" of the material world left an indelible mark on true Jewish and Christian doctrine. From time to time certain heretics would teach that the flesh, human sexuality, and all worldly desires are evil. While the reality of the Fall (Gen. 3) enables these created realities to be abused, God insists that creation as it came from His hand is the friend of humanity, not an evil.

Evangelistic Emphasis

After the first chapter of Genesis, we are told little about God's work of creation and the way He controls the universe. But if we will closely observe nature, we should be convinced of God's hand in the world (Rom. 1:18-23).

However, mankind has tended to look at God's creation and reach the wrong conclusions. From very early times, people worshiped pieces of carved wood, stone or metal or imagined gods and goddesses on a mountain or in the sea.

During New Testament times, people in Athens, Greece, were very involved in worshiping idols. They had temples and altars to every god they had ever heard of. They even had one inscribed, "To the Unknown God." This outrageous display of idolatry disturbed the Apostle Paul when he was visiting the city. So, using their "unknown god" as the beginning point, he challenged the people to worship the one true God, who was truly "unknown" to them. Some believed because of his preaching.

It is now popular to ridicule the Bible story of creation and reject the idea of God and His role in bringing the world into existence. We should not be ashamed to tell people what the Bible says about God. Many who declare they are unbelievers are really uninformed about what the Bible says. If they are patiently and lovingly taught what God has revealed, they may believe and receive His blessings.

• • • • • • •

Memory Selection

And God saw every thing that He had made, and, behold, it was very good.—*Genesis 1:31a*

As God's Spirit moved upon the face of the dark waters, God said, "Let there be light!" Suddenly light appeared. We are told that God created everything else into existence by simply speaking His desire to have it appear. As God finished creating each major component of the world and its various forms of life, He pronounced it "good." Having completed His creation at the end of that glorious week of work, He said, "It is very good!"

The Creation was actually perfect. The world was exactly like God wanted it. No pollution had taken place. There was no sin in the world. All was very good.

God still has a place where everything is perfect. We call it "heaven." One of these days, He has promised to welcome every one there who has prepared in this life to be with Him.

Weekday Problems

Jimmy's teacher said the creation story was fiction, that God didn't really make the world, and Adam and Eve weren't created. The teacher even showed them "proof" in the science textbook.

This incident presented a crisis in Jimmy's mind. He had been taught at home and Sunday School that the Bible is true, that God created the world and all that is in it, including the first man and the first woman. The teacher and the science textbook are equally firm in the account they give. Whom is he to believe?

This is a problem facing almost all families whose children attend the public schools of our communities. Nearly everywhere in America, there is a conflict between the teachings in science classrooms and the teachings of the church.

What is a parent to do? Let the child learn what is said in public school and in the Sunday School and leave it to the child to sort out the truth? Tell the child, "Learn what the teachers require in order to pass the tests, but do not change your belief in the Word of God?" Approach the secular schools at the school level or higher and urge them to abandon their anti-Biblical teachings?

* Which of these approaches is right?

* How would you explain your belief in the Bible account of creation?

* How should church leaders deal with conflicts between school and church teachings?

Natural Disasters

As a special treat, the teacher took her class to visit the museum of natural history. The children returned home excitedly, and on rushing into his house one of the little boys greeted his mother: "What do you think we did today, Mom? The teacher took us to a dead circus!"

* * *

On the way home from church the little girl asked, "Mommy, is it true that we are all made of dust?"

"Yes it is."

"And do we go back to dust again when we die?"

"Yes we do."

"Well Mommy, when I said my prayers last night and looked under the bed, I found someone who is either coming or going."

* * *

Young man to maid: Ah, see that calf rubbing noses with its mama? Makes me want to do the same.

Maid: Well, go ahead. It's your cow.

This Lesson in Your Life

In Genesis 1:1 we are told that God created the heavens and the earth. We do not know how much planning He did before performing this stupendous feat. We do not know how much energy He expended. We do know that God was satisfied with the outcome.

When God created light, He said it was good. When He separated the waters and formed seas and dry land, He said it was good. When He created plants and trees, He saw that it was good. In like manner, He considered His work good when He set the sun, moon and stars in the heavens. When He made fish and birds and similar animals, He was able to declare those creations good. When He reached the end of His six days of creation, He judged the creation of land animals and mankind to be good. In fact, as our Memory Selection indicates, He considered the whole creation "very good."

What would happen if we took God's handiwork as a standard for our own work? When you come to the end of the day, are you able to say to yourself, "Today I did good work"? When the week draws to a close, are you confident in saying, "This week I did *very* good work"?

God was the best judge of the quality of His work. He is all-wise, unbiased. He knew before He performed His creative acts exactly what He wanted to do. He did it perfectly. You also are in a unique position to judge your own performance in whatever you set out to do. Only you know your intentions, your motivation. Perhaps you are also able to set aside bias or prejudice in assessing the quality of your work. When we were children, we depended on others to tell us how well we were doing. The teachers assigned grades to our work; our parents complimented or criticized us. As adults, we are expected to be self-motivated and self-correcting in our pursuit of success.

Are you self-employed? Then you know that the success of your business, your reputation, depends on how well you do your work. Even if the customer does not complain, you will know if you failed to do a good job.

Is your job to accomplish tasks set for you by someone else? Perhaps that person will judge your work, but whether that person is satisfied or not, only you will know whether you did your best.

God expects us to do our work with excellence. Servants are instructed to work "in singleness of your heart, as unto Christ . . . with good will doing service, as to the Lord" (Eph 6:5-7). Again, serve "heartily, as to the Lord, and not unto men" (Col. 3:23). But more than doing our secular work well, God calls us to be perfect in our service to Him (Heb. 13:21). This goal is always before us, though our human nature interferes with attainment.

At the end of the day can we say of both our secular work and our service to God that we have followed God's pattern of doing well?

Seed Thoughts

1. When did creation take place?

2. Who was/were present at creation?

3. What method did God use to create?

4. Having finished creation, what did God think of the results?

5. Did creation end on the sixth day?

6. Name the order of creation according to Genesis 1.

7. Why should we be grateful for God's creation?

8. What is meant by the phrase, "we are the offspring of God?" (See Acts 17:29.)

9. Why do cows reproduce cows, birds reproduce birds and people reproduce people?

10. Name some of the reasons we should consider God's creation "good."

1. When did creation take place?

In the beginning. No one knows when that was.

2. Who was/were present at creation?

God, Christ and the Holy Spirit. (See Gen. 1:1,2,26; John 1:1,14,15,29.)

3. What method did God use to create?

God *spoke* everything into existence, except for mankind. He fashioned Adam from the dust of the earth and Eve from his rib (Gen. 2:7,22).

4. Having finished creation, what did God think of the results?

He saw every thing that He had made, and, behold, it was very good (Gen. 1:31).

5. Did creation end on the sixth day?

Yes, God rested on the seventh day (Gen. 2:2).

(Continued next page)

399

In the beginning. No one knows when that was.

God, Christ and the Holy Spirit. (See Gen. 1:1,2,26; John 1:1,14,15,29.)

God *spoke* everything into existence, except for mankind. He fashioned Adam from the dust of the earth and Eve from his rib (Gen. 2:7,22).

He saw every thing that He had made, and, behold, it was very good (Gen. 1:31).

Yes, God rested on the seventh day (Gen. 2:2).

(1) Light; (2) firmament; (3) dry land and plants; (4) sun, moon, stars; (5) birds, sea animals; (6) land animals, mankind.

He has provided for us and for all the living things. (See Psalm 104:27-28.)

Since God created us in His own image (Gen. 1:27) and breathed into his nostrils the breath of life (Gen. 2:7), we are His children.

God said that each kind should reproduce after its own kind (Gen. 1:21, 25).

He set the world in just the right order to make life sustainable (light, water, food, heat and cold, provided food for all, etc.).

6. Name the order of creation according to Genesis 1.

(1) Light; (2) firmament; (3) dry land and plants; (4) sun, moon, stars; (5) birds, sea animals; (6) land animals, mankind.

7. Why should we be grateful for God's creation?

He has provided for us and for all the living things. (See Psalm 104:27-28.)

8. What is meant by the phrase, "we are the offspring of God?" (See Acts 17:29.)

Since God created mankind in His own image (Gen. 1:27) and breathed into his nostrils the breath of life (Gen. 2:7), we are His children.

9. Why do cows reproduce cows, birds reproduce birds and people reproduce people?

God said that each kind should reproduce after its own kind (Gen. 1:21, 25).

10. Name some of the reasons we should consider God's creation "good."

He set the world in just the right order to make life sustainable (light, water, food, heat and cold, provided food for all, etc.).

God's Purpose for His People

*A*nd the LORD God formed man of the dust of the ground, and breathed into his nostrils the breath of life; and man became a living soul.

8 And the LORD God planted a garden eastward in Eden; and there he put the man whom he had formed.

9 And out of the ground made the LORD God to grow every tree that is pleasant to the sight, and good for food; the tree of life also in the midst of the garden, and the tree of knowledge of good and evil.

Genesis 2:7-9, 15-25

15 And the LORD God took the man, and put him into the garden of Eden to dress it and to keep it.

16 And the LORD God commanded the man, saying, Of every tree of the garden thou mayest freely eat:

17 But of the tree of the knowledge of good and evil, thou shalt not eat of it: for in the day that thou eatest thereof thou shalt surely die.

18 And the LORD God said, It is not good that the man should be alone; I will make him an help meet for him.

19 And out of the ground the LORD God formed every beast of the field, and every fowl of the air; and brought them unto Adam to see what he would call them: and whatsover Adam called every living creature, that was the name thereof.

20 And Adam gave names to all cattle, and to the fowl of the air, and to every beast of the field; but for Adam there was not found an help meet for him.

21 And the LORD God caused a deep sleep to fall upon Adam, and he slept: and he took one of his ribs, and closed up the flesh instead thereof;

22 And the rib, which the LORD God had taken from man, made he a woman, and brought her unto the man.

23 And Adam said, This is now bone of my bones, and flesh of my flesh: she shall be called Woman, because she was taken out of Man.

24 Therefore shall a man leave his father and his mother, and shall cleave unto his wife: and they shall be one flesh.

25 And they were both naked, the man and his wife, and were not ashamed.

Memory Selection
Genesis 2:7

Background Scripture
Genesis 2:4-25

Devotional Reading
Ephesians 5:21-33

Printed Scripture
Genesis 2:7-9, 15-25

Teacher's Target

Lesson purpose: *To discern the basic responsibilities of being human, and of living in relationship, taught in Genesis' account of the creation of mankind.*

"Life is cheap," we say, in these times when a youngster may be shot if he is wearing a pair of athletic shoes someone else wants. There is no better antidote for the devaluation of human life than reading the Genesis story of the creation of man and woman.

Emphasize in this lesson that people are the direct creation and reflection of the living God; that they live and breathe by the living breath of God; that they are strong enough to be expected to live within moral boundaries, and to be responsible for caring for creation; and that a man and woman can have no more worthy goal than to function harmoniously as husband and wife.

Human life must not be devalued, but glorified by living in harmony with God's purpose.

Lesson Introduction

Genesis has already treated us to a glimpse of the glory of humanity when it said people were created "in the image of God" (1:26-27). It is often said that from 2:4 we are given another, different account of humanity's origin. However, the present material can also be viewed as an expansion of the earlier account, offering some detail about what it means to be created in the image of God.

Chapter 1 is like a wide-angle photo of mankind in the context of the entire creation. It shows the man and the woman at home in a natural world with its plants and animals. Chapter 2 is a "close-up" of the humans in the first picture. The second photo reveals that while man and woman share many traits with the animals, they have a special glory—and a special responsibility. They are not only children of nature, but of the Spirit—the very breath of God. Their being made in His image becomes also their challenge—to rise above mere "nature," and to partake of grace by choosing to obey their Creator.

Teaching Outline	Daily Bible Readings
I. Created for a Garden—7-9	**Mon.** God Planted a Garden *Genesis 2:4-14*
A. Of dust and Spirit, 7	**Tue.** A Man Clings to His Wife *Genesis 2:15-25*
B. The Goodness of Eden, 8-9	**Wed.** Husbands, Love Your Wives *Ephesians 5:21-23*
II. Challenged by Commands—15-17	**Thu.** Honor Father and Mother *Matthew 15:1-9*
A. The challenge of work, 15	**Fri.** Keep the Commandments *Matthew 19:16-22*
B. Living within limits, 16-17	**Sat.** Created Male and Female *Mark 10:1-9*
III. Completed by Companions—18-25	**Sun.** Perishable to Imperishable *1 Corinthians 15:42-49*
A. Naming the animals, 18-20	
B. The Companion that Fits, 21-25	

Verse by Verse

I. Created for a Garden—7-9

A. Of dust and Spirit, 7

7 And the Lord God formed man of the dust of the ground, and breathed into his nostrils the breath of life; and man became a living soul.

This simple verse is a valuable commentary on 1:26-27, and what it means for man to have been made "in the image of God." Even though the animals live and breathe, nowhere is it said that God breathed into them "the breath of life." The Hebrew word for "breath" here (*ruach*) can also mean "spirit"; so we conclude that in breathing life into mankind God also places a dimension of His divine Spirit in them, giving them both a special glory and a unique responsibility over the animals. Unlike animals, people are given the capacity to respond to God's will, as will be illustrated in verses 16-17.

B. The Goodness of Eden, 8-9

8 And the Lord God planted a garden eastward in Eden; and there he put the man whom he had formed.

9 And out of the ground made the Lord God to grow every tree that is pleasant to the sight, and good for food; the tree of life also in the midst of the garden, and the tree of knowledge of good and evil.

Unlike the creation accounts of many surrounding peoples, Genesis dares both to describe the surroundings in which the first man and woman were placed, and (in vss. 10-14) the very area in which it was located.

"Eden" means "delight" in Hebrew. The word is used in 2 Samuel 1:25 to describe the delightful things brought to the people during the reign of King Saul (see also Neh. 9:25). No wonder so many people even today find "delight" in having a garden. "Eden" is in our spiritual genetic code!

The most important plants God provided in Eden were the tree of life and the tree of the knowledge of good and evil. Regarding the first, mankind was apparently not created to live forever apart from this miraculous tree. God expelled Adam and Eve from the Garden after they sinned partly so they would not eat of the tree of life "and live forever" (3:22). The role of the second tree will be noted in connection with verses 16-17.

II. Challenged by Commands—15-17

A. The challenge of work, 15

15 And the Lord God took the man, and put him into the garden of Eden to dress it and to keep it.

Note that it was not God's purpose to place the man and the woman in the garden to loaf in the shade, but to tend it. This reminds us of the truth that was rediscovered by Martin Luther, John Calvin, and other Reformers: work is a vocation or calling to be done as unto the Lord. It is not a curse. It was only after the Fall that the ground of a garden grew cranky, and caused cranky gardeners (3:17-19).

B. Living within limits, 16-17

16 And the Lord God commanded the man, saying, Of every tree of the garden thou mayest freely eat:

17 But of the tree of the knowledge of good and evil, thou shalt not eat of it: for in the day that thou eatest thereof thou shalt surely die.

Now the man and woman are tested at the level of the "spirit," the dimension of conscience that makes them distinct from the animal world. They are given a direct command not to eat of the tree of the knowledge of good and evil. This does not imply that the tree would impart a sense of conscience to the man and woman, or the mere knowledge that there are such things as good and evil. They had to know that much in order to disobey God's command. "Knowledge" here is, instead, the in-depth, knowing-by-doing experience of good such as God has, and of evil such as Satan has (3:22).

In its simplist form, "death" means "separation"—separation from life. Sure enough the very "day" Adam and Eve partook of the forbidden tree they were separated from God in being driven from the Garden. The story becomes a powerful prophecy also, promising that all who live in deliberate sin face the same judgment (see Rom. 5:12).

III. Completed by Companions–18-25
A. Naming the animals, 18-20

18 And the Lord God said, It is not good that the man should be alone; I will make him an help meet for him.

19 And out of the ground the Lord God formed every beast of the field, and every fowl of the air; and brought them unto Adam to see what he would call them: and whatsover Adam called every living creature, that was the name thereof.

20 And Adam gave names to all cattle, and to the fowl of the air, and to every beast of the field; but for Adam there was not found an help meet for him.

"Meet" in the original is an adjective, meaning "opposite," "complementary," or "appropriate." The man had no help that was "fit." It was only through the odd coincidence that "meet" sounds like "mate" in English that enabled the two words to be collapsed into the noun "helpmeet" (or helpmate). The point in Genesis is that man alone was incomplete, and that despite the creation of animals they were not a "fit help" for him.

Verse 19 does not contradict the order of creation already given in chapter 1 (animals, then man), but simply comments that none of the animals that had been created could serve as the complement the man needed. Although a dog may be man's best friend, it is still an "it"— leaving most men to seek out a woman for the kind of companionship they really need.

Yet there is a word here for singles, too. While seeking a fit help is the general rule, Adam lived alone before sin entered the world. God apparently had no word of judgment against him for being the world's first single person.

Verses 19-20 portray the first man as also the first zoologist, or cataloger of animal life. In the ancient world, naming something was a sign of authority. Thus God takes it upon Himself to rename Abram "Abraham," Sarai "Sarah," and Isaac "Israel." In Eden, Adam is given the authority to name the animals to reinforce his right—and duty—to "have dominion" over the animal world and to care for it as a precious, God-given resource (1:26).

The naming scene strikes a note of familiarity between man and beast, but verses 18 and 20 repeat the theme that something else is needed to satisfy the man's need for intimacy.

B. The Companion that Fits, 21-25

21 And the Lord God caused a deep sleep to fall upon Adam, and he slept: and he took one of his ribs, and closed up the flesh instead thereof;

22 And the rib, which the Lord God had taken from man, made he a woman, and brought her unto the man.

23 And Adam said, This is now bone of my bones, and flesh of my flesh: she shall be called Woman, because she was taken out of Man.

24 Therefore shall a man leave his father and his mother, and shall cleave unto his wife: and they shall be one flesh.

25 And they were both naked, the man and his wife, and were not ashamed.

Chapter 2 closes with the moving and poetic description of the man's being provided with a counterpart and intimate companion. As has often been said, particularly at weddings, the woman is not taken from the man's head, that she should dominate him; nor from his foot, that she should be dominated or walked on; but from his side, where the two can walk side-by-side as intimate partners.

There is a tone of joy and excitement as the man extends his task of naming of the animals to naming the new companion taken from his very body. He is, in the Hebrew, *ish,* a male, while she is *ishbah*, "taken from the male." (The woman will not be called "Eve" until 3:20). An African creation story echoes the exuberance Adam feels at being provided with such a complementary and ideal companion: "The two looked at each other and began to laugh, whereupon God sent them into the world."

This memorable scene is also used by our Lord to show the basis for marriage, and to teach the ideal of the permanent man-woman relationship in marriage, in Mark 10:6-9.

The dramatic chapter closes with an affirmation of the sacredness of the sexual relationship in marriage. Adam and Eve are "one flesh" even before it is explicitly stated that they united sexually (4:1); and, in their pre-Fall state, their nakedness before each other, and God, is perceived to be totally natural and without shame. It is only after sin enters the world that nudity becomes associated with illicit sexuality.

405

Evangelistic Emphasis

The story of the creation of mankind is placed at the beginning of the Bible. This place at the beginning tells us that God's action for the redemption of Israel has implications for all people. The love of God is for all God's children. All have received the breath of life. All are precious in God's sight.

Our task is to share the gospel with all people. The great commission, "Go therefore and make disciples of all nations," spells out the universal implications of this story . The placement of man's creation at the beginning of the story of God's saving acts makes it plain that this story concerns all humankind.

Our churches should be open houses where Jesus stands at the door to welcome all who come. Our charge is to share the gospel with all, not just those we like, who look and dress and think like we do. Jesus' ministry included the outcasts and neglected of his day. The children wasted by hunger, growing up in refugee camps, the poor in the slums of great cities, the prisoners who live out their lives behind bars are persons who have received the breath of life, God's Spirit. It is our privilege to share God's love with the least of them. In ministry to them, we may in truth be serving Christ. "Truly I tell you just as you did it to one of the least of those who are members of my family you did it to me" (Matt. 25:40).

● ● ● ● ● ● ●

Memory Selection

The Lord God formed man of the dust of the ground , and breathed into his nostrils the breath of life; and man became a living soul.—*Genesis 2:7*

There are two ways of visualizing this breath of life, which God breathed into the human creature God had formed from the earth. One way is to think of breath filling up a balloon. It is held there, captured, tied up and sealed. It is held for a time, but sooner or later the air leaks out, or the balloon bursts. A second image suggests a dynamic relation. It is the image of windmill. The wind blows continually. It is caught for an instant and moves on. It is a continuing, ongoing, moment-by-moment relationship. The wind is not given once and for all, a limited quantity. It is renewed each moment. So by the breath (wind) of God we are sustained and renewed moment by moment. Like the process of respiration, we inhale God's breath and breathe out God's praise.

Weekday Problems

Pat Ryan tells the story of Clara McDuff.

Clara prided herself on the way she used her time. She was exceptionally efficient. She would say to herself each time she completed a task within the allotted time, "exceptionally efficient."

She filled her time to the very brim. One would never find Clara just sitting. Even when she watched television, Clara would be busy polishing the silver, darning socks or addressing envelopes for her latest fund raising project.

Her schedule was organized to the least detail. Clara even kept a list of special things to do just in case there was a last minute opening in her time.

Yes indeed, one would never find Clara MacDuff just sitting.

One morning while she was ironing her permanent press sheets and listening to a radio program on improving vocabulary, someone knocked at her door. "Good morning," he said. "I'm looking for Clara McDuff. "Who?" she said.

* Do you know persons like Clara MacDuff?

* Do you see yourself in this fable?

* Do we lose our soul in staying too busy?

Your Questions Answered
About Adam and Eve

Q: At what time of day was Adam created?
A: A little before Eve.

* * *

Q: How did Adam have such a good thing going?
A: When he said something, he knew know one had said it before.

* * *

Q: When was radio first mentioned in the Bible?
A: When the Lord took a rib from Adam and made a loud speaker.

* * *

Q: Why is Adam known as a famous runner?
A: Because he was first in the human race.

* * *

Eve: Adam, do you love me?
Adam: Who else?

This Lesson in Your Life

The vivid image of God breathing into us the breath of life is captured by James Weldon Johnson's masterpiece, *God's Trombones:* "This Great God, like a mammy bending over her baby, kneeled down in the dust, toiling over a lump of clay till he shaped it in His own image; Then into it He blew the breath of life and man became a living soul."

After a season of rush our shallowness begins to show. Our prayers are empty, our relationships superficial. Our life has no direction. Our decisions reveal more expediency than integrity. We wither. We go through the motions but the breath has gone out of us. The self is hollow. We lose touch with the source of life.

The Hebrew word for "breath" is the same as the word for spirit. The story of God breathing His Spirit into us calls us to acknowledge another dimension of our being. Something there is in us that is restless, until it finds its rest in God. We are dust of the earth, but something more. Dust plus divinity! Matter and Spirit! Dirt of the earth plus the breath of God.

It is all too easy for us to neglect, ignore this dimension of our being. We live for days, even weeks, in only one dimension of life., thinking of salaries, and promotions, of houses and boats, of new cars and clothes, as if this were the whole of life. We are dust, flesh and blood, and these concerns are important. But we are more than what we wear and we are more than what we eat. Too often we get caught up in the rush and bustle of our daily routine. Every hour is crammed full. Each day's schedule is stretched to the bursting. There are never enough hours in the days or days in the week. Yet we often neglect the most important. We take no time to reflect, to seek , to wait, to pray, to be still, to be open, to let the breath of God fill us and renew us.

The story calls us back to the source of life and helps us to pray again: "Breathe on me, Breath of life, fill me with life anew."

In Genesis 2:16 the man who has received the breath of life is also given a vocation. He is to till the earth and keep it. The bountiful garden is provided but the human is called to be its gardener, and steward. Through these words of the Creator to Adam we are called to preserve the good earth, cherishing its beauty, protecting it from pollution of air and water and resisting the wanton waste of limited resources. Taking care of the earth is the common vocation of us all.

The words to the man are also words of permission to eat of the trees of the garden. There is a goodness in creation. So for us every meal is a reminder of our dependence upon God and a call for giving thanks to Him who sustains us day by day.

Finally, in God's charge to the man is the simple prohibition that reminds him that he is a creature not the Creator, that he is steward and not owner. In Genesis 3 we read how Adam and Eve defied this prohibition. They overreached themselves, assuming they knew more about what was good for their well being than did God. The act of rebellion, trusting in self, refusing to obey, is repeated in every life.

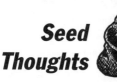

Seed Thoughts

1. What two trees are mentioned as being in the Garden of Eden?

The tree of life (Gen. 2:9) and the tree of the knowledge of good and evil (Gen. 2:9, 17).

2. What are the names of the four branches of the river that flowed out of Eden?

The names of the four rivers are: Pishon, Gihon, Tigris, and Euphrates.

3. Which of the four rivers can be found on a map of the Middle East today?

The Tigris and Euphrates.

4. What did God say would be the consequence of eating of the tree of the knowledge of good and evil?

"In the day that you eat of it, you shall die" (Gen. 2:17).

5. What was man's responsibility in the garden of Eden?

He was to till it and keep it (Gen. 2:15).

---

1. What two trees are mentioned as being in the Garden of Eden?

2. What are the names of the four branches of the river that flowed out of Eden?

3. Which of the four rivers can be found on a map of the Middle East today?

4. What did God say would be the consequence of eating of the tree of the knowledge of good and evil?

5. What was man's responsibility in the garden of Eden?

6. Compare the King James, "I will make him a help meet for him" (Gen. 2:18), with other versions.

7. Who provided the names for the animals?

8. What part of the man was used by the Lord God to make woman?

9. Why did the man call the partner God made "woman"?

10. How is the covenant between the man and woman expressed?

(Continued next page)

The tree of life (Gen. 2:9) and the tree of the knowledge of good and evil (Gen. 2:9, 17).

The names of the four rivers are: Pishon, Gihon, Tigris, and Euphrates.

The Tigris and Euphrates.

"In the day that you eat of it, you shall die" (Gen. 2:17).

He was to till it and keep it (Gen. 2:15).

NASB: "a helper as his partner." NIV: "a helper suitable for him." NEB: "a partner for him," Moffat: "a helper to suit him."

Whatever the man called every living creature, that was its name (Gen 2:19).

The Lord God took one of the ribs and made it into a woman.

"This one shall be called Woman, for out of Man this one was taken" (Gen. 2:23).

"Therefore a man leaves his father and mother and clings to his wife and they become one flesh" (Gen. 2:24).

6. Compare the King James, "I will make him a help meet for him" (Gen. 2:18), with other versions.

NASB: "a helper as his partner." NIV: "a helper suitable for him." NEB: "a partner for him," Moffat: "a helper to suit him."

7. Who provided the names for the animals?

Whatever the man called every living creature, that was its name (Gen 2:19).

8. What part of the man was used by the Lord God to make woman?

The Lord God took one of the ribs and made it into a woman.

9. Why did the man call the partner God made "woman"?

"This one shall be called Woman, for out of Man this one was taken" (Gen. 2:23).

10. How is the covenant between the man and woman expressed?

"Therefore a man leaves his father and mother and clings to his wife and they become one flesh" (Gen. 2:24).

Consequences of Sin

And Adam knew Eve his wife; and she conceived, and bare Cain, and said, I have gotten a man from the LORD.

2 And she again bare his brother Abel. And Abel was a keeper of sheep, but Cain was a tiller of the ground.

3 And in process of time it came to pass, that Cain brought of the fruit of the ground an offering unto the LORD.

4 And Abel, he also brought of the firstlings of his flock and of the fat thereof. And the LORD had respect unto Abel and to his offering:

5 But unto Cain and to his offering he had not respect. And Cain was very wroth, and his countenance fell.

6 And the LORD said unto Cain, Why art thou wroth? and why is thy countenance fallen?

7 If thou doest well, shat thou not be accepted? and if thou doest not well, sin lieth at the door. And unto thee shall be his desire, and thou shalt rule over him.

8 And Cain talked with Abel his brother: and it came to pass, when they were in the field, that Cain rose up against Abel his brother, and slew him.

9 And the LORD said unto Cain, Where is Abel thy brother? And he said, I know not: Am I my brother's keeper?

10 And he said, What hast thou done?

Genesis 4:1-15

the voice of thy brother's blood crieth unto me from the ground.

11 And now art thou cursed from the earth, which hath opened her mouth to receive thy brother's blood from thy hand;

12 When thou tillest the ground, it shall not henceforth yield unto thee her strength; a fugitive and a vagabond shalt thou be in the earth.

13 And Cain said unto the LORD, My punishment is greater than I can bear.

14 Behold, thou hast driven me out this day from the face of the earth; and from thy face shall I be hid; and I shall be a fugitive and a vagabond in the earth; and it shall come to pass, that every one that findeth me shall slay me.

15 And the LORD said unto him, Therefore whosoever slayeth Cain, vengeance shall be taken on him sevenfold. And the LORD set a mark upon Cain, lest any finding him should kill him.

Memory Selection
Genesis 4:7
Background Scripture
Genesis 4
Devotional Reading
1 John 3:11-17
Printed Scripture
Genesis 4:1-15

Teacher's Target

Lesson purpose: *To reflect on the Bible's account of the growth of the cancer of sin upon the earth in the form of the first murder, and its consequences.*

What could be more true to life than this ancient account of the consequences of Adam and Eve's sin? Its basic elements—jealousy, disobedience, violence, shame, punishment, and protests against the stern consequences of wrong-doing—are repeated and reported daily in modern news media.

In fact, using current events to illustrate these elements is an effective way to present the lesson. You may also want to involve members of the group in a discussion of the marked contrast we often see among children in the same family, as the biblical account describes the differences between Cain and Abel. Your group will recognize that this classic narrative is not just the story of Cain and Abel, but of humankind itself.

Lesson Introduction

Modern scholars sometimes dismiss ancient stories like this account of the first murder as "etiological myths." The Greek word *aitios* meant "cause"—and it is often assumed that the ancients looked around them at an existing fact of life and invented a story to explain its cause or origin.

Yet there is no reason to dismiss as myth all stories about causes and backgrounds. For example, the nomadic life-style is said in Genesis 4:20 to have originated with one "Jabal." Why should this statement be disregarded? When modern science explains that the "etiology" or cause of a disease is a virus we do not reject the claim as myth.

The fact is that the elements of this story of the first cause of violence on the earth ring true both because they have the authority of Scripture and because they are attested in crimes of passion today. If we are interested in probing the true "etiology" or cause of such wrongs, we will take this account seriously instead of dismissing it.

Teaching Outline	Daily Bible Readings
I. The First Children—1-2	**Mon.** Sin Lurks at the Door *Genesis 4:1-7*

II. The First Sacrifices—3-7
  A. Unacceptable worship, 3
  B. Acceptable worship, 4-7
	Tue. Cain Murders His Brother
	Genesis 4:8-16

III. The First Murder and Its Consequences—8-16	**Wed.** The Birth of Enoch and Seth *Genesis 4:17-26*

A. The blood cries out, 8-10
  B. The curse is assigned, 11-12
  C. Protection is promised, 13-15
	Thu. The Barrier of Sin
	Isaiah 59:1-15

	Fri. The Way to Mercy *Proverbs 28:9-14*
	Sat. 'But I Say to You . . .' *Matthew 5:21-26*
	Sun. The Blessing of Forgiveness *Psalm 32:1-11*

Verse by Verse

I. The First Children—1-2

1 And Adam knew Eve his wife; and she conceived, and bare Cain, and said, I have gotten a man from the LORD.

As in the use of the word "know" regarding Adam and Even knowing sin (3:5, 22), the term here implies the intimacy of personal experience. In this case it refers to "knowing" each other body and soul in sexual intercourse.

The influential Christian teacher Augustine noted in the fourth century that this sexual union did not occur until after the Fall (Gen. 3). Ever since, many Christians have associated some degree of shame with intercourse. This notion has also been accompanied by the idea that celibacy is somehow a holier lifestyle than marriage. All this ignores the biblical teaching that "marriage is honourable . . . and the bed undefiled" (Heb. 13:4). It was only because of the "present distress" and uncertainties of being a Christian in a time of persecution that the apostle Paul recommended celibacy (1 Cor. 7:25-40).

Eve gives her firstborn the name "Cain" because it sounds like the Hebrew *qana,* to get, and she is overjoyed at having "gotten a man (child) from the Lord." This tradition of attaching such meanings to a child's name often reappears, especially in the naming of the

twelve sons of Jacob, who become the leaders of the twelve tribes of Israel.

2 And she again bare his brother Abel. And Abel was a keeper of sheep, but Cain was a tiller of the ground.

The second-born child's name (Heb. *habel)* simply means "son." However, a similiar form of the word means "vanity," and it is possible that he receives a "prophetic" name in anticipation of his murder and the vain or useless wasting of his life.

Note that even this early in the story of human origins the two life-styles of the shepherd and the farmer are anticipated. There is no hint here that God favors one occupation over the other, or one son over the other.

II. The First Sacrifices—3-7
A. Unacceptable worship, 3

3 And in process of time it came to pass, that Cain brought of the fruit of the ground an offering unto the LORD.

It is commonly held that Cain's offering was unacceptable to God because it was not a "blood sacrifice," as was Abel's, offered in anticipation of the sacrifice of Christ, "the Lamb of God." This view reads more into the text than is actually here. Unless God explicitly called for an animal sacrifice (see comments below), Cain appropriately offers the fruits of his labor, as Abel will do. Grain offerings, or "the fruit of the ground," will be as acceptable as blood offerings under the Law of Moses. ("Meat offerings" in passages such as Exod. 29:41 is misleading; see the NIV "cereal offering" and the RSV "grain offering.") The difference in these first sacrifices is to be found in the spirit in which they are offered, more than in the content.

B. Acceptable worship, 4-7

4 And Abel, he also brought of the firstlings of his flock and of the fat thereof. And the LORD had respect unto Abel and to his offering:

5 But unto Cain and to his offering he had not respect. And Cain was very wroth, and his countenance fell.

6 And the LORD said unto Cain, Why art thou wroth? and why is thy countenance fallen?

7 If thou doest well, shat thou not be accepted? and if thou doest not well, sin lieth at the door. And unto thee shall be his desire, and thou shalt rule over him.

We must rely on the New Testament for an explanation of why God "had respect" for Abel and his offering, and not for Cain's. The Hebrew writer says that the difference was a matter of *faith* (Heb. 11:4). The most likely explanation is that Abel was more aware of his need for forgiveness, and more trusting that God would grant it. It is also possible, since "faith cometh by hearing, and hearing by the word of God" (Rom.

10:17), that God had called for an animal sacrifice, and that Cain rebelliously brought what he wished. The apostle John will comment that Cain killed Abel "because his own works were evil" (1 John 3:12).

The fact that God "had respect" (NIV "looked with favor") on Abel's sacrifice brought out the worst in Cain. His jealousy is satanically human, fueled by one of the most demeaning and damaging—but most common—of human emotions. Every parent of more than one child knows the struggle to prevent the demon of envy from rupturing harmonious family relationships.

God places the responsibility for Cain's downcast demeanor squarely on his own shoulders. It is because Cain has not "done well," not because God has arbitrarily favored Abel. Again, the NIV makes the meaning of verse 7b clearer: "If you do not do what is right, sin is crouching at your door; it desires to have you, but you must master it."

III. The First Murder and Its Consequences—8-16

A. The blood cries out, 8-10

8 And Cain talked with Abel his brother: and it came to pass, when they were in the field, that Cain rose up against Abel his brother, and slew him.

9 And the LORD said unto Cain, Where is Abel thy brother? And he said, I know not: Am I my brother's keeper?

10 And he said, What hast thou done? the voice of thy brother's

lood crieth unto me from the ground.

Cain's talking with his brother may have been a deliberate attempt to lure him into the field, away from their parents, where the murder is committed. Just as God confronted Adam and Eve with the question "Where are you?" (3:9), although He well knew, so He confronts Cain with questions. "Where is your brother?" and "What have you done?" are questions for the murderer, not for God's information.

Cain's reply has been deservedly installed as a classic in all languages and literature. Although asking, "Am I my brother's keeper?" was intended to avoid responsibility, the line actually indicts all who would try to hide behind indifference to escape responsibility for tending to the needs of others.

Cain's pretended ignorance fails. His deed is so horrible that it evokes from God the figure of speech of Abel's blood "crying out" from the ground. It is like the over-loud, haunting heart-beat that gives away the murderer in Edgar Allen Poe's classic story, "The Telltale Heart." The cry begs for punishment, unlike the blood of Jesus, which speaks of grace (Heb. 12:24).

B. The curse is assigned, 11-12

11 And now art thou cursed from the earth, which hath opened her mouth to receive thy brother's blood from thy hand;

12 When thou tillest the ground, it shall not henceforth yield unto thee her strength; a fugitive and a vagabond shalt thou be in the earth.

Cain's "curse" is that he will be banned from the society of decent people who occupy the earth that drank Abel's blood. Like the curse that resulted from the sin of Adam and Even, the earth will also fail to cooperate with man's attempts to make it yield harvests (3:17).

C. Protection is promised, 13-16

13 And Cain said unto the Lord, My punishment is greater than I can bear.

14 Behold, thou hast driven me out this day from the face of the earth; and from thy face shall I be hid; and I shall be a fugitive and a vagabond in the earth; and it shall come to pass, that every one that findeth me shall slay me.

15 And the Lord said unto him, Therefore whosoever slayeth Cain, vengeance shall be taken on him sevenfold. And the Lord set a mark upon Cain, lest any finding him should kill him.

Along with many a convicted felon, Cain believes his punishment is unjust. His protest is accompanied by the fear that "everyone that findeth me shall slay me," envisioning the rapid growth of the earth's population.

Oddly, "the mark of Cain" God promises has been interpreted as a visible racial blight on his descendants. Instead, God seems to be graciously saying that He will "mark" Cain in the sense of "noting" him, taking special care that he will not be unduly hunted down for his deed. Vengeance belongs not to man, but to God (Rom . 12:19).

415

Evangelistic Emphasis

"Am I my brother's keeper?" Cain meant it sarcastically. Am I the shepherd's shepherd? Am I a nursemaid to my younger brother? Indeed the Lord is the one who keeps Israel (Ps. 121:4, 5). The Lord is the good shepherd (Ps. 23). God should be watching out for this fragile, wayward brother.

Cain's focus is too narrow. His vision is centered only on himself. Deny it or not, his brother Abel is his responsibility. The rivalry between brothers not withstanding, Abel is his responsibility.

We are children of one God, Father of us all. We cannot deny our kinship with others without separating ourselves from God.

The command to "make disciples of all nations" includes the children in poverty, the criminals in prison. It includes persons with whom we have strong differences, personal, political, theological. That commission to share the gospel includes persons similar to us, toward whom we feel animosity and resentment. That commission to share the gospel includes those of different nations, classes, races and life style. It includes our rivals, our competitors even our enemies.

When we pick and choose whom we will welcome to the Lord's house, we only exclude ourselves from the table of the Lord. "So if when you are offering your gift at the altar, and there remember that your brother or sister has something against you, leave your gift there before the altar; first go and be reconciled to your brother or sister, and then come and offer your gift" (Matt. 5:23-24).

Memory Selection

If thou doest well, shalt thou not be accepted? and if thou doest not well, sin lieth at the door. And unto thee shall be his desire, and thou shalt rule over him.—*Genesis 4:7*

The King James Version "thou shalt rule over him" sounds like a promise to Cain of his ultimate triumph over the sins that "lieth at the door." Other translations suggest not the certainty or inevitability of Cain's ruling over sin, but the possibility. You must or you can master it.

The passage reminds us that life is not fair. For some persons life is full of tragedy and sorrow. Accident, illness, unemployment or war impose circumstances that limit and frustrate us. We cannot control what happens. We are given freedom to choose how we will respond. We may give in to anger, dejection, and let sin have control over us. Or by God's grace we may choose to seek a reconciliation.

The temptation to strike back, to lash out is close at hand. It is a power that can consume us, take over our thinking, our feeling and our acting. We may give into that power of evil and be destroyed ourselves. But we can overcome it. In the long run how we respond to what happens to us is more important than what happens to us.

Weekday Problems

The Monday morning Women's Circle is meeting. Someone mentions that Betty is not here today and she was not at church yesterday. She usually comes, and they wonder why she is absent. Emma says that she lives near her and sees her quite often. She will run by after the circle meeting.

When Emma gets to Betty's house and knocks, Betty does not open the door all the way. Emma wants to know what is the matter. Then Emma gets a glimpse of Betty's face. It is bruised and her eyes are puffy. "What happened?" Betty asks. After some pause Betty invites Emma in . Betty tells her that her husband has beaten her up again.

Emma responds: "You don't have to take that! Why don't you go to the doctor or to the pastor or somebody?" Betty answers, "I'm afraid of John and what he will do."

* Am I my sister's keeper? Am I my brother's keeper? What would you do? How can the church help Betty? How can the church help John?

* What is the line between unwelcome interference in a private, family affair and responsible intervention to protect the well being of the victim?

* What resources are available in your community to abused women? What help is available for the abusing husband?

Ready and Abel

Did you hear about the ape who overheard visitors at the zoo discussing evolution? The next morning his keepers found this question scrawled on the concrete in front of the ape's cave: *"Am I my keeper's brother?"*

* * *

Fay: How long did Cain hate his brother?
Ray: As long as he was Abel.

* * *

Cain: A snake just snapped at me!
Abel: Snakes don't snap. They coil and strike.
Cain: Well, this one must've been a garter snake.

* * *

Cain: I don't know about this cow the Lord made. She only gives buttermilk.
Abel: So? Have you ever heard of a cow that gives anything but-her-milk?

This Lesson in Your Life

Two men go to worship the Lord. They are brothers, sons of the same parents. But they are different. One is a farmer and one is a shepherd. The two brothers are in two different kinds of work. Both need each other. Each is able to provide what the other needs. Yet Cain sees Abel as a rival, a threat and a competitor for land, for their father's blessing, for God's favor.

In our life together today we get divided into different groups: management and labor, rich and poor, black and white, conservationist and energy developers. The rivalry where each wants a bigger piece of the pie is intensified when inflamed by national pride. We forget that we are brothers and sisters, children of one God, all part of one human family. Each of us needs what the other has to offer.

Even in the church family there are clashes of special interests: between the dreamers and the doers, the spenders and the savers, the innovators and traditionalists, the prophets and the nurturers, the "Marthas" and the "Marys." All are needed in the community of faith. We get locked into conflict where it seems one must win and the other lose. The fabric of society is shredded. The common values that make us a family seem less important than the interests which divide. Tragic is the hurt, waste and destruction when persons and groups can't co-exist side by side and cooperate with each other.

The story of Adam and Eve eating the fruit of the forbidden tree in the Garden of Eden in defiance of God's clear command (Gen. 3) suggests that the root of the trouble between the brothers may be Adam's disobedience and consequent estrangement from God. Until humans are set right with God, we will not be in right relations with each other. The jealousy, the insecurity, the anger that erupts in violence will not finally be cured until we are reconciled to God. Through Christ we come to know that all are winners, all are precious, all are loved. We need not prove our superiority over others. Our offerings at worship are not a contest with our brother. Differences can be a blessing and not a threat. Secure in God's love we can affirm and encourage others, and rejoice in the good that others do. Like Cain and Abel we live east of Eden but we live on this side of the Cross.

In one sense conflict with our brother comes from not being right with God. That chasm separating us from God is bridged by Christ. "God was in Christ reconciling the world unto himself" (2 Cor. 5:19). In another sense, it is our enmity with our brother that blocks our living in harmony with God. Jesus reminds us that true worship is blocked when we are alienated from our neighbor. We are admonished to leave our very gift at the altar and first go and be reconciled to the brother who has something against us. Then we can offer our gift at the altar (Matt 5:23-24). Cain's only alternative , when his offering is not acceptable to God, is to seek reconciliation with his younger brother. "If you do well," God said (Gen. 4:7). "If you turn to your brother and are reconciled" (Matt 5:24). But Cain chose not to do well. Reconciliation, the one thing required, was too much.

Seed Thoughts

1. What was the punishment for Cain's killing his brother?

The ground would not yield him strength and he would be a fugitive and wanderer on earth (Gen. 4:12).

2. Where did Cain go?

He settled in the land of Nod, east of Eden (Gen. 4:16).

3. What was Cain's son's name?

Enoch.

4. Who were the descendants of Cain named in the fourth chapter of Genesis?

Enoch, Irad, Mehujael, Methushael, Lamech, Jabal, Jubal, Tubal-cain, Naamah (Gen. 4:17-22).

5. What was the name of Adam's third son?

Adam's wife named the son Seth, for "God has appointed for me another child instead of Abel" (Gen. 4:25).

1. What was the punishment for Cain's killing his brother?

2. Where did Cain go?

3. What was Cain's son's name?

4. Who were the descendants of Cain named in the fourth chapter of Genesis?

5. What was the name of Adam's third son?

6. What was the name of Seth's son?

7. What offering did Cain bring to the Lord?

8. What was Abel's offering?

9. What were the occupations of Cain and Abel?

10. Which of the sons of Adam and Eve was the older?

Continued next page)

The ground would not yield him strength and he would be a fugitive and wanderer on earth (Gen. 4:12).

He settled in the land of Nod, east of Eden (Gen. 4:16).

6. What was the name of Seth's son?
Enosh (Gen. 4:26).

Enoch.

7. What offering did Cain bring to the Lord?
Cain brought an offering of the fruit of the ground (Gen. 4:3).

Enoch, Irad, Mehujael, Methushael, Lamech, Jabal, Jubal, Tubal-cain, Naamah (Gen. 4:17-22).

8. What was Abel's offering?
Abel brought the firstlings of his flock and their fat portions (Gen. 4: 4).

Adam's wife named the son Seth, for "God has appointed for me another child instead of Abel" (Gen. 4:25).

9. What were the occupations of Cain and Able?
Abel was a keeper of sheep and Cain a tiller of the ground (Gen. 4:2).

Enosh (Gen. 4:26).

Cain brought an offering of the fruit of the ground (Gen. 4:3).

10. Which of the sons of Adam and Eve was the older?
Cain was Adam and Eve's eldest son.

Abel brought the firstlings of his flock, and their fat portions (Gen. 4: 4).

Abel was a keeper of sheep and Cain a tiller of the ground (Gen. 4:2).

Cain was Adam and Eve's eldest son.

Judgment and New Beginning

*A*nd GOD saw that the wickedness of man was great in the earth, and that every imagination of the thoughts of his heart was only evil continually.

6 And it repented the LORD that he had made man on the earth, and it grieved him at his heart.

7 And the LORD said, I will destroy man whom I have created from the face of the earth; both man, and beast, and the creeping thing, and the flows of the air; for it repenteth me that I have made them.

8 But Noah found grace in the eyes of the LORD.

7:1 And the LORD said unto Noah, Come thou and all thy house into the ark; for thee have I seen righteous before me in this generation.

2 Of every clean beast thou shalt take to thee by sevens, the male and his female: and of the beasts that are not clean by two, the male and his female.

3 Of fowls also of the air by sevens, the male and the female; to keep seed alive upon the face of all the earth.

4 For yet seven days, and I will cause it to rain upon the earth forty days and forty nights; and every living substance that I have made will I destroy from off the face of the earth.

9:12 And God said, This is the token of

the covenant which I make between me and you and every living creature that is with you, for perpetual generations:

13 I do set my bow in the cloud, and it shall be for a token of a covenant between me and the earth.

14 And it shall come to pass, when I bring a cloud over the earth, that the bow shall be seen in the cloud:

15 And I will remember my covenant, which is between me and you and every living creature of all flesh; and the waters shall no more become a flood to destroy all flesh.

16 And the bow shall be in the cloud; and I will look upon it, that I may remember the everlasting covenant between God and every living creature of all flesh that is upon the earth.

17 And God said unto Noah, This is the token of the covenant, which I have established between me and all flesh that is upon the earth.

Genesis 6:5-8; 7:1-4; 9:12-17

Memory Selection
Genesis 9:15

Background Scripture
Genesis 6:5–9:17

Devotional Reading
Deuteronomy 7:7 -11

Printed Scripture
Genesis 6:5-8; 7:1-4; 9:12-17

421

Teacher's Target

Lesson purpose: *To explore the Genesis account of the Great Flood as a pattern both of how God holds us accountable for sin, and offers redemption.*

Some months ago, pictures and models of Noah's Ark became a hot new item at many Christian book stores. Old Noah and the two-by-two procession of animals have never appeared so cute.

Lead your group to see that the reali behind this spate of merchandise is mor serious than cute. The Genesis account tel of the awful reality of sin and its inevitabl consequences. Yet this grim part of the stor is followed, after all, by an outpouring grace that the models and pictures cel ebrate. Noah's Ark is a symbol both of th seriousness with which God takes sin, an of His providence in preserving the faithf through His grace.

Lesson Introduction

Like the Creation account, Genesis' story of the Great Flood may prompt question about how literal we are to take it. These issues usually center around (1) Whether th flood was universal or only "all the earth" envisioned in the earliest chapters of Genes (the "cradle of civilization). (2) The adequacy of the ark to preserve pairs of animal necessary for repopulating the earth. (3) Reports that the remains of what appears to b a huge boat have been found in the mountains of southeast Turkey, perhaps corrobora ing the biblical story of the ark. (3) Similarities and differences between the biblica account and flood stories from other ancient cultures.

Reading an article on "The Flood" in a good Bible dictionary will help you prepar for these and other questions that may arise during the lesson. Yet the discussion wi prove most helpful if the focus centers on the text, and the theological "point" of judg ment and redemption it makes.

Teaching Outline	Daily Bible Readings

I. Evil Gone to Seed—6:5-7
  A. Effects of the Fall, 5
  B. Plan for punishment, 6-7
	Mon. A Corrupt Earth
	  Genesis 6:5-22
	Tue. One Righteous Man
	  Genesis 7:1-16

II. Electing a Remnant—6:8, 7:1-4
  A. Noah found grace, 6:8, 7:1
  B. Preserving life, 2-3
  C. Destroying life, 4
	Wed. God Remembered Noah
	  Genesis 7:17–7:5
	Thu. The Waters Dry Up
	  Genesis 8:6-22

III. Establishing a Covenant—9:12-17
  A. The bow in the cloud, 12-13
  B. The covenant affirmed, 14-17
	Fri. Noah's Family Blessed
	  Genesis 9:1-7
	Sat. The Covenant with Noah
	  Genesis 9:8-17
	Sun. A Curse from Noah
	  Genesis 9:18-28

Verse by Verse

I. Evil Gone to Seed—6:5-7

A. Effects of the Fall, 5

5 And GOD saw that the wickedness of man was great in the earth, and that every imagination of the thoughts of his heart was only evil continually.

While many people today debate the question of mankind's *evolution*, the Genesis account describes an opposite trend: *devolution.* The moral quality of life seems to have been on a downhill slide since Adam and Eve partook of the forbidden fruit—with the trend broken only momentarily by Enoch "who walked with God" (5:22).

Otherwise, from the first murder, when Cain took his brother Abel's life, the "wickedness of man" has now worsened to the point that people seem to be plotting and imagining evil at every waking moment. Some interpreters speculate that the intermarriage of "the sons of God" and "the daughters of men" in 6:2 describes a race of fallen angels that contributed to the decline in morality.

B. Plan for punishment, 6-7

6 And it repented the LORD that he had made man on the earth, and it grieved him at his heart.

7 And the LORD said, I will destroy man whom I have created from the face of the earth; both man, and beast, and the creeping thing, and the flows of the air; for it repenteth me that I have made them.

In its purest form, "repentance" means to change one's mind; only secondarily does it mean sorrow for sin. It is in the primary sense that a sinless God can be said to have "repented" about having created man (see NKJV "The LORD was sorry"). Apparently creating persons with free will was worth the risk that they would turn out wrong.

The decision to sweep the earth clean of its wickedness reminds us that God will one day have enough of present-day evil as well, and bring another round of destruction to the earth. The divine judgment here will be tempered only by the exception of Noah, sea life, and enough animals to begin repopulating the earth.

II. Electing a Remnant—6:8, 7:1-4

A. Noah found grace, 6:8, 7:1

6:8 But Noah found grace in the eyes of the LORD.

7:1 And the LORD said unto Noah, Come thou and all thy house into the ark; for thee have I seen righteous before me in this generation.

Noah was introduced in 5:28-32 as the son of Lamech. God's recognition of Noah's righteousness establishes a pattern that can be traced throughout the Bible: regardless of how evil seems to rule, God chooses a "remnant," a minority, to be saved.

The "grace" these remnants find in the eyes of God will become the one essential of the several "covenants" to follow (see below). The ark becomes a type of the place in which God protects the remnant—the family of Abraham in the case of the covenant at Sinai, and the Church in the case of the New Covenant. The waters of the flood that save those in the safety ark will be compared to the water of baptism under the New Covenant (1 Pet. 3:20-21).

The fact that God chooses a remnant to be saved does not show their "worthiness" so much as God's intention to vindicate His having created people of free will by choosing to save some. Noah and the pairs of beasts share the distinction of being "seed" for the regeneration of the earth after the Flood cleanses it of its wickedness.

B. Preserving life, 2-3

2 Of every clean beast thou shalt take to thee by sevens, the male and his female: and of the beasts that are not clean by two, the male and his female.

3 Of fowls also of the air by sevens, the male and the female; to keep seed alive upon the face of all the earth.

These verses repeat God's plan outlined in 6:19-20, with the additional break-down of the ratio of clean and unclean animals to be taken aboard the ark. It is noteworthy that this distinction existed long before it was included in the Law of Moses (Lev. 11). It ha long been recognized that classifying scavengers and pigs, for example, a "unclean" safe-guarded the health o God's people. This reference shows tha He was looking after their welfare ever before implementing the dietary laws o the Jews.

C. Destroying life, 4

4 For yet seven days, and I wil cause it to rain upon the earth fort days and forty nights; and every liv ing substance that I have made wil I destroy from off the face of the earth.

Although Noah has only a week t gather the animals into the ark as God instructed, 6:3 indicates that he ma have had 120 years to build the ark. Th wicked people about him who have al ready earned the judgment of God tool little notice, so the flood came as a sud den surprise (Matt. 24:37-39). Th planned destruction of life "from off th face of the earth" reminds us that sea life is apparently exempt.

III. Establishing a Covenant— 9:12-17

A. The bow in the cloud, 12-13

12 And God said, This is the to ken of the covenant which I make between me and you and every liv ing creature that is with you, fo perpetual generations:

13 I do set my bow in the cloud and it shall be for a token of a cov enant between me and the earth.

The important word "covenant" appears for the first time in 6:18, in the same context of Noah and the ark. The Hebrew word for covenant, *berith*, survives even today in the name of the Jewish men's group, "B'nai Berith" (Sons of the Covenant.)

God's covenant with Noah is the first of three great biblical covenants—the second being His covenant with Abraham (ratified through Moses in the giving of the Law), and the third the New Covenant given through Christ. Additionally, God makes covenants with others such as David regarding the perpetual kingship of his descendants; and individuals make covenants with each other such as the bond made between David and Jonathan.

The three major covenants seemed to have been patterned after treaties made by ancient Bedouins in the Arabian desert. There a great king would make a treaty with smaller tribes, promising to protect them in return for their loyalty. Typically the covenant would be ratified over a meal, a tradition reflected in the Passover in the covenant with Israel, and the Lord's Supper under the New Covenant.

Each of the three major covenants also have a "token" or sign. Here it is the rainbow; in the covenant with Abraham it is circumcision; and in the New Covenant it is usually considered to be baptism.

B. The covenant affirmed, 14-17

14 And it shall come to pass, when I bring a cloud over the earth, that the bow shall be seen in the cloud:

15 And I will remember my covenant, which is between me and you and every living creature of all flesh; and the waters shall no more become a flood to destroy all flesh.

16 And the bow shall be in the cloud; and I will look upon it, that I may remember the everlasting covenant between God and every living creature of all flesh that is upon the earth.

17 And God said unto Noah, This is the token of the covenant, which I have established between me and all flesh that is upon the earth.

Some have seen in the rainbow a promise that God has laid aside the "bow" and arrows of His wrath in allowing the waters to subside. It is more likely that it is a sign that the darkness of God's judgment in sending the flood is relieved by the contrasting brightness of the rainbow. It is this imagery of beauty, rather than the bow as a weapon, that is picked up in Revelation 4:3 and 10:1 when the glory of God's throne and the crown of His Son are described.

The symbol of the rainbow against the dark clouds has become not only a reminder that God will never again destroy the earth by water, but that times can never grow so difficult that God's people cannot find a rainbow or silver lining amid the darkness.

Evangelistic Emphasis

The ancient story of the flood portrays God as one who grieves. God grieves for the wickedness He sees on the earth, "that every inclination of the thoughts of their hearts was only evil continually" (Gen. 6:5). The Lord was sorry he made man.

Have you ever known a parent like that? The parents had such high hopes for this child of their love. It was as though the baby was welcomed with a standing ovation. But one by one their dreams were shattered. There is a grief that won't be healed, although there is a love that won't quit. There is a caring that hurts. There is a compassion that suffers.

Humankind is not changed by the flood.

The inclination of the human heart is still evil (Gen. 8:21). God is not simply resigned to evil. God must find a new way of engaging evil. God takes the route of suffering. Opening up the divine heart to the world means that God continues to grieve. God remembers Noah floating on the flood waters. More than that, God promises never again to destroy every living creature with a flood. God approaches creation with an unlimited patience and forbearance. The change in God is to a suffering love. The full meaning of that love is seen on the cross. The destruction of the flood is followed by hope of a new world. The holiness of judgment is balanced by redeeming love. The story anticipates the prophet's promise: "Fear not, for I have redeemed you; I have called you by name, you are mine. When you pass through the waters . . . they shall not overwhelm you" (Isa. 43:1-2).

● ● ● ● ● ● ●

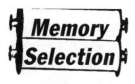

Memory Selection

And I will remember my covenant, which is between me and you and every living creature of all flesh; and the waters shall no more become a flood to destroy all flesh.—*Genesis 9:15*

The covenant made with Noah is a continuing theme of the Bible. The covenant made with Noah is with all creatures of the earth. A covenant is an agreement. It is a contract between two parties. It is a promise. God makes a covenant with Abraham, and through Moses with the Hebrews in the wilderness. Jeremiah speaks of a new covenant written on hearts. (Jer. 31:31) As Jesus shares the cup of wine with the Twelve at the last supper, he declares: "Drink from it all of you, for this is my blood of the covenant, which is poured out for many for the forgiveness of sins." (Matt. 26:27-28)

God is glimpsed in the story as One who makes a promise, "never again." God promises that never again will God give up on the human family. God's will is no longer in doubt. "If God is for us, who can be against us? Nothing can separate us from the love of God in Christ Jesus Our Lord." (Rom. 8:35,39) The rainbow is a sign to remind God of the covenant.

Weekday Problems

Martha learned she could trust the promises of God. Rev. Kelly was her high school teacher and her pastor in that small town in Virginia. When he asked Martha what he intended to do after graduation, Martha replied she would have to go to work in the nearby factory. It was what everybody did. But Rev. Kelly had seen other gifts in her. The pastor encouraged her to go to college. No one in her family had ever gone to college. No one in her small Afro-American congregation had ever gone to college. Martha said she couldn't go. She needed to get a job to help support her mother, grandmother and her little sister. There was no way she could afford college. But they agreed to pray about it.

Rev. Kelly promised her that if she decided to go, that if the Lord meant for her to go, a way would be provided. There was a singing group from that little church that traveled through several counties. Wherever they went, Pastor Kelly asked the congregation to pray for Martha that a way would be found for her to go to college. At every service of the small congregation, Wednesday night and Sunday morning , they prayed for Martha. Martha sent applications to schools across Virginia. One day she got a letter back offering a scholarship to cover tuition and a part time job to help with expenses. As they were carrying her things into the college dormitory her 80-year-old grandmother, a former slave, began to sing: "Amazing grace, how sweet the sound."

Some months later Rev. Kelly received a call from Martha. She was in tears, tears of joy. She reported: "I traveled with the drama group to Atlanta. I had a lead in the play. When it was over, the audience gave me a standing ovation."

Oh, No, Noah!

God: Noah, gather all the animals into the ark.
Noah: Oh no, now I've herd everything.

* * *

Teacher: Do you know who built the ark?
Student: No-ah, that is . . . .
Teacher: Correct.

* * *

Noah was standing at the gangplank of the ark when three camels tried to go aboard. "Wait!" he commanded. "Two is the limit. One of you will have to stay behind."

"Not me," said the first camel. "I'm the camel whose back is broken by the last straw."

"Not me," said the second. "I'm the camel people will have to swallow while straining at a gnat."

"I'm needed, too," said the third. "I'm the camel that shall pass through the eye of a needle sooner than a rich man shall enter heaven."

"I give up," said Noah. "The world is going to need all of you."

This Lesson in Your Life

"God remembered Noah" (Gen. 8:1) . . . and his little family and his menagerie floating on the waters, waiting, waiting, waiting. Then God remembered Noah.

In the popular musical "1776" George Washington sent repeated reports to the Continental Congress with pleas for supplies, equipment, troops. His pleas went unheeded. He has the feeling of being isolated, forgotten, forsaken. Washington concluded one message, "Is anybody there? Does any body care?" Noah must have felt that way, waiting day after day, night after night. Even when the rains had stopped, there were weeks when there was no land in sight. He did not know when the waters would subside. He did not know if the waters would recede. He had nothing to do but to wait and trust that God would remember him.

It is the plea of the psalmist time and again. "Remember thy congregation, which thou hast gotten of old" (Ps. 74:2). "Why has thou forgotten me?" (Ps. 42:9). "My God, my God, why has thou forsaken me?" (Ps. 22:1).

In Job's protest to the Lord, he calls upon the Lord to remember, "Thy hands fashioned and made me; and now thou dost turn about and destroy me. Remember that thou hast made me out of clay and wilt thou turn me to dust again? " (Job 10:8-9). The dying thief upon the cross has one request of Jesus: "Remember me" (Luke 23:42). "Do Lord, O do Lord, O do remember me." And God remembered Noah.

The prophet Isaiah voices the fear of the people: "But Zion said, 'The Lord has forgotten me.'" Through the prophet the Lord responds: "Can a woman forget her sucking child, that she should have no compassion on the son of her womb? Even these may forget, yet I will not forget you" (Isa. 49:14-15).

There are times when we feel ourselves adrift on flood waters. We wonder if God has just forgotten us. Events remind us that the big issues of life are not under our control. We did not will our birth and do not control our dying. We have a measure of responsibility for our health, diet, exercise, weight control and smoking. But disease is not ours to invite or to dismiss. We can do our work well with competence and even excellence and still find ourselves passed over, retired early, dismissed. Some circumstances are beyond our control. We have to live in trust that God remembers us. Our hope is that the One who created us has not forgotten us.

And God remembered Noah. It may not immediately change the circumstance, but still it helps to know that God knows. We are not lost out here among the stars, set adrift, forgotten, heading toward sheer nothingness. God remembered Noah.

Centuries later Peter, who had been nourished on these stories from Genesis, sees in Noah's experience of the flood a pre-figuring of baptism. As Noah came through the flood waters to make a new beginning, so the Christian goes through the flood waters of baptism to be purified and cleansed. "And I cannot help pointing out what a perfect illustration this is of the way you have been admitted to the safety of the Christian 'ark' by baptism, which means , of course, far more than the mere washing of a dirty body; it means the ability to face God with a clear conscience" (1 Pet. 3: 21, *Phillips*).

Seed Thoughts

1. What kind of person was Noah?
He was righteous, blameless and he walked with God (Gen. 6:9).

2. Who were the sons of Noah?
Shem, Ham, and Japheth (Gen. 6:10, 9:19).

3. How big was the ark?
The ark was 450 feet long, 75 feet wide, 435 feet tall (Gen. 6:15).

4. Why did the Lord regret having made human kind?
The Lord saw the wickedness of humankind was great in the earth, and that every inclination of the thoughts of their hearts was only evil continually (Gen. 6:5).

5. How long did it rain?
It rained forty days and forty nights (Gen. 7:4; 7:11; 7:17).

---

1. What kind of person was Noah?

2. Who were the sons of Noah?

3. How big was the ark?

4. Why did the Lord regret having made human kind?

5. How long did it rain?

6. How old was Noah when the flood waters came on earth?

7. What did the dove bring back in its beak the second time Noah sent it out?

8. What was the significance of the olive leaf brought back to Noah by the dove?

9. How old was Noah when he died?

10. What is the significance of the rainbow?

(Continued next page)

He was righteous, blameless and he walked with God (Gen. 6:9).

Shem, Ham, and Japheth (Gen. 6:10, 9:19).

6. How old was Noah when the flood waters came on earth?

He was 600 years old (Gen. 7:6; 7:11)

The ark was 450 feet long, 75 feet wide, 435 feet tall (Gen. 6:15).

7. What did the dove bring back in its beak the second time Noah sent it out?

The dove brought back a fresh olive leaf (Gen. 8:11).

The Lord saw the wickedness of humankind was great in the earth, and that every inclination of the thoughts of their hearts was only evil continually (Gen. 6:5).

It rained forty days and forty nights (Gen. 7:4; 7:11; 7:17).

8. What was the significance of the olive leaf brought back to Noah by the dove?

Noah knew by the olive leaf that the waters had subsided from the earth (Gen. 8:11).

He was 600 years old (Gen. 7:6; 7:11).

The dove brought back a fresh olive leaf (Gen. 8:11).

9. How old was Noah when he died?

Noah was 950 years old when he died (Gen. 9:28).

Noah knew by the olive leaf that the waters had subsided from the earth (Gen. 8:11).

10. What is the significance of the rainbow?

It is a reminder of the covenant made between God and the earth (Gen. 9:13).

Noah was 950 years old when he died (Gen. 9:28).

It is a reminder of the covenant made between God and the earth. (Gen. 9:13)

Lesson 5

God's Call to Abram

*A*nd Terah took Abram his son, and Lot the son of Haran his son's son, and Sarai his daughter in law, his son Abram's wife; and they went forth with them from Ur of the Chaldees, to go into the land of Canaan; and they came unto Haran, and dwelt there.

32 And the days of Terah were two hundred and five years: and Terah died in Haran.

12:1 Now the Lord had said unto Abram, Get thee out of thy country, and from thy kindred, and from thy father's house, unto a land that I will shew thee:

2 And I will make of thee a great nation, and I will bless thee, and make thy name great; and thou shalt be a blessing:

3 And I will bless them that bless thee, and curse him that curseth thee: and in thee shall all families of the earth be blessed.

4 So Abram departed, as the Lord had spoken unto him; and Lot went with him: and Abram was seventy and five years old when he departed out of Haran.

5 And Abram took Sarai his wife, and Lot his brother's son, and all their substance that they had gathered, and the souls that they had gotten in Haran; and they went forth to go into the land of Canaan; and into the land of Canaan they came.

6 And Abram passed through the land unto the place of Sichem, unto the plain of Moreh. And the Canaanite was then in the land.

7 And the Lord appeared unto Abram, and said, Unto thy seed will I give this land: and there builded he an altar unto the Lord, who appeared unto him.

8 And he removed from thence unto a mountain on the east of Bethel, and pitched his tent, having Bethel on the west, and Hai on the east: and there he builded an altar unto the Lord, and called upon the name of the Lord.

9 And Abram journeyed, going on still toward the south.

Genesis 11:31–12:9

July 4

Memory Selection
Genesis 12:1-2

Background Scripture
Genesis 11:27–12:9

Devotional Reading
Hebrews 11:8-12

Printed Scripture
Genesis 11:31–12:9

Teacher's Target

Lesson purpose: *To trace the beginnings of "the people of God" with "Father Abraham," emphasizing the importance of faith like his.*

The Old Testament portrays a strong sense of family that is missing in many modern societies. Of course God also dealt individually with people such as Adam and Eve, Cain and Noah, and, here, Abram (whose name will later be changed to Abraham). Yet in all these instances there are important implications for the families of these "main characters."

This emphasis becomes especially clear in this lesson, as Abram's famous pilgrimage of faith involves his entire family. Here are the roots of the biblical emphasis on "the people of God." In presenting the lesson, note that people today—including singles—have their own family of faith, consisting of people who, like Abraham, have faith in God.

It will also be helpful to use a Bible map to trace Abram's travels from Ur to Haran and Canaan.

Lesson Introduction

This lesson opens an important new chapter in "salvation history" or "the scheme of redemption." The first 11 chapters of Genesis do not portray the family of man making impressive moral progress. Instead of sending another flood, however, God now singles out a particular family through whom to offer His grace to the whole world.

In choosing Abraham and His descendants, God intends to mold for Himself a people to uphold the lofty ideal that there is one God, and that He expects people's lives to reflect His goodness. Through this family He will give the Law, through Moses. Long years later, it will also be through this people that He will send the Messiah. Little did Abraham know, when he was first called, the full meaning of God's promise that "in thee shall all families of the earth be blessed" (12:3).

Teaching Outline	Daily Bible Readings
I. People of the Promise—11:31-32	**Mon.** Settling in Ur *Genesis 11:27-32*
II. Promise of Nationhood—12:1-3	**Tue.** God Calls Abram *Genesis 12:1-9*
A. Called to a pilgrimage, 1	**Wed.** Abram's History Recalled *Acts 7:1-8*
B. Called to be a blessing, 2-3	**Thu.** God Calls Samuel *1 Samuel 3:1-10*
III. Pilgrimage to Canaan—4-6	**Fri.** God Calls Amos *Amos 7:10-15*
IV. Promise Renewed—7-9	**Sat.** God Calls Saul *Acts 9:1-9*
A. The seed promise, 7a	**Sun.** Jesus Calls Disciples *Mark 1:16-20*
B. Worshiping the Promiser, 7b-9	

432

Verse by Verse

I. People of the Promise—11:31-32

31 And Terah took Abram his son, and Lot the son of Haran his son's son, and Sarai his daughter in law, his son Abram's wife; and they went forth with them from Ur of the Chaldees, to go into the land of Canaan; and they came unto Haran, and dwelt there.

32 And the days of Terah were two hundred and five years: and Terah died in Haran.

The story of the call of Abram begins with his lineage. The writer is careful to trace Abram's family tree back to Noah (see 11:10ff.), which of course also connects him to Adam. Remembering that the word "adam" also means "mankind," we are to understand that any saving grace extended to Abram has the potential of affecting the whole world—which is exactly what God will promise. Thus it is highly appropriate when Abram's name is changed to Abraham, which means "the father of many" (Gen. 17:5). To this day, he is revered by Jews, Christians and Muslims alike.

Abram's father Terah begins the pilgrimage from his home in "Ur of the Chaldees" —in an area with such ancient evidence of human dwellings that it has been called "the cradle of civili-

zation." Archeologists have discovered that Ur, located in what is now southeastern Iraq, had been an advanced, thriving metropolis some 500 years before Abram's day (about 2,000 B.C.). It was a center of worship for the moon god (Nannur), and, as Joshua 24:2 notes, Abram had taken part in such pagan worship. Perhaps God chooses him to learn the truth about the one God Yahweh because, in His sovereignty, He can see unique potential for Abram's rising above his idolatrous background.

Instead of going directly to Canaan, Terah and his family go far to the northwest, to Haran, an area which was roughly connected to Ur by the long Euphrates River. Haran may have been Terah's original home since one of his sons bore the same name. We may speculate that the family stopped for some time there on the way to Canaan because Terah was getting old, and wanted to die in his homeland.

II. Promise of Nationhood—12:1-3

A. Called to a pilgrimage, 1

1 Now the LORD had said unto Abram, Get thee out of thy country, and from thy kindred, and from thy father's house, unto a land that I will shew thee:

Apparently Abram had received the

call to go to Canaan while still at Ur (see also Acts 7:2-4), and Haran was merely a detour on the way. We can only imagine the towering faith it took for Abram to turn from many gods to the One God he could not see and to leave his homeland at the true God's command. He is appropriately included in the New Testament's famous list of giants of faith, as one who "went out, not knowing whither he went" (Heb. 11:8).

The promise of a land seems to have been an essential part of God's plan to provide His chosen people a place to live under His rule, separate from surrounding pagan nations. This promise is basic to the landmark covenant God makes with Abram (although it is not explicitly called a "covenant" until 15:18). Like other covenants of the day, the arrangement consists of both a promise and a duty. Abram's duty is to leave his present homeland and to journey to the land God promises will be his.

B. Called to be a blessing, 2-3

2 And I will make of thee a great nation, and I will bless thee, and make thy name great; and thou shalt be a blessing:

3 And I will bless them that bless thee, and curse him that curseth thee: and in thee shall all families of the earth be blessed.

The repetition of the words "bless" and "blessing" shows that God is choosing Abram for the benefit of other peoples, not merely to become a spe-

cially favored nation in God's eyes. Although Abram's descendants, the Israelites, will often falter in this calling, God intends for them to model what it is like for a people to live under His rule. For this reason, God promises that people who bless this chosen race will be blessed, while those who curse them will be cursed.

Many years later the apostle Paul said that this blessing consists of believing in Christ as the Messiah, just as Abraham believed in God (Gal. 3:6-9).

III. Pilgrimage to Canaan—4-6

4 So Abram departed, as the Lord had spoken unto him; and Lot went with him: and Abram was seventy and five years old when he departed out of Haran.

5 And Abram took Sarai his wife, and Lot his brother's son, and all their substance that they had gathered, and the souls that they had gotten in Haran; and they went forth to go into the land of Canaan; and into the land of Canaan they came.

6 And Abram passed through the land unto the place of Sichem, unto the plain of Moreh. And the Canaanite was then in the land.

Both Lot and Sarai (whose name was later changed to Sarah, Gen. 17:15) will later become important in the story of Abram. Sarai was apparently Abram's half-sister (Gen. 20:12); and archeological discoveries have shown that this kind of marriage was not unusual. Lot,

Abram's nephew, will separate from his uncle over a quarrel about pasturage, and wind up living in the infamous city of Sodom.

The "substance" Abram had accumulated in Haran no doubt included large herds and flocks. The "souls" (an Old Testament word for "persons") consisted of slaves he inherited when his father Terah died, herdsmen to care for his large flocks and herds, along with their families, and what was apparently a small army (14:14). The picture is of a significant migration of an entire nomadic clan to Canaan, which lay to the southwest of Haran.

The immigrant family arrives at Sichem (elsewhere "Shechem"), an important center of worship and trade in a strategic spot (about 40 miles north of Jerusalem) to control a fertile valley to the east where Abram no doubt stopped to graze his flocks and herds. This important city would later be the site where the Israelite general Joshua renews the very covenant Abram had received from God (Josh. 24).

IV. Promise Renewed—7-9
A. The seed promise, 7a

7a And the LORD appeared unto Abram, and said, Unto thy seed will I give this land:

Another monument to Abram's faith is the fact that he relied on God's promise that his "seed" or descendants—not Abram himself—would inherit the land. As we shall see, Abram merely "sojourned" in Canaan, then headed south,

and eventually wound up in Egypt to escape a famine (12:10). Although he later returned to Canaan (13:1), it would be left to his seed, the twelve tribes of Israel, to settle there. Abram is thus among those who "died in faith, not having received the promises, but having seen them afar off, and were persuaded of them" (Heb. 11:13).

B. Worshiping the Promiser, 7b-9

7b and there builded he an altar unto the LORD, who appeared unto him.

8 And he removed from thence unto a mountain on the east of Bethel, and pitched his tent, having Bethel on the west, and Hai on the east: and there he builded an altar unto the LORD, and called upon the name of the LORD.

9 And Abram journeyed, going on still toward the south.

Now Abram begins to model the new faith to which he has been called by building altars and, presumably, offering sacrifices upon them to this mysterious, invisible God who is leading him on such a fantastic journey. Although both Shechem and Bethel were already well-established centers of pagan worship, Abram boldly establishes Yahweh worship there. Like the early Spanish explorers who knelt on the shores of the new world, Abram, as it were, is raising a flag claiming the land for the God who promised it to his descendants, and who alone is worthy of worship.

Evangelistic Emphasis

Abram is called, chosen for a special task. As the story unfolds in Genesis chapters 12–25 it is plain that Abram is no paragon of virtue. He is even willing to pass his wife, Sarai, off as his sister, offering her body for the pleasures of the Pharaoh of Egypt to save his own neck (Gen. 12:-20. He is chosen to play a part in God's redemptive plan because of God's grace, not because of his own merit. We are saved not because of any good work but through the grace of God.

In one sense with the story of Abraham we seem to move from the world stage, creation and the first human family (Genesis 1–11), to a particular place, and family and person. Yet from the start it is clear that the calling of Abraham, and the promise of descendants, land and fame are for a wider purpose: "In you all the families of the earth shall be blessed" (Gen. 9:3)."

It was often forgotten by Israel that her being chosen was for the sake of a wider mission "to be a light to the nations, that my salvation may reach to the end of the earth" (Isa. 49:6). Likewise, the mission of the Church is sometimes forgotten in our zeal to build more beautiful buildings, develop more efficient organizations and instigate programs to nurture each other. As worthwhile as these endeavors may be, we cease to be the Church if we cease to make disciples of Jesus Christ. The Church exists for mission as a fire exists for burning. If we lose that mission, we may be a cozy social club, a helpful service agency, a respected museum of art and history but we are not the Church that God sends to all the families of the earth.

• • • • •

Memory Selection

Now the Lord had said unto Abram, Get thee out of thy country, and from thy kindred, and from thy father's house, unto a land that I will shew thee: And I will make of thee a great nation, and I will bless thee, and make thy name great; and thou shalt be a blessing.—*Genesis 12:1-2.*

Incredible! If I had been there, I'd have asked for a little more information. Just where is it you want me to go, Lord? I'd like to get a few maps. Maybe I should check it out before I move, then come back for the family and the furniture. I don't know what the job opportunities are. I don't know what the climate is like. I don't know what language they speak. I don't even know where you want me to go. At my age it's a little late to be starting all over in a strange land."

But Abram went as the Lord told him. Abram had to leave everything that was important to him. The land was viewed as sacred. It was passed on from generation to generation. Even more important to Abram was the family, the clan. Identity, meaning and security were bound up with that larger family. Abram was called to leave everything that was familiar and dear. He was to leave everything and take his family into another land, trusting only the promise of God.

Weekday Problems

Davis was in his late 30s, married, and had four children, a good job and a house mortgage. He made a good living selling sports equipment to schools. He served a small congregation on the weekend. For some years he had been struggling with a call to go into pastoral ministry full time. His denomination would expect him to finish college and go to seminary for three years.

He had been out of school so long he didn't know if he could do graduate work. He didn't know what part-time work he might find. He didn't know if his wife could find a teaching position in another state, and he agonized over whether to leave his mother, who was dying. Even if he finished seminary he didn't know to what church he might be sent.

Many pastors in his denomination worked full-time and received considerably less than he was now earning. He could barely make his mortgage payments now. Could he afford to live on a pastor's salary? Yet his greatest joy came from his weekend work with his small church, which was growing under his leadership. Should he should wait until he had some savings built up? Perhaps he should wait until he retired and had his pension and social security to fall back on. Perhaps he should wait until his ailing mother died.

* What advice would you give Davis?

* If you were he, what would you do?

Psalms of Faith and Pilgrimage

The faith of the head is the faith that is dead;
   The faith of the heart is better in part.
But the faith of the hand is the faith that will stand.
    For the faith that will do must include the first two.
                —Anonymous

* * *

Is not one's life itself an act of daring,
   A voyage of hazards, without chart or lee;
A risk of tempest, vanquishing or sparing
   Our precious argosy?
                —Francis Greenwood Peabody

* * *

So I go on, not knowing,
   —I would not, if I might—
I would rather walk in the dark with God
   Than go alone in the light;
I would rather walk with Him by faith
   Than walk alone by sight.
                —Mary Gardner Brainard

This Lesson in Your Life

To us the call comes to leave the familiar and secure, to journey by faith into a new land, trusting only in God's promises. There is a risk in leaving the familiar and secure. But there is a greater risk in living only by our fears. The choice is to live by our fears or by our faith. The one way seems to promise safety and security. In reality that safe way is the way to slow death, a life without purpose.

In varied ways God's call comes to launch out, to journey in faith, to go to a new country. For some it means college, for others it 's marriage, or starting a family, leaving home, making a career change, taking on a new responsibility, standing up for an abused person or getting involved in an unpopular cause.

When we choose the safe, the comfortable, the secure route we may forfeit a much greater joy. Jesus declares: "For those who want to save their life will lose it, and those who lose their life for my sake , and for the sake of the gospel, will save it " (Mark 8:35).

Flo McCarthy shares a fable about a swan who found and hatched three eggs.* The first was an eagle, the second a dove and the third a sparrow. When they were ready to fly the swan took them on the cliff of a high mountain. She told them she would have to leave for a while. But she would return and take them on a wonderful trip. While she was away, they must learn to fly. "There's nothing to it. This is all you have to do." With that she spread her wings, threw herself into space and soared off gracefully over the mountains. They stood there for a long time, peering over the edge into empty space.

The eagle was the first to take the plunge. He spread his wings and threw himself out over the void. At first he seemed to be falling but then gained control. He flew around in circles, then rejoined them. "There's really nothing to it," he said, and he flew off again.

Soon the dove took the plunge. She returned shortly and echoed what the eagle had said. Soon the eagle and the dove were flying freely. But the little sparrow refused to take the plunge. She clung stubbornly to the ledge. She had discovered a patch of soil rich in worms. She was growing fatter with each day that passed. The fatter she got the lazier she got. The lazier she got the less the idea of flying appealed to her.

Then one day the swan returned. "Are you ready to come with me?" she asked.

"Yes !" cried the eagle.

"Yes!" cried the dove.

"I can't," said the sparrow. I never learned to fly."

"What?" exclaimed the swan. You never learned to fly? You neglected the one thing that makes a bird a bird."

So off they flew the swan, the eagle and the dove. The sparrow looked at his two comrades. "Are you not coming home again?" it called.

"We're *going* home," they replied. The sparrow watched them as they flew away, growing smaller and smaller in the sky. Then he knew real loneliness with no company but the worms. The one who had never left home now had no home to go to.

To live by faith is to shape our existence on the basis of the promises of God. "By faith Abraham obeyed when he was called to go out to a place which he was to receive as an inheritance; and he went out, not knowing where he was to go" (Heb. 11:8).

---

*Adapted from *And the Master Answered*, pp. 127-132.

Seed Thoughts

1. What did the Lord promise Abram?
God promised to make of Abram a great nation, to bless him and to make his name great so he would be a blessing (Gen. 12:1-2).

2. How old was Abram when he left Haran?
Abram was 75 years old (Gen. 12:4).

3. Who did Abram take with him?
He took his wife Sarai and his brother's son Lot. (Gen. 12:5)

4. Who was Abram's father?
Terah was the father of Abram (Gen. 11:26, 31).

5. Abram's father Terah moved with his family from what place to what place?
Terah went from Ur of the Chaldeans and settled in Haran (Gen 11: 31).

---

1. What did the Lord promise Abram?

2. How old was Abram when he left Haran?

3. Who did Abram take with him?

4. Who was Abram's father?

5. Abram's father Terah moved with his family from what place to what place?

6. Where did Abram settle?

7. At the time of God's promise to Abram to make of him a great nation, how many children did he have?

8. Where did Abram build the first altar to the Lord?

9. Where did Abram build the second altar to the Lord?

10. Toward what region was Abram traveling?

(Continued next page)

God promised to make of Abram a great nation, to bless him and to make his name great so he would be a blessing (Gen. 12:1-2).

Abram was 75 years old (Gen. 12:4).

He took his wife Sarai and his brother's son Lot (Gen. 12:5).

Terah was the father of Abram (Gen. 11:26, 31).

Terah went from Ur of the Chaldeans and settled in Haran (Gen 11: 31).

He set forth to go to the land of Caanan (Gen. 12:5).

None.

Shechem.

Between Bethel on the west and Ai on the east (Gen. 12:8).

Abram journeyed on by stages toward the Negeb (Gen. 12:9).

6. Where did Abram settle?
He set forth to go to the land of Caanan (Gen. 12:5).

7. At the time of God's promise to Abram to make of him a great nation, how many children did he have?
None.

8. Where did Abram build the first altar to the Lord?
Shechem..

9. Where did Abram build the second altar to the Lord?
Between Bethel on the west and Ai on the east (Gen. 12:8).

10. Toward what region was Abram traveling?
Abram journeyed on by stages toward the Negeb (Gen. 12:9).

A Promise Fulfilled

*A*fter these things the word of the LORD came unto Abram in a vision, saying, Fear not, Abram: I am thy shield, and thy exceeding great reward.

2 And Abram said, Lord GOD, what wilt thou give me, seeing I go childless, and the steward of my house is this Eliezer of Damascus?

3 And Abram said, Behold, to me thou hast given no seed: and, lo, one born in my house is mine heir.

4 And, behold, the word of the LORD came unto him, saying, This shall not be thine heir; but he that shall come forth out of thine own bowels shall be thine heir.

5 And he brought him forth abroad, and said, Look now toward heaven, and tell the stars, if thou be able to number them: and he said unto him, So shall thy seed be.

6 And he believed in the LORD; and he counted it to him for righteousness.

17:17 Then Abraham fell upon his face, and laughed, and said in his heart, Shall a child be born unto him that is an hundred years old? and shall Sarah, that is ninety years old, bear?

18 And Abraham said unto God, O that Ishmael might live before thee!

19 And God said, Sarah thy wife shall bear thee a son indeed; and thou shalt call his name Isaac: and I will establish my covenant with him for an everlasting covenant, and with his seed after him.

20 And as for Ishmael, I have heard thee: Behold, I have blessed him, and will make him fruitful, and will multiply him exceedingly; twelve princes shall he beget, and I will make him a great nation.

21 But my covenant will I establish with Isaac, which Sarah shall bear unto thee at this set time in the next year.

21:1 And the LORD visited Sarah as he had said, and the LORD did unto Sarah as he had spoken.

2 For Sarah conceived and bare Abraham a son in his old age, at the set time of which God had spoken to him.

Genesis 15:1-6; 17:17-21; 21:1-2

Memory Selection
Genesis 17:19

Background Scripture
Genesis 15:1–18:15; 21:1-7

Devotional Reading
Deuteronomy 7:7-11

Printed Scripture
Genesis 15:1-6; 17:17-21; 21:1-2

Teacher's Target

Lesson purpose: *To reaffirm, through the story of the birth of Isaac, our faith in the reliability of God's promises.*

This familiar story shows God to be greater than our greatest need. The lesson can be effectively introduced by asking the group to share moments when they themselves have experienced light amid darkness, or had "impossible" prayers answered.

Care should be taken to hear out those who have other kinds of stories to share—unanswered prayers, disappointments, dead ends, times when God was silent. Accept such experiences in the same light as the very human doubt expressed by Abraham and Sarah. Yet reaffirm the biblical truth that God's sovereign will isn't always worked out in this life; and reinforce the basis for optimism and faith in His promises that is laid by this account of the giving of "the son of promise."

Lesson Introduction

This account poses two great forces against each other: *nature* and *grace*. Since Abraham and Sarah were past the *natural* time to bear children they questioned whether God's covenant promise would be fulfilled. They learned that God's *grace* can overwhelm such natural barriers.

This confrontation becomes a pattern that is repeated throughout Scripture. The nature of Israel as a small nation made it doubtful they could conquer Canaan; but God's grace enabled them to do so. The natural cycle of birth and death was interrupted by grace in the resurrection of Christ. Our natural but inadequate tendency to atone for sin by works is overcome by God's grace in giving His Son.

Nature is not evil, since God pronounced the natural world "very good." However, in Adam nature "fell"; and it is now simply inadequate to fulfill all our needs, hopes and dreams. Not to fear, however: "the grace of God that bringeth salvation hath appeared unto all men" (Tit. 2:11).

Teaching Outline	Daily Bible Readings
I. Faith Amid Doubt—15:1-6	**Mon.** An Heir from His Body *Genesis 15:1-6*
A. A natural barrier, 1-3	**Tue.** The Covenant with Abram *Genesis 15:12-20*
B. A supernatural promise, 4-6	**Wed.** Hagar Bears a Son *Genesis 16:1-6*
II. Faltering Faith—17:17-21	**Thu.** Your Name Is Abraham *Genesis 17:1-4*
A. A natural alternative?, 17-18	**Fri.** Sarah Shall Be Her Name *Genesis 17:15-27*
B. A reaffirmed promise, 19-21	**Sat.** Sarah Laughs to Herself *Genesis 18:1-15*
III. Fulfillment of the Promise—21:1-2	**Sun.** Sarah Bears a Son *Genesis 21:1-8*

Verse by Verse

I. Faith Amid Doubt—15:1-6

A. A natural barrier, 1-3

1 After these things the word of the Lord came unto Abram in a vision, saying, Fear not, Abram: I am thy shield, and thy exceeding great reward.

2 And Abram said, Lord God, what wilt thou give me, seeing I go childless, and the steward of my house is this Eliezer of Damascus?

3 And Abram said, Behold, to me thou hast given no seed: and, lo, one born in my house is mine heir.

"After these things" may refer to the several events that have occurred since God called Abram to go into Canaan, and promised to make of him a great nation. He sojourned briefly in Egypt during a famine (12:10-20). He and his nephew Lot parted ways, resulting in Lot's disastrous choice to live in Sodom, and Abram's rescue when foreign kings overran Sodom and Gomorrah (13–14). Abram received a blessing from the mysterious Melchizedek, king of Salem (later Jerusalem; 14:18-20). Now the story returns to a crucial issue: although God had promised to make of Abram a great nation, he remains childless.

God's reassurance that He is Abram's divine "shield" and "reward" was especially timely after the warfare described in chapter 14. Abram, however, is more concerned to know how he can become the "father of many nations" without having a son. Perhaps, he suggests, God can use Abram's chief servant, Eliezer. Archeologists have confirmed that it was common for tribal chieftains of other cultures of the day to adopt foreign slaves as their children when they had none of their own.

The NIV solves the difficulty of Eliezer being both "of Damascus" and "born in my house" by translating the latter phrase, "a servant in my household." Perhaps Eliezer joined the clan when they trooped by Damascus on the way from Haran to Canaan.

B. A supernatural promise, 4-6

4 And, behold, the word of the Lord came unto him, saying, This shall not be thine heir; but he that shall come forth out of thine own bowels shall be thine heir.

5 And he brought him forth abroad, and said, Look now toward heaven, and tell the stars, if thou be able to number them: and he said unto him, So shall thy seed be.

6 And he believed in the Lord; and he counted it to him for righteousness.

Just as in the case to be considered in the section to follow, God has supernatural plans instead of following Abram's suggestion. His heir will not be Eliezer, but will come from Abram's own body (which the NIV renders "bowels"). Then, as a powerful illustration of the divine plan, God shows Abram that from this heir the clan will grow as numerous as the stars. Later, the apostle Paul will qualify the promise by warning that only believers in Christ compose Abram's true descendants (Rom. 9:6-9; see also Jesus' statement in John 8:37-42).

The simple line in verse 6 affirming Abraham's faith, following so closely on the heels of his questions, will become an important part of New Covenant teaching. It is quoted twice by Paul (Rom. 4:3; Gal. 3:6), to show that the principle of salvation by faith instead of law-keeping or works originated with Abraham and thus takes precedent over the Law of Moses, which came centuries later.

II. Faltering Faith—17:17-21

A. A natural alternative?, 17-18

17 Then Abraham fell upon his face, and laughed, and said in his heart, Shall a child be born unto him that is an hundred years old? and shall Sarah, that is ninety years old, bear?

18 And Abraham said unto God, O that Ishmael might live before thee!

The scene has changed from the time Abraham asked God if his servant Eliezer might be the promised heir. At the suggestion of his wife Sarai, Abram has taken Sarai's servant Hagar as a concubine. Unlike Sarai, Hagar becomes pregnant immediately and bears Abram's first son, who is named Ishmael.

Now, with Abram's name changed to Abraham and Sarai's to Sarah, God renews the promise of peoplehood. Since Abraham has gone to such lengths in taking Hagar for a concubine, he is perhaps surprised when God affirms that the promise will be fulfilled through Sarah (17:16). With Sarah age 90 and Abraham 100, the patriarch finds God's persistent choice of Sarah so outlandish that he laughs. (Later [18:12], Sarah will also laugh at the "preposterous" suggestion that she and old Abraham were young enough to have a child.)

Instead of God's going to the supernatural length of resetting his and Sarah's aging biological clocks, Abram thinks he has a better idea. Why not fulfill the promise through Ishmael, Hagar's son, causing him to "live" in the sense of perpetuating the tribe and the covenant? (As a matter of fact, the Koran, the "Bible" of Islam, holds that Ishmael, rather than Isaac, was the child of promise and the ancestor of Abraham's "true" followers, the Muslims. The Koran also holds that it was Ishmael whom Abraham almost sacrificed in the test God administered in Genesis 22.)

B. A reaffirmed promise, 19-21

19 And God said, Sarah thy wife shall bear thee a son indeed; and thou shalt call his name Isaac: and I will establish my covenant with him for an everlasting covenant, and with his seed after him.

Insisting that the child of promise will come through Sarah, not Hagar, God goes so far as to name the unborn child. "Isaac" means "laughter," for, as Sarah will exclaim when the child is finally born, "God hath made me to laugh" (21:6).

Three major ways of interpreting the term "everlasting covenant" have been suggested. (1) "Everlasting" is to be taken at face value, meaning that God's covenant with Abraham's seed is still valid. This interpretation is held by Zionists and others who believe the Jews as a race still have a claim on the land of Israel. (2) "Everlasting" (Heb. *'olam*) means "until the end of the age" here, as it does in Leviticus 16:34, not eternal, meaning that the covenant expired when a majority of the Israelites broke God's covenant (as Isaiah charged in Isa. 24:5, or in the rejection of Jesus as Messiah). (3) The covenant has been "spiritualized," meaning that the covenant with Abraham was transferred to spiritual Israel (Christians), who inherit a spiritual kingdom instead of the land of Canaan.

20 And as for Ishmael, I have heard thee: Behold, I have blessed him, and will make him fruitful, and will multiply him exceedingly;

twelve princes shall he beget, and I will make him a great nation.

21 But my covenant will I establish with Isaac, which Sarah shall bear unto thee at this set time in the next year.

Although God insists that His covenant will be fulfilled through Isaac, He does not turn his back on Ishmael. Indeed, He had required that the lad be named Ishmael because it means "God shall hear"—implying that God will hear his and his mother's appeal for help. This God provides when the two are driven from Abraham's camp (21:9-21). The "twelve princes" predicted here (listed in 25:13-15) established themselves in the Arabian peninsula.

III. Fulfillment of the Promise—21:1-2

1 And the LORD visited Sarah as he had said, and the LORD did unto Sarah as he had spoken.

2 For Sarah conceived and bare Abraham a son in his old age, at the set time of which God had spoken to him.

True to His promise, God blesses Abraham and Sarah with a son, Isaac, in their old age. In doing so, He affirms His miraculous power to bless and guide His people as He wills, not being limited to the natural "helps" concocted by Abraham and Sarah. The second of the three primary patriarchs of the Jewish nation, Isaac will be succeeded by his son Jacob in the line that produces the 12 tribes of Israel.

Evangelistic Emphasis

Abraham "believed the Lord; and the Lord reckoned it to him as righteousness" (Gen. 15:6). We are justified by faith. Paul recalls this story in his letter to the Romans as he reminds the church there that it is through trust in God's promises that Abraham is counted as righteous. Hoping against hope, Abraham believed he would become the father of many nations. He did not weaken in faith when he considered his own body, which was already as good as dead or when he considered the barrenness of Sarah's womb. No distrust made him waver concerning the promise of God. He was fully convinced that God was able to do what God had promised. Therefore his faith was reckoned to him as righteousness (Rom. 4: 1-24).

Our salvation does not depend on being good enough. We cannot do enough good deeds to earn everlasting life as a reward. We cannot fulfill the demands of the law, especially the radical demands of the law as interpreted by Jesus. We cannot by our own will and decision love others as we are loved by God. The good news is that being right with God, being accepted as God's child, being reconciled to God, being made whole, being forgiven, does not depend on works of human righteousness. What is asked is trust, a full reliance upon the promise of God. It was this belief that God would do what God has promised that was counted to Abraham as righteousness. This is our hope and joy. This is the good news that we share. "For by grace you have been saved through faith. It is the gift of God" (Gal. 2:8).

Memory Selection

And God said, Sarah thy wife shall bear thee a son indeed; and thou shalt call his name Isaac: and I will establish my covenant with him for an everlasting covenant, and with his seed after him.— *Genesis 17:19.*

The promise of God was all that Abraham had to go on. It was this promise that led him from his father's land into a new and unknown country. It was a promise he sometimes doubted. He and his wife Sarah were so old that at one point Abraham laughed to himself at the thought of becoming parents at their age. He sometimes thought to take matters into his own hands. He thought of adopting his servant Eliezer's son as his own son in order to have an heir. At Sarah's suggestion he had a child by her slave, Hagar. But Ishmael, Hagar's son is not the promised heir.

Abraham struggled to trust the promise of the Lord: The promise is clear. " Sarah thy wife shall bear thee a son indeed." (Gen. 17:19). Paul comments: "Hoping against hope, he believed that he would become the father of many nations. He did not weaken in faith when he considered his own body, which was already as good as dead . . . No distrust made him waver concerning the promise of God . . . being fully convinced that God was able to do what He had promised" (Rom. 4: 18-21).

Weekend Problems

A small group gathered at the church. One of them had been reading about the plight of refugees from Laos. The refugees were crowded into camps. They lived in tents, lined up for food once a day. There was little to do all day. Because of the war there was no chance of ever returning home. Their only hope for a new life was that a family or a church in America would sponsor them. This small group at church decided to ask their church to be a sponsor.

There was great excitement the day the family arrived. An apartment was rented, furniture was gathered, the pantry was filled. The church helped provide transportation for medical care, English classes and job interviews.

In extending a warm welcome to the Laotian family the church itself was blessed. It helped the church to break out of its narrow concerns for its building and its members. They gained a sense of being part of global family. The misfortune of this family displaced by war reminded church families of their blessing. They realized they were blessed to be a blessing.

Long ago Abraham and Sarah had welcomed strangers into their home (Gen. 18:1-15), only to discover they had "entertained angels without knowing it" (Heb. 13:2). So when we show hospitality to strangers, we find Jesus' words fulfilled: "I was a stranger and you welcomed me. Inasmuch as you did it to one of the least of these who are members of my family you did it to me" (Matt. 25:35, 40).

More Q's and A's

Q: What do you call two fat men having a chat?
A: A heavy discussion.

Q: What lies on the ground 100 feet in the air?
A: A centipede trying for a suntanned tummy.

Q: How did Moses part the Red Sea?
A: With a sea saw, of course.

Q: Why did the priest giggle?
A: Mass hysteria, I guess.

Q: What do you call great bodies of water filled with grape juice?
A: The Grape Lakes.

Q: What ballet do squirrels like best?
A: The Nutcracker.

Q: What's a pig's favorite ballet?
A: Swine Lake.

This Lesson in Your Life

Laughter is a theme that runs through the story of Abraham, Sarah and Isaac. It is the laughter of disbelief. When Sarah and Abraham are told that in their old age they are finally to have a child, it sounds too good to be true. It's a disbelief with hope "You gotta be kidding!" The Bible is full of such disbelief at incredible good news, promises too good to be true. The Red Sea parts and the Hebrew runaway slaves march through. The Lord provides manna everyday. Joshua leads the troops of Israel around the walled city of Jericho every day for seven days, and the walls come tumbling down. The women on Easter morning run from the tomb to tell the disciples what they have seen and heard. But their report seemed to the disciples as an idle tale.

We know this kind of laughter, the laughter of disbelief. The dreamers speak of a day when wars will be no more, and the lion and the lamb shall lie down together. We laugh in disbelief. The dreamers tell of a day when there shall be enough to eat for all of God's children. No way, we say. The skeptics laugh, saying it will never be.

But the day comes when there is another kind of laughter. It is a laughter of joy, delight, incredible wonder. It was Sarah's laughter when despite all reasonable calculations she held that baby in her arms. It was the laughter of the man born blind, who through Jesus came to see. It was the laughter of Mary Magdalene when in the garden she recognized her risen Lord. It is the laughter of a mother who holds her newborn child. It is the laughter of a people who celebrate the ending of a war. It is the joy when people long separated by race discover they are one in Christ. It is the joy of persons who have long cherished resentments and bitterness find reconciliation as they break bread together at the Lord's table. James Harnish puts it : "It is the laughter that wells up within us when we discover that we are loved not because we have earned it or deserve it but simply because we are children of God."

"Is anything too hard for God?" (Gen. 18:14). It is the question the Lord puts to Abraham, in response to the laughter of disbelief at news too good to believe. It is the question asked of Abraham to refute the the old couple's hopelessness. Yet it is not a proclamation but a question. A decision each of us must answer, as Sarah and Abraham must answer. How it is answered determines everything else. Walter Bruggemann observes that if the question of the Lord is answered Yes, some things are too hard, impossible for God," then God is something less than God. If it is answered "No, nothing is impossible for God," then God is free to exercise God's will.

Though everything is possible, not everything is promised. In the garden Jesus prayed, "Father, for you all things are possible; remove this cup from me; yet not what I want but what you want" (Mark 14:36). The one thing God will not do is to avoid the reality of suffering, the necessity of the cross.

One's trust in God to fulfill God's promise does not avoid suffering. It makes possible through trusting obedience for God's will to triumph through us. God's ultimate will for the salvation of the world is not in doubt. Alleluia!

Seed Thoughts

1. **How many descendants were promised to Abraham?**
   As many as the stars (Gen. 15:1).

2. **What was the name of Sarai's Egyptian slave?**
   Hagar (Gen. 16:11, 15).

3. **What is the name of Hagar's son?**
   Ishmael (Gen. 16:11, 15).

4. **What is the meaning of the change of name from "Abram" to "Abraham"?**
   Abram means exalted father, while Abraham means father of many (Gen. 17:5).

5. **What was the sign of the covenant between Abram and God?**
   Circumcision (Gen. 17:9-10).

1. How many descendants were promised to Abraham?

2. What was the name of Sarai's Egyptian slave?

3. What is the name of Hagar's son?

4. What is the meaning of the change of name from "Abram" to "Abraham"?

5. What was the sign of the covenant between Abram and God?

6. What was Abraham's response to the promise of God that Sara would have a baby?

7. What was the name of Sarah and Abraham's son?

8. What did Abram serve his guests as a sign of hospitality?

9. What was Sarah's response when she overheard the visitors prophesy that she would have a son?

10. What is the significance of Isaac's name?

(Continued next page)

As many as the stars (Gen. 15:1).

Hagar (Gen. 16:11, 15).

Ishmael (Gen. 16:11, 15).

Abram means exalted father, while Abraham means father of many (Gen. 17:5).

Circumcision (Gen. 17:9-10).

Abraham fell on his face and laughed (Gen. 17:17).

Isaac (Gen. 17:19; 21:3).

Bread, curds, milk and lamb (Gen. 18:6-8).

Sarah laughed to herself (Gen. 18:12).

Isaac means "He laughs." Sarah said, "God has brought laughter for me; everyone who hears will laugh with me" (Gen. 21:6).

6. What was Abraham's response to the promise of God that Sara would have a baby?

Abraham fell on his face and laughed (Gen. 17:17).

7. What was the name of Sarah and Abraham's son?

Isaac (Gen. 17:19; 21:3).

8. What did Abram serve his guests as a sign of hospitality?

Bread, curds, milk and lamb (Gen. 18:6-8).

9. What was Sarah's response when she overheard the visitors prophesy that she would have a son?

Sarah laughed to herself (Gen. 18:12).

10. What is the significance of Isaac's name?

Isaac means "He laughs." Sarah said, "God has brought laughter for me; everyone who hears will laugh with me" (Gen. 21:6).

A Test of Faith

*G*od did tempt Abraham, and said unto him, Abraham: and he said, Behold, here I am.

2 And he said, Take now thy son, thine only son Isaac, whom thou lovest, and get thee into the land of Moriah; and offer him there for a burnt offering upon one of the mountains which I will tell thee of.

3 And Abraham rose up early in the morning, and saddled his ass, and took two of his young men with him, and Isaac his son, and clave the wood for the burnt offering, and rose up, and went unto the place of which God had told him.

Genesis 22:1-14

4 Then on the third day Abraham lifted up his eyes, and saw the place afar off.

5 And Abraham said unto his young men, Abide ye here with the ass; and I and the lad will go yonder and worship, and come again to you.

6 And Abraham took the wood of the burnt offering, and laid it upon Isaac his son; and he took the fire in his hand, and a knife; and they went both of them together.

7 And Isaac spake unto Abraham his father, and said, My father: and he said, Here am I, my son. And he said, Behold

the fire and the wood: but where is the lamb for a burnt offering?

8 And Abraham said, My son, God will provide himself a lamb for a burnt offering: so they went both of them together.

9 And they came to the place which God had told him of; and Abraham built an altar there, and laid the wood in order, and bound Isaac his son, and laid him on the altar upon the wood.

10 And Abraham stretched forth his hand, and took the knife to slay his son.

11 And the angel of the LORD called unto him out of heaven, and said, Abraham, Abraham: and he said, Here am I.

12 And he said, Lay not thine hand upon the lad, neither do thou any thing unto him: for now I know that thou fearest God, seeing thou hast not withheld thy son, thine only son from me.

13 And Abraham lifted up his eyes, and looked, and behold behind him a ram caught in a thicket by his horns: and Abraham went and took the ram, and offered him up for a burnt offering in the stead of his son.

14 And Abraham called the name of that place Jehovah-jireh: as it is said to this day, In the mount of the LORD it shall be seen.

July 18

Memory Selection
Genesis 22:12
Background Scripture
Genesis 22:1-19
Devotional Reading
Daniel 3:16-26
Printed Scripture
Genesis 22:1-14

Teacher's Target

Lesson purpose: *To emphasize God's challenge to put Him first, through the story of Abraham's willingness to sacrifice his son Isaac.*

This challenging lesson can be effectively introduced by asking group members, "What do people sometimes give up to show their loyalty to God?" Believers regularly give up a portion of their finances . . . perhaps some bad habits they are better off without anyway . . . at times, their reputation . . . and in some extreme instances, as in the case of martyrs, their very life.

Now we are ready to go one step farther by entering into the heart of Abraham. God has already called him to give up his home and his old religion. Now he is asked to offer his very son.

Because the idea is so remote from our thinking, and because we know how the story turns out, we must make considerable effort to ask the crucial question of ourselves: *How would I respond?*

Lesson Introduction

Many people see several remarkable parallels between the near-sacrifice of Isaac and the story of the sacrifice of Christ on the Cross.

Jesus was the Son of God, just as Isaac was Abraham's son. The costly decision to offer a son in behalf of others must have been wrenching both to Abraham and to God.

Isaac bore the wood that was to be the means of his own death, just as Jesus bore the Cross to Calvary. Both bore their burden in supreme submission.

The hill of Calvary, in fact, where Jesus was crucified, in the area of Moriah, where Abraham went to sacrifice Isaac.

Jesus was a substitute sacrifice for sinners, dying in our stead, just as the ram caught in the thicket was made a substitute for Isaac.

The trip to Mt. Moriah took three days, just as Christ was three days in the tomb.

Abraham's confidence that "I and the lad will . . . come again" (22:5) reminds us of Christ's resurrection.

Teaching Outline	Daily Bible Readings
I. Exceptional Demand—22:1-2	**Mon.** 'Offer Your Son' *Genesis 22:1-8*
II. Expedition to Moriah—3-5	**Tue.** Abraham Obeys *Genesis 22:9-14*
A. Preparation and journey, 3-4	
B. Aim and expectation, 5	**Wed.** 'I Will Bless You' *Genesis 22:15-19*
III. Excelling in Faith—6-10	**Thu.** 'We Will Not Bow Down' *Daniel 3:16-26*
A. Questions and answers, 6-9	
B. A leap of faith, 10	**Fri.** 'Remove This Cup' *Mark 14:32-42*
IV. Example of Grace—11-14	**Sat.** One Who Was Tested *Hebrews 4:14—5:4*
A. Proof of allegiance, 11-12	
B. A ram, not a son, 13-14	**Sun.** The Greatest Is Love *1 Corinthians 13:1-13*

Verse by Verse

I. Exceptional Demand—22:1-2

1 And it came to pass after these things, that God did tempt Abraham, and said unto him, Abraham: and he said, Behold, here I am.

2 And he said, Take now thy son, thine only son Isaac, whom thou lovest, and get thee into the land of Moriah; and offer him there for a burnt offering upon one of the mountains which I will tell thee of.

Since James 1:13 says that God does not actually tempt anyone, it is better to accept the NIV reading of *test* here. God often puts His people to such tests to bring out (for them) their real mettle or feelings. For example, the psalmist prays, "Test me, O LORD, and try me, examine my heart and my mind" (Ps. 26:2, NIV). Although God already knows Abraham's heart, the patriarch himself needs to be put in touch with what he values most—that is, who or what will be "God" to him.

And what could have been a more demanding test? After waiting so long for Isaac to be born as heir to the promise, was the heir now to be slain? Recalling that Abraham had only a few short years earlier been an idol worshiper (Josh. 24:2), it is yet another monument to his faith that he would listen to such a command from this invisible God.

Moriah was apparently an ancient name for the area where the city of Salem (later Jerusalem) was located. "Mt. Moriah" would later be identified as one of the hills on which Jerusalem was built, the place where God appeared to David at the threshing floor of Ornan, and the site of the Temple built by Solomon (2 Chron. 3:1). The Jews believed the altar in the Temple was on the very spot where Abraham was told to go and sacrifice his son; and the area is very near Golgotha, where Christ was crucified. God could not have directed Abraham to a more significant and sacred site.

II. Expedition to Moriah—3-5
A. Preparation and journey, 3-4

3 And Abraham rose up early in the morning, and saddled his ass, and took two of his young men with him, and Isaac his son, and clave the wood for the burnt offering, and rose up, and went unto the place of which God had told him.

4 Then on the third day Abraham lifted up his eyes, and saw the place afar off.

Not knowing what kind of timber might be available for the wood of an altar of sacrifice, Abraham takes care to bring his own kindling. "Blood offerings" like the one he is prepared to make are as old as human history, the first recorded in Scripture being Abel's (Gen. 4:4). The earliest offerings seem to have been born in a spontaneous and instinctive need to give something of worth to God. The fact that blood was shed may indicate also a sense of guilt and a kind of "substitutionary atonement"—the animal's life for the worshiper's. In Abraham's case, however, there is no such felt need; he is responding to the sheer command of God.

B. Aim and expectation, 5

5 And Abraham said unto his young men, Abide ye here with the ass; and I and the lad will go yonder and worship, and come again to you.

Why would Abraham lead the men with him to expect his *and* Isaac's return, if indeed he was ready to offer the lad up as God had commanded? Perhaps because, as the New Testament would later say, he believed "that God was able to raise him up, even from the dead" (Heb. 11:19). Since the idea of an after-life at the time of Abraham was more of a hope than a confident expectation, we can only marvel once again at the depth of Abraham's faith and courage.

Verse 5 is the first time the word "worship" appears in the Bible. The fact that Abraham's serious mission is termed "worship" shows that all worship is to be taken as a heart-felt offering to God.

III. Excelling in Faith—6-10

A. Questions and answers, 6-9

6 And Abraham took the wood of the burnt offering, and laid it upon Isaac his son; and he took the fire in his hand, and a knife; and they went both of them together.

7 And Isaac spake unto Abraham his father, and said, My father: and he said, Here am I, my son. And he said, Behold the fire and the wood: but where is the lamb for a burnt offering?

8 And Abraham said, My son, God will provide himself a lamb for a burnt offering: so they went both of them together.

9 And they came to the place which God had told him of; and Abraham built an altar there, and laid the wood in order, and bound Isaac his son, and laid him on the altar upon the wood.

Perhaps Abraham leaves his servants behind so they will not misunderstand that what he is about to do is a sacrifice instead of a murder. We wonder what he would have told the young men had he returned without his son. With Isaac now bearing the wood, Abraham carries glowing embers or a pot of burning oil with which to light the fire of the sacrifice.

For the first time we see that Isaac is beginning to question the nature of this unusual journey. Surely his father was unable to meet the lad's eyes as he mutters that "God will provide." His words must have been forced out by the sheer iron will of a faith that was dedicated not just to *believing* but to *doing* as well. In fact, James says that Abraham's grim determination amounted to having done the deed: "Was not Abraham our father justified by works, when he had offered Isaac his son upon the altar?" (James 2:21).

There is no mention of any protest from Isaac. His apparent calm submission may indicate his own growing faith, or sheer obedience to his father. His attitude has been compared with that of Christ, who "was led as a sheep to the slaughter; and like a lamb dumb before his shearer, so opened he not his mouth" (Acts 8:32).

B. A leap of faith, 10

10 And Abraham stretched forth his hand, and took the knife to slay

his son.

The time is past now for Isaac's questions, and for Abraham's evasive answer that God will somehow provide the offering. The high point of the test has arrived. Abraham faces his moment of truth, the point at which he must indicate whether his first loyalty is to his beloved son, and the family he believed God would bless, or to the God who promised the blessing in the first place. In one of the most dramatic scenes in all literature, we can see Abraham's arm raised, knife in hand, ready to take the swift, awful stroke.

IV. Example of Grace—11-14
A. Proof of allegiance, 11-12

11 And the angel of the Lord called unto him out of heaven, and said, Abraham, Abraham: and he said, Here am I.

12 And he said, Lay not thine hand upon the lad, neither do thou any thing unto him: for now I know that thou fearest God, seeing thou hast not withheld thy son, thine only son from me.

How relieved Abraham must have been to hear God call his name in the instant before the knife came flashing down to take his son's life. The voice from heaven not only releases the lad, but is full of affirmation for Abraham for passing the test.

B. A ram, not a son, 13-14

13 And Abraham lifted up his eyes, **and looked, and behold behind him a ram caught in a thicket by his horns: and Abraham went and took the ram, and offered him up for a burnt offering in the stead of his son.**

14 And Abraham called the name of that place Jehovah-jireh: as it is said to this day, In the mount of the Lord it shall be seen.

God's providence was never so welcome as Abraham spies the ram God had prepared to take Isaac's placed on the altar. The whole event calls forth a worthy name for the site. "Jehovah-jireh" is derived from verse 8, where Abraham affirms that "God will provide"—or, as the KJV indicates, "It will be seen (that God will provide)."

Postscipt: Some scholars say that since God has never condoned human sacrifice (see 2 Kings 16:3; Micah 6:6-7), He did not actually tell Abraham to offer Isaac. They suggest that the outcome of the story was concocted to challenge pagan practices that *did* call for human offerings?

Such a view ignores the significance of the account as a "test." As in the test Job faced, God no doubt knew how it would turn out. The test is more for the examinee's benefit. God wanted Abraham also to know whether he loved anything or anyone more than Him. To discount the story would void the test. As C. S. Lewis wrote, "The apparent absurdity . . . is precisely the one we must not ignore." For Abraham's test is also ours.

Evangelistic Emphasis

The continual struggle of faith is to put God first. The call to discipleship is a call to love God with all one's heart, mind, soul and strength. The first commandment is "You shall have no other gods before me" (Ex. 20:3). It is a matter of priorities. No matter what creed we profess with our lips, whatever or whoever is first in our love is really the god we serve. The temptation is always to elevate something good in itself and find our meaning or security in it. The call of God is always to put our trust, our reliance in God, and in God alone.

God put Abraham to the test. Had Abraham come to love his son too much? Had Abraham made an idol of his son? Was Isaac the source of his hope, his meaning, his life?

Jesus put a similar test to the rich young ruler. "What must I do to inherit eternal life?" the young man asks. Jesus reminds him of the commandments. He replies "All these I have done."

"One thing you need," Jesus replies. For the rich young ruler this was the crucial test, the crux of the matter, the cross roads for him, the cross to take up. Seeing that the source of the man's security was what he owned, He said, "Sell all you have, give it to the poor, and come and follow."

The call to discipleship still comes. "Come away from all that would take first place in your heart. Take up your cross and follow Me."

• • • • • • •

Memory Selection

And he said, Lay not thine hand upon the lad, neither do thou anything unto him: for now I know that thou fearest God, seeing thou has not withheld thy son, thine only son from me. —*Genesis 22:12*

Even with God, the faith is expressed in our decisions and actions. Hymns of praise, affirmation of faith, public testimony and spoken prayers are ways of expressing our loyalty and devotion. But the clearest expression of what we believe is how we live. In crucial choices our first love is revealed. God who knows our hearts, who sees the inner conflicts raging there, who understands the struggles for first place puts Abraham to the test. Only in the choice does Abraham resolve the struggle for competing loves. Thus only in the willingness to sacrifice is ultimate trust placed in God.

The test confirms for God that Abraham deeply trusts that God has his best interests at heart so that he will follow where God's command leads. The story teller means to suggest that up to that point, with Abraham's struggle between faith and unfaith, God did not really know where he stood with Abraham. There is a yet larger purpose to be fulfilled, affecting all the nations of the earth. Only a faithful Abraham can carry that purpose along. But now God knows.

Weekday Problems

Brad was obsessed with being as "successful" as his prominent preacher father. He was driven to excel his father's achievements. His father had earned a master's degree. He would go for a Ph.D. His father pastored a large city church. He would serve a bigger one. His father wrote articles for national religious journals. He would publish books. His father had a weekly radio broadcast. He would buy time on television.

One day he realized that he was not called to be successful, as the world measures success. His faithfulness had nothing to do with his obsessive comparison with his father. He was called to preach, to care for the souls of those in his charge, to make disciples. When he gave up the idol of success, he found a new peace in being faithful. If others saw Christ through him, that was "success" enough. If he could be with people through suffering and death, that was a holy privilege. If he could touch a young life in a positive way, that was reward enough. If he could help a congregation reclaim a mission beyond its own survival, he would find a confirmation of his calling.

He saw that he had made an idol of his "career" and had forsaken his calling. In offering his successful career on the altar he was free to be used as an instrument of God's redemptive purpose.

* What is most important in your life?

* If Jesus said to you "One thing is needful" what would it be?

* If it interfered with putting God first, would you be willing to put it aside?

Closing the Doors

I have closed the doors on Doubt.
I will go by what light I can find,
And hold up my hands and reach
   them out
To the glimmer of God in the dark,
   and call,
"I am Thine, though I grope and
   stumble and fall,
I serve, and Thy service is kind."

I have closed the door on Fear.
He has lived with me far too long.
If he were to break forth and
   reappear,
I would lift my eyes and look at the
   sky,

And sing aloud and run lightly by;
He will never follow a song.

I have closed the door on Gloom.
His house has too narrow a view.
I must seek for my soul a wider
   room,
With windows to open and let in the
   sun,
And radiant lamps when the day is
   done,
And the breeze of the world
   blowing through.

—*Irene Pettit McKeehan*

457

This Lesson in Your Life

The wonderfully told story of Abraham and his near sacrifice of Isaac tells us something about God. God is portrayed as One who *tests* and as One who *provides*.

The picture of God as one who tests us is not a familiar way of imagining God. When Abraham leaves his father's land and his father's people not knowing where he was to go, it was a high point in his absolute trust in God who called him. But not far into his journey he grows fearful. He passes off his wife, his beloved Sarah, as his sister. He lets her be taken into Pharaoh's harem. He thinks that if he is to survive to have descendants he had better rely upon his own wit and resources. God wants to know where he really stands with Abraham. God is a jealous God. "Thou shalt have no other gods before me."

Who is first with us? On whom do we rely? In whom or in what do we put our trust? To whom do we give our first allegiance? We often pray in the prayer that Jesus taught, "Lead us not into temptation." We have some trouble imagining that God would tempt us to go astray. Some translations suggest that the meaning of the word is "test." Jesus is teaching us to pray "Do not put us to the test." If the test is a test of where our true faith lies, like the test of Abraham's faith, it gives new meaning to those familiar words.

The other glimpse of God revealed in the story is that of a God who provides. The eyes of Abraham were opened to see that God had already provided for the sacrifice. A ram was there and waiting. The root meaning of the word "provide" comes from the Latin *pro* meaning before or ahead and *video* meaning to see. The video tapes we make of significant family events, the videos we rent to view a movie and those made of history-making events around the world help us to see. The God who "provides" (*pro-video*) is one who sees, who sees ahead, who sees the possibility before it is yet realized. To Isaac's innocent question, "Behold the fire and the wood, but where is the lamb for a burnt offering?" Abraham replies "God will provide himself with a lamb for the burnt offering my son."

Glimpsing God who tests and provides in the story of Abraham, we recognize God's shape and reality in the story of Jesus. There is a parallel in the stories.

Jesus is both Abraham and Isaac. His Moriah is called Golgotha. In Gethsemane he struggles with the test. "Let this cup pass from me." He has been called as Messiah, as Savior, as Redeemer. His disciples are slow to understand. The practice of the Kingdom life has been so slowly grasped. The full dimensions of loving neighbor have not yet been demonstrated. Now arrest, trial, crucifixion and death loom before him. The crucifixion appears to others as the end. Perhaps it seemed to Jesus as the defeat of all he hoped to do, of all he was called to do. "Let this cup pass from me, nevertheless not my will but thine be done" (Mark 14:32-36). In this story there is no ram nearby. Jesus is the lamb who is slain, the Passover lamb of sacrifice, the lamb of God.

Yet God provides. God sees ahead. God knows the possibilities beyond death. God sees suffering made redemptive. God sees ahead to Christ's resurrection, his victory over sin, his victory over death. Jesus trusts that not even death can separate him from God.

We find that often the cloud we dread proves to be a means of grace. Out of evil, we find good. Out of suffering we find healing. Out of death there comes new life. In what seems to us as hopeless, God sees new possibilities. The Lord provides.

Seed Thoughts

1. Where was Abraham to go to sacrifice Isaac?
To the land of Moriah.

2. How many days did it take Abraham and Isaac to reach the mountain where the sacrifice was to take place?
Three days.

3. What did Abraham carry to the mountain for the sacrifice?
Wood, fire and a knife.

4. What did Isaac ask his father?
"Where is the lamb for the burnt offering?"

5. What was Abraham's reply?
God himself would provide.

---

1. Where was Abraham to go to sacrifice Isaac?

2. How many days did it take Abraham and Isaac to reach the mountain where the sacrifice was to take place?

3. What did Abraham carry to the mountain for the sacrifice?

4. What did Isaac ask his father?

5. What was Abraham's reply?

6. What did the angel say to Abraham that caused him to stop the sacrifice of Isaac?

7. What did Abraham see caught in the thicket?

8. What did Abraham call that place?

9. What did God promise to Abraham?

10. Where did Abraham go after this experience?

(Continued next page)

459

To the land of Moriah.

Three days.

6. What did the angel say to Abraham that caused him to stop the sacrifice of Isaac?

The angel said not to harm Isaac, since Abraham had demonstrated he loved God above all (Gen. 22:12).

Wood, fire and a knife.

"Where is the lamb for the burnt offering?"

7. What did Abraham see caught in the thicket?

He saw a ram caught in the thicket by his horns.

God himself would provide.

The angel said not to harm Isaac, since Abraham had demonstrated he loved God above all (Gen. 22:12).

8. What did Abraham call that place?

"Jehovah Jireh," or "The Lord will provide."

He saw a ram caught in the thicket by his horns.

9. What did God promise to Abraham?

Multitudes of descendants, the cities of his enemies, and offspring that would bless the nations (Gen. 22:17-18).

"Jehovah Jireh," or "The Lord will provide."

Multitudes of descendants, the cities of his enemies, and offspring that would bless the nations (Gen. 22:17-18).

10. Where did Abraham go after this experience?

Beersheba.

Beersheba.

Deceit and Blessing

*A*nd when her days to be delivered were fulfilled, behold there were twins in her womb.

25 And the first came out red, all over like an hairy garment; and they called his name Esau.

26 And after that came his brother out, and his hand took hold on Esau's heel; and his name was called Jacob.

29 And Jacob sod pottage: and Esau came from the field, and he was faint:

30 And Esau said to Jacob, Feed me, I pray thee, with that same red pottage; for I am faint: therefore was his name called Edom.

31 And Jacob said, Sell me this day thy birthright.

32 And Esau said, Behold, I am at the point to die: and what profit shall this birthright do to me?

33 And Jacob said, Swear to me this day; and he sware unto him: and he sold his birthright unto Jacob.

34 Then Jacob gave Esau bread and pottage of lentiles; and he did eat and drink, and rose up, and went his way: thus Esau despised his birthright.

27:15 And Rebekah took goodly raiment of her eldest son Esau, which were with her in the house, and put them upon Jacob her younger son:

16 And she put the skins of the kids of the goats upon his hands, and upon the smooth of his neck:

17 And she gave the savoury meat and the bread, which she had prepared, into the hand of her son Jacob.

Genesis 25:24-26, 29-34; 27:15-19, 30-33

18 And he came unto his father, and said, My father: and he said, Here am I; who art thou, my son?

19 And Jacob said unto his father, I am Esau thy firstborn; I have done according as thou badest me: arise, I pray thee, sit and eat of my venison, that thy soul may bless me.

30 And it came to pass, as soon as Isaac had made an end of blessing Jacob, and Jacob was yet scarce gone out from the presence of Isaac his father, that Esau his brother came in from his hunting.

31 And he also had made savoury meat, and brought it unto his father, and said unto his father, Let my father arise, and eat of his son's venison, that thy soul may bless me.

32 And Isaac his father said unto him, Who art thou? And he said, I am thy son, thy firstborn Esau.

33 And Isaac trembled very exceedingly, and said, Who? where is he that hath taken venison, and brought it me, and I have eaten of all before thou camest, and have blessed him? yea, and he shall be blessed.

July 25

Memory Selection
Genesis 27:35-36

Background Scripture
Genesis 25:19-34; 27:1-40

Devotional Reading
Luke 16:1-19

Printed Scripture
Genesis 25:24-26, 29-34;
27:15-19, 30-33

461

Teacher's Target

Lesson purpose: *To reflect on the implications of God's selection of Jacob, deceitful son of Isaac, to be the heir of the covenant through Abraham.*

The story of Jacob's theft of his older brother's birthright shows how God can use even a flawed character to accomplish His will. Jacob would go on to gain deceitfully at the expense of his father-in-law, Laban. Yet eventually his character is remolded and he becomes the father of the 12 tribes of Israel.

Do members of your group have similar experiences illustrating how people can "grow into the high standards expected of them by love? Have they known of a child with low self esteem who was transformed when a parent or teacher "elected" them, or showed them unconditional love? Of the irresponsible who have changed when they were given responsibility? The untrustworthy transformed when trusted?

Jacob is an outstanding example in a long line of people who have "leaned into their election," becoming more than they otherwise could have been simply because someone "chose" them to love.

Lesson Introduction

God's selection of Jacob over his brother Esau to be the bearer of the covenant promise is of crucial significance. First, it highlights God's sovereignty in "electing" Esau—for it is either divine sovereignty or gross injustice to say, beforehand, "Jacob have I loved, but Esau have I hated" (Rom. 9:13).

In His foreknowledge, God must have seen potential in Jacob that He did not see in Esau. In His compassion He compensated for Esau's having been his father Isaac's favorite. In choosing the second-born, God continues the pattern of election that caused Abraham to be singled out to bear the covenant promise that would one day result in the coming of the Messiah . . . and in the election of those who are "born again" as His followers.

This event was also a defining moment for the later Arab nations, since Esau aligned himself with the Ishmaelites and became one of their forefathers.

Teaching Outline	Daily Bible Readings
I. The Surprising Twins—25:24-26	**Mon.** Twins Are Born *Genesis 25:19-26*
A. Esau the Hairy, 24-25	**Tue.** Esau Sells His Birthright *Genesis 25:27-34*
B. Jacob the Supplanter, 26	**Wed.** Rebekah Plots with Jacob *Genesis 27:1-17*
II. The Sale of the Birthright—29-34	**Thu.** Jacob Deceives Isaac *Genesis 27:18-29*
A. Edom the Red, 29-30	**Fri.** Esau Laments His Loss *Genesis 27:30-40*
B. Despising a heritage, 31-34	**Sat.** Shrewdness Commended *Luke 16:1-9*
III. The Sham to Deceive Isaac—27:15-19	**Sun.** Clean Hands, Pure Hearts *Psalm 24:1-6*
IV. The Stolen Blessing—30-33	

Verse by Verse/

The Surprising Twins—25:24-26
Esau the Hairy, 24-25

24 And when her days to be delivered were fulfilled, behold there were twins in her womb.

25 And the first came out red, all over like an hairy garment; and they called his name Esau.

Like her mother-in-law Sarah, Rebekah had at first been unable to have children (vs. 21). In answer to prayer, however, she not only has one child, but twins. Her discomfort while carrying them signals a struggle between their descendants (vss. 22-3), which has certainly been fulfilled in the conflict between Jews and Arabs.

Esau, barely the first-born, was apparently born with red hair covering his body. He will have two names, with the first one, here, being a pun made by swapping the first two letters of the Hebrew word *se'ar,* hairy. Already we can see that the biblical writer is preparing us for Jacob's famous deception with the goat skins.

Jacob the Supplanter, 26

26 And after that came his brother out, and his hand took hold on Esau's heel; and his name was called Jacob.

The second-born child's name is a forecast of his primary role in life. The Hebrew *ya'qov* means "heel," then "one who is at your heel"—an apt description of the second-born twin clinging to his brother's heel as though to supplant him as first-born, which indeed he will.

II. The Sale of the Birthright–29-34
A. Edom the Red, 29-30

29 And Jacob sod pottage: and Esau came from the field, and he was faint:

30 And Esau said to Jacob, Feed me, I pray thee, with that same red pottage; for I am faint: therefore was his name called Edom.

"Sod" is a King James word meaning to boil, or cook in water (cp. our word "sodden" for drenched). Verse 27 has said that Jacob was a homebody, so it is not surprising to find him tending a cooking fire when his outdoorsman-brother Esau comes in from the hunt.

Famished, Esau sees the red pottage (a thick soup), and—no doubt overstating his distress—asks for some. (In Hebrew the language is much like a southwesterner calling for a bowl of chili: "I gotta gulp down a bowl of that red!") Verse 34 says the soup was made of "lentiles" (lentils, of the bean family), some varieties of which turn a deep brownish-red when cooked. All this leads to Esau's second name, "Edom," which sounds much like the Hebrew word for red. Esau will later settle in southeastern Palestine, and his descendants will become enemies of Israel, Jacob's descendants.

B. Despising a heritage, 31-34

31 And Jacob said, Sell me this day thy birthright.

32 And Esau said, Behold, I am at the point to die: and what profit shall this birthright do to me?

33 And Jacob said, Swear to me this day; and he sware unto him: and he sold his birthright unto Jacob.

34 Then Jacob gave Esau bread and pottage of lentiles; and he did eat and drink, and rose up, and went his way: thus Esau despised his birthright.

Jacob's bent for being a schemer first appears here, in a hard bargain that acts out his birth, when he reached out a little hand as though to restrain Esau from being born first. Neither he nor his brother are following a high moral road in this landmark incident.

As in many ancient cultures, and some even today, a family's first-born male had many privileges. He received twice as much of his father's inheritance as the other children. More significantly, among the patriarchs the first-born would have been the "priest" or spiritual leader of the clan. Esau is apparently more interested in satisfy-

ing his immediate needs than assuming this kind of responsibility. No wonder the biblical writer scorns his willingness to "sell out" as despising his birthright. Hebrews 12:16 has the same opinion, calling Esau "profane" because he sold the priceless birthright for "one morsel of meat" (food).

III. The Sham to Deceive Isaac—27:15-19

15 And Rebekah took goodly raiment of her eldest son Esau, which were with her in the house, and put them upon Jacob her younger son:

16 And she put the skins of the kids of the goats upon his hands, and upon the smooth of his neck:

17 And she gave the savoury meat and the bread, which she had prepared, into the hand of her son Jacob.

18 And he came unto his father, and said, My father: and he said, Here am I; who art thou, my son?

19 And Jacob said unto his father, I am Esau thy firstborn; I have done according as thou badest me: arise, I pray thee, sit and eat of my venison, that thy soul may bless me.

For Jacob to secure the birthright he must not only wrest it from Esau; it must also be transferred from the first-born by Father Isaac. At this point, Mother Rebekah, who has always favored Jacob as Isaac favored Esau, steps up with a plan to trick her husband into using his customary "blessing" as a vehicle to transfer the birthright from Esau to her favorite son Jacob.

Chapter 27 began with the important information that old Isaac was losing his eyesight. If Jacob is wearing Esau's clothes, and if his skin is somehow made to appear hairy, Isaac might be fooled to mistake Jacob for his firstborn at the important "passing the blessing" feast Isaac planned before his death (27:3-4).

Despite his mild protest (vss. 11-12), Jacob seems all to willing to go along with his mother's ruse, not foreseeing that it would result in his having to leave home (see Lesson 9). Although Jacob's lying and cheating cannot be defended, there is something plaintive about his request that his father "sit and eat of my venison." Clearly he wants more than the birthright. He yearns for something of the love his father has chosen to give to Esau.

IV. The Stolen Blessing—30-33

30 And it came to pass, as soon as Isaac had made an end of blessing Jacob, and Jacob was yet scarce gone out from the presence of Isaac his father, that Esau his brother came in from his hunting.

31 And he also had made savoury meat, and brought it unto his father, and said unto his father, Let my father arise, and eat of his son's venison, that thy soul may bless me.

32 And Isaac his father said unto him, Who art thou? And he said, I am thy son, thy firstborn Esau.

33 And Isaac trembled very exceedingly, and said, Who? where is he that hath taken venison, and brought it me, and I have eaten of all before thou camest, and have blessed him? yea, and he shall be blessed.

Both Isaac and Esau are understandably shocked and disappointed to find that Jacob has successfully won the blessing by impersonating his brother. Apparently it was the custom to seal the passing of the birthright at a kind of "covenant meal" (in this case, one similar to that which sealed God's covenant with Abraham—see 18:1-8). The content of the birthright and the blessing are therefore identical.

Although Isaac regrets his mistake, there is something final about his insistence that "he (Jacob) *shall* be blessed." He seems to realize at last that his favoritism for Esau was against God's plan that "the elder shall serve the younger" (25:23). As for Esau, we may wonder how deep his sorrow goes, recalling the ease with which he traded his birthright. At any rate, his grief cannot erase what has happened, for once the transaction had been celebrated by the meal, it was irrevocable: "Afterward, when he would have inherited the blessing, he was rejected: for he found no place of repentance, through he sought it carefully with tears" (Heb. 12:17).

465

Evangelistic Emphasis

Esau made a bad bargain. He sold his birthright for a bowl of soup. Hebrews 12:16 describes Esau as profane, unspiritual, worldly minded, a godless and immoral person. He had no sense of the special privilege of being in that blessed family tree through whom God works to bring salvation and healing to all nations. All that was his, yet he lightly traded it off for a bowl of hot soup when he was tired and hungry. The birthright was an idea, a privilege, a promise. He wanted something he could hold and taste and touch.

Like Esau, we are often "rich in things and poor in soul." We are glutted with gadgets, comforts and conveniences but discover that in acquiring these things we have neglected the unique, special person we are. Our schedules are filled with good causes, significant meetings, gala parties. We run ragged from dawn until well after dark, strangely proud of our overfilled schedule as though being harried and busy were some badge of honor. All the while we neglect the things of the spirit. As children of God each of us is given a special birthright. There is given to each of us a capacity for communion with God. We have the potential of being aware of God's presence. We have the possibility of being at one with God's Spirit.

Today is a new day. Some foolish bargains we have to live with. Some years are wasted. Some opportunities lost beyond recall. But today is the first day of the rest of your life. May God grant us the wisdom of maturity and the wonder of a child to choose how we shall use the precious gifts of God this day.

● ● ● ● ●

Memory Selection

And he said, Thy brother came with subtilty and hath taken away thy blessing. And he said, Is not he rightly named Jacob? for he hath supplanted me these two times: he took away my birthright, and behold, now he hath taken away my blessing. And he said, Hast thou not reserved a blessing for me? —*Genesis 27:35-36*

The memory selection is like the tip of an iceberg. The actions of several persons intersect in Isaac's giving the blessing to Jacob. Esau had early traded away his birthright, the privilege of being the first born son. He was indifferent to the larger promise of being the one through whom God's promise to Abraham was fulfilled. Jacob was clever and deceptive. He cheated his brother out of the blessing the aged father meant to give to Esau. He took advantage of his father's blindness and played him for a sucker.

Rebekah, the twins' mother, had a clear favorite. Though a woman in a male dominated society, she devised a way to have her will carried out. Isaac knew he had not long to live. He wanted to get his affairs in order. He would give the blessing to his favorite son, the first born son. The voice sounded like Jacob...but the touch, the smell . . . the taste were more like Esau's. He just wasn't sure, but he was too proud to admit he didn't know.

Through these less than perfect humans, despite their faults, God is at work. God uses imperfect people to fulfill his purpose of bringing blessing to all the families on earth.

Weekday Problems

Tad grew up on a farm, the eldest of six sons. As an adult, with children of his own, he worked the small farm. his portion of the land which he had inherited from his father. The family all called the old patriarch "Pa." Pa mostly spoke to pass judgment, to pronounce his evaluation on everything and everyone. He had a fixed opinion on all subjects.

It seemed to Tad that he was clearly outside of Pa's affection. On Sundays when all the sons and their families gathered at the old home place, Tad felt he was ignored. It's like he wasn't even there. Pa always had a smile, a word, perhaps a story for all the sons, except for Tad. All his life Tad seemed driven by the compulsion to make his father acknowledge him, recognize his worth through his outstanding achievements. The truth is even if Tad had become the owner of the largest farm in the state, or been elected governor of the state he would never had gained his father's approval and blessing. Tad's whole life was driven by trying to win his father's blessing.

* Have you ever felt "unblessed" by a person significant to you—a parent, a boss, a person in authority over you?

* Did your parents have a favorite? Was it you? If not were you driven to win their approval? How else might you respond?

* Is the unmerited grace of God, mediated through persons who love you with no expectation of return, a way to heal that hurt?

* Is your church that kind of healing place? Are you that kind of loving person?

Promises, Promises

A promise is the one thing you can keep after giving it.

* * *

Two sailors were adrift on a raft in the ocean. They had just about given up hope of rescue, when one began to pray: "O Lord, I've led a worthless life. I've been unkind to my wife, and I've neglected my children, but if you'll save me, I promise that . . . ."

"Hold it!" the other sailor interrupted. Watch what you say. I think I see land."

* * *

"I promise to be honest about this house," the real estate salesman said. "It has good and bad points."

"What are the bad points?" the prospect asked.

"There's a chemical plant just to the north and a slaughterhouse to the south."

"And the good points?"

"You can always tell which way the wind's blowing."

This Lesson in Your Life

Many can identify with Esau's sense of having been left out. "Have you not reserved a blessing for me?" (Gen. 27:38). With all the effort of conscientious parents to be fair and equal in their love, many children know that their parents have favorites. The piano lessons, the orthodontic trips, the Christmas gifts, the personal time is carefully and equally apportioned. But ask the brothers and sisters of many families and the children will tell you who is mother's favorite, who is the apple of daddy's eye. This perception often colors one's whole approach to life.

The unblessed child may spend a lifetime trying to get a blessing. He is the dutiful, obedient, conforming child, doing everything that's expected. He is the one who stands close by, who tends the parent who is sick and dying. Always he hopes to win by faithful and dutiful service the blessing bestowed upon a brother or sister.

Sometimes the unblessed one tries to win the blessing from his heavenly Father. He takes on all manner of good works, hoping that one day the much-sought blessing will be earned. Myron Madden observes: "Our striving for what we can't get becomes our curse. We get hooked by our need for approval. It all amounts to giving away our power, thereby allowing ourselves to be controlled by the parent or whoever withholds approval" (*Blessing and the Gift of Power*).

Jesus told a parable of a father who had two sons (Luke 15:11-32). The younger son claimed his share of the family inheritance and went away to a far land. There he wasted his share of the family inheritance in riotous living. He came to his senses and returned home in penitence. His father ran to welcome him, and gave a great party to celebrate his homecoming. Everyone was happy except the elder son. He had dutifully stayed at home all those years, faithfully doing what was expected of him. He refused to go in and share in the party. The son who goes away is the blessed one. He is the child so secure in his father's love that he is free to go out on his own, free to mess up, free to return. The son who stays at home feels unblessed. No matter how early he gets up and how long he works he will never make it. Insecure and self hating, he tries to earn what can only be freely given.

Karl Olsson observes, "The human family is divided into these two groups: the blessed and the unblessed, the favored and the unfavored, those who have come to the party and those who haven't." Olsson says that people fall into four categories: 1. those who doubt there is a party; 2. those who believe that there is a party somewhere but they're not invited; 3. those who believe there is a party and they're invited but they don't deserve to stay; 4. those who are invited and go and stay" (*Come to the Party*).

The blessing of God is always a gift. It cannot be earned, nor is it related to our accomplishments. Luckily for Jacob and for us, God doesn't love people because of who they are but because of who God is. It is by grace that Jacob became the father of the twelve tribes of Israel and the many times grandfather of Jesus of Nazareth. It is by God's grace that Jesus of Nazareth was born into the world at all. Old Isaac had but one blessing to give. The good news is that God's blessing is available to all.

Seed Thoughts

1. Whom did Isaac marry?
   Rebekah (Gen. 25:20).

2. What did Isaac and Rebekah name the twins?
   Esau and Jacob (Gen . 25:25-26).

3. Which twin was born first?
   Esau.

4. Which of the twins was Isaac's favorite?
   Esau (Gen. 25:27).

5. Which of the twins was Rebekah's favorite?
   Jacob (Gen. 25:27).

---

1. Whom did Isaac marry?

2. What did Isaac and Rebekah name the twins?

3. Which twin was born first?

4. Which of the twins was Isaac's favorite?

5. Which of the twins was Rebekah's favorite?

6. What did Esau get in exchange for privileges that went with being the first born, his birthright?

7. Who proposed to Jacob the scheme to deceive Isaac and get the blessing?

8. Why was Jacob reluctant to try to trick Isaac?

9. Which of the five senses (seeing, hearing, touching, tasting and smelling) did Jacob use in deceiving Isaac?

10. What was the blessing Isaac bestowed on Jacob?

(Continued next page)

Rebekah (Gen. 25:20).

Esau and Jacob (Gen . 25:25-26).

Esau.

Esau (Gen. 25:27).

Jacob (Gen. 25:27).

Bread and pottage of lentils (a bowl of soup; Gen. 25:33-34).

Rebekah (Gen. 27:5-13).

If the deception were discovered, he might receive a curse instead of a blessing (Gen. 27:12).

Touch (goatskin on his hands); smell (Jacob wore Esau's clothes, smelling of the fields); taste (Rebekah prepared a stew as Esau would have prepared wild game).

Richness (fatness) of the earth, corn (grain) and wine, and the service of the peoples of all nations, including his own brothers (Gen. 27:28-29, 37).

6. What did Esau get in exchange for privileges that went with being the first born, his birthright?

Bread and pottage of lentils (a bowl of soup; Gen. 25:33-34).

7. Who proposed to Jacob the scheme to deceive Isaac and get the blessing?

Rebekah (Gen. 27:5-13).

8. Why was Jacob reluctant to try to trick Isaac?

If the deception were discovered, he might receive a curse instead of a blessing (Gen. 27:12).

9. Which of the five senses (seeing, hearing, touching, tasting and smelling) did Jacob use in deceiving Isaac?

Touch (goatskin on his hands); smell (Jacob wore Esau's clothes, smelling of the fields); taste (Rebekah prepared a stew as Esau would have prepared wild game).

10. What was the blessing Isaac bestowed on Jacob?

Richness (fatness) of the earth, corn (grain) and wine, and the service of the peoples of all nations, including his own brothers (Gen. 27:28-29, 37).

Lesson 9

Jacob's Flight and Vision

*A*nd Esau hated Jacob because of the blessing wherewith his father blessed him: and Esau said in his heart, The days of mourning for my father are at hand; then will I slay my brother Jacob.

28:10 And Jacob went out from Beersheba, and went toward Haran.

11 And he lighted upon a certain place, and tarried there all night, because the sun was set; and he took of the stones of that place, and put them for his pillows, and lay down in that place to sleep.

Genesis 27:41; 28:10-22

12 And he dreamed, and behold a ladder set up on the earth, and the top of it reached to heaven: and behold the angels of God ascending and descending on it.

13 And, behold, the LORD stood above it, and said, I am the LORD God of Abraham thy father, and the God of Isaac: the land whereon thou liest, to thee will I give it, and to thy seed;

14 And thy seed shall be as the dust of the earth, and thou shalt spread abroad to the west, and to the east, and to the north, and to the south: and in thee and in thy seed shall all the families of the earth be blessed.

15 And, behold, I am with thee, and will keep thee in all places whither thou goest, and will bring thee again into this land; for I will not leave thee, until I have done that which I have spoken to thee of.

16 And Jacob awaked out of his sleep, and he said, Surely the LORD is in this place; and I knew it not.

17 And he was afraid, and said, How dreadful is this place! this is none other but the house of God, and this is the gate of heaven.

18 And Jacob rose up early in the morning, and took the stone that he had put for his pillows, and set it up for a pillar, and poured oil upon the top of it.

19 And he called the name of that place Bethel: but the name of that city was called Luz at the first.

20 And Jacob vowed a vow, saying, If God will be with me, and will keep me in this way that I go, and will give me bread to eat, and raiment to put on,

21 So that I come again to my father's house in peace; then shall the LORD be my God:

22 And this stone, which I have set for a pillar, shall be God's house: and of all that thou shalt give me I will surely give the tenth unto thee.

Aug. 1

Memory Selection
Genesis 28:15
Background Scripture
Genesis 27:41–28:22
Devotional Reading
Psalm 121:1-8
Printed Scripture
Genesis 27:41; 28:10-22

Teacher's Target

Lesson purpose: *To sketch the next chapter in the story of God's covenant promise through Jacob, showing that God can use each of us despite our flaws.*

This lesson can be effectively introduced by reminding the group that God has often used flawed specimens of humanity to accomplish His perfect will. There was David, who, despite his sin with Bathsheba, was "a man after God's own heart." There was Solomon, who, despite his infatuation with many pagan wives, was crowned with wisdom and riches. There was impetuous Peter, who, despite his denial of Christ, was graced with the commission, "Feed my sheep."

In this lesson there is Jacob, who, despite having just cheated his brother out of the birthright, sees a vision confirming that God will reshape him into the bearer of the covenant with Abraham.

Despite our own flaws, what can God do with us?

Lesson Introduction

Although God's covenant with Abraham remains sure and certain, the path toward fulfillment takes some surprising twists and turns along the way. Lesson 8 dealt with the unusual selection of Jacob over Esau as bearer of the promise, the second-born over the first. Now the path of the promise takes another surprising turn as Jacob actually leaves the land of promise and retraces the steps his grandfather Abraham had taken when he came out of Haran at God's call.

In another dramatic scene, the lesson records Jacob's vision of the ladder (or stairway) to heaven, along with some important footnotes about the ancient use of "stelae" or pillars of stone as religious monuments.

It may also come as a surprise to learn that as third in the line of patriarchs of the promise (after Abraham and Isaac), Jacob exhibits a less mature faith than did Abraham. While Jacob set terms and conditions for his faith, Abraham answered God's call without setting any terms at all.

Teaching Outline	Daily Bible Readings
I. Vengeance Plotted—27:41	**Mon.** Esau Hated Jacob *Genesis 27:41-46*
II. Vision Experienced—28:10-15	**Tue.** Jacob Flees Genesis 28:1-5
A. Jacob's ladder—10-12	**Wed.** Jacob's Dream at Bethel Genesis 28:6-17
B. Renewal of the promise, 13-15	**Thu.** 'If God Be with Me' *Genesis 28:18-22*
III. Vows Made—16-22	**Fri.** Jacob Meets Rachel Genesis 29:1-4
A. Monument at 'God's House,' 16-19	**Sat.** Laban Tricks Jacob Genesis 29:15-30
B. Plans and promises, 20-22	**Sun.** God's Faithfulness *Deuteronomy 30:1-5*

Verse by Verse

I. Vengeance Plotted—27:41

41 And Esau hated Jacob because of the blessing wherewith his father blessed him: and Esau said in his heart, The days of mourning for my father are at hand; then will I slay my brother Jacob.

Jacob's wrath at losing the blessing is not surprising, in view of the anguish he had expressed in 27:33-36. On the one hand he has good reason to be angry, since Jacob won the prize with deceit and treachery. On the other hand, Esau himself was partly responsible since he had not prized the birthright more than his temporary appetite. In any case, he was fighting the sovereign will of God, who had predetermined that Jacob would be the bearer of the covenant promise.

Apparently the idea of killing Jacob occurred to Esau during the specified and sacred, period of mourning. This was a seven-day observance, if the custom at this time was the same as when Jacob's sons mourned his own death (see Gen. 50:10).

Verses 42-45 indicate that the death threat against Jacob prompted his mother Rebekah to arrange to have him flee. When she actually brings the idea to Isaac, however, the reason has changed to wanting Jacob to marry someone other than "the daughters of Heth" (the Hittites). The two Hittites that Esau had married had not endeared themselves to either Rebekah or Isaac (26:35). It is uncertain whether Rebekah honestly thought that Jacob would need to remain in Haran only "a few days" (27:44, cp. NIV "a while"). As it happened, Jacob would be gone 20 years, and Rebekah would never see her favorite son again.

II. Vision Experienced—28:10-15
A. Jacob's ladder—10-12

10 And Jacob went out from Beersheba, and went toward Haran.

11 And he lighted upon a certain place, and tarried there all night, because the sun was set; and he took of the stones of that place, and put them for his pillows, and lay down in that place to sleep.

12 And he dreamed, and behold a ladder set up on the earth, and the top of it reached to heaven: and behold the angels of God ascending and descending on it.

The "certain place," as we shall see, was the ancient religious center of Bethel, where Father Abraham had first stopped in his pilgrimage from Haran to Canaan (12:8). Bethel is west of the Jordan River, just north of Jerusalem. Since Beersheba is far to the south, it would have taken Jacob several days to reach Bethel.

As remarkable as Jacob's famous vision or dream is, we are given few explicit clues as to its meaning. The most likely guess is that the dramatic vision of angels ascending and descending between heaven and earth was designed to reassure Jacob that he is being attended by divine powers on his journey. Jesus spoke of angels performing a similar service for Him (John 1:51).

The vision is described in terms reminiscent of the "ziggurats" of Babylon, Abraham's homeland. These towers were also considered to reach heaven, as in vs. 12, and had ramps or "stairways" (NIV for the KJV "ladders") to the top.

B. Renewal of the promise, 13-15

13 And, behold, the LORD stood above it, and said, I am the LORD God of Abraham thy father, and the God of Isaac: the land whereon thou liest, to thee will I give it, and to thy seed;

14 And thy seed shall be as the dust of the earth, and thou shalt spread abroad to the west, and to the east, and to the north, and to the south: and in thee and in thy seed shall all the families of the earth be blessed.

15 And, behold, I am with thee, and will keep thee in all places whither thou goest, and will bring thee again into this land; for I will not leave thee, until I have done that which I have spoken to thee of.

That the vision was to reassure and encourage Jacob is made even more likely by the word from God that accompanied it. God appears in a "theophany" (divine appearance or manifestation) much like those in which the covenant was first announced with Abraham, and renews the promise with Jacob. We can imagine how timely the event must have been. He was no doubt lonely, and may have brooded over having been forced to leave his home and family. He may also have begun to feel some guilt over his treachery in seizing Esau's blessing. God's appearance illustrates that "Where God guides, God provides."

Specifically, God renews both the *posterity* (seed) and the *land* promise. This time, instead of the heirs of the promise being as numerous as the stars in the sky, they will be as widespread as the dust of the earth. As noted in previous lessons, a literal interpretation identifies this promise with the scattering of the Jews themselves, then their regathering in Palestine. A spiritual or figurative interpretation sees the promise fulfilled in the worldwide presence of Christians, or "spiritual Israel" (Gal. 6:16), who inherit the "land" of the Kingdom, or salvation.

III. Vows Made—16-22

A. Monument at 'God's House,' 16-19

16 And Jacob awaked out of his sleep, and he said, Surely the LORD is in this place; and I knew it not.

17 And he was afraid, and said,

How dreadful is this place! this is none other but the house of God, and this is the gate of heaven.

18 And Jacob rose up early in the morning, and took the stone that he had put for his pillows, and set it up for a pillar, and poured oil upon the top of it.

19 And he called the name of that place Bethel: but the name of that city was called Luz at the first.

The vision of the stairway to heaven and the reaffirmation of the covenant struck Jacob with a sense of awe. The word for "dreadful" (vs. 17) can imply either horror or reverence; Jacob probably felt some of both. Turning an oblong stone on end to make a monument or "stele" of it was a common practice in many religions, as was anointing it with oil (see Lev. 8:10; Num. 7:1).

Although Jacob had no way of knowing that the place had been used for years as a religious center both by Abraham and pagans, his own experience prompts him to name it Beth-el, "the house of God." The biblical author injects the explanation that the place's original name was Luz.

Bethel was one of the first places to which Jacob returned after his sojourn in Haran (35:1-3). Long years later, after Israel came under the rule of the Law of Moses, the ark of the covenant was placed at Bethel. Unfortunately the place became a center of idolatry when Jeroboam, king of the northern kingdom of Israel, set up a golden calf for the people to worship instead of going to Jerusalem to worship Yahweh (1 Kings 13:1-2).

B. Plans and promises, 20-22

20 And Jacob vowed a vow, saying, If God will be with me, and will keep me in this way that I go, and will give me bread to eat, and raiment to put on,

21 So that I come again to my father's house in peace; then shall the LORD be my God:

22 And this stone, which I have set for a pillar, shall be God's house: and of all that thou shalt give me I will surely give the tenth unto thee.

Despite the faith of Isaac and Abraham, Jacob has not inherited a faith strong enough to serve God unconditionally. Yahweh will be his God *"if . . . ."* Abraham's decision to leave Ur and Haran and go wherever God would lead included no such qualifications. However, it should be noted that each "if" in verses 20-21 precisely matches the promises God had made in the vision: to (a) be with Jacob; (b) keep or protect him wherever he went; and (c) bring him again the promised land.

Giving a tithe or tenth was a religious practice long before it was incorporated into the Law of Moses. The Bible first mentions it when Abraham paid tribute to Melchizedek, king of Salem (Gen. 14:18-20). By the time of Christ, the Pharisees had made tithing such a centerpiece of the Jewish faith that it was applied to tiny details, to the neglect of "weightier matters" (Matt. 23:23).

Evangelistic Emphasis

Jacob made an important discovery. The God he so much needed was not to be found among the memories of the past, though those traditions were important. It was not in ruminating on a past that could be remembered but not relived that he would find God. He was poised on the brink of a new and unknown future. He had no way of telling what that future might hold in store for him. He had high hopes of family, of flocks, of descendants , of land, of returning home. But he could not live in the future. All that he was given was that brief moment between the past and the future, the no longer and the not yet. The present moment was all he had.

The present moment is all we ever have. This present moment can be the time when God draws near. "This is the day which the Lord hath made."

Sometimes we try to bury ourselves in the past. We endlessly relive its great moments. We burden ourselves with regrets over what might have been. It is a past we cannot change. Sometimes we live in the future imagining what we will do when . . . when we finish school, when we have a family, when the children leave home, when we get the next promotion, when we retire.

But we can never live in the future. Life comes to us one day at a time. This day, this hour can be that moment when you become aware of God's holy presence. Jesus said to the woman at the well "The hour is coming and now is when the true worshipers will worship the Father in spirit and truth" (John 4:23). This day could be the day when you make a new commitment to Christ as Lord and Savior. Of this day and hour you may exclaim with Jacob: "Surely the Lord is in this place and I did not know it" (Gen. 28:16).

• • • • • •

And, behold, I am with thee, and will keep thee in all places whether thou goest, and will bring thee again unto this land; for I will not leave thee, until I have done that which I have spoken to thee of.— *Genesis 2:15*

The Lord promises Jacob in the dream that "I am with you." In this very ordinary place, in this barren, lonely wilderness, this place between the father's house you have left and your uncle's land you are to find, I am with you. It is the promise implicit in the name of the Messiah "Immanuel" which means God with us (Isa.14; Matt.1:23). It was the promise of the risen Christ as he leaves his disciples: "Lo, I am with you always even to the close of the age" (Matt. 28:20).

In the Lord's words to Jacob there was also a second promise: " I will keep you wherever you go." It is the image of a shepherd who will protect Jacob. The psalmist also reflects these words: "The Lord will keep your going out and your coming in" (Ps. 121:8).

There is also the promised homecoming, "I will bring you back to this land." There will be a time of exile but it will come to an end. In these words there is the promise of God's accompaniment, protection, and homecoming. All are based simply on God's word of promise: "I will not leave thee until I have done that which I have spoken to thee of."

Weekday Problems

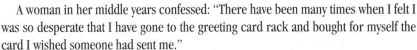

Jacob found God in a lonely place. He was miles from home, from anyone. He felt forsaken, forgotten and alone. Who of us has not known such time of loneliness.

Don Selby reports on instances of loneliness. One young man put it this way: "You want to put your head on someone's lap and feel a closeness that is not physical or mental but spiritual."

A woman in her middle years confessed: "There have been many times when I felt I was so desperate that I have gone to the greeting card rack and bought for myself the card I wished someone had sent me."

One man yearns so much to have someone speak to him that he dials his telephone to hear a recorded voice say, "The time is . . . ."

We know what it is to desire to be home, to have a place where we belong, to be with persons who know us and care for us.

Speaker of the House Sam Rayburn, near the end of his life, discovered how ill he was. He surprised his colleagues in Congress by announcing that he was going home to Bonham, Texas, for medical tests and treatment. Some asked why he did not remain in Washington, D.C., where he would have access to the most advanced medical treatment. Rayburn replied: "Bonham is a place where people know it when you're sick and where they care when you die."

Sometimes it is in that very lonely place that we find God. Sometimes we discover we are closest to God in the midst of difficulties. We discover God is with us when we are most alone.

An Awesome God

Experiencing God as awe-inspiring, as did Jacob, is as important in the Bible as knowing Him personally:

"It came to pass, when the flame went up toward heaven from off the altar, that the angel of the Lord ascended in the flame of the altar. And Manoah and his wife looked on it, and fell on their faces to the ground. . . And Manoah said unto his wife, We shall surely die, because we have seen God" (Judg. 13:210-22).

"In thoughts from the visions of the night, when deep sleep falleth on men, Fear came upon me, and trembling, which made all my bones to shake. Then a spirit passed before my face; the hair of my flesh stood up . . . There was silence, and I heard a voice, saying, Shall mortal man be more just than God?" (Job 4:13-17).

"In the year that king Uzziah died I saw also the Lord sitting upon a throne, high and lifted up, and his train filled the temple . . And the posts of the door moved at the voice of him that cried, and the house was filled with smoke. Then said I, Woe is me! for I am undone . . . for mine eyes have seen the King, the Lord of hosts" (Isa. 6:1-5).

477

This Lesson in Your Life

It was a very ordinary place, where Jacob found God. He might have looked for God in a holy shrine, a place hallowed by tradition. He might have looked for God in the palace of a king. He might have looked for God in a place of spectacular beauty. Jacob found God in a most unlikely place. Here in the wilderness. Nothing special, nothing grand, nothing sacred made it seem like the place of an encounter with God. In that ordinary place Jacob meets God and receives God's awesome promises. Jacob declares: "Surely the Lord is in this place and I did not know it. How awesome is this place! This is none other than the house of God and this is the gate of heaven" (Gen. 28:16-17).

God comes to us in the commonplace, the everyday, the ordinary, if we but have the eyes to see it. Elizabeth Barrett Browning wrote:

Earth's crammed with heaven,
and every common bush afire with God:
But only he who sees takes off his shoes,
the rest sit round it and pick blackberries."

George Washington Carver was one of the first Afro-Americans to make a name for himself in the field of science. He helped renew the economy of the South as he developed a heartier strain of sweet potatoes, and found a score of uses for the common peanut. There was no need to import exotic plants or to move to more fertile lands. The Lord had provided all that was needed in what was already given, in the common and the ordinary. The peanut thrived in that red clay of Alabama. The devout scientist prayed, "Mr. Creator, tell me what's in the peanut." To which the answer came "George, I made the peanut. Now you find out what's in it." So he did! His motto was "Dip down in your bucket where you are." Another version of the saying is "Bloom where you are planted."

The blessedly unpretentious saint, Brother Lawrence, was a cook in a monastery. He reflects: "It is not necessary for being with God to be always at church. We may make a (chapel) of our heart, wherein to retire from time to time to converse with him in meekness, humility and love. The time of business does not with me differ from the time of prayer, and in the noise and clatter of my kitchen, while several persons are at the same time calling for different things, I possess God in as great tranquillity as if I were upon my knees at the Blessed Sacrament."

In our daily round, our common tasks, our every day work, at home and school, in the store, at the plant, in the fields, in the laboratory , in the library, in all of these ordinary places God can be found. Of these common places where God is found, encountered in our daily round, we can declare: "Surely the Lord is in this place. This is none other than the house of God, and this is the gate of heaven."

Seed Thoughts

1. What was the name of Rebekah's brother?

Laban (Gen. 27:43, 28:2; 28:5).

2. According to Rebekah how long should Jacob stay with Laban?

"Until your brother's anger against you turns away, and he forgets what you have done to him" (Gen. 27:45).

3. What reason did Rebekah give Isaac for sending Jacob away?

If Jacob stays he might marry a Hittite woman (Gen. 27:46).

4. Where did Jacob go?

Paddan-Aram (Gen. 28:5).

5. What was Jacob's dream described this lesson?

He dreamed there was a ladder set up on the earth, the top of it reaching to heaven and the angels of God were ascending and descending on it (Gen. 28:12).

---

1. What was the name of Rebekah's brother?

2. According to Rebekah how long should Jacob stay with Laban?

3. What reason did Rebekah give Isaac for sending Jacob away?

4. Where did Jacob go?

5. What was Jacob's dream described this lesson?

6. What promises did God make to Jacob at Bethel?

7. What did Jacob say when he woke from his sleep?

8. What did Jacob call that place?

9. What did Jacob promise in his vow to the Lord?

10. What conditions did Jacob lay out for God to meet before he (Jacob) would fulfill his vow?

(Continued next page)

Laban (Gen. 27:43, 28:2; 28:5).

"Until your brother's anger against you turns away, and he forgets what you have done to him" (Gen. 27:45).

If Jacob stays he might marry a Hittite woman (Gen. 27:46).

Paddan-Aram (Gen. 28:5).

He dreamed there was a ladder set up on the earth, the top of it reaching to heaven and the angels of God were ascending and descending on it (Gen. 28:12).

(a) I will give you this land; (b) your offspring will be many ; (c) all the families of the earth shall be blessed in you; (d) I am with you and will keep you.

That the Lord was in that awesome place, and that it was the house of God and the gate of heaven (Gen. 28:16, 17).

He called the place Bethel (the house of God; Gen. 28:19).

The Lord would be Jacob's God, the stone would be God's house, and Jacob would tithe to God (Gen. 28:21-22).

God must be with him, provide him with food and clothing, and bring him back to his father's house in peace (Gen. 28:21).

6. What promises did God make to Jacob at Bethel?
(a) I will give you this land; (b) your offspring will be many ; (c) all the families of the earth shall be blessed in you; (d) I am with you and will keep you.

7. What did Jacob say when he woke from his sleep?
That the Lord was in that awesome place, and that it was the house of God and the gate of heaven (Gen. 28:16, 17).

8. What did Jacob call that place?
He called the place Bethel (the house of God; Gen. 28:19).

9. What did Jacob promise in his vow to the Lord?
The Lord would be Jacob's God, the stone would be God's house, and Jacob would tithe to God (Gen. 28:21-22).

10. What conditions did Jacob lay out for God to meet before he (Jacob) would fulfill his vow?
God must be with him, provide him with food and clothing, and bring him back to his father's house in peace (Gen. 28:21).

Jacob's Struggle at Peniel

And Jacob said, O God of my father Abraham, and God of my father Isaac, the LORD which saidst unto me, Return unto thy country, and to thy kindred, and I will deal well with thee:

10 I am not worthy of the least of all the mercies, and of all the truth, which thou hast shewed unto thy servant; for with my staff I passed over this Jordan; and now I am become two bands.

11 Deliver me, I pray thee, from the hand of my brother, from the hand of Esau: for I fear him, lest he will come and smite me, and the mother with the children.

24 And Jacob was left alone; and there wrestled a man with him until the breaking of the day.

25 And when he saw that he prevailed not against him, he touched the hollow of his thigh; and the hollow of Jacob's thigh was out of joint, as he wrestled with him.

26 And he said, Let me go, for the day breaketh. And he said, I will not let thee go, except thou bless me.

27 And he said unto him, What is thy name? And he said, Jacob.

28 And he said, Thy name shall be called no more Jacob, but Israel: for as a prince hast thou power with God and with men, and hast prevailed.

29 And Jacob asked him, and said, Tell me, I pray thee, thy name. And he said, Wherefore is it that thou dost ask after my name? And he blessed him there.

30 And Jacob called the name of the place Peniel: for I have seen God face to face, and my life is preserved.

33:1 And Jacob lifted up his eyes, and looked, and, behold, Esau came, and with him four hundred men. And he divided the children unto Leah, and unto Rachel, and unto the two handmaids.

2 And he put the handmaids and their children foremost, and Leah and her children after, and Rachel and Joseph hindermost.

3 And he passed over before them, and bowed himself to the ground seven times, until he came near to his brother.

4 And Esau ran to meet him, and embraced him, and fell on his neck, and kissed him: and they wept.

Genesis 32:9-11, 24-30; 33:1-4

Aug. 8

Memory Selection
Genesis 32:10

Background Scripture
Genesis 32:3–33:17

Devotional Reading
Matthew 18:21-25

Printed Scripture
Genesis 32:9-11, 24-30; 33:1-4

Lesson purpose: *To trace the events marking Jacob's return to Canaan, and how making peace with God finally settled the warfare in Jacob's scheming heart.*

We have noted that the name "Jacob" means first "heel," then "one who is at the heel" in the sense of "dogging" or trying to overtake or supplant. Jacob seems to have spent most of his life up to now struggling with something or someone, not just Esau, from whom he stole the birthright. In this lesson he returns from Padan-aram (or Haran) and 20 years of scheming against his father-in-law Laban.

Ask your class to share issues or events with which people typically struggle. They may list career and job situations . . . children . . . marriage relationships. Now note that conflicts with God often lie behind such struggles, and ask how Christ can help speak peace to such inner conflict.

All this points to the events in Jacob's life in this lesson. They are capped by the night he fought God all night long—a battle which marked the end of his ever feeling that he had to be a schemer.

Lesson Introduction

Jacob has spent 20 eventful years in Padan-aram (Haran) since our last lesson. His scheming against Esau has been matched by the deceit of Laban, his father-in-law. Laban agreed to give his daughter Rachel to Jacob in marriage if Jacob would work for him seven years. However, Laban substituted Leah, Rachel's sister in the marriage ceremony at the last moment. In order to get his beloved Rachel, Jacob had to work seven additional years for both wives.

In turn, Jacob became an expert livestock breeder. Apparently with God's help he contrived to make Laban's breeding stock bear young with markings showing they belonged to Jacob, thus repaying Laban for his treachery in the marriage of his daughters.

The present lesson portrays Jacob returning to Canaan. Faced with having to square things with Esau, Jacob has a strange experience that marks the end of his deceitful ways.

Teaching Outline	Daily Bible Readings

I. Praying for Deliverance—32:9-11
   A. A penitent spirit, 9-10
   B. In fear of Esau, 11
 	
II. Wrestling with God—24-30
   A. Struggling for a blessing, 24-26
   B. A new name, 27-30
 	
III. Reunion with Esau—33:1-4
	Mon. Jacob Seeks Reconciliation
	Genesis 32:3-8
	Tue. Jacob Prepares Gifts
	Genesis 32:9-21
	Wed. Jacob's Wrestling Match
	Genesis 32:22-32
	Thu. The Great Reunion
	Genesis 33:1-11
	Fri. Going Separate Ways
	Genesis 33:12-17
	Sat. Jesus on Human Relations
	Matthew 5:21-26
	Sun. Forgive Indefinitely!
	Matthew 18:21-35

Verse by Verse

I. Praying for Deliverance—32:9-11

A. A penitent spirit, 9-10

9 And Jacob said, O God of my father Abraham, and God of my father Isaac, the Lord which saidst unto me, Return unto thy country, and to thy kindred, and I will deal well with thee:

10 I am not worthy of the least of all the mercies, and of all the truth, which thou hast shewed unto thy servant; for with my staff I passed over this Jordan; and now I am become two bands.

We noted in the previous lesson that as Jacob fled from Esau's wrath he promised loyalty to God in return for protection and blessing (Gen. 28:20-21). His success during 20 years in Padan-aram has apparently convinced Him that God would fulfill His promise; and in return Jacob will worship Him.

It is significant that Jacob re-enters the land with a prayer that addresses God in terms that show renewed awareness of Yahweh and His true nature. He confesses that He is the God of the covenant with Grandfather Abraham and Father Isaac. He even uses God's personal name "Yahweh" (indicated by the caps-and-small-caps printing of "the Lord). Jacob will never again confuse

Yahweh with pagan deities.

Verse 10 reflects the fact that Jacob had crossed the Jordan with only his staff when he had fled Esau, in contrast to his returning a wealthy man, with massive flocks and herds, wives and servants. His crediting God for his blessings shows a humble and penitent spirit. Much of his wealth had been gained by deceit (recall the deception required to gain more of the striped and spotted livestock than was his due—30:41-43). Yet God had blessed him even in his nefarious ways—perhaps because his father-in-law Laban was even more deceitful! At any rate, in giving God the credit for his prosperity instead of his own shrewdness, Jacob shows signs of a crack in his previous scheming personality.

B. In fear of Esau, 11

11 Deliver me, I pray thee, from the hand of my brother, from the hand of Esau: for I fear him, lest he will come and smite me, and the mother with the children.

Jacob had sent scouts up ahead to seek out his brother Esau, testing the waters for whether Esau is still angry at Jacob for stealing his birthright (32:3-5). Jacob was "greatly afraid and distressed" when he learned that Esau was coming to meet him with a large contingency of soldiers (vss. 6-7). Now he lays his fear before the Lord. He fears not only for his own life, but for "the mother" (a general term for all the women with children in his company) and their children.

Jacob may have been concerned for all these people not only because they were his responsibility but because he wanted to preserve them as the people God had promised to give him (28:14). While in Padan-aram, he had apparently fathered all the sons but Benjamin who were destined to become heads of "the 12 tribes of Israel." (See the summary in 35:22b-26; Benjamin was born after Jacob's return to Canaan, 35:16-18).

II. Wrestling with God—24-30

A. Struggling for a blessing, 24-26

24 And Jacob was left alone; and there wrestled a man with him until the breaking of the day.

25 And when he saw that he prevailed not against him, he touched the hollow of his thigh; and the hollow of Jacob's thigh was out of joint, as he wrestled with him.

26 And he said, Let me go, for the day breaketh. And he said, I will not let thee go, except thou bless me.

Here, in one of the strangest stories in all of Scripture, Jacob seems to reach a turning point in his life. As he and his large company of people approach Canaan, he sends them all ahead while he is left alone, camped by the brook Jabbok. He may have been playing the coward, postponing the inevitable mee[t]ing with Esau. Or perhaps he wants t[o] spend one last night alone reflecting o[n] his past life, and what might be ahea[d]

The "man" in verse 24 was actuall[y] God in human form (see vs. 30), thu[s] perhaps an angel. It is as though a[ll] Jacob's previous struggles, as exempl[i]fied in his relationship with Isaac, Esa[u] and Laban, have pointed to this one su[-]preme struggle. The strange wrestlin[g] match shows that Jacob's restlessnes[s] of soul stems from his uneasiness abou[t] his relationship with God more tha[n] with other people in his life. A perso[n] who has settled *this* struggle feels les[s] need to "supplant" anyone or to gras[p] at wealth in their insecurity.

For a divine Being with superhuma[n] strength not to be able to "prevail" ove[r] Jacob shows that God was condescend[-]ing to struggle merely on a human leve[l] The Being gains an advantage by crip[-]pling Jacob in the thigh (prompting a[n] explanation about one aspect of "ko[-]sher" slaughtering in verse 32). Jacob['s] recognition that he was struggling wit[h] a divine Being is indicated by his ap[-]peal for his opponent to bless him.

B. A new name, 27-30

27 And he said unto him, Wha[t] is thy name? And he said, Jacob.

28 And he said, Thy name shal[l] be called no more Jacob, but Is[-]rael: for as a prince hast tho[u] power with God and with men, an[d] hast prevailed.

29 And Jacob asked him, an[d] said, Tell me, I pray thee, thy name

484

nd he said, Wherefore is it that
1ou dost ask after my name? And
e blessed him there.

30 And Jacob called the name
f the place Peniel: for I have seen
od face to face, and my life is pre-
erved.

The blessing the angel gives Jacob is
change in names. Instead of being
nown by a name ("Supplanter") that
1dicated his devious desire to get more
1an was his, Jacob will now be known
s "Striver" (Israel), or one noble
1ough (as a "prince," KJV) to have
triven with God. From this point on,
1e former deceiver will try to live up to
1e royal nature of his new name.

In return, Jacob ask his opponent's
ame, for in the ancient world being
ble to name supernatural forces was
1ought to give people power over them,
ither in prayer for blessings or curses
) curtail their power. God declines to
eveal His name, since He is subject to
o one's control. With the battle finally
ver as the day dawned, Jacob gives the
lace an appropriate name—a word-
lay on Jacob's feeling that he had "seen
od face to face." Actually, "No man
ath seen God" in his essence (John
:18), but Jacob has certainly seen His
ngel "up close and personal."

II. Reunion with Esau—33:1-4

1 And Jacob lifted up his eyes,
nd looked, and, behold, Esau
ame, and with him four hundred
1en. And he divided the children
nto Leah, and unto Rachel, and
nto the two handmaids.

2 And he put the handmaids and
their children foremost, and Leah
and her children after, and Rachel
and Joseph hindermost.

3 And he passed over before
them, and bowed himself to the
ground seven times, until he came
near to his brother.

4 And Esau ran to meet him, and
embraced him, and fell on his
neck, and kissed him: and they wept.

Jacob perhaps organizes his wives
and children in this fashion as a kind
of "who's who" for Esau, helping him
discern what children belong to which
wife. Jacob may also have put them in
the vanguard of the procession to meet
Esau as a defense to show his brother
he is a family man whose dependents
would suffer if harm came to him.

The latter reason proved to be un-
necessary. The years have mellowed
Esau and melted his resentment. After
all, he has become a mighty man and a
wealthy *sheik* in his own right, without
the blessing of the first-born.

Still, being careful not to overdo a
good thing, Jacob will decline to have
Esau and his troops accompany him further (33:12-17). Instead, Esau turns toward his home in Seir (also known as
Edom), and Jacob and his family, servants, and livestock on toward Canaan.
He has striven not only with God but
with others, and with himself; and has
finally fought his way to peace in all directions. Now he is ready for the next
chapter in the saga of God's covenant
people.

Evangelistic Emphasis

In the struggle with the mysterious night-time visitor, the stranger asks Jacob his name. Names in the Bible are often more than they seem to be. They represent the being, the inner self, the essence of a person. To give your name is to share with another who you are. The request of the stranger, "Tell me your name," was more than an easy conversation opener. For Jacob to give his name was like making a confession of the constant theme of his life, "My name is Jacob." The name means "heel/trickster/over-reacher/supplanter." Each description was true but none was flattering.

The stranger gave Jacob a new name. "Your name shall no more be called Jacob but Israel" (Gen. 32:28). Some scholars say the name "Israel" means "one who strives with God." The name fits. Jacob realizes that his mysterious visitor is not a human visitor. He has seen God face to face. Other scholars suggest that "Israel" means "God rules, God preserves, God protests." A new being has been created, a new man out of the old, so he is given a new name. If Jacob, who has relied so much on his own skills and cleverness, now trusts in God, he is indeed a new creature. He can now trust that the One with whom he strives is ultimately the One who saves. Here is an anticipation of the gospel in which Jesus gives new names to his disciples. Simon becomes Peter, the rock. Impetuous Peter became as steadfast as his name. Saul, the persecutor of the church becomes Paul, apostle to the Gentiles.

The good news for Jacob is good news for us. Paul declares "If anyone is in Christ, he is a new creation; the old has passed away, behold the new has come (2 Cor. 5:17-18)."

• • • • • •

Memory Selection

I am not worthy of the least of all the mercies, and of all the truth, which thou has showed unto thy servant; for with my staff I passed over this Jordan and now I am become two bands.—*Genesis 32:10*

Jacob has reached the end of his rope. He is in a situation from which his cleverness, his fast talk, his tricks cannot save him. The brother he has cheated is coming to meet him, with 400 men. What kind of welcome committee is that? Like many of us, when Jacob's own resources are at an end, he turns to God for help. He is not bargaining with God. He simply throws himself on the mercy of God. He trusts himself to God's steadfast love and faithfulness.

In the ritual for the Lord's Supper in many traditions there is a prayer: "We do not presume to come to this thy table, trusting in our own righteousness but in thy manifold and great mercies. We are not worthy so much as to gather up the crumbs under the table."

Jacob counts his blessings. He has crossed the Jordan with nothing, only a staff in his hand. Now he returns, blessed with family, servants, flocks of sheep and cattle. Now he realizes these were not so much the fruit of his ingenuity but the blessing of God. Like every sinner before and after him, he simply throws himself on the mercy of God. "I am not worthy . . . deliver me, I pray."

Weekday Problems

When Jacob comes to the Jabbok river, he is all alone. He has sent on ahead his servants, his flocks, his family. Tomorrow he shall meet Esau. He doesn't know what the future holds for him. In this crisis at the midpoint of his life, I wonder if he did not struggle with questions like we have.

Sometimes such soul-searching questions often come when we realize we are past fifty. Many of our dreams will not be realized. On the eve before major surgery, or the day before an appointment with a doctor when he shares the results of medical tests, when one is forced to make a job change, when the last child leaves home, when one faces retirement . . . in such times of change and crisis we reflect on life's meaning.

What have we accomplished in life? What is the real meaning of our work and struggle? What of lasting consequence has come? What have we done with the years granted to us? If we had to give a final accounting today to God for our stewardship of time and training and opportunity, what can we show for all these years? Are their signs that our discipleship has been fruitful? Have we been faithful to our calling to follow Jesus?

For some, that time of taking stock can be a frightening encounter with God's Truth. In gaining material wealth and financial security have we anything that will live after us.

* Have we made our life count for something beyond our own survival and comfort?

* Is the world a better place because we've lived?

* If we are granted a few more years to live, what would we do differently?

* What would it mean for us to put first things first?

This and That

We're constantly amazed at these young things with their fancy hairdos and skintight pants. And the girls are even worse.

* * *

Teacher: Really, Tommy, your handwriting is terrible! You must learn to write better.
Tommy: Well, if I did, you'd just find fault with my spelling.

* * *

He: Did the movie have a happy ending?
She: Yes, everyone was happy it was over.

* * *

True believer: In hell there will be weeping, wailing, and gnashing of teeth among the wicked.
Doubting Thomas: What about those of us who don't have any teeth?
Believer: God will provide. Teeth will be handed out to all who don't have them.

This Lesson in Your Life

The God glimpsed in the story of Jacob at the Jabbok River is a God who blesses, but not always as expected. The God portrayed is One who responds to prayers, but not always in the terms we ask. Jacob is blessed, he is given a new name, he learns to trust; but he is permanently disabled. He will forever carries a sign of his all-night struggle with God.

Up to this encounter Jacob thought himself to be self sufficient, quite able to take care of himself. In that long and lonely night at the Jabbok River he discovered there were forces he could not control. He could only cross that river in trust and faith. Jacob needed Someone greater than himself. The limp would go with him all his days to remind him of his need for God's power and grace. The limp was a mark of his struggle with God. His weakness led to a strength beyond his own.

In John's gospel we read the story of the disciples gathered behind locked doors (John 26:19-29) Jesus comes and stands among them, but Thomas is not present. Thomas can't believe their excited reports of the resurrected Lord. Eight days later they are gathered in the same place. This time Thomas is there. Again Jesus comes and stands among them. He shows to Thomas the wound in his side, the print of the nails in his hands. The risen Christ is recognized by the wounds left by his suffering and death.

James Harnish reports that in the language for the deaf, the sign for Jesus is to point with the third finger of one hand to the palm of the other and vice versa. The Christ is identified by the nail scars on his hands. Those wounds become signs of God's goodness and love

Charles Colson was a powerful figure in the Nixon White House. A young, bright attorney , he rose quickly to a position of influence and power. At the height of his power he was convicted for his part in the Watgergate cover up and went to prison. In prison he became a Christian. Since then he has been an instrument in bringing hundreds, even thousands of prison inmates to new life in Christ through his "Prison Ministries Fellowship."

He learned that one needs more than job skills, a brilliant mind and good training, as important as they are. One has to be remade, reborn. A new person needs a new center for his life. Colson said that what amazed him most about his new life dedicated to ministry to those in prison was that God did not choose to use his strengths, his law degree, his political influence, his contacts in Washington. God chose to use his weakness. God took his defeat, even his shame and public humiliation, his years in prison and used these in a redemptive way.

Paul writes: "God chose what is weak in the world to shame the strong, God chose what is low and despised in the world to bring to nothing things that are, so that no human being might boast in the presence of God" (1 Cor. 1:27-28). Three times Paul asked God to remove his "t horn in the flesh." But God said, "My grace is sufficient for you, for my power is made perfect in weakness."

Seed Thoughts

1. Why did Jacob send messengers to Esau with a report of his wealth in livestock and slaves?

He sent them in order that he might find favor in Esau's sight (Gen. 32:5).

2. Why was Jacob afraid of Esau?

Jacob had stolen the blessing from Esau, and Esau had vowed to kill Jacob (Gen. 27:41).

3. What report did the messengers bring to Jacob?

They reported that Esau was coming to meet Jacob with 400 men (Gen. 32:6).

4. What gifts did Jacob send to Esau?

Over 550 animals, including 200 female goats, 20 male goats, 200 ewes, 20 rams, 30 camels with colts, 40 cows, 10 bulls, 20 female donkeys and 10 male donkeys.

5. What is the name of the river or stream where Jacob was left alone?

Jabbok (Gen. 32:22).

---

1. Why did Jacob send messengers to Esau with a report of his wealth in livestock and slaves?

2. Why was Jacob afraid of Esau?

3. What report did the messengers bring to Jacob?

4. What gifts did Jacob send to Esau?

5. What is the name of the river or stream where Jacob was left alone?

6. What new name was given to Jacob and what does it mean?

7. What did Jacob call that place ?

8. What does the name Peniel mean?

9. Where did Jacob go after his meeting with Esau?

10. What is the difference in Jacob's motive between his first and second offering of gifts to Esau?

(Continued next page)

He sent them in order that he might find favor in Esau's sight (Gen. 32:5).

Jacob had stolen the blessing from Esau, and Esau had vowed to kill Jacob (Gen. 27:41).

They reported that Esau was coming to meet Jacob with 400 men (Gen. 32:6).

Over 550 animals, including 200 female goats, 20 male goats, 200 ewes, 20 rams, 30 camels with colts, 40 cows, 10 bulls, 20 female donkeys and 10 male donkeys.

Jabbok (Gen. 32:22).

The new name was Israel, which means "one who strives with God."

Jacob called the place Peniel (Gen. 32:30).

It means "the face of God."

Jacob journeyed to Succoth (Gen. 33:17).

The first gifts were to appease Esau. The second was to express thanks "since you have received me with such favor and because God has dealt graciously with me."

6. What new name was given to Jacob and what does it mean?
The new name was Israel, which means "one who strives with God."

7. What did Jacob call that place ?
Jacob called the place Peniel (Gen. 32:30).

8. What does the name Peniel mean?
It means "the face of God."

9. Where did Jacob go after his meeting with Esau?
Jacob journeyed to Succoth (Gen. 33:17).

10. What is the difference in Jacob's motive between his first and second offering of gifts to Esau?
The first gifts were to appease Esau. The second was to express thanks "since you have received me with such favor and because God has dealt graciously with me."

Favored Son to Slave

N ow Israel loved Joseph more than all his children, because he was the son of his old age: and he made him a coat of many colours.

4 And when his brethren saw that their father loved him more than all his brethren, they hated him, and could not speak peaceably unto him.

17b And Joseph went after his brethren, and found them in Dothan.

18 And when they saw him afar off, even before he came near unto them, they conspired against him to slay him.

Genesis 37:3-4, 17b-28

19 And they said one to another, Behold, this dreamer cometh.

20 Come now therefore, and let us slay him, and cast him into some pit, and we will say, Some evil beast hath devoured him: and we shall see what will become of his dreams.

21 And Reuben heard it, and he delivered him out of their hands; and said, Let us not kill him.

22 And Reuben said unto them, Shed no blood, but cast him into this pit that is in the wilderness, and lay no hand upon him; that he might rid him out of their hands, to deliver him to his father again.

23 And it came to pass, when Joseph was come unto his brethren, that they stript Joseph out of his coat, his coat of many colours that was on him;

24 And they took him, and cast him into a pit: and the pit was empty, there was no water in it.

25 And they sat down to eat bread: and they lifted up their eyes and looked, and, behold, a company of Ishmeelites came from Gilead with their camels bearing spicery and balm and myrrh, going to carry it down to Egypt.

26 And Judah said unto his brethren, What profit is it if we slay our brother, and conceal his blood?

27 Come, and let us sell him to the Ishmeelites, and let not our hand be upon him; for he is our brother and our flesh. And his brethren were content.

28 Then there passed by Midianites merchantmen; and they drew and lifted up Joseph out of the pit, and sold Joseph to the Ishmeelites for twenty pieces of silver: and they brought Joseph into Egypt.

Aug. 15

Memory Selection
Genesis 27:3

Background Scripture
Genesis 37:1-35

Devotional Reading
1 Samuel 18:1-9

Printed Scripture
Genesis 37:3-4, 17b-28

Teacher's Target

Lesson purpose: *To recount the story of Jacob's favoritism for his son Joseph, and the circumstances that led to Joseph's being taken captive to Egypt.*

Abraham and his descendants, through whom God gave the covenant promise, shared a remarkable—and, on the other hand, a very common—trait with modern families: they were flawed. Abraham tried to "help" God by taking Hagar as a wife; Isaac's favoritism for his son Jacob led to hatred and family estrangement; and now Jacob's favoritism for Joseph leads to strife among his sons, and eventually to the Egyptian Captivity.

Introduce this lesson by recounting just how similar these family frailties are to families today. Then note that just as God continued to work through the flaws of being human in patriarchal times, He can use families today despite their being less than perfect.

Lesson Introduction

Since our last lesson, Jacob has settled in the promised land "wherein his father (Isaac) was a stranger" (Gen. 37:1). Most of Jacob's twelve sons have grown to be heads of their own families, and God has blessed the family with prosperity.

Yet all has not been well among them. Jacob has had to exhort his sons to "put away the strange gods"—the idols worshipped by the nations about them (Gen. 35:2-4). Furthermore, Joseph, the next-to-youngest son, was a tattle-tale, bringing "evil reports" to Jacob about several of his half-brothers (37:2). He also made the mistake of sharing his dreams of superiority with his father and brothers.

Setting the stage for today's lesson, and bringing all this dissension to the breaking point, is the fact that Jacob's favoritism toward Joseph created jealousy among his eleven brothers. His visit to them in the field provides them with an opportunity for revenge.

Teaching Outline	Daily Bible Readings	
I. The Price of Favoritism—3-4	**Mon.**	Tattler and Dreamer *Genesis 37:1-11*
II. The Plot Against Joseph— 17b-20	**Tue.**	Jealous Brothers *Genesis 37:12-24*
A. Journey of mercy, 17b	**Wed.**	Sold into Slavery *Genesis 37:25-28*
B. Vengeance for dreams, 18-20	**Thu.**	Jacob Mourns Joseph *Genesis 37:29-36*
III. The Plan Enacted—21-28	**Fri.**	Saul Is Jealous, Too *1 Samuel 18:1-9*
A. Death sentence commuted, 21-22	**Sat.**	First Workers Jealous *Matthew 20:1-16*
B. Attack against Joseph, 23-24	**Sun.**	Who Is the Greatest? *Luke 14:14-27*
C. Sold into slavery, 25-28		

Verse by Verse

I. The Price of Favoritism—3-4

3 Now Israel loved Joseph more than all his children, because he was the son of his old age: and he made him a coat of many colours.

4 And when his brethren saw that their father loved him more than all his brethren, they hated him, and could not speak peaceably unto him.

Like the saying about the deeds of Jesus, "the world would not hold the books" that could be written about the tragic outcome of showing favoritism to one family member over another. Sometimes the family favorite is the firstborn. Here Jacob favors Joseph, his next-to-youngest son, because he was born late in Jacob's life when many men have ceased being able to have children (Gen. 30:22-24).

The phrase that yields the famous "coat of many colours" is also translated "richly ornamented robe" (NIV), "long robe with sleeves" (RSV) or "coat of many pieces." In 2 Samuel 12:18, the same term is used to describe the robe of the daughters of a queen. Whatever the exact nature of the robe, it was far fancier than shepherds normally wore, and was a continuous and irritating reminder of Joseph's favored status. This evidence of Jacob's partial treatment, along with Joseph's dreams to be noted below, were a predictable source of jealousy and hatred among the other 11 sons of Jacob.

II. The Plot Against Joseph—17b-20
A. Journey of mercy, 17b

17b And Joseph went after his brethren, and found them in Dothan.

In a land such as Canaan there were no fences and few stone walls marking boundary lines of private property. A herdsman like Jacob lived a semi-nomadic life, following the rains and the resulting improved grazing conditions. Here Joseph's brothers had taken their flocks north from their headquarters at Hebron (Gen. 35:27), to Shechem (37:13). Apparently they either found no suitable grazing there, or had too much competition from other flocks and shepherds; so they moved on to Dothan, in what is now central Palestine. Joseph was sent to see to their needs, in a mission similar to that of young David, who visited his own brothers in King Saul's army (1 Sam. 17:17-18).

B. Vengeance for dreams, 18-20

18 And when they saw him afar off, even before he came near unto them, they conspired against him to slay him.

19 And they said one to another, Behold, this dreamer cometh.

493

20 Come now therefore, and let us slay him, and cast him into some pit, and we will say, Some evil beast hath devoured him: and we shall see what will become of his dreams.

The dreams that had so angered Joseph's brothers are described in verses 7-9. In one, the brothers were in the fields binding sheaves ("shocking feed," in American parlance). Joseph's sheaf stood upright, and the sheaves of his brothers gathered around it and bowed down before it. In another dream, the sun, moon, and eleven stars—apparently standing for Joseph's parents and brothers—all bowed down before Joseph.

While the dreams were no doubt from God, and accurately portrayed the future (see Lesson 13), Joseph showed poor judgment in sharing them with his brothers. Predictably, they took it all as evidence of Joseph's youthful conceit instead of a message from God. Even old Jacob rebuked the young dreamer (vs. 10). In their anger, the brothers plot to slay Joseph, throw his body in a pit, and tell his father that he had been killed by beasts like those that regularly took their toll of flocks in the area.

III. The Plan Enacted—21-28
A. Death sentence commuted, 21-22

21 And Reuben heard it, and he delivered him out of their hands; and said, Let us not kill him.

22 And Reuben said unto them, Shed no blood, but cast him into this pit that is in the wilderness, and lay no hand upon him; that he might rid him out of their hands, to deliver him to his father again.

The death plot against Joseph did not please Reuben, Jacob's firstborn through his wife Leah (29:32). Perhaps, as the eldest son, Reuben had a greater sense of responsibility than his brothers and half-brothers. Years later, when Joseph has the power of life and death over his brothers, Reuben will remind them that he had warned of dire consequences from harming Joseph (42:21-22).

For the moment, Reuben recommends not killing Joseph, but just casting him in a pit and leaving him to die. Secretly, however, he plans to rescue Joseph and restore him to Jacob. Here is one among the 11 who is big enough to rise above his normal resentment at his younger brother's arrogance.

B. Attack against Joseph, 23-24

23 And it came to pass, when Joseph was come unto his brethren, that they stript Joseph out of his coat, his coat of many colours that was on him;

24 And they took him, and cast him into a pit: and the pit was empty, there was no water in it.

Apparently willing to take Reuben's advice, the brothers attack Joseph, stripping from him the special robe that had been an ever-present reminder of their father's favoritism. Ironically, years later the prophet Elisha will also be at Dothan when he and his servant will see that "they that be with us are more than they that be with them" (2 Kings 16). Although Joseph cried out in anguish at his treatment (Gen. 42:21), and al-hough he did not have the benefit of Elisha's perception, future events will show that God's forces were also with him over the evil intent of his brothers.

C. Sold into slavery, 25-28

25 And they sat down to eat bread: and they lifted up their eyes and looked, and, behold, a company of Ishmeelites came from Gilead with their camels bearing spicery and balm and myrrh, going to carry it down to Egypt.

26 And Judah said unto his brethren, What profit is it if we slay our brother, and conceal his blood?

27 Come, and let us sell him to the Ishmeelites, and let not our hand be upon him; for he is our brother and our flesh. And his brethren were content.

28 Then there passed by Midianites merchantmen; and they drew and lifted up Joseph out of the pit, and sold Joseph to the Ishmeelites for twenty pieces of silver: and they brought Joseph into Egypt.

With supreme indifference to the discomfort they have caused Joseph, his brothers sit down to a meal while contemplating their next move. Reuben, who had planned to rescue Joseph, is apparently absent, perhaps having been called away temporarily to see to some problem with his flocks.

Dothan was on a well-traveled caravan route from Gilead, east of the Jordan, and points farther East, to Egypt; so the abrupt appearance of these trad-ers would not have surprised the plotters. The account calls these merchants both Ishameelites and Midianites; but we learn from Judges 8:22-24 that the Midianites were in fact also descendants of Ishmael. The two terms are apparently used interchangeably here. They traded in spices, used in food preparation and incense; and balm, used as medicine—a science that was highly developed in ancient Egypt.

In Reuben's absence another brother, Judah, expresses similar concern at shedding Joseph's blood. His intervention is based both on concern for slaying a member of the family, and on purely commercial grounds. They would gain nothing by killing their brother, but could make 100 percent profit by selling him as a slave—a booming business in most parts of the ancient world.

The twenty pieces of silver the brothers receive for Joseph remind some interpreters of some parallels between Joseph and Jesus. Both were sold out for a fee (although it was thirty pieces of silver in Jesus' case); designated to be the deliverer of their people; rejected by those very people; yet eventually were used by God to work His will despite such treatment.

Evangelistic Emphasis

The story of Joseph is a story of God bringing good out of evil. Joseph's brothers were jealous of the father's showing such preference for Joseph. The gift of the "coat of many colors" seemed to flaunt that favoritism every time Joseph strutted around in his new coat. Their jealousy and rage is expressed in a plot to get rid of their father's favorite. They sold him into slavery and thought that was the end of Joseph. That was their intention, born of their hate.

God uses their evil intentions for God's own plan for the redemption of the world. God's chosen people are to be a light to the Gentiles—to all nations. They are shaped into a people of the covenant through the event of the exodus, the miraculous deliverance in crossing the Red Sea, the provision of manna day by day, the giving of the law. The great liberating event of the exodus, by which the nation is formed and shaped, requires a sojourn in Egypt. That stay in Egypt, the prelude to the birth of a nation, was brought about not *despite* the brothers' evil plan but even *through* that hatred. The wrath of men is made to praise God. Through the selling of Joseph as a slave, eventually all Israel will find a haven from the famine in the land of Egypt.

The Joseph story is echoed in the story of Jesus. The cross was the product of the evil designs of men. The chief priests, the Pharisees, the Roman officials conspired together to be rid of Jesus. But it was precisely through His suffering and death on the cross that God brings salvation to us all.

● ● ● ● ● ● ●

Memory Selection

Now Israel loved Joseph more than all his children, because he was the son of his old age; and he made him a coat of many colors.—*Genesis 27:3*

The coat of many colors expressed old Jacob's love for Joseph. The splendid robe set Joseph apart from his brothers. The same coat which conveyed Jacob's affection for his son at the same time aroused the envy of Jacob's other sons. Joseph wears the coat when he goes to find his brothers. After they plot to sell Joseph into slavery, they dip the robe in goat's blood and bring the coat to old Jacob. For him the blood soaked coat was the confirmation of Joseph's death.

In Jesus' story of the prodigal son (Luke 15:32) the younger son is welcomed home. The father bids the servant to bring the best robe and put it on him, for he was lost and now is found, he was dead and is alive again. In John's vision of the holy city he sees "a great multitude, that no one could count, from every nation . . . standing before the throne and before the Lamb, robed in white" (Rev. 7:9).

The old spiritual puts it: "All God's children got robes, and when I get to heaven, gonna put on my robe and walk all over God's heaven." Paul exhorts, "Lay aside the works of darkness and put on the armor of light . . . put on the Lord Jesus Christ" (Rom. 13:12, 14).

Weekday Problems

Suzie had always been jealous of her sister Alice. It seemed to Suzie that Alice was the favorite of their parents. It was a favoritism hard to prove, but strongly felt. There was no flagrant show of partiality as with Jacob's gift of the special coat to Joseph. Suzie had stayed at home to take care of her parents. Alice traveled the world, worked in exciting cities.

When Alice occasionally came home for a visit there was a twinkle in the eyes of her parents. All the special dishes were prepared. The feeling of jealousy came to a head when both parents died and the will was read. While each girl received an equal share of the modest estate, on small personal items it seemed to Suzie that Alice got the real treasures. Suzie got the microwave and toaster but it was Alice who received the old dining table, around which the family had gathered for special days. The will gave to Suzie the new recliner bought for Dad on last father's day, but the high chair which had been used by four generations went to Alice. So it seemed throughout the will. Possessions were equally divided in financial terms, but the pieces that Suzie especially cherished went to Alice. Suzie was hurt, disappointed, angry. She vowed to cut off all contact with Alice, never to visit, never to write, never to call. She would live as if Alice were dead.

* What would you do if your were Alice?

* What advice might you give to Suzie?

Clothes Calls

Male shopper—I want to look at the cheapest suit in the house.
Sales clerk—You're wearing it, sir.

* * *

Clothes seem to suffer a sea-change when they get on to me. They look quite promising in the shop, and not entirely without hope when I get them back into my wardrobe. But then, when I put them on, they tend to deteriorate with a very strange rapidity and one feels so sorry for them.—*Joyce Grenfell,* Stately as a Galleon

* * *

From the cradle to the coffin, underwear comes first.—*Bertolt Brecht,* The Threepenny Opera

* * *

You have got to be a Queen to get away with a hat like that.—*Anna Loos,* Gentlemen Prefer

* * *

Where is the man could ease a heart
Like a satin gown?
                    —*Dorothy Parker,* Enough Rope

This Lesson in Your Life

Violence is not a stranger to the Bible. Joseph is sent by Jacob to see if "it is well" with them. The word is "*shalom.*" *Shalom* is hard to come by in the story of Israel. The brothers of Joseph agree to kill him. Later their plan is changed to sell their brother as a slave to be rid of "the dreamer." The book of Genesis relates the story of Cain's murder of his brother Abel (Gen. 4); the rape of Dinah, daughter of Jacob and Leah, by Shechem, the Hivite; the killing by Jacob's sons of all the males in Shechem's city (Gen. 34); the hanging of the Pharaoh's chief baker (Gen. 40:22).

Shalom, peace and justice among people is also hard to come by in our day. We live in a violent society. Every two hours a child is killed by gunfire in the United States. Between 1967 and 1991, 50,000 American children died from guns. Homicide is now the third leading cause of death of American children ages five to fourteen. Within a fifteen-year period as many children died from guns in America as there were American Soldiers killed in the Vietnam war. Almost 3 million children were reported abused or neglected in 1992, one every eleven seconds. On the average, a U.S. child will have witnessed 18,000 murders on television by the time she or he is eighteen years old. Every eighteen seconds a woman is beaten. Three to 4 million women are battered each year. Every hour sixteen women confront rapists; a woman is raped every six minutes.

Dorothy Prothrow-Sith suggests the causes of violence, "I think there is a convergence of factors. It is like a slot machine where you have to get five oranges before you hit the jack pot. One window is the widening gap of poverty over the last decade or so and the creation of an underclass. Another window includes alcohol use and other drugs. Another window is the increase in guns and their availability. Another window has to do with family problems and issues. Then I add one that I call our 'make my day' ethic—the way we encourage and celebrate violence. You add all that up and you've got an epidemic of youth violence."

What is the Christian response to violence? How can we seek *shalom*, the well-being of our brothers and sisters, and especially the children and youth of our communities? Among the responses some churches have made are: an after-school program for children and youth; a house for battered women and their children; parenting courses for adults and teenagers; restriction of the sale of violent pornography; alternative programs for inner city youth; literacy programs to tutor adults and young adults in reading skills; prison ministry that offers counseling, rehabilitation, Bible study and worship; ongoing prayer support for victims of violence and injustice.

We know that God plans a different way for people to live together. This vision and hope can make all the difference. God seeks the well-being (*shalom*) of all God's children. Jesus said, "Blessed are the peacemakers, for they shall be called children of God" (Matt. 5:9).

Seed Thoughts

1. Why did Joseph's brothers hate him?

Because their father loved him more than them, because Joseph brought bad reports of them to their father, and because Joseph told of his dreams of superiority

2. Where were the flocks of Jacob grazing?

They were near Shechem (Gen. 37:2), and later they were moved to Dothan (Gen. 37:17).

3. What was the initial plan of Joseph's brothers concerning Joseph?

To kill him, throw him into a pit and say that a wild animal had devoured him (Gen. 37:20).

4. Who objected to the plan to murder Joseph?

First Reuben, then Judah (Gen. 37:21-26).

5. What was the brothers' second plan concerning Joseph, the plan which they followed?

They would sell him to the Ishmaelites (Gen. 37:25-27) / Midianites (Gen. 37:28) on their way to Egypt.

---

1. Why did Joseph's brothers hate him?

2. Where were the flocks of Jacob grazing?

3. What was the initial plan of Joseph's brothers concerning Joseph?

4. Who objected to the plan to murder Joseph?

5. What was the brothers' second plan concerning Joseph, the plan which they followed?

6. Who suggested selling Joseph into slavery instead of killing him?

7. For what price did the sons of Jacob sell their brother to the Ishmaelites?

8. How did the brothers deceive their father Jacob?

9. What was Jacob's reaction?

10. To whom did the Ishmaelites/ Midianites sell Joseph?

(Continued next page)

499

Because their father loved him more than them, because Joseph brought bad reports of them to their father, and because Joseph told of his dreams of superiority

They were near Shechem (Gen. 37:2), and later they were moved to Dothan (Gen. 37:17).

To kill him, throw him into a pit and say that a wild animal had devoured him (Gen. 37:20).

First Reuben, then Judah (Gen. 37:21-26).

They would sell him to the Ishmaelites (Gen. 37:25-27) / Midianites (Gen. 37:28) on their way to Egypt.

Judah (Gen. 37:26-27).

For twenty pieces of silver (Gen. 37:28).

They took the "coat of many colors," dipped it in goat's blood so that Jacob would think Joseph had been killed by a wild animal (Gen. 37:31-33).

Jacob tore his robes, put sackcloth on his loins, and mourned for his son many days (Gen. 37:34).

They sold Joseph in Egypt to Potiphar, one of the Pharaoh's officials the captain of the guard.

6. Who suggested selling Joseph into slavery instead of killing him?
Judah (Gen. 37:26-27).

7. For what price did the sons of Jacob sell their brother to the Ishmaelites?
For twenty pieces of silver (Gen. 37:28).

8. How did the brothers deceive their father Jacob?
They took the "coat of many colors," dipped it in goat's blood so that Jacob would think Joseph had been killed by a wild animal (Gen. 37:31-33).

9. What was Jacob's reaction?
Jacob tore his robes, put sackcloth on his loins, and mourned for his son many days (Gen. 37:34).

10. To whom did the Ishmaelites/ Midianites sell Joseph?
They sold Joseph in Egypt to Potiphar, one of the Pharaoh's officials the captain of the guard.

Opportunity to Serve

7hen Pharaoh sent and called Joseph, and they brought him hastily out of the dungeon: and he shaved himself, and changed his raiment, and came in unto Pharaoh.

15 And Pharaoh said unto Joseph, I have dreamed a dream, and there is none that can interpret it: and I have heard say of thee, that thou canst understand a dream to interpret it.

16 And Joseph answered Pharaoh, saying, It is not in me: God shall give Pharaoh an answer of peace.

25 And Joseph said unto Pharaoh, The dream of Pharaoh is one: God hath shewed Pharaoh what he is about to do.

26 The seven good kine are seven years; and the seven good ears are seven years: the dream is one.

27 And the seven thin and ill favoured kine that came up after them are seven years; and the seven empty ears blasted with the east wind shall be seven years of famine.

34 Let Pharaoh do this, and let him appoint officers over the land, and take up the fifth part of the land of Egypt in the seven plenteous years.

35 And let them gather all the food of those good years that come, and lay up corn under the hand of Pharaoh, and let them keep food in the cities.

36 And that food shall be for store to the land against the seven years of famine, which shall be in the land of Egypt; that the land perish not through the famine.

37 And the thing was good in the eyes of Pharaoh, and in the eyes of all his servants.

38 And Pharaoh said unto his servants, Can we find such a one as this is, a man in whom the Spirit of God is?

39 And Pharaoh said unto Joseph, Forasmuch as God hath shewed thee all this, there is none so discreet and wise as thou art:

40 Thou shalt be over my house, and according unto thy word shall all my people be ruled: only in the throne will I be greater than thou.

Genesis 41: 14-16, 25-27, 34-40

Memory Selection
Genesis 41:39-40

Background Scripture
Genesis 39–41

Devotional Reading
John 6:1-13

Printed Scripture
Genesis 41:15-17, 25-27, 34-40

Aug. 22

501

Teacher's Target

Lesson purpose: *To show God's providence and Joseph's grit in "turning captivity captive" by wresting positive outcomes from being a slave in Egypt.*

An effective way to introduce this lesson is to ask the group to share stories—from Scripture or everyday life—of people of courage turning tragedy into triumph. The story of Jo-

seph maintaining his faith through the "impossible" days of Egyptian captivity, and eventually rising to rulership, is surely near the top of such a list.

As a slave, Joseph had no rights. Being accused of attacking Potiphar's wife did nothing to improve his situation. Being forgotten by the prisoner he befriended could have dimmed all hope.

Yet Joseph persevered, and was finally rewarded by being elevated to a position second only to Pharaoh. In "hanging tough," Joseph showed himself to be an able heir to God's covenent with his great-grandfather, Abraham.

Lesson Introduction

This lesson begins what many Bible surveys call "The Descent into Egypt," since Joseph's captivity will lead to the entire clan's following him in a few years. Although the patriarchs have previously been in and out of this ancient land, it is at this point that their "sojourn" there becomes a captivity lasting more than 400 years.

New Testament writers found in the cycle of Israel's descent into and subsequent release from Egypt a pattern of what happened to the infant Jesus. The phrase, "Descent into Egypt," is also often applied to the infant Jesus' being taken there to escape Herod's mad designs; and Israel's release from captivity is paralleled with Jesus' return: "Out of Egypt have I called my son" (Matt. 2:15).

Earlier, some scholars believe that "the descent into Egypt" was confirmed by references in secular records to the "Habiru," from which the word "Hebrew" was thought to be derived. Now this connection is widely doubted.

Verse by Verse

I. Pharaoh Sends for Joseph—14-16

A. Joseph's reputation, 14-15

14 Then Pharaoh sent and called Joseph, and they brought him hastily out of the dungeon: and he shaved himself, and changed his raiment, and came in unto Pharaoh.

15 And Pharaoh said unto Joseph, I have dreamed a dream, and there is none that can interpret it: and I have heard say of thee, that thou canst understand a dream to interpret it.

Much has happened in Joseph's life since he was sold into Egyptian captivity. He had become a trusted servant in the house of his master Potiphar, captain of Pharaoh's personal troops. Unfortunately, Potiphar's wife unjustly accused Joseph of seducing her, and he landed in jail. Even there, God was with him, and he gained favor with the prison keeper (39:21).

Also while in prison, Joseph gained a reputation as an interpreter of dreams (chap. 40). Pharaoh's butler and baker had also been sentenced to prison for some real or imagined offense. Joseph interpreted their dreams to mean that the baker would lose his head, but the butler would regain his post—and events proved him correct. Although the butler promised to remember Joseph to Pharaoh, he forgot it until Pharaoh himself was troubled by a strange dream. That prompted the butler's memory, and it was through him that Pharaoh "heard say" that Joseph could interpret dreams.

B. Deferring to God, 16

16 And Joseph answered Pharaoh, saying, It is not in me: God shall give Pharaoh an answer of peace.

We remember that Joseph would be on familiar ground on the subject of dreams, since he himself was a dreamer. As in other ancient cultures, the Egyptians were given to turning to various kinds of "seers" and magicians for the interpretation of dreams. Pharaoh had turned to these sources without success (vs. 8; remarkably, the magicians either did not lie and produce a manufactured interpretation, or Pharaoh saw through such ruses). No doubt Pharaoh now seeks to discover whether this imprisoned Hebrew slave has superior magic or insight.

Joseph, however, places himself in a different league. It is neither magic, occult powers, or his own wisdom, but God who gives him the meaning of dreams.

Although God often used dreams and visions as a means of communicating with people, as in Joseph's case, they were not always considered a reliable source of information. In the prophet Jeremiah's day, people were concocting dreams to contain what they wanted to hear (Jer. 29:8). The prophet urged the people to distinguish clearly between such dreams and genuine revelation (23:26-28).

II. Pharaoh's Dream Interpreted—25-27

A. God's providence, 25

25 And Joseph said unto Pharaoh, The dream of Pharaoh is one: God hath shewed Pharaoh what he is about to do.

After listening to Pharaoh recount his dream (vss. 17-24), Joseph perceives that God is at work through it. Although not all natural phenomena occur at the direct intervention of God, Joseph perceives that He will be responsible for an approaching famine.

The Egyptians would have been more inclined to blame an evil god for such an event. Despite his youth, Joseph is already grounded firmly in monotheism, and realizes that all events can ultimately be traced either to his ideal or permissive will. God will later say through the prophet Isaiah that "I form the light, and create darkness: I make peace, and create evil" (Isa. 45:7). In this case, the "evil" of the famine will actually be used for the good of reconvening Jacob's clan in God's ongoing plan to develop a covenant people.

B. Famine Ahead—26-27

26 The seven good kine are seven years; and the seven good ears are seven years: the dream is one.

27 And the seven thin and ill favoured kine that came up after them are seven years; and the seven empty ears blasted with the east wind shall be seven years of famine.

The King James word "kine" was the plural of "cow" (as in the NIV). God shows Joseph that Pharaoh's two dreams, one about cows and the other about corn (NIV "grain"), were about the same event—an approaching agricultural cycle. Seven good years of bountiful harvest would be followed by a seven-year famine.

It is significant that in his dream Pharaoh finds himself beside "the river," from which the cattle emerge (vss. 1-2). This no doubt refers to the Nile River, which controls to a large degree all agriculture in Egypt. Its seasonal flooding spreads fertile silt over the farmland along its borders, and it was used for irrigation from earliest known times. Apparently for the next seven years the Nile would be fed by plenty of rainfall at its source far to the south, only to be followed by scarce rains during the next second seven-year cycle.

III. Formula and Reward—34-40

A. Plan for the Famine, 34-36

34 Let Pharaoh do this, and let him appoint officers over the land, and take up the fifth part of the land of Egypt in the seven plenteous years.

35 And let them gather all the food of those good years that come, and lay up corn under the hand of Pharaoh, and let them keep food in the cities.

36 And that food shall be for store to the land against the seven years of famine, which shall be in the land of Egypt; that the land perish not through the famine.

Joseph's upbeat attitude and aggressive spirit, even after spending years in jail for something he did not do, is amazing. He does not stop with interpreting Pharaoh's dreams, but suggests a solution to the problem they raise. He recommends levying a 20 percent per year tax, in the form of grain, the commodity that will be in the shortest supply. This grain was to be warehoused during the seven years of plenty, then distributed to the people during the seven years of famine. (Sound though the plan was, Joseph might not have won a public election for tax collector!)

B. Joseph is promoted, 37-40

37 And the thing was good in the eyes of Pharaoh, and in the eyes of all his servants.

38 And Pharaoh said unto his servants, Can we find such a one as this is, a man in whom the Spirit of God is?

39 And Pharaoh said unto Joseph, Forasmuch as God hath shewed thee all this, there is none so discreet and wise as thou art:

40 Thou shalt be over my house, and according unto thy word shall all my people be ruled: only in the throne will I be greater than thou.

Pharaoh knows a good thing when he sees it. Despite Joseph's humility in crediting God with the interpretation of the dream, Pharaoh knows that it takes a wise person both to admit he is not the source of divine wisdom and to perceive what God is saying. Pharaoh's attendants join him in admiring this new figure in the Egyptian palace.

Although Pharaoh would have understood his acclamation of "the Spirit of God" (vs. 38) and "God" (vs. 39) in a pagan sense, some 300 years after the time of Joseph Pharaoh Akhenaton did teach that there was only one God—Aton (or Aten), represented by the sun. It was a short-lived religious experiment, and ancient Egyptian religion is otherwise consistently polytheistic. Here, Pharaoh would have simply meant that Joseph's dream interpretation indicated that the spirits and the gods were with him in a special way. (The original language has no capitals, as in the KJV.)

Apparently Pharaoh makes Joseph a "vizier"—something like the Vice President or at least the Secretary of Agriculture in our own country. Joseph is now only 30 years old (vs. 46), and he has been brought in a few short years from a slave to second in command over all Egypt. His story is the ultimate exception to the cynical rule that "Nice guys finish last."

Evangelistic Emphasis

Joseph might have been filled with bitterness. His own brothers sold him into slavery. Here he was thrust from being his father's favorite to being a stranger in a foreign land. He was a slave. He had no rights. What had he ever done to deserve this? Life is not fair! But the Lord was with him. His master Potiphar trusted him. He was in charge of his household and his lands. Things were going well for this young man, until he was thrown into prison on the unjust charges of Potiphar's wife.

His world comes crashing down. A slave, a foreigner, in jail! What hope had he? But Joseph refuses to be consumed by his resentments. He does not go through life whining about what might have been. He bides his time. A new opportunity comes. He could not control the circumstances, but he could control how he would respond to them.

Every person has disappointments, frustrations, failures Everyone has asked, "Why me?" Every one can cry, "Life is not fair!" What ultimately matters is not what happens to us but what we do with it when it happens. God does not promise us an easy road, a life of comfort and security. God does promise that God will be with us. God will work with us and through us to bring good out of evil, growth out of suffering, wisdom from mistakes, strength out of weakness, life out of death. The one freedom that God has given, which no one can take away, is the freedom to choose how we will respond to the circumstances of life that come. The boasting, self-centered, spoiled teenager became a man of wisdom and discernment. The change came not despite his hard knocks, but because he chose to learn from them. That choice is ours as well.

● ● ● ● ● ●

Memory Selection

And Pharaoh said unto Joseph, Forasmuch as God hath showed thee all this, there is none so discreet and wise as thou art: Thou shalt be over my house, and according unto thy word shall all my people be ruled: only in the throne will I be greater than Thou.—*Genesis 41:39-40*

The Pharaoh of Egypt did not know much about the God of Abraham, Isaac, and Jacob. But he knew the interpretation of his dreams were not simply due to Joseph. Joseph made it plain to the pharaoh that it was not by his wisdom or power that he was able to interpret dreams. The pharaoh recognized in Joseph something which was lacking in his own advisors. He recognized in Joseph the Spirit of God. The talent of discernment was divinely given. There was no one like Joseph in all of Egypt. Joseph rises from a foreign slave in prison to the second in command in all of Egypt. The Pharaoh advances him over men twice his age, with decades of experience in the king's service. He raises him over native born Egyptians steeped in the history and culture of the nation. The pharaoh recognizes there is not a leader like Joseph in the land. He is chosen to lead Egypt through the years of plenty and the years of famine.

Weekday Problems

Joe had worked hard to learn the art of graphic design. He had some lean years in developing clients to keep himself financially afloat in his new business. Then the casino came to town. There was a need for newspaper ads, TV spots, billboards, flyers. It was the sort of job he had dreamed of. They paid well. They would be around for years. It was his big break. However, personally he disapproved of casinos. He would not want his son to read his ads and waste his money in gambling. He felt they were ripping off people who could least afford to lose it. But the casino was coming whether he wanted it or not. They would spend hundreds of thousands of dollars in advertising. He could have a piece of the action if he wanted it. He wasn't sure he wanted his gifts and training to be used to persuade people to gamble.

Bob had been raised in a Christian home. He had been taught to respect the sacredness of marriage vows. As a rising young executive he lived in a fast paced business world that seemed to operate on values different from his. The company president had great confidence in him and had given him opportunities to prove his abilities.

* Should he compromise his long term dreams for short term success?

* What principles can guide us in deciding between maintaining our integrity and making necessary compromises?

Optimism and Opposite-ism

An optimist is a guy who grabs a fishing pole when he discovers that his basement is flooded.

* * *

A pessimist is a person who, when opportunity knocks, complains about the noise.

* * *

Both optimists and pessimists raise buildings to the sky. Optimists build air castles and pessimists build dungeons.

* * *

Always borrow from a pessimist. He never expects it back anyhow.

* * *

The pessimist thinks he has to take a chance. An oppimist is glad for the chance to grab an opportunity.

* * *

An optimist is the guy who goes into the restaurant without a dime, but plans to pay for his meal with the pearl he'll find in an oyster.

This Lesson in Your Life

Joseph emerged as a leader in Egypt. The pharaoh recognized his gifts of discernment and wisdom and gave him authority. "Authority can be given. Leadership must be earned," according to Lovett Weems. "The final test for all leaders is whether someone is following."

The leaders needed today in the church are persons of vision and commitment. First a leader must have a vision, a guiding purpose. The leader's task is to give expression to an overarching vision in which all the people share. Joseph led the Egyptians to save a fifth of their grain each year, in the years of plenty, so that they might have enough and enough to spare in the years of famine which were to follow.

The necessity of vision in leadership is suggested by the dialogue between Alice and the Cheshire-Puss in Lewis Caroll's classic *Alice's Adventures in Wonderland*: Alice asks of the cat, "Would you tell me please, which way I ought to go from here?"

"That depends a good deal on where you want to get to," said the cat.

"I don't much care where," said Alice.

"Then it doesn't matter which way you go," said the Cat.

" . . . so long as I get somewhere," Alice added as an explanation.

"Oh, you're sure to do that," said the Cat, "if you only walk long enough."

The church needs leaders, leaders with vision. It is important to have good managers. A manager helps an organization move efficiently. No waste of money, time or energy. Managers do the thing right. Leaders do the right thing. We need good managers. But there is a greater need for leaders who have vision of what God calls the church to do and to be.

A second mark of leadership needed in the church today is passionate commitment. This is leadership which takes risk. This is costly discipleship. By the standards of the world there is a sort of madness to it. It is a servant leadership, where the goal is not to gain more power, more prestige for the leader . The single focused goal is to move the vision one step closer to being realized. One church volunteer is suing his denomination for five million dollars because, he claims, the denominational officials did not warn him that mission service could be hazardous to his safety. The leaders needed in the church today are those passionately committed to the kingdom, and willing to take up the cross to follow Jesus. The Belgian priest Henri Nouwen wrote, "The way of the Christian leader is not the way of upward mobility in which our world has invested so much, but the way of downward mobility ending on the cross."

Where are these leaders? They may be in your church, in your class, in your family. You may be that leader whom God is calling. "Whom shall I send and who will go? " May God give us grace to answer, "Here am I, Lord, send me."

Seed Thoughts

1. Why did Joseph refuse the entreaties of Potiphar's wife?

Potiphar had entrusted him with everything he owned and Joseph would not betray that trust; also, it would be a sin against God (Gen. 39:9-10).

2. Who were the king's servants imprisoned when Joseph was in prison?

The king's cup bearer and baker (Gen. 40:1).

3. What favor does Joseph ask of the cup bearer?

He asked the cup bearer to remember him before the Pharaoh and get him out of prison (Gen. 40:14).

4. Whose dreams did Joseph interpret?

The dreams of the king's cup bearer, the king's baker, and the dreams of Pharaoh the king.

5. What was Joseph's interpretation of the Pharaoh's dream?

There would be seven years of abundance followed by seven years of famine.

---

1. Why did Joseph refuse the entreaties of Potiphar's wife?

2. Who were the king's servants imprisoned when Joseph was in prison?

3. What favor does Joseph ask of the cup bearer?

4. Whose dreams did Joseph interpret?

5. What was Joseph's interpretation of the Pharaoh's dream?

6. How old was Joseph when he entered the service of the Pharaoh?

7. What reason did the Pharaoh give for appointing Joseph to be in charge?

8. What are the names and what is the significance of the names given to Joseph's sons?

9. What symbols of Joseph's new office as "prime minister" in Egypt did the Pharaoh give him?

10. When the Egyptians cried to the Pharaoh for food, what did he say to them?

(Continued next page)

Potiphar had entrusted him with everything he owned and Joseph would not betray that trust; also, it would be a sin against God (Gen. 39:9-10).

The king's cup bearer and baker (Gen. 40:1).

He asked the cup bearer to remember him before the Pharaoh and get him out of prison (Gen. 40:14).

The dreams of the king's cup bearer, the king's baker, and the dreams of Pharaoh the king.

There would be seven years of abundance followed by seven years of famine.

Joseph was thirty years old when he entered the service of Pharaoh, king of Egypt (Gen. 41:46).

God had shown Joseph the meaning of the dream, and there was no one so discerning and wise as Joseph.

Manasseh ("God has made me forget all my hardship"), and Ephraim ("God has made me fruitful in the land of my misfortune" (Gen. 41:51-52).

His signet ring from his hand, garments of fine linen, a gold chain around his neck, and riding in the chariot of the second in command (Gen. 41:42-43).

"Go to Joseph; what he says to you, do" (Gen. 41:55).

6. How old was Joseph when he entered the service of the Pharaoh?

Joseph was thirty years old when he entered the service of Pharaoh, king of Egypt (Gen. 41:46).

7. What reason did the Pharaoh give for appointing Joseph to be in charge?

God had shown Joseph the meaning of the dream, and there was no one so discerning and wise as Joseph.

8. What are the names and what is the significance of the names given to Joseph's sons?

Manasseh ("God has made me forget all my hardship"), and Ephraim ("God has made me fruitful in the land of my misfortune" (Gen. 41:51-52).

9. What symbols of Joseph's new office as "prime minister" in Egypt did the Pharaoh give him?

His signet ring from his hand, garments of fine linen, a gold chain around his neck, and riding in the chariot of the second in command (Gen. 41:42-43).

10. When the Egyptians cried to the Pharaoh for food, what did he say to them?

"Go to Joseph; what he says to you, do" (Gen. 41:55).

Forgiven and Reunited

hen Judah came near unto him, and said, Oh my lord, let thy ser-vant, I pray thee, speak a word in my lord's ears, and let not thine anger burn against thy ser-vant: for thou art even as Pharaoh.

19 My lord asked his servants, saying, Have ye a father, or a brother?

20 And we said unto my lord, We have a father, an old man, and a child of his old age, a little one; and his brother is dead, and he alone is left of his mother, and his father loveth him.

Gen. 44: 18-20, 33-45:7; 46:5-6

33 Now therefore, I pray thee, let thy servant abide instead of the lad a bondman to my lord; and let the lad go up with his brethren.

34 For how shall I go up to my father, and the lad be not with me? lest peradven-ture I see the evil that shall come on my father.

45:1 Then Joseph could not refrain him-self before all them that stood by him; and he cried, Cause every man to go out from me. And there stood no man with him, while Joseph made himself known unto his brethren.

2 And he wept aloud: and the Egyptians and the house of Pharaoh heard.

3 And Joseph said unto his brethren, I am Joseph; doth my father yet live? And his brethren could not answer him; for they were troubled at his presence.

4 And Joseph said unto his brethren, Come near to me, I pray you. And they came near. And he said, I am Joseph your brother, whom ye sold into Egypt.

5 Now therefore be not grieved, nor an-gry with yourselves, that ye sold me hither: for God did send me before you to preserve life.

6 For these two years hath the famine been in the land: and yet there are five years, in the which there shall nei-ther be earing nor harvest.

7 And God sent me before you to pre-serve you a posterity in the earth, and to save your lives by a great deliverance.

46:5 And Jacob rose up from Beersheba: and the sons of Israel carried Jacob their father, and their little ones, and their wives, in the wagons which Pharaoh had sent to carry him:

6 And they took their cattle, and their goods, which they had gotten in the land of Canaan, and came into Egypt, Jacob, and all his seed with him.

Memory Selection
Genesis 45:5
Background Scripture
Genesis 42–45
Devotional Reading
Psalm 105:7-22
Printed Scripture
Genesis 44:18-20,

Aug. 29

Teacher's Target

Lesson purpose: *To show, through the story of Joseph's being reunited with his family, how God can work through restored family relationships.*

Members of your study group may have family relationships that range from harmonious to just short of open warfare. Although a Bible study group is not always an appropriate scene to share traumatic family ties, discuss in a general way how disastrous they can be. Note that the families of God's chosen people were no different. Jacob and Esau competed for their father's favor. Joseph's arrogance made his brothers so jealous they sold him into Egyptian captivity. God's people are human.

God, however, has a plan that is greater than family quarrels. This lesson will show the power of forgiveness, and how healed relationships offer God fertile ground for witnessing to His love.

Lesson Introduction

This final lesson in our series on the origins of God's covenant with Abraham and his descendants shows His providence at work among the clans that became the Jewish nation. There was no evil—from family feuds to Joseph's being sold into slavery and imprisoned on a false charge—that God could not redeem and use for His purposes and the good of His people. Specifically, had Joseph's brothers not sold him into slavery, he would not have been in a position to rescue his family from starvation.

Some scholars believe that references in secular history to the "Hyksos" kings in Egypt confirm the Genesis account of the immigration of the children of Abraham. The Hyksos were a class of Middle Eastern rulers who wrested control of Egypt from about 1667–1559 B.C. It is possible that the Pharaoh who promoted Joseph to second in command was a part of this ruling class, and that for this reason he welcomed old Jacob and his family as fellow Middle Easterners.

Teaching Outline	Daily Bible Readings
I. Desperate Plea—44:18-20, 33-34	**Mon.** Journey to Buy Grain *Genesis 42:1-17*
A. 'Here's What Happened,' 18-20	**Tue.** Plan to See Benjamin *Genesis 42:18-38*
B. 'My life for his,' 33-34	**Wed.** Jacob Consents *Genesis 43:1-15*
II. Disclosure of Identity—45:1-7	**Thu.** A Meeting Arranged Genesis 43:16-34
A. 'I am Joseph,' 1-4	**Fri.** Bejamin Threatened *Genesis 44:18-34*
B. 'God arranged this!' 5-7	**Sat.** Judah Offers Himself *Genesis 45:1-28*
III. Descent into Egypt—46:5-6	**Sun.** 'I Am Joseph' *Genesis 45:1-28*

Verse by Verse

I. Desperate Plea—44:18-20, 33-34

A. 'Here's What Happened,' 18-20

18 Then Judah came near unto him, and said, Oh my lord, let thy servant, I pray thee, speak a word in my lord's ears, and let not thine anger burn against thy servant: for thou art even as Pharaoh.

19 My lord asked his servants, saying, Have ye a father, or a brother?

20 And we said unto my lord, We have a father, an old man, and a child of his old age, a little one; and his brother is dead, and he alone is left of his mother, and his father loveth him.

Joseph's eldest brother Judah summarizes the complex chain of events described in chapters 42–44. The famine that had been forecast in Pharaoh's dream struck Canaan as well as Egypt. Hearing that conditions were better in Egypt, old Jacob was driven to send 10 of his sons there to buy grain. By God's providence they appeared before none other than the "Secretary of Agriculture," their brother Joseph. While he recognized them, no doubt he had become an Egyptian in appearance; and his brothers did not recognize him.

Joseph treated his brothers gruffly at first, even imprisoning them on the pretext that they were spies. He wanted to test them to see if they were still as hard-hearted as when they sold him into slavery. As other tests, he put his brother Simeon in bonds as surety against his demand that Benjamin be brought to him; and he had the money they had paid for the grain put into the grain sacks, as though to have cause to arrest them again.

As the long famine ground on, Jacob and his family had to return to Egypt for more grain. This time Jacob reluctantly allowed Benjamin, "a child of his old age," to go with his brothers as Joseph had demanded. Jacob also sent twice the amount of money the men had found in their sacks after the first trip.

Joseph broke down upon seeing his beloved younger brother, but managed to disguise his tears of joy and frustration. Devising another ruse, this time in order to detain Benjamin, Joseph had his own personal drinking cup, made of silver, tucked away in Benjamin's sack of grain. Joseph's steward then overtook the brothers as they made their way back to Canaan, charged them with stealing the cup, and of course "found" it in Benjamin's sack.

Jacob's sons returned sorrowfully to Egypt, feeling sure they would face the wrath of this man who ranked next to Pharaoh. As spokesman, Judah confessed with not a little bewilderment that they had been found out, and had no excuse. Joseph could do with them what he thought best.

Continuing his charade, Joseph says he will not punish the entire group, but will place Benjamin in bondage (44:17). It is this threat that prompts Judah to give the explanation above.

B. 'My life for his,' 33-34

33 Now therefore, I pray thee, let thy servant abide instead of the lad a bondman to my lord; and let the lad go up with his brethren.

34 For how shall I go up to my father, and the lad be not with me? lest peradventure I see the evil that shall come on my father.

Now Joseph sees the positive results of the rigorous tests he has required his brothers to undergo. He has already overheard them speaking with remorse over their crime against him years earlier (42:21-24). Now Judah, who, along with Reuben, had been opposed to killing Joseph, shows how he has grown even more in character by offering to take Benjamin's place as Joseph's servant. If the youngest brother is not allowed to return to Canaan, it could easily be the death of their father.

II. Disclosure of Identity—45:1-7
A. 'I am Joseph,' 1-4

1 Then Joseph could not refrain himself before all them that stood by him; and he cried, Cause every man to go out from me. And there stood no man with him, while Joseph made himself known unto his brethren.

2 And he wept aloud: and the Egyptians and the house of Pharaoh heard.

3 And Joseph said unto his brethren, I am Joseph; doth my father yet live? And his brethren could not answer him; for they were troubled at his presence.

4 And Joseph said unto his brethren, Come near to me, I pray you. And they came near. And he said, I am Joseph your brother, whom ye sold into Egypt.

Joseph has seen and heard enough to know his brothers have repented of their crime against him. He can restrain himself from revealing his identity no longer. Commanding all others to leave the room, he makes himself know to his brothers, amid many tears.

It is hard to imagine the brothers' shock at this revelation. Hearing this "Egyptian" official speak their own language, then perhaps barely discerning his resemblance to the brother they had thought dead, strikes them dumb for a moment.

B. 'God arranged this!' 5-7

5 Now therefore be not grieved, nor angry with yourselves, that ye sold me hither: for God did send

me before you to preserve life.

6 For these two years hath the famine been in the land: and yet there are five years, in the which there shall neither be earing nor harvest.

7 And God sent me before you to preserve you a posterity in the earth, and to save your lives by a great deliverance.

The brothers have suffered enough. Now Joseph would release them from their grief and guilt by pointing out the way a sovereign God has taken the deed they intended for evil and transformed into good. The family could not have survived the famine that still has five years left on its lease had not Joseph somehow wound up in Egypt, and in a position to help. As Joseph will say years later, after the death of Jacob, "You intended to harm me, but God intended it for good to accomplish what is now being done, the saving of many lives" (50:20, NIV).

III. Descent into Egypt—46:5-6

5 And Jacob rose up from Beersheba: and the sons of Israel carried Jacob their father, and their little ones, and their wives, in the wagons which Pharaoh had sent to carry him:

6 And they took their cattle, and their goods, which they had gotten in the land of Canaan, and came into Egypt, Jacob, and all his seed with him.

Hearing that Joseph has been re-united with his estranged family, Pharaoh graciously urges Joseph to bring them to Egypt and to make it their home. He even supplies them with the wagons in which to move. Loading his brothers with rich gifts, Joseph sends them back to Canaan to bring their father Jacob (here called both Jacob and Israel), and their families to Egypt (45:16-24).

Old Jacob's heart is almost unable to bear the good news that his son Joseph is alive (vss. 25-28). He and his sons and all their families and servants total 66 people (vs. 26. Along with their livestock, they made a sizable caravan as they headed for Goshen, the area in Egypt Pharaoh had designated for them, on the rich delta where the Nile empties into the Mediterranean Sea. Along with Joseph's own wife and two children, 70 people of the family of Abraham are now in Egypt.

As grateful as Jacob and his family must have been to find relief from the famine, we may wonder whether they felt that the covenant promise had been postponed once again. Particularly as Pharaohs arose who "knew not Joseph" (Exod. 1:8), and as the Israelites were reduced to slavery in Egypt, their faith would be tested. It was their challenge to affirm, with Joseph, that God meant their fate for good, and not evil.

Evangelistic Emphasis

The story of Joseph and his brothers is a story of the power of God's grace to bring change. God brings transformation to persons and their relationships. The change is seen in Judah . Where once he joined his brothers in resenting Joseph, now he offers himself as a slave to his younger brother, volunteering to take the place of Benjamin, his father's favorite son.

We see a maturing in Joseph. As a young teenager he had flaunted his role as the father's favorite son. As the second most powerful person in Egypt, he does not remain as a lord demanding obeisance from his brothers. Rather he reveals himself as a brother, embracing them with tears and kisses, and providing for them in the Land of Egypt. Although he had ample opportunity to take revenge, he rises above vengeance and provides for them and for their families. Joseph came to the faith that God was in all of these deeds, working to preserve the family of Abraham.

To claim "You can't change human nature" flies in the face of the whole witness of the Bible, which tells the story of persons whose lives are changed: Paul and Peter, Mary Magdalene and Zacchaeus . . the list goes on and on. Scripture is full of testimonies to the power of God to transform human life.

God is still in the redemption business God is at work to replace estrangement with reconciliation, hate with love, hostility with unity, division with harmony . When we see these signs of life rather than death we know that God has been at work in human affairs. John sums it up: "We love because he first loved us" (1 John 4:19).

● ● ● ● ● ● ● ●

Now, therefore be not grieved, nor angry with yourselves, that ye sold me hither: for God did send me before you to preserve life.—*Genesis 45:5*

Joseph's brothers were dismayed, dumbfounded, terrified when they realize that the high Egyptian official who held their fate in their hands was in fact their younger brother Joseph, whom they had sold into slavery. Joseph comforts them with a faithful way of understanding these events. Though Joseph himself did not see it this way when he was made a slave and sent to a strange land, now he sees God at work in and under and through these strange events. God could take even the evil deeds of the brothers, and use them for a larger purpose. Joseph reaffirms his trust in divine providence when he declares at the story's end: "Even though you intended to do harm to me, God intended it for good, in order to preserve a numerous people" (Gen 50:20). Paul expresses a similar view of divine providence when he writes: "We know that in everything God works for good with whose who love Him, who are called according to His purpose" (Rom. 8:28).

516

Weekday Problems

Kay could not believe it. The X-ray examination showed what ooked like a tumor. The biopsy indicated malignancy. The surgery howed the cancer was widespread. The prognosis was not good. 'rolonged chemotherapy was called for. There was no assurance f a cure. She had so much to live for.

For a time she denied it, fantasizing that the lab reports were mixed up. Then she was ngry, with her self for not going sooner to the doctor, with the medical team because hey could not bring a quick cure, with God for letting her life be filled with illness and ain. It just wasn't fair. Her well-meaning friends who called did not help. They told her God always has a reason for everything." "Don't worry; everything always works out for he best." Her friends seemed to believe that God has absolute control over every detail f her life. They spoke as though God had caused the cancer, and was responsible for er pain, for the loss of her job, for her approaching death. .

Through talking with her pastor, Kay came to a different faith perspective. In the vords of James Harnish: "While there may be circumstances over which God does not ave absolute control, and "things" that God does not cause, there is nothing that God annot turn into good. There is nothing that God cannot use in some way for good."

Kay was drawn closer to her family. She discovered in a deeper way the support and ove of her friends at church. She reassessed her values and how she spent her life. In act she felt God's presence in a way she had not known before. She began to under-tand Paul's words, "We know that in all things God works for good with those who love im, those whom he has called by his purpose" (Rom. 8:28).

All in the Family

Father of teenage son to neighbor: Junior's at that awkward age—too old for a spanking and too young for analysis.

* * *

Son: Dad, the Bible says if you don't let me have the car, you hate me.
Dad: Oh, really? Where does it say that?
Son: Proverbs 13:24—"He that spareth the rod hateth his son."

* * *

Co-ed: Daddy, the girl who sits next to me in class has a dress just like mine.
Dad: So I guess you want a new dress?
Co-ed: Well, it would be cheaper than changing colleges.

* * *

Mom: Son, how could you be so rude as to tell your sister she's stupid? Tell her you're sorry.
Son: OK, Sis, I'm sorry you're stupid.

This Lesson in Your Life

The major theme of the Joseph story is the mysterious providence of God. It is the good news of the Bible that God could use the envy and violence of Joseph's brothers, the false accusations of a frustrated woman and the faulty memory of an ungrateful wine steward in His larger design of providing for His people. The family of Abraham with whom God had made a holy covenant are to be a blessing to the nations. Although he years of famine seemed to threaten all of that, through God's providence a remnant is preserved. In retrospect it seemed as though God sent this favored son ahead, to prepare the way. When the time was right, Joseph sent for his extended family to come and ride out the years of famine in a place where there was enough, enough to spare, enough to share.

The lesson for our lives today in the ancient story of Joseph is that God can take the events of our lives and weave them into God's larger purposes, in ways we cannot imagine, predict or understand. It is not that God causes all events to happen. Despite the language of insurance policies, earthquakes and hurricanes, flood waters and mud slides are not the acts of God. Nor was it by God's act that Hitler built his gas chambers, or that the Klan bombed churches filled with little children, or that in a world of plenty children starve for want of food. It is the message of the Bible that in all these events God is at work, bringing healing out of pain, good out of evil, redemption out of suffering, life out of death. Joseph declares to his brothers "You meant it for evil but God used it for good" (Gen. 50:20).

John Gunther in *Death Be Not Proud*, the moving story of his son's illness and death, cries out to God, "Is there nothing I can do for my boy?" There was no improvement. He tries again with a new direction. "Is there nothing you can do for my boy?" There was no improvement. And then, one day, the boy suggests to his father "Maybe God is doing something for you."

The Joseph story, read in the Christian community, read in the light of the Cross, seems a kind of dim anticipation of the story of the Savior. Joseph was a savior for his people. In the midst of famine, he provided for them. Despite the evil they had done him, he welcomed them to this strange land. He promised to care for them.

Yet he would never have come to this place if he had not been the victim of their jealousy, if he had not been sold into slavery, if he had not been thrown into prison. There was for Joseph, in being sent as a slave into a strange land, a kind of death. Jacob grieved because he thought he was dead. Yet through this "death" there was provided life for Israel. This evil deed God used for good, just as He used the death of Christ as the means of our salvation.

The God revealed in Christ does not take away the mystery of suffering. The reason for pain and evil is not explained. But the biblical story does witness that human barriers are God's opportunities, our endings are God's beginnings. Out of evil, God brings good. Out of death is born new life. The Joseph story anticipates this gospel: "Even though you intended to do harm to me, God intended it for good."

Seed Thoughts

1. When Jacob sent his sons to Egypt to buy grain, which son did he keep at home and why?

Benjamin, the one remaining son of his beloved wife Rachel. Jacob was afraid Benjamin might come to harm (Gen. 42:3).

2. What dreams were fulfilled when the ten brothers bowed down before Joseph? (Gen. 42:6; 43:26-28).

Joseph's dreams, in which his brother's sheaves and the stars bowed down before him (Gen. 37:6-9).

3. What was Joseph's first proposal to test the truthfulness of Jacob's other sons?

One brother was to return to Canaan and bring back Benjamin, while the other nine remained in prison in Egypt (Gen. 42:15).

4. What was Joseph's second plan, the one which was followed?

One brother would remain in Egypt and the others would go home with grain, then return with their youngest brother (Gen. 42:18-19).

5. Which brother stayed in Egypt while the others carried grain to alleviate the famine back home?

Joseph picked Simeon to stay in prison in Egypt (Gen. 42:24).

---

1. When Jacob sent his sons to Egypt to buy grain, which son did he keep at home and why?

2. What dreams were fulfilled when the ten brothers bowed down before Joseph? (Gen. 42:6; 43:26-28).

3. What was Joseph's first proposal to test the truthfulness of Jacob's other sons?

4. What was Joseph's second plan, the one which was followed?

5. Which brother stayed in Egypt while the others carried grain to alleviate the famine back home?

6. Who offered his life for Benjamin's?

7. Why do you think Joseph put his brothers to the test?

8. What did Joseph say to Benjamin?

9. How did Joseph's brothers respond when he said to them "I am Joseph!"

10. According to Judah what would happen to Jacob if the brothers return without Benjamin?

(Continued next page)

519

Benjamin, the one remaining son of his beloved wife Rachel. Jacob was afraid Benjamin might come to harm (Gen. 42:3).

Joseph's dreams, in which his brother's sheaves and the stars bowed down before him (Gen. 37:6-9).

One brother was to return to Canaan and bring back Benjamin, while the other nine remained in prison in Egypt (Gen. 42:15).

One brother would remain in Egypt and the others would go home with grain, then return with their youngest brother (Gen. 42:18-19).

Joseph picked Simeon to stay in prison in Egypt (Gen. 42:24).

Judah: "Please let your servant remain as a slave to my lord in place of the boy (Gen. 44:33).

To determine whether the brothers had changed.

"God be gracious to you, my son!" (Gen. 43:29).

They were troubled (KJV), terrified (NIV), dismayed (NRSV), dumbfounded (NEB) (Gen. 45:3).

When Jacob sees that the boy (Benjamin) is not with them, he would die (Gen. 44:30).

6. Who offered his life for Benjamin's?

Judah: "Please let your servant remain as a slave to my lord in place of the boy (Gen. 44:33).

7. Why do you think Joseph put his brothers to the test?

To determine whether the brothers had changed.

8. What did Joseph say to Benjamin?

"God be gracious to you, my son!" (Gen. 43:29).

9. How did Joseph's brothers respond when he said to them "I am Joseph!"

They were troubled (KJV), terrified (NIV), dismayed (NRSV), dumbfounded (NEB) (Gen. 45:3).

10. According to Judah what would happen to Jacob if the brothers return without Benjamin?

When Jacob sees that the boy (Benjamin) is not with them, he would die (Gen. 44:30).